AF714490

The Nobel Laureates and their Legacies:
A Survey of Contributions to Economic Thought

VOLUME - II

The Nobel Laureates and their Legacies: A Survey of Contributions to Economic Thought

VOLUME - II

Professor B.S.R. Rao

BSP BS Publications
An Imprint of **BSP Books Pvt. Ltd.**
4-4-309/316, Giriraj Lane,
Sultan Bazar, Hyderabad - 500 095

The Nobel Laureates and their Legacies: A Survey of Contributions to Economic Thought, Volume II
***by* Professor B.S.R. Rao**

© 2025 *by B.S.R. Rao*

All rights reserved. No part of this book or parts thereof may be reproduced, stored in a retrieval system or transmitted in any language or by any means, electronic, mechanical, photocopying, recording or otherwise without the prior written permission of the author.

Published by

BSP BS Publications
An Imprint of **BSP Books Pvt. Ltd.**
4-4-309/316, Giriraj Lane, Sultan Bazar,
Hyderabad - 500 095
Phone: 040 - 23445688
e-mail: info@bspbooks.net
www.bspbooks.net

ISBN
Volume I : 978-93-95038-94-2
Volume II : 978-93-95038-82-9

DEDICATED TO

MY PATERNAL GRAND PARENTS

BALANTRAPU RAMAYYA

BALANTRAPU SURAMMA

Dr. C. Rangarajan
Former Chairman, Economic Advisory Council to the PM
Former Governor, Reserve Bank of India

FOREWORD

Prof. BSR Rao has undertaken the painstaking work of bringing together in two volumes a gist of the contributions made by the Nobel Laureates in Economics. The Nobel Award for economics was instituted only in 1969. Economics is a growing science. It is difficult for anyone to be an expert in all the sub disciplines. However, every student and teacher in economics must have some understanding of the developments in every field of economics. All the Nobel Laureates in economics have been well known names in their fields. Their writings have contributed immensely to the development of economics as a discipline. This book will give to every student of economics a brief insight into various developments. For a deeper understanding of the developments in any field, the student however will have to go to the original seminal articles. Prof. Rao instead of going chronologically has grouped the Nobel Laureates in terms of their contributions to the various subfields. This book should serve as an appetizer for further study. Prof. Rao has done a signal service to the students and teachers of economics by bringing out this compendium.

Chennai
November 10, 2014

C. RANGARAJAN

PREFACE

The unstructured and inadequate teaching in our colleges and many universities in our country of even the significant and major developments in economics - both theoretical and empirical – during the later part of the last century puts the Indian students at a disadvantageous position for pursuing advanced studies including the choice of a contemporary relevant topic for research. To partly alleviate the situation a reasonably comprehensive history of modern economic analysis encompassing the major contributions to various branches of the subject is called for. Such a work would facilitate interested students and teachers to update their knowledge and further help who would like to deepen and widen their intellectual base. This would hopefully help in improving the standard of post graduate teaching of economics as also enriching the research work on contemporary economic problems.

The present work is a humble and modest attempt in that direction. It summarizes major contributions of sixty-seven winners of Nobel Memorial Prize for economic sciences during 1969 through 2010. A brief biographical note on each of the winners is provided to make the reader note and appreciate the progress achieved by each of them including in some cases the hardships and privations they had to pass through in order to indicate the difficulties to be faced to reach the top. To enable interested readers make further reading, select bibliography of the work of each Nobel laureate is appended.

The award of a research project – History of Modern Economic Analysis: Contributions to Economics by Nobel Laureates – by the University Grants Commission, New Delhi, provided the initial impetus to this work. I took up the research work, acutely conscious of the daunting task what with the difficulty in collecting vast material and scrutinising it single handed. The project was completed and the draft report submitted to the sponsors in 2005. This has whetted my appetite; encouragement of professional friends made me decide to continue the work with the objective of bringing out a volume spanning the contributions of Laureates up to 2010. This meant revising and updating the earlier work. When I completed the work in 2013, I heaved a sigh of satisfied and delighted relief.

This work has been a long time in writing. I have accumulated debt of gratitude to many persons. However, first I sincerely thank the University Grants Commission that was instrumental in igniting my interest in the work by awarding a research project.

My deepest sense of gratitude is to the members my family who gave unstinted support to my research effort all along, putting up with my neglect of all other activities. I cannot adequately thank my wife, Seshasayi Balantrapu, who cheerfully took care of all family responsibilities, leaving me free to concentrate on my intellectual effort. My two sons and two daughters and their families were quite helpful in the completion of the work.

In writing this book, I have greatly depended on the websites of Noble Foundation such as its Archives. The photographs of the Laureates are given in the work. My sincere thanks to the Foundation. For providing valuable material, I have acknowledged it by specific reference to it at appropriate places. It would not be redundant if I once again express here my gratitude to Nobel Foundation.

Some of the material I have used here was supplied to me by one of my former students, Madhusudan Kalimipalli, currently Associate Professor at Wilfried Laurier University, Waterloo, Ontario, Canada. My profound thanks to him.

Two visits to the USA by me and my wife were very helpful in completing the work. Our stay at Irvine, Dulles, with my younger son, Krishna Balantrapu, was memorable and very fruitful. I was provided by him and my daughter-in-law, Sunita Balantrapu, besides warm and affectionate hospitality, conducive conditions for completing the work. In the second visit, Krishna has helped me improve the computer presentation and in finalising the manuscript for publication.

I have to acknowledge with thanks the help and co-operation of the library, librarian and staff of Ratan Tata Library, Delhi School of Economics, New Delhi of Gokhale Institute of Politics and Economics, Pune, of Jayakar Library, University of Pune, Pune and Library of Department of Economics, Osmania University, Hyderabad. I express my grateful thanks to Ms. N. Srilekha for the computer help in regard to a part of the work.

Last, but not the least, my gratitude to Messrs Nikhil Shah and Anil Shah, Directors of BSP Books Pvt. Ltd., Hyderabad for undertaking the publication of the work and to Mr. Mohit Singha, for introducing them to me.

Professor B. S. R. Rao
Hyderabad.

CONTENTS

Volume - II

Section - IV

GENERAL EQUILIBRIUM THEORY

Chapter 33

Kenneth Joseph Arrow

(1921 –)

Chapter 34

Gerard Debreu

(1921 – 2004)

Chapter 35

Maurice Allais

(1911 – 2010)

Section-V

MICROECONOMIC THEORY

Chapter 36

George Joseph Stigler

(1911 – 1991)

Chapter 37

James Alexander Mirrlees

(1936 –)

Chapter 38

William Spencer Vickrey

(1914 – 1996)

Chapter 39

George Arthur Akerlof

(1940 –)

Chapter 40

Andrew Michael Spence

(1943 –)

Chapter 41

Joseph Eugene Stiglitz

(1943 –)

Section - VI

INTERDISCIPLINARY RESEARCH

Chapter 46

Gunnar Myrdal

(1898 – 1987)

Chapter 47

Herbert Alexander Simon

(1916 – 2001)

Chapter 48

James McGill Buchanan Jr.

(1919 – 2013)

Chapter 49

Ronald Harry Coase

(1910 – 2013)

Chapter 50

Gary Stanley Becker

(1930 – 2013)

Chapter 51

Robert William Fogel

(1926 – 2013)

Chapter 52

Douglass Cecil North

(1920 –)

Chapter 53

Amartya Sen

(1933 –)

Chapter 54

Daniel Kahneman

(1934 –)

Chapter 61

Robert John Aumann

(1930 –)

VOLUME - I

SECTION - I

MACROECONOMICS

Chapter 1

Milton Friedman

(1912 – 2006)

Chapter 2

Bertil Gotthard Ohlin

(1899 – 1979)

Chapter 3

James Edward Meade

(1907 – 1995)

Chapter 4

Theodore Wilhain Schultz

(1902 – 1998)

Chapter 5

Sir William Arthur Lewis

(1915 – 1991)

Chapter 6

Lawrence Robert Klein

(1920 – 2013)

Chapter 7

James Tobin

(1918 – 2002)

Chapter 8

Franco Modigliani

(1918 – 2003)

Chapter 11

Robert Alexander Mundell

(1932 –)

Chapter 12

Finn Erling Kydland & Edward Christian Prescott

(1943 –) & (1940 –)

Chapter 13

Edmund Strother Phelps Jr.

(1933 –)

SECTION-II

FINANCIAL ECONOMICS

Chapter 16

Harry Max Markowitz

(1927 –)

Chapter 17

William Forsyth Sharpe

(1934 –)

Chapter 18

Merton Howard Miller

(1923 – 2000)

Chapter 19

Robert C Merton & Myron Samuel Scholes

(1944 –) & (1941 –)

SECTION - III

NEW METHODS OF ECONOMIC ANALYSIS: ECONOMETRICS ETC

Chapter 20

Ragnar Anton Kittel Frisch

(1895 – 1973)

Chapter 21

Jan Tinbergen

(1903 – 1994)

Chapter 22

Wassily Wassilyovich Leontief

(1906 – 1999)

Chapter 23

Leonid Vitaliyevich Kantorovich

(1912 – 1986)

Chapter 24

Tjalling Charles Koopmans

(1910 – 1985)

Chapter 25

Sir John Richard Nicholas Stone

(1913 – 1991)

Chapter 28

Daniel Little Mcfadden

(1937 –)

Chapter 29

Clive William John Granger

(1934 – 2009)

Chapter 30

Robert Fry Engle III

(1942 –)

INTRODUCTION

The Sveriges Riksbank Prize in economic sciences in memory of Alfred Nobel was instituted by the central bank of Sweden to mark its tercentenary celebration in 1968. The award, based on an economic commitment by the bank in perpetuity, is given by the Royal Swedish Academy of Sciences according to the same principles as for the Nobel Prizes that have been awarded in Physics, Chemistry, Medicine/Physiology, Literature and Peace since 1901. The procedure that is followed for selecting the laureates in Economic Sciences is the same as for the other subjects.

The procedure that is followed for the selection of the laureate(s) is described by Assar Lindbeck. According to him each year the Royal Swedish Academy receives roughly 200-300 nominations, covering about one hundred nominees. The Economics Prize Selection Committee of the Academy (with 5 to 8 members) commission expert studies of the most prominent candidates. The prize committee presents its award proposal to the Social Science Class of the Academy in the form of a report including all solicited expert studies. This forms the basis for the class to suggest a Laureate or a shared prize between two or, at most, three laureates. Finally the entire Academy at its meeting takes the final award decision usually in October every year.

The Royal Academy started awarding the prize in 1969. In the first 42 years (1969 - 2010, the period covered in this work) the laureates totalled sixty seven. It is proposed to attempt a bird's eye view of the type of awards given so far under a rather arbitrary classification, drawing heavily from Lindbeck's article "The Sveriges Riskbank Prize in economic sciences in memory of Alfred Nobel 1969 – 2007; Nobel Prize. Org".

I. General Equilibrium Theory

Paul A. Samuelson (1970)

John R. Hicks, Kenneth J. Arrow (1972)

Gerard Debreu (1983)

Maurice A. Allais (1988)

The economists included in this category have basically studied analytical structure of theoretical economic models, specifying the conditions for consistency, equilibrium, stability and efficiency of the economic system. Their contributions also analysed how equilibrium positions change when changes occur in exogenous factors (comparative static analysis). General equilibrium theory has emerged as a basic approach in theoretical economic analysis as a result of their efforts.

Hicks was awarded the prize for formulating multi-market stability conditions, extending the applicability of static analysis to several periods. Hicks was the first economist to attempt a rigorous dynamic analysis of capital accumulation. Another notable feature of Hicks's work was his anchoring it in microeconomic theories of behaviour of individual households/families and firms which helped the study of consequences of changes in various parameters. He also presented a widely-used and celebrated aggregate general equilibrium model with four markets – commodities, labour, money and credit – the well-known IS-LM model.

Samuelson's work is considered both continuation of the contributions by Hicks as also a break-through, specially in terms of analytical sophistication. It is widely accepted: Samuelson "single-handedly re-wrote considerable parts of central economic theory, microeconomic theory, static and dynamic, partial and general equilibrium theory, as well as welfare economics." Further, using simple mathematical models and employing second-order conditions of maximization procedures, he established important results that are treated now as classical theorems of economics.

Arrow and Debreu used powerful mathematical methods (for example theory of convex sets) to obtain more general results in general equilibrium theory. They were able to define broadly the concept of a good so that they can use it in static equilibrium analysis as well as in inter-temporal analysis, spatial distribution of production and consumption activities and in the analysis of decision-making under uncertainty. Arrow has also formulated well-known "impossibility theorem"- difficulties in deriving social welfare functions from preferences of individuals.

Maurice Allais's work has great similarities with the work of Samuelson and Arrow and Debreu. A particularly interesting aspect of Allais's work is his showing that an economy's path to equilibrium as a process by which competition exhausts all surpluses in firms. He is credited with demonstrating that returns to scale in production result in natural monopolies.

II. Macroeconomics

Milton Friedman (1976)

Franco Modigliani (1985)

James Tobin (1981)

James Meade and Bertil Ohlin (1977)

Robert Mundell (1999)

Lawrence Klein (1980)

Robert E. Lucas (1995)

Robert Solow (1987)

Arthur Lewis and Theodore Schultz (1979)

Finn Kydland and Edward S. Prescott (2004)

Edmund S. Phelps (2006)

Paul Krugman (2008)

Peter Diamond, Dale Mortensen and Christopher Pissarides (2010)

A number of prizes (13 prizes to 18 economists) have been awarded to macroeconomics. It is a branch of economic analysis that seeks to explain the behaviour of the whole national economy in terms of broad aggregates such as private consumption, investment, exports, government expenditure on goods, services etc. Some of the awards, however, were given to contribution in studies relating to some specific sectors.

The prize in 1976 was given to Milton Friedman for his contribution to consumption analysis, monetary history and theory. In his book A Theory of the Consumption Function, he joined together formal consumption theory and empirically applied it to a specific sector of the U.S. economy. His extensive and robust empirical study of monetary history of the U.S together with Anna Schwartz is a prime example of pure empirical research. The study is regarded as a monetary interpretation of macroeconomic fluctuations in the country (U.S.A).

Franco Modigliani who was awarded the prize for 1985 is specially known for two important building blocks, namely, sub models of private consumption and financial sector, in macroeconomic models. His analysis of the consequences for household saving of changes in demography and economic growth in his life-cycle theory of saving (together with Brumberg and Albert Ando) is particularly noteworthy. Together with Merton Miller, he pioneered the field of what has come to be known as corporate finance. The Modigliani-Miller theorem specifies the conditions under which the value of a firm in the stock market is not influenced (or influenced) by the way the firm finances its investment through equity capital or borrowed funds and by its dividend policy.

James Tobin was given the prize (in 1981) for his analysis of "financial markets and their relation to expenditure decisions, employment, production and prices." The award was for his theoretical contributions relating to specific sectors in the national economy. Tobin's approach modelling interactions between financial and real sectors in the economy received wide acceptance and got integrated into macro models of national economies. In this, "Tobin's q" – important role played by the relation between the market value of a capital asset and its reproduction costs – played an important role. Furthermore, Tobin's portfolio model has gained acceptance as a useful analytical tool for analyzing direct effects on product prices of changes in money supply.

James Meade and Bertil Ohlin shared the 1977 prize for their contributions to the theory of international trade and international capital movements. The award is another example of a contribution concerning the sector of foreign transactions. The award to Ohlin is for his development of a theory of international and interregional trade – referred to as Heckscher-Ohlin model – which seeks to explain both the causes and consequences of trade. Ohlin showed that the proportions of available factors of production, namely labour and capital, determine the trade pattern of individual countries. He further demonstrated that international trade tends to equalize the return to these factors among countries. Meade anticipated the theory of "second best" resource allocation by analysing trade policy in a world market with various market distortions. He also pioneered the theory of open-economy macroeconomics and worked on the analysis of the relation between internal and external balance and the relation between targets and instruments of economic policy.

Robert Mundell carried Meade's work further and has laid the foundation for today's theory of open-economy macroeconomics – the so-called Mundell-Fleming model. He is the recipient of 1999 Prize. Mundell is reputed for introducing foreign trade and global capital movements into Hicks's IS-LM model for a closed economy. Taking inspiration from David Hume's work, he showed that the effects of fiscal and monetary policy crucially depend upon international capital mobility. Mundell did creditable work on optimum currency areas, delineating the advantages and disadvantages for countries giving up their monetary sovereignty in favour of common currency.

Robert Klein did important macroeconomic research work for national economies and even regarding interaction among several national economies for which he is given the 1980 award. The prize citation specifically mentions his "creation of econometric models and their application to the analysis of economic fluctuations and economic policies". He employed statitical model simulation for analyzing the effects of economic policies. His contributions to developing forecasting techniques are noteworthy. It is also observed that initially Klein used Keynesian type of macro theories; however, over time they became eclectic and more detailed.

Robert Lucas (who received the 1995 prize) further strengthened macroeconomic model building with particular emphasis on the important role of expectations. He is especially remembered for developing consequences of "rational expectations" among agents. According to him the agents exploit all available information and do not make any systematic expectational mistakes. Lucas showed the way the policies of government and central bank change in response to changes in the economy. He has become well-known for his criticism of traditional macroeconomic estimation – the so-called "Lucas critique" – and ways of obviating the problem.

Robert Solow received the prize in 1987 for his work on the theory of long-term macroeconomic growth by building a simple mathematical model demonstrating how capital accumulation process raises productivity in an economy. The prices of capital and labour determine the capital intensity of production. He is also known for his pioneering work in "growth accounting."

Arthur Lewis and Theodore Schultz shared the 1979 prize for their research on "economic development with particular consideration of the process of developing countries". The award to Lewis particularly mentions his two long-term growth models for developing countries, laying stress upon the consequences of an elastic supply of labour and the determinants of the terms of trade exporting tropical products. In the case of Schultz, the award is for his analysis of the role of investment in human capital for economic development, particularly in agriculture. He made specific reference to the seeming efficiency in the agricultural sector in less developed countries in the context of resource and knowledge constraints in those countries. Lewis analysed the situation in that these countries are characterised by large, stagnant agricultural sector and a dynamic capitalist sector (as almost an economic enclave). Both Lewis and Schultz have not used formalised statistical or econometric techniques.

The award for 2004 was shared by Finn Kydland and Edward Prescott for showing that economic policies are often afflicted with problems of "time consistency." Without prior commitment to a specific policy rule, economic policy makers may find it convenient not to pursue a policy which they initially thought to be the best one. Even when price stability is the desired objective of monetary policy, national economies get caught in high inflation. Kydland and Prescott's research highlighted the need for economic research into the issue of the credibility and feasibility of economic policy. Their work also moved the discussion of economic policy from isolated policy measures to the institutional mechanism of policy making. Another important aspect of their contribution relates to joining together the analysis of short-term economic fluctuations with analysis of long-term economic growth – earlier considered separate fields. They also underlined the role of supply shocks or productivity disturbances in studies of short-term macroeconomic fluctuations in addition to the analysis of economic growth. This insight was integrated by subsequent studies relating to the role of aggregate demand shifts and wage – and price – rigidities while explaining short-term and long-term economic development.

Another prize awardee in macroeconomics was Edmund Phelps (2006). He has provided a number of previous missing pieces to the macroeconomic problem which helped in greater understanding of the relation between short-run and long-run effects of economic policy. Phelps was considered the first economist who challenged successfully the so-called Phillips curve explanation of a stable trade-off between inflation and unemployment. He contended that inflation is affected by the structure and functioning of the labour market.

Phelps demonstrated when changes in the saving rate confer inter-temporal benefits, benefits across all generations. He underlined the key role human capital plays in encouraging economic growth through diffusion of new technology.

Paul Krugman was awarded the 2008 prize for his research in international trade and economic geography. After Second World War, traditional foreign trade theory could not satisfactorily explain the emerged pattern of trade. In 1979 Krugman presented a new model which provided a convincing explanation for the observed foreign trade patterns. He made assumptions of presence of economies of scale in manufacturing industry and also that consumers desire to have product diversity in consumption.

Krugman's award was also for his presentation of a new model of economic geography. He developed a comprehensive theory of location of labour and firms.

The 2010 Nobel Memorial Prize in Economics was awarded jointly to Peter Diamond, Dale Mortensen and Christopher Pissarides for their "analysis of markets with search frictions." The real world markets are quite different from their idealized verison as put forward by classical economists. The real world markets are search and matching markets. From out of the work of the three economists on search and matching theory emerged the Diamond – Mortensen – Pissarides model or DMP model. The DMP model has been found useful to analyse the process of transmission of aggregate shocks to the labour market that would result in fluctuations in unemployment in the economy, job vacancies and employment flows. The theory has been used extensively to study a number of economic issues in consumer theory, inventory theory, financial economics among others.

III. Microeconomic Theory

George Stigler (1982)

James Mirrlees and William Vickrey (1996)

George Akerlof, Michael Spence and Joseph Stiglitz (2001)

Leonid Hurwicz, Roger Myerson and Eric Maskin (2007)

Vernon Smith (2002)

Contributions of researchers in microeconomic theory devoted to decision-making by individual households and firms and allocation of resources among different uses and production sectors received a total of five awards to ten economists.

George Stigler was awarded the prize (in 1982) for his studies of "industrial structures, functioning of markets and causes and effects of public regulation." By analysing how economic regulations are managed by political leaders and public administrators, he showed, for example, that it results in "regulatory capture" – that is, those who are supposed to be regulated dominate the regulators. His contributions to the history of economic analysis is widely recognised and appreciated. Like Friedman, Stigler belonged to positivist tradition, laying particular stress on analytical simplicity and significance of empirical application. He pioneered the field of information economics, bringing information costs specifically into his analysis.

James Mirrlees and William Vickrey shared the prize (in 1996) for their work in information economics with particular focus on consequences of limitations in individuals' information, including information asymmetries among economic agents. Such information asymmetries play an important role in the functioning of markets such as financial markets. Mirrlees did important work on results for taxation of asymmetric information between tax payers and government. Vickrey did valuable work on various types of auctions. His analytical insights have significant impact on developing efficiently – functioning auction of rights to broadcast, airport landing permits, television rights and privatisation of government assets.

A more general theory of asymmetric information was developed by George Akerlof, Michael Spence and Joseph Stiglitz for which they shared the 2001 Prize.

Akerlof studied markets where sellers of products have more information than buyers about product quality. He showed that low quality products may squeeze high-quality products in such markets and that prices of high quality products may suffer as a result. The analysis helps explain, for instance, extremely high borrowing rates in poor countries and the difficulties for broad markets for health care insurance to emerge. Spence and Stiglitz analysed various types of spontaneous adjustment mechanisms in such markets. Spence showed how better informed agents may improve the market outcome by taking costly actions for the purpose of transmitting information to poorly informed agents. Important examples of such 'signalling' are education as a signal of individual in labour markets and dividend payments to signal high profitability of individual firms. Stiglitz however, analyzed the role of 'screening' in markets with asymmetric information. Relevant examples include attempts by insurance companies to partition contracts into risk classes, thus offering different types of contracts among which customers can choose. He has also shown how a number of market phenomena may be explained by the theory of asymmetric information such as unemployment, credit rationing, and share cropping contracts in agricultural sector in some developing countries.

The role of information asymmetries has been further probed by theorists studying alternative allocation mechanisms – Leonid Hurwicz, Roger Myers and Eric Maskin. They shared the 2007 prize.

Hurwicz defined allocation mechanisms as a game in which the participants act as if they send messages to each other, or to a hypothetical "message centre". He also emphasised the importance that an allocation mechanism is "incentive compatible" in the sense that the predicted, or desired, outcome is consistent with all agents' economic incentives to act. Other important roots of the theory of mechanism design are Mirrlees's optimisation analysis and Vickrey's analysis of auction markets, referred to earlier. A number of authors, in particular Myerson and Maskin have generalised and developed the insights of Hurwicz, Mirrlees and Vickrey. Through a calculation algorithm called the "Revelation Principle", they have simplified the analysis of alternative allocation mechanisms. Generally speaking, this mechanism states that the researcher can restrict his attention to a subset of hypothetical mechanisms, denoted "direct mechanisms", that satisfy the condition of incentive compatibility. Myerson has applied the method, for instance, to auction markets and regulation. Since one and the same mechanism in some cases turns out to generate several different equilibria (multiple equilibria) the task remained to develop methods to find an optimum equilibrium. Maskin has developed analytic tools for this purpose, what he calls "implementation theory". He has also classified the importance of monotonocity of the preference ordering among individuals when attempting generation of efficient allocation mechanisms.

Traditionally, economics has been a non-experimental discipline, till the emergence of the work of Vernon Smith who has shared the Prize in 2002 with Daniel Kahneman. To help understand economic behaviour, Smith has developed methods for conducting laboratory experiments in economics. He demonstrated that interaction of sellers and buyers in laboratory experiments often yielded prices that were quite close to market prices predicted by traditional supply-demand theory.

Smith has also developed the theory underlying the auction markets and enriched literature in this regard.

IV. Financial Economics

Harry Markowitz, William Sharpe and Merton Miller (1990)

R. Merton and M.Scholes (1997)

In recent years, financial economics became an important and rapidly growing field. As mentioned earlier, Modigliani and Tobin built vital financial building blocks to macro-economic theory. The real foundations of financial economics were laid in the 1950s and 1960s by Harry Markowitz, Merton Miller and William Sharpe who were jointly awarded the prize in 1990. Markowitz's main contribution was in formulating a micro theory of portfolio management of individual wealth holders. Equilibrium analysis in financial markets was primarily developed by Miller and Sharpe. Miller's main work was in the field of corporate finance (in the beginning, his work was in collaboration with Franco Modigliani). He is credited with underlining the factors that determine share prices in the market and capital costs of firms. Sharpe's pioneering work is in the development of a general theory for the pricing of financial assets in the market.

Subsequently R. Merton and M. Scholes were given the prize (in 1997) for their analysis of price formation of so-called derivative instruments such as options, which are claims on underlying financial instruments including shares and financial assets. (The late F. Black, cooperating with Scholes, was also instrumental for this achievement). These contributions were a necessary condition for the subsequent development of today's huge markets for various types of derivative instruments. These markets have increased the possibility for individual agents to choose appropriate risk levels according to their own preferences, regardless whether they choose low or high exposure to risk.

V. Interdisciplinary Research

James Buchanan (1986)

Gary Becker (1992)

Ronald Coase (1991)

Herbert Simon (1978)

Oliver Williamson and Elinor Ostrom (2009)

Simon Kuznets (1971)

Robert Fogel and Douglass North (1993)

Amartya Sen (1998)

Friedrich Hayek and Gunnar Myrdal (1974)

Daniel Kahneman (2002)

These are economists who have widened the domain of economic analysis to new areas.

J. Buchanan got the prize (1986) for his research on the boundary between economics and political science, or more specifically, "for his development of the contractual and constitutional basis for the theory of economic and political decision-making." This research made him one of the founding fathers of the 'Public Choice' school which analyses the driving forces behind political decisions and tries to endogenise political behaviour in models of national economies. The Public Choice school assumes that politicians are motivated by considerations similar to those explaining the behaviour of other agents, including the striving for personal benefit and a desire for power.

G. Becker had worked on the borderline between economics and sociology, in particular in his research about the family, e.g, he studied the household's role as a combined producer and consumer of goods and services. He had, however, not only analysed the economic behaviour of families – labour supply, consumption, household production and household saving – but also behaviour that has not earlier been considered by economists, such as education, marriage, child birth and divorce. He had both shown how economic considerations influence choice in these areas and analysed "social interaction" between individuals outside the market system, reflected in the prize citation (1992): "for having extended the domain of microeconomic analysis to a wide range of human behaviour and interactions including non-market behaviour." Becker's influence today extends far outside economics, in particular the so-called 'rational choice' school of sociology.

R. Coase (1991 award winner) made important contributions on the borderline between economics, law and organization. In particular, he showed which factors determine the size of firms. He also clarified conditions under which voluntary contracts between private agents can resolve problems with "external effects" of production, important example being pollution. These contributions are reflected in the Prize citation: "for his discovery and clarification of the significance of transaction costs and property rights for the institutional structure and functioning of the economy". Coase's concept of transaction costs has become an important foundation for the theory of contracts and for the whole field of law and economics.

H. Simon's prize citation (1978) refers to his research on "the decision-making process within economic organizations". He challenged some basic building blocks of microeconomic theory, in particular the maximisation principle and the assumption about full ("unbounded") rationality. He argued that the decision-makers are content with a "satisfactory" outcome – satisficing behaviour. This is an important contribution in the field of administrative (management) science.

Oliver Williamson, who shared the 2009 Nobel Prize with Elinor Ostrom has carried further the work of Herbert Simon and Ronald Coase. Accepting Simon's view that human behaviour is boundedly rational and Coase's work on the importance of transaction costs in any study of firm and market organisation, Williamson analysed the issue of economic governance. He has studied the rationale for the existence of markets and hierarchical organizations in, say, resolving conflicts of interest. The resolution of such conflicts crucially depend upon the complexity of transactions and costs of transactions. Williamson is recognised as the founder and chief developer of what has come to be known as 'Transaction Cost Economics'.

Elinor Ostrom who shared the 2009 prize with Williamson, was awarded the prize "for her analysis of economic governance, especially the commons". The contributions of Williamson and Ostrom are complementary. While the former concerns himself with the problem of regulating transactions, Ostrom's focus was on the issue of enforcement of rules. The work of Ostrom, a political scientist, was associated with the new institutional economics. By her work she was responsible for the resurgence of political economy.

S. Kuznets (1971 award winner) made empirical research on the borderline between economics and history; the citation states "for his empirically founded interpretation of economic growth." The award to Kuznets is an example of an award for inductive rather than deductive analysis. His important contributions include the celebrated "Kuznets curve" of the U-shaped relation between GDP and income inequality as well as his findings that the long-run average propensity to consume out of income tends to be constant in time series data whereas it tends to fall in cross-section data. He used very long-term data to identify regularities by characterizing economic growth and the distribution of income in different nations at different times.

The concentration of R. Fogel and D. North (1993) again lie in the boundary between economics and history. The Academy cited them "for having renewed research in economic history by applying economic theory and institutional change." Fogel's main contributions have been to clarify the role of railways for the development of the national economy in the U.S. and the economic role of slavery. By comparing the factual development with a counter-factual benchmark, Fogel has concluded that previous studies of economic-growth in the U.S. had vastly over estimated the importance of railways. He also concluded that slavery was not abolished because of falling profitability of the slave system, but rather because of humanitarian considerations.

North has shed new light on the economic development in Europe and the U.S. before and in connection with the industrial revolution including the roles of sea transport and changes in the pattern of regional specialisation and interregional trade. He has also been a pioneer in analysing the role of institutions (property rights), for economic development as well as the importance of different types of transaction costs. In these fields he developed and applied the ideas of Ronald Coase.

Amartya Sen's (1998) research is on the borderline between economics and philosophy; the citation says: "for his contributions to welfare economics". He scrutinised the philosophical foundations of collective decisions and welfare evaluations, including problems of evaluating the distribution of income and wealth. He has also constructed influential indices to measure income distribution and poverty. Sen has also analysed the determinants and consequences of starvation in a number of less developed countries. These empirical studies of actual famines show that reduced aggregate supplies of food has not always been the most important factor for starvation catastrophes, which, in some cases, have instead been caused by redistribution of income to the disadvantage of the poor.

While the early contributions of Friedrich Hayek and Gunnar Myrdal (award in 1974) in the 1930s related to business cycles and monetary phenomena, their works from early 1940s dealt with the interrelation between economic, social and political processes. Hayek is particularly known for his emphasis on information and incentive content of the price system. He bestowed special attention to individual behaviour, to the institutional framework for economic decisions, especially the political constitution and the legal rules that define contracts and property rights. In addition, he is remembered for his emphasis on the significance of "spontaneous" social order in contrast to planned institutional designs.

Myrdal showed how interaction of economic, political and social forces often generate virtuous circles. He claimed that his methods of analysis of "mutual causation" was a generalisation of Knut Wicksell's "cumulative process in monetary theory." In this context, a reference is to be made to his study of the Negro problem in the United States in his work An American Dilemma which has undoubtedly influenced social science research generally; it was referred to by the U.S. Supreme Court when outlawing segregation. A similar approach was employed by Myrdal in his subsequent work on poverty and economic development in South Asia.

Research in psychology has influenced economic research in recent years which is reflected in the award to Daniel Kahneman (2002) who, in cooperation with Amos Tversky has made significant contribution to decision-making under uncertainty. They developed an alternative theory – Prospect Theory – to the traditional theory of choice under uncertainty. Tversky died in 1996. They have specifically shown how choice of individuals is systematically influenced by their perception of alternatives and by the exact "framing" of these alternatives.

VI. New Methods of Economic Analysis: Econometrics etc.

Jan Tinbergen and Ragnar Frisch (1969)

Trygve Haavelmo (1989)

Leonid Kantorovich and Tjalling Koopmans (1975)

James Heckman and Daniel Mcfadden (2000)

Clive Granger and Robert Engle (2003)

Wassily Leontief (1970)

Richard Stone (1984)

The very first-award in 1969 jointly to Ragnar Frisch and Jan Tinbergen is a case in point. The award to them was for their pioneering work on Econometric Model building. The prize citation says "for having developed and applied dynamic models for the analysis of economic processes." Frisch is credited with developing general methods of dynamic and econometric analysis. Tinbergen had applied them empirically, besides developing rigorous statistical tests to empirically verify alternative business cycle theories. They both developed a formalized theory of the relation between instruments and targets of economic policy – paralleling Meade's analysis of similar issues.

The award to Haavelmo (in 1989) was "for his clarification of the probability theory foundation of econometrics and his analysis of simultaneous economic structures." He showed that complex economic relations, if estimated simultaneously, could lead to avoiding misleading interpretations of partial relations between economic variables.

The 1975 award jointly to Kantorovich and Koopmans was for their methodological contributions in theory. Kantorovich developed the concept of efficient resource use in individual enterprises and for the whole economy. He also showed the theoretical link between resource allocation and the price system. Koopmans, through the development of activity analysis, demonstrated the correspondence between efficiency in production and existence of a system of "accounting prices." Both Kantorovich and Koopmans demonstrated the theoretical possibility of decentralised decision-making in a centrally planned economy being linked to the existence of an efficient price system, including a uniform accounting price of capital for making investment decisions. One can see how this analysis is related to the achievements in general equilibrium theory by Arrow and Debreu. Kantorovich and Koopmans also made vital contributions to the mathematical technique of linear programming.

The breakthrough in econometrics achieved by James Heckman and Daniel Mcfadden, namely development of microeconometrics, was recognised by the award of the prize to them jointly in 2000. Their contributions have importantly facilitated analysis of data relating to large groups of individual agents – households as well as firms.

Heckman had developed methods to obviate biased statistical estimates in situations in which the sample data being analyzed are non-random – the well-known Heckman Correction (the Heckit method). Examples include studies of wage formation and return on education, since individuals who do not work and do not have the type of education that is being studied are outside the sample.

Mcfadden has developed methods for analysing discrete choice by individuals. Prominent examples include choice of profession, occupation, residence and means of transportation.

Conditional logit analysis is a significant contribution by Mcfadden. This method, besides utilising observable facts about individual agents and available alternatives, exploits unobservable differences among individuals and among alternatives. They are represented by random error terms.

The 2003 award jointly to Clive Granger and Robert Engle is in regard to their work (separately and jointly) on analysis of time series data.

Granger had developed and applied new statistical methods based on "cointegration" to differentiate between short-term fluctuations and long-term trends and combine them. This is vital in the case of analysis of "non-stationary" time series. For instance, when temporary disturbances in aggregate production have long-lasting effects; that is, when time series reflect a "stochastic trend." Granger made his contributions partly in association with Engle. Cointegration has now become a central aspect in time series analysis in economics.

Engle is best known for his work involving study of the volatility properties of many time series in economics, for example in financial markets. For this purpose, he applied the concept of ARCH (autoregressive conditional heteroskedasticity). His method is particularly useful in clarifying market developments where turbulent periods marked by large fluctuations are followed by calmer periods, with modest fluctuations.

Wassily Leontief was awarded (1970) the prize for the development of the input-output method or inter-industry analysis. His work highlighted in quantitative form, the interdependencies between different sectors of the economy. The analysis is also found suitable for analysing short-term effects of shocks in one sector on the other sectors of the economy. He not only formulated the method but also applied it to empirical data.

Richard Stone, who received the award for 1984, got it for his "fundamental contributions to the development of systems of national accounts." It is hard to imagine empirical analysis in macroeconomics without comprehensive systems of national accounts. In this regard, a reference has to be made to the earlier work by Ragnar Frisch, Erik Lindahl, Colin Clark and Simon Kuznets. Leontief-style input-output tables also formed a useful component of this type of work.

VII. Game Theory

John Nash, John Harsanyi and Reinhard Selten (1994)

Thomas Schelling and Robert Aumann (2005)

John von Neumann and Oskar Morgenstern pioneered the development of game theory in 1940s. A couple of awards were made to contributors in this area. The award for 1994 was made to John Nash, John Harsanyi and Reinhard Selten "for their pioneering analysis of equilibrium in the theory of non-cooperative games." Nash draws a distinction between cooperative games, in which obligatory agreements can be made, and non-cooperative games, where such agreements are not feasible. He is well known for developing an equilibrium concept for predicting the outcome of non-cooperative games that later came to be known as Nash equilibrium. By providing theoretical foundation for predicting outcomes of games characterised by incomplete information, Harsanyi provided the needed impetus to further development in the field of information economics following the lead of Stigler, Vickrey and Mirrlees.

The concept of Nash equilibrium was refined by Reinhard Selten which was helpful in analysing dynamic strategic interaction among different agents. He applied these refinements in the analyses of markets with a few sellers. Selten's refinements helped in excluding a number of theoretically possible but unstable or irrelevant equilibria.

After a gap of over a decade, the prize for 2005 was awarded in game theory to Robert Aumann and Thomas Schelling, the former for his theoretical work and the later for his work involving important social, political and economic problems. Both of them analysed conflict and cooperation through game-theoretic methods.

Aumann pioneered comprehensive formal analysis of infinitely repeated games, laying stress upon the types of outcomes that can be maintained over time in the context of long-run economic relations. His analysis has many practical applications such as price wars among business firms, and trade wars among nations. Aumann's approach is found useful for understanding the emergence of institutions such as those for wage negotiations and international trade agreements.

Schelling's analysis of strategic commitments has found to be useful in explaining a wide range of phenomena, from competitive strategies of firms to delegation of political decision-making power to administrative agencies. He showed that an agent may strengthen its position in bargaining by openly worsening its own options and that the ability to retaliate can be more useful than the capacity to attack. Schelling also demonstrated how under certain circumstances uncertainty about retaliation strengthens one's position than certainty about retaliation. He is instrumental in making game theory a unifying framework for all social sciences.

VOLUME - II

Section - IV
General Equilibrium Theory

CHAPTER 31

PAUL ANTHONY SAMUELSON

(1915 – 2009)

The Royal Academy of Sciences while announcing its decision to award the Alfred Nobel Memorial Prize in Economic Sciences for 1970 to Professor Paul Anthony Samuelson makes a particular mention of "the scientific work through which he has developed static and dynamic economic theory and actively contributed to raising the level of analysis in economic science." The Committee on Economic Science of the Royal Academy of Sciences notes that, "Professor Samuelson's extensive production, covering nearly all areas of economic theory, is characterised by an outstanding ability to derive important new theorems, and to find new applications for existing ones. By his many contributions, Samuelson has done more than any contemporary economist to raise the level of scientific analysis in economic theory."

31.1 A BRIEF BIOGRAPHICAL NOTE: PAUL SAMUELSON

Paul Anthony Samuelson was born in Gary, Indiana, U.S.A. on May 15, 1915. His parents were Frank Samuelson and Ella(Lipton)Samuelson. He received his B.A. from University of Chicago in 1935 and received M.A. and Ph.D. from Harvard University in 1936 and 1941 respectively. He was appointed Assistant Professor of Economics and Associate Professor of Economics at Massachusetts Institute of Technology (MIT) in 1940 and 1944 respectively. For a year – 1945 – Samuelson worked as Professor of International Economic Relations at Fletcher School of Law and Diplomacy, Tufts University. He returned in 1947 to the Massachusetts Institute of Technology (MIT), Cambridge, U.S.A. as Professor of Economics, where he remained ever since. In 1966 he was appointed as Institute Professor there, the position he held for two decades till 1986, when he became Institute Professor, Emeritus. For a year (1989), he accepted Vermon F. Taylor visiting Distinguished Professorship at Trinity University.

During Second World War, Samuelson served as a consultant for the National Resources Planning Board, the War Production Board and the Office of War Mobilization and Reconstruction. After the war, he worked as a consultant for the US Treasury, the Bureau of the Budget and the Rand Corporation.

He was awarded the David A. Wells Prize for his dissertation in 1941 by Harvard University and the first John Bates Clark Medal by the American Economic Association in 1947, as the living economist under forty "who has made the most distinguished contribution to the main body of economic thought and knowledge."

Samuelson received a number of fellowships including Guggenheim Fellowship (1948-1949), Ford Faculty Research Fellowship (1958-1959) and Reflective Year Fellowship from Carnegie Foundation (1965-1966). He was a fellow of British Academy, The American Philosophical Society, a member of the National Academy of Sciences (U.S.A.), The American Academy of Arts and Sciences, The American Economic Association (President 1961), Econometric Society (President 1951), and International Economic Association (President 1966-1968, honorary President 1968-till death). Samuelson received honorary degrees from a number of Universities including University of Chicago, East Anglia University and University of Michigan.

He wrote in a 1986 collection "Lives of the Laureates": "one honour leads to another. After the first dozen honorary degrees, all it takes is longevity to double the number."

The Royal Swedish Academy citation refers to his best-known work – Foundations of Economic Analysis, 1947 (a printed version of his Ph.D. dissertation from 1941) – and states that in this work as also in a large number of articles he had rewritten large parts of main economic theory. He had put forward significant results in several areas, which now rank among theorems of economics. Specific reference is made to Samuelson's "Correspondence Principle" which attempts at integrating statics and dynamics, to his model of economic fluctuations by combining the mechanism of multiplier and accelerator, and to his "theory of revealed preferences" which has reformed the foundations of consumption theory. In the theory of international trade, he has developed and improved important theorems such as the factor price equalization theorem. Reference is also made to Samuelson's development of the theory of inter- temporal efficiency and his formulation of what has come to be known as "turnpike theorem" – a growth path with a maximal rate of growth and to his clarification of the role of collective goods or public goods in the theory of optimum resource allocation.

Samuelson's pursuing economics was the result of an "accidental blind chance." He states that all his life he was at the right place at the right time. For undergraduate studies, Samuelson joined University of Chicago, which was at that period the top centre for "old fashioned neo classical microeconomic study." Samuelson admits that he, however, did not know that. His reason for entering University of Chicago was its closeness to his school and home. For the pursuit of graduate studies, he had to choose between Harvard and Columbia Graduate School. He was advised by his teachers at Chicago--Frank Knight, Jacob Viner, Henry Simons and Paul Douglas-- "without exception" to choose Columbia. According to Samuelson, "Never one to blindly accept adult advice, I picked Harvard, I picked it by miscalculation, expecting that it would be a little oasis on rolling green hills." However, it turned out to be a wise choice. Samuelson observed: "Thanks to the evils of Adolf Hitler, my 1935-40 sojourn at Harvard coincided with its economics renaissance under Joseph Schumpeter, Wassily Leontief, Gottfried Haberler, and the 'American Keynes,' Alvin Hansen...contemporary Harvard graduate students came to match in brilliance with the new Harvard faculty. Richard Musgrave, Wolfgang Stolper, Abram Bergson, Joe Bain, Lloyd Metzler, Richard Goodwin, Robert Triffin, James Tobin, Robert Solow,...-all of them my pals – became the 1950—2000 era stars in world frontier economics. Harvard made us, yes." His remark regarding the contribution of the universities such as Harvard to the victory in Second World War is worth recalling: "The Duke of Wellington said 'The battle of Waterloo' was won on the playing fields of Eton: I can say, 'World War II was won in the seminar rooms of Cambridge, Princeton and Los Alamos.'"

In an autobiographical essay presented by Samuelson at Trinity University in San Antonio, he asserted that 1932 was a great time to be born as an economist. He remarked: "The sleeping beauty of political economy was waiting for the enlivening kiss of new methods, new paradigms, new hired hands, and new problems." The year was the bottom point of the Great Depression and "from the rotten soil was belatedly begot the new subject that today we call macroeconomics." Samuelson acknowledged how outside influences during the period commencing with 1932 was favourable to the professional economist "in that it was an epoch of tremendous university expansion and job opportunity...my generation of economic activity was buoyed along by the great wave of a Kondratieff expansion."

31.2 A SUMMARY OF PAUL SAMUELSON'S CONTRIBUTIONS

By his own admission, Samuelson is primarily a theorist. Early in life, he discerned that mathematics was to revolutionise modern economics; he, therefore, proceeded to learn mathematics. At the same time his 'first and last allegiance' is to the facts. Assar Lindbeck, one of the members of the Committee on Economic Science of the Royal Academy of Sciences, identifies two distinct branches in the development of economic theory in the second half of the last century. The first one was econometrics, designed for immediate statistical application--pioneers in this development were Frisch and Tinbergen (their contributions have been covered in chapters 20 and 21) along with others-- while the second branch is 'pure' theory, which is directed more towards basic theoretical research, with no intentions of immediate statistical testing or estimation. Samuelson and Hicks can be considered to belong to the latter branch. They are primarily responsible for the development of the branch and wielded enormous influence on it. "Even if Samuelson himself has hardly made any contributions to empirical research, he has usually tried to find operational concepts and to derive non-trivial, 'meaningful' theorems, which have served as a basis for empirical testing and estimation by others."

Samuelson's writings cover a very large number of areas in economics-- almost the entire subject. His published articles were collected into five volumes some years ago. He continued publishing papers even after that. In fact, Samuelson's research spanned more than seven decades; he continued publishing into his 90s. Even while a graduate student at Harvard, he had won international renown and had made important theoretical contributions. Besides, one has to mention the books authored by him or jointly with others. His first major work, indeed considered by most economists as his magnum opus was Foundations of Economic Analysis published in 1947, won the David A Wells Prize at Harvard. The Foundations helped him receive the first John Bates Clark Medal of the American Economic Association awarded for scholarly promise before the age of forty. At that time Economics was characterised as "the laborious literary working over of essentially simple mathematical concepts such as is characteristic of much modern economic theory is not only unrewarding from the standpoint of advancing the science, but involves as well mental gymnastics of a particularly depraved type." What had then been a largely verbal discipline, Samuelson declared "an Augean stable full of inherited contradictions, overlaps, and fallacies." Samuelson insisted that mathematics was essential to proper understanding of economics. His 1958 work Linear Programming and Economic Analysis written in collaboration with Robert Dorfman and Robert Solow and sponsored by a grant from the Rand Corporation is a good text on the subject of linear programming. His Economics: An Introductory Analysis, first published in 1948, has become the best selling text book of all time on the subject. It is translated into a number of languages (about forty, including Arabic, Korean, Polish and Portuguese)and is reported to have sold more than 4 million copies. New editions continue to appear--the book is on its 19th edition in English. Since the 12th edition in 1985, Samuelson had a co-author, William D. Nordhaus. On many college campuses in America, "studying economics was just synonymous with studying Samuelson's textbook."

George Stigler, referring to Samuelson's 1947 Foundations and his newly published (in 1948) best selling textbook Economics introduced him with the words, "Samuelson, having achieved fame, now seeks fortune." J. K. Galbraith accurately prophesied in a Fortune review, that a new generation would receive its economics from a beginning text-Economics: An Introductory Analysis. Samuelson had this to say about the textbook Economics: An Introductory Analysis: "Writing book is hard work. But its rewards have been tremendous and I do not mean simply pecuniary rewards. Contact with hundreds of thousands of minds of a whole generation is an experience like no other that a scholar will ever meet."

It is clearly not possible to even briefly summarise the most important original contributions of Samuelson in a single essay with reasonable self-imposed space constraints. However, as most critics agree one can say with no fear of contradiction that Samuelson had contributed "to great order, logic and analytical sophistication in a large number of different fields in economic theory... his demonstration of the unity of methodology and theoretical structure in various fields... [as] diverse as production economics, consumer behaviour, international trade, public finance and macro analysis. In most of these fields maximization (minimization) under constraints and the exploitation of second-order conditions for reaching unambiguous conclusions, were shown fundamentally to play the same analytical role.... [He] has also helped us understand the relation between endogenous variables, parameters and constants and the methodology and meaning of analytical techniques such as comparative statics, dynamics, partial equilibrium and general equilibrium theory etc."

Despite his voluminous work, we are tempted to identify the significantly most important and original contributions for a little detailed discussion here. They are:

1. Theory of Consumer Behaviour, Index Theory and Welfare Economics;
2. Public Goods;
3. Dynamic Economic Theory and Stability Analysis;
4. General Equilibrium Theory and its Various Applications;
5. Theory of Capital and Interest and Inter- temporal Efficiency and issues relating to Optimality;
6. Macroeconomics, and
7. Theory of Finance.

31.2.1 THEORY OF CONSUMER BEHAVIOUR, INDEX THEORY AND WELFARE ECONOMICS

Samuelson, through his revealed preference analysis sought to reconstruct the theory of consumer behaviour. If the consumer's tastes do not change, observation of his behaviour in the market furnishes all the required data. The one vital assumption underlying the revealed preference theory is that of transitivity. If a consumer buys some collection of goods A, rather than the available collections B, C, etc., and that none of the latter i.e. B, C etc. is more expensive than A, it is said that collection A has been revealed preferred to the others, namely B, C etc. According to Samuelson, the 'Fundamental Theorem of Consumption Theory' states that the demand for a commodity always moves in the same direction as that of a change of the consumer's income. Positively sloped income curves invariably imply negatively sloped demand curves. A brief exposition of revealed preference theory may be in order here.

Let us assume that there are 'n' commodities in the market. Further, assume that a particular set of prices, p_{01}, p_{02}, ..., p_{0n} denoted by P_0 prevails in the market. At that set of prices, a consumer purchases a quantity basket denoted by Q_0. Then, the consumer's aggregate expenditure equals P_0Q_0 obtained as the sum of his total expenditure on the commodities; that is

$$\sum_{i=1}^{n} p_{0i}q_{0i}$$

That results in

$$P_0Q_0$$

Assume another batch of commodities Q_1 that is available in the market which the consumer could have purchased but did not. The total cost of Q_1 at the price set P_0 must be no greater than the total cost of purchase of Q_0. That is,

$$P_0Q_1 \leq P_0Q_0$$

We can state that the commodity combination Q_0 is revealed to be preferred to Q_1 as the consumer has declined to choose the basket Q_1 though Q_0 is at least as expensive a commodity basket as Q_1.

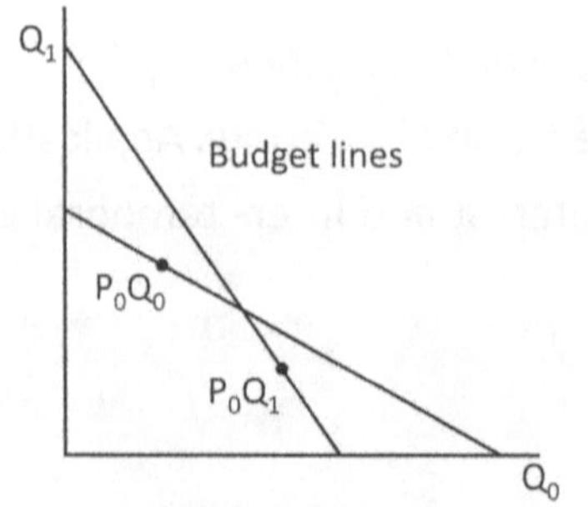

Fig. 31.1 Weak Axiom of Revealed Preference

Samuelson's weak axiom of revealed preference asserts that if a commodity combination Q_0 is revealed to be preferred to Q_1, then Q_1 must never be revealed preferred to Q_0. The meaning of this axiom becomes clear by the accompanying diagram (Fig. 31. 1), which illustrates a two-commodity case. When the prices were given by P_0, the consumer purchased commodity basket Q_0. When prices were, however, given by P_1, he purchased commodity combination Q_1. He could have purchased Q_1 at the P_0 prices because Q_1 lies below the line P_0. Given this choice of the consumer, the weak axiom of the revealed preference theory asserts that Q_0 could not have been obtained when he purchased Q_1 – that is, Q_0 must lie above the price line P_1.

Strong Axiom of Revealed Preference: If Q_0 is revealed to be preferred to Q_1, which is revealed to be preferred to Q_2, which is revealed to be preferred to Q_s, Q_s must never revealed to be preferred to Q_0. The strong axiom guarantees the transitivity of revealed preferences of the consumer.

From the revealed preference theory put forward by Samuelson, a number of familiar theorems can be proved, such as, that the substitution effect is negative, the demand functions of zero degree in prices and incomes are homogeneous and the cross-substitution effects are equal. Lindbeck is of the view that "even if economists such as Frisch and Haberler had already demonstrated the connection between utility theory and index theory, it is probably fair to say that the theory of revealed preferences gave us a new, powerful and empirically fruitful formulation of the issue, by inferring preferences directly from observable behavior." Kenneth Arrow in his review of Samuelson's Collected Works in the Journal of Political Economy (1967) suggests that the Revealed Preference theory provides a useful bridge between neoclassical utility theory and Gustav Cassel's behaviouristic formulation of price theory, thereby linking the market behaviour of the consumer to the principle of utility maximisation.

Welfare economics is concerned with evaluating the social desirability of alternative economic states. Each economic state is marked by a different resource allocation and different distribution of rewards for economic activity. As such, welfare economics deals itself mostly with economic policy issues, which arise out of the society's allocation of resources, namely distribution of inputs in the production of various commodities and the distribution of commodities among various consumers. The welfare of a society is dependent upon the satisfaction level of all its consumers. However, the alternatives that have to be judged will have some favourable impact on some consumers and unfavourable effects on others. It would be simple to make welfare comparisons if only we can get a single aggregate utility function by aggregating utilities of individuals in a society. This cannot be done because it is not possible to make interpersonal comparisons of utility.

The status of welfare economics in 1938 when Bergson's 1938 Quarterly Journal of Economics article putting forward for the first time the idea of social welfare function was written (while he and Samuelson were graduate students they had extensive discussion on it) as outlined by Arrow was: economic policy followed by a state was not generally defended by an appeal to fundamental principles; however, if it was defended it was based on utilitarian principle and the Pareto principle – the latter is not useful for discussing issues concerning income distribution as it ignores the question of income distribution.

Chapter VIII of Samuelson's Foundations of Economic Analysis deals with the concept of social welfare function. He asserted that the social welfare is drawn up for a given society, the members of which have given preferences. In Arrow's opinion "[Bergson – Samuelson formulation of social welfare function] brought us to a confrontation and in certain aspects a reconciliation of two themes in economic thinking about individual economic behaviour and the choice of policies: the utilitarian tradition of normative analysis and the much more recent parsimonious description of economic behaviour usually referred to as Ordinalism." He further comments: "His [Samuelson's] accomplishments both close chapters and open new vistas." Samuelson in his Nobel lecture "Maximum Principles in Analytical Economics" stated: "...One of my abiding concerns over the years has been the field of Welfare Economics. Along with my close friend, Abram Bergson of Harvard, I have tried to understand what it is that Adam Smith's 'invisible hand' is supposed to be maximizing."

31.2.2 PUBLIC GOODS

Paul Samuelson's development of the modern theory of Public Goods is considered a major breakthrough in the theory of public finance.

In two short papers, one in 1954 and the other in 1955 ("The Pure Theory of Public Expenditure" and "Diagrammatic Exposition of a Pure Theory of Public Expenditure"), Samuelson had raised and partly given solution to the main problems in the normative theory of public expenditure. As is well known, one case of market failure is that of the presence of public goods. A public good is defined as any good that is both joint-in-consumption (or nontrivial-in-consumption) and not excludable. To be categorised as a public good, a good must possess both these characteristics.

Samuelson raised the following questions:

How do we define those goods, which are consumed collectively and for which there is no clear and meaningful distinction between individual and total consumption?

How does one characterise an optimal resources allocation to the production of such goods?

How can one design an efficient and equitable tax system that will finance the expenditures of the public sector?

A good is 'joint in consumption' if the consumption of the good by one individual does not lower the amount of the good available to others. Further, the marginal cost of providing the good to one additional user is exactly zero. For example: a radio broadcast. However, in case of an impure public good, it is a public good in some situations but not in others. A good is considered non-excludable if it is impossible or prohibitively costly to exclude from consumption those who are not willing to pay the price for the good. If there is a potential for 'free riding' by the users of the good, it clearly shows that it is a source of potential market failure in the case of a public good.

Samuelson formulated a model that suggested an integrated solution to the above three questions.

Samuelson's solution does not assume that the benefits derived from the supply of the public good are not equal to all, even though availabilities are the same. This formulation does not also assume that the benefits from the public goods are independent of quantities consumed of the private goods.

The condition (referred to as 'Samuelsonian condition') for efficient provision of a public good is the sum of the marginal rates of substitution across all individuals must be equal to the marginal cost of production of the good.

31.2.3 DYNAMIC ECONOMIC THEORY AND STABILITY ANALYSIS

The development of dynamic economic theory and stability analysis has taken place particularly in 1920's and 1930's with significant contributions coming from, among others, Frisch, Tinbergen, Hicks and noted Polish economist, Kalecki. Samuelson's Foundations has richly contributed to the field, specifically to short-run dynamics and stability analysis. We have to mention the link Samuelson provided between comparative statics and dynamics and the development of the analysis of dynamic stability of an economy. His emphasis on the need to specify the behaviour of an economy when it is outside the equilibrium, particularly whether prices in the market respond to excess demand as was argued by Walras or the response is in quantity of output produced in the face of the discrepancy between demand price and supply price as contended by Marshall is especially noteworthy. Samuelson had thrown his weight behind Walrasian approach (namely that prices in the market change in response to excess demand for a commodity and, specifically, the rate of change in price is an increasing function of excess demand) has become part of the received economic theory.

Samuelson's stability analysis led to his development of the well-known "correspondence principle." In his Foundations, he asserted that the stability of equilibrium is linked to comparative static theorems. It was shown that in the absence of specific formulation of the behaviour of the model in a disequilibrium situation, it is not possible to determine its comparative static effects. That is, how the presence of excess demand in the market affects the prices and changes in market price impacts the excess demand for the commodity. Samuelson had demonstrated how sufficient condition for local stability in a Walrasian system is, by and large, the same as the conditions for an autonomous change in excess demand to have a clear effect on equilibrium quantity and price. Samuelson's contribution in this direction is considered "an application of analogy between economic processes and dynamic systems in classical mechanics."

Another notable contribution of Samuelson is the extension of the dynamic analysis and stability at micro level (i.e. individual commodity markets) to the macro models, such as stability analysis of simple Keynesian macroeconomic models. A celebrated example that comes to one's mind is the development by Samuelson of the interaction between the multiplier and the accelerator. Alvin Hansen's verbal exposition of the interaction between multiplier and accelerator in terms of impact of change in investment leading to change in national income which, in turn, impacts aggregate investment in an economy was formulated by Samuelson in a logical way. The significance of Samuelson's contribution can be gauged by the observation of Lindbeck that "...such multiplier accelerator mechanism – (further developed by ...Hicks and Kalecki)- now-a-days constitute the theoretical backbone of most mathematical and econometric macro-economic models of short-run fluctuations."

31.2.4 GENERAL EQUILIBRIUM THEORY

The effort at simplifying the Walrasian general equilibrium theory is considered one of the useful contributions of Samuelson in general equilibrium theory in contradistinction to partial equilibrium theory. Samuelson had in his work very often used models encompassing the whole economy in growth theory and theory of capital, international trade and macroeconomics. This has the desirable effect of facilitating analysis of concrete problems for arriving at operationally meaningful solutions, instead of the traditional approach of counting equations and unknowns to determine whether or not a solution exists. Samuelson's effort in this direction was indicated by his statement in the introductory chapter in the Foundations: "We [economic theorists] are like highly trained athletes, who never run a race." To this assertion may be added his statement elsewhere, discussing his methodology: "I am primarily a theorist. But my first allegiance is to the facts.... The facts don't tell their own story. You can't enunciate all the facts."

While one has to acknowledge Hicks's contribution to general equilibrium theory in his Value and Capital, which is similar to Samuelson's contribution, one basic difference between the two has to be noted. Hicks used a rather highly aggregated general equilibrium model in his effort to converting Keynesian macroeconomics consisting of four markets, namely commodities market, labour market, money market and bond market, into general equilibrium theory. It was essentially developed to analyse the macroeconomic problems that are particularly useful for designing and implementing an appropriate stabilisation policy. On the other hand, Samuelson's effort was to 'concretize' the Walrasian system with the purpose of dealing with resource allocation problems.

Another example where Samuelson's efforts to concretize the Walrasian general equilibrium system yielded useful results is in the determination of relative commodity prices in simple models which employ one or two productive factors. Leontief's model of input-output analysis essentially deals with production and takes into account the interdependence of production and activities of production units in an economy. Theory of demand plays almost no role in the open model of input-output analysis. The assumption of input-output analysis that the production is characterised by fixed technological coefficients – that is, to produce one unit of output, it takes, say, x hours of labour and y units of raw materials of a particular type - is crucial. The firm has no choice here;there is no other input proportion that the firm can choose, such as labour-saving devices. Samuelson, in his article in Koopmans's edited Activity Analysis of Production and Allocation, had demonstrated that in some situations this assumption is not as restrictive as it appears. Even where it is possible for the firm to vary the input proportions, it will never be advantageous for the firm to alter the input proportions when there exists only one scarce input, constant returns to scale and no joint products. That is, according to Samuelson, the fixed input proportions are dictated by reasons of productive efficiency rather than unchanging technological requirements. According to Samuelson, in a closed one-factor model (labour being the lone factor of production) characterised by constant returns to scale and with no possibility of joint production, the conditions on the production side alone determine the long-run relative commodity prices. In such a stationary equilibrium, demand side does not play any role. However, in a two-factor case (the two factors being, say, labour and capital) the demand side comes into its own, through its effect on interest rate. That is, in conditions of stationary equilibrium, for each level of interest rate, there is a unique set of relative commodity prices – the well-known non-substitution theorems of Samuelson.

The field of international economics has greatly benefited from Samuelson's work in general equilibrium theory. R. W. Jones describes the significant impact of Samuelson on international trade theory in Paul Samuelson and Modern Economic Theory. Specific mention may be made of Samuelson's celebrated factor price equalization theorem (conditions under which international trade in commodities leads to complete equalisation of factor rewards between the countries participating in trade) which influenced the pioneering works of Heckscher and Ohlin and Samuelson's joint article with Stolper "Protection and Real Wages" analysing the effects of tariff on the income distribution in a country. It has shown that an imposition of tariff on a commodity results in an increase in its price as also an increase in the real reward for a factor which is relatively intensively used in the production of the commodity but a fall in real reward for other factor inputs. Another contribution of Samuelson in this area was his 1939 article 'The Gains from International Trade', which demonstrated as to how free trade under certain conditions is 'better' than no trade as well as restricted trade. The analysis in the article used the familiar "Compensation Criteria" in that it pays those who desire 'more' free trade to 'bribe' those who do not want it as they would lose in conditions of free trade.

Stanley Fischer while evaluating Samuelson's contributions to trade theory observes: "the contributions are basic, the models are tractable and fecund, the problems come from the real world as well as the literature, the articles continue to reward the reader. And they continue to be read."

31.2.5 CAPITAL THEORY AND INTERTEMPORAL EFFICIENCY

The theory of capital is perhaps the most controversial field, more controversial than most other parts of economic theory. This can be seen from the "continuing polemics between Cambridge, England (Joan Robinson, Sraffa, Pasinetti among others) and Cambridge Mass, U.S.A. (Samuelson, Solow and others). Samuelson had made significant contributions to capital theory- starting with the 1943 Schumpeter Festschrift paper, 'Dynamics, Statics and Stationary State' – sometimes alone and sometimes in joint authorship with Robert Solow, another Nobel Laureate from MIT. In the 1943 contribution, discussing the properties of a steady state, Samuelson showed the possibility of the existence of a steady state with a zero real interest rate provided that the rate of time preference of 'infinitely lived' individuals is zero – a situation in which the marginal product of capital can be driven to zero.

It is interesting to note that two of Samuelson's first three published papers relate to the theory of capital and interest. Lindbeck divides Samuelson's most important contributions to capital theory into two categories: (1) the concept of capital within the theory of allocation and growth; (2) the theory of efficiency and optimality in growth. In his 1956 article (together with Solow) and in his 1962 article which developed the surrogate production function, Samuelson had shown that though there is no satisfactory way of defining an aggregate capital stock, it is still possible to talk about a well-defined price of capital. He used here the concept of factor price frontier, which has the same properties as in the one-sector growth model with the slope of the frontier equal to the capital-labour ratio. The implication is to demonstrate the feasibility of developing a capital theory that yields results for factor income distribution without depending upon the concept of aggregate capital. He had demonstrated in a later article that the problem of substitution between the two factors, namely, capital and labour may be formulated as a 'dual' problem in terms of real return on each of the factors. In this context, Fischer's observations on the re-switching controversy need to be quoted fully: "Under more general conditions, the famous result may occur in which a given technique of production that has been used at a low interest rate comes back into use again at a higher interest rate.... Re-switching implies that the one-sector neo-classical production function cannot be viewed as a general 'as if' construct that describes the behaviour of economies with several techniques of production. Cambridge (England) critics of neo-classical capital theory viewed re-switching as a confirmation of the view that marginal productivity had nothing to do with distribution, since the same techniques of production might be used with two (or more) different distributions of income."

One of Samuelson's important contributions in this area relates to the derivation of a variety of turnpike theorems. The fully worked out turnpike theorem (in his 1958 book with R. Dorfman and R.M. Solow, Linear Programming and Economic Analysis) emphasised the importance of the initial position – what is called 'initial assets' – and analysed the movement of the economy to and from the maximal growth path. Samuelson also showed that for a distant time horizon (independent of the initial position and with specified terminal conditions), the efficient path lies close to the von Neumann ray. Lindbeck comments: "This seems to have been the basis of the celebrated Turnpike theory, which in a very general formulation says that it is always possible to conceive of such a distant time horizon that it pays to follow a growth path with a maximum rate of growth – the Turnpike – even if neither the point where we start nor the point to which we go is located on this growth path."

In mid-sixties, many economists, of whom Samuelson was a prominent one, studied 'Turnpike properties' of different consumption profiles over time, thus linking Turnpike theory to the golden rule of growth. By taking into account more than one capital good in the economy, Samuelson along with Robert Solow generalised Ramsey's theory of optimal saving.

Solow has this to say in regard to Samuelson's work on the theory of capital: "[It] shares the characteristics of his work elsewhere in economics: energy, ingenuity, the distinct air... of having been written by a person and not a computing machine, a belief that economics is an important and beautiful subject, an acquaintance with everything that has ever been written on it...."

31.2.6 MACROECONOMICS

Samuelson's work on multiplier-accelerator model in which he underscored the empirical importance of the accelerator and which he described as algebraic generalisation of Alvin Hansen's numerical example is referred to in an earlier section (Dynamic Theory and Stability Analysis). James Tobin described the neo-classical synthesis as the greatest contribution of Samuelson to macroeconomics. Samuelson considered aggregate demand as the key determinant of output in an economy as evidenced by the famous 45-degree diagram popularised in his Economics textbook. In his 'Theory of Pump-priming Re-examined', Samuelson categorically stated that "...the basic features of the private economy forming the environment within which governmental action must take place...--- (1) The economic system is not perfect and frictionless so that there exists the possibility of unemployment and underutilization of productive resources...."

Samuelson presented his neo-classical synthesis in a number of articles he wrote in early fifties and also in his Economics text book. The essence of the synthesis is the possibility of keeping the economy close to full employment by monetary and fiscal policies and a judicious mix of monetary – fiscal policies to determine the rate of investment. In Fischer's view the neo-classical synthesis of Samuelson "represents the views of mainstream macroeconomics in the Fifties and Sixties and perhaps in the Seventies and even the Eighties. Its activist spirit was evident in the Kennedy administration. Its acceptance must have been helped by the wide-spread use of Samuelson's Economics...."

Samuelson-Solow's 1960 article "Analytic Aspects of Anti-Inflation Policy" which presented Phillips curve for the United States is widely interpreted as society's long-run trade off between inflation and unemployment. A careful reading of the article does not lend support to this interpretation. The authors categorically stated that the discussion pertains to short-term and that it is erroneous to believe that the Phillips curve "will maintain its same shape in the longer run."

Another notable contribution of Samuelson is the Consumptions Loan Model, 'An Exact Consumption Loan Model of Interest with or without Social Contrivance of Money' (1958) which could have been discussed in the section on capital theory. However, it is considered appropriate to discuss here as it is concerned with the analysis of inter-temporal allocation and optimisation of consumption in an economy where old people are supported by inter-generational borrowing. Assuming that people live for two periods, with utility functions defined over consumption in the two periods and assuming further that inter-temporal transactions with nature are not possible as production of commodities cannot be saved or redistributed over time, inter-temporal reallocation of consumption can occur only by lending and borrowing consumption. The current young will give part of their endowment to the current old in return for the endowment to be received next period from the then young. Double coincidence of wants and bilateral trade possibilities are assumed away. The apparent point of the model is that trade becomes possible with the introduction of money, thus bringing about a Pareto – improving change, given the initial endowment pattern. The strength of the "Consumption Loans Model lies in the elegance and robustness with which it captures the essential point that finitely lived individuals exist in an infinitely lived economy (we are each but not all dead in the long run)." Samuelson had also shown through this model how in the context of an infinite time horizon, limitations in efficiency may occur in a model of perfect competition.

31.2.7 THEORY OF FINANCE

Samuelson's contributions to the theory of finance appeared as he turned fifty. In financial economics of Samuelson, rational man 'reigns supreme.' In Paul Samuelson and Modern Economic Theory, Merton in the article titled 'Financial Economics' evaluates six of Samuelson's papers in the field of finance starting with his 1952 paper on "Expected Utility and the Independence Axiom." Two Samuelson's papers 'Proof that Properly Anticipated Prices Fluctuate Randomly' and 'Rational Theory of Warrant Pricing' are generally considered to be of significant importance. The objective of the first paper is to explore the consequences of market efficiency for speculative prices. He was profoundly influenced by Bachelier's idea of the random character of price movements in financial markets; that is, security prices are as likely to go up as they are to go down and that, with the passage of time, the range of their fluctuations would expand according to the square root of time. Samuelson characterised such views of random movements as ridiculous... absurdities because security prices cannot fall below zero (zero down-side limit). According to Samuelson there can be no symmetry of expectations in the participants of security markets when the upside is infinity and the downside is zero. He was of the view that the non- predictability of future security prices from past and present prices "is the sign, not of failure of economic law, but the triumph of economic law after the competition has done its best." Samuelson could see that stock prices presented "...as an unexplored variation on a theme that runs throughout economic theory – the difference between price and value." Market prices gyrate around 'true value.' The reason stock prices fluctuate so much and the reason shares or stocks are considered a risky investment is that there is nothing clear about their value.

Samuelson attempted an answer by introducing the expression 'shadow prices' to characterise the so-called 'true values' or what Keynes in his General Theory had termed as 'prospective yield.' Samuelson's shadow prices are, of course, theoretical prices – "prices never seen on land or sea outside of economics libraries; however, we must assume that they exist – there is such a thing as intrinsic value."

In Samuelson's view the best estimates of shadow prices are the prices set in the market place, every minute of every trading day. "We would expect people in the market place, in pursuit of avid and intelligent self-interest, to take account of those elements of future events that in a probability sense may be discerned to be casting their shadows before them. (Because past events cast 'their' shadows after them, future events can be said to cast their shadows before them)." The prices thus set in the marketplace may not be precisely equal to the shadow prices but no other estimate of intrinsic value is likely to be more accurate than what buyers and sellers agree on in the marketplace.

Samuelson, like many other writers in economics and finance, emphasised the importance of information. Investors in stocks, buyers of commodities for future delivery, and lenders and borrowers of funds need information for arriving at decisions. As Jack Treynor has observed, that you may not get rich by using all the available information, but you surely will get poor if you don't. While new information brings about a change in prices in the market, it arrives with no predictable pattern. As such, properly anticipated prices fluctuate randomly. In Samuelson's opinion, an investor who is investing in an asset under these conditions can expect to earn a return of zero or "no easy pickings, no sure thing gains." This is, of course, something of an oversimplification. When Samuelson, echoing Louis Bachelier, stipulated that the expected return will be zero, he meant that the excess return over the minimum return is likely to be zero; it is zero, on the average and in the long run. Furthermore, it is the allocation of the excess return that is likely to be random. Bernstein observes: "The unpredictability of speculative prices is proof that they are predictions of themselves." Samuelson remarked: "This theorem is so general, that I must confess to having oscillated over the years between regarding it as trivially obvious (and almost trivially vacuous) and regarding it as remarkably sweeping. Such perhaps is characteristic of basic results."

Many serious students of financial markets have been taking lively interest in the evidence of violations of Samuelson's proposition that speculative prices will fluctuate randomly but will best reflect intrinsic values. Fischer Black's presidential address to the American Finance Association in 1986 titled 'Noise' demonstrates how far real world markets, even competitive markets, fall short of Samuelson's conditions. He contrasts information with noise. The latter arises as market participants buy and sell on what they believe is information but is really rumour; badly analysed information, misinformation or even hunch. Black points out "Noise is what makes our observations imperfect." Many people trade on noise believing that they are trading on reliable information. This state of affairs has two major consequences. Noise stands in the way of rational decision-making, which is bad. Black opines: "Because there is so much noise in the world, people adopt rules of thumb. They share their rules of thumb with each other.... In the end, a theory is accepted not because it is confirmed by conventional empirical tests, but because researchers persuade one another that the theory is correct and relevant." At the same time, we have to observe that noise trading is the primary motivation for market activity. Noise trading imparts liquidity and liveliness to markets.

The second important paper is 'Rational Theory of Warrant Pricing.' Warrants are similar to options contracts, which give the owner to buy a pre-specified number of shares at an agreed price during a specified time period. As with options, there is no obligation on the part of the owner of the warrant to exercise the right. However, while investors create options and sell them to one another, warrants are issued by corporations for sale to investors. Additionally, options run for a short time period before they expire; warrants typically run for a much longer time. Samuelson, who was familiar with Bachelier's 1900 work on continuous time stochastic calculus calculation of rational option prices, supervised Richard Kruizenga's 1956 Ph.D. dissertation on the very same subject. Samuelson's paper almost succeeded in solving the valuation problem but as Merton remarks, it is a "near miss." Samuelson was aware that "the results of the paper were not obvious...(he)was not sure how they would come out until the work was done." Specifically, Samuelson formulated a partial differential equation for the option price, which depends, inter alia, on the expected return on the stock and the required rate of return on the option. Later, Black-Scholes solution, however, shows that the rational price of the warrant depends on risk-free rate of return and not on the expected return on the share.

Samuelson's contributions to the field of finance included papers on diversification and the conditions under which Markowitz's mean-variance analysis can be justified.

31.3 CONCLUDING OBSERVATIONS

The review of Samuelson's work attempted here does not claim to be even a cursory summary of a good fraction of his total output. It is just a 'miniaturized' Samuelson Sampler. His contributions touch almost every major field of economics. As Robert C. Merton states "His theoretical contributions have been ecumenical and his ramified influence on the whole of economics has led economists in just about every branch of economics to claim him as one of their own." A survey of Samuelson's main research areas also becomes a survey of many of the great economic problems of our time. In this context, we may refer to an unconfirmed anecdote which has it that at the end of Samuelson's dissertation defence Schumpeter turned to Leontief (the co-examiner) and asked, "well, Wassily, Have we passed?"

Samuelson was a prolific writer. By the time he was 25, he was already famous for publishing more articles than he was years old: Bernstein writing in 1992 reports that Samuelson's Collected Scientific Papers which include his work from 1937 to 1986 runs into five volumes. They include 388 articles filling 4,665 pages – and a sixth volume is on its way. Paul Samuelson and Modern Economic Theory, a celebration of his contribution to economic theory written by his contemporaries, extols his accomplishments in ten fields of economics: welfare, consumption, international trade, money, capital theory, policy, Ricardo, Marx and finance. In an autobiographical note, Samuelson observed: "In this age of specialization, I sometimes think of myself as the last 'generalist' in economics." Though he classified himself as a theorist, he had been busy in the work-a-day world also. In his own words, he had given "economic tutorials" to the likes of Adlai Stevenson, Averill Harriman and, especially, John F. Kennedy. His column in Newsweek for over 15 years from 1966 to 1981 was very informative, educative and was well received.

Fischer refers to the extraordinary success of Samuelson's Economics and remarks that it "is something of a mystery, for the book is not easy.... Depending on what students retain from their economics courses, Economics may have done much to raise the level of public discourse about economic policy."

While discussing the factors that led to his great achievements in the field of economics, Samuelson observed: "Perhaps more important than casual role of luck was the salutary fact that economics was just right for me. This field was entering a mathematical phase in both theory and statistics. As a precocious youngster I had always been good at logical manipulations and puzzle solving IQ tests. So if economics was made for me, it can be said that I too was made for economics. Never underestimate the vital importance of finding early in life the work that for you is play. This turns possible underachievers into happy warriors."

His reminiscences also contain his transformation over time. "My Chicago-trained mind resisted tenaciously the Keynesian revolution; but reason won out over tradition and dogma. So after all, as I look back in my ninth decade over my long career in economics, I realize that all those incidents of good luck have to be understood against the background of fundamental trends in economic history.... Bliss it was to be in the forefront of the revolutions that have changed economics forever. Always I have been overpaid to do what has been pure fun."

This observation must end on a remarkable note penned by Stanley Fischer, which is worth quoting. "Samuelson was described in 1967 as 'Knocking on the door of the pantheon of the greats.'.... He may have been let in by now." But the final word has to be that of Franco Modigliani, who, after the speeches at the 1983 party at which Samuelson was presented with the Brown-Solow Festschrift, walked over to the seated Samuelson, wagged his finger at him and said 'You' and after a pause "You have enriched our lives."

Paul Krugman had this to say when Samuelson's death was announced: "He had a long good life; yet he will be sorely missed. It is hard to convey the full extent of Samuelson's greatness. Most economists would love to have written even one seminal paper.... Samuelson wrote dozens: from international trade to finance to growth theory to speculation to well, just about everything, underlying much of what we know is a key Samuelson Paper that set agenda for generations of scholars."

31.4 SELECT BIBLIOGRAPHY OF PAUL SAMUELSON'S WORKS

31.4.1 BOOKS

1947 Foundations of Economic Analysis, Harvard University Press, Cambridge, MA. Expanded Edition, 1983.

1948 Economics: An Introductory Analysis, McGraw-Hill, New York. (with W.D. Nordhaus) since 1985. 19th Edition.

1958 (with R. Dorfman and R. M. Solow), Linear Programming and Economic Analysis, McGraw-Hill, New York.

1966-2011 The Collected Scientific Works of Paul A Samuelson (J.E. Stiglitz et al., eds.) MIT Press, Cambridge. MA.

1981 "Bergsonian Welfare Economics," in Economic Welfare and the Economics of Soviet Socialism, S. Rosefield (ed.), Cambridge.

2007 (with W. A. Barnett) Inside the Economist's Mind: Conversations with Eminent Economists, Blackwell, London.

31.4.2 ARTICLES

1952 "Economic Theory and Mathematics; An Appraisal," AER, Vol.42, No.2.

1972 "Maximum Principles in Analytical Economics," Nobel Lecture, AER, Vol.62, No.3.

31.5 WORKS OF OTHERS

Brown, E.C. and R. M. Solow (eds.), (1983), Paul Samuelson and Modern Economic Theory, McGraw-Hill, New York.

Fischer, S. (1987) "Samuelson, Paul Anthony," The New Palgrave: A Dictionary of Economics, Macmillan, London.

Houthakker, H.S. (1950), "Revealed Preference and the Utility Function," Economica, N.S. Vol.17, May.

CHAPTER 32

SIR JOHN RICHARD HICKS

(1904 – 1989)

Professor John Richard Hicks of All Souls College, Oxford, England and Professor Kenneth J. Arrow of Harvard University, Cambridge, Mass, U.S.A. were jointly awarded the Alfred Nobel Memorial Prize in Economic Sciences for 1972 by the Royal Swedish academy of Sciences. The award was made "for their pioneering contributions to general economic equilibrium theory and welfare theory."

The official announcement of the Royal Academy notes that the transformation of general equilibrium theory is marked by the 'pioneering works' of Sir John Hicks and of Kenneth Arrow. Mark Blaug in his Economic Theory in Retrospect observes "... before World War I, general equilibrium...was generally greeted with unmitigated hostility from the economics profession because it was thought to be too mathematical, too abstract and too impractical. And then from this virtual state of oblivion began the rise which has brought general equilibrium theory to the front ranks of economic theory in our own times. It was Schultz, Hicks, Hotelling, Lange and Samuelson who were responsible in the golden decade of the 1930's in bringing about this revival of general equilibrium theory... by the time we get to Debreu's Theory of Value (1959) or Arrow and Hahn's General Competitive Analysis (1971), general equilibrium theory is explicitly defended as a purely formal representation of the determination of economic equilibrium in a decentralized competitive economy, having no practical value whatsoever."

The award announcement refers to opening up of new productive paths by Hicks and Arrow for research in the area of general equilibrium and "thereby made fundamental contributions to the renewal of the theory." Hicks initiated this recreative process in the 1930's and Arrow provided it with fresh nourishment in the 1950's and 1960's. The official announcement observes: "As the distance in time between these contributions indicates, Hicks and Arrow belong to two different generations of scientists, a fact which can be traced in their choice of problems and methods of analysis." General equilibrium theory at the time of Walras's death in 1910 was dismissed as abstract and remote from life in the great centres of academic economics in England, Germany and Austria. Hicks's Value and Capital first published in 1939, "put Walras on the map of the general equilibrium theory as one of the great economists of all times."

Hicks presented a complete equilibrium model with aggregated markets for commodities, factors of production, credit and money. The construction of this general equilibrium model by Hicks involved a number of innovations, such as a further development of the old theories of production and consumption, the setting up of multi-market stability conditions, an extension of the applicability of the static method of analysis to include multi- period analysis and the introduction of a theory of capital under assumption of profit maximisation. Through his model, Hicks formulated a number of economically interesting theorems. His model succeeded in providing a link between general equilibrium theory and the then current theories of business cycles.

From general equilibrium theory to welfare theory is but a short step. Contributions to welfare theory by Hicks include his analysis of criteria for comparisons between different economic situations and his revision of the concept of consumer's surplus. The latter has had a great impact within the field of cost-benefit analysis.

While Hicks employed as his mathematical tool, the traditional differential analysis, Arrow applied the modern mathematical theory of convex sets, providing the basis for a radical reformulation of the traditional equilibrium theory, resulting in the general equilibrium theory gaining both generality and simplicity. The model presented in Arrow's 1954 pioneering paper authored jointly with Gerhard Debreu became the starting point for the major part of further research in the field. Arrow made significant contributions in a number of fields including the development of the theory of uncertainty and its incorporation within the frame of general equilibrium theory. Another outstanding contribution of Arrow relates to the analysis of the possibilities for decentralised decisions in a society where a system of prices is fixed by the central authority. This analysis was made in collaboration with Leonid Hurwicz.

In the field of welfare theory, Arrow's contributions include generalisation of the well-known theorem about Pareto optimality of a competitive equilibrium. Further, he has also demonstrated that there exist general tendencies towards 'inoptimality' in the allocation of resources between research and investments in real capital. His demonstration that it is impossible to construct a social welfare function out of individual preference functions – Arrow's so-called 'possibility theorem' – is considered the most important of his many contributions to welfare theory.

The citation of the Nobel Committee on Economic Sciences refers to Hicks's and Arrow's other important contributions (besides general equilibrium theory and welfare theory) to monetary theory and business cycles theory in the case of Hicks and to growth theory and to decision theory by Arrow.

The main contributions of Sir John Hicks are summarised in this chapter while those of Kenneth Arrow are surveyed in the next chapter.

32.1 A BRIEF BIOGRAPHICAL NOTE: JOHN HICKS

Born in 1904 at Warwick, England, Hicks was educated at Clifton College and at Balliol College, Oxford – 'an expensive education financed by mathematical scholarships.' Though a mathematical specialist during his school days and in his first year at Oxford, he was "not contented with mathematics." His move in 1923 to Philosophy, Politics and Economics was not a success. He finished with a second-class degree. His first teaching post was at the London School of Economics where he was a lecturer from 1926 to 1935. Hicks was appointed Fellow at Gonville and Caius College in Cambridge in 1935 where he remained till 1938. During those years, Hicks was mainly occupied in writing Value and Capital. From 1938 to 1946, he was Professor at the University of Manchester where he did his main work on welfare economics. In 1946, he returned to Oxford, first as a research fellow of Nuffield College (1946-52), then as Drummond Professor of Political Economy (1952-1965) and finally as a research fellow of All Souls College (1965-1971).

Hicks was a member of the Royal Commission on the Taxation of Profits and Income in 1951. He became a fellow of the British Academy in 1942 and was knighted in 1964. Hicks himself stated that within the nine years he taught at the London School of Economics (LSE), he "passed from the state of appalling ignorance, from which I started, to my first theoretical achievements; the invention of the elasticity of substitution (Theory of Wages, 1932), the distinction between income and substitution effects ("Reconsideration of the Theory of Value" in collaboration with Roy Allen) and the liquidity spectrum ('A Suggestion for Simplifying the Theory of Money'). Already, before I left LSE, I had done what I still feel to be some of my best work."

As Christopher Bliss remarks "Hicks is the product of a generation which was last to produce in abundance all round economic theorists – economists who could turn their minds to almost any theoretical problem."

Sir John Hicks died in New York City in 1989.

32.2 A SURVEY OF JOHN HICKS'S CONTRIBUTIONS

Hicks's contributions span a number of fields in economics and cover a host of theoretical areas. No one can hope to cover all his rich and extensive work in a limited essay such as the present one. His contributions to value theory and welfare economics are the fields which would have made him a great economist, even if he had done nothing else. The Nobel Committee acknowledges: Hicks was first and foremost a value theorist but he never neglected monetary theory – an area to which he was to frequently return.

We outline his contributions under the following heads:

1. Theory of Value and Theory of Demand;
2. Welfare Economics;
3. Consumer's Surplus;
4. Macroeconomics and Money;
5. Term Structure of Interest Rates;
6. Dynamic Analysis; and
7. Economic History.

32.2.1 THEORY OF VALUE AND THEORY OF DEMAND

Two works of Hicks, Value and Capital (1939) – a work rich in ideas – and A Revision of Demand Theory (1956) were devoted largely to the field of the theory of value. Value and Capital covers a number of topics in value theory such as consumer equilibrium, equilibrium of the firm, theory of interest, wage theory and the general equilibrium of the economic system. In that work he showed that the main results of consumer theory could be obtained from ordinal utility. Earlier in 1934, Hicks and Allen showed that the concept of indifference curves can be employed to 'reconstruct' the theory of consumer behaviour on the basis of ordinal utility. As the indifference curve approach is an essential part of the received doctrine, it is not necessary to make a detailed recapitulation here. A brief exposition would be in order.

The indifference curve approach makes an assumption that an individual consumer can consistently rank his or her preferences. We actually observe one point on the indifference curve at which the slope of the price line of two goods, x and y, equals the ratio of the marginal utilities of x and y. But we 'infer' that at other hypothetical ratios of exchange between x and y, the individual could choose a combination of x and y such that his or her level of total utility would be the same. Thus, an indifference curve of an individual depicts the various combinations of x and y that yield the same level of total satisfaction.

As Hicks put it in Value and Capital: "...we can translate the marginal utility theory into terms of indifference curves: but, having done that, we have accomplished something more remarkable than a mere translation." Instead of an abstract cardinal marginal utility, Hicks used indifference curves to represent consumer's preferences and by using a ratio of marginal utilities, he identified substitution and income effects. Hicks and Allen showed that changes in prices generate an income effect whose direction cannot be predicted from the weak maximisation assumption. Once we separate income effects, it is possible to study effectively the substitution effects in demand. From Slutsky's important discovery referred to as Slutsky effect, we know that the substitution effect (of a change in the price of x upon the quantity of x purchased by a consumer) will always be negative. Further, Hicks deduced a number of propositions – what Hicks called "the secondary substitution theorems." For example, that the substitution effect of a change in the price of y must be exactly equal to the effect of a change in the price of y on the purchase of x. Going beyond these secondary substitution theorems, utilising the compensated demand curve (the demand curve along which the consumer's income is readjusted so that the individual's level of utility remains unchanged as he moves along the curve), Hicks demonstrated the limitations of Marshall's concept of consumer's surplus). He also described the circumstances under which the concept can be confidently used and indicated its relation to the concept of index numbers.

In the course of his work on consumer theory, Hicks enriched the formal procedures of comparative statics. The comparative statics methods, which he developed, were later to prove essential for the work of Paul Samuelson, Lloyd Metzler, Don Patinkin and many others. Regarding the mathematical methods of comparative statics, Baumol points out,

"Hicks and Allen developed the method fully, showing how total differentiation of the first order conditions produces a set of equations linear in the differentials of the variables, once we recognize that the requirement that the decision-maker be in equilibrium both before and after the change requires each of the total differentials to be equal to zero. The solution of the system of simultaneous equations can then be compared directly to the second order conditions to derive qualitative conclusions about the response of the decision variables of the system to changes in the values of the system's parameters. This, in effect, takes us half-way to the correspondence principle."

By common consent, it was in parts III and IV of Value and Capital that Hicks showed the full extent of his originality. We have to recognise that Value and Capital laid the foundations of general equilibrium theory "and it made his name;" it stands out as one of the central books of twentieth century economics. Harrod wrote in 1939 in the Economic Journal: "Professor Hicks, his place in the first rank of economic theorists long since secure, establishes by this volume his claim to admission to a narrow circle – the economists with a distinctive and distinguished style of writing...." Samuelson, in an article in New York Times (October 26, 1972) summarising Hicks's contribution states: "Value and Capital established for the first time the general properties of the economic market system.... Sir John...showed what could and what could not be predicted for a general equilibrium system." Hicks's analysis of consumer behaviour and general equilibrium theory, which is in the first part of the book, develops in the tradition of Walras and Pareto the ordinal theory of demand and the static general equilibrium model. In the second part, Hicks presented a theory of economic dynamics in the tradition of Myrdal and Lindahl. Hicks's assumption in this part of instantaneous adjustment (which is not fully 'in time') is considered restrictive. In this part of Value and Capital, Hicks relaxed the unrealistic way of not taking time into account by early economic theorists and attempted to bridge the gap between statics and dynamics and specially to extend static methods to dynamic cases. He defined dynamics as economic theory under which every quantity must be dated. In the mathematical appendix in Value and Capital, Hicks demonstrated the general equilibrium method to its full potential, though he was "well aware of its limitations and well aware of the cost of imposing the required assumptions."

As has been commented by historians of the subject, the important idea here was the concept of temporary equilibrium. It is defined as current market equilibrium, determined by the behaviour of economic agents in the current markets, which was indirectly influenced by the future markets through the agents' expectations regarding the future. From this idea had emerged the concept of elasticity of expectations, which proved to be very influential in later work in macroeconomic theory.

32.2.2 WELFARE ECONOMICS

Hicks's contribution to the field of welfare economics essentially comprised his work on four closely connected fields of interest, namely, the foundations of welfare economics which include the well-known compensation test, the valuation of social income, the definition and measurement of Marshallian consumer's surplus and measurement of capital. Hicks is widely regarded as one of the pioneers of the 'new welfare economics' along with Kaldor. With the marginal revolution, welfare economics has emerged as the central concern of applied economics. However, it has concerned itself with aspects of public policy dealing with partial adjustments rather than with aggregate policy. Hicks realised that the difficulties arising from the definitions employed by Pigou could be obviated by the employment of the concept of Paretian optimality. Besides defining the Paretian optimality conditions, Hicks attempted at extending the analysis to deal with cases not only of Pareto improvement but also where redistribution was involved wherein there were both gainers and losers. The issue of inter-personal comparisons of utility had been completed.

Hicks suggested a solution, the same as suggested by Kaldor, namely a compensation test. A reform should be treated as improvement if the gainers could afford to compensate the losers and still be better off. The crucial question of whether compensation must actually be paid for the improvement to count became crucial with the example posed by Scitovsky which showed that the Hicks-Kaldor rule could lead to contradictory recommendations if compensation were not paid. I.M.D. Little proposed a well-argued solution to the problem, which showed the need to make explicit value judgments regarding whether or not distribution of income resulted in improvement in a movement from one position to another. This vitiates the original purpose of the whole exercise, namely differentiating between scientific propositions and value judgments and excluding value judgments from welfare economics.

The main issue of welfare economics was the concern of Classicals with the measurement of real income. Hicks discussed the method of social accounting in The Social Framework and the question of valuation of social income in a paper in Economica. In his 1940 paper in Economica, Hicks noted that there were two approaches to this problem – the utility approach and the cost approach or production possibility approach – and that the two measures were in general different and were germane to address different questions. The issue of the treatment of indirect taxation and government expenditure on goods and services in the valuation of social income was the key element that arose out of this distinction. Hicks, working on the twin problems of social accounting and welfare economics, clearly stated the dichotomy – that the question of welfare has to be separated from the issue of productivity. The Kuznets controversy reflected the gradual and slow absorption of the dichotomy in late 1940's. The general practice is to measure prices at factor cost and to value public services at actual cost. Bliss summarises Hicks's original position in this regard: As market test is not applicable to public goods, the government's taxation that pays for them is not a reliable measure of their value to the consumer; and it is appropriate to use marginal costs rather than average costs as price weights even if it is assumed that the consumers implicitly choose public expenditures as they choose private expenditure.

32.2.3 CONSUMER'S SURPLUS

Consumer surplus and change in its level represented one way of comparing welfare. Economic policies could be compared by reference to consumer surplus. Between 1941 and 1946, Hicks published a number of papers in the Review of Economic Studies. When it seemed that the concept of consumer's surplus lost its validity with measurable utility losing its general acceptability, Hicks with these articles helped substantially in reviving interest in the concept. Hicks in Value and Capital remarked: "The doctrine of consumer's surplus has caused more trouble and controversy than anything else in the book (iii) of Marshalls' Principles... the best way of looking at consumer's surplus is to regard it as a means of expressing, in terms of money income, the gain which accrues to the consumer as a result of a fall in price. Or better, it is the compensating variation in income, whose loss would just offset the fall in price, and leave the consumer no better off than before...."

We may outline Hicks's contribution to the field adopting Baumol's presentation in the Scandinavian Journal of Economics. The figure given below demonstrates the concept as Hicks had developed it.

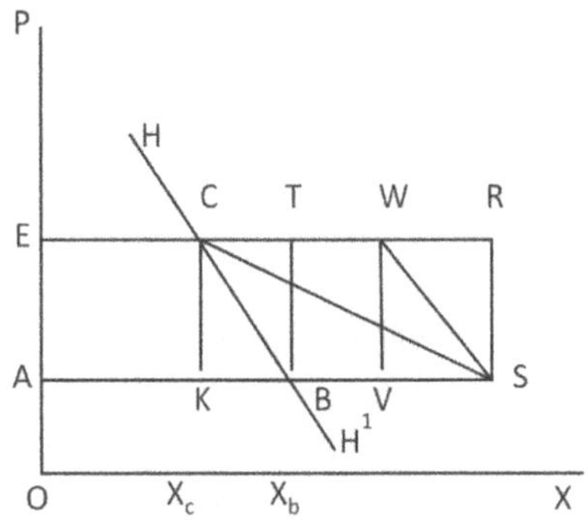

Fig. 32.1 Consumer's Surplus

HH^1 is a Hicksian compensated demand curve. Assume that the price of commodity x has fallen from E to A. If the consumer continues to purchase the same quantity of x as he bought prior to decline in the price (x_c), the area AKCE represents the amount of money he would save. Since the consumer always has the option of continuing the purchase of x_c, the compensating variation in income must at least be equal to this amount. However, the compensating variation must be equal to or greater than AKCE as, after a fall in price, he will normally buy a different amount consequent to a fall in price, which must be his preferred choice. Now, if we assume that the price of the commodity has shown a rise from A to E, it can be shown that the compensating variation in income must be less than or equal to ABTE. This position receives support from the argument that the consumer could always continue to purchase the same quantity as before (x_b) by paying the extra amount. In the limit, the compensation variation for the price rise, EA, is equal to ABCE, the area to the left of the compensated demand curve (HH^1) between the two price levels.

The demand curve CS in the diagram is the Marshallian (uncompensated) demand curve. Supposing x is not an inferior good, the consumer will purchase more of x when price of x falls. Hence point S must lie to the right of B (as shown in the diagram). It is clear that BS is the income effect of the price fall while KB is the substitution effect. Demand curve SW depicted in the above figure is a compensated demand curve when there is a rise in the price of x from A to E. It is obtained if one starts from point S, the quantity of commodity that is bought at the lower price A and price has now risen to E.

According to Hicks, as we discussed above, there are three measures of the effect of a change in price on consumer's surplus. They are the following.

1. ABCE: Compensating Variation;
2. ASCE: Marshallian Measure—to the left of the uncompensated demand curve;
3. ASWE: To the left of the compensated curve through S.

32.2.3.1 The Compensating Variation ABCE and Marshallian Measure ASCE

The area ASWE which Hicks called "the equivalent variation" as it represents that rise in income that would move the consumer to point W in the diagram. It is clear that this puts the consumer in a position "equivalent to" (equally desirable with) the lower price positions.

Hicks, in addition, showed two measures that serve as lower and upper bounds to the desired consumer's surplus. These two correspond to the Laspeyers and Paasche index numbers.

The lower bound rectangular area AKCE which provides the Laspeyers measure – price change weighted by the initial purchase quantity EC. The upper bound rectangular area ASRE provides the Paasche measure – change in price weighted by the final purchase quantity. As Hicks stated: "This is all that is necessary in order to establish the important consequences in the theory of taxation which follow from the consumer's surplus principle."

32.2.4 MACROECONOMICS AND MONEY

Hicks saw very early (in 1935) that his consumer theory can be applied to the theory of the demand for money. His 1935 essay "A Suggestion for Simplifying the Theory of Money" is basically a statement of the micro foundations of monetary theory. In this paper, Hicks took the fundamental concepts of his utility theory and applied them, with suitable modification, to monetary theory. This essay gives the line of approach that Hicks used in most of his subsequent monetary analysis. Hicks maintained that money is one of the assets in a continuum of various types of assets or spectrum of assets that differ from each other in regard to return and risk or in degree of liquidity. Money, in a world of stable prices, represents the one asset that is perfectly liquid, riskless and bearing no rate of return. Thus, he suggested that there are various interest-bearing assets possessing varying degrees of liquidity. It is, therefore, appropriate to analyse the demand for money as a choice of a portfolio comprising a combination of assets that best meets the requirements of the assets-holder rather than as a choice between money and 'other things.' Hicks in this essay argued that money held partly as a store of value should be considered a type of capital asset on the lines of Walras who treated money balances as a capital good whose service of availability generates utility to individuals. In the 'Simplifying' essay, Hicks suggested that the demand for money equation must include as explanatory variables, the individual's aggregate wealth and expected rates of return on assets other than money. Furthermore, as individuals can very well choose to hold their entire portfolio of wealth in the form of liquid cash, the wealth variable represents the budget constraint on holdings of money. Thus, individuals can be viewed as treating the demand for money as a problem of balance sheet equilibrium among the assets analysed.

Adoption of this approach called for an explanation as to why anyone would desire to hold zero interest-bearing money when interest-bearing assets are available and an analysis of the basis of an appropriate combination of assets in a chosen portfolio. Hicks's analysis showed that the holding of liquid cash by economic agents depends upon three phenomena: the imperfect coordination of receipts and payments, cost in effecting transactions and the presence of risk. The rationale for holding money, even though it bears zero rate of return, is its being the only asset which can be used readily (and in a non-inflationary world without loss in value) to purchase goods and services the time of which cannot be confidently foreseen or to make unanticipated purchases. Even in a situation where there is no risk, it pays to hold some cash to avoid transactions costs, particularly when they are high. Hicks's observation that when the transaction cost is rather high, it would not pay anyone to purchase now an interest-bearing security and later sell it when the payment is due, say a month later. This formed the basis for the development of the inventory theoretic model (of Tobin and Baumol) of the transactions demand for cash.

Hicksian portfolio theoretic approach to monetary analysis received further elaboration and refinement at the hands of Tobin, Markowitz and Hicks himself, among others. Most of the development of the portfolio theory was based on the characterisation of any asset in terms of its two parameters, namely mean (expected earnings of the asset) and variance (variance of the asset's earnings) as a measure of the asset's risk. This approach neither considers money as a unique item of the portfolio of assets nor does it employ the motives for holding money, such as transactions demand and precautionary demand. In his later work, Hicks brought out the limitations of portfolio-theoretic approach based on the first two moments of the probability distribution of asset returns, namely expected return and variance of return. He pointed out how such analysis can lead to the inclusion of some anomalous portfolios in the computed efficiency locus and demonstrated how the inclusion of the third moment of the probability distribution as a measure of asymmetry affects the nature of the efficiency locus.

Observers have noted that Hicks's development of monetary theory in his earlier writings was influenced by Keynes's A Treatise on Money, his formulation of the theory of consumer behaviour on the challenge presented by Hayek's notion of 'neutral money.' Hicks came through money to liquidity left incomplete by Keynes, via risk. In his view, liquidity is a problem of temporal coordination, since risk and uncertainty reflect an 'imperfection of knowledge.' Hicks stressed that money is an imperfect institution and it is not an equilibrium phenomena. In his Critical Essays in Monetary Theory, he stated that his conception of monetary theory at that time had been reached over a long period. "All the while I have been learning.... I have realized that truth is many sided. An uniform presentation could only be a photograph from one angle; by changing my approach I hope that I have achieved something more stereoscopic."

Hicks is best remembered for his response to Keynes's General Theory of Employment, Interest and Money in his expository piece "Keynes and the Classics" in Econometrica (1937). Working with a two-sector model, Hicks introduced a framework that resulted in the now famous IS-LM diagram (in the original, the curves were labelled IS-LL). The economy was sub-divided into a goods market and money market through the mechanism of IS (goods market) and LM (Money Market) curves. This Hicksian approach, which is called "macro general equilibrium analysis," has predecessors in Francois Quesnay and Karl Marx. In the Hicks's IS-LM framework, the rate of interest in the money market and the level of output in the goods market were simultaneously determined by the equality of the demand for and supply of money on one hand and the equality of saving and investment on the other. While there are many economists who have interpreted Keynes's General Theory, Hicks's 1937 paper "Keynes and 'Classics'" became one of the half-dozen or so most frequently cited papers of twentieth century economics. Furthermore, IS-LM diagram has become an essential part of the standard Macroeconomics textbooks.

It is not as though Hicks's interpretation of Keynes's General Theory in regard to what Keynes really meant has been generally accepted. There had been different appraisals by economists. However, there is general agreement that the basic message of the General Theory is the proposition that the macroeconomic equilibrium between saving and investment (with investment being the active factor and saving the passive factor) is brought about by changes in the aggregate output. Still, the debate continues unabated as to what the essence of Keynesian economics is. The debate received a fresh jolt in 1968 when A.Leijonhufvud published On Keynesian Economics and Economics of Keynes in which he argued that the IS-LM framework of Hicks (or income-expenditure theory as Leijonhufvud calls) does justice "neither to the letter nor to the spirit of the General Theory." More specifically, he claimed that (1) Keynes's economics is not equilibrium economics; (2) Keynes assumed a world of less than perfect information, in consequence of which markets adjust to disturbances first by variations in quantities and only later by variations in prices, extending to macroeconomics what Marshall had argued with respect to microeconomics; (3) Keynes does not assume rigid money wages but rather that (money) wages and prices change only slowly; and (4) Keynes's model is essentially a two-sector model in which the basic cause of unemployment is the 'relative prices are wrong' – interest rates are too high and long-term asset prices too low to generate full employment. The competitive economy suffers from 'inter-temporal coordination failure.'

Hicks in a paper "IS-LM : An Explanation" in the Journal of Post-Keynesian Economics had changed his position somewhat (perhaps partly in response to the development of a variety of alternative interpretations of Keynes's General Theory). He categorically stated in the paper "The IS-LM diagram, which is widely, though not universally accepted as a convenient synopsis of Keynesian theory, is a thing for which I cannot deny that I have some responsibility. I have, however, not concealed that, as time has gone on, I have myself become dissatisfied with it." Discussing the importance of 'Time' in Economics, Hicks in his 1975 paper had emphasised the importance of the principle of irreversibility of time. Time just goes on, never goes back. One of the principal consequences of the irreversibility of time is that past and future are different. You cannot turn past into future or future into past. The past cannot be changed. Furthermore, knowledge of the past is incomplete. Thus, the time-relations can be quite complicated.

Hicks further elaborated: "... in a stationary state one moment of time is just like another. The stationary state is out of time; time has stood still." The holding of liquid reserves is a matter of provision against an uncertain future – not passive provision (like insurance), but active provision, providing oneself with the ability to take action to meet emergencies that may arise in the future, and which are such that their particular shape cannot be accurately foreseen.... There can be no question of liquidity...in a stationary state. Liquidity is a problem of the economy in time." Hicks observed that Keynes's theory has one leg which is in time, but another which is not. It is a 'hybrid concept.' Keynes divided his theory into two parts. The theory concerning the Marginal Efficiency of Capital and Liquidity Preference is in time while the Multiplier theory is out of time. In the latter, Keynes employs the old tools of equilibrium economics – demand curves, supply curves and cost curves. A state of equilibrium is a state in which there are no surprises. "A state of equilibrium, by definition, is a state in which...something relevant is not changing, so the use of an equilibrium concept is a signal that time...has been put to one side." Hicks categorically admitted that IS-LM diagram (or IS-LL in the "Classics" paper) reduces the General Theory to equilibrium economics; it is not really in time.

Hicks further clarified that "mine was a flex price model, a perfect competition model, in which all prices were flexible, while in Keynes's the level of money wages (at least) was exogenously determined. So Keynes's was a model that was consistent with unemployment, while mine, in his terms, was a full employment model." Hicks noted a fundamental difference between the two models – it concerns the length of the period. Keynes's was a short-period model-say, a year. Hicks's was an "ultra-short-period;" he called it a week. It is clear that much more can happen in a year than in a week. Hicks wanted to avoid "so much happening, so that my (flex price) markets could reflect propensities (and expectations) as they are at a moment."

Hicks posited that the intersection of IS and LM curves determined the equilibrium of the system as a whole; but in IS-LM (following Keynes) the labour market is not cleared; there is excess supply of labour. It is only the point of intersection of IS-LM curves which makes any claim to representing what actually happened. Other points are only theoretical constructions. Hicks concluded the paper "IS-LM: An Explanation" that "the only way in which IS-LM usefully survives – as anything more than a classroom gadget, to be superseded, later on, by something better – is in application to a particular kind of causal analysis, where the use of equilibrium methods...is not inappropriate...when one turns to questions of policy, looking towards the future instead of the past, the use of equilibrium methods is still more suspect." After a change in policy, when the economy moves to a new equilibrium (from the existing equilibrium), there must always be a problem of traverse. For the study of a traverse, "one has to have recourse to sequential methods of one kind or another."

32.2.5 TERM STRUCTURE OF INTEREST RATES

Hicks contributed to the theory of interest implicitly in his 'Portfolio Analysis', in the papers "Suggested Interpretation..." and "Keynes and the Classics" as also in the volume Capital and Growth. One contribution that is specifically to be mentioned here because of its influence on other writers is his model of the structure of interest rates developed in Value and Capital. Hicks's explanation of the maturity structure of interest rates was based on the expectations hypothesis. He argued that the interest rate at which people can expect to borrow or lend for short periods will depend upon their anticipations of the future course of market rates; "it will be less than the current market rate if the market rate is expected to rise, greater than the market rate if the market rate is expected to fall." Based on expectations about the future course of short rates, Hicks postulated that the long rate of interest (say, the n period rate) must in equilibrium equal the geometric mean of the expected short rates for the long period of the same duration (that is, short rates for the next n periods).

Hicks's explanation of the maturity structure of interest rates has given rise to a substantial literature on the subject. For example, Culbertson's 'Segmentation Hypothesis', Meiselman's 'Error-Learning Expectations Model' and Malkiel's analysis taking into account transaction costs which will prevent perfect adjustment warranted in the Hicksian analysis and the fact that expectations of different investors will vary from one another.

32.2.6 DYNAMIC ANALYSIS

While Hicks employed various types of dynamic analysis, which add to the complexities of analysis, one finds almost every type of dynamics has appeared in one writing or the other of Hicks. However, an understanding of the dynamic methods is necessary to properly understand his theories on money, growth and trade cycle.

Economic Dynamics is defined by Hicks as the theoretical analysis of the process of economic change. So defined, the subject includes the study of fluctuation as well as that of growth; it includes the study of change in particular markets as well as in the whole of the economy.

One of the advantages of this definition of dynamics is that it rehabilitates statics. Static economics is perfectly valid economics; it is economics arranged for the comparison of states, not for the analysis of processes.

Some writers identify four stages in the development of dynamics by Hicks – the IS-LM Model, the position he had taken in Value and Capital, (his reaction to the method of dynamics adopted by Harrod and finally flex price/fix price models. The last one was further developed) in Capital and Growth. The essence of dynamic models lies in analysing processes rather than static outcomes; it is a relation between capital and time. In some of his later writings, Hicks suggested that statics is concerned with stationary processes whereas dynamics deals with situations that are undergoing change. Baumol is of the opinion that one feels uncomfortable with Hicksian views on the term 'dynamics'. He prefers the point of view adopted by Ragnar Frisch and Paul Samuelson: "They distinguish between statics and dynamics not in terms of the stationariness or non-stationariness of the economy studied, but upon the degree of emphasis of the analysis upon the process of change." Adopting this criterion, Hicks's "A Contribution to the Theory of Trade cycle" can be considered dynamic as it deals with the process of change. Likewise, the method of analysis followed in Capital and Growth is dynamic as it is concerned with growth equilibrium and the optimality of the growth trajectory.

In Capital and Growth, Hicks stated that growth theory is a branch of Economic Dynamics; or better, it is one of the methods of Economic Dynamics. The dynamic theory is the analysis of the processes by which certain key variables change. His focus in the book was on the study of optimal growth paths, turnpike theory and other related matters. It was Hicks's personal response to the widespread interest in growth theory that was witnessed in 1960's. He endeavoured to apply the framework for dynamic analysis that he had developed in Value and Capital to the construction of a model of growth.

Hicks argued that steady state growth theory which has been put forward by many economists in 1960's is nothing but an extension of the concept of stationary state in conditions of rising population and increasing savings in the framework of variable product proportions and variable production techniques. He considered it an analogue of the static problem outlined in Part I of his Value and Capital. In a stationary state one moment of time is just like another. Time stands still. The stationary state is out of time. In a stationary state, net saving as well as net investment must by definition equal zero. In the steady state, though quantities of inputs and outputs do not remain unchanged over time, the ratios do. In ratio terms, the steady state is quite stationary. It was just as much 'out of time' as the stationary state. However, the interesting question is the passage of time and the dynamic adjustment to equilibrium. That is, how does an economy move from one steady growth path to another? He solved the problem by using the approach of 'traverse.' Traverse captures the history of the movement of an economy from one steady state to another. As Bliss points out, Hicks's approach to growth theory did not exert much influence on the profession. In Capital and Growth, Hicks introduced a number of analytically useful concepts such as fix-price and flex-price models and stock equilibrium and flow equilibrium.

Another notable work of Hicks is Capital and Time in which he attempted at perceiving the growth theory from the Austrian angle. The Austrian approach to capital theory always held particular attraction to him because of its treatment of the relations of capital and time. Hicks was strongly influenced by Hayek (when the former was at LSE). This can be traced back to Carl Menger, whom Hicks had always held in high esteem. Austrians, particularly the two progenitors of the school, namely Menger and Bohm-Bawerk, stressed the importance of time in economics even while adopting the marginalism of the late nineteenth century. Menger's theory is an economics in time; for Menger, time never stood still. Essentially, the steady state model used in Capital and Growth is presented in Capital and Time adopting the Austrian approach. In the latter, the concept of impulse is introduced, a shock with a series of consequences flowing from the potential of a major new invention.

A more explicit treatment of time is available in Hicks's later article "Time in Economics." In the article, he particularly emphasized the simple principle of irreversibility of time; time just goes on, never goes back. One of the consequences of the irreversibility of time is that past and future are different. We can have knowledge of the past, knowledge of facts – may be incomplete knowledge. As far as the future is concerned, the knowledge that we have, at best, is no more than knowledge of probabilities. While the time-relations can be complicated, it is easy to slip into ways of thinking which treat past and future alike. But its consequences for economics are quite far reaching. Hicks then discussed the consequences in respect of a few applications in economics, such as in social accounting and in consumer theory; turning to wider questions, he remarked: "The parts of economics where the distinction with which I began is of greatest importance are the theory of capital and...the theory of markets."

32.2.7 ECONOMIC HISTORY

Economic history has always been of great interest to Hicks though he turned to it at a much later stage of his research work. However, one can witness his interest in the subject by the footnotes that were sprinkled throughout his works. His foray into economic history can be viewed as a logical extension of a concern for the passage of time in economic theory. For instance, when Hicks draws a distinction of fix-price and flex-price markets and the development over time of markets from flex-price to fix-price, Hicks was required to trace the evolution of markets and the eventual dominance of fix-price over flex-price markets. As the flex-price market is, by nature, an unorganised market, an intermediary is required for the market to function and the merchant is such an intermediary. Hicks's A Theory of Economic History is, in part, a theory of the evolution of the merchant as an institution facilitating clearing of markets while an auctioneer in the Walrasian system only registers prices at which trading takes place. Hicksian merchant actually trades in the market with progress of time--there appear more organised and administered markets, tending towards fix-price variant.

In this volume, (A Theory....), Hicks has a 'fascinating' chapter on the finances of sovereign. In what he called a 'middle period,' the sovereign was perpetually short of funds. This poverty of sovereign was explained by Hicks as a consequence of absence of economic activities that could easily be taxed. This situation was changed, according to Hicks, with the invention of joint stock company which has, of necessity, to keep records for its shareholders. The kings found it difficult to resort to public borrowing. In the absence of higher authority which could help the debtor recover the money, the king was a very bad lending risk. Government borrowing became easy with the founding of central banks and the establishment of republics. From all this analysis, Hicks tried to explain why inflations in modern times have been so much sharper and how inflations have become an instrument which increased the real income of treasury.

Baumol takes the view that "as a set of insights and a new way of looking at a body of facts...most readers will agree that the Hicksian view of history is a most substantial piece of work."

32.3 CONCLUDING OBSERVATIONS

A much longer and more substantial review of Hicks's work would have included discussion on his writings on economic policy, on history of economic analysis, on international trade, on the theory and practice of public finance (much of it written jointly with his wife, Lady Ursula Hicks), on the theory of monopoly and what Bliss calls "the most audacious of Hicks's expeditions far from the mainstream of economic theory, namely, Causality in Economics."

Hicks's economics has been considered predominantly theoretical, developed with an eye on application. Well-meaning critics point out that in every field in which he has worked, the contribution of Hicks has "almost always become a pivotal element in the literature, and has often led to a major redirection of research in the area." Hicks's mastery of general equilibrium methods is considered the major strength of his theoretical work. He is counted as one of a small band of economists who has taken the general equilibrium approach beyond the process of counting of variables and equations or beyond the more sophisticated approaches toward the testing of the existence and uniqueness of a solution. In the words of Assar Lindbeck "Because it [the work of Hicks] was deeply anchored in microeconomic theories of the behavior of individual consumers and firms, the models developed by Hicks offered far better ways to study the consequences of change in various parameters than did earlier general equilibrium models (such as Leon Walras'general equilibrium system of equations)." Further, "that current general equilibrium analysis is no longer a purely formal exercise is in no small part a tribute to the success of Hicksian analysis."

Another important feature is the work of others that has been inspired by Hicks's writings. Such writings constitute an eloquent tribute to his accomplishment.

Before closing this essay it is fitting to recall Christopher Bliss's mention of two special qualities of Hicks. "First, he writes beautifully, in a style that is very correct from the formal point of view yet almost conversational in its flow and ease. Secondly, he is the most approachable of men, never pulling rank or flaunting his formidable distinction."

32.4 SELECT BIBLIOGRAPHY OF SIR JOHN HICKS'S WORKS

32.4.1 BOOKS

1932, 1963 The Theory of Wages, Macmillan, London.

1939 Value and Capital, Clarendon Press, Oxford.

1942 The Social Framework, Clarendon Press, Oxford.

1950 A Contribution to the Theory of Trade Cycle, Clarendon Press, Oxford.

1956 a A Revision of Demand Theory, Clarendon Press, Oxford.

b Essays in World Economics, Clarendon Press, Oxford.

1965 Capital and Growth, Clarendon Press, Oxford.

1967 Critical Essays in Monetary Theory, Clarendon Press, Oxford.

1969 A Theory of Economic History, Clarendon Press, Oxford.

1973 Capital and Time, Clarendon Press, Oxford.

1974 The Crisis in Keynesian Economics, Basil Blackwell, Oxford.

1977 Economic Perspectives, Clarendon Press, Oxford.

1979 Causality in Economics, Basil Blackwell, Oxford.

1981-1983 Collected Essays on Economic Theory, Basil Blackwell, Oxford.

32.4.2 ARTICLES

1934 (with R.G.D. Allen) "A Reconsideration of the Theory of Value," Parts I & II, Economica (n.s.), Vol.1, Feb and May.

1935 "A Suggestion for Simplifying the Theory of Money," Economica,(n.s.), Vol.2, Feb.

1937 "Mr. Keynes and the 'Classics', " Econometrica, Vol.V, April.

1939 "The Foundations of Welfare Economics," EJ, Vol.49, Dec.

1940 "The Valuation of the Social Income," Economica, Vol.7, May.

1961 "Measurement of Capital in Relation to the Measurement of Other Economic Aggregates," in The Theory of Capital, F.A. Lutz and D.C. Hague (eds.), Macmillan, London.

32.5 WORKS OF OTHERS

Baumol, W. J. (1972), "John R. Hicks' Contribution to Economics," Swedish JE, Vol.74, No.2.

Bliss, C. (1987), "Hicks, John Richard," The New Palgrave: A Dictionary of Economics, Macmillan, London.

Helm, D. (ed.) (1984), The Economics of John Hicks, Selected and Edited with an Introduction, Basil Blackwell, Oxford.

Rao, B. S. R. (1974), Book Review of "Capital and Time: A Neo-Austrian Theory," Clarendon Press, Oxford, Economic Times, Sep 1, 1974.

CHAPTER 33

KENNETH JOSEPH ARROW

(1921 –)

Kenneth Arrow shared the 1972 Alfred Nobel Memorial Prize in Economic Sciences with John R. Hicks for pioneering contributions to general equilibrium theory and welfare economics. In the citation announcing the award, the Royal Academy of Sciences, Sweden, states: "As his mathematical tool Hicks used traditional differential analysis. When later on more modern mathematical methods were introduced in economic sciences, Arrow applied those methods in his studies of general equilibrium systems. In a series of papers, which preferentially treated the properties of solubility and stability of such systems, he provided the basis for a radical reformulation of the traditional equilibrium theory." Through this reformulation using mathematical theory of convex sets, Arrow brought about simplicity and generality to the general equilibrium theory. His development of the theory of uncertainty and its incorporation within the framework of general equilibrium theory is another notable contribution of Arrow. In collaboration with Leonid Hurwicz (2007 Nobel Laureate), Arrow analysed the possibilities of decentralised decisions in a society where the price system is fixed by the central authority, such as the erstwhile Soviet Union.

Like Hicks, Arrow made significant contributions to welfare economics. Generalising Pareto-optimality theorem of a competitive equilibrium, Arrow has shown that there exist general tendencies towards 'inoptimality' in resource allocation of a society between research and investments in real capital. His significant and well-known contribution to welfare theory is his startling thesis (built on elementary mathematics)--the "impossibility theorem" (or Arrow's theorem) which holds that under certain conditions of rationality and equality, it is impossible to guarantee that "a ranking of societal preferences will correspond to rankings of individual preferences when more than two individuals and alternative choices are involved." In an early (1951) article, he demonstrated that a competitive economy in equilibrium is 'efficient.' He also showed in an economy, an efficient resource allocation could be reached if a government employs lumpsum taxes to transfer wealth and allow the market to function towards equilibrium. One important implication of Arrow's findings is that it is advisable for the government to directly redistribute income rather than use price regulations that could hamper the functioning of free market. His early work on equilibrium is one of the prime reasons of many economists' opposition to price controls. Arrow has also made important contributions to decision theory and growth theory.

33.1 A BRIEF BIOGRAPHICAL NOTE: KENNETH ARROW

Kenneth Arrow was born in the city of New York, USA, on August 23, 1921. He had his undergraduate studies at the City College of New York. He graduated in 1940 with a degree of Bachelor of Science in Social Sciences, but a major in Mathematics – "a paradoxical combination that was prognostic of my future interests," as Arrow observes in his autobiographical sketch written at the time of the award and later published in Nobel Lectures. He entered Columbia University for graduate study and received an M.A. in Mathematics in June 1941. However, he changed to the Economics Department for subsequent graduate work under the influence of the well-known statistician – economist, Harold Hotelling. Arrow's graduate study was interrupted by World War-II. During 1942-1946, he served as a weather officer in the US Army Air Corps, rising to the rank of captain. His assignment was exclusively in research field. A result of the outgrowth of that work was his first published paper, "On the Optimal Use of Winds For Flight Planning." After return from the war, he spent the years 1946-1949, partly as a graduate student at Columbia University and partly as a research associate of the Cowles Commission for Research in Economics at the University of Chicago, where he held the rank of Assistant Professor of Economics in 1948-1949. The brilliant intellectual atmosphere of the Cowles Commission, "with eager young econometricians and mathematically-inclined economists" under the able guidance of Tjalling Koopmans (who was also a recipient of Nobel Memorial Prize in Economic Sciences,1975) and Jacob Marschak was 'a basic formative influence' for Arrow. The summer of 1948 and subsequent years at Rand Corporation in the "heady days of emerging game theory and mathematical programming deeply" influenced him. Arrow's work on social choice and Pareto efficiency dated from this period.

Arrow was appointed Acting Assistant Professor of Economics and Statistics at Stanford University in 1949 where he remained until 1968 becoming eventually Professor of Economics, Statistics and Operations Research. In 1968 he accepted an appointment as Professor of Economics at Harvard University. He was a Social Science Research Fellow, 1952, a Fellow of the Center for Advanced Study in the Behavioral Sciences, 1956-57, Economist on the staff of the United States Council of Economic Advisors, 1962, Fellow of Churchill College (Cambridge, U.K.), 1963-64 and again in 1970 and Guest Professor, Institute for Advanced Studies, Vienna, in 1964 and again in 1971.

Arrow became a Professor Emeritus at Stanford University in 1991.

Arrow received numerous honours and awards including the John von Neumann Theory Prize, 1986, for notable contributions to Operations Research and Management Science and National Medal of Science, 2004, the highest scientific honour in the U.S. He received the John Bates Clark Medal of the American Economic Association, 1957, elected member of the National Academy of Sciences and the American Philosophical Society. He is a

Fellow of the Econometric Society, the American Statistical Association, the Institute of Mathematical Statistics and of the American Academy of Arts and Sciences. He was awarded Honorary Doctorate Degree by University of Chicago (1967), by the University of Vienna (1971) and the City University of New York (1972). Arrow is associated with several academic and professional societies including the Econometric Society, the American Economic Association, the Institute of Mathematical Statistics and the American Association for the Advancement of Science. He was President of the Econometric Society in 1956, the Institute of Management Sciences in 1963 and of the American Economic Association for 1972.

33.2 A SUMMARY OF KENNETH ARROW'S CONTRIBUTIONS

While Arrow's contributions to economics have been of decisive character in several fields, including general equilibrium and efficiency theory, social choice and individual values which is concerned with Welfare Economics, Mathematical Programming and Statistical Decision Theory, Economics of Uncertainty and Information Economics including Insurance and Social Policy Issues, such as health and medical care. In the limited space available to us, it is proposed to analyse some of the more important contributions which have been cited by the Royal Swedish Academy and which have helped the advancement of economic theory.

Arrow's contributions are briefly summarised under five heads.

1. General Equilibrium and Efficiency of the Economic System;
2. Social Choice and Individual Values;
3. Economics of Uncertainty;
4. Theory of Production and Technical Progress; and
5. Optimisation in the Context of Inter-temporal Allocations.

33.2.1 GENERAL EQUILIBRIUM AND EFFICIENCY OF THE ECONOMIC SYSTEM

Since the time of Adam Smith's Wealth of Nations (1776), one recurrent theme of economic analysis has been the remarkable degree of coherence of individual economic decisions. It is widely noticed that the economic system adjusts with a considerable degree of smoothness and rationality to variations in the fundamental facts within which it operates. However, one has to contend with the problematic nature of economic coordination in a free enterprise economy and even in a socialist or planned economy. All societies are characterised by the diversity of information about productive methods simply because the information acquisition is expensive. It, therefore, becomes necessary to have a coordination mechanism.

The way in which the activity of coordination takes place has been the main focus of economic theory since Adam Smith. A satisfactory answer to the issue was provided in 1870's with the work of Jevons, Menger and, more importantly, Walras. The coordination of the system is performed by the market price mechanism and the balancing of supply and demand is referred to as equilibrium. Arrow observes that the adjective, 'general' (in general equilibrium) refers to the overall equilibrium of the economy which cannot be decomposed into separate equilibria for individual commodities since supply and demand in any one market depends on the prices of commodities in other markets.

It is well recognized that prices alone may not convey adequate information to the individual economic agents for the achievement of equilibrium. One line of criticism placed greater emphasis on quantities (rather than prices) as signals (e.g. Keynes, Leijonhufvud and Kornai). This line of criticism has not provided a genuine alternative model of resource allocation in a society. The important question remains: "how does an overall total quantity, say demand, as in the Keynesian model, get transformed into a set of signals and incentives for individual sellers?" Rationing is a non-price coordinating mechanism with which all of us are familiar. At this point, the focus of discussion shifts from coordination to that of efficiency. For a long time, a view is held that competitive equilibrium is optimal or efficient unlike rationing. Pareto (and later Hotelling and Bergson) clarified the issue of optimality. An allocation of resources is said to be Pareto efficient or Pareto optimal, if there is no other feasible allocation which makes everyone at least as well off and at least one member of the society better off. It is also stated that a competitive equilibrium necessarily yielded a Pareto efficient resource allocation.

The next stage in the development of general equilibrium model is due to the contributions of Hicks and Samuelson (discussed in the respective chapters). Despite these developments, Arrow argues that there are several directions in which the structure of general equilibrium theory was "either incomplete or inconsistent with doctrines which have strong currency in economic theory."

The most serious unresolved problem (problem 1) is the proof that there exists a solution to the general equilibrium. That is, whether there exists a set of prices at which excess demand in each and every market is zero.

The system assumed constant returns to scale in production. In such a situation, there cannot be a unique profit-maximising position for any set of prices. That is, under constant returns to scale, there is never a single-valued function defining inputs and outputs as a function of prices; there is no profit-maximising input-output vector or else there is a whole ray of such vectors. This situation warrants a redefinition of the notion of equating supply and demand.

There is no clear formulation of the relation between Pareto-efficient allocation and competitive equilibria. To take care of corner maxima, the condition for individual optimisation (equating marginal rates of substitution to price ratios) required some modification. It is commonly observed that for each individual, there are some or many commodities of which he consumes nothing. Likewise, for every firm, there are some commodities, which are neither inputs to nor outputs of the same. In such a situation, the condition that the marginal rate of substitution must equal to price ratio for each individual breaks down. Arrow concludes: "since marginal rates of substitution do not have to be equated across individuals either for competitive equilibria or for Pareto-efficient allocations, the relation between the two concepts was seen to need further study."

Another issue, which needs an answer, is whether supply and demand are necessarily equal. While demand cannot exceed supply as there would be unfulfilled demands, the situation on supply side is different. For example, free goods as opposed to scarce goods. "Equilibria in which there are free goods are referred to as corner equilibria."

In the evolution of general equilibrium theory, there is a shift from local to global analysis. From a local viewpoint, the list of scarce goods can be taken as given. However, the existence of equilibrium prices [problem (1) stated earlier] cannot be handled at all except from a global viewpoint. "The realisation of the possibility of corner equilibrium turned out to be an indispensable step in the development of an existence proof."

Arrow clarifies that Hicks and Samuelson, who have contributed significantly to the general equilibrium theory, are interested primarily "in the laws of working of the general equilibrium system...than in the questions of existence and the like."

Arrow's interest in the field initially centred on the relation between Pareto efficiency and competitive equilibrium. Working independently, both Arrow and Debreu (awarded Nobel Memorial Prize in 1983) started applying Kakutani's fixed point theorem to the issue of the existence of equilibrium. The development of the subject was greatly assisted by the use also of saddle point theorems, and theorems on convex sets which were proved in game theory and mathematical programming by von Neumann, Dantzig, Kuhn, Tucker and Nash. Using these tools, Arrow and Debreu presented more general and much simpler existence theorems for general equilibrium models in 1954. Independent of Arrow and Debreu's work, Lionel Mckenzie proved in 1954 the existence of equilibrium. For this purpose, he just assumed the existence of demand and supply functions instead of analysing them in terms of the underlying consumption and production structures.

The existence of general equilibrium was proved by Arrow and Debreu by making the following assumptions.

That production sets of firms are well-defined, do not possess increasing returns to scale, do not suffer from indivisibilities and are irreversible.

That consumption sets of individuals or households are bounded from below; they possess well-defined preferences, that their ordinal utility function is continuous and quasi-concave.

That every consumer has sufficient initial endowments, which enables him or her to supply each commodity in a positive amount – an unrealistic assumption.

Some of the assumptions of the authors to prove existence of general equilibrium have been weakened since or rendered superfluous.

Arrow and Hahn's book General Competitive Analysis which appeared in 1971, contained a few new results or new and simpler proofs for existing results. Particular mention may be made of the existence of equilibrium for a model with externalities, for a model of monopolistic competition and an inter-temporal model with no futures markets.

In a series of papers (mostly co-authored), Arrow discusses questions concerning stability of general economic equilibria. In an outstanding paper published in 1959 Econometrica, Arrow, Hurwicz and Block show that the stability of the tatonnement process is ensured "if all commodities are gross substitutes, or if the market satisfies weak axiom of revealed preference or if the matrix of partial derivatives of the excess demand functions has a dominant diagonal" or if one of the commodities is chosen as a numeraire. The paper proves global stability. According to Weizsacker "the results of this paper have remained the basic results concerning stability of tatonnement processes [and it] is until today the starting point concerning the stability of multi-market equilibria."

In a paper included in the 1959 publication, The Allocation of Resources, edited by M. Abramovitz, Arrow points out the absence of a disequilibrium price theory in the traditional theory. According to him, the theory of perfect competition is only valid in equilibrium situations; in disequilibrium conditions exchange contracts must be influenced by monopoly situations, though they may be transitory.

In his 1951 paper "An Extension of the Basic Theorems of Classical Welfare Economics," Arrow, employing the theory of convex sets, proves that under fairly general conditions the absence of external economies and diseconomies implies Pareto-optimality of market equilibrium. He proves the converse theorem: given the choice of appropriate distribution of initial resources, the market forces can yield any Pareto-optimality resource allocation. In a 1961 paper written in collaboration with Hurwicz, Arrow, employing a utility function and constraints (undertaking a large number of activities) that are concave and using the Kuhn-Tucker theorem, shows the existence of a price system such that maximisation can be achieved with decentralised decision procedures. The manager of each activity has to maximise the profits of his activity. This paper gives, for the first time, a sound mathematical foundation to the widely known Taylor-Lange-Lerner theory of market socialism.

33.2.2 SOCIAL CHOICE AND INDIVIDUAL VALUES

Arrow's name has been established very early in his career by the 1951 book Social Choice and Individual Values. He has developed satisfactory mechanisms for arriving at social choices. General competitive equilibrium discussed above shows the extent to which a social resource allocation can be achieved by market coordinated independent private decisions. Such an allocation is shown to be Pareto efficient. However, there is nothing in this which ensures that it is a just distribution. The distribution of initial supplies and ownership of firms determine the final social allocation of resources. Arrow contends that "if we want to rely on the virtues of the market but also to achieve a more just distribution, the theory suggests the strategy of changing the initial distribution rather than interfering with the allocation process at some later stage. There is, therefore, a need or desirability of replacing market by collective decision-making. In the context of social choice, it may be assumed that each individual has a preference ordering over all possible social states. Such ordering expresses not only the individual's choice for his own consumption but also social attitudes. The preference of each individual is given the same weight. The society comprises a finite number of individuals."

Arrow states that the formation of welfare judgements is 'logically equivalent' to what he calls a constitution which is defined as a rule which associates to each possible set of individual preference orderings a social choice rule. A social choice rule is simply a rule for selecting a socially preferred action out of a set of feasible alternatives. He then lays down the conditions to be imposed on the constitution. They are listed below.

Social choices must be transitive or consistent. That is, if A is decided in preference to B, B in preference to C, then C will not be decided in preference to A.

The process of social choice shall never yield an outcome if there is another feasible alternative which everyone prefers according to his preference ordering. In other words, an alternative which would otherwise have been chosen by society must never be rejected just because some individuals come to regard it more favourably.

Condition of non-dictatorship: That is, the social choice must not be dictated by any one individual in the community or by anyone outside the community. In Arrow's formulation, this condition is: "The constitution shall not be such that there is an individual whose preferences automatically become those of society regardless of anyone else's preferences."

Condition of Independence of Irrelevant Alternatives: The social preference as between two alternatives A and B must depend only on orderings of individuals of just these two alternatives – A and B – and not on any other alternative which does not happen to be immediately relevant. Arrow observes that any form of voting clearly satisfies this condition; the preferences of voters as between non-candidates are never asked for or taken into account.

At first glance, it may appear that these requirements for social choice appear to be reasonable or appropriate. However, they are mutually contradictory. It would seem that social choice must be in a sense inconsistent or undemocratic. This is referred to in literature as Arrow's 'possibility theorem' which is a great challenge to those who are interested in the foundations of welfare economics.

33.2.3 ECONOMICS OF UNCERTAINTY

In a 1992 article titled 'I know a Hawk from a Handsaw' which appeared in Eminent Economists: Their Life and Philosophies, edited by M. Snerberg, Arrow sounds a warning: "To me our knowledge of the way things work in society or in nature comes trailing clouds of vagueness. Vast ills have followed a belief in certainty.... When developing policy with wide effects for an individual or society, caution is needed because we cannot predict the consequences." He underlines the importance of taking account of uncertainty, characteristic of the real world situation. His experience as an Air Force weather forecaster during World War II has prompted him to add that the natural world is also unpredictable. In his 1953 paper, Arrow develops, in a cohesive manner, the general equilibrium theory of choice to uncertain outcomes. Adopting the 'state of the world model' (the meaning of uncertainty is that the agent does not know the state of the world), he incorporated uncertainty into a general equilibrium model by developing a concept of a contingent commodity. The same physical commodity in different states of the world is considered as economically different commodities. Commodities in the ordinary sense are replaced by promises to buy or sell a given commodity if and only if a certain state of the world occurs. The market will then determine contingent prices. This concept of contracts in contingent commodities has real world counterparts; for example, insurance contracts, lottery tickets etc.

Arrow surveys important aspects of economics of uncertainty in his 1971 publication, Essays in the Theory of Risk Bearing. The rationale for a special theory to explain behaviour under uncertainty arises, according to Arrow, from two considerations listed below.

1. Subjective feelings of imperfect knowledge when certain types of choices, typically involving commitments over time, are made;
2. The existence of certain observed phenomena, of which insurance is the most conspicuous example, which cannot be explained on the assumption that individuals act with subjective certainty.

As mentioned above, Arrow introduces the concept of the state of the world, to formalise the theory of choice under uncertainty. For a rational theory of uncertainty, it is essential to consider the influence of experience on beliefs. After laying axiomatic foundations of behaviour under conditions of uncertainty, leading to the familiar expected utility theorem, he asserts that any utility function which satisfies the conditions of Expected Utility Theorem must be "bounded both from above and from below."

Stating that since the time of Bernoulli, it is argued that

(a) individuals tend to display aversion to the taking of risks, and

(b) that risk aversion, in turn, is an explanation for many phenomena observed in the economic world, Arrow defines a risk averter as one who, "starting from a position of certainty is unwilling to take a bet which is actuarially unfair (a fortiori, he is unwilling to take a bet which is actuarially unfair to him)." Gambling, which tells against the prevalence of risk aversion, is explained by Arrow as consistent with risk aversion where the risks are understood subjectively and also by citing Friedman-Savage hypothesis. Furthermore, Arrow states that the durability of risk aversion hypothesis is because of its success in providing a qualitative explanation of otherwise puzzling examples of economic behaviour; for example insurance, equity investment, cost-plus and other forms of risk-sharing contracts. Another example is the holding of money by the public which depends in part on the motive of avoiding risks.

Arrow discusses the well-known distinction between absolute risk aversion and relative risk aversion of Pratt. He shows that avoidance of paradoxes such as St. Petersburg Paradox implies a tendency for increasing relative risk aversion with the rise of individual's wealth or income. This analysis has significant implications for the theory of demand for money (for example, as put forward by Friedman, Latane, Meltzer and Selden) and Portfolio Selection of Markowitz and Tobin. Arrow, in association with Hahn, has discussed in General Competitive Economic Analysis, the relationship between money, contracts and uncertainty. A contract would not be written in terms of money "if we consider an economy without a past or a future." Arrow provides a very useful and scintillating discussion of institutions facilitating risk-shifting and risk-spreading, such as insurance and equity shares as also the problem of moral hazard hampering the proper functioning of these institutions. He takes up these issues in some of the public policy fields, such as "Welfare Economics of Medical Care." He says that the special economic problems of medical care can be explained as "adaptations to the existence of uncertainty in the incidence of disease and in the efficacy of treatment." He compares the actual medical-care market and the competitive model which economists usually use. He emphasises that risk and uncertainty are significant elements in medical care. Arrow contends that medical doctors and hospitals generally do not maximise profits. He lists the factors, such as the nature of demand, behaviour expected of sellers of medical care (say, physicians), uncertainty as to the quality of the product supply conditions, pricing practices (e.g. extensive price discrimination by income) and attitudes of medical profession or absence of price competition, which distinguish it from the usual commodity of economics text books. Arrow then compares the operations of actual medical care market with those of an ideal system "in which not only the usual commodities but also insurance policies against all conceivable risks are available." The absence of ideal insurance is noted. Hence there arises institutions which offer substitute guarantees –- setting up of a relationship of trust and confidence in the ability of the physician. A consequence of such trust relation is that the physician "cannot act or at least appear to act, as if he is maximizing his income at every moment of time. As a signal to the buyer of his intentions to act as thoroughly on the buyer's behalf as possible, the physician avoids the obvious stigmata of profit-maximizing." This special relation between the patient and the physician brings about various forms of ethical behaviour and the unimportance of profit-making in hospitals. In conclusion, Arrow suggests that the failure of the market to insure against uncertainties has created many social institutions in which the usual assumptions of the market are to some extent contradicted.

In his presidential address delivered to the International Meeting of the Institute of Management Sciences titled "Control in Large Organizations," Arrow analyses the problem of control in a large organisation by applying economic theory of uncertainty. The problem of control in large organisations is closely allied to the problems of information and consequently of uncertainty. Dwelling on the issue of centralisation or decentralisation in a large corporation, Arrow states that under a centralised system, the operating rules take the form of "do this or that" while under a decentralised system they rather take the form, "do whatever is necessary to maximize a certain objective function."

The central problem of organisation control arises when two conditions mentioned below hold.

The objective of the organisation is a function of a number of interrelated decision variables pertaining to individual activities;

Different members of the organisation have different bodies of knowledge.

"Uncertainty is simply the complement of knowledge." Different bodies of knowledge referred to above indicate different uncertainties.

As an example of control in an organisation, one can refer to the conflict of interest between owners (shareholders) of the firm and its managers in regard to the choice of risky investments. As the risks involved in risky investments chosen by a firm are independent of other risks present in the economy, shareholders would like the company to take any risks with positive expected money value, as the shareholders may as well resort to portfolio diversification. However, managers would not like to take up such risky investment projects as they do not have such possibilities to shift and spread the risks because of the problem of moral hazard or incentives. Wizesacker observes: "This analysis sheds light, for example, on the limited applicability of the Modigliani-Miller theorem on the corporate finance structure."

Arrow speculates about an imaginary insurance company or any other risk-sharing institution that would "insure against any loss of any kind and of any magnitude, in a complete market." Arrow comes to the conclusion that the world would be a better place if we could insure against 'any future possibility' with the existence of a complete market. Then people would show greater willingness to take risk, facilitating economic progress. In practice, insurance is available only in cases where the law of large numbers is observed. The law is applicable if the risks insured are large in number as well as independent of one another.

33.2.4 THEORY OF PRODUCTION AND TECHNICAL PROGRESS

One of the most widely quoted and empirically tested papers of Arrow (written jointly with Chenery, Minhas and Solow) is "Capital Labour Substitution and Economic Efficiency" that has put forward the concept of Constant Elasticity of Substitution (CES) Production Function. It provided for the first time a means of measuring the elasticity of substitution between capital and labour. The empirical isolation of the elasticity of substitution between capital and labour provided support to the practical relevance of marginal productivity theory of income distribution. The CES production function has been useful for theoretical and empirical studies of economic growth.

In the 1962 NBER paper "Economic Welfare and Allocation of Resources for Invention," Arrow deals with the problems which a market economy faces with respect to the production of technical progress because of public goods properties of inventions. He is concerned here with the welfare theoretical implications of the existing patents system. He also explores the possible alternatives.

Yet another significant contribution of Arrow in this field is his 1962 article in the Review of Economic Studies titled "The Economic Implications of Learning by Doing." In this, he discusses a case of market failure. That is, in the process of production, society learns how to produce efficiently. In the event of the failure of single individuals or corporates to appropriate this social learning process by means of appropriate payment to them who cause it to take place, government intervention becomes necessary.

33.2.5 OPTIMISATION IN THE CONTEXT OF INTERTEMPORAL ALLOCATIONS

The contributions in this field essentially relate to optimal inventory policy and the issue of optimal accumulation. The early contribution was a 1951 Econometrica paper "Optimal Inventory Policy" written by Arrow in collaboration with Harris and Marschak. Weizsacker comments: It has become "one of the classic references in the literature on optimal inventory problems. This paper...for the first time...makes use of the recursive nature of inter-temporal decision problems...the paper can also be considered a forerunner to the theory of dynamic programming as it was then developed by Bellman."

A 1958 volume on the mathematical theory of inventory and production edited by Arrow together with Karlin and Scarf contains a number of research papers with Karlin and Beckmann as co-authors on the deterministic models of optimal production scheduling and related problems. In the same volume with the same co-authors, Arrow has written a paper on problems of optimal capital investment by private firms. An important paper in this field by Arrow appeared in Hicks's Festschrift edited by J. N. Wolfe. The paper is devoted to the consideration of the irreversible capital investment, employing Pontryagin's maximum principle.

Arrow has also contributed to the field of criteria for public investment projects. He argues for selection of public investment projects by using an explicit optimisation model. Another publication in this area to which reference has to be made is the book by Arrow (co-authored with Kurz) Public Investment, the Rate of Return and Optimal Fiscal Policy. The authors make extensive use of Pontriyagin's maximum principle in this book which is considered an important step towards "close interaction between the theory of public finance and the modern theory of inter-temporal decision-making."

33.3 CONCLUDING OBSERVATIONS

The above write up attempts at touching and briefly surveying the more important contributions in the fields mentioned above. Arrow's other contributions include outstanding surveys marked by lucidity, comprehensiveness and balanced judgment. Among such surveys, we have to mention "Alternative Approaches to the Theory of Choice in Risk- Taking Situations," "Economic Equilibrium" in the International Encyclopaedia of the Social Sciences, "The Measurement of Price Changes," "Applications of Economic Theory to Economic Growth" and "The Organization of Economic Activity: Issues Pertinent to the Choice of Market versus Non-market Allocation."

In addition, Arrow has contributed to statistical decision theory and to the field of mathematical programming. He has also made comprehensive evaluation of the work of fellow economists, among whom should be mentioned Ragnar Frisch and Paul Samuelson. His wide interests are shown by his papers on a number of divergent fields -- economic development, problems relating to management science and urban crisis, among others.

Critics particularly mention that the "broad scope and the analytic depth of Arrow's scientific work is quite outstanding in economic sciences." We may conclude this by quoting Bernstein from his work Against the Gods: The Remarkable Story of Risk. He sumps up in regard to choice under conditions of uncertainty: Arrow "... focuses on how we make decisions we have made. He has brought us to the point where we can take a more systematic look at how people tread the path between risks to be faced and risks to be taken. ...Arrow is the father of the concept of risk management as an explicit form of practical art."

33.4 SELECT BIBLIOGRAPHY OF ARROW'S WORKS

33.4.1 BOOKS

1951 Social Choice and Individual Values, Wiley, New York. 1963 Yale University, New haven, Conn.

1958 (with S. Karlin and H. Scarf eds.), Studies in the Mathematical Theory of Inventory and Production, Stanford University Press, Stanford, CA.

1959 (with S. Karlin and P. Suppes eds.), Mathematical Methods in the Social Sciences, Stanford University Press, Stanford, CA.

1970 (with M. Kurz), Public Investment, the Rate of Return, and Optimal Fiscal Policy, John Hopkins University Press, Baltimore, Maryland.

1971 a Essays in the Theory of Risk-Bearing, North Holland, Amsterdam.

b (with F. H. Hahn) General Competitive Analysis, Holden Day, San Francisco, CA.

1978 (with L. Hurwicz eds.) Studies in Resource Allocation Processes, Cambridge University Press, Cambridge.

1986 (with H. Raymand eds.) Social Choice and Multicriterion Decision-Making, MIT Press, Cambridge, MA.

1989 (with H. Uzawa eds.) Preference, Production and Capital, Cambridge University Press, Cambridge.

1990 Advances in Spatial Theory of Voting, Cambridge University Press, Cambridge.

1993 (with M. D. Intriligator eds.) Handbook of Mathematical Economics, Edition 4, Vol.2, No.2, Elsevier, New York.

1997 (with R. Arnott et al. eds.) Public Economics. Real Author-Name: Vickrey, William, Cambridge University Press, Cambridge.

2000 (with M. D. Intriligator eds.) Handbook of Mathematical Economics, edition 4, Vol.1, No.1. Elsevier, New York.

2002 (with A. K. Sen and K. Suzumura eds.) Handbook of Social Choice and Welfare, edition 1, Vol.1, No.1. Elsevier, New York.

2005 a (with H. Uzawa eds.) Preference, Production and Capital, Cambridge University Press, Cambridge.

b (with M. D. Intriligator eds.), Handbook of Mathematical Economics, edition 2, Vol.3, No.3, Elsevier, New York.

2007 (with L. Hurwicz eds.) Studies in Resource Allocation Processes, Cambridge University Press, Cambridge.

2008 Advances in Spatial Theory of Voting (J.M. Enelow and M.Hinich eds.), Cambridge University Press, Cambridge.

2011 (with A. K. Sen and K. Suzumura eds.), Handbook of Social Choice and Welfare, edition 1, Vol.2, No.2, Elsevier, New York.

33.4.2 ARTICLES

1950 "A Difficulty in the Concept of Social Welfare," JPE, Vol.58, No.4.

1951 (with T.E. Harris and J. Marschak), "Optimal Inventory Policy," Econometrica, Vol. 19, No.3.

1954 (with G. Debreu), "Existence of Equilibrium for a Competitive Economy," Econometrica, Vol.22, No.3.

1956 (with A. C. Enthoven), "A Theorem on Expectations and the Stability of Equilibrium," Econometrica, Vol. 24,No.3.

1958 a (with M. Nerlove), "A Note on Expectations and Stability," Econometrica, Vol.26, No.1.

b "Measurement of Price Changes," in Joint Economic Committee, The Relationship of Prices to Economic Stability and Growth, Washington D.C.

1959 (with H.D. Block and L. Hurwicz), "On the Stability of Competitive Equilibrium," Econometrica, Vol.27, No.1.

1960 (with Hurwicz), "Some Remarks on the Equilibria of Economic Systems," Econometrica, Vol. 28, No.3.

1961 (with H. R. Chenery, B. Minhas and R. M. Solow) "Capital-Labor Substitution and Economic Efficiency," REStat, Vol.43, No.3.

1962 a "The Economic Implications of Learning by Doing," RES, Vol. 29, No.3.

b "Economic Welfare and the Allocation of Resources for Invention," in The Rate and Direction of Inventive Activity, National Bureau of Economic Research, Princeton, University Press, Princeton.

1963 "Uncertainty and the Welfare Economics of Medical Care," AER, Vol.53, No.5.

1967 "Samuelson Collected," JPE, Vol.75, pp.730 on.

1968 a "Economic Equilibrium," in International Encyclopaedia of the Social Sciences, Vol.4, Free Press, New York.

b "Optimal Capital Policy with Irreversible Investment," in Value, Capital and Growth, J. N. Wolfe (ed.) Edinburgh.

1969 a (with M. Kurz) "Optimal Consumer Allocation over an Infinite Horizon," JET, Vol.1, No.1.

b (with D. Levhari) "Uniqueness of the Internal Rate of Return with Variable Life of Investment," EJ, Vol.79, No.315.

c "Classificatory Notes on the Production and Transmission of Technical Knowledge," AER, Vol.59, No.2.

d (with M. Kurz) "Optimal Public Investment Policy and Controllability with Fixed Private Savings Ratio," JET, Vol.1, No.2.

1970 a (with M. Kurz) "Optimal Growth with Irreversible Investment in a Ramsey Model," Econometrica, Vol.38, No.2.

b (with R.C. Lind) "Uncertainty and the Evaluation of Public Investment Decisions," AER, Vol.60, No.3.

1973 "Higher Education as a Filter," JPubE, Vol.2, No.3.

1974 a "General Economic Equilibrium: Purpose, Analytic Techniques, Collective Choice," (Nobel Lecture), AER, Vol.64, No.3.

b "Environmental Preservation, Uncertainty, and Irreversibility," QJE, Vol.88, No.2.

1975 "Vertical Integration and Communication," BellJE, Vol.6, No.1.

1977 "Extended Sympathy and the Possibility of Social Choice," AER, Vol.67, No.1.

1979 "Allocation of Resources in Large Teams," Econometrica, Vol.47, No.2.

1982 (with C. Sheldon) "Optimal Pricing, Use, and Exploration of Uncertain Natural Resource Stocks," Journal of Environmental Economics and Management, Vol.9, No.1.

1985 "Information Structure of the Firm," AER, Vol.75, No.2.

1986 "Rationality of Self and Others in an Economic System," JB, Vol. 59, No.4.

1991 "Ricardo's Works as Viewed by Later Economists," Journal of History of Economic Thought, Vol.13, No.1.

1994 "Methodological Individualism and Social Knowledge," AER, Vol. 84, No. 2.

1996 "The Theory of Risk-Bearing: Small and Great Risks," JRU, Vol.12, Nos.2-3.

1997 "Invaluable Goods," JEL, Vol.35, No.2.

1998 "What Has Economics to Say about Racial Discrimination?" JEP, Vol.12, No.2.

1999 a (with F. Hahn) "Notes on Sequence Economies, Transaction Costs and Uncertainty," JET, Vol.86, No.2.

b Amartya K Sen's "Contributions to the Study of Social Welfare," ScandJE, Vol.101, No.2.

2001 a "John C. Harsanyi 1920-2000," EJ, Vol.111, No.475.

b "The Five Most Significant Developments in Economics of the Twentieth Century," European Journal of History of Economic Thought, Vol.8, No.3.

2003 (with P. Dasgupta and K.G. Maler) "The Genuine Savings Criterion and the Value of Population," Economic Theory, Vol.21, No.2.

2009 a "A Note on Uncertainty and Discounting in Models of Economic Growth," JRU, Vol.38, No.2.

b "Some Developments in Economic Theory Since 1940: An Eyewitness Account," Annual Review of Economics, Annual Review, Vol.1, No.1.

c (with P. Dasgupta) "Conspicuous Consumption, Inconspicuous Leisure," EJ, Vol.119, No.541.

2011 (with B. D. Bernheim et al.) "100 Years of the American Economic Review: The Top 20 Articles," AER, Vol.101, No.1.

33.5 WORKS OF OTHERS

Bernstein, P. L. (1990), "Against the Gods: The Remarkable Story of Risk," Wiley, New York.

von Weizsacker, C. C. (1972), Kenneth Arrow's "Contribution to Economics," Swedish JE, Vol.74, No.2.

CHAPTER 34

GERARD DEBREU

(1921 – 2004)

The Royal Swedish Academy of Sciences has awarded the 1983 Prize in Economic Sciences in Memory of Alfred Nobel to Professor Gerard Debreu, University of California, Berkley, U.S.A., for having incorporated new analytical methods into economic theory and for his rigorous reformulation of the theory of general equilibrium. The award was made for his "penetrating basic research" in one of the central fields of economic science, viz., the theory of general equilibrium.

In a decentralised market system, individual consumers and firms make decisions on purchase and sale of goods and services essentially on the basis of self-interest. Since the time of Adam Smith, economists have been concerned as to how these decisions, apparently independent of one another, are coordinated and result in a situation whereby consumers realise their planned consumption and sellers usually find markets for their planned production. The desired coordination of individual sellers' and consumers' plans is automatically brought about, according to Adam Smith, by the price system, given flexibility of wages and prices.

Towards the end of the 19th century, Leon Walras, a Frenchman, formulated this idea in mathematical terms as a system of equations to represent the demand of consumers for goods and services, supply of producers of these same goods and services and their demand for factors of production and finally equality between supply and demand; that is, equilibrium in each market. This system of equations was not scrutinised for a long time to find out whether it had an economically meaningful solution; that is, whether this theoretical structure of crucial importance for understanding the market system was "logically consistent."

The major achievement of Gerard Debreu was his work in proving the existence of equilibrium-creating prices. In collaboration with Kenneth Arrow (who received the 1972 Nobel Memorial Prize in Economic Science for his work in this field and other related fields), Debreu's first fundamental contribution came in the early 1950s.

Arrow and Debreu formulated a mathematical model of a market economy where producers planned their output of goods and services and the related demand for factors of production in such a way that their profit was maximised. In this way, connections were generated within the model between the supply of goods and demand for factors of production on the one hand and all prices on the other. By making additional assumptions, regarding the behaviour of consumers, Arrow and Debreu generated demand functions or "correspondences;" that is, relation between prices and quantities demanded and supplied. In their model, Arrow and Debreu managed to prove the existence of equilibrium prices. That is, they confirmed the internal logical consistency of Adam Smith's and Leon Walras's model of the market economy.

Since then, there have been considerable development and extensions of such proofs, with Debreu in the forefront. His book Theory of Value had become a classic, both for its universality and for its elegant analytical approach. In this study, Debreu defined the concept of "goods" so broadly that the theory may be used in pure static equilibrium analysis, the analysis of the spatial distribution of production and consumption activities, inter-temporal analysis and the analysis of uncertainty. In one model, Debreu's general equilibrium theory "integrates the location theory, capital theory and the theory of economic behaviour under uncertainty."

Another important issue relating to the market economy and which can also be traced back to Adam Smith is the normative properties of the market allocation of resources. The issue concerns whether the fulfilment of self-interest through the "invisible hand" of the market mechanism leads to efficient utilisation of society's resources. Another concern that needs to be considered is whether the resources are used and production adapted so as to result in a situation where any attempt to make one individual better off necessarily means taking away from other individuals; that is, a situation with no waste whatsoever. It has long been known that, in certain circumstances, market price formation has such efficiency properties (Pareto optimality) but the exact nature and full extent of the conditions that must be satisfied in order to guarantee them had not been determined. These conditions have been clarified and a detailed analysis conducted through the work of Debreu and his successors.

The idea of the market economy is also concerned with stability of equilibrium. An interesting property of stability involves the question whether it would be profitable for any group of market agents to withdraw completely from the market economy so as to ensure independently, improvement of the agents' own economic position. Debreu had made permanent contributions in this field in a joint paper with Herbert Scarf and through subsequent major accomplishments. He had demonstrated that in very large economies (that is, with numerous market agents), it will not be profitable for any group to stop trading in the markets. Thus, in this respect, the market equilibrium will be stable.

In addition, Debreu had also made significant contributions to the theory of consumer behaviour. He had shown possible representations of consumer preferences in terms of utility functions. Further, he had also studied the feasibility of consistently aggregating individual demand functions over groups of individuals.

34.1 A BRIEF BIOGRAPHICAL NOTE: GERARD DEBREU

Gerard Debreu was born in Calais, France, on July 4, 1921. All his schooling to the Baccalaureat took place in the College of City of Calais. He was a graduate in mathematics at the University of Paris. During the period 1946-1948, Debreu was a research associate at the Centre National de la Recherche Scientifique, Paris. In the summer of 1948, he attended for several weeks the Salzburg Seminar in American Studies where Wassily Leontief was a faculty member. Debreu obtained a Rockefeller Fellowship that permitted him in 1949 to visit Harvard University, the University of California at Berkley, the University of Chicago, and Columbia University, and during the first four months of 1950, to visit the University of Uppsala and the University of Oslo. He was research associate at the Cowles Commission for Research in Economics, University of Chicago, Chicago (1950-1955).

In his autobiographical note Debreu stated: "The Cowles Commission in the early fifties proved itself to be more than I had hoped for. It seemed to be a focal point for mathematical economics.... In that exceptionally supportive environment, in which almost all my time was devoted to research, my work on Pareto optima, on the existence of a general economic equilibrium, and on utility theory made quick progress." In the Nobel Memorial lecture in 1983, titled "Economic Theory in the Mathematical Mode," Debreu referred to the supportive environment of Cowles Commission: "To be associated at that time [Debreu joined the Cowles Commission on June 1, 1950] with a strongly interactive group which provided the optimal environment for the type of research that I wanted to do was an exceptional privilege." In the summer of 1955, the Cowles Commission moved from the University of Chicago to Yale University and in that new environment Debreu completed an article on market equilibrium and his monograph, Theory of Value, whose purpose was an axiomatic analysis of the theory of general equilibrium. He also studied several problems in the theory of cardinal utility, notably, "the additive decomposition of a utility function defined on a Cartesian product of sets."

Debreu obtained his doctorate from the University of Paris in 1956 and then worked at Yale University, the Cowles Foundation and Stanford University before joining the faculty of the University of California at Berkley as Professor of Economics in 1962 and Professor of Mathematics in 1975. Debreu was Visiting Professor at CORE, University of Louvain (1968-1969 and 1971-1972).

In the autobiographical note, Debreu traced his later research interests as follows: "My later research interests in Berkley in the seventies and the early eighties centred mainly on the study of differentiable utility functions, on the characterization of the excess demand function of an economy, on the rate of the convergence of the core of an economy to its set of competitive equilibria, on the problem of least concave utility functions, and (in collaboration with Tjalling C. Koopmans) on the question of additively decomposed quasi-convex functions."

Debreu received a number of honours and fellowships including Guggenheim Fellowship, Distinguished Fellow of the American Economic Association, Erskine Fellowship and Officer de la Legion d' Honneur. He served as Vice- President and President of the Econometric Society (1969-1971) and as President of the American Economic Association (1990). He became a U.S. citizen in 1975.

Gerard Debreu died in Paris on December 31, 2004.

34.2 A BRIEF SUMMARY OF GERARD DEBREU'S CONTRIBUTIONS

Hal Varian observed in 1984 that "for at least two decades the name of Debreu has been virtually synonymous with mathematical economics. His works have not only contributed to this area of study; they have set the standards for others to follow." Debreu is one of those economists who contributed significantly to the present understanding of the many vital fields of economic theory such as production, consumption and general equilibrium.

The other contemporary economists who made this possible include Arrow, Gale, Hurwicz, Koopmans, McKenzie and Samuelson – four of them were awarded Nobel Memorial Prize in Economics.

The study of economic theory has benefited by the development of topological and set-theoretic foundations of the basic concepts of microeconomics. In this effort, the contributions of Debreu and the economists associated with Cowles Foundation are noteworthy. The adoption of topological and set-theoretic approach led to an important change in the emphasis in the study of economic theory.

The works of Debreu, Arrow and others in the field of general equilibrium analysis has helped in bringing about a unifying framework for much of microeconomic theory, capital theory, location theory, theory of finance, international trade and macroeconomic theory. Furthermore, the axiomatic approach used by Debreu and others received wide acceptance of the profession in that this approach was employed in general equilibrium theory, theory of production and utility theory. The axiomatic methods were used in macroeconomics, public finance, industrial organisation among other fields in the 1980's. In this context one must mention Debreu's opinion that the axiomatic methods form the basis of economic analysis, whether the investigation is conducted using symbols of mathematics, or by employing graphical method or through verbal reasoning.

Varian classifies Debreu's work into the following five major categories which is adopted here for the purpose of our survey.

1. Mathematical Methods;
2. Utility and Demand Theory;
3. Equilibrium Theory;
4. Core Theory; and
5. Welfare Theory.

34.2.1 MATHEMATICAL METHODS

In his Nobel lecture, Debreu had given the motivation for the type of research he wanted to undertake when he joined the Cowles Commission. The motivation was the study of the theory of general economic equilibrium. "Its goals were to make the theory rigorous, to generalize it, to simplify it, and to extend it in new directions. The execution of such a program required the solution of several problems in the theory of preference, utility and demand. It led to introduction into economic theory of new analytical techniques borrowed from diverse fields of mathematics. Occasionally it made it necessary to find answers to purely mathematical questions." His work on quadratic forms and non-negative matrices presented theorems and proofs of results which were hitherto not generally accessible. He made them available to a wider range of the profession and facilitated deeper and more general applications to problems in economics.

The classical mathematics, whose development was largely stimulated by problems of physics, generally dealt with single valued functions as the main objective for mathematical analysis. This approach was not particularly suitable to problems in economics as economics has to consider functions that can take on a whole range of values. For example, the supply function of a firm in a perfectly competitive market, experiencing constant returns to scale is necessarily a multi-valued function or correspondence. Debreu's work on correspondence in later 1960's and 1970's was considered "profound in nature in that it developed new tools of analysis by generalizing the classical constructions of measure theory to set valued functions."

34.2.2 UTILITY AND DEMAND THEORY

Debreu, in his Nobel lecture stated: "Intimately linked with the contemporary development of the theory of general economic equilibrium was that of the theory of preferences, utility and demand. New results in the latter were in some cases required, in others motivated by the former." His 1954 paper "Representation of a Preference Ordering by a Numerical Function" is generally considered a classic. He further stated: "To say that an agent has preferences similar to that of another means for a mathematical economist that a topology has been introduced on the set of preferences.... The topology on the set of preferences was at the basis of the theory of the core in Hildenbrand's work." The question whether the preference relation can be represented by a utility function was studied by using topological methods by Debreu. His work presented the fundamental topological conditions that a preference ordering must possess to be represented by an additive utility function. This formulation by Debreu was accepted as a marked improvement over differential conditions. Debreu also contributed to the foundations of expected utility theory and "clarified the relationship of this particular cardinalization to other types of cardinalizations."

Another example from the theory of preferences, utility and demand concerned the problem of characterisation of the excess demand function of an economy. The aggregate excess demand function of an economy, under weak standard assumptions is (1) continuous, and (2) satisfies Walras's Law. Hugo Sonnenschein in two of his papers "Market Excess Demand Functions" and "Do Walras' Identity and Continuity Characterize the Class of Community Excess Demand Functions" raised the question, whether these two properties characterise the aggregate excess demand function. He asked a question concerning the restrictions that utility theory placed on aggregate demand behaviour. It is common knowledge that demand functions derived from individual utility maximisation must satisfy Slutsky conditions. Sonnenschein asked whether "there were any analogous conditions which restricted the behavior of aggregate excess demand functions." He conjectured that the answer was affirmative and made the first attack on the problem. Rolf Mantel in his 1974 article titled "On the Characterization of Aggregate Excess Demand" provided the proof for Sonnenschein's conjecture in the case of continuously differentiable demand functions. Debreu resolved this issue in a general framework by showing that there were no such restrictions on aggregate excess demand behaviour.

Debreu in his Nobel lecture pointed out that the proof appearing in his 1974 article "Excess Demand Functions" rests on the representation of the excess demand function as a vector-field on the strictly positive part of the unit sphere. This characterisation, Debreu claimed, has several applications in general economic equilibrium analysis. Varian observes that "Debreu's recent work in utility theory concerning 'least concave utility functions'...has yet to be incorporated into the general set of tools of the profession. But I believe that it is likely to prove to be useful. For example, when one models consumer choice among many goods under conditions of uncertainty, a common trick is to write the expected utility function as v [u(x)] where u(x) represents the purely ordinal preferences among the goods in question and v(u) represents the attitude towards risk summarized in the von-Neumann – Morgenstern expected utility frame work. The analysis [of Debreu] can be used to show that such a decomposition is not only meaningful, but it is actually canonical in that all concave utility functions" can be viewed as being monotonic transformation of a least concave function.

34.2.3 EQUILIBRIUM THEORY

One of the earliest and most lasting interests of Debreu and the field with which he was most closely associated is the equilibrium theory. His early work in this area is reflected in his 1953 paper "A Social Equilibrium Existence Theorem" which generalised the concept of Nash equilibrium. In this paper, Debreu examined the conditions that need to be verified to ensure the existence of a social equilibrium. By applying fixed point techniques to the issue of the existence of an equilibrium, Debreu presented "a useful and powerful result for analyzing many sorts of game-theoretic and economic models."

This led to his seminal and renowned paper authored jointly with another Nobel laureate Kenneth Arrow titled "Existence of an Equilibrium for a Competitive Economy." In the words of John Geanakoplos "it is not easy to separate the significance and influence of the Arrow-Debreu model of general equilibrium from that of mathematical economics itself." Arrow and Debreu individually and jointly have shown that two of the oldest and most important questions of neo-classical economics, namely, the viability and efficiency of the market system, are susceptible to analysis in a model fully faithful to the neoclassical methodological premises of individual rationality, market clearing, and rational expectations through elegant arguments, using two key techniques of convexity and fixed point theory. The two writers who derived the most fundamental properties of the model, have also provided the very significant economic interpretations.

To quote Geanakoplos again: "the greatest triumph of Arrow-Debreu model was to lay out explicitly the conditions under which it is possible to claim that a properly chosen price system must always exist that, like the invisible hand, can guide diverse and independent agents to make mutually compatible choices...it was Arrow-Debreu that spelled out precise microeconomic assumptions at the level of individual agents that could be used to show the model was consistent. The axiomatic and rigorous approach that characterized the formulation of general equilibrium by Arrow-Debreu has been enormously influential. It is now taken for granted that a model is not properly defined unless it has been proved to be logically consistent. Much of the clamor for 'microeconomic foundations of macroeconomics,' for example, is a desire to see an axiomatic clarity similar to that of Arrow-Debreu model applied to other areas of economics."

The first fruit of the more precise formulation of equilibrium by Debreu and Arrow was the "transparent demonstration" of the first and second welfare theorems. Particularly significant and noteworthy is the proof that every equilibrium is Pareto optimal.

Debreu's classic work, The Theory of Value, contains the most detailed of his writings concerning the existence of a competitive equilibrium. The book, after reviewing the basic mathematical tools, discusses the concepts of commodities and prices, producer behaviour, consumer behaviour, the question of the existence of an equilibrium, the relationship between equilibrium and Pareto Optimality and finally of uncertainty.

As Debreu rightly emphasised, the general equilibrium approach, encompassing as it does a theory of market allocation across space, time and states of nature, "unifies and extends" location theory, capital theory and theories of behaviour under uncertainty. It provides a normative standard against which other allocative mechanisms can be compared. Furthermore, the notation and terminology employed by Debreu in the chapter devoted to the mathematic material needed for understanding the rest of the book have been adopted as standards by later economic theorists.

After describing the notion of a commodity, a fundamental primitive concept in economic theory, as characterised by its physical properties, the date and the location at which it will be available, Debreu classified commodities into goods and services. He then discussed prices and extensions of the concept of prices such as interest rates, discount rates and exchange rates. In this context, we have to note that objects, such as financial assets may be traded but they are not commodities. One chapter each is devoted to analysing producer behaviour and consumer behaviour. In the chapter on consumer behaviour, he introduced two important topics, namely, the indirect utility functions and the concept of expenditure minimisation, which have become hallmarks of the "new" approach to consumer theory through duality.

The chapter on equilibrium brings together the producers and consumers and is the heart of the book. By employing Kakutani's fixed point theorem, Debreu proved the existence theorem. The next chapter states and proves the two fundamental theorems of welfare economics; first, that every equilibrium is Pareto optimal and second, that every Pareto efficient allocation is an equilibrium for some distribution of wealth.

The last chapter in The Theory of Value is a generalisation of the earlier discussion of an economy operating under conditions of uncertainty. His treatment of uncertainty has had an important influence in the study of financial markets and insurance markets among others.

34.2.4 CORE THEORY

Edgeworth had furnished a persuasive argument in support of the common belief that markets become more competitive as the number of agents increases in such a way that each one of them tends to become negligible. Debreu stated: "He [Edgeworth] had specifically shown that his 'contact curve' tends to the set of competitive equilibria in a two-commodity economy with equal numbers of consumers of each one of two types. His brilliant contribution stimulated no further work until Martin Shubik...linked Edgeworth's contract curve with the game-theoretical concept of the core...." The core is defined as follows: An allocation is said to be in the core of an economy if there is no group of agents that can improve their lot by withdrawing from the rest of the economy and simply trade among themselves. Debreu was interested in the economic applications of the concept of the 'core' of a game. It is quite easy to demonstrate that all competitive equilibrium allocations are in the core; however, the core contains many other allocations.

The first extension of Edgeworth's result is due to Herbert Scarf and the complete generalisation to the case of an arbitrary number of commodities and of types of consumers was given by Debreu in association with Scarf in their paper "A Limit Theorem on the Core of an Economy." They had shown that the core and the competitive equilibrium coincided in the limit, as the economy became infinitely large. Debreu and Scarf collaborated again on a refinement of their earlier work.

34.2.5 WELFARE ECONOMICS

Debreu's first published paper in Econometrica was "The Coefficient of Resource Utilization" in which he presented an alternative concept for the classical notion of "dead weight loss." For the purpose of measuring the degree of inefficiency in an economy, Debreu recommended using the value of resources that could be discarded and still permit the economy to attain the same configuration of levels of utility.

He employed his measure of utilisation of resources in another paper "A Classical Tax-subsidy Problem," with the purpose of investigating the measurement of loss of welfare due to taxation policies of government. In another paper "Valuation Equilibrium and Pareto Optimum," Debreu put forward the relationship between resource allocations that maximise value with respect to a price system and those allocations that are Pareto efficient. The paper used the separating hyper plane theorem of mathematics in a general setting in order to establish the equivalence of these two concepts.

34.3 CONCLUDING OBSERVATIONS

Halo Varian while mentioning that Debreu's written works may be few in number recalls Gauss's motto "Few fruits, but ripe" and states that "each is a gem of clear, succinct exposition of a topic of fundamental importance." Evaluating the significant influence of Debreu on economics and the economics profession, Varian observes: One can hardly read an issue of the American Economic Review or the Journal of Political Economy without finding a reference to Debreu or other authors influenced by Debreu.

Regarding Debreu as a teacher, Varian has this to say: "I was fortunate to attend his lectures on mathematical economics. ...Each lecture was carefully prepared and delivered; and each lecture was characterized by the elegance of presentation.... Indeed it is Debreu's role as a teacher and as an exponent of the interest and importance of mathematical economics that must remain one of the most satisfying accomplishments." There can be no higher tribute for a good teacher!

34.4 SELECT BIBLIOGRAPHY OF DEBREU'S WORKS

34.4.1 BOOKS

1959 Theory of Value; An Axiomatic Analysis of Economic Equilibrium, Wiley, New York. Reprinted by Yale University Press, Newhaven, CT. 1971.

1983 Mathematical Economics: Twenty Papers of Gerard Debreu, Econometric Society Monograph, Cambridge University Press, Cambridge.

34.4.2 ARTICLES

1951 "The Coefficient of Resource Utilization," Econometrica, Vol. 19, No.3.

1952 "A Social Equilibrium Existence Theorem," Proceedings of the National Academy of Sciences, Vol.38.

1954 a "A Classical Tax-Subsidy Problem," Econometrica, Vol.22, No.1.

b (with K. J. Arrow), "Existence of an Equilibrium for a Competitive Economy," Econometrica, Vol.22, No.3.

c "Valuation Equilibrium and Pareto Optimum," Proceedings of the National Academy of Sciences, Vol. 40. Reprinted in K. J. Arrow and T. Scitovsky (eds.), Readings in Welfare Economics, R. D. Irwin, Homewood, IL.

d "Representation of Preference Ordering by a Numerical Function," in R. M. Thrall et al.(eds.), Decision Processes, Wiley, New York, reprinted in P. Newman (ed.) Readings in Mathematical Economics: I:Value Theory, John Hopkins Press, Baltimore, MD.

1956 "Market Equilibrium," Proceedings of the National Academy of Sciences, Vol.42.

1960 "Topological Methods in Cardinal Utility Theory," in K. J. Arrow et al.(eds.) Mathematical Methods in the Social Sciences, Stanford University Press, Stanford, CA.

1962 "New Concepts and Techniques for Equilibrium Analysis," IER, Vol.3, No.3.

1963 (with H. Scarf), "A Limit Theorem on the Core of an Economy," IER, Vol.4, No.3.

1970 "Economies with a Finite Set of Equilibria," Econometrica, Vol.38, No.3.

1974 "Excess Demand Functions," JMathE, Vol. 1, No.1.

1975 "The Rate of Convergence of the Core of an Economy," JMathE, Vol.2, No.1.

1976 a "Regular Differentiable Economies," AER, Vol.66, No.2.

b "Least Concave Utility Functions," JMathE, Vol.3, No.2.

1982 "Existence of Competitive Equilibrium," Chapter 15, in K. J. Arrow and M. D. Intriligator (eds.), Handbook of Mathematical Economics, Vols. I to III, North Holland, Amsterdam.

1984 "Economic Theory in the Mathematical Mode," Nobel Lecture, ScandJE, Vol.86, No.4.

1986 "Theoretical Models: Mathematical Forms and Economic Content," Econometrica, Vol.54, No.6.

1991 "The Mathematization of Economic Theory," AEA Presidential Address, AER, Vol.81, No.1.

1993 "Existence of Competitive Equilibrium," in K. J. Arrow and M. D. Intriligator (eds.) Handbook of Mathematical Economics, edition 4, Vol.2, North Holland, Amsterdam.

34.5 WORKS OF OTHERS

Geanakoplos, J. (1987), "Arrow-Debreu Model of General Equilibrium," The New Palgrave: A Dictionary of Economics, Macmillan, London.

Hildenbrand, W. (1974), Core and Equilibria of a Large Economy, Princeton University Press, Princeton, NJ.

Hildenbrand, W. (1982), "Core of an Economy," Ch.18, in K. J. Arrow and M. D. Intriligator (eds.) Handbook of Mathematical Economics, Vol.I to III, North Holland, Amsterdam.

Mantel, R. (1974), "On the Characterization of Aggregate Excess Demand," JET, Vol.7, No.3.

Shubik, M. (1959), "Edgeworth Market Games," Contribution to the Theory of Games, Vol. IV, Annals of Mathematical Studies, Princeton University Press, Princeton, NJ.

Sonnenschein, H. (1972), "Market Excess Demand Functions," Econometrica, Vol.40, No.2.

Sonnenschein, H. (1973), "Do Walras' Identity and Continuity Characterize the Class of Community Excess Demand Functions," JET, Vol.6, No.4.

Varian, H. R. "Gerard Debreu's Contributions to Economics," ScandJE, Vol.86, No.1.

CHAPTER 35

MAURICE ALLAIS

(1911 – 2010)

Professor Maurice Allais, Ecole Nationale Superieure des Mines, Paris, was awarded the 1988 Alfred Nobel Memorial Prize in Economic Sciences by the Royal Swedish Academy of Sciences for his "pioneering contributions to the theory of markets and efficient utilization of resources."

Since the days of Adam Smith, a main task of basic research in economics has been concerned with formulating a rigorous model of equilibrium in markets and examine the efficiency of this equilibrium. Adam Smith in his Wealth of Nations put forward the theory of 'invisible hand' which coordinated a chaotic structure (to all appearances) consisting of a multitude of independent individual decisions rooted in self-interest. Paradoxically, from out of this chaos emerges a coordinated equilibria based on market prices. Production decisions of firms would correspond to planned consumption of consumers.

Adam Smith formulated his theory in verbal and somewhat expository manner that was common in the social sciences during the latter part of the 18th century. Scholars belonging to the later half of the nineteenth century tried to reformulate Smith's basic problems in mathematical terms. As a result, modern price theory, as it emerged from out of these efforts in the 19th century, differed radically from the previous conceptions of "just" prices or prices based exclusively on labour theory of value.

The missing link in the development of a more rigorous theory was provided in 1870s by the French economist, Leon Walras. He formulated his model of the economic system as a large system of equations which described individuals' demand for goods and services and their supply of labour and other productive inputs along with firms' demand for various factors of production and their supply of goods. A set of prices which gave rise to equilibrium between demand and supply could be regarded as a solution to the extremely large and complex system of equations. Later on, Walras's model was developed further by, among others, the Italian economist and sociologist, Wilfred Pareto. The Swedish economist, Gustav Cassel, formulated a simplified version that had a significant international impact.

Maurice Allais's outstanding contribution was made in the 1940s when he continued to develop the work of Walras and Pareto by providing increasingly rigorous mathematical formulations of market equilibrium and the efficiency properties of markets. On the basis of the mathematical models of households' and firms' planning and choice, Allais introduced a very general formulation of the conditions for market equilibrium. The Award citation refers to the two pioneering works of Allais in French, A la Recherché d'une Discipline Economique – Premiere Parlie - L'Economie Pure (The Question of an Economic Discipline – Part One – Pure Economics) published during World War II in 1943 and Economique et Interet (Economy and Interest) published in 1947. A second edition of the first book appeared in 1952 as Traite d'Economie Pure (Treatise on Pure Economics). The citation mentions that each of these studies is extensive: the first book comprised about 900 pages (in Gerard Debreu's words "the massive array of formulas (of) more than 900 oversize pages") and the second approximately 800 pages.

The second edition of the first book, Traite d'Economie Pure, contained a general and rigorous formulation of the two principal propositions of welfare economics. An economic situation with equilibrium prices is socially efficient in the sense that no one can become better off without someone else becoming worse off. In addition, under certain reasonable conditions, each such socially efficient situation can be achieved through redistribution of initial resources and a system of equilibrium prices. These two propositions are important not only as results of basic research, but also as guidelines for planning in, for example, the public sector units by means of prices instead of direct regulation.

Allais is credited with formulating a generalisation which covered the case where various kinds of returns to scale may give rise to natural monopolies. The press release of the Royal Swedish Academy announcing the award states that through his analysis of market equilibrium and social efficiency, Allais laid the foundations for the school of post-war French economists who not only analysed the conditions for efficient use of resources in large public monopolies (such as Electricite de France or SNCF, the state-owned railroad), but also in many instances applied the theory to business management.

Allais's two monumental works also contained many results, which represented very early contributions in areas that were not explored until much later on. He used new mathematical methods to analyse the stability of market equilibria; that is, the conditions under which an economy, after a disturbance, will return to equilibrium through price formation. In his 1948 study, Allais also anticipated important results in research, which led to the modern theory of economic growth in the late 1950's and early 1960's.

Allais's "distinguished contribution" can be regarded as a parallel to two important works published around the same time in the Anglo-Saxon research community: Value and Capital (1939) by Sir John Hicks and Foundations of Economic Analysis (1947) by Paul A. Samuelson. Hicks was awarded the Nobel Memorial Prize in Economic Sciences in 1972 and Samuelson in 1970. The similarity of the works of the three lies primarily in the objective of providing a comprehensive and rigorous interpretation of economic theory. The main difference, according to Nobel Award citation, is perhaps that Allais's formulation is more general and includes an analysis of, for example, long-run or inter-temporal planning of households and firms. Moreover, the work of Allais served as a basis for the analysis of market equilibrium and social efficiency using more advanced mathematical methods, carried out by his pupil, Gerard Debreu (who was awarded the 1983 Nobel Memorial Prize), concurrently and sometimes in collaboration with Kenneth Arrow – Nobel Laureate in 1972.

Allais's outstanding achievements were characterised as basic research in economics. By his links to an older French tradition in economic research, Maurice Allais is rated as the most prominent figure in modern economic research in France as regards basic theory and applications to public sector planning. As Allais's early research work was mostly available in French, his impact on the profession has been indirectly through younger French economists who have been strongly influenced by his work.

In this context, Paul Samuelson's comment needs to be quoted. "Had Allias's earliest writings been in English, a generation of economic theory would have taken a different course."

Allais had also made pioneering and original contributions in other areas of economic research. He carried out, at an early stage, theoretical and empirical studies on the significance and determinants of the volume of money and thus he is regarded as an initiator of monetary macro dynamic analysis. He is perhaps best known for his outstanding studies of risk theory and the so-called Allais' paradox. He had shown that the theory of maximisation of expected utility which has been generally accepted for over forty years does not hold true to many empirically realistic decisions under conditions of risk and uncertainty.

In his later work, Allais had attempted generalisation of market theory by emphasising its dynamic aspects. The impetus for economic behaviour of consumers and producers consists of their efforts to use any surpluses that may arise in an economy through previously unexploited exchange opportunities. Equilibrium in the economy is reached only when these surpluses have been exhausted. Allais had summarised many of his research contributions in La Theorie Generale des Surplus (The General Theory of Surpluses) published in 1981.

35.1 A BRIEF BIOGRAPHICAL OUTLINE: MAURICE ALLAIS

Maurice Allais was born in Paris in 1911. He came from a working class family; his parents owned a small cheese shop. His father's death as a prisoner of war in Germany in 1915, directly and indirectly influenced his life. He states in his autobiographical note: "Albeit often in difficult conditions, I was nevertheless able to pursue my secondary studies and entered Ecole Polytechnique in 1931" where he graduated at the top of his class in 1933. After a year of military service and two years at the Ecole Nationale Superieure des Mines in Paris, Allais started as an engineer in the mines public service in October 1936.

Beginning in 1937, with a brief interruption for active service during the war, he worked in the French State-owned mine administration. In 1944, he became Professor of Economic Analysis at the Ecole Nationale Superieure des Mines and director of the school's economic research institute. A few years later he was also appointed director of research at the National French Research Council, Centre Nationale de la Recherché Scientifique.

During 1947-1968, Maurice Allais was Professor of Theoretical Economics, Institute of Statistics, University of Paris, and between 1970 and 1985, he was Director, Seminar of Monetary Analysis at the University of Paris-X. For over three decades (i.e. between 1946-1980), Allais was a member of the National Committee of the National Centre for Scientific Research. During 1967-1970, he worked as Professor of Economics, at the Graduate Institute of International Studies, Geneva.

Alongside his predominant activities as teacher and researcher, Allais had served the French government in many capacities. He was honoured with many academic distinctions and was the first economist to be awarded the Gold Medal of the Centre de la Recherche Scientifique in 1976. He was named Officer of the Legion of Honor in 1977. Allais was a member of the International Statistical Institute, elected Fellow of the International Econometric Society in 1949, elected Fellow of the New York Academy of Sciences in 1956 and Fellow of the Operational Research Society of America in 1958. He also served as a member of the Editorial Board of Econometrica (together with Ragnar Frisch, Milton Friedman, Tjalling Koopmans, Wassily Leontief and Richard Stone – all Nobel Laureates) for a decade between 1959 and 1969. He was a member of the Council of Econometric Society between 1960 and 1965 and was elected honorary member of the American Economic Association in 1976. Allais also received Doctor honoris causa from University of Groningen in 1964.

Maurice Allais died at his home in Paris at the ripe old age of 99 on October 9, 2010.

35.2 A BRIEF SUMMARY OF MAURICE ALLAIS'S CONTRIBUTION TO ECONOMICS

In his Nobel Prize lecture, Maurice Allais dwelt upon the motivation of his career as an economist and stated: "What could be a better way of preparing for the aftermath of the war than to find a solution to the fundamental problem of any economy, namely how to promote the greatest feasible economic efficiency while ensuring a distribution of income that would generally be accepted. Thus my vocation as an economist was not determined by my education but by circumstances." He was no more than self-taught. He read the fundamental works of Leon Walras, Wilfred Pareto and Irving Fisher, "the three great economists who have had the deepest influence on my thought." Allais added: "... I was guided, although unwittingly, by the fundamental principle set forth by Abel, "To read only the great masters in their original works."

Jacques H. Dreze observes that during the first decade immediately following World War II, the "French Marginalist School" started work on development and implementation of an operational theory of efficient resource allocation. The work covered the following.

(i) the general statement of the theory of efficient resource allocation and its extension to new areas not previously investigated, especially in areas such as inter-temporal allocation and problems linked with increasing returns to scale or uncertainty;

(ii) the translation of general principles into operational guidelines for public policy, particularly for the management of public utilities, implementation of marginal cost pricing in situations involving peak loads or indivisibilities and defining efficient pricing and investment decisions simultaneously; and

(iii) the actual application of these guidelines in the French Public sector.

Dreze's assessment of Maurice Allais and his work is revealing: Maurice Allais could be clearly identified as the intellectual father and the leader of the French Marginalist School, as the person "whose vision, writings, teachings and applied work were instrumental" in the development of the work of the school and whose own contributions embody all the distinguishing features of the school as well as "an additional feature which was quite specific to him, i.e., concern for positive empirical verification."

Maurice Allais, in his Prize lecture, stated that his contributions to fundamental economic analysis belong to essentially five fields, all related to the search for the conditions of the greatest possible economic efficiency and to the analysis of the income distribution it implies, fields in which he had been working continuously since 1941. They are:

1. The theory of economic evolution and "economic calculus;"
2. The theory of inter-temporal processes and maximum capitalist efficiency;
3. The theory of choices under uncertainty and the criteria to be considered for rational economic decisions;
4. The theory of money, credit and monetary dynamics; and
5. Probability theory, as well as the analysis of time series and their exogenous components.

Allais asserted: "In each of these fields, I believe, I have freed myself from current conceptions, opened up original paths, and brought out new perspectives."

The contributions of Maurice Allais in each of these fields are briefly outlined here.

35.2.1 THEORY OF ECONOMIC EVOLUTION AND GENERAL EQUILIBRIUM, OF MAXIMUM EFFICIENCY, AND OF THE FOUNDATIONS OF ECONOMIC CALCULUS

Allais's work in this field had developed in two successive phases – from 1941 to 1966 and since 1967. His 1943 book <u>A la Reserche d'une Discipline Economique</u> and 1945 book

Economie Pure... contained the proof of two fundamental propositions or basic theorems of welfare economics (i) under local non-satiation conditions, a competitive equilibrium is Pareto efficient; and (ii) under certain assumptions, one can associate with every Pareto-efficient allocation, a price system and a distribution of initial resources which sustain this allocation as a competitive equilibrium. Allais had combined the above two theorems of welfare economics into a single proposition, namely that existence of competitive prices and of an adequate distribution of income provides a necessary and sufficient condition for Pareto efficiency. In proving this proposition, Allais had built on Pareto's work. He recognised the limitations of the proof offered by Pareto; instead, he provided two proofs – the first one in the spirit of Aba Lerner's independent work and the second one similar to the approach developed independently roughly at the same time by the Polish economist, Oscar Lange. It may be pertinent to point out that a more general and elegant proof based on convex analysis was developed in 1951 by Debreu and independently by Kenneth Arrow. Debreu acknowledges: "To nobody is my debt greater than to Maurice Allais, whose interest in this kind of question is the origin of mine." Dreze comments: "The classic paper of Debreu is definitely an outgrowth of Traite d'Economie Pure."

In the 1943 book, the proof offered by Allais was of great generality for an economy considered at a given time, while taking the future into account. The formulation of discounted value appeared as a condition of maximum efficiency. Allais claimed that he introduced four new concepts: Surface of maximum possibilities in the hyperspace of preference indices of the consumption units; Distributable surplus corresponding to a feasible modification of the economy from a given situation; loss, defined as the maximum distributable surplus for all feasible modifications of the economy which leave the preferences unchanged; surfaces of equal loss in the hyperspace of preference indices.

From the winter of 1966-1967, Allais became more and more dissatisfied with the neo-classical paradigm, which led him to discard the Walrasian model characterised by a single price system, the same for all the operators which he considered "a completely unrealistic hypothesis." He therefore embarked on an important theoretical work on entirely new bases resting "on the concept of distributable surplus" and on a new model, "the model of the economy of markets (in the plural)." It resulted in the publication in 1978 of La Theorie Generale des Surplus (The General Theory of Surpluses). Grandmont opines: "This study may be interpreted as an effort to construct rigorous foundations for the theory of the disequilibrium economics of a capitalist decentralized economy."

Moving from one feasible state of the economy to another generates individual welfare gains or losses which Allais proposed to measure by the amount of an always desired commodity that should be given to, or taken from, each individual to generate the same gain or loss. The sum of all corresponding positive or negative variations of the commodity would then measure the global potential surplus corresponding to the move. When no surplus can be achieved, then there is general economic equilibrium and maximum efficiency.

Allais's theory outlined here is, to recall, based on the fundamental concepts of distributable surplus, loss, and surfaces of maximum efficiency and equal loss. Besides, it permits the integration of money into the theory of general economic equilibrium and maximum efficiency. His theory of surpluses was, according to Allais, a synthesis of marginalist approach of causality and the Walrasian approach of functional interdependence, two complementary approaches. Furthermore, the theory lends itself to the analysis of international trade as it does to the analysis of national economies and just as well to the analysis of Eastern and Third World economies as to the analysis of Western economies. Finally, Allais considered that his general theory of surpluses constituted "very considerable progress, and is indeed quite revolutionary, by comparison not only with all previous theories but also with all contemporary theories." However, in the opinion of Grandmont, Allais's arguments are complicated and his General Theory of Surpluses has perhaps not been studied and exploited to the extent that it should have. "But it does seem to provide the foundations for a general theory of dynamics of a capitalistic economy out of equilibrium, where returns to scale may be increasing and exchanges take place at (not necessarily unique) prices out of equilibrium."

35.2.2 THEORY OF INTER-TEMPORAL PROCESSES AND OF OPTIMAL CAPITALIST STRUCTURE

In the other monumental work, Economie et Interet (Economy and Interest) published in 1947, Allais presented a general theory of the efficiency of inter-temporal processes with "two particularly significant original contributions: the extension of the theory of maximum efficiency to the case where one considers the different generations and the theory of productivity of capital." He made a systematic theoretical analysis of inter-temporal allocation, investment and money in a closed competitive economy under conditions of perfect foresight.

When future generations are taken into account, the analysis revealed that, while the uniqueness of interest rate is a condition of efficiency in the production sector, it is not so for the economy as a whole. It followed that the Classical theory, according to which an equilibrium of the supply of and the demand for capital leads to an intrinsic optimum was unacceptable. Further, in particular, a policy of compulsory saving for old age is perfectly compatible with conditions of inter-temporal maximum efficiency. Thus, Allais is recognized as the first to develop the "overlapping generations model" in the study of dynamic processes, eleven years before Samuelson. The model was later "rediscovered" and popularised by Samuelson (1958) and has been extensively used ever since. Grandmont gives a useful outline of Allais work relating to the overlapping generations model. "...in Appendix 2 of the book (Economie et Internet), Allais proceeded to a detailed mathematical analysis of a specific model, the structure of which is indeed close to the familiar one. The household sector was composed of overlapping generations of identical individuals who live for two periods, supply inelastically one unit of labor when young and consume a single good in both periods of their lives; Allais chose their utility function to be

Cobb-Douglas for analytical tractability.... On the production side, production of the consumption good could be achieved directly from labor and land, again with a Cobb-Douglas technology. Allais introduced an additional complication by assuming that the productive service of land could be replaced by a production (capital) good, produced from labor one period earlier with constant returns to scale. He assumed perfect foresight and, for the most part, no propensity to bequest." In the later part of the work Allais relaxed the no-bequest assumption and non-monetary economy by explicitly considering money and banks.

Malinvaud has recently established Allais's priority in developing the overlapping generations model and gave a simplified account of the model and some of Allais's main results. Malinvaud categorically states: "if they had been placed side by side, Allais's appendix and Samuelson's independent article would have complemented each other...."

The second significant original contribution of Allais, namely the theory of the maximum productivity of capital, attempted at analysing the influence of the more or less indirect character of production processes on the level of real national income, itself related to the real rate of interest. According to Allais himself, this theory had provided for the first time, a rigorous proof that in a non-monetary economy with a constant population, a stationary state in which welfare or output per capita is maximum. Such a state Allais called "maximum maximorum," "capitalistic optimum" or "maximum of social productivity," characterised by a zero real rate of interest.

The theory, according to Allais, rested on two new concepts: that of primary income (overall value of wages and land rents) and that of the characteristic function (representing the inter-temporal production processes). This theory formed the basis of all subsequent work of Allais. Dreze comments: "Allais was the first among contemporary theorists to treat analytically the possibility of alternative efficient programs, associated with alternative levels of capital accumulation." In the process, Allais formulated a first statement of the golden rule of accumulations which was later rediscovered and popularised by Phelps, Swan and others. Allais, in the first Walras – Bowley lecture of the Econometric Society, generalised the arguments to the case of a growing economy, by showing that optimality required equality of the real rate of interest and the rate of growth. In his Nobel Prize lecture, Allais claimed: "To my knowledge, of all the theories of dynamic capitalist processes, the one I have presented is the only one which lends itself to numerical applications. It is fully confirmed by empirical data."

35.2.3 THEORY OF CHOICE UNDER UNCERTAINTY AND THE CRITERIA FOR RATIONAL ECONOMIC DECISIONS

Allais's contribution, which is very well-known, concerned the theory of decision-making among risky prospects; that is, in situations where economic agents are able to assign well-defined subjective or objective probabilities to the states of nature that describes their unknown environment. He had two objectives in undertaking the work – the desire to extend the theories of general equilibrium and maximum efficiency to an economy characterised by uncertainty; and a critical analysis of the 1947 Theory of Games of von Neumann and Morgenstern, the criteria for making rational economic decisions.

The standard way of dealing with the issue of decision-making by economic agents under conditions of uncertainty is to portray them as "maximizing an index that is linear in probabilities": that is, expected utility hypothesis. The theory devised by von Neumann and Morgenstern postulated that, in order to be rational, an economic agent must maximise mathematical expectation of neo-Bernoullian utility index or expected utility.

This "stance" struck Allais as unacceptable because "it amounts to neglecting the probability distribution of psychological values around their mean, which precisely represents the fundamental psychological element of the theory of risk." Allais strongly believed that in the social sciences as in the natural sciences, abstract theory should always be confronted with facts. In order to test empirically the conflicting doctrines regarding rational behaviour in face of uncertainty, he carried out a survey involving about a hundred respondents with good training in and knowledge of the theory of probability so that they could be considered to behave rationally. The results of the survey were partially reported in a Memoir at an International Symposium. His experiments showed that actual individual behaviour systematically violated the expected utility hypothesis. This fact, which is known to economists as the Allais Paradox has generated substantial research work – both theoretical and empirical -especially in recent years. Allais commented in his Prize lecture: "... the Allais Paradox is paradoxical in appearance only, and it merely corresponds to a very profound psychological reality, the preference for security in the neighbourhood of certainty."

These experimental violations have been confirmed again and again in a variety of contexts, for example, by Morrison and Raiffa. "These findings have been confirmed and extended by a host of experiments conducted by psychologists;" for example Kahneman and Tversky. To account for the experimental evidence, increasing amounts of theoretical research work has been done. Allais as well as other writers had suggested incorporation of not only the mean of the distribution of utilities generated by a risky prospect, as is done in the expected utility hypothesis, but also other characteristics of the distribution, such as its dispersion, its lower bound or the probabilities of ruin. As Grandmont comments: "...these theoretical developments have not yet led to a new and accepted paradigm.... On this important matter, again, Allais was a precursor."

35.2.4 THE THEORY OF MONEY, CREDIT AND MONETARY DYNAMICS

From 1941 onward, Allais started thinking over monetary phenomena, money, credit and economic fluctuations, as experience (the great Depression of 1929-1934) has shown that "there can be neither economic efficiency nor equitable distribution of income in an economy with monetary instability...." In two papers in the 1950's, he demonstrated, using the theory of non-linear difference equations, the possibility of limit cycles in macroeconomic models of the economy. He did this shortly after Hicks had made pioneering studies of theory of trade cycle (in "A Contribution to the Theory of the Trade Cycle"). These two papers are the basic foundations on which, Allais constructed his general theory of monetary dynamics in all its later developments. In a number of papers presented after 1965, he specified the demand functions for money and the supply functions of money in a novel way. His formulation is "hereditary" in so far as it determines the present as a function of the past, and it is "relativistic" in the sense that such dependence is "invariant" when physical time is replaced by psychological time. It postulated that "the past is forgotten in the same way as the future is discounted. This implies that at any given moment in time the common value of the rate of forgetfulness (of the past) and the rate of interest is itself an invariant functional variation of global expenditure."

Allais's theory of monetary dynamics rested on some of the ideas applicable to many fields, such as Economics, Psychology, Sociology and Political Science. They are: "the fundamental analogy between forgetting the past and discounting the future; the hereditary psychological process of forgetfulness; the consideration of psychological time; the hereditary conditioning of men by past events; the hereditary propagation of monetary phenomena with a gradual weakening through time; the concept of lagged regulation implying the existence of limit cycles." He had also introduced some new concepts, such as "psychological rate of interest," the "rate of forgetfulness" and the "reaction time" whose values vary according to the economic situation; "coefficient of psychological expansion," representing the average appraisal of the economic situation by all economic agents; "psychological time," the referential of psychological time being such that the laws of monetary dynamics remain unchanged therein.

Allais claimed that the empirical verifications of the new theory are "very remarkable." There has, of course, been controversy regarding the reasons underlying the empirical success, such as possible automatic correlations between the aggregates constructed by Allais and about the possible circularity of the argument. He further claimed that by revealing the existence of invariant effects of a hereditary and relativistic type in social phenomenon, the new approach opens up wide unsuspected perspectives. His results showed that humans are conditioned by their past and "they open up new perspectives in the general debate on determinism and free choice."

35.2.5 PROBABILITY THEORY AND THE ANALYSIS OF TIME SERIES

Allais had critically analysed the concept of chance and of probability theories as a result of his reflection on the theory of choice under uncertainty and the search for the fundamental factor underlying the fluctuations of time series, especially the variation of the residuals of the best empirically verified models. This search led to the proof of a new theorem, the "T Theorem" and to the introduction of a new concept, the "X Factor," representing the exogenous physical influence on time series.

Allais contended that the mathematical theories of chance actually ignore chance, uncertainty and probability. Instead, the models are purely deterministic. The models study quantities that are mathematical frequencies of particular configurations, among equally possible configurations. In reality, no axiomatic definition of chance is conceivable. According to the "X Factor" hypothesis, we can largely explain the structure of fluctuations of time series that seem to be so incomprehensible, such as, those in stock exchange quotations or fluctuations in sunspots. In fact, these fluctuations present all the features of an almost periodic structure.

Allais stated: "To such a structure there corresponds an almost periodic function, defined as the sum of sinusoidal components of which certain have incommensurable periods." It follows from the "T-Theorem" that under very general conditions, the successive values of an almost periodic function are normally distributed. It is thus established that the deterministic vibratory structure of the universe can bring about seemingly random effects, and that determinism can generate what is commonly referred to as chance.

35.3 CONCLUDING OBSERVATIONS

In his Prize lecture, Allais summed up the principles, which he constantly followed in his work ever since the publication of his first book in 1943.

They are outlined here.

1. The prerequisite of any science (and economics is a science) is the existence of regularities which can be analysed and forecast. All science is based on models and every scientific model consists of three distinct stages: statement of well-defined hypotheses; deduction of all the consequences of these hypotheses; and confrontation of these consequences with observed data. Economists are interested in the first and third stages: the second stage is tautological and is only of mathematical interest. Allais categorically stated: Any theory, whatever, if it is not verified by empirical evidence, has no scientific value and should be rejected.
2. All the general theories have always to be illustrated through specific models for which all calculations can be carried out explicitly. There is no general theory which can be comprehensively understood if it is not illustrated by its application to particular cases.
3. Allais's work has been marked by an increasing concern for numerical applications based on empirical data. He has been led to a two-fold conviction: human psychology remains fundamentally unchanged at all times and all places and the present is determined by the past according to invariant laws. Thus, the whole human economic activity is a search for, and the realisation and distribution of surpluses, according to fundamentally invariant processes. Now, an important conclusion of Allais: "...human societies, within very different contexts – whether

they correspond to current situations, either inflationary or deflationary, or to hyperinflations, to capitalist or communist countries, either today or a century ago – behave in a similar way."

4. Allais had constantly used mathematics in all the cases where ordinary logic was manifestly insufficient for the analysis of economic phenomena, which are essentially quantitative and often very complex. He sounded a useful warning: "...mathematics is not and cannot be anything more than a tool.... The use of even the most sophisticated forms of mathematics can never be considered as a guarantee of quality."

5. One should never hesitate to question commonly accepted theories when they appear to be founded on hypotheses which implied consequences incompatible with observed data. Allais was of the view: "...it is only through the constant questioning of 'established truths' and the blossoming of new ideas suggested both by empirical evidence and by creative intuition that a science can truly progress." All genuine scientific progress, however, comes up against the tyranny of the dominant ideas generated by the "establishment."

Allais's concluding observations bear quoting in full: "...it is essential to subject 'established truths' constantly to a critical analysis without indulgence, while always bearing in mind Pareto's statement: 'The history of science boils down to the history of errors of competent men. Whatever the price he might pay for it in his career, the scientist should never steer his course according to the fashions of the day, or of the approval or disapproval of his contemporaries. His sole concern must be with the quest for truth.'"

Maurice Allais is rated high and is universally regarded as one of the most powerful and brilliant economists of his generation. He is identified as the intellectual father and leader of the French Marginalist School. According to Grandmont Allais's style of writing is not always easy to penetrate as is often the case regarding original inventors. He further observes: Some of his views as well as his expressions are controversial. In the words of Dreze "even when Allais is not convincing, he is neither dull nor commonplace, and his critics stand to learn a great deal."

35.4 SELECT BIBLIOGRAPHY OF MAURICE ALLAIS'S WORKS (in ENGLISH)

35.4.1 BOOKS

1979 (with Ole Hagen eds.), Expected Utility Hypothesis and the Allais Paradox. Contemporary Discussion of Decisions under Uncertainty with Allais Rejoinder, Reidel Publishing Co., Dordrecht.

1989 a Cardinal Utility: History, Empirical Findings and Applications, Fourth International Conference on the Foundations and Applications of Utility,

Risk and Decision Theory, Budapest, June 1988, Kulwer Academic Publishers, Dordrecht.

b Scientific Papers on Risk and Utility Theory: Theory, Experience and Applications, Kulwer Academic Publishers, Dordrecht.

35.4.2 ARTICLES

1953 a "Extension of the Theories of General Economic Equilibrium and Economic Efficiency to the Case of Risk," Econometrica, Vol.21, No.2.

b "Rational Behavior under Risk-Criticism of the Postulates and Axioms of the American School," Econometrica, Vol.21, No.4.

1956 "Explanation of Economic Cycles by a Non-linear Model with Lagged Relations," Metroeconomica, Vol.8, Fasc.1.

1962 "The Influence of the Capital Output Ratio on Real National Income," Walras-Bowley Lecture, American Meeting of the Econometric Society, New York, Dec 1961, Econometrica, Vol.30, No.4. Republished in Readings in Welfare Economics (with an Additional Note), American Economic Association, Vol.XII, 1969.

1963 "Some Analytical and Practical Aspects of the Theory of Capital," Memoir Presented to the Cambridge Conference of the International Economic Association, July, Published in Activity Analysis in the Theory of Growth and Planning (E. Malinvaud and M. Bacharach, eds.), St. Martin's Press, New York, 1967.

1966 "A Restatement of the Quantity Theory of Money," (Very Abridged English Version of the 1965 Memoir), AER, Vol. LV1, No.5.

1968 a "Growth and Inflation," American Bankers Association, Conference of University Monetary Economists, Ditchloy Park, Sep 1968, JMCB, 1969, Vol.1, Aug.

b "The Conditions of Efficiency in an Economy," Economia Internazionale, Vol. XX1, No.3.

1972 "Forgetfulness and Interest," JMCB, Vol.4, Feb.

1974 "The Psychological Rate of Interest," JMCB, Vol.6. No.3.

1975 "The Hereditary and Relativistic Formulation of the Demand for Money," AER, Vol.65, No.3.

1977 "Theories of General Equilibrium and Maximum Efficiency," in Equilibrium and Disequilibrium in Economic Theory, D. Reidel Publishing Co., Dordrecht.

1983 "Frequency, Probability and Chance," in Foundations of Utility and Risk: Theory with Applications, (B.F.Stigum and F.Wenstop, eds.), D. Reidel Publishing Co. Dordrecht.

1984 "The Foundations of the Theory of Utility and Risk," in Progress in Decision Theory, (O.Hagen and F.Wenstop, eds.), D. Reidel Publishing Co., Dordecht.

1985 "The Concepts of Surplus and Loss, and the Reformulation of the General Theory of Economic Equilibrium and Maximum Efficiency," in Production and Exchange: The Foundations of Economic Knowledge (M. Baranzini et al.) Blackwell, Oxford.

1987 a "Economic Surplus and the Equimarginal Principle," The New Palgrave: A Dictionary of Economics, Macmillan, London.

b "The Allais Paradox," The New Palgrave: A Dictionary of Economics, Macmillan, London.

c "The General Theory of Random Choices in Relation to the Invariant Cardinal Utility Function and the Specific Probability Function, The (U.O) Model. A General Overview," in Risk, Decision and Rationality, (B.Munier, ed.), D.Reidel Publishing Co., Dordrecht.

d "A New Neo-Bernoullian Theory: The Machina Theory – A Critical Analysis," in Risk, Decision and Rationality, (B. Munier, ed.), D.Reidel Publishing Co., Dordrecht.

e "The Credit Mechanism and its Implications," in Arrow and the Foundations of the Theory of Economic Policy, (G.R. Feiwel, ed.), Macmillan, London.

f "Some Remarkable Properties of the Determination of a Continuous Distribution by its Moments," in Risk, Decision and Rationality, (B. Munier, ed.), D. Reidel Publishing Co., Dordrecht.

1988 "An Outline of My Main Contributions to Economic Science," Nobel Lecture, AER, Vol.87, No.6.

35.5 WORKS OF OTHERS

Dreze, J. H. (1989), "Maurice Allais and the French Marginalist School," ScandJE, Vol.91, No.1.

Grandmont, J.M. (1989), "Report on Maurice Allais' Scientific Work," Scand JE, Vol.91, No.1.

Hicks, J. (1950), A Contribution to the Theory of the Trade Cycle, Oxford University Press, Oxford.

Kahneman, D. and A. Tversky (1979), "A Prospect Theory: An Analysis of Decision under Risk," Econometrica, Vol.47, No.2.

Lange, O. (1942), "The Foundations of Welfare Economics," Econometrica, Vol.10, No.3.

Lerner, A. (1946), The Economics of Control, Macmillan, New York.

Malinvaud, E. (1987), "The Overlapping Generations Model in 1947," JEL, Vol.25, Mar.

Morisson, D. (1967), "On the Consistency of Preferences in Allais' Paradox," Behavioral Science, Vol.12, No.5.

Neumann, von J. and O. Morgenstern, Theory of Games and Economic Behavior, Princeton University Press, Princeton, NJ.

Phelps, E. (1961), "The Golden Rule of Accumulation: A Fable for Growthmen," AER, Vol.51, No.4.

Samuelson, P. A. (1958), "An Exact Consumption-Loan Model of Interest with or without the Social Contrivance of Money," JPE, Vol. 66, No.6.

SECTION - V
MICROECONOMIC THEORY

CHAPTER 36

GEORGE JOSEPH STIGLER

(1911 – 1991)

Professor George Joseph Stigler, University of Chicago, U.S.A., was awarded the 1982 Alfred Nobel Memorial Prize in Economic Sciences. The announcement regarding the decision of the Royal Swedish Academy of Sciences to award the prize to Stigler refers to "his seminal studies of industrial structures, functioning of markets and causes and effects of public regulation."

The announcement states that George Stigler, through long and extensive research with strong empirical orientation, had made "fundamental" contributions to the study of processes of the market and the analysis of the structure of industries. In this process, he had investigated as to how economic legislation affects markets. His work devoted to the examination of forces that give rise to regulatory legislation had opened up a fresh area of economic research.

Stigler's achievements established him as a leader in applied research on markets and industrial structure – a field commonly referred to as industrial organization. On the basis of particular features of his research, Stigler is generally recognised as the founder of the fields, "economics of information," and "economics of regulation." He had pioneered research in the "inter- section" of economics and law.

The basis of Stigler's research effort was that while basic economic theory, in spite of strong simplifications, had been helpful in explaining and predicting the important market events, it had left unexplained many individual market phenomena. As such, Stigler through his research effort had sought explanations for the distinctive features and peculiarities of markets and structural developments. He tried to accomplish this task "within the framework of basic theoretical assumptions" about optimising behaviour of firms and households and the interaction between supply and demand.

This is particularly exemplified in Stigler's studies of the role of information in market processes. Traditional theory hypothesised that the result of optimisation and market processes lead to a situation where every commodity is sold at a unique price everywhere in the market, except for transport costs. However, the real world situation is in conflict with the theoretical stipulation. In practice, in most markets we observe price variation. Stigler demonstrated that the explanation for this phenomenon lay in the costs of search for and diffusion of information about commodities and prices. The basic properties of the traditional theory are not to be challenged; we have to incorporate in the model, search and information costs, along with production and transport costs.

A market participant's lack of knowledge about goods and prices can be remedied by collecting and furnishing information. The quantum of information a household or firm acquires is guided by comparison of costs and benefits as in the case of production of a commodity. That is, information is collected until the expected utility of further search no longer outweighs additional search costs. The information an economic agent acquires is consciously chosen. "Conversely – and more provocatively – even a lack of market information is rationally and deliberately chosen."

These and similar achievements of Stigler serve as a necessary complement to traditional basic theory. Subsequent research has demonstrated that some of the essential features of market processes such as price rigidity, queuing, unutilised resources and variations in delivery periods can be satisfactorily explained within the framework of principal economic assumptions. These cannot be categorised as unwarranted market imperfections requiring government intervention. Stigler's research results had also contributed to an explanation of inflation and unemployment in the economy. The official announcement of the Royal Swedish Academy of Sciences acknowledges that Stigler was not only the foremost originator of economics of information but also one among those who have provided the basic postulates for contemporary research on the theoretical foundations of macroeconomics.

In another significant study, Stigler investigated the traditional theoretical prediction in microeconomics/industrial economics that differences in rates of return are rapidly eroded through shift of capital and labour from low-yield to high-yield firms. This is one of the cornerstones of neo-classical concept of market mechanism. Making a pioneering effort in the field of economic statistics by compiling extensive data on earnings and capital of American firms, Stigler showed that differences in rates of return earned by firms were effectively equalised, even if the process took as long as a decade. Stigler observed that an industrial sector is profitable or unprofitable in a year may at best indicate its remaining so for a short period of the subsequent 2 to 3 years but it says "hardly anything whatsoever about the condition of the sector after 7/8 years. Sluggishness can postpone equalization, but it will emerge eventually." Differences in rates of return between firms or industrial sectors may appear to persist. This is often because 'new,' highly productive firms and sectors come up while old firms and sectors which were profitable, fall. Indications are there that these tendencies have been reinforced in recent years by increased globalisation of the economic system. These processes appear to be equally prevalent in many countries as they are in the U.S.A.

In yet another study, Stigler demonstrated that, in practice, clear cut conclusion regarding scale economies and similar phenomena could not be drawn on the basis of traditional cost data in order to determine an optimal size firm in an industrial sector. Cost conditions in production do not reveal adequately a firm's vitality and development capacity. The latter are dependent on various factors that are difficult to observe. Therefore, Stigler suggested what is called the "survivor principle." It states: (1) It is necessary to determine those categories of firms which actually exhibit an ability to survive; (2) then, we have to identify the factors which provide this ability.

Stigler also made other empirical studies of markets and industry structure such as survey of pricing behaviour in American industry and the significance of monopoly and oligopoly market structures.

Another area which received early attention of Stigler was the regulatory legislation and its effects. He studied the effects of some features of U.S. regulatory legislation since 1940s, particularly rent controls and minimum wage legislation. His contention was that far-reaching unintended side effects might come about alongside the primary, desired effects. In a later study, he found that regulation of electricity rates completely lacked clear observable effects.

In other studies of regulatory legislation conducted later, Stigler had emphasised its "causes" rather than its "effects." Preliminary observations, which received firm empirical support, led Stigler to hypothesise that, in practice, some regulations protect producers' interests (firms, organisations and occupational and professional groups) rather than achieving the stated objective of protecting the general public. To the extent that this is so, legislation is no longer "exogenous" price but an endogenous part of the economic system itself.

This approach of Stigler marks a further step towards extending the sphere of application for the basic assumption of economic theory.

Stigler's studies have opened up another new area of economic research – economics of regulation. This has led to research into forces, purposes and effects of different aspects of legislation. These achievements have also made Stigler one of the pioneers in another new field of research – law and economics.

36.1 A BRIEF BIOGRAPHICAL NOTE: GEORGE STIGLER

George Joseph Stigler was born in Renton, a suburb of Seattle, in Washington State on January 17, 1911. He attended schools in Seattle through the University of Washington, from which he graduated in 1931. He spent the next year at North Western University and took a business degree in 1932. He obtained his doctorate in economics from the University of Chicago in 1938. At the University of Chicago, he came under the influence of three economists, "each remarkable in his own way." They are Frank H. Knight, "a powerful, skeptical philosopher, at that time vigorously debated Austrian Capital theory;" Jacob Viner, "logical disciplinarian, and equally the omniscient student of history of economics;" and Henry Simons, "passionate spokesperson for a rational, decentralized organization of the economy." Stigler was also influenced by two fellow students, W. Allen Wallis and Milton Friedman.

Stigler taught at Iowa State College (1936-1938). In 1938 he went to University of Minnesota from where he was on leave for several years during the war as a member of the Statistical Research Group at Columbia University. After the war, he returned to Minnesota; from there he moved to Brown University and a year later to Columbia University where he remained from 1947 to 1958. In 1958, he joined University of Chicago as a Distinguished University Professor. Stigler was a senior research staff member of the National Bureau of Economic Research (NBER) since 1947. Two longest-held academic positions of Stigler were at Columbia University (1947-1958) and at the University of Chicago (1958-1991).

He was President of the American Economic Association in 1964.

Stigler's entire Presidential address was devoted to the topic of regulation, arguing that economists should study the effects of regulation rather than just assuming them.

George Stigler died on December 1, 1991.

36.2 A BRIEF SURVEY OF GEORGE STIGLER'S CONTRIBUTIONS

Stigler is reputed for his fundamental contributions to several fields of economics though he is rated as a leading authority in microeconomic theory, industrial organisation and the history of economic thought. He had written a number of influential and pioneering papers in diverse fields of economics. Schmalensee is of the view that Stigler ranks with Joe Bain as "a founder of modern industrial economics." Furthermore, he "stands alone" as the inspiration for most exciting work on government regulation. His contributions to the following fields in economics are covered here.

1. Microeconomic Theory;
2. Theory of Markets;
3. History of Economic Thought;
4. Industrial Organization/Industrial Economics; and
5. Public Regulation.

36.2.1 MICROECONOMIC THEORY

Stigler, in his early work, made significant contributions to microeconomic theory. He had extended the scope of analysis of microeconomic theory by adapting and enhancing it to make it useful for studying a wide range of real world economic phenomena. He argued that firms could build in flexibility into short-run cost functions. He recognised that the traditional principle of diminishing returns does not preclude introduction of qualitative changes in the so-called fixed factors of production in the short run. Stigler defined short run as a period within which some of the inputs are "freely" variable while others are fixed. He made a distinction between variable and fixed factors on the criterion that while variable factors are variable without an impact on the price, fixed factors can be varied only "at a considerable cost of increase in price." According to Stigler, these are matters of degree; the dichotomy of short-run and long-run is a "crude substitute" for a continuum of runs or cost conditions that depend upon the speed of change. The rate of expansion of fixed factors is influenced not only by the cost of rapid change but also the time period for which output is expected to stay at a high or a low rate. Stigler specified that responses to expected or unexpected changes in demand are different. The type of response elicited by the expected changes in demand, depend upon whether such changes are anticipated to be of a temporary nature or long-lasting.

Stigler's interest lay not only in modifying the existing theories or in formulating new theoretical frameworks but also in applying the theories to analyse and explain the real life problems. In this respect, we have to mention his attempt at testing the law of diminishing returns which implies that the short-run marginal cost curves are upward sloping. Stigler tested this proposition by posing the following question: Does variation in output come about mainly through changes in number of plants (as implied by the inverted L-shaped estimates) or through a change in the rate of operation of existing plants? He found empirical support to the latter case as implied by the upward-sloping short-run marginal cost curves.

Stigler was not satisfied with the explanation that because of constant returns to scale, we observe in an industry a considerable range of sizes of firms at a given time and persist over long periods of time. He had offered a different explanation for this observed phenomenon. That is, even within an industry there are differences among firms in optimal size which are a result of differences in ownerships of resources, locational differences and differential managerial capabilities. The different size classes of firms operating in the region of constant or rising long-run marginal cost must be equally efficient. He proposed what has come to be known as the "survival principle" according to which scale economies can be evaluated by observing the sizes of plants that survive and prosper indefinitely in competition with other firms of other sizes in the market place. This is a comprehensive all inclusive empirical test. It takes into consideration the ability of the firm to introduce new technology at an appropriate rate, cope with changes in consumer preferences and tastes and adapt to changing geographical market, besides producing goods efficiently.

In Stigler's essay titled "The Division of Labour is Limited by the Extent of the Market," he pioneered an analysis of the factors determining the structures and boundaries of firms. In this essay, he reconciled Adam Smith's theorem (which is the title of the article) with observed real world market structures. He had also demonstrated that what firms produce, just as the quantum of output they produce, is an issue amenable to economic analysis. Stigler's analysis in the paper was "rich in implications about relations between functional and geographical structure of firms, and the effect of industrial development on production costs."

Richard Schmalensee observes: "One can see Stigler's approach to economic theory quite clearly in his elegant and influential text, The Theory of Price. In it...he is clearly willing to sacrifice theoretical generality and mathematical rigor in order to stress the development of empirically relevant, testable propositions." Another notable comment: "Paging through the classic microeconomics text, The Theory of Price, one is struck by how many principles of economics are illustrated with real data rather than hypothetical examples. Stigler deserves a great deal of credit for getting economists to look at data and evidence."

36.2.2 THEORY OF MARKETS

The distinction familiarly drawn between the abstract theoretical model of perfect competition and the "substantive conditions" for which it is essentially useful is because of George Stigler. There are a number of conditions to be fulfilled for a market to be characterized as perfectly competitive: an extremely large number of firms, divisibility of products, perfect knowledge on the part of buyers and sellers and absence of barriers to entry and exit of firms. Stigler in his book, The Organization of Industry, stated that these conditions are stronger than are actually needed. The only necessary condition is the existence of a large number of firms competing with each other in the market. This condition is adequate for producing economic incentives which reduce ignorance and indivisibilities. Further, the activities producing divisibility and providing information can introduce competition in the same sense that there are many producers, producing each product. Stigler concluded that these prices bring about efficient markets though they do not bring about a tendency toward perfect competition.

In this context, some commentators view his theoretical analysis, as supplying a substantive formulation for J. M. Clark's concept of "workable competition." If we accept this argument, Clark's concept should be basically distinguished from Joan Robinson's "Imperfect Competition" or Edwin Chamberlin's "Monopolistic Competition." Stigler agreed that the merit of the theory of monopolistic competition is its focus on the problems of defining commodities and industries. Yet, Stigler rejected the Chamberlinian theory as "...it has not been useful in the concrete analysis of economic problems, in the sense that it does not contain more accurate or more comprehensive implications than neo-classical theory. The downward sloping demand curve is essentially correct, but the real question is how steep is it?"

Stigler's scientific positivism of which the critique of monopolistic competition is an outstanding example can be gauged from his following succinct statement: "The purpose of the study of economics is to permit us to make predictions about the behavior of economic phenomena under specified conditions. The sole test of the usefulness of an economic theory is the concordance between its predictions and the observable course of events. Often a theory is criticized or rejected because its assumptions are 'unrealistic.' But it is quite impossible to determine whether assumption A is more realistic than assumption B, except by comparing implications with facts.... Different theories, each with its particular assumptions, can be applied to the same phenomenon to answer different questions."

Stigler had made a valuable contribution to the extension of the neo-classical theory of the firm. In the article "Economics of Information," he explored the economic implications of imperfect information on market processes, particularly labour markets. In his view, the problem is one of search: workers search for wage offers and employers search for wage demand until expected marginal returns and costs are equalised. He argued that even in industries with a "going wage," variances in wage rates still exist. He posited that the unemployed are as much information seekers as job seekers. His theory is now referred to as theory of search unemployment. Later, a number of economists, like Spence and Stiglitz, further extended the analysis.

In an article "The Theory of Oligopoly," Stigler attempted an explanation of the behaviour of oligopolists. Assuming that firms operating in an oligopolistic market structure aim, by means of collusion, at maximising joint profits, he tried to establish factors that influence the success of their efforts. His analysis focused wholly on the problem of "policing" a collusive agreement in regard to price structure which the oligopolists must somehow reach. Stigler's article is considered a land mark in the theory of industrial organization and in the practice of antitrust. According to S. Peltzman and D. Carlton "Stigler's theory of oligopoly remains a central pillar in merger policy in most, if not all, antitrust regimes around the world."

36.2.3 HISTORY OF ECONOMIC THOUGHT

For his doctoral degree which he received in the year 1938 from the University of Chicago, Stigler wrote a dissertation on production and distribution theories under the supervision of Professor Frank H. Knight. This scholarly work was published in 1941, including an additional essay on John Bates Clark, under the title Production and Distribution Theories: The Formative Period. It is a critical evaluation of contributions of ten outstanding neo-classical economists, Stanley Jevons, Philip Wicksteed, Alfred Marshall, Francis Y. Edgeworth, Carl Menger, Friedrich von Wieser, Eugene von Bohm-Bawerk, Leon Walras, Knut Wicksell, and John Bates Clark to the theories of value and distribution and has helped generations of students of economics in getting a proper understanding and critical appreciation of an important part of neo-classical theory.

Stigler is highly regarded as economic historian. He wrote numerous articles on the history of economic ideas. His journal articles on Ricardo are ranked "landmark analyses of that special and difficult system of thought." He had also given a modest amount of attention on some of the contemporary economists such as Edwin Chamberlin and John Kenneth Galbraith "though quite possibly more than they wished" as remarked by Thomas Sowell. Analyzing John Stuart Mill's work Stigler observed: "if we cannot associate a catchword with the man, we are inclined to deny him originality." In Stigler's opinion, Mill deserved much more credit. He considered Mill one of the most original economists in the history of the profession on the basis of Mill's introduction into the subject of such original concepts as non-competing groups, joint products and alternative costs.

In Stigler's contributions to the history of economic thought, mention should be made of his scholarly analysis of particular concepts such as perfect competition and Giffen Paradox. Another broad theme which Stigler dealt with related to the influence of economists on events and of events on economists and their thinking. He did not share the view of many economists that external events generally shape the development of economic theory. As an instance, he pointed out that classical economists treated the state of technology as given at the height of the industrial revolution. He also noted that neo-classical marginal utility revolution did not reflect any "discernible environmental change." In the same way as Stigler regarded the influence of contemporary events on economists as exaggerated, he also considered the influence of economists on contemporary events as equally exaggerated. In this connection, Sowell observes: "The economic purist can expect to have little effect on current policy.... [However] it is the purist, who fights on his own ground and unfurls an unsullied banner, who has the long-run prospect of attracting disciples who may ultimately prevail in a changed climate of opinion. The repeal of the Corn Laws long after Ricardo's death is an example."

36.2.4 INDUSTRIAL ORGANISATION/INDUSTRIAL ECONOMICS

Stigler's path-breaking work, Capital and Rates of Return in Manufacturing Industries, provided comprehensive and fairly detailed data on capital stock and rates of return in all U.S. manufacturing industries, spanning two decades (1937-1957). His analyses of the data were equally interesting and important in that they threw light on three of the traditional problems of economics. They are:

- the tendency to equality of rates of return on capital in different industries as a consequence of market competition;
- factors determining the rate of investment in industries; and
- the relationship between capital and labour and between their respective rates of remuneration.

His findings on the first question were in conformity with the classical economic theorem that, under competition, rates of return on capital employed in different industries tend to be equal. On the second issue, the data revealed that annual rates of investment were volatile not only for aggregate investment in all industries, but also for individual industries. Among the economic factors influencing investment in industries, Stigler found shifts in consumer demand and technological change, the most important. His results lent support to the hypothesis that firms tend to leave slow-growing industries (often declining industries) and enter the most rapidly growing industries.

The division of the total net product after taxes between the two productive agents, namely capital and labour, gave rise to some important issues of public policy. Further, the allocation of capital and labour among industries was equally important in relation to the productive process. Stigler's analysis showed that the average wage rates did not differ greatly among U.S. industries during the period of study and so the functional distribution of income was dominated by the amount of capital per worker in various industries. In addition, as differences among industries in the relative use of capital persisted over a long period of time, the share of wages in total income had a stable industrial pattern. There was also evidence to show that capital per worker in industries was "highly responsive to wage rates."

36.2.5 PUBLIC REGULATION

Stigler wrote extensively on the government regulation of economic activity and its causes and consequences. In his first seminal paper in this area, Stigler strongly challenged the contemporary view of economic regulation in the U.S. in the early 1960s. He was one of the first to study directly the effects of regulation. His conclusion was that the early state regulation of electric utilities in the U.S. had no effect on electricity prices. Stigler's views on regulation may be gleaned from his articles on the subject, particularly his 1964 paper titled "Public Regulation of the Securities Markets" in which he examined the report of the special study of the Securities and Exchange Commission (SEC) and policy proposals made therein for tightening the controls over securities markets in the U.S.A. He concluded that public regulation of securities markets had not achieved its stated goal of benefiting investors. He made a scathing attack on the proposals made in the report and, in his characteristic bluntness termed them "a promiscuous collection of conventional beliefs and personal prejudices" for which he earned the retort from Irwin Friend et al. (of Wharton School, University of Pennsylvania) that "Stigler's paper represents a triumph of ideology over scholarship." Stigler devoted his entire 1964 Presidential address to the American Economic Association to the topic of regulation and advised fellow economists to study the effects of regulation and not simply assume them. He expressed the view:

"The economic role of the state has managed to hold the attention of scholars for over two centuries without arousing their curiosity." He further observed: "Economists have refused either to leave the problem alone or to work on it."

Later in his 1971 seminal essay, "The Theory of Economic Regulation," Stigler had put forward a supply and demand theory of regulation in which industries were held to be demanding regulation to protect their own interests by sheltering them from competitive market forces and in which the government was the supplier of regulation. Stigler's conclusion that regulation generally "exists to serve the regulated has stimulated a wide examination" of the origin and effects of regulatory institutions in the U.S. As Schmalensee remarks: "Economists simply cannot look at regulatory policy or at many other government policies, as they did before 1971. Stigler had made us all a bit more cynical, but, in exchange, opened up a broad new field of economic research."

36.3 CONCLUDING OBSERVATIONS

Besides the fields in which Stigler's contributions have been outlined above, he contributed to many other fields. In one of his early papers "The Cost of Subsistence" (1954), Stigler examined the problem of minimum cost diet which belonged to what came to be known later as Linear Programming problems and as such he is considered one of the pioneer writers in this field. As observed by Mincer, "this article is a classroom illustration of linear programming predating its formal appearance in economics."

Many economists consider Stigler's famous essay 'The Economics of Information' as having a "profound and lasting impact" on many fields of economics. Schmalensee in his sum up of Stigler's contributions says: "Throughout his long and productive career, Stigler has concentrated on the development and use of microeconomic theory as a tool for understanding real phenomena.... His writings do not display the sort of advanced mathematical technique that has become increasingly common in economics journals. Rather, they exhibit Stigler's extraordinary ability to pose important questions and his exceptional economic insight and ingenuity. They are distinguished as well by his rigorous insistence on testing the predictions of theory, by his clear and incisive prose, and by brilliant flashes of his justly famous wit."

Overall, George Stigler is rated as one of the most influential applied micro economists of the last several decades.

Milton Friedman in "A Personal Reminiscence" observes: "His [Stigler's] quickness of mind, cleverness of repartee, and unmatched capacity for smart cracks, always with a point, enlivened every encounter, yet belied his seriousness of purpose." Stigler was well-known for his pungent wit and biting sarcasm. The essay may be closed by quoting a couple of them.

"Smith's intellectual heirs did little to strengthen his case for laissez-faire, except by that most irresistible of all the weapons of scholarship, infinite repetition."

"When a good comedian and a production of [the play] Hamlet are on rival channels, I wish I could be confident that less than half the professors were laughing."

36.4 SELECT BIBLIOGRAPHY OF GEORGE STIGLER'S WORKS

36.4.1 BOOKS

1941 Production and Distribution Theories, Macmillan, New York.

1946 The Theory of Price, Macmillan, New York.

1947 Trends in Output and Employment, NBER, New York.

1950 Five Lectures on Economic Problems, Macmillan, New York.

1952 (with K. E. Boulding eds.), Readings in Price Theory, R.D. Irwin, Homewood, Ill.

1962 The Intellectual and the Marketplace: Selected Papers No.3, University of Chicago Press, Chicago, Ill.

1963 a Capital and Rates of Return in Manufacturing Industries, NBER, Princeton University Press, Princeton, NJ.

	b	The Intellectual and the Market Place and Other Essays, Free Press, Glencoe, Ill.
1965		Essays in the History of Economics, University of Chicago Press, Chicago, Ill.
1968		The Organization of Industry, R. D. Irwin, Homewood, Ill.
1975		The Citizen and the State, University of Chicago Press, Chicago, Ill.
1981		Economics or Ethics: Tanner Lectures on Human Values, Vol. 2, University of Utah Press, Salt Lake City.
1982		The Economist as Preacher and Other Essays, University of Chicago Press, Chicago, Ill.
1985		Memoirs of an Unregulated Economist: Autobiography, Basic Books, New York.

36.4.2 ARTICLES

1937		"The Essence of Carl Merger," JPE, Vol.45, Apr.
1939		"Production and Distribution in the Short Run," JPE, Vol.47, June.
1940		"Notes on the Theory of Duopoly," JPE, Vol.48, Aug.
1945		"The Cost of Subsistence," Journal of Farm Economics, Vol.27, May.
1947	a	"Notes on the History of Giffen Paradox," JPE, Vol.55, Apr.
	b	"The Kinky Oligopoly Demand Curve ad Rigid Prices," JPE, Vol.55, Oct.
1950	a	"The Development of Utility Theory," Part 1, JPE, Vol.58, Aug.
	b	"The Development of Utility Theory," Part 2, JPE, Vol.58, Oct.
1951		"The Division of Labor is Limited by the Extent of the Market," JPE, Vol.59, June.
1952		"The Ricardian Theory of Value and Distribution," JPE, Vol.60, June.
1953		"Sraffa's Ricardo," AER, Vol.43, Sep.
1954		"Schumpeter's History of Economic Analysis," JPE, Vol.62, Aug.
1955		"The Nature and Role of Originality in Scientific Progress," Economica, Vol.22, No.88.
1956		"The Statistics of Monopoly and Merger," JPE, Vol.64, Feb.
1957		"Perfect Competition, Historically Contemplated," JPE, Vol.65, Feb.
1958	a	"Ricardo and the 93% Labor Theory of Value," AER,Vol.48, No.3.
	b	"The Economies of Scale," JLawE, Vol.1, Oct.
1960	a	"The Influence of Events and Policies on Economic Theory," AER, Vol 50, No. 2.

b "Prometheus Incorporated: Conformity or Coercion," in Social Control In a Free Society, R. Spiller (ed.), Benjamin Franklin Lectures, University of Pennsylvania Press, Philadelphia, PA.

1961 a "The Economics of Information," JPE, Vol.69, June.

b "Economic Problems in Measuring Changes in Productivity," in Input, Output, and Productivity Measurement, Studies in Income and Wealth, Vol.25, Princeton University Press, Princeton, NJ.

1962 a "Administered Prices and Oligopolistic Inflation," JB, Vol.35, No.1.

b (with Claire Friedland), "What Can Regulators Regulate? The Case of Electricity," JLawE, Vol.5, Oct.

1964 a "A Theory of Oligopoly," JPE, Vol.72, Feb.

b "Public Regulation of the Securities Markets," JB, Vol. 36, Apr.

1965 "The Dominant Firm and the Inverted Umbrella," JLawE, Vol.8, Oct.

1967 "Imperfections in the Capital Market," JPE, Vol.75, June.

1968 a "Price and Non Price Competition," JPE, Vol.76, Jan/Feb.

b "Competition," "Henry L. Moore," International Encyclopaedia of Social Sciences, Vol.3; David L. Sills (ed.), Macmillan, New York.

1971 "The Theory of Economic Regulation," Bell Journal of Economics and Management Sciences, Vol.2, Spring.

1972 "The Evolution of the Marginal Utility Theory," HOPE,Vol.4, Fall.

1974. "Price System," Encyclopaedia Britannica, 15th ed.

1976 a "The Xistence of X-Efficiency," AER, Vol.66, Mar.

b "The Successes and Failures of Professor Smith," JPE, Vol.84, Dec.

1978 "The Literature of Economics; The Case of the Kinked Oligopoly Demand Curve," Econ Inq, Vol. 16, No. 2.

1983 a "The Process and Progress of Economics," Nobel Lecture, JPE, Vol.91, No.4.

b (with C. Friedland), "The Literature of Economics: The Case of Berle and Means," JLawE, Vol.26, No.2.

1984 a "Economics-The Imperial Science?" ScandJE, Vol.86, No.3

b "History of Economic Society Distinguished Fellow," JHET, Vol.5, No.1.

1985 (with R. A. Sherwin), "The Extent of the Market," JLawE, Vol.28, No.3.

1988 "Palgrave's Dictionary of Economics," JEL, Vol.26, No.4.

1990 "Ricardo or Hollander? [Ricardian Growth Theory: A Resolution of Some Problems in Textual Interpretation]" OEP, Vol.42, No.4.

1991 "Charles Babbage (1791+200=1991)," JEL, Vol.29, No.3.

1992 "Law or Economics," JLawE, Vol.35, No.2.

1995 (with S.M. Stigler and C. Friedland), "The Journal Of Economics," JPE, Vol.103, No.2.

2010 "Theory of Oligopoly," CPI Journal, Vol.6.

36.5 WORKS OF OTHERS

Friend, I. and E.S. Herman (1964), "Comment on S.E.C. through a Glass Darkly," JB, Vol. 36, Oct.

Mincer, J. (1983), "George Stigler's Contribution to Economics," ScandJE, Vol.85, No.1.

Peltzman and D. Carlton (2010), "Introduction to Stigler's in Theory of Oligopoly," Contemporary Policy International, Vol.6.

Rao, B.S.R. (1982), "Stigler: Professor and Prolific Writer," Science Today, December.

Schmalensee, R. (1983), "George Stigler's Contributions to Economics," ScandJE, Vol. 85 No.1.

Schmalensee, R. (1987), "George Stigler's Contributions to Micro economics and Industrial Economics," The New Palgrave: A Dictionary of Economics, Macmillan, London.

Sowell, T. (1987), "George Stigler's Contribution to History of Economic Thought," The New Palgrave: A Dictionary of Economics, Macmillan, London.

CHAPTER 37

JAMES ALEXANDER MIRRLEES

(1936 –)

Professor James Alexander Mirrlees, University of Cambridge, U.K., and Professor William Vickrey, Columbia University, New York, USA, were jointly awarded the 1996 Nobel Memorial Prize in Economic Sciences. The Royal Swedish Academy of Sciences decided to award the prize to them "for their fundamental contributions to the economic theory of incentives under asymmetric information."

Traditional economics assumes that all decision- makers in the market have the same information. In recent years, this assumption is questioned and one of the important and lively areas of economic research addresses situations where decision-makers have different sets of information. In real world, such informational asymmetries are commonly observed in a great many contexts. A number of examples can be cited. An insurance company may not have all the information about the person's health who may have been issued a health insurance policy. A bank does not have full information regarding the future income of a person to whom it has lent funds. Likewise, the shareholders of a corporate unit cannot have the same detailed information relating to costs and competitive conditions as its managing director. An auctioneer may not have complete information about the willingness and ability to pay of potential buyers. The government of a country has to devise an income tax system without adequate knowledge about the productivity of individual citizens and so on.

Incomplete and asymmetrically distributed information has very important consequences as such informational advantage can be exploited strategically. Research on the economics of information has crucially focussed on the issue of designing contracts and institutions to deal with different incentive and control problems. This research has facilitated a better understanding of insurance markets, credit markets, auctions, the internal organization of firms, tax systems, social insurance, competitive conditions, political institutions, etc.

William Vickrey and James Mirrlees laid the foundation for examining these areas through their analytical work on issues where the key component is informational asymmetries. Vickrey's work is concerned with the properties of different types of auctions, and the best way in which they can be designed to generate economic efficiency. His efforts have helped in laying the basis for a lively field of research which, more recently, has found practical applications such as auctions of treasury bonds and band spectrum licenses. One of Vickrey's works is his formulation of a model of income tax in late 1940's to attain a balance between efficiency and equity.

The principles of income taxation have been studied for a long time by economists, political scientists and philosophers. In a classical essay published in 1897, Francis Y. Edgeworth, an Oxford Professor, adopted a utilitarian welfare perspective. His conclusion in the essay is that all differences in income should be neutralised, which requires strong progressive tax rates. The work in 1940's of Vickrey's emphasised that a progressive tax schedule would impinge on an individuals' incentives to exert himself. He reformulated the problem taking into account both incentive problems and concerns of asymmetrical information. Incentive problems relate to each individual taking the tax schedule into consideration when choosing the work effort while the problems of asymmetric information is concerned with the lack of knowledge in practice on the part of government of the productivity of individuals. He formulated a solution to the problem in principle, but did not succeed in coming to terms with its mathematical complications.

James Mirrlees, who reconsidered the problem after a lapse of twenty-five years, solved it in a way that has established a paradigm for analysing a broad spectrum of economic issues where asymmetric information is a key feature. Mirrlees identified a critical condition (what has come to be known as single crossing) which also proved to contain the "germ of a general principle: the revelation principle." According to this principle, the solution to incentive problems under incomplete information belongs to the relatively limited class of so-called allocation mechanisms which induce all individuals to reveal their private information truthfully, in a way which does not conflict with their own self-interest. The application of this principle makes it easy to design optimal contracts and other solutions to incentive problems. This has had a large bearing on the treatment of many issues of economic theory.

One of the important issues relating to the insurance industry is the question of moral hazard. For example, damage to insured property depends not only on external factors such as weather and attempted theft, but also on the care taken by the policyholder, which is expensive and difficult for an insurance company to monitor. Such moral hazard problems arise regarding different kinds of social insurance and disability insurance. Generous insurance coverage can exaggerate risk-taking and affect the way individuals care for themselves and their property. Principal-agent problems are another example involving moral hazard.

Many other two-party relations involve an outcome that is observable to both parties, where the outcome depends on one party --- the agent - which cannot be observed by the other party --- the principal, as well as on random factors. For instance, the relation between the owner of a firm (principal), and the management of a firm (the agent), the action of the agent such as the executive's work effort would determine the outcome-- the firm's profit --and the random variable could be the firm's market conditions or production conditions. The owners of the firm want to choose terms of compensation, a "contract," which gives the agent incentives to act in accordance with the principal's interests, say, by maximising the owner's expected profits.

The technical difficulties encountered in analysing these so-called moral hazard problems are similar to the income tax problems referred to earlier. In the mid-1970's, by a simple reformulation of the problem, Mirrlees paved the way for powerful analysis. He noted that an agent's actions indirectly imply a choice of the probabilities of occurrence of different outcomes. The conditions for the optimal terms of compensation thus provide "probability information" about the agent's choice and the extent to which insurance protection has to be restricted in order to provide the agent with suitable incentives. In designing an incentive scheme, the principal has to consider the costs of giving the agent incentives to act in line with the interests of the principal. The higher the agent's sensitivity to punishment and the larger the amount of information about the agent's choice contained in the outcome, the lower these costs, which are stipulated in a contract. The agent bears part of the cost of undesirable outcomes or receives a part of profits from favorable outcomes. For instance, the insurance policyholder takes care of the insured object almost as if it was uninsured, and the executive of the insurance company manages the firm as if it were his own.

In auctions, where potential buyers have limited knowledge about the value of the asset or rights up for sale, asymmetrical information is an essential component. Vickrey attempted analysis of the properties of different kinds of auctions. He attached special importance to the second-price auction or, as it is often referred to as, the Vickrey auction. In such an auction, an object is auctioned off in sealed bidding, where the highest bidder gets to buy the item, but only pays the next highest price offered. This kind of auction is socially efficient. The object goes to the person with the highest willingness to pay, and the person in question pays the social opportunity cost which is the second highest bid. Vickrey's analysis has not only been momentous for the theory of auctions; it has also conveyed fundamental insights into the design of resource allocation mechanisms aimed at providing socially desirable incentives. While Mirrlees's work is covered in this chapter, Vickrey's contributions are surveyed in the next chapter.

37.1 A SHORT BIOGRAPHICAL NOTE: JAMES MIRRLEES

Professor James Alexander Mirrlees was born on July 5, 1936, in Minnigaff, Kirkcudbrightshire, Scotland. His father was a bank teller in Scotland. James Mirrlees went to school in Newton Stewart. While at primary school he was quick at mental arithmetic, he also "acquired glasses." Childhood illnesses gave Mirrlees time to read. He passed the "control," the examination at age eleven to decide who could go on to the high school, The Douglas Ewart. In his autobiographical note, Mirrlees states: "By the age of fourteen I had acquired a strange enthusiasm for mathematics.... The head mathematics teacher somehow gave me individual tuition during classes, and I raced ahead.... When asked by the Rector (the headmaster) what I wanted to do in life, I gave the obvious answer: be a professor of mathematics."

Mirrlees thought of trying for the Cambridge scholarship but could not take the examination because of serious illness. Instead, he went in 1954 to Edinburgh "...which I did not mind then, and do not regret now." According to him, mathematics was easy in those years in Edinburgh, and did not take much time. As a result, he was able to engage in many cultural activities. In the final examination, he got the Napier medal. He had taken Cambridge Scholarship in early 1957. In that year, at the age of twenty-one, he left Scotland, "like many before and since..." In Trinity College, Cambridge, which he had joined, Mirrlees was taught by the best mathematician one could hope to find. Mirrlees duly became a wrangler. There he was guided by his mathematics teacher to Piero Sraffa in economics. Mirrlees wanted to do economics because "... poverty in what were then called the underdeveloped countries, seemed to me what really mattered in the world, and that meant economics." His tutor at college managed to get Mirrlees, a three year award to do Ph.D. in economics. David Champernowne was his first teacher in Trinity.

David Champernowne advised Mirrlees to read Keynes's General Theory. Mirrlees remarks: "That may not have been the best advice, but it did no great harm, and one day I hope to finish it." His reading was haphazard. The lectures and seminars of the notable Cambridge names, Kahn, Kaldor and Joan Robinson were highly "idiosyncratic, but it was a stimulating time." Mirrlees's official supervisor to guide his research was Richard Stone. At the end of first year, Stone associated Mirrlees in his Growth Project – a project aimed at simulating realistically the long-term growth of an economy, particularly the UK. The guiding star was "indicative planning." According to Mirrlees, "Stone pointed me to Ramsey on optimal saving...and at some point in all this I had discovered Samuelson and mathematical economics." Mirrlees wrote some research papers during this period; in this effort he received encouragement from Frank Hahn, who became another unofficial supervisor and "great mentor." Later, after marriage, Mirrlees started doing a fellowship dissertation for Trinity College. He was sure that there were no contributions in his work; still, he preserved a copy of the work, Contributions to a Theory of Economic Planning.

Not satisfied with the work, in the context of his mathematical culture, Mirrlees was hoping for "an inspiration for a real idea" which, according to him, came on one day in November 1961. He felt that the idea of uncertainty was neglected and tried to think about how uncertainty should affect the optimal rate of saving in an economy. Setting up a model to answer these questions, he could show that quite commonly...greater uncertainty is a reason for saving more, not less, contrary to the prevalent opinion then. He started using Wiener processes and "...discovered the Ito calculus for myself."

The preparation of his Ph D was delayed because of his assignment as a research assistant to Nicholas Kaldor who was writing a paper on growth (in the end Mirrlees was made a co-author). Another reason for delay was his association with the India project run by Paul Rosenstein-Rodan for the MIT Center for International Studies at the suggestion of Amartya Sen. Mirrlees spent three months along with his wife at MIT where he met Paul Samuelson and Robert Solow. Mirrlees gave a seminar at MIT on optimum growth under uncertainty.

In 1962 on his way from MIT to India, Mirrlees worked out the theory of efficiency-wage equilibria. When in India working on the India Project, he wrote many little papers, particularly about investment appraisal, and efficiency wages. His work on investment appraisal, including ideas about uncertainty, led on, after some years, to work with Ian Little on criteria for cost-benefit analysis in developing countries. Mirrlees adds "I fear I did not do as much for the Planning Commission as had been hoped or intended. I learned an immense amount, both from the country and from its many fine economists. In these days Jagdish Bhagwati, T. N. Srinivasan and [late] Sukhomoy Chakravarty were all there too, and Amartya Sen was about to return."

Trinity College, Cambridge, offered him a teaching fellowship in economics to be taken up in 1963, which he accepted. He submitted his Ph. D thesis on Optimum Accumulation under Uncertainty in September 1963. Kenneth Arrow was visiting Cambridge that year, and was one of Mirrlees's two examiners. In the autobiographical note Mirrlees states: "He [Arrow] tried very hard to find the mistakes and failed. But I have still never been able to solve the main problem the thesis addressed, at least to my satisfaction." Later he published a small paper on the subject. The stimulus of teaching at Trinity took Mirrlees in some new directions, as he thought increasingly about general welfare economics, conceived as a general theory of economic policy. In the next few years he worked on optimal taxation in collaboration with Peter Diamond. Mirlrres observes: "I followed the main principle for academic success: get a good co-author (and also the second: get another)." His thinking on the question of taxation led to contemplation about non-linear tax schedules, still referred to as optimal income tax theory. After almost leaving Cambridge, he took the vital step towards a more general conception of relationships between principal and agent in economic contracts.

At the age of thirty-two, in 1968, Mirrlees was offered a professorship of economics by Oxford University. He comments in his autobiographical note "...Cambridge was increasingly suffering from shrill doctrinal, almost religious, squabbles (mainly then with the rest of the economic world)." After leaving Cambridge and before joining Oxford University, Mirrlees spent a sabbatical at MIT; he began work on non- linear incentive relationships. Before joining Oxford, Ian Little got Mirrlees to do A Manual on Cost Benefit Analysis with him.

At Oxford he had "several superb" Ph. D students; He found himself almost invariably with at least one, often several, research students of the highest class. He states: "I have always supervised research much more diverse than what I do myself.... It was only quite loosely a school of optimal taxes and welfare and incentives. I am proud that in due course industrial economics and game theory flourished in Oxford. ....I have long lost count of the number of my students who hold full professorships, but I like to think they are numerous as well as able."

Mirrlees worked as advisor, MIT Centre for International Studies, India project, New Delhi, was visiting professor of economics at University of California at Berkley and at Yale

University. He was fellow of Trinity College between 1963 and 1968 and since 1995 and fellow of Nuffield college of Oxford University between 1968 and 1995.He is currently Emeritus Professor of Political Economy, University of Cambridge. He was knighted in 1998. He was elected Fellow of Econometric Society. Mirrlees is known as co-creator, with Peter Diamond, of the Diamond Mirrlees Efficiency Theorem developed in 1971. He is currently the Distinguished Professor—at—Large of the Chinese University of Hong Kong. Mirrlees is a member of Scotland's Council of Economic Advisors. His students have included eminent academics: Lord Nicholas Stern and Sir Partha Dasgupta.

37.2 A BRIEF SUMMARY OF JAMES MIRRLEES'S CONTRIBUTIONS

As a background to the work of Mirrlees, one may refer to his Nobel lecture: "Information and Incentives : The Economics of Carrots and Sticks," which essentially deals with ignorance. Quoting from Adam Smith's The Theory of Moral Sentiments in which Smith stated that the rich are led by an invisible hand to make nearly the same distribution of necessities of life which would have been made, had the earth been divided into equal portions among all its inhabitants, Mirrlees expresses his view that "this is far from the later conception of an economic equilibrium that is 'optimal' in Pareto's sense." Mirrlees also says Smith's claim is not "very plausible." However, it sets the major themes; first, the working of the economy as a system, and second, the good or otherwise, for everyone, that can flow from it.

Mirrlees opines that in the Wealth of Nations, Smith had argued correctly that individual profit maximisation implies maximisation of national income. Smith did not talk about possible advantage to the poor – nothing about distribution of gains at all. Mirrlees identifies two parts to the doctrine of invisible hand. First, an economic equilibrium is Pareto optimal. Second, any Pareto- optimal allocation can be an economic equilibrium. This proposition makes assumptions about the nature of technological possibilities such that a perfectly competitive equilibrium can occur. It excludes economies of scale; or, production levels in those industries experiencing scale economies have to be determined in some other way, as, for example, by some kind of planning.

Mirrlees agrees with those economists who pointed out serious defects of the theory. The competitive model ignores important deviations from the standard assumptions. For example, a number of economic transactions are characterised by monopoly power on at least one side of the market in view of the presence of search costs, switching costs and uncertainty about the future performance of contracts such as in credit markets. The other important drawback of the theory concerns the asset distribution. There has to be a particular distribution of assets which would result in equilibrium that is good. Mirrlees comments: "That requirement, when properly understood, was plainly impossible to fulfil." He observes that a strong case can be made for thinking that transfer from richer to poorer was an improvement; carrying that to the logical extreme, riches of the earth should be distributed equally. This, he considers is not a popular policy. A perfectly equalising policy would eliminate the incentive to work. Mirrlees remarks: "From each according to his abilities, to each according to his needs (Karl Marx, Criticism of the Gotha Programme) is not thought to be feasible, even if desirable."

The problem, according to Mirrlees, is the government does not have and could not obtain the information required for redistribution of assets. The main problem could be identified as information asymmetries. Workers have better knowledge of their abilities than their employers. Government knows less than taxpayers about the latter's actual and potential income. According to standard economic theory, the price system automatically fully aggregates the dispersed information. In perfectly competitive markets with a large number of buyers and sellers, the economic transactions are anonymous and have features that the traditional theory cannot explain. A clear example is bilateral bargaining. A commercial bank lending funds to a corporate unit is exposed to default risk from that unit. An employer who is employing a group of workers trying to secure a better effort from them is not operating in an anonymous labour market. Avinash Dixit and Timothy Besley argue that some such relationships may be competitive ex ante. An employer may have a choice to make from among a number of applicants for the job; likewise, a worker may choose among several jobs. Similarly, in the capital market there are many potential lenders as also borrowers. They argue: "...once the deal is struck, the relationship becomes bilateral and non- anonymous.... When private information bears on transactions that are not anonymous, each participant has the opportunity and the natural incentive to manipulate his information to his own advantage." For instance, a life insurance applicant may not reveal all the information that has a bearing on the risk being transferred to the insurance company. If the insured risk occurs, the claimant may try to conceal his failure to take the precautionary measures.

It is, of course, possible for the other party to the transaction to improve the information set and make information symmetric. For example, a bank that has lent funds to a corporate unit may get represented on the board of directors, if only to monitor the use of sanctioned funds. In the case of medical and health insurance, the insurer may subject the prospect to a medical examination. Likewise, tax authorities conduct periodic audits. Such independent checks by one side of the transactions are rather imperfect besides being costly. It is, therefore, suggested that use must be made of devices that rely on the informed parties' own incentives. Dixit and Besley summarise the idea: [It] is to structure the terms of the contract between the two asymmetrically informed parties in such a way that concealment becomes less possible or more costly for the informed party." Reverting to the insurance example, we find common use of devices such as deductibles and co-insurance, where a part of the loss is borne by the insured. The foundations of the general theory of the design of incentives have been laid by Mirrlees's work.

Further, it is possible to see the application of non-cooperative game theory in information economics what with the opportunities for specifically manipulating the information by parties to a transaction in the backdrop of the importance of private information and absence of anonymity in transactions. Dixit and Besley remark: "... it is this combination of game theory and theory of information that has produced some of the most exciting and fruitful research in economics during the last two decades." This is evidenced by the award of 1994 Nobel Memorial Prize in Economic Sciences "to three game theorists and the award of this year's prize to Vickrey and Mirrlees, the two pioneers of information economics."

In the initial stages of the study of information, economists treated information as an economic commodity. This approach was found to be less fruitful. Instead, the focus of attention shifted to the issue as to how the availability and the dispersal of information relating to economic commodity would affect the working of the markets as also mechanisms for allocation of those commodities. Kenneth Arrow pioneered the work on economic analysis of asymmetric information. His work dealt with issues of adverse selection and moral hazard, very major issues in insurance economics. Though Arrow's analysis was mainly informal, a large amount of research work was conducted on those two basic concepts. In regard to the problem of adverse selection, the work of George Akerlof is well-known. In respect of a second-hand or used car market, he had demonstrated how the market could collapse because of the adverse selection problem. However, it is observed that while many markets may suffer from some adverse selection, most of them continue to exist. The markets try to tackle the problem of asymmetric information by devising contracts and other incentives.

The theory that has developed over time to cope with the problem is generally classified into two streams. The first one while dealing with the issue of asymmetric information distinguishes between market interactions and non- market ones. According to Dixit and Besley, the conceptually more basic approach "... classifies the problems according to whether the initiative for coping comes from the less informed party or the more informed."

Screening devices are methods used by less informed party to obtain desired information or action from the more informed party. Screening by self- selection refers to schemes that change the informed party's own incentives in the desired direction. The foundations for latter, which is of special relevance in non-market situations such as a firm's internal organisation or government's economic policy are provided by the work of Vickrey and Mirrlees. Rothschild and Stiglitz presented a model for insurance markets representing screening by self-selection in market contexts. Incidentally, it may be mentioned that A.M Spence pioneered the work relating information to more informed party revealing the true information to the less informed party in the transaction, if this will work to its advantage. Spence calls such action "signals." In market interactions, signalling is of special importance.

The contributions of Mirrlees relate to designing incentive mechanisms for screening dealing with cases of adverse selection and moral hazard.

37.2.1 ADVERSE SELECTION: GOVERNMENT TAXATION

Adverse selection in information economics is of direct relevance in an insurance context. If an insurance company cannot determine the risk class of an individual because of non-observance of some of his innate characteristics, an insurance policy will selectively attract clients in bad risk classes. "More generally, the term [adverse selection] refers to a situation where one party to an economic relationship has adverse private information about some parameter that affects the payoff from the relationship."

An important application of the concept of adverse selection concerns redistributive taxation. The government actions, according to Mirrlees, are a function of only what it could observe--only observations of individual consumer's behaviour. It is widely recognised that Mirrlees's 1971 article in the Review of Economic Studies, for the first time presented a general analysis of optimal income tax policy design that considered specifically the problem of informational asymmetry. In his Nobel lecture, Mirrlees states that in case of income taxation, tax can be a highly complicated function of income. While income of an individual consists of several elements such as labour income and income from capital, Mirrlees's model specifically deals with labour income. He states that labour income can be taxed non-linearly and fully non-linear taxation is, like linear taxation, incentive-compatible. The computation of tax is based on the publicly observable behaviour of the consumer. Mirrlees contends that non-linearity will be advantageous as it is more general than linear taxation.

One, of course, could not tell in advance how advantageous linearities might be as in many countries there are elements in social insurance etc., that are more like a form of income taxation. Mirrlees observes that the typical real tax system has "high marginal tax rates for low incomes and for high incomes, and low marginal tax rates in the intermediate range." For the design of the optimum income-tax system, he suggests thinking about allocation of real commodities and labour. It is necessary because in welfare terms incentive-compatibility is added to the original constraint that the allocation of commodities should be feasible. Then a question needs to be asked: What allocations of commodities are possible if policy has to be incentive-compatible?

Mirrlees assumes that individual consumers can decide about the quantum of labour supply. The situation of each consumer is described by two variables: consumption and labour supply. Each consumer type is defined by a single parameter, productivity or equivalently the person's wage rate. The government knows the distribution of wage rates in the economy. The total product of each individual can be observed by the government as it is the product of the wage rate and the amount worked, though it cannot observe either of these alone. This assumption is in line with the tax systems which relate to total income of an individual and not to wage rates.

Assuming that the government wishes to maximise a standard utilitarian welfare function subject to the market constraints or equivalently a total resource constraint, one has to find the real distributions of consumption and work in the population that are incentive-compatible. Through a diagram depicting incentive-compatibility and showing before tax income on the horizontal axis and after-tax income on the vertical axis and further assuming that people with higher wage rates always find it easier to produce more income by working than those with smaller, Mirrlees demonstrates incentive-compatible consumption/income allocations. This assumption means that different people's indifference curves cross one another once only. The condition is known as the single-crossing property (or sometimes called the Spence-Mirrlees condition). The comment of Dixit and Besley on this is: "The single crossing property underlies virtually all models of adverse selection, and Mirrlees was the first to recognize it and pinpoint its role."

Mirrlees further states "... the original optimal income tax problem could now be converted into something very like a standard control-theory problem with utility as the state variable, income the control variable.... An exciting feature of this analysis was its validity.... The use of fully non-linear taxation does solve one problem that has troubled tax theorists."

In his Nobel lecture, Mirrlees states that the analysis of asymmetric information is applicable to many economic relationships that are of the principal/agent type, particularly employer/employee relationships. The type of Mirrlees's analysis outlined above applies "...when the agent's performance is observable and measurable, but the agent knows more than the principal, for example, about the relationship between unobservable effort and performance." He further states that an optimal payment system, with asymmetric information "could well have an authoritarian character, if it showed pay rising rapidly with performance over some range, low at lower incomes, and not rising much further at higher." However, Mirrlees does not think such a harsh relationship is optimal in realistic cases of asymmetric information. Other fields of application of asymmetric information include control of firms by regulators and pricing by public utilities. One way of thinking about regulation is to have an output variable, tax; then the methods of analysis suggested by Mirrlees can be employed. According to Mirrlees, in such areas of application, however, the time dimension is potentially important.

37.2.2 SITUATIONS OF MORAL HAZARD AND INCENTIVES

Individual economic agents may be also uncertain about their taxes and ability, when they make decisions. The extreme case where the agent is no better informed than the principal--referred to as moral hazard in insurance. According to Dixit and Besley, the essence of moral hazard is that one party to an economic relationship takes an action that cannot be observed or deduced by another affected party. If the behaviour of the agent cannot be observed, it is generally not possible to infer from performance in situations where the link between action and performance is uncertain. Many relationships can be cited: medical care, share cropping with farmers paying for the use of land with a share of income or profits.

Dixit and Besley explain this problem as follows:

Let an observable outcome x be a function of two unobservables; 'a' and 'Θ'. That is, $x = g(a,\Theta)$, where a denotes action and Θ is state of nature. The action is decided before the state of nature is realised. In the context of insurance, 'a' could be the care exercised by the insured and 'x', the amount of loss when the insured event happens. In principal–agent relationship, 'a' is the effort of the agent and 'x' is the aggregate profit or surplus for the pair. In each case, 'Θ' is a random variable that affects the outcome, making it impossible to infer 'a' accurately by observing 'x.'

Problems relating to moral hazard are generally analysed assuming that people try to maximise their expected utility. Mirrlees observes that incentives will have to be set up so that people will make an optimal effort. For solving the problem it is to be ensured that the marginal effect of effort on the expected utility of consumption takes some particular value. "At the same time, government is constrained by the total consumption that is going to be available when people do that amount of effort. Subject to these two constraints, it wants to maximise expected utility." Mirrlees further states that when the right incentives are set, some consumption levels will be low, perhaps at lower income levels. The probability of this outcome can be avoided by greater effort at lower income levels. On the other hand, incentives will be imposed by reducing consumption though it lowers expected utility. He states: "... reduce consumption at observed output levels where the incentive improvement is greatest, relative to utility loss, i.e. where the elasticity of output probability with respect to effort is great." He draws a simple rule: reduce consumption at output observed levels where effort has a large proportional effect on the probability of that level.

Mirrlees's model suggests that government can realise a satisfactory outcome, "almost as though the incentive constraint could be ignored," by instituting very low consumption at very low incomes. However, this solution is unacceptable for various reasons. Low consumption when there is a very poor outcome, which is appropriate in principal/agent situations with moral hazard, is what Mirrlees says, incentives by means of punishments. He however, remarks that he does not persuade himself that the solution is correct. Nevertheless, he believes that in employment relationships where a heavy punishment cannot be imposed on the agent, "...dismissal will happen in a range of bad outcomes, and then rewards may rise rather rapidly over a range of outcomes." He illustrates the solution with the following diagram.

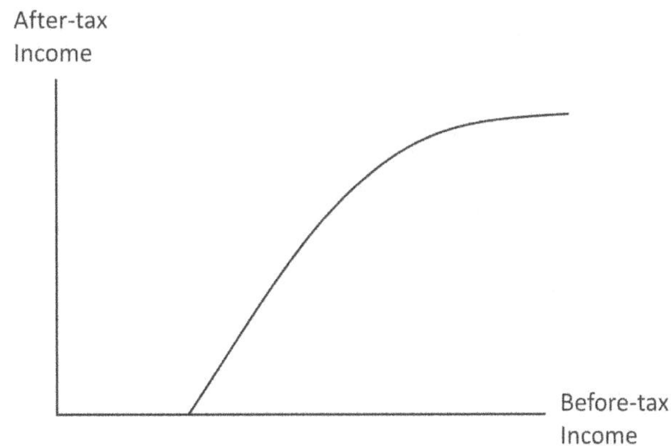

Fig. 37.1 Optimal Pay Schedule under Moral Hazard

The shape of the payment schedule may be given by the marginal utility of payment related to the elasticity of probability with respect to effort. According to Mirrlees, the method of solution to the problem does not always work. With the complications present in the issue, Mirrlees finds it "hard to give any general rules as to what we would want or expect payment schedules to look like when the relationship between principal and agent involves moral hazard." The sharply rising middle section of the payment curve in Fig. 37.1 is by no means universal.

Mirrlees has applied the general model of incentives under moral hazard to study the internal organisation of firms, especially the use of incentive wage schedules and the role of hierarchies. Dixit and Besley are of the opinion that "...this is an important contribution to the formation of Coase's idea that the size of the firm is determined by trading off the costs of internal control against the costs of using the market." A particularly intriguing result in Mirrlees's paper, according to Dixit and Besley, is that "payment schedules at lower levels of the firm's internal hierarchy should be more like fixed wages for following particular instructions, and at higher levels there should be more profit-sharing incentives."

Mirrlees in the last part of his Nobel lecture observes as to how one can think of ways of creating incentives in principal/agent situations. He acknowledges how the theory and practice of the design of economic mechanisms or contract theory or principal/agent problems have progressed in recent years. In his view it is the asymmetry of responsibilities, with the principal moving first and the agent following that has made the problem easier. He concludes his lecture with the following: "... anonymous market relationships are only a part of economic reality; perhaps not even the largest part. Most economic problems and possibilities involve instead, relationships between and among individual agents, whether taxes, contracts and bargains, fights and thefts, learning and research. It is a world still only imperfectly explored."

37.3 CONCLUDING OBSERVATIONS

Mirrlees's contributions relating to information and incentives are fundamental to the foundations of economic theory. In the economics profession he is better known for his particular contributions to public economics and development economics. In collaboration with Peter Diamond he made notable contributions to commodity taxation: "...the Diamond Mirrlees model now stands as the definitive statement and analysis of this branch of public economics." Their treatment of the subject is considered an advance over the work of Frank Ramsey and Paul Samuelson.

It is generally agreed that Mirrlees's work has improved our understanding of a host of problems. His work which usually starts with applications and not with the avowed goal of developing general theories, is commented upon and commended by economists. Dixit and Besley sum up the importance of this approach; "...his attempts to put the welfare economics of government policy on a rigorous footing stem from an intrinsic interest in providing policy guidance." Finally they state: "...while one learns a great deal about economic analysis in general form studying his contributions, one is also reminded of the vision that one reason for doing economics is the possibility of making the world a better place."

37.4 SELECT BIBLIOGRAPHY OF JAMES MIRRLEES'S WORKS

37.4.1 BOOKS

1969 (with I M D Little), Manual of Industrial Project Analysis in Developing Countries, Vol. II , Social Cost Benefit Analysis, OECD, Paris.

1974 (with I.M.D. Little), Project Appraisal and Planning for Developing Countries, Heinemann, London, and Basic Books, New York.

2006 Welfare, Incentives and Taxation, Oxford University Press, Oxford.

2011 (with S Adam et al.), Tax by Design: The Mirrlees Review, Oxford University Press, Oxford.

37.4.2 ARTICLES

1962 (with N. Kaldor), "A New Model of Economic Growth," RES, Vol.29, June.

1967 "Optimum Growth When Technology is Changing," RES, Vol.34, June.

1969 a "The Dynamic Non substitution Theorem," RES, Vol.36, Jan.

b "The Evaluation of National Income in an Imperfect Economy," Pakistan Development Review, Spring.

1971 a "An Exploration in the Theory of Optimum Income Taxation," RES, Vol.38, April.

	b	(with P. A. Diamond), "Optimal Taxation and Public Production I & II, Production Efficiency and Tax Rules," AER, Vol.61, Nos.1 and 3.
1972	a	"On Producer Taxation," RES, Vol.39, Jan.
	b	(with N. H. Stern), "Fairly Good Plans," JET, Vol.4, Apr.
1973	a	(with P. J. Hammond), "Agreeable Plans," in Models of Economic Growth, Mirrlees and Stern (eds. for IEA), Macmillan, London.
	b	(with P. A. Diamond), "Aggregate Production with Consumption Externalities," QJE, Vol.87, No.1.
1974	a	"Optimal Accumulation under Uncertainty: The Case of Stationary Returns to Investment," in Allocation under Uncertainty, J. Dreze (ed.), Macmillan, London.
	b	"Notes on Welfare Economics, Information and Uncertainty," in Essays in Equilibrium Behavior under Uncertainty, M. Balch, D. McFadden, and S. Wu (eds.), North Holland, Amsterdam.
1975	a	"Optimal Taxation in a Two-Class Economy," JPubE, Vol.4.
	b	(with Avinash Dixit and N. H. Stern), "Optimum Saving with Economies of Scale," RES, Vol.42, No.3.
	c	"A Pure Theory of Underdeveloped Economies, using a Relationship between Consumption and Productivity," in Agriculture in Development Theory, L. Reynolds (ed.) Yale University Press, New Haven, CO.
1976	a	"Optimal Tax Theory: A Synthesis," JPubE, Vol. 6, No.4.
	b	(with P. A. Diamond), "Private Constant Returns and Public Shadow Prices," RES, Vol. 43, No. 1.
	c	"The Optimal Structure of Incentives and Authority within an Organization," Bell JE, Vol.7, No.1.
1978		(with P. A. Diamond), "Model of Social Insurance with Retirement," JPubE, Vol. 10, No. 3.
1980		(with P. A. Diamond and L. J. Helms), "Optimal Taxation in a Stochastic Economy: A Cobb- Douglas Example," JPubE, Vol. 10, No. 3.
1982	a	"The Economic Uses of Utilitarianism," in Utilitarianism and Beyond (A. K. Sen and Williams, eds.) Cambridge University Press, Cambridge,
	b	"Migration and Optimal Income Taxes," JPub E, Vol.18, No.3.
1985		(with P. A. Diamond), "Insurance Aspects of Pensions, Labor, and Individual Choice," NBER, New York.

1986 a "The Theory of Optimal Taxation," in Handbook of Mathematical Economics, K. J. Arrow and M. D. Intriligator (eds.), Vol. III, North-Holland, Amsterdam.

b (with P. A. Diamond), "Payroll-Tax Financed Social Insurance with Variable Retirement," ScandJE, Vol. 88, No.1.

1990 "Taxing Uncertain Incomes," OEP, Vol. 42, No.1.

1992 (with P. A. Diamond), "Optimal Taxation of Identical Consumers when Markets are Incomplete," in Economic Analysis of Markets and Games, P. Dasgupta et al. (eds.) MIT Press, MA.

1994 "Optimal Taxation and Government Finance," in Modern Public Finance, Quigley and Smolensky (eds.) Harvard University Press, Cambridge, MA.

1997 "Information and Incentives: The Economics of Carrots and Sticks," Nobel Lecture., EJ, Vol. 107, No.444.

1999 "The Theory of Moral Hazard and Unobservable Behaviour: Part I," RES, Vol. 66, No.1.

2005 "The Theory of Optimal Taxation," in Handbook of Mathematical Economics, (K. J. Arrow and M. D. Intriligator eds.), Ed 2, Vol.3, Elsevier, Amsterdam.

37.5 WORKS OF OTHERS

Arrow, K. J. (1963), "Uncertainty and the Welfare Economics of Medical Care," AER, Vol.53, No.5.

Dixit, A. and T. Besley (1997), "James Mirrlees's Contributions to the Theory of Information and Incentives," ScandJE, Vol.99, No.2.

Ramsey, F. P. (1927), "A Contribution to the Theory of Taxation," EJ, Vol.37, No.145.

Spence, M. (1973), "Job Market Signaling," QJE, Vol.87, No.3.

CHAPTER 38

WILLIAM SPENCER VICKREY

(1914 – 1996)

The 1996 Sveriges Riskbank Prize in Economic Sciences in Memory of Alfred Nobel was awarded by the Royal Swedish Academy of Sciences jointly to Professor William Vickrey, Columbia University, New York, U.S.A. and to Professor James A. Mirrlees, University of Cambridge, U.K., for their fundamental contributions to the economic theory of incentives under asymmetric information. Asymmetric information has important effects on decision-making by economic units. In recent years, the focus of economic research has turned to situations where all decision-makers do not have the same information. Information asymmetries occur in great many contexts. For example, an insurance company does not have information about the medical history if the prospect had suffered from any serious illness before issuing a life insurance policy whereas the prospect has all this information. A bank which is granting a loan to a customer does not have complete information regarding the future income of the borrower and his repayment capacity. The owners or shareholders of a firm may not have the same detailed information about costs and competitive conditions in the market as the managing director; an insurer cannot fully observe how far the policyholder is discharging his responsibility for insured property and managing external events which impact the risk of damage; an auctioneer does not possess all the information regarding the potential buyer's willingness and ability to pay; the government has to design an income tax code without much knowledge relating to the productivity of individual citizens; and so on.

Important consequences arise from incomplete and asymmetrically distributed information. The press release states that an informational advantage can often be exploited strategically. It is therefore not surprising that research on economics of information has been devoted to the issue of how contracts and institutions can be designed to deal with different incentive and control problems. This research focus has helped in better understanding of financial markets including insurance markets and credit markets, social insurance, tax systems, wage forms, auctions, internal organization of firms, competitive conditions, and political institutions and so on.

The award notification specifically mentions that the two laureates have laid a firm foundation for examining these seemingly quite disparate areas through their analytical work on questions essentially characterised by informational asymmetries. It particularly mentions the specific contribution of the two to economics. In the case of Vickrey, the press release mentions that an essential part of his research was concerned itself with the properties of different types of auctions and generate economic efficiency by suitably designing them. This work was done by Vickrey in early 1960s. His research provided a basis for a lively field of research. In recent years, the field of research has tried to cover practical applications such as auction of treasury bonds and band spectrum licenses.

In the late 1940's, Vickrey formulated a model suggesting how income taxation can be so framed so as to achieve a balance between efficiency and equity. Interest in this model was renewed by the work of James Mirrless after a quarter of a century. Mirrlees put forward a more thorough solution to the problems relating to optimal income taxes. Mirrlees realised soon that the method developed by him could also be applied to many other similar problems. It has become an important component of the modern analyses of complex information and incentive problems. Mirrlees's approach has been particularly found useful in situations where it is not possible to observe the actions of another agent, the so-called moral hazard problem.

William Vickrey's contributions are summarised here; the contributions of Mirrlees are covered in the earlier chapter.

38.1 A BRIEF BIOGRAPHICAL SKETCH: WILLIAM VICKREY

William Spencer Vickrey was born in Victoria, British Columbia, Canada, in 1914. His elementary and secondary educations were in Europe and the United States, with graduation from Phillips Andover Academy in 1931. He attended Yale University, obtaining a B.S. degree in mathematics in 1935 and then went to Columbia University for graduate work in economics, obtaining an M.A. in 1937. Vickrey then worked for the National Resources Planning Board in Washington and the Division of Tax Research in the U.S. Treasury Department.

A conscientious objector (he was a Quaker), Vickrey, during the second world war, spent part of his alternate service designing a new inheritance tax for Puerto Rico. Columbia University awarded him the Ph.D. degree in economics in 1948. His 496-page doctoral dissertation, "Agenda for Progressive Taxation," was included in 1972 among the REPRINTS OF ECONOMIC CLASSICS.

Vickrey joined the faculty of Columbia University in 1946 as a lecturer in economics and never left the University, except for a few sabbaticals. He became a full professor in 1958 and was named Mc Vickar Professor of Political Economy in 1971. He was Chairman of the Department of Economics from 1964 to 1967 and retired as Mc Vickar Professor Emeritus in 1982. He devoted 60 years of his life to economics, including 50 years on the Faculty of Columbia University. Vickrey's working life was devoted mostly to teaching and research, publishing several books and over 140 articles. In fact, he wrote an article—"Fifteen Fatal Fallacies of Financial Fundamentalism: A Disquisition on Demand Side Economics," in 1996, one week before his death. In addition, he did also a significant amount of advisory and consulting services on behalf of public institutions and utilities, and none too small amount of non-specialist writing and lecturing. It is observed that Vickrey'seconomic philosophy was influenced by Keynes and Henry George.

His long career of research covered a wide range of subjects. The first of much research work involving efficient pricing of public utilities done in 1939 and 1940 for the Twentieth Century Fund dealt with electric power. In 1951, he did the famous study of sub-way fares in New York City for the Mayor's Committee for Management Survey. He was a member of the Carl Shoup Mission that developed a comprehensive programme for revising the tax system of Japan. This was followed by a number of tax missions, notably to Puerto Rico, Venezuela and Liberia. In 1959, Vickrey studied the problem of traffic congestion in Washington. Further studies on urban planning and transportation took him to India, Argentina and Venezuela. In this context it is pertinent to mention an Indian economist's remark: "Of all foreign economic advisers, Vickrey had been the most directly helpful because he had produced new railway schedules that permitted substantial energy saving and improved service." Vickrey also spent a year as an adviser on fiscal matters for the United Nations, working in a number of countries including Singapore, Malaysia, Iran, Zambia and Libya. Over the years, he developed ideas for efficient pricing of electricity, telephone services, urban transportation, airlines, street and road use and municipal services. It is reported that he also kept up with every conceivable technological development in these areas. Vickrey's pursuit of maintaining and improving efficiency of public services made him a crusader, advocating innovations not only through lectures for the National Tax Association, National Bureau of Economic Research, Public Utility Conferences and Transportation Symposia, but also through testimony at hearings and letters to newspapers. Vickrey had special interest in ethics and philosophy which led to several publications by him in these fields. Interdisciplinary contacts always appealed to him, especially through seminars. It should also be mentioned that Vickrey supervised Kenneth Arrow's doctoral dissertation "Social Choice and Individual Values."

Vickrey had received many honours and awards, besides the Nobel Prize. He was a distinguished fellow of the American Economic Association and served as its President in 1992. He was elected Fellow of the Econometric Society. He was elected to the National Academy of Sciences. He was a past president of the Metropolitan Economic Association and the Atlantic Economic Association. Among various honours Vickrey received were the F. E. Seidman Distinguished Award in Political Economy and a doctor of humane letters degree from the University of Chicago.

William Vickrey died on October 11, 1996, three days after the announcement of the Nobel Memorial Prize in Economic Sciences.

38.2 A BRIEF SUMMARY OF WILLIAM VICKREY'S CONTRIBUTIONS

The Royal Swedish Academy of Sciences has made specific mention of the fundamental contributions of William Vickrey and James Mirrlees to the economic theory of incentives under asymmetric information. The laureates' complementary contributions to the theory of optimal income taxation, Vickrey's pioneering work on auctions and Mirrlees's work on the issue of moral hazard are "privileged examples of the development of incentive-compatible allocation mechanisms." Reference is also made to other complementary topics of second best indirect taxation and pricing of public services. The Academy particularly emphasises the unusual talent of Vickrey and Mirrlees in following up theoretical contributions to practical application.

While his research work is varied and voluminous, Vickrey's contributions in the following five areas are summarised here.

1. Economic Incentives;
2. Auction Theory;
3. Taxation;
4. Marginal Cost Pricing; and
5. Urban Transportation.

38.2.1 PIONEERING WORK ON ECONOMIC INCENTIVES

The economics of incentives is concerned with the design of rules and institutions with a view to inducing economic agents to make all efforts and to reveal truthfully all socially relevant information they possess. Laffont considers this an advance over Jacob Marschak's 1955 work on theory of teams. As incentive theory, Marschak's work emphasised the decentralisation of information in multi-agent situations. However, unlike game theory, the theory of teams neglects strategic behaviour. Laffont observes: "From a theoretical perspective incentive theory corresponds to a simple case of game theory with incomplete information in which bargaining has been eliminated by attributing to an economic agent, the principal, all the ability to design the rules of the games played by the other agents, under the only constraint that they must be induced to participate." As is clear, the principal designs rules to maximise his expected utility (in the backdrop of the handicap of asymmetric information) anticipating the strategic behaviour of the agents for the rules proposed by him.

Laffont distinguishes three types of results in the incentive theory with reference to the above-mentioned principal-agent model.

(i) At one extreme, Vickrey identifies Gibbard-Salterthwaite's impossibility theorem. This theorem demonstrates that if the principal does not have any information on the preferences of the agents, very little can be achieved by him with dominant strategy mechanisms; that is, mechanism for which each agent has a unique best strategy, irrespective of the other agents' strategies. For example, if we assume that the principal is a constitutional designer organising the production of public goods, only dictatorial mechanisms that make no use of the other agents' information are possible.

Vickrey in his 1960 paper, after clearly explaining Arrow's possibility theorem, commented upon social welfare functions that do not satisfy the independence axiom. He then discussed strategic misrepresentation of preferences and made a conjecture: "...if a function is to be immune to strategy and be defined over a comprehensive range of admissible rankings, it must satisfy the independence criterion.... Immunity to strategy and independence are thus at least closely similar requirements if not actually logically equivalent." Vickery suggested, in the article, the route to the impossibility of non-manipulative, non-dictatorial voting mechanisms through Arrow's theorem. It was only in 1973 that Gibbard provided the proof confirming Vickrey's conjecture.

(ii) At the other extreme, the principal can use the class of so-called Clarke-Grover dominant strategy mechanisms. In the example given in (i) above relating to public goods, if the principal knows that the agents have quasi-linear utility functions (this is indeed a strong assumption on agents' preferences) the dominant strategy mechanisms yield the first best up to "some imbalance of the budget." Laffont conjectures: For quadratic utility functions the budget may even be balanced so that the exact first best can be achieved despite asymmetric information.

In <u>The Economics of Control</u>, Aba Lerner makes a suggestion that where markets are imperfectly competitive, a state agency, through counter speculation, might be able to create conditions whereby the marginal conditions for efficient resource allocation could be maintained. Taking the cue from this, Vickrey explored the possibility of organising such mechanisms. To impose the competitive price or determine the optimal allocation, Laffont quotes Vickrey: "...what the marketing agency needs...is an unbiased report of the marginal cost curves of the sellers and of the marginal value curves of the purchasers. The problem is then for the marketing agency to behave in such a way as to motivate the buyers and the sellers to furnish such unbiased reports. One method, though an expensive one, is to arrange to purchase the commodity from suppliers and to sell it to purchasers on terms that are dependent on the reported supply and demand curves in such a way that the suppliers and purchasers will maximise their profits, individually at least, by reporting correctly, so that any misrepresentation will subject them to risk of loss (or at least offer no prospect of gain)."

Vickrey then explicitly outlined such a method in these words: "The agency would first aggregate the reported supply and demand curves to determine the equilibrium marginal value, and apply this value to the individual demand and supply curves to determine the amounts to be supplied and purchased by the various individual buyers and sellers. The amount to be paid seller 'i' would, however, somewhat exceed the amount calculated by applying this marginal value to his amount supplied; in effect, for the rth unit supplied, seller 'i' would have an amount equal to the equilibrium price that would have resulted if seller 'i' had had restricted his supply to 'r' units, all other purchasers and sellers behaving competitively." Vickrey gives a graphical proof that such a mechanism induces truthful revelation. Laffont comments: These mechanisms were reinvented ten to twelve years later by Clarke in 1971 and Grover in 1973 in the context of public goods.

Vickrey was quite sceptical about this mechanism since it requires an external source of funds. The solution would permit optimum allocation of resources if there were a source of public funds that has no adverse impact on resource allocation in other directions. Further, Vickrey was of the view that all modifications that would result in reducing the cost of the scheme either imply the use of some external information or reintroduction of a direct incentive for misrepresentation. He also admitted the possibility of collusive behaviour. He therefore suggested the method of auctions – the second price-sealed bid option – where the seller was going to be the external agency required to achieve Pareto optimality. He further showed that truthful bidding is a dominant strategy. Laffont observes: "To compare the first price and second price auction and obtain a first version of the revenue equivalence theorem, he [Vickrey] computed Bayesian equilibria (for particular distributions) many years before the formal definition of Harsanyi (1967-68) and explored the still quite unknown territories of asymmetric auctions and repeated auctions."

(iii) The third type of result which lies between (i) and (ii) above is: there are a large number of second best problems in which the principal, who maximises his expected utility under conditions of asymmetric information, strikes a trade off between efficiency and the allocation of informational rents to the agents.

The application of economics of incentives by Vickrey can, in fact, be traced to his work on optimal income tax problem. Employing the insights of von Neumann and Morgenstern, Vickrey modelled the optimal income tax problem as a principal-agent problem – the tax authority is the principal and tax payers are the agents. Vickery stated: "If utility is defined as that quantity the mathematical expectation of which is maximized by an individual making choices involving risk, then to maximize the aggregate of such utility over the population is equivalent to choosing that distribution of income which such an individual would select were he asked which of various variants of the economy he would become a member of, assuming that once he selects a given economy with a given distribution of income he has an equal chance of landing in the shoes of each member of it."

Taking this as the objective function, Vickrey formulated optimal income taxes as follows: "It is generally considered that if individual incomes were made substantially independent of individual effort, production would suffer and there would be less to divide among the population. Accordingly, some degree of inequality is needed in order to provide the required incentives and stimuli to efficient cooperation of individuals in the production process. The question of the ideal distribution of income, and hence of the proper progression of the tax system, becomes a matter of compromise between equality and incentives."

Formalising the issue as a problem of calculus of variation, Vickrey concluded that even in the simplified form, the problem does not yield any facile solution. Laffont remarks: "The Pontryagin principle was far away and twenty six years were needed to obtain Mirrlees' 1971 solution." Laffont further observes, that Vickrey formulated and solved incentive problem in partial equilibrium contexts. His work on incentives was "totally ignored until the development of the game theory under incomplete information because of the dominance of general equilibrium theory in the 1950s and 1960s."

In 1945, while working on the issue of guidelines for progressive taxation, Vickrey was concerned with the use of cardinal utility measures. After reviewing the approach of Irving Fisher and Ragnar Frisch among others based on the assumption of additive preferences and the technical property that an additive representation of additive preferences is unique up to linear transformations, Vickrey argued: "As a basis for determining the proper progression of the tax structure, an independence utility function has no demonstrable competence." He explained the relevance to welfare economics of cardinal utility as measured from choices among uncertain prospects. Vickery made significant contributions in these three directions "...10 to 25 years before anyone else in the economics profession. It is to the credit of Mirrlees that he provided necessary and sufficient conditions outlining the constraints imposed by the decentralization of information on resource allocation."

38.2.2 AUCTION THEORY

After emphasising the link between incentives and information, the Swedish Academy refers to the importance of that link in "lively developments of contemporary economic research," particularly relative to Vickrey's work on auctions. The Academy states that asymmetric information is also an essential component of auctions, where potential buyers have limited knowledge about the value of an asset or rights up for sale. Vickrey analysed the properties of different kinds of auctions in two papers in 1961 and 1962. He attached particular importance to the second-price auction or, as it is now called, the Vickrey auction.

Prior to Vickrey's work on auctions, economic theory relating to markets did not pay attention to the detailed rules that determine who trades how much with whom and at what price. Classical economists as well as modern economists of neo-classical persuasion like Hicks, Samuelson, Debreu and Arrow had, in their analysis, focussed on the supply and demand conditions, which they assumed, determine market conditions. Milgrom observes: The [neo-classical] theory implicitly assumes that the particular rules governing how bids and offers are combined to determine prices and allocations ultimately has no effect on market outcomes."

This doctrine of neo-classicals was rejected by Vickrey. Instead, in his analysis he paid particular and detailed attention to the rules of the market and contended that these rules could crucially determine the level of prices, the quantities traded and identities of traders. His papers on auction theory specifically included the first formal analysis using theory to devise new auction rules to ensure efficient outcomes. According to Milgrom, the term auction broadly refers to any market process in which the identities of the buyers or sellers and the terms of trade, particularly including prices, are determined by an explicit comparison of bids or offers. Further, the term is inclusive of both "open auctions" and "sealed tenders."

Vickrey's 1961 paper is perhaps his most cited article and "Vickrey auction" is now an accepted technical concept.. That paper is an outcome of his investigation of methods that bring out Pareto efficiency in non-competitive situations. The motivation for this work is also the idea put forward by Lerner in his Economics of Control, referred to earlier. In the case of divisible commodities, Vickrey came to a pessimistic conclusion regarding Pareto-efficient allocation. In contrast, he finds in situations in which a single indivisible item is to be allocated, the common or progressive type of auction generally results in Pareto allocation, with the object purchased by the bidder to whom it has the highest value, at a price only slightly above the second highest value. In contrast, the so-called Dutch auction, characterised by the announcement of prices in descending sequence until a first bid is made, is not generally Pareto efficient.

In this context, Vernon Smith has to say the following: "Auctions may be classified according to the different institutional rules governing the exchange. Since the seminal work of Vickrey (1961), it has been recognized that these rules are important because they can affect bidding incentives, and therefore the terms and the efficiency of an exchange...following Vickrey, it has become standard to distinguish four primary types of auctions which can be used either in single object or multiple (identical or non-identical) unit auction." They are English auction, Dutch auction, First Price auction and Second Price auction.

About auctions, Vickrey observed: "A considerably greater degree of importance attaches, not to auctions as such, but to cases in which a contract is to be let on the basis of competitive sealed tenders.... Actually, the usual practice of calling for the tender of bids on the understanding that the highest or lowest bid as the case may be, will be accepted and executed in accordance with its own terms is isomorphic with the Dutch auction...." Vickrey, as mentioned earlier, favoured the second-price auction. This type of auction is advantageous to the successful bidder, besides being socially efficient. In Vickrey's own words: "...it is of interest to inquire whether there is not some sealed-bid procedure that would be logically isomorphic to the progressive auction. It is easily shown that the required procedure is to ask for bids on the understanding that the award will be made to the highest bidder, but on the basis of the price set by the second highest bidder." Given this procedure, the optimal strategy for each bidder, assuming no collusion among bidders (this assumption is necessary in the analysis of progressive auctions) is to make his bid equal to the full value of the article or contract to himself. Unlike other kinds of auctions, this mechanism also gives each bidder a dominant strategy, namely, to bid its own value (A dominant strategy is generally designed as a strategy that is best for the bidder, regardless of the strategies of the other bidders). This is an example of a mechanism that elicits an individual's true willingness to pay. It represents the highest amount he could afford to pay without incurring a net loss or to that price at which he would be on the margin of indifference as to whether he obtains the article or not. Vickrey further elaborated: "Bidding less than this full value could then only diminish his chances of winning at what would have been a profitable or at least not unprofitable, price and could not, collusion aside, affect the price he would actually pay if he were the successful bidder. Bidding more than the full value, on the other hand, would increase his chances of winning, but only under circumstances that would involve him in an unprofitable transaction, the price to be paid, greater than his value."

Jacques Dreze comments on Vickrey's 1961 article: "There it is: ...the isomorphism of the Dutch and first-price auctions: the efficiency and incentive compatibility of the second-price auction: and the starting point for what has become the most important area of auction theory." The literature on the subject that has developed since Vickrey's work, is in Arrow's words "devoted to maximizing seller's revenues, rather than social welfare in some broader sense." It is also seen that the "second-price" in an auction corresponds exactly to Vickrey's notion of "marginal social costs," being in this case a measure of the loss inflicted on the rest of the society.

Vickrey's work has led to a major intellectual event of 1970's in public economics, namely, demand revelation mechanism. That mechanism was developed by eliciting individual "willingness to pay" (WTP) for social outcomes by announcing the two-step process. (i) Selection of the outcome with the maximum aggregate of individual WTPs, and (ii) each individual player, say i, will have to contribute the difference between the total WTPs of the other participants for the selected outcome and for the outcome that would have been chosen if i's preferences have been ignored. The mechanism, of course, is not self-financing, which is its main drawback. Vickrey subsequently considered the applicability of the mechanism to international disputes. Later, there have been practical applications of his auctions theory such as auctioning of pure public goods – say, wavelengths for personal communication services, like pocket telephones or networks of wireless computers, and Macmillan's analysis in his paper "Selling Spectrum Rights." However, Vickrey was sceptical of the usefulness of his work on the topic as "one of my digressions into abstract economics, at best of minor significance in terms of human welfare."

38.2.3 TAXATION

The award citation makes specific reference to Vickrey's work on income taxation. The press release notes the extensive study of principles of income taxation by economists, philosophers and political scientists. In this connection, reference may be made to the classic work of Edgeworth, 'an Oxford adopted Professor,' that was published in 1897 which took a utilitarian welfare perspective. He suggested neutrality of all income differences which requires strongly progressive tax rates. Vickrey's earliest writings were on taxation. His graduate training at Columbia in the mid-1930's in public finance under Robert Haig and Carl Shoup and in theory under Harold Hotelling and his work in the Tax Research Division of the U.S. Treasury were helpful in the designing of a tax system and were instrumental in his important and mature contributions to the theory of tax policy. Vickrey thought of a progressive income tax with a base in comprehensive lifetime income. His 1939 paper "Averaging of Income for Tax Purposes" envisaged computation of a cumulative (present value) tax liability with inputs regarding his tax age and his cumulative income. The current year's tax liability would be calculated as the difference between his current cumulative tax liability and his previous year's cumulative tax liability brought forward one year.

Such a tax system was considered horizontally equitable, in that two individuals of the same tax age with the same present value of income would pay the same present value of taxes, independent of the timing of income. In contrast, a progressive tax system, with annual income of the tax payer as the base, taxes more heavily those who have an uneven stream of income. Be that as it may, the concept of income averaging for income tax purposes has not become popular despite its appeal on grounds of both equity and efficiency, perhaps because of practical difficulties in implementation and the failure of cumulative averaging in terms of comprehensibility.

In a later paper, Vickrey developed the idea of optimal income taxation, a reference to which has been made by the Nobel Prize citation. "Vickrey stated: Assuming that the marginal utility of money declines with increasing income, maximizing the total utility derived by a population from a given fixed aggregate income implies that this income be distributed equally, due allowance being made for varying needs.... But the aggregate amount of income to be distributed cannot in practice be considered independent of the way in which it is distributed. It is generally considered that if individual incomes were made substantially independent of individual effort, production would suffer and there would be less to divide among the population. Accordingly, some degree of inequality is needed to provide the required incentives and stimuli to efficient cooperation of individuals in the production process – the question of the ideal distribution of income, and hence of the proper progression of the tax system, [then] becomes a matter of compromise between equality and incentives."

Vickrey, therefore, reformulated the problem with respect to asymmetric information (government is not in the know of the productivity of individuals) and problems of incentives (when choosing work effort, each individual takes the tax schedule into account). He derived a solution to the problem in principle, "but did not succeed in mastering its mathematical complications." The problem was subsequently solved by Mirrlees a quarter-century later.

Another issue which is important concerns the taxation of inter-generational transfers. There is general recognition that the tax payable on an estate can be greatly reduced through good tax management and that the wealthy taxpayer will always be one step ahead of the tax authorities. Vickrey had also importantly contributed to the question of taxation of inter-generational transfers by his two papers published in 1944. The papers dealt with problems involving design of the taxation of inter-generational transfers in such a way as to be neutral in regard to "generation-skipping" and at the same time be progressive with respect to the wealth of the recipient. Arnott remarks: "To my knowledge, no such exercise had been performed before nor has a similar exercise been performed since. While Vickrey's particular scheme has had little if any impact on actual succession taxation, he is to be credited both for advocating the rationalization of succession taxation and for proposing an essentially axiomatic approach to the design of a coherent succession tax system."

Before concluding the section, reference has to be made to Vickrey's Ph.D. thesis, "Agenda for Progressive Taxation," published in 1947, considered his "crowning achievement" in the field of taxation. The book has a comprehensive approach and suggested an implementable progressive tax system. We may cite here Arnott's assessment of the book: "While no one will agree with all of Vickrey's decisions concerning the compromise between theoretical and practical considerations, one cannot but admire his attempt to design as coherent and rational a tax system as is practicable...while few of Vickrey's specific proposals have been adopted, his method of deriving a tax system from basic principles has been influential, and many of the principles he employed have since guided tax reform efforts."

38.2.4 MARGINAL COST PRICING

Jules Dupuit is credited with first recognising in the 1840's, the efficiency of marginal cost pricing of public utilities. The principle was well established because of the work of many economists including Vickrey's teacher at Columbia, Harold Hotelling. Vickrey was reported to have written some forty articles on the subject, many of them giving specific application of marginal cost pricing to electricity, urban transportation, water supply, telephone service and air travel. In his papers on the subject we come across two important ideas, namely:

Efficiency requires the price be set equal to short-run marginal cost; and

Random fluctuations in demand may be taken care with responsive pricing.

While pricing public utilities, one has to take into account the issue of systematic as well as random fluctuations in demand. According to Vickrey, who was the first to address this issue, pricing has to be on the basis of expected short-run marginal cost, where the expectation is conditioned on the information available to the user of the utility at the time he undertakes his usage decision. He illustrated this principle through the example of ticket sales for an airline flight. If the price is set ex ante, there may be empty seats or overbooking of tickets, both of which are inefficient. However, ongoing spot market for tickets for a particular flight ensures efficient rationing of seats by price.

Responsive pricing may be used effectively for electricity, water and telephone usage. The usage decision is taken on the basis of current spot price. However, Vickrey recognised the drawbacks of responsive pricing. It is not invariably the most efficient method of dealing with demand fluctuations. In certain cases, for example, city bus travel, transaction costs associated with implementing responsive pricing may exceed efficiency gains. In other cases, the demand characteristics and the nature of congestion technology may make other mechanisms (other than responsive pricing) more effective.

A prominent application of the principle of marginal cost pricing was in regard to his study relating to New York subway fares. The study resulted in Vickrey's "Proposal for Revising New York's Sub-way Fare Structure," a well known "Classic." His study had emphasised the influence of the fare upon the utilisation of the transit system by the riding public. For the purpose of the study, he collected cost data and apportioned costs among different traffic parameters. He also computed arc-elasticities of demand using data on the recent fare increase. Utilising the information so collected, Vickrey could evaluate the consequences for efficiency and revenues, of alternative fare structures. He recognised very early that the actual application of marginal cost pricing demands a detailed knowledge of congestion technology; Vickrey therefore informed himself of the technology of each public utility he considered. His first degree from Yale which was in mathematics and electrical engineering was of considerable help in this regard. For example, his 1959 study of auto congestion in Washington D.C. was concerned with the technological implementation of "Congestion Pricing." It is an independent derivation of Ramsey-Boiteux pricing of public utilities. Vickrey also wrote papers which dealt with non-pricing aspects of efficient provision of public utilities services, as, for example his study of efficient scheduling of trains in India. Arnott notes that while Vickrey's name was associated with pricing solutions to congestion, "...he clearly recognized the importance of applying economics in the design of public utility capacity and in scheduling. In his ideal world, engineering economics would occupy a position of prominence and efficient pricing would be only one element – albeit a central one – of good engineering practice."

Critics have noted that Vickrey, in his application of the principle of marginal cost pricing, did not consider the interaction between capacity and pricing, "...in particular to the simultaneous determination of efficient pricing and optimal capacity, though he clearly understood the issues," as also lack of attention to second-best issues, even though "...he was the first to articulate them in the context of urban transportation!"

Vickrey admitted that he "...kind of hipped on the idea of marginal cost pricing; the use of pricing as a device for improving the efficiency with which we use various facilities." In this context, we may refer here to Vickrey's interest and his work on marginal cost pricing by his entry on the subject for the New Palgrave Dictionary of Economics.

38.2.5 URBAN TRANSPORTATION

As mentioned earlier, Vickrey was assigned by Carl Shoup and Robert Haig, Directors of a study in the early 1950's of New York City's finances to study and suggest a transit fare structure for the city. His study was rated as pioneering and "the first modern work in urban transport economic policy analysis." In the study, he emphasised the efficiency of marginal cost pricing; he applied the theory for estimation of marginal cost of trips by origin-destination as also time of day of the trip. He not only worked out the schedule of first-best fares but also made second-best adjustments to it to take care of costs of collection, equity, distortionary financing of the deficit etc. In addition, he looked into the mechanics of collection of fares. In the opinion of Arnott, Vickrey's New York Sub-way fare study was "path breaking and much of the subsequent work in urban transport economic theory has entailed elaborating and formalizing its insights and conceptual framework. Despite the theoretical strength, the article [1955] has had little impact on transit pricing practice." Vickrey's other works in transportation economics include a study of urban transportation problems with specific reference to Washington D.C. Another outstanding study in urban transport economics is Vickrey's 1969 paper "Congestion Theory and Transport Investment." Prior to this paper, urban transport economists treated traffic congestion as a flow congestion. This approach was subject to criticism. Arnot comments: "In a stroke of genius, Vickrey captured the essence of the transport engineering approach, while dramatically simplifying it thereby permitting economic analysis, by modeling congestion as a queue behind a bottleneck." Vickery went further and developed an analysis of the dynamic equilibrium of rush-hour auto congestion. His paper showed that worsening congestion results in a lengthening of the rush hour and strengthened the case for congestion pricing and indicated the potential gains from charging time-varying tolls.

Critics have extracted the principles of efficient congestion pricing and how to implement such pricing for roads and parking. A few of them are given here.

Charges should reflect as closely as possible the marginal cost of each trip in terms of impact on others. There is no valid reason for charges below marginal social cost.

Charges should vary smoothly over time. This will work as an incentive for people to shift the time of travel, if only by small amounts, away from the peak.

Efficient charges have to be determined taking into account the impact of an individual trip on other traffic from the time the trip is made until the end of the congestion period.

All vehicles should be charged without exception in order to preserve the integrity of the market pricing principle.

Curb parking, if permitted, has to be charged on the basis of clearing the market.

Use of parking cards is a simple and inexpensive way of collection of the charges.

No political interference or bureaucratic bungling should be allowed.

38.3 CONCLUDING OBSERVATIONS

Besides the fields discussed above in which Vickrey made important contributions, he had also contributed to other fields in economics such as micro and macroeconomics. He published graduate text books in them. He viewed generation of persistent unemployment as fundamentally wrong with any economic system as he was concerned with waste and loss of dignity caused by unemployment. He frequently remarked that there is nothing natural about the natural rate of unemployment. In this connection, the following observations from his last article, "Fifteen Fatal Fallacies of Financial Fundamentalism: A Disquisition on Demand Side Economics" (written a week before his death) are worth quoting: "These fallacious notions which seem to be widely held in various forms by those close to the seats of economic power are leading to policies that are not only cruel but unnecessary and self-defeating in terms of their proposed objectives.... We will not get out of the economic doldrums as long as we continue to be governed by fallacious notions that are based on false analogies, one-sided analysis, and an implicit underlying counterfactual assumptions of an inevitable level of unemployment."

Dreze makes specific reference to Vickrey's substantial contribution to the field of public economics "...all the way from the foundations rooted in social choice theory, through the quest for efficiency in both revenue raising and resource allocation, down to the implementation of inventive practical proposals. To each of these aspects, Vickrey has brought the benefits of a global viewpoint and a masterful command of principles, but also of an unfailing imagination in his unique determination to extend theoretical research toward practical application."

Arnott notes Vickrey's "breadth of conceptualization, inventiveness, subtlety of thought, depth of intellect, and generosity of spirit." He also observes that Vickrey's style of writing is distinctive, curious and distinguished; "it is also clear, literate, engaging, entertaining and eminently quotable." Arnott also comments that full appreciation of a Vickrey paper requires repeated reading. He finds that Vickrey had the cast of mind of a theorist but interests in public policy. Vickrey's corpus of research is distinctive and unusually broad in scope. He observes: "Vickrey, the scholar, is there in print. Vickrey, the man is far more elusive. Some obituaries portrayed him as a cross between Albert Einstein and the Nutty Professor. He was brilliant, eccentric and other worldly.... He was a moral philosopher."

We may close this essay with a quote from the citation of the American Economic Association on Vickrey's election as a distinguished fellow: "Some great scholars receive recognition from the beginning, but, inscrutably with others it takes a little longer. His [Vickrey's] numerous works, in all leading journals in economics, law, operations research, finance, and taxation contain many seminal contributions, and many more that would have been seminal but for the fact that the profession was not yet ready for his ideas."

38.4 SELECT BIBLIOGRAPHY OF WILLIAM VICKREY'S WORKS

38.4.1 BOOKS

1947 Agenda for Progressive Taxation, Ronald Press, New York.

1964 a Microstatics, Harcourt, Brace and World, New York.

b Metastatics and Macroeconomics, Harcourt, Brace and World, New York.

1994 Public Economics: Selected Papers by William Vickrey (Arnott, R., A. B. Atkinson, K. Arrow and J. H. Dreze, eds.), Cambridge University Press, New York.

38.4.2 ARTICLES

1939 "Averaging of Income for Income Tax Purposes," JPE, Vol. 47, pp.379-397.

1944 "The Rationalization of Succession Taxation," Econometrica, Vol.12, No.3-4.

1945 a "Measuring Marginal Utility by Reactions to Risk," Econometrica, Vol.13, No.4.

b "The Effect of Averaging on the Cyclical Sensitivity of the Yield of the Income Tax," JPE, Vol.53, pp.275-288.

1948 "Some Objections to Marginal Cost Pricing," JPE, Vol.56, pp.218-238.

1949 "Resource Distribution Patterns and the Classification of Families," Studies in Income Wealth, Vol.10, NBER, New York.

1950 "Ethics and Economics: An Exchange of Questions between Economics and Philosophy," in Goals of Economic Life, A. Ward (ed.) National Council of Churches.

1955 "A Proposal for Revising New York's Sub-way Fare Structure," Journal of Operations Research Society of America, Vol.3, pp.38-68.

1960 "Utility, Strategy, and Social Decision Rules," QJE, Vol.74, No.4.

1961 "Counterspeculation, Auctions and Competitive Sealed Tenders," JF, Vol.16, No.1.

1962 "Auctions and Bidding Games," in Recent Advances in Game Theory, Princeton University Press, Princeton, NJ.

1963 "Pricing in Urban and Suburban Transport," AER, Vol.53, No.2.

1969 "Congestion Theory and Transport Investment," AER, Vol.59, No.2.

1971 a "Responsive Pricing of Public Utility Services," BellJE, Vol.2, No.1.

b "Maximum Output or Maximum Welfare? More on the Off-Peak Pricing Problem," Kyklos, Vol.24, No.2.

c (with R. M. Solow), "Land Use in a Long Narrow City," JET, Vol.3, No.4.

1972 a "Cumulative Averaging after 30 years," in Modern Fiscal Issues: Essays in Honor of Carl S. Shoup (Bird, R. M. and J. G. Head, eds.), University of Toronto Press, Toronto.

1985 "The Fallacy of Using Long-run Cost for Peak-Load Pricing [Heterogeneous Users and the Peak-load Pricing Model]," QJE, Vol.100, No.4.

1987 "Progressive and Regressive Taxation," The New Palgrave: A Dictionary of Economics, Macmillan, London.

1992 a "Today's Tasks for Economists," AER, Vol. 82, No.1.

b "An Updated Agenda for Progressive Taxation," AER, Vol.82, No.2.

c "Chock-Full Employment without Inflation: A Proposal for Marketable Mark up Warrants," AER, Vol.82, No.2.

d "Meaningfully Defining Deficits and Debt," AER, Vol.82, No.2.

e "Efficient Pricing of Electric Power Service: Some Innovative Solutions," Resources and Energy, Vol.14, No.1-2.

1993 a "My Innovative Failures in Economics," Atlantic Economic Journal, Vol.21, pp.1-19.

b "Today's Tasks for Economists," AER, Vol.83, No.1.

c "Disarmament, Unemployment, Budgets, and Inflation," Journal of Asian Economics, Vol. 4, No.1.

1999 (with S. P. Anderson and M. R. Braid), "Spatial Competition, Monopolistic Competition and Optimum Product Diversity," International Journal of Industrial Organisation, Vol.17, No.7.

2001 "Site Value Taxes and the Optimal Pricing of Public Services," American Journal of Economics and Sociology, Vol. 60, No.5.

38.5 WORKS OF OTHERS

Arnott, R. (1997), "William Vickrey's Contributions to Public Policy," ScandJE, Vol.99, No.2.

Clarke, E. G. (1971), "Multipart Pricing of Public Good," Public Choice, Vol.88. Feb.

Dreze, J. H. (1997), "Research and Development in Public Economics: William Vickrey's Inventive Quest of Efficiency," ScandJE, Vol.99, No.2.

Grover, T. and M. Loeb (1975), "Incentives and Public Inputs," JPubE, Vol.4, No.3.

Lerner, A.P. (1944), The Economics of Control, MacMillan, New York.

Marschak, J. (1955), "Elements for a Theory of Teams," Management Science, Vol.1, No.2.

Mirrlees, J. (1971), "An Exploration in the Theory of Optimum Income Taxation," RES, Vol.38, April.

Ramsey, F. P. (1927), "A Contribution to the Theory of Taxation," EJ, Vol.37, No.145.

CHAPTER 39

GEORGE ARTHUR AKERLOF

(1940 –)

The Bank of Sweden Prize in Economic Sciences for 2001 in Memory of Alfred Nobel was awarded jointly to three American economists. The Royal Swedish Academy of Sciences while announcing the award to them, specifically states that it is "for their analyses of markets with asymmetric information." The winners are George A. Akerlof, University of California at Berkeley, A. Michael Spence, Stanford University, and Joseph E. Stiglitz, Columbia University.

Adam Smith's argument in The Wealth of Nations that free markets would lead to efficient outcomes, "as if by an invisible hand," has played a key role in the debates of economists. The essence of the argument is that we could largely rely on free markets without government intervention to lead to efficient outcomes. Government has a limited role, at best. As Stiglitz remarks problems of information-- whether incomplete or asymmetric information--- are very important to understand market economics besides political economy. The ideas of Adam Smith have been undermined by Information Economics, which has suggested that the reason that the hand may be invisible is "that it is simply not there – or at least if it is there, it is palsied."

The analyses of this year's three laureates, i. e., analyses of Akerlof, Spence and Stiglitz form the core of modern information economics. The thinking of economists about the functioning of markets has been transformed by the work of these laureates. Perfect market models, which dominated in teaching of economics and most of the research in the subject for over five decades, have been shown by the prize-winners as flawed and quite misleading as they ignore information economics. According to Stiglitz these models are flawed even for developed countries, such as U.S.A and countries in Europe; more importantly they are truly inappropriate for developing countries. The latter countries are known to be characterised by features such as imperfect information, absence of markets and pervasive and persistent dysfunctional institutions such as share cropping.

Akerlof observes that prior to late 1960's, microeconomic theory was essentially concerned with analysing the purely competitive, general equilibrium model based upon maximisation of utility by consumers and profit maximisation by firms. The prevalent macroeconomics of the day, referred to as "neoclassical synthesis," applied a fixed money wage to such a general equilibrium system. Departures from full employment and business cycle fluctuations are sought to be explained by the sticky money wages. Blanchard and Fischer are of the view that was put forward in 1989 in their Lectures on Macroeconomics that "on the surface, macroeconomics appears to be field divided among schools, Keynesians, Monetarists, new Classical, new Keynesian, and no doubt others." Further they observe: "We believe that its [macroeconomics] inherent difficulties stem from the need to draw from all branches of micro economics...." Since 1970's, both micro economics and macroeconomics have developed a number of models that are formulated to incorporate into economic theory a whole variety of realistic behaviours. The new models have incorporated markets with asymmetric information and imperfect and incomplete information. The press release of Royal Swedish Academy states that for more than two decades, the theory of markets with asymmetric information has been a vital and lively field of economic research. Models with imperfect information are "indispensable instruments" in the tool box, of researchers in economics. It notes of innumerable applications extending from traditional agricultural markets in developing countries to modern financial markets all over the world including developed economies. A number of issues that arise in the markets characterised by the asymmetric information include the following which are highlighted by the press release.

Why are interest rates often excessively high on local lending markets in Third world countries? Why do people who want to buy a good used car turn to a dealer rather than a private seller? Why does a corporate unit pay dividends even if they are taxed more heavily than capital gains? Why is it advantageous for insurance companies to offer policy owners a menu of contracts where higher deductibles can be exchanged for lower premiums? Why do rich landowners not bear the entire harvest risk in contracts with poor tenants? Each of these and other similar questions that illustrate familiar phenomena has posed a challenge to economic theory. This year's winners of the Economics prize put forward a common explanation and extended the theory by augmenting it with the realistic assumptions of asymmetric information: economic agents on one side of the market have much better information than those on the other side. Repayment prospects are better known to the borrowers than lenders in the credit market. In a used car market, the seller knows more about the quality of his car than buyers. The CEO and Board of Directors have better knowledge than the shareholders about the firm's profitability. Insureds know more than the insurer about their accident risk. Tenants of land know better than the landowner about their work effort and harvesting conditions.

The award announcement specifically highlights the significant contributions of each of the three Laureates. For instance, Akerlof demonstrated that informational asymmetries may result in adverse selection on markets. As a result of imperfect information on the part of prospective car buyers or lenders, sellers of low-quality cars or borrowers with weak repayment prospects crowd out everyone else from the market. Spence showed that under certain conditions, well-informed agents can improve the market outcome by signalling their private information to poorly informed agents. To signal high profitability, the management of a firm can incur additional tax burden of dividend payments. Among other things, Stiglitz showed that an uninformed agent can sometimes capture the information of a better informed agent through screening, for example by providing choices from a menu of contracts for a particular transaction. Thus, insurance companies are able to classify their clients into risk classes by offering different policies, where lower premiums can be exchanged for a higher deductible.

It is proposed to cover in this chapter major contributions to economics by Akerlof; the significant contributions of Spence and Stiglitz are briefly surveyed in the subsequent two chapters.

39.1 A BRIEF BIOGRAPHICAL SKETCH: GEORGE AKERLOF

George Akerlof was born on June 17, 1940 in New Haven, Connecticut, U.S.A. His father who was a chemist on the faculty of Yale University and who was born in Sweden in 1898, had come to the United States on a fellowship to obtain a Ph.D. at the University of Pennsylvania, Philadelphia. The elder Akerlof moved to Yale in 1928 when his thesis adviser received an appointment at that university. The elder Akerlof who was appointed as instructor, later became assistant professor, and then associate professor at Yale. George Akerlof's mother was a housewife, whose mother and father were of German and Jewish descent.

George Akerlof had his schooling in Pittsburgh, Pennsylvania. He was interested in "social things:" history and economics. In his autobiographical note, Akerlof says: "These early years...were partly defining, but they were comfortable and happy." His schooling continued in Washington and later in a small private school in Princeton. Akerlof states that when he was 11 or 12, his father lost his job. "I remember one of my first significant thoughts about economics.... Although slightly wrong, I had understood the foundation of Keynesian economics." The exploration of the reasons for unemployment and the defence of Keynesian macroeconomics have dominated his work as an economist. He continued his college education at Yale. While Akerlof's first two years at Yale were essentially spent in taking liberal arts courses, the last two years were utilised in learning economics and mathematics.

For graduate studies, Akerlof entered MIT in the fall of 1962, and was surprised that his background in both mathematics and economics was "better than that of almost everyone else in my class. I was surprised because previously I had not been impressed by the economics that I learned at Yale." His study of algebraic topology in his first year of graduate school bolstered his suspicion that many of the results of the economic theory of the time were due to economists' lack of (mathematical) knowledge rather than to the truth of their arguments. Akerlof formed an opinion that "standard economic theory was based on mathematics that failed to capture a good portion of economic reality. Richer structure would give a more realistic picture." Akerlof reminisces. At MIT, everyone learned growth theory, which was the core of the curriculum. He found Solow's growth models, and Arrow's "learning by doing" model were very interesting. From growth theory he has learned as to how to model issues that were much closer to the heart of economics, which is how markets worked. The key chapter in his Ph. D. thesis demonstrated the stability of a putty-clay model without technical change. Akerlof used the techniques derived there for his article, "Market for Lemons" which was cited by the Nobel Memorial Award. He attempted to derive a theory of employment in another chapter and the third one dealt with leads and lags as a result of monetary policy changes. Akerlof observes that these last two papers were "... the beginnings of an attempt to base Keynesian economics on sound microeconomic foundations." Socially, MIT was also a great deal of fun. He made many friends there, including Joseph Stiglitz, Bill Nordhaus, Mrinal Datta Chaudhuri, Tom Weisskopf, Steve Marglin, Karl Shell, Mike Rothschild and Eytan Sheshinski, and many others.

After graduating from MIT in 1966, he was appointed as assistant professor by University of California at Berkeley, where in his first year he wrote "The Market for Lemons." At the same time, he continued his work on Keynesian macroeconomics. In 1967-68, Akerlof took leave from Berkeley to spend a year at the Indian Statistical Institute (ISI) in New Delhi. He was a member (an extra according to Akerlof himself) of a team that was attempting to develop a programme to allocate the waters of the Bhakra-Nangal dam. By joining the group Akerlof thought that he would gain a first-hand view of why India was "so poor." In that year, Planning in India was suspended temporarily because of the bad monsoons, and Akerlof's paper on "Federal-State Fiscal Policy in India" suggested principles for planning if it should be revived. During his stay in India he revised "Lemons" paper and included in it examples of incomplete markets from the readings of Indian economic history.

For his intellectual development, Akerlof's trip to India was important as it confirmed for him that non-standard analyses were needed to understand many economic transactions. He wished to explore "the fundamental problem in economics," the reason for unemployment which involves, above all, a gap between supply and demand. According to Akerlof "in India, the caste system for centuries has interposed itself between supply and demand." He felt that similar gaps might exist in labor markets in Western countries. What he learned in India became the "keystone" for his later contributions to the development of an efficiency wage theory of unemployment in Western countries. He states: "This theory unfolded over the next twenty years."

Akerlof served as a Senior Economist at the Council of Economic Advisers to the U.S. president in 1973-1974. His stint there helped him in learning how to do empirical research. After leaving Berkeley as a result of his being denied full professorship by the University, Akerlof spent a year at Federal Reserve Board in Washington after which he accepted a professorship (Cassel Professor of Economics) at the London School of Economics, from where he returned to Berkeley in 1980. Akerlof's focus of research which hitherto was concerned with the exploration of the consequences for macroeconomics of different microeconomic structures, such as staggered contracts, target–threshold monitoring and asymmetric information, subtly shifted to examining the effects of different assumptions regarding fairness and social customs on unemployment. Akerlof is of the view that there are two leading problems in macroeconomics. First, existence of or non–existence of involuntary employment; second, whether with complete information monetary policy could have real economic effects. In regard to the first problem, Akerlof has developed the concept of efficiency wages and presented a sociologically-based efficiency wage theory of unemployment. As regards the second problem, he jointly with Janet Yellen (his wife) devised a theory which argues that sticky wages and prices in an economy with monopolistic competition and efficiency wages would be near-rational and would explain why monetary policy would be effective.

Akerlof continues to be at Berkeley and is working on both macroeconomics and poverty. He was appointed as Richard and Rhode Goldman Distinguished Professor by the University in 1997. Akerlof received a number of awards and honours including Guggenheim Fellowship and Fulbright Fellowship. He was elected Fellow of the Econometric Society and Fellow American Academy of Arts and Sciences. He was elected President of the American Economic Association, 2007. He is a trustee of the Economists for Peace and Security. He is in the Advisory Board of the Institute for New Economic Thinking.

39.2 A SUMMARY OF AKERLOF'S CONTRIBUTIONS

Akerlof's 1970 article "The Market for Lemons," according to the press release of the Royal Swedish Academy of Sciences, is probably the single most important contribution to the literature on information economics. The paper has all the typical features of truly seminal contribution. It addresses a simple but profound and universal idea, with numerous interesting implications and widespread applications. In his Nobel lecture, Akerlof says that for him the study of asymmetric information was a first step towards the realisation of a dream, namely, development of behavioural macroeconomics in the original spirit of Keynes's General Theory. The General Theory emphasised the role of psychological and sociological factors, such as cognitive bias, reciprocity, fairness, herding and social status. Akerlof deals with the deficiencies in the New Classical macroeconomics which was based on the competitive general equilibrium model and has incorporated price and wage decisions as explicit micro foundations. However, the behavioural assumptions were so primitive that it could not satisfactorily specifically deal with the following macroeconomic phenomena.

1. Existence of involuntary unemployment;
2. Impact of monetary policy on the real variables of output and employment;
3. Failure of deflation to accelerate when there is high unemployment in the economy;
4. Prevalence of under saving for retirement needs by individuals;
5. Excessive volatility of share prices relative to their fundamentals; and
6. Stubborn persistence of a self-destructive underclass.

He observes: "The theory cannot account for persistent and extreme poverty coupled with high incidence of drug and alcohol abuse, out-of-wedlock births, single-headed households, high welfare dependency, and crime." Hence Akerlof considers income distribution as an important topic in macroeconomics. He then refers to how behavioural macroeconomics, incorporating realistic assumptions based in psychological and sociological observation, has produced models that account for each of the above macroeconomic phenomena.

Contributions made by Akerlof may conveniently be covered under two broad heads.

1. Microeconomics; and
2. Macroeconomics.

39.2.1 MICROECONOMIC CONTRIBUTIONS

Akerlof's interest in asymmetric information arose when he was investigating a major cause for fluctuations in output and employment, that is, large variations in the new car sales. He surmised that illiquidity, due to the fact that sellers of used cars know more than the buyers of used cars might explain the high volatility of new car purchases. He further surmised that problems of asymmetric information that are present in the used car (colloquially referred to as "lemons") market were potentially present to an extent in other markets as well. While asymmetric information problems can be solved in some markets by repeat sales and reputation, it is not so in some other markets, such as insurance markets, credit markets and labour markets. Serious market breakdowns result from such information problems. He provides a few examples of market breakdowns. Minorities are likely to experience statistical discrimination in labour market as people are "lumped together into categories of those with similar traits." Elderly experience difficulty in getting health insurance. Small business enterprises tend to be credit-rationed. He observes that one of the prime reasons for a country's under development is the failure of credit markets. Further, if some mechanisms to overcome problems of asymmetric information are developed, such institutions become an important determinant of market structure.

Economists, by and large, prior to early 1960's, constructed models, neglecting specific market characteristics or unique institutions, despite Chamberlin's monopolistic competition and Robinson's imperfect competition revolution. Growth models developed at that time, however, contained specialised technological features, such as putty-clay, vintage capital and learning by doing. Such models had not violated established price-theoretic norm. Akerlof's article "The Market for Lemons" was the first application of a new economic orientation in which models are constructed with particular attention to realistic macroeconomic detail--incorporation of asymmetric information in markets.

The article analyses the market for a product (used cars or lemons) where sellers are better informed than buyers about the quality of a good. The information given by the Nobel press lease provides a simple example. Assume that a good is sold in indivisible units and is available in two qualities-high and low in fixed proportion, λ and 1-λ. Each buyer is potentially interested in buying one unit, but cannot observe the difference between the two qualities at the time of purchase. Further, assume that all buyers have the same valuation of the two qualities: one unit of low quality worth w^L to the buyer, while one high quality unit is worth w^H, $w^H > w^L$ dollars. Each seller knows the quality of the unit he sells and values low quality units at $v^L < w^L$ dollars and high quality units at $v^H < w^H$ dollars.

If separate markets exist for low and high quality product, transactions which would be beneficial to both parties would take place, low quality at every price between v^L and w^L; likewise, for high quality product at every price between v^H and w^H. This is a socially efficient outcome since all gains from trade would be realised. However, in practice, if markets were not regulated, the two markets would merge into a single market with the one and the same price for all units of the product-- both low quality and high quality. Suppose that this occurs and that the sellers' valuation of the high quality product is higher than the average valuation of the buyers, i.e., $v^H > \overline{w}$ [where $\overline{w} = \lambda\, w^L + (1-\lambda)\, w^H$]. If trade took place, assuming that buyers are risk averse or risk neutral, the market price for the product could not exceed $\overline{w}$. This would lead to the exit from the market of sellers of high quality product, leaving only an adverse selection of low quality products or lemons. Akerlof remarks that Gresham's law has made "a modified appearance. For most cars traded will be the 'lemons' and good cars may not be traded at all. The "bad" cars tend to drive out the good.... But the analogy with Gresham's Law is not quite complete." It is rather impossible for a buyer to distinguish between a good and a bad car although bad cars sell at the same price as good cars while the seller knows which a good car is and which a bad car is. In Gresham's Law "presumably" both buyer and seller can tell the difference between a good coin and bad coin, the analogy is "intrusive, but not complete."

Akerlof concludes: "... Ignoring the asymmetric information problem, classical economic analysis would (wrongly) predict that products of both qualities would be sold on the market, at a price close to the buyers' average valuation. Lofgren, Persson and Weibull observe: "Adam Smith's invisible hand is not always as effective as traditional economics had us believe."

Further, Akerlof in his paper argues how private information may lead to the malfunctioning of markets. He illustrates the problem with difficulties for elderly people in buying individual medical or health insurance. He appropriately quotes the following statement in an insurance text book written at the Wharton School of Finance and Commerce, University of Pennsylvania, U.S.A. "There is potential adverse selection in the fact that healthy term insurance policyholders may decide to terminate their coverage when they become older and premiums mount. This action could leave an insurer with an undue proportion of below average risks and claims might be higher than anticipated. Adverse selection appears (or at least is possible) whenever the individual or group insured has freedom to buy or not to buy, to choose the amount or plan of insurance, and to persist or to discontinue as a policyholder." The principle of adverse selection is potentially present in all lines of insurance. Akerlof comments in his article: "... medical insurance is least available to those who need it most, for the insurance companies do their own 'adverse selection'."

The next issue he takes up for illustrating the Lemons Principle is the employment of minorities. Employers might not offer certain types of jobs to members of minority groups, not because of irrationality or prejudices but because race may serve as a good "statistic" for the applicant's social background, quality of schooling and general job capabilities. Good quality schooling could be a substitute for this statistic. As T.W Schultz remarked, the educational institution "discovers and cultivates" potential talent. The certifying institution must enjoy credibility. Akerlof remarks: "the unreliability of slum schools reduces the 'economic possibilities' of their students. The disadvantaged minority groups suffer as employers cannot distinguish those with good job qualifications from those with bad qualifications." As a result, reward for work in slum schools tends to accrue to the group as a whole-- in raising its average quality rather than to the individual. Further, if only information in addition to race is used, then there is incentive for minority groups to undergo training. Akerlof makes some useful comments on the costs of dishonesty, applying the Lemons Model. The major cost of dishonesty is in terms of dishonest dealings driving honest dealings out of market. That is, the cost of dishonesty does not lie in the amount by which the customer or the purchaser is cheated; but the cost must include loss occasioned from driving legitimate and honest business out of existence. In regard to the situation in the developing countries, he comments that dishonesty being a serious problem, the models delineate the nature of the "external" economies involved. Talking of the situation in India he comments: "In India...under the Export Quality Control and Inspection Act of 1963, about 85 percent of Indian exports are covered under one or the other type of quality control. Indian housewives must carefully glean the rice of the local bazaar to sort out stones of the same colour and shape which have been intentionally added to the rice."

Akerlof in his article provides an example of adverse selection drawn from credit markets in India in the 1960's, where indigenous moneylenders charged interest rates twice as high as the rates in large cities-- "extortionate rates." He provides this explanation for the phenomenon: The answer to this seeming paradox is that credit is granted only where the granter has (1) easy means of enforcing his contract, or (2) personal knowledge of the character of the borrower. The middleman who tries to arbitrage between the rates of the moneylender and the central bank is apt to attract all the "lemon" and thereby make a loss.

An important insight Akerlof furnishes is the emergence of a number of institutions to counter the effects of quality uncertainty, such as guarantees. Most consumer durables carry guarantees to assure the buyer of some normal expected quality. In this case, risk is borne by the seller rather than the buyer. Another institution that serves the same purpose is creation of brand name. Hotel chains or restaurant chains are similar to brand names. Licensing practices (in regard to doctors and lawyers etc) also reduce quality uncertainty. He concludes the article (which is cited by the Nobel Prize Award Committee) by stating that adverse selection may explain many economic institutions and may in fact be one of the more important aspects of uncertainty.

39.2.2 CONTRIBUTIONS TO MACROECONOMICS

In his Nobel lecture, Akerlof summarises the essential ingredients of the new Keynesian macroeconomics. New classical economics considers involuntary unemployment as a logical impossibility. Akerlof states that efficiency wage theories, which first appeared in the 1970's and 1980's, make the concept of involuntary unemployment meaningful. Efficiency wages which are paid by employers for reasons such as fairness, morale or asymmetric information, are higher than market clearing, so that some workers cannot obtain jobs and are involuntarily unemployed. He states that data on U.S. workers earnings reveal that industries with higher pay have also lower quit rates suggesting that there are "good jobs" and "bad jobs," making the concept of involuntary unemployment meaningful. He explains: Unemployed workers are willing to accept, but cannot obtain, jobs identical to those currently held by workers with identical ability. At the same time, workers who are involuntarily unemployed may not accept the available lower-paying or lower skilled jobs. The definition of involuntary unemployment implicit in efficiency wage theory is consistent with facts. An important first step forward in reconstructing the foundations of economics of Keynes lies in having a meaningful concept of involuntary unemployment.

The explanation for firms paying efficiency wages (higher than a rock bottom wage) can be sought in anthropology or psychology or sociology. Akerlof mentions three explanations- reciprocity, fairness, or theory of group formation. The insider-outsider model is Akerlof's favourite version of efficiency wages. That is, insider workers prevent the firm from hiring outsiders at a market clearing wage that is lower than what the insiders are currently receiving. He concludes: "Collusion by insiders against outsiders is an important factor that prompts many firms pay higher than market clearing wages." In this context, it may be mentioned that Stiglitz offers an alternative version of efficiency wage theory based on asymmetric information. It will be discussed in the chapter devoted to Stiglitz's contributions. Thus, it is clear that apart from his work on asymmetric information, Akerlof has enriched economic theory with insights from sociology and social anthropology.

In his Nobel lecture, Akerlof examines the issue of effectiveness of monetary policy in the context of hypothesis of the New Classical economics that fully anticipated monetary policy can have no impact on output or employment in an economy. Akerlof considers that the major contribution of behavioural macroeconomics is to show that under "sensible" behavioural assumptions monetary policy does affect real outcomes. The New Classical economists have criticised the inertial wage behaviour put forward in neoclassical synthesis and termed it "as irrational, costly for workers and firms, hence implausible." Behavioural economists have argued that rules of thumb involving money "illusion" are sensible in that the losses from following such rules are very small. This result was shown in Akerlof's joint work with Janet Yellen in the context of a model with efficiency wages and monopolistic competition. This is an important result as it shows that near-rational price stickiness is sufficient to demonstrate the important power of monetary policy. Surveying the results of other economists, Akerlof concludes that there are many forms of near-rational rule of thumb behaviour that renders monetary policy efficacious. Further he contends: "Near rational rule–of–thumb models solve the great puzzle posed by Robert Lucas regarding the effectiveness of monetary policy with rational expectations." While New Classical economics is unable to explain a "fleeting relation" between money and output, the behavioural economics yields a "robust relation" between changes in supply of money and output changes.

Phillips curve, which posited trade-offs between inflation and unemployment, is perhaps the most important and highly controversial macroeconomic relationship. In 1968 both Milton Friedman and Edmund Phelps argued that workers bargain for real not nominal wage increases. Further, pricing policies of firms translate wage inflation into price inflation. They denied a durable unemployment inflation trade-off. Instead, they demonstrated a unique "natural" rate of unemployment consistent with a stable inflation. The long-run Phillips curve is vertical since only at the "natural rate of unemployment" is actual rate of inflation equal to the expected inflation rate. Akerlof observes that economists accepted quickly the natural rate hypothesis, particularly because of the following factors among others. First, the hypothesis seemed to explain well the inflation-unemployment experience of the U.S. and Europe in 1960's and 1970's. Second, empirical estimates of the Phillips curve showed that the sum of the coefficients of the past inflation was not statistically different from unity. From this evidence, the researchers drew the inference that the lagged inflation terms in the estimates correspond to past inflation.

Akerlof is critical of the ready acceptance of the natural rate hypothesis by a large body of economists, particularly in the context of both theoretical and empirical objections. He particularly cites econometric evidence suggesting that the natural rate theory rests on "shifty sand rather than bedrock." Akerlof cites the "Prospect Theory" put forward by Kahneman and Tversky. The theory developed by them postulates that individuals evaluate changes in their situations according to the gains they make or losses they sustain relative to some reference point. If workers take current nominal wage as a reference point in measuring gains and losses, downward wage rigidity can be easily and satisfactorily explained by the Prospect Theory. Their evidence shows that individuals do not like to sustain losses rather than making gains.

Akerlof further argues in his Nobel lecture that if workers are averse to money wage cuts, then at low inflation there exist a long run trade-off between output and inflation. Moreover, the benefit of a little inflation is that it 'greases the wheels of the labour market.' Econometric estimates of Phillips curve allowing the possibility that past inflation has a different impact on current inflation when inflation is high than when it is low are in accord with this hypothesis. At high inflation, the sum of coefficients of past inflation is closer to unity, while at low inflation the sum of coefficients of past inflation is much closer to zero. The demonstration by behavioural macroeconomics that very low inflation coincides with high unemployment and low output has important implications for central bankers. Akerlof advises central bankers: "They should follow the advice of Oliver Cromwell to the General Assembly of the Church of Scotland: 'I beseech you in the Bowels of Christ, think it possible you may be mistaken'." The central bankers should resist the temptation to be overconfident in their monetary policy stance.

It is generally observed that people save too little. Financial assets of most households fall very much short of their post-retirement consumption needs. New Classical economics do not accept this as it clearly contradicts the assumptions of the models, since saving is the result of individual utility maximisation. In contrast, behavioural macroeconomics argues that individuals may maximise a utility function that is independent of maximisation of "true welfare." Akerlof argues: "The hyperbolic discount function, which has been used to study inter-temporal saving choices, can be used to formalise the distinction between the utility function that measures the actual saving behaviour and the utility function that measures the welfare resulting from that behaviour. The hyperbolic function captures the difficulty people have in exercising self- control.... Because present consumption is more salient than future consumption, individuals procrastinate about saving."

In Akerlof's opinion Keynes's General Theory was the progenitor of the modern behavioural finance view of asset markets. Stock markets are highly volatile and respond quickly to news. In contrast, the efficient markets model contends that stock prices reflect the present value of future risk- adjusted returns. Shiller has established in his major work Irrational Exuberance that stock market bubbles are common, which is referred to by Akerlof who contends that asset markets are important, particularly because they impact the macro economy through "at least three channels." First, the value of assets affects wealth, which, in turn, influences consumption. Second, the price of existing assets relative to the price of new capital (what is referred to in literature as Tobin's q ratio) affects investment. This is so because investment can be considered as an arbitrage between new capital stock and claims to similar existing assets. Third, firms face bankruptcy threat from changes in asset values. Due to this threat, firms may find it difficult to borrow from the market.

Taking income distribution as an important topic in macroeconomics, behavioural economics offers a satisfactory insight to the important problem in the U.S.A; namely, disparity in income and social conditions between white Americans (majority of the population) and the African – American minority. On the other hand, standard economic theory offers no explanation or cannot explain the observed behaviour of the poorest African-Americans as regards high rates of crime, addiction to drugs and alcohol, out of wedlock births, female-headed households and dependence on state provided welfare measures. In this connection, Akerlof makes reference to the models he developed jointly with Rachael Kranton in order to understand the persistence of African-American "disadvantage." He claims that his identity–based theory suggests that large negative externalities from imprisonment may outweigh the short –run gains from combating crime by deterrent punishment as argued by neo classical economic theory. Furthermore, the externalities involved in identity formation suggests that what is required is some affirmative action because, as Akerlof states ".... It is a symbol of welcome for African-Americans into the white society that has rejected them for so long."

Akerlof rates Keynes's General Theory as the greatest contribution to behavioural economics before the present era. Keynes had put blame for market failures at the door-step of psychological propensities as in consumption, and irrationalities as in share market speculation. The economics profession translated Keynesian economics into the "smooth" mathematics of classical economics. Akerlof expresses his view that if there is any subject in economics which should be behavioural, it is macroeconomics. In sum, he states: "I have argued that reciprocity, fairness, identity, money illusion, loss aversion, herding, and procrastination help explain the significant departures of real world economies from the competitive general equilibrium model. The implication, to my mind, is that macroeconomics *must* be based on such behavioural considerations" (Emphasis in the original). He concludes his Nobel lecture stating that modern behavioural economics has rediscovered the "wild side" of macroeconomic behaviour.

39.3 CONCLUDING OBSERVATIONS

Akerlof, besides what is surveyed above, has also made important contributions to Monetary Economics. Lofgren, Persson and Weibull in their article in Scandinavian Journal of Economics, evaluating the contributions of this year's laureates to economic sciences observe that the work of Akerlof, Spence and Stiglitz on markets and information asymmetries is "fundamental" to modern microeconomic theory. Their research work is helpful in understanding market phenomena that could not be explained by traditional neoclassical theory. More importantly, the models developed by the three laureates have been extensively employed to explain the emergence of many social institutions that counteract the negative effects of informational asymmetries. The models have found fruitful application in other areas, such as, financial economics, industrial organisation, labour economics and development economics.

39.4 SELECT BIBLIOPHY OF GEORGE AKERLOF'S WORKS

39.4.1 BOOKS

1984 An Economic Theorist's Book of Tables, Cambridge University Press, Cambridge.

1986 (with J. Yellen, eds.), Efficiency Wage Theories of the Labour Market, Cambridge University Press, Cambridge.

2005		Explorations in Pragmatic Economics, Oxford University Press, Oxford.
2009		(with R.J Shiller), Animal Spirits: How Human Psychology Drives the Economy, and Why It Matters for Global Capitalism, Princeton University Press, Princeton, NJ.

39.4.2 ARTICLES

1967	a	"Stability, Marginal Products, Putty and Clay," in K. Shell, (eds.), The Theory of Optimal Economic Growth, MIT Press, Cambridge, MA.
	b	(with W. Nordhaus), "Balanced Growth--A Razor's Edge?" IER, Vol.8, Oct.
1969	a	"Structural Unemployment in a Neoclassical Framework," JPE, Vol.77, No.3.
	b	(with J. Stiglitz.), "Capital, Wages, and Structural Unemployment," EJ, Vol.79, No.314.
	c	"Relative Wages and the Rate of Inflation," QJE, Vol. 83, No.3.
	d	"Centre-State Fiscal Relations in India," Indian Economic Review, Oct.
1970	a	"The Market for Lemons: Quality Uncertainty and the Market Mechanism," QJE, Vol.84, No. 3.
	b	(with E. Burmeister), "Substitution in a General Equilibrium Framework," JET, Vol.2, No.4 .
1973		"The Demand for Money: A General-Equilibrium Inventory-Theoretic Approach," RES, Vol.40, No.1.
1976	a	"Inflationary Tales Told by Static Model: The Case of Price Setters," AER, Vol.66, No.2.
	b	"The Economics of Caste and the Rat-Race and Other Woeful Tales," QJE, Vol. 90, No.4.
1978	a	"The Economics of Tagging as Applied to the Optimal Income Tax and Other Things," AER, Vol.68, No.1.
	b	"The Micro foundations of a Flow of Funds Theory of the Demand for Money," JET, Vol.18, No.1.
	c	(with R. Milbourne), "New Calculations of Income and Interest Elasticities in Tobin's Model of the Transactions Demand for Money," RES, Vol.60, No.4.
1979	a	"Irving Fisher on His Head: The Consequences of Target-Threshold Monitoring of Bank Accounts," QJE, Vol.93, No. 2.
	b	"The Case Against Conservative Macroeconomics: An Inaugural Lecture," Economica, Vol.46, No.183.

1980 a (with H. Miyazaki), "The Implicit Contract Theory of Unemployment Meets the Wage Bill Argument," RES, Vol. 47, No.2.

b "A Theory of Social Customs, of which Unemployment May be One Consequence," QJE, Vol.94, No.4.

c (with R. Milbourne), "Irving Fisher on His Head II: The Consequences of the Timing of Payments for the Demand for Money," QJE, Vol.95, No.1.

d (with B. Main), "Maximum Likelihood Estimation with Pooled Observations – An Example from Labor Economics," IER, Vol.21, No. 3.

e (with B. Main), "Unemployment Spells and Unemployment Experience," AER, Vol.70, No.3.

f (with R. Milbourne), "The Short Run Demand for Money," EJ, Vol. 90, Dec.

1981 (with B. Main), "An Experience- Weighted Measure of Employment and Unemployment Durations," RES, Vol. 71, No.5.

1982 a "The Short-Run Demand for Money: A New Look at an Old Problem," AER, Vol. 72, No.2 .

b (with W. Dickens), "The Economic Consequences of Cognitive Dissonance," AER, Vol. 72, No.3.

c "Labor Contracts as Partial Gift Exchange," QJE, Vol.97, No.4.

1983 "Loyalty Filters," AER, Vol.73, No.1.

1984 "Gift Exchange and Efficiency Wage Theory: Four Views," AER, Vol.74, No.2.

1985 a "Discriminatory, Status-Based Wages among Tradition-Oriented, Stochastically Trading Coconut Producers," JPE, Vol.93, No.2.

b (with J. Yellen), "Unemployment Through the Filter of Memory," QJE, Vol.100, No. 3.

c (with J. Yellen), "Can Small Deviations from Rationality Make Significant Differences to Economic Equilibria?" AER, Vol.75, No.4.

d (with J. Yellen), "A Near Rational Model of the Business Cycle with Wage and Price Inertia," QJE, Vol. 100, No. 5.

1987 (with J. Yellen), "Rational Models of Irrational Behavior," AER, Vol.77, No. 2.

1988 a (with J. Yellen), "Fairness and Unemployment," AER, Vol.78, No.2.

b (with A. Rose and J. Yellen), "Discussion" of "The New Keynesian Economics and the Output-Inflation Trade-off," BPEA, Vol. 19, 1988:I.

	c	(with A. Rose and J. Yellen), "Job Switching and Job Satisfaction in the U.S. Labor Market," BPEA, No. 19, 1988:II.
1989		(with L. F. Katz.), "Do Deferred Wages Eliminate the Need for Involuntary Unemployment as a Worker Discipline Device?" in Advances in the Theory and Measurement of Unemployment, Y. Weiss and G. Fishelson, (eds.), MacMillan, New York.
1990	a	(with J. Yellen), "The Fair Wage-Effort Hypothesis and Unemployment," QJE, Vol.105, No.2.
	b	(with J. Yellen), "Discussion of An Aging Society: Opportunity or Challenge?" BPEA, 1990:I.
1991	a	(with J. Yellen), "How Large are the Losses from Rule of Thumb Behavior in Models of the Business Cycle?" in Money, Macroeconomics and Economic Policy: Essays in Honor of James Tobin, (W. Brainard, et al. eds.), MIT Press, Cambridge, MA.
	b	"Procrastination and Obedience," The Richard T. Ely Lecture, AER, Vol.81, No.2.
1993		(with P. Romer), "Looting: The Economic Underworld of Bankruptcy for Profit," BPEA, Vol. 24, 1993:II.
1994		(with J. Yellen), "Gang Behavior, Law Enforcement and Community Values," in Values and Public Policy, (H. Aaron, et al. eds.) Brookings Institute, New York.
1996	a	(with J. Yellen and M. Katz), "An Analysis of Out-of-Wedlock Births in the United States," QJE, Vol.111, No. 2.
	b	(with W. Dickens and G. Perry), "The Macroeconomics of Low Inflation," BPEA, Vol. 24, 1996:1.
1997		"Social Distance and Social Decisions" (The Fisher-Shultz Lecture at the 1995 World Congress of the Econometric Society), Econometrica, Vol.65, No. 5.
1998		"Men without Children," EJ, Vol.108, No. 447.
2000	a	(with R. Kranton), "Economics and Identity," QJE, Vol.115, No.3.
	b	(with W. T. Dickens and G. L. Perry), "Near-Rationality and the Long-Run Phillips Curve," BPEA, Vol.31, 2000:1.
2002	a	"Behavioral Macroeconomics and Macroeconomic Behavior," Nobel Lecture, AER, Vol.92, No.3.
	b	(with R. Kranton), "Identity and Economics of Organizations," JEP, Vol. 19, No. 1.

2006 (with J. Yellen), "Stabilization Policy: A Reconsideration," Economic Inquiry, Vol. 44, No.1.

2007 a "The Missing Motivation in Macroeconomics," AER, Vol.97, No.1.

b "The New Case for Keynesianism," Challenge, Vol. 50, No.4.

2008 (with R. Kranton), "Identity, Supervision, and Working Groups," AER, Vol. 98, No.2.

39.5 WORKS OF OTHERS

Arrow, K. J. (1963), "Uncertainty and the Welfare Economics of Medical Care," AER, Vol.53, No. 5.

Friedman, M. (1961), "The Lag in Effect of Monetary Policy," JPE, Vol.69, Oct.

Friedman, M. (1968), "The Role of Monetary Policy," AER, Vol.58, No.1.

Kahneman, D and A. Tversky (1979), "Prospect Theory: An Analysis of Decision under Risk," Econometrica, Vol.47, Mar.

Keynes, J. M. (1936), "The General Theory of Employment, Interest and Money," Macmillan, New York.

Lofgren, K. G., T. Persson and J. Weibull (2002), "Markets with Asymmetric Information: The Contributions of George Akerlof, Michael Spence and Joseph Stiglitz," ScandJE, Vol.104, No.2.

Mirrlees, J. (1971), "An Exploration in the Theory of Optimum Income Taxation," RES, Vol. 38, No.2.

Phelps, E. S. (1968), "Money Wage Dynamics and Labor Market Equilibrium," JPE, Vol. 76, part 2. July/Aug, Part-2.

Phelps, E. S. (1969), "The New Microeconomics in Inflation and Employment Theory," AER, Vol. 59, No.2.

Stigler, G. J. (1962), "Information in the Labor Market," JPE, Vol. 70, No.5, Part 2.

CHAPTER 40

ANDREW MICHAEL SPENCE

(1943-)

Andrew Michael Spence shared the 2001 Nobel Memorial Prize for Economic Sciences with George A. Akerlof and Joseph E. Stiglitz for their analyses of markets with asymmetric information. Akerlof's contributions were covered in the preceding chapter while Stiglitz's contributions are summarised in the next chapter.

40.1 A SHORT BIOGRAPHICAL SKETCH: MICHAEL SPENCE

Spence was born in Montclair, New Jersey, U.S.A. on November 7, 1943. His father was a member of the (Second World) War Time Prices and Trades Board. Spence grew up in Canada during and after the war until leaving for college in the United States; he was an American by birth. He noted his parents were "wonderful." His father, senior Spence, was intellectual by instinct. He had a Ph.D. from Northwestern University in Commerce and Finance. The junior Spence had learned from his father "to love precision in thought, the power of abstraction and the use of symbols to capture structures and relationships." Spence's mother was strong-willed, demanding and very supportive, all at the same time. According to Spence, he inherited from his mother "a kind of tenacity (sometimes referred to as stubbornness) that served me well. It partially filled gaps when sheer intellectual horsepower (of which others had much more than I) proved insufficient." The overall effect of his parents' upbringing was to provide a great sense of security, a great sense of self-confidence, and an equally great sense of intellectual adventure. Spence believes that the greatest gifts to him from his parents were the sense of freedom and the confidence to try to use it.

His family moved to Winnipeg in 1946 and to a farm outside Toronto, Canada. His school education started in 1950 and from 1955 he attended schools, which were part of University of Toronto. In 1962 Spence graduated from High School, University of Toronto, and went as a freshman to Princeton University. In 1966, he graduated from Princeton University majoring in Philosophy. In the same year, he received Canadian Rhodes Scholarship and went to Magdalene College, Oxford. With encouragement from his parents, Spence decided to try an academic career. He majored in Mathematics at Oxford University and graduated from there in 1968. He returned to U.S.A. and entered Ph.D. programme in Economics at Harvard University in Fall 1968, with a Danforth Fellowship.

He functioned as Rapporteur in Faculty Seminar in Kennedy School of Government at Harvard. The seminar participants included his Ph.D. thesis advisors, Kenneth Arrow, Thomas Schelling and Richard Zeckhause. Spence states his thesis advisors are "very gifted." Arrow taught him mathematical economics and general equilibrium theory. Thomas Schelling had an "extraordinarily original mind." His curiosity seemed endless and his capacity to shed light "remarkable." Spence wrote his first paper with Richard Zeckhause on insurance markets, moral hazard and adverse selection. Spence notes "[Zeckhause's] tremendous breadth of his interests and his intuitive grasp of complex phenomena." Spence began teaching analytical methods at Kenney School in 1971. He received Ph.D. degree in 1972 and moved to Stanford University as Associate Professor in 1973. There he taught and did research in Applied Microeconomic Theory and Industrial Organization. In 1975 he returned to Harvard as Professor. Bill Gates was his student in the graduate theory course.

From 1975 to 1990, Spence served as Professor of Economics and Business Administration at Harvard University, holding a joint appointment in its Business School and the Faculty of Arts and Sciences. In 1983, he was named Chairman of the Economics Department and George Gund Professor of Economics and Business Administration. For a period of six years, from 1984 to 1990, Spence served as the dean of Faculty of Arts and Sciences at Harvard. From 1990 to 1999, Spence served as Philips H. Knight Professor and dean of the Stanford Business School.

Spence received a number of honours and awards, including David A. Well's Prize for outstanding doctoral dissertation at Harvard University in 1972, John Kenneth Galbraith Prize for excellence in teaching in 1978, John Bates Clark Medal of the American Economic Association in 1981 awarded then to economists under 40 for a "significant contribution to economic thought and knowledge." From 1977 to 1979, Spence was a member of the Economics Advisory Panel of National Science Foundation and in 1979 served as a member of the Sloan Foundation Economic Advisory Committee. He has been a member of the American Economic Association and a Fellow of the Econometric Society and American Academy of Arts and Sciences. At various times, Spence has served as a member of the editorial boards of American Economic Review, Bell Journal of Economics, Journal of Economic Theory, and Journal of Public Policy.

Spence is a senior Fellow at Hoover Institution and Philips H. Knight Professor Emeritus of Management in the Graduate School of Business of Stanford University. He is Chairman of an independent Commission on Growth and Development created in 2006 and is focussed on growth and poverty reduction in developing countries.

40.2 A SUMMARY OF MICHAEL SPENCE'S CONTRIBUTIONS

The press release from the Royal Swedish Academy of Sciences refers to Michael Spence's most important work that demonstrates how agents in a market can use signalling to counteract the effects of adverse selection. Signalling here refers to observable actions taken by economic agents to convince the opposite party of the value or quality of their products. He has identified an important aspect of adjustment by individual market participants, where the better informed take costly actions in an attempt to improve on their market outcome by credibly transmitting information to the poorly informed. He has also shown when such signalling will actually work. His own research has emphasised education as a productivity signal in job markets. However, subsequent research widened the area of applications, such as, how corporate units may use dividends to signal their profitability to agents in the stock market.

In his Nobel lecture, Spence explains how he started research work in information economics. One of his thesis advisors brought to Spence's attention of Akerlof article "The Market for Lemons" and advised him to read it. He states: "I always did what my advisers told me to do and hence followed up immediately. It was quite electrifying." Spence found in the article a clear and plausible analysis of the performance characteristics of a market with incomplete and asymmetrically located information. He observes: "That, combined with my puzzlement about several aspects of the discussion of the consequences of incomplete information in job markets, pretty much launched me on a search for things that I came to call signals...." Spence says that he noticed that there are many markets with informational gaps, such as markets for most consumer durables, virtually all job markets, many financial markets, markets for various types of food and pharmaceuticals. These informational gaps might change some of the performance characteristics as well as institutional structure of markets in which they appear.

Reference is made to Spence's 1973 seminal paper on job market signalling and his book Market Signaling both of which deal with education as a signal in the labour market. If an employer cannot distinguish between high productivity and low productivity labour at the time of hiring new workers, labour market might collapse into market where only low-productivity workers are hired at a low-wage. This phenomenon is analogous to the adverse selection outcome in Akerlof's market where only lemons remain. Adverse selection problem is commonly applied to insurance markets.

The idea is that there are attributes of potential employees which cannot be observed by the employer. These attributes impact the employee's productivity on the job and is therefore of vital importance to the employer. The way out of this situation was suggested by Spence through signalling – a slight modification and extension of the example suggested by Akerlof. Suppose the sellers in the labour market, i.e., job applicants can acquire education prior to entering the labour market. Assume that workers can be divided into only two groups--low productivity workers (w^L) and high productivity workers (w^H). Further $w^L < w^H$. The population of the two groups are λ and 1-λ respectively. However, it is not possible for buyers or employers to directly observe the productivity of the workers they propose to employ; the level of education of workers can be ascertained. Education is measured on a continuous scale, $s \geq 0$. Further, the cost of education, in terms of expenses, effort, and time to reach each level of education is lower for higher productivity workers or individuals. As Spence's focus is on signalling aspect, he assumes that education has no impact on productivity of workers and has no consumption value for them. Ceteris Paribus the job applicant has every reason to choose as little education as possible. In traditional theory, that is, under perfect information, perfect competition and constant returns to scale, each job applicant tends to choose minimal educational level, i.e., $s = 0$. The productivity of each applicant will determine the wage he is paid. However, under conditions of asymmetric information, to signal their superior ability, high productivity workers may acquire education.

Let us assume that employers in general expect all job applicants who possess a minimum level of education say $s^H > 0$ to have high productivity whereas the rest of the applicants to have low productivity. Under perfectly competitive conditions and constant returns to scale, all applicants with a level of education equal to or higher than s^H are offered a wage equal to their expected productivity, w^H and those with educational level lower than s^H are offered the wage, w^L. Lofgren, Persson and Weibull demonstrate such a wage setting by step-wise schedule in Fig. 40.1. Given the wage schedule as shown in the Figure, each job applicant would choose either $s^L = 0$ (i.e., lowest possible education) and settle for the low wage, w^L, or s^H, the higher education level, and obtain w^H, the higher wage. The other options are not attractive. Any education between s^L and s^H, would not give him a wage higher than w^L but costs more. Likewise, an education above s^H costs more but does not give a wage higher than w^H.

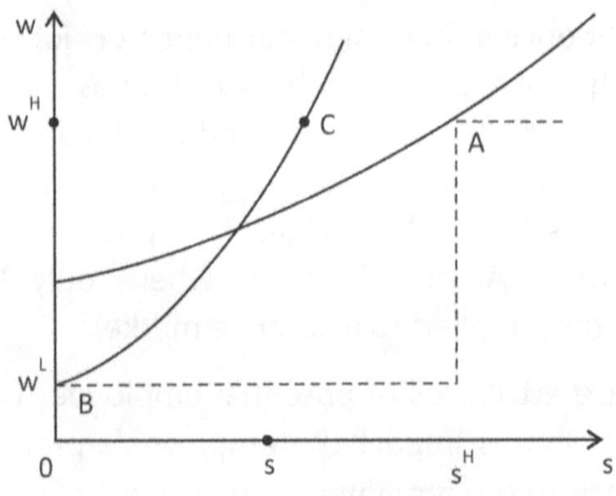

Fig. 40.1 Steep indifference curve for low- productivity job applicants; Flat indifference curve for high-Productivity job applicants.

In the above Fig. 40.1, preferences of job applicants are represented by two indifference curves based on the assumption that education costs less for high productivity applicants. Those education-wage combinations (s, w) that high productivity individuals consider equally good as their expected education-wage pair-- s^H w^H are represented by the flatter curve passing through point A. Those education—wage combinations that low—productivity individuals find equally attractive as the minimum level of education $s^L = 0$ and wage w^L are shown by the steeper curve, passing through B.

The authors state that with the above-mentioned preferences, high productivity individuals choose educational level, s^H, and receive the higher wage; it is clear that alternative A gives them a preferred outcome than alternative B. The optimal choice of the other group, namely, low-productivity individuals, is at B, the minimum education level. At point A, the group is worse off, as the higher wage they can obtain does not compensate them for the higher cost of education they have to incur. Lofgren, Persson and Weibull assert: "'Employers' expectations that workers with different productivity choose different educational levels are indeed self- fulfilling in this signalling equilibrium. Instead of a market failure, where high–productivity individuals remain outside of the market (e. g., by moving away or setting up their own business), these workers participate in the labour market and acquire a costly education solely to distinguish themselves from low-productivity job applicants."

Spence suggests that a certain signalling equilibrium is socially most efficient in which high productivity workers choose the minimum education for the purpose of distinguishing themselves from those with low- productivity. In Fig. 40.1, high-productivity workers choose the combination given by C. Low productivity workers, however, are indifferent between the education-wage combinations at point C (s, and w^H) and the combination at their chosen point B (0, w^L).

In his Nobel lecture, Spence provides a simple job market signalling model which might be helpful for a better understanding of the problem. Suppose there are two groups of people—Group 1 and Group 2. Further, suppose there is something called education, denoted by E, that can be invested in by the labour. However, it is assumed that education does not affect individual's productivity. Spence assumes that cost of E years of education for group 1 is E whereas the cost for individuals belonging to group 2 is E/2. Equilibrium in a situation like this has two components. First, given the costs of and return to education, individuals in the two groups make rational investment choices with respect to education. Second, employers entertain beliefs about the relation between the signal and the individual's underlying productivity. Spence asserts that in equilibrium the beliefs must be consistent, or, the beliefs must be accurate. The wages that the employers offer at various levels of education are determined by the beliefs or expectations of employers. In turn, the wage offers determine the returns to individuals from investments in education which influence the individual's investment decisions with respect to education, that is, the actual relationship between worker's productivity and education that is observed by employers in the marketplace. Thus, Spence argues that in equilibrium the employers' beliefs are "self- confirming" which gives rise to the potential presence of "multiple equilibria" in the market.

Continuing the above example, Spence argues that suppose for group 1 individuals $E_1 = 0$ and group 2 individuals set $E_2 = E^*$ (where E^* is the signalling level of education). Assuming that employers who individually do not influence individuals' investment decisions in education, believe that if $E < E^*$, then productivity is 1 and if $E \geq E^*$, then productivity is 2. Spence observes that individuals in group 1 will rationally set $E = 0$, provided that

$$2 - E^* < 1.$$

Members of group 2 will rationally set $E = E^*$, provided that

$$2 - E^*/2 > 1.$$

Spence asserts that the choices of the two groups will be rational and the expectation confirmed in the market if

$$1 < E^* < 2.$$

He draws a few general properties of signalling equilibria from this model. First, there is a continuum of equilibrium. There is more investment in the signal in each equilibrium than there would be in a world of full information. Second, the result is "inefficient" as investment in the signal, thereby squandering resources with no productivity improvement. Third, the equilibria are orderable by the Pareto criterion. Everyone is either no better off or worse off as you move from one equilibrium to another. However, the signal actually distinguishes low productivity and high productivity workers, a characteristic that is of value to employers. Spence observes: "The equilibrium indicates a schedule that gives the returns to education; that is, wage for each level of education, and optimizing choices (given that schedule) by individuals in the two groups."

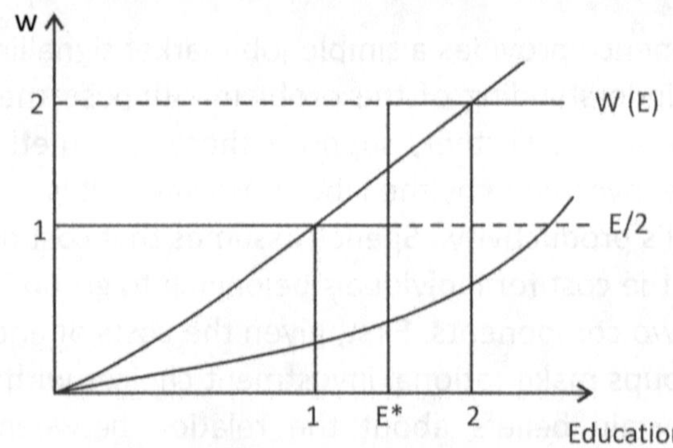

Fig. 40.2 Education-Wage Combination

Spence in his Nobel lecture gives the above Fig. 40.2 that depicts the equilibrium. He explains: "The wage schedule is the dark line and jumps from wage level 1 to a wage level 2: E^* which is between 1 and 2 is the signaling level of education. Group 1 opts for educational level 0 while group 2 chooses E^*. There is a spectrum of equilibria of which Spence remarks probably the most interesting is the one in which $E^* = 1 + \delta$ where δ may be taken as a small positive number. In this equilibrium

$w_1 = N_1 = 1$, and

$w_2 = 2$, and

$$N_2 = 1.5 - \delta/2$$

where N_i is income net of signalling costs for group 1.

Spence then explores the possibility of finding an equilibrium in the Pareto sense (that is, every one is better off) than the one outlined above. His answer is positive sometimes. "It involves pooling and it depends on the relative sizes of the two groups." Further, he states that "in general with discrete groups, pooling with lower level groups becomes attractive if they are relatively small...." Spence also demonstrates in his Nobel lecture that one can get rid of the inefficiency and keep the signalling and informational content of the signals, with an appropriate tax on the signalling activity. It results in redistributing income in a way that reproduces the results of the pooling equilibrium. Furthermore, if the information the signal carries is itself productive, the equilibrium should be a separating one.

In his Nobel lecture, Spence covers a number of other scenarios such as two group model when education results in improvement of human capital, serving at the same time as a potential signal and a model in which there is both pooling and separating components of the equilibrium. The lecture also deals with a general continuous model and establishes some reasonably general properties of signalling models. He concludes his lecture with discussion of the development of interest and the changing informational structure of markets. Furthermore, Spence's signalling work has been used in research fields other than job markets. For example, firms use dividends to signal their profitability to agents in the stock market.

40.3 SPENCE'S OTHER IMPORTANT CONTRIBUTIONS

While the Nobel Committee specifically mentions Spence's work with regard to education as a productivity signal in job market, there are other significant contributions by Spence to the field of industrial organisation. In the new industrial organisation theory, he was reckoned as pioneer in the game-theoretic inspired work. Mention has to be made of some of his work in this broad area, namely monopolistic competition and market entry by new firms. Economists working in growth theory and international trade have been influenced by the model of market equilibrium under monopolistic competition developed by Spence.

40.4 CONCLUDING OBSERVATIONS

While Spence is well known for his outstanding work in connection with the crucial role signalling plays in job market, he is generally credited with significant research in what is called "economics of information." His work has inspired further research effort such as how corporate dividend announcements and payments provide useful signals to participants in the stock markets as to the expected profitability performance of the corporate units, helping them make informed decisions. His major research interests include, besides economics of information, Economic Policy in emerging markets and impact of leadership on economic growth.

His latest work titled "The Next Convergence: The Future of Economic Growth in a Multispeed World" is rated high dealing as it does with recent growth experience of developing countries and how it is leading to a convergence with the developed world. He tries to analyse some important issues relating to the post-crisis world economy such as the following, among others.

Can we learn over time to manage the emerging and evolving complex global economy characterised by rising interdependence and complexity of the economies?

Is the experience of managing the world economy during the last quarter of the twentieth century helpful in managing it in future?

Can we envisage continuation of the fourfold increase in the ranks of the relatively wealthy or is it unlikely that what is true and possible for "a few" will not be possible for the many. The work is well received as can be gathered from the two following comments.

"Rarely does one find a book that is so powerful in its analysis, timely in its topic, relevant in its thinking and clear in its exposition." (A corporate Chief and author of a book in marketing).

We may close this note by this comment by a leading academic, none other than Robert Solow.

"If you are looking for a lucid, readable, consistent, unprejudiced picture of what has been happening and what might happen next in the world economy, this is an excellent place to find it."

40.5 SELECT BIBLIOGRAPHY OF A. MICHAEL SPENCE'S CONTRIBUTIONS

40.5.1 BOOKS

1974 Market Signaling: Informational Transfer in Hiring and Related Processes, Harvard University Press, Cambridge, MA.

1980 (with R.E Caves and M.E. Porter), Industrial Organization in an Open Economy, Harvard University Press, Cambridge, MA.

1983 (with S. Hayes and D. Marks), Competitive Structure in Investment Banking, Harvard University Press, Cambridge, MA.

2011 The Next Convergence: The Future of Economic Growth in a Multispeed World, Farrar, Straus and Giroux, New York.

40.5.2 ARTICLES

1971 (with R. Zeckhause), "Insurance, Information, and Individual Action," AER, Vol. 61, No. 2.

1973 a "Job Market Signaling," QJE, Vol.87, No.3.

b "Time and Communication in Economic and Social Interaction," QJE, Vol.87, No.4.

1974 "Competitive and Optimal Responses to Signals: An Analysis of Efficiency and Distribution," JET, Vol. 7, No.3.

1975 a (with D. Starrett), "Most Rapid Approach Paths in Accumulation Problems," IER, Vol. 16, No.2.

b "The Economics of an International Organization: An Introduction," BellJE, Vol. 6, No.1.

c "Monopoly, Quality, and Regulation," BellJE, Vol.6, No. 2.

1976 a "Competition in Salaries, Credentials, and Signaling Prerequisites for Jobs," QJE, Vol.90, No.1.

b "Product Differentiation and Welfare," AER, Vol. 66, No.2.

c "Product Selection, Fixed Costs, and Monopolistic Competition," RES, Vol.43, No.2.

d "Informational Aspects of Market Structure: An Introduction," QJE, Vol. 90, No.4.

e (with M. J. Roberts), "Effluent Charges and Licenses under Uncertainty," JPubE, Vol.5, No.3- 4.

1977 a (with B. Owen), "Television Programming, Monopolistic Competition, and Welfare," QJE, Vol. 91, No.1.

b "Non-Linear Prices and Welfare," JPubE, Vol.8, No.1.

c "Consumer Misperception, Product Failure and Producer Liability," RES, Vol.44, No.3.

d "Non-Price Competition," AER, Vol.67, No.1.

e "Entry, Capacity, Investment and Oligopolistic Pricing," BellJE, Vol.8, No.2.

1978 a "Tacit Coordination and Imperfect Information," Canadian JE, Vol.11, No.3.

b "Product Differentiation and Performance in Insurance Markets," JPubE, Vol.10, No.3.

1979 "Investment Strategy, and Growth in a New Market," BellJE, Vol. 10, No.1.

1980 a "Multi-Product Quantity-Dependent Prices and Profitability Constraints," RES, Vol.47, No.5.

b "Notes on Advertising, Economies of Scale, and Entry Barriers," QJE, Vol.95, No.3.

1981 a "The Learning Curve and Competition," BellJE, Vol.12, No.1.

b "Signaling, Screening and Information," in Studies in Labor Markets, NBER, New York.

1983 "Contestable Markets and the Theory of Industry Structure: A Review Article," JEL, Vol.21, No. 3.

1984 "Cost Reduction, Competition, and Industry Performance," Econometrica, Vol.52, No.1.

1985 a (with P. Ghemawat), "Learning Curve Spillovers and Market Performance," QJE, Vol.100, No.5.

b "Capital Structure and the Corporation in Product Market Environment," in Corporate Capital Structure in the United States, NBER, New York.

2002 "Signaling in Retrospect and Informational Structure of Markets," Nobel Lecture, AER, Vol.92, No.3.

2009 "The Financial and Economic Crisis and The Developing World," Journal of Policy Modelling, Vol.31, No.4.

2010 (with P. Collier et al.), "Managing Resources Revenues in Developing Economies," IMF Staff Papers, Vol.57, No.1.

2011 (with R. Zagha), "Restoring Inclusive Growth in Advanced Economies: A Conversation with Economists and Policy Makers from the G 20," Corporative Economic Studies, Vol. 53, No.3.

40.6 WORKS OF OTHERS

Arrow, K. J. (1943), "Higher Education as a Filter," JPubE, Vol.2, No.3.

Bedard, K. (2001), "Human Capital Versus Signaling Models, University Access and High School Dropouts," JPE, Vol.109, No.4

John, K. and J. Williams (1985), "Dividends, Dilution and Taxes, A Signaling Equilibrium," JF, Vol.40, No.4.

Lofgren, K.G., T. Persson and J. W. Weibull (2002), "Markets with Asymmetric Information: The Contributions of George Akerlof, Michael Spence and Joseph Stiglitz," ScandJE, Vol. 104, No.2.

Riley, J. (1979), "Testing the Educational Screening Hypothesis," JPE, Vol.87, No.5.

CHAPTER 41

JOSEPH EUGENE STIGLITZ

(1943 –)

Joseph Eugene Stiglitz shared the 2001 Nobel Memorial Prize in Economic Sciences with George A. Akerlof and A. Michael Spence. The award was given to them for their analyses of markets with asymmetric information. The press release of the Royal Swedish Academy announcing the award states that many markets are characterised by asymmetric information in the sense that participants on one side of the market have much better information than those on the other side of the market. It also recognises that for over two decades, the theory of markets with asymmetric information has been an important and lively field of economic research. Further, models incorporating imperfect information are necessary and vital instruments in the researcher's tool box. Such models are applied extensively from traditional agricultural markets in developing countries to sophisticated modern financial markets in developed economies. Contributions of Akerlof and Spence to the field were covered in the previous two chapters. Major contributions of Stiglitz are summarised in this chapter.

The information provided by the Royal Swedish Academy cites one of Stiglitz's classical articles co-authored with Michael Rothschild that considered the issue of what uninformed agents can do to improve their outcome in a market characterised by asymmetric information. The article demonstrates how information problems can be dealt with on insurance markets where insurers do not have information on the risk situation of individual insured. Stigltz shows that an uninformed agent can sometimes capture the information of a better-informed agent through screening, for example, by providing choices from an array of contracts for a specific transaction. Insurance companies are thus able to classify their clients into risk classes by offering different policies, where lower insurance premiums can be exchanged for a higher deductible.

Stiglitz and his co-authors have time and again substantiated that those economic models disregarding informational asymmetries may be quite misleading. The underlying message in this work has been that in the perspective of asymmetric information many markets take a completely different guise, as do the conclusions relating to appropriate forms of government intervention and regulation. Stiglitz is credited with analysing the implications of asymmetric information in many different contexts, ranging from unemployment to the design of an optimal tax system. More importantly, his articles have provided opportunities for launching further research.

A highly significant work of Stiglitz co-authored with Andrew Weiss relates to analysis of credit markets with asymmetric information. Banks report credit rationing steps while meeting demand for loans. Stiglitz and Weiss demonstrate that it may be optimal for bankers to ration the volume of loans instead of raising the lending rate. This is done with the aim of reducing losses from bad loans. These insights are helpful in developing a more realistic theory of credit markets. There have been also other applications in macroeconomics, monetary theory and corporate finance.

Efficiency of financial markets is a vital issue on which there are theoretical differences. More importantly, it has significant policy implications. Stiglitz in collaboration with Sanford Grossman analysed the efficiency question. Their key result is referred to as Grossman–Stiglitz paradox: if a market is informally efficient in the sense that market prices reflect all relevant information, then no single agent would have any incentive to gather information on which prices are based.

Stiglitz is considered an important founder of modern development economics. He argues that asymmetric information and economic incentives are not mere academic abstractions. They have significant explanatory value in analysis of institutions and market conditions in developing economies. In this context, reference needs to be made to one of the early works of Stiglitz relating to problems of information dealt with a common, but an ancient, form of contracting, namely share cropping. He considers share cropping is an optimal solution to the risk exposure involved for the tenant as well as land owner or land lord.

The Royal Swedish Academy observes that Joseph Stiglitz's many contributions have transformed the way economists think about the working of markets in an economy.

41.1 A BRIEF BIOGRAPHICAL NOTE: JOSEPH STIGLITZ

Joseph E. Stigltz was born on February 9, 1943 in Gary, Indiana. His parents were born within six miles of Gary and lived in the area for nearly a century. In his autobiographical note, Stiglitz remarks that there must have been something in the air of Gary that led one into economics-such as the poverty, the discrimination and the episodic unemployment. An enquiring youngster has a number of questions in regard to these; why did these exist and what could be done about them. Stiglitz's father was an independent insurance agent. His mother's family was one belonging to New Deal Democrats. Stiglitz comments that he grew up in a family in which political issues were often discussed and debated intensely.

Stiglitz studied in public schools. The public school system in Gary was integrated though the city - like most American cities at that time- was racially segregated. He had the "good fortune of having dedicated teachers, who in spite of relatively large classes, provided a high level of individual attention." The extracurricular activity in which he was most engaged (because of his attraction to ideas) namely debating, helped shape his interests in public policy. He reminisces. "Every year, a national debating topic is chosen. One year, it was the reform of the agricultural support programs, an issue which I had to grapple with almost forty years later in Clinton Administration." According to him, the intellectually most formative experiences occurred to him during the three years 1960-1963, when he was a student at Amherst College, a liberal arts college at Boston. Stiglitz laments in his autobiographical note that the notion that every well educated person would have a mastery of at least the basic elements of the humanities, sciences, and social sciences is a far cry from the specialised education that most students today receive, particularly in the research universities. He observes that what distinguished Amherst was not only what was taught, but how it was taught, and the close relationship the students had with teachers. A most revealing statement from him about higher education: "The best teachers still taught in a Socratic style, asking questions, responding to the answers with still another question.... We were taught that what mattered most was asking the right question - having posed the question well, answering the question was often a relatively easy matter."

Stiglitz loved all the courses he studied at the college but had an irresistible attraction of economics. His freshman history class in which a major theme for discussions of the encounters between different civilisations helped shape his thinking about globalisation more than three decades later. He decided to major in economics late in the third year of undergraduate programme as he wanted to combine his interest in history and in writing, besides his desire to apply his interest and abilities in mathematics to important social problems. He left Amherst for MIT to pursue graduate studies "without a degree, or without any promise of one." He comments: "It was before I had done my work on the economics of information, and I think I didn't grasp the information that might be conveyed by having a degree.... Later, Amherst gave me a degree, and still later, in 1974, they gave me an honorary doctorate." Amherst was pivotal in Stiglitz's intellectual development; MIT in his development as a professional economist. He recalls that he had at least four Nobel Prize winners as professors--Samuelson, Solow, Modigliani and Arrow. Stiglitz's first paper presented at an academic meeting, to the econometric society, was co-authored with another graduate student - George Akerlof, who shared 2001 Nobel prize. "He recollects: The students and faculty at MIT were highly interactive."

After Stiglitz's first year as a graduate student, he was offered a "wonderful opportunity," editing Paul Samuelson's collected papers. He observes: "I often took Paul as a role model, the expansiveness of his learning, the breadth of his work, its originality and penetration." After two years at MIT (he did his generals in a year and a half and then began writing thesis). Stiglitz received a Fulbright fellowship to Cambridge for 1965-1966. He remarks that at that time, there were three "High Churches" in the economics profession: "Chicago on the right and Cambridge, U.K. on the left, with MIT being in the center. Cambridge was still basking in the reflected glory of Keynes. Lord Kahn, Joan

Robinson, Nicholas Kaldor, James Meade, David Champernowne and Piero Sraffa were among the gods that populated the colleges of Cambridge."

Stiglitz's research in this period centred on growth, technical change, and income distribution. Further, the subject of the causes and consequences of income inequality remained one of his abiding concerns. He returned from Cambridge to take up a one-year appointment as an assistant professor at MIT, from which he went to Yale. During this period, Stiglitz continued his work on economic dynamics, and began his research on the economics of uncertainty, which, in turn, led to the work on the economics of information. His research on dynamics was concerned with the stability of the market economy in the absence of futures markets, extending infinitely far into the future. Co-authoring with Karl Shell, Stiglitz showed that a competitive economy with futures markets extending to an arbitrarily large finite number of periods into the future would, in general, exhibit dynamic instabilities. The subject was central to the efficiency of the capitalist economy. Assuming that individuals live finitely, there are overlapping generations. Stiglitz showed, there exist a multiplicity of equilibria both in the short run and in the long run. Further, the economy could be trapped in a "bad" equilibria. In addition, in some cases, some individuals are better off in one equilibrium, some worse off, but in other cases, one equilibrium could Pareto dominate others.

Apart from exploring the logic of economic models, Stiglitz attempted to reconcile the models with every day observation. He tried to examine what would happen to the standard results in the absence of complete set of risk markets as postulated by Arrow and Debreu in their analysis of competitive equilibrium. His early work in this area showed how sensitive not only were the "results" of the standard model to the clearly unrealistic assumptions posited, but even the reasonableness of the assumed behaviour. As his work progressed, the discrepancies between the kind of behaviour implied by the standard model and actual behaviour also became increasingly clear.

Further, to Stiglitz's mind, models, which suggested that there was not such a thing as unemployment, or that it was at most short lived, was suspect. He was critical of economists who like "startling theorems" and results which run counter to conventional wisdom. In this context, Stiglitz refers to, Modigliani and Miller's well-known corporate finance article suggesting irrelevance of corporate financial policy and questions their assumption of rational behaviour when there was ample evidence of market irrationality. He also questions their neglect of two important assumptions, namely bankruptcy and lack of perfect information. In his work, he explored the consequences of these assumptions, not only for the theories of corporate finance, but also for corporate governance including takeovers and macroeconomics. In this connection, he refers to the failure of the IMF to take on board fully the consequences of these assumptions that led to their policy failures thirty years later.

Stiglitz's research work on the economics of uncertainty led naturally to the work on information asymmetries, and more generally, imperfect information. He recognises that information is, in many respects, like a public good. Further, it is unlikely that the private market would provide efficient resource allocation wherever information was endogenous. His later work was an attempt at defining more precisely the nature of market failures. In the development of his ideas on economics of information, the time Stiglitz spent in Kenya was important. He felt that sharecropping was a peculiar institution which very much weakens the incentives for workers to work hard. Another topic in which he has interest from the high school days was economic organisation. The market economy seemed to be plagued by repeated periods of unemployment, and to leave large sections of the population in poverty. As a consequence, one of the key foci of his research was concerned with understanding the limitations of the market or market failures.

Stiglitz considered the neglect of technical change, by the standard model which played such an important role in the U.S development unacceptable. In his view Schumpeter had asked the right question but did not provide the right answer, several of the accepted results of Schumpeterian competition were not valid; for example, that there would necessarily be a succession of short lived monopolies. Instead, Stiglitz showed that a monopoly, once established, could be "persistent," that Schumpeterian competition was not, in general, "efficient," and that the incumbent firm would take actions which deterred entry of new firms, "that potential competition" would in general, not ensure a rapid and efficient pace of innovation. Furthermore, potential competition would not be able to limit the abuses of monopoly.

In his autobiographical note Stiglitz observes that the failure of socialist economies like East European countries and the Soviet Union had reinforced his belief in the inadequacy of the competitive equilibrium model. He is convinced that the standard competitive equilibrium model had failed to recognise the complexity of the information problem facing the economy, such as the socialists had. Here, his concern was not with asymmetries of information but with how different economic organisational structures in effect "aggregated" the disparate and limited information of different individual market participants.

In one of the widely cited papers co-authored with Avinash Dixit, Stiglitz argues that monopolistic competition describes far better many of the real world markets in the economy rather than models of pure competition, pure monopoly, or oligopoly. He found himself to be dissatisfied with rational expectations/representative agent model which was "in ascendency" during the 1970's and 1980's. He showed that it was not just wage and price rigidities, which could give rise to macroeconomic problems. Incomplete contracts, by bringing about unanticipated changes in wages and prices, give rise to "large distributional effects with correspondingly large consequences."

In 1992, Stiglitz moved to Washington to join in 1993 as Chairman of the President's Council of Economic Advisers which he left in 1997. He considers the experience there "wonderful." He asserts: "I was pleased to see how ideas that I had helped formulate only a few years earlier, like adverse selection and moral hazard, were now part of the everyday language of the policy debate in health care."

He joined World Bank in 1997 as its senior vice president for development policy and its chief economist. Stiglitz realised soon that the IMF was using models which ignored the work on imperfect information and incomplete markets. He felt that IMF used its economic power effectively to "force" countries to adopt those policies that are undermining democratic processes. He argued against these policies: those within the World Bank broadly agreed. He, however, made little headway with IMF. In a way, Stiglitz was somewhat frustrated and left World Bank in January 2000. According to him, the experiences during the seven years in Washington have helped shape Stiglitz's activities since then. He accepted a joint appointment to a Chaired Professorship at Columbia Business School, the Graduate School of Arts and Sciences (in the Department of Economics) and the School of International and Public Affairs. He was the first Joel M. Stern Faculty Scholar of Columbia Business School until spring 2001.

Stiglitz has received a large number of honours and awards. He was recipient of the prestigious John Bates Clark Medal of the American Economic Association. He was a Fulbright Scholar. He was elected Fellow of the Econometric Society at a very young age of 29. He is also a member of the National Academy of Sciences, U.S.A. Stiglitz also served as President of the International Economic Association (IEA). He is co-founder and co-president of the Initiative for Policy Dialogue (IPP). He authored a large number of books and over 300 articles.

41.2 A SUMMARY OF JOSEPH STIGLITZ'S MAIN CONTRIBUTIONS

A number of contributions of Stiglitz are covered very briefly in the biographical sketch outlined above. His contributions, particularly relating to the economics of information are summarised in this section. His rather comprehensive Nobel lecture "Information and the Change in the Paradigm in Economics" is an excellent source for this purpose. This summary heavily draws from the lecture. A summary of Stiglitz's discussion of the New Theory of the Firm and Foundations of Modern Economics is also given.

41.2.1 INFORMATION ECONOMICS

Stiglitz provides in his lecture an historical backdrop to the impact information economics has had on how economics is approached today and how information economics represents a fundamental change in extant paradigm within economics. The reigning paradigm-- the neoclassical model--assumed perfect information and ignored the possible effect on the analysis of the problem of imperfect information "perhaps because they could not see how to embrace [it].... In their seemingly precise models, perhaps doing so would have led to incompatible conclusions about the efficiency of markets." He cites Adam Smith's statement that as firms raises interest rates, the best borrowers drop out of the market. This anticipates the later discussion of adverse selection, which has important consequences. Stiglitz brings to the fore a number of paradoxes or puzzles which are difficult to reconcile with the standard theory. From microeconomics, he cites the following examples: Tax paradoxes such as why firms do not take actions to minimise their tax liabilities; security market paradoxes such as high volatility in asset prices; behaviour puzzles such as the ways in which firms respond to risks significantly different from those predicted by the theory. In regard to macroeconomics, he gives the following examples: cyclical variations of many key macro variables, such as consumption, inventories, real wages and interest rates, which cannot be reconciled with the standard theory. The widely accepted models have not been able to explain a number of phenomena and institutions, such as the reasons for IPOs being sold at discount, the limited role equities play in financing new investment since equities provide far better diversification of risk than debt. Information was considered just a transaction cost.

Despite the bouts of unemployment plaguing capitalism, practical economists talked of the neoclassical synthesis which had enormous intellectual influence. However, it came under attack in 1970s and 1980s with regard to its lack of micro-foundations. Another group placed the blame for unemployment in an economy at the doorstep of government intervention, advocating more flexible markets. Stiglitz, in association with Greenwald, put forward an alternative perspective – massive unemployment is the tip of the iceberg of more pervasive market inefficiencies. The economy must be malfunctioning much of the time. The economics of information bolstered this view.

Stiglitz contends that the traditional model was not robust – even slight departures from the underlying assumptions of perfect information has serious consequences. In traditional economic literature, education was assigned the role of adding to human capital and influencing labour productivity, whereas in developing countries (Stiglitz cites Kenya as an example) education enhanced the probability of getting a good job, and yield a higher return, though social return for education may decline. One of the key issues in information economics is the "difficulty of appropriating the returns." If the employer has a way of screening among the job applicants and if he could keep that information private, he will be able to appropriate the return to the information. On the other hand, if the employee knew his ability (a case of asymmetric information), he has an incentive to convince the employer of his ability. But someone at the bottom of the ability distribution has an incentive not to have the information revealed. The question Stiglitz raises is how do the forces for secrecy and information disclosure get balanced. Leibenstein earlier postulated that in very poor countries, higher wages lead to higher productivity. Stiglitz observes that whenever information and contracting were imperfect, productivity might depend on wages. In that case he argues, firms might pay a higher than minimum wage necessary to hire labour, i.e., efficiency wages; Stiglitz states: "The efficiency wage theory meant that there could exist unemployment in equilibrium." The traditional competitive market equilibrium analysis which posits that the market had to clear is, according to Stiglitz, not true if information were imperfect. He shows that in equilibrium there had to be unemployment: "Unemployment was the discipline device that forced workers to work." In this context it is appropriate to discuss the Shapiro-Stiglitz model.

Stiglitz was instrumental in developing the Shapiro-Stiglitz model to explain why there exists unemployment even in equilibrium, why wages are not pushed down sufficiently by job seekers (assuming there is no minimum wage stipulation). The model explains why unemployment is driven by the information structure of employment.

In the model of efficiency wages (see Figure 41.1), workers are paid at a level that "dissuades" them from shirking work, preventing wages from declining to market clearing levels. Full employment cannot be achieved as workers would shirk work if the workers were not threatened with the possibility of unemployment. Because of this, the curve for the non-shirking condition, labelled NSC in the diagram, goes to infinity at full employment.

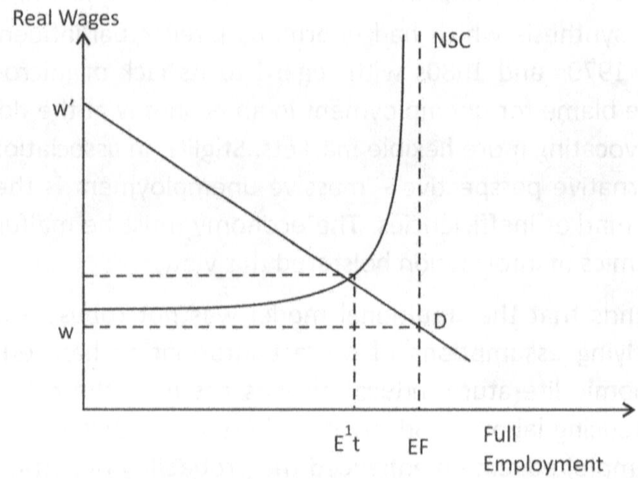

Fig. 41.1 Shapiro-Stiglitz Model

His experience, noticing the disparities between the models used and the world that Stiglitz saw, had motivated search for a paradigm that serves as an alternative to the competitive general equilibrium model. Stiglitz comments: The latter virtually made economics a branch of engineering. According to Stiglitz, in the standard paradigm, "there were no shocks, no unanticipated events: at the beginning of time, the full equilibrium was solved, and everything from then on was an unfolding over time of what had been planned in each of the contingencies." In the real world, the critical question is how, and how well do markets handle information problem when the model assumes perfect information?

Further, in the standard model institutions did not matter, wealth distribution did not matter and history did not matter. These premises are difficult to accept. Stiglitz's work on the economics of information has started by questioning each of these. With imperfect information and the cost of acquiring it, these implausible assumptions cannot be accepted. He showed that "there was a fundamental concavity in the value of information;" in other words, it does not pay to buy just a little bit of information. In another co-authored work it has been demonstrated that the domain of law of diminishing returns to be "more limited" than had been previously realised. In yet another work co-authored with M. Rothschild, it has been shown that equilibrium does not exist in a competitive market with imperfect information, even in the face of a small amount of imperfection. Further, in models put forward by Spence, a full equilibrium never existed. Stiglitz states: "Non-convexities naturally give rise to discontinuities, and discontinuities to problems of existence, but the non-convexity that Rothschild and I had uncovered was a different and more fundamental nature." Furthermore, the foundations of competitive equilibrium analysis were undermined by the new information paradigm. They include basic laws of economics such as law of demand and supply (equilibrium by market clearing), law of a single price, law of competitive price (equilibrium price equals marginal cost) and efficient market hypothesis. As actions including choices convey information, market participants know this which affects their behaviour; markets with imperfect information differ from the traditional paradigm.

The reason for this is not far to seek. For example, the willingness of an insured to take an insurance policy with a large deductible conveys information to the insurance company that he is prepared to bear the risk as he considers the likelihood of an accident is low. The efficiency and overall performance of the economy is impaired by the absence of some markets such as markets for risk. More importantly, unlike in the old paradigm, in imperfect information paradigm, markets are almost never Pareto efficient.

It is rather difficult to construct an (alternative) impact information paradigm, particularly because while there is a single way in which information is perfect, there are an infinite number of ways in which information can be imperfect; besides, information imperfections are pervasive in the economy, run deeper and are largely asymmetric. Some of the information asymmetries are inherent; such as, the individual naturally knows more about himself than does anyone else. Economic processes may generate some of the asymmetries such as in labour market, or insurance market. Stiglitz also gives instances of informational externality such as in oil exploration business.

In his Nobel lecture, Stiglitz discusses the ways by which information asymmetries are dealt with and how they can be overcome. He considers instances in which actions of persons may convey information. For example, the quality of the guarantee offered by a firm can convey information about the quality of the product. The guarantee is desirable because it reduces risk; more importantly, it conveys information. Likewise, the number of years of schooling may convey information about the productivity of an individual. The size of the deductible an insured chooses conveys information about his perception of the likelihood of and/or the size of the accident he anticipates. The fact that such actions may convey information influences behaviour. While some individuals may wish to convey information some individuals may wish not to have information conveyed. In either case, actions conveying information lead people to alter their behaviour which may change the functioning of markets. Stiglitz asserts: That is why information imperfections have such "profound effects." Two results follow from the recognition that actions convey information. First, in making decisions persons will consider not what they like (as in the traditional economics) but how it will affect others beliefs' about them. Second, individuals have an incentive to lie. Self-selection mechanism works if a mechanism is devised by which the groups can be easily separated. As for example, people who know they are less likely to have an accident will be more willing to accept an insurance policy with a high deductible; an insurer can offer two policies one at a high premium and no deductible and the other with a low premium and high deductible, to sort out high risk and low risk persons and separate them into identifiable categories. Stiglitz expresses the view that a situation of a monopolist is easy to analyse in this way by structuring the entire choice set, pricing his customers. He is able to put forward "a general theory of price discrimination" by monopoly. The economics of information is credited with providing "the first coherent theory of monopoly."

The analysis of full competitive equilibrium by Stiglitz and Rothschild in their 1976 paper shows that equilibrium might not exist; the competitive equilibrium model is not robust and how the fact that actions convey information affects the equilibrium. Further, the work provided insights in the functioning of an important set of markets and also that there exists important elements of insurance in many transactions. Stiglitz cites some examples like the relationship between the landlord and tenant (share – cropping), or the employer and employee (in the labour market).

Dealing with screening and signalling concepts, Stiglitz states: "In equilibrium, both buyers and sellers, employees and employers, insurance companies and insured, lender and creditor are aware of the informational consequences of their actions.... In the case, where, say, the insurance company or employer or employee takes the initiative for sorting out applicants, self–selection is an alternative to examination as a sorting device. In the case where the insured or employee or borrower, takes initiative for identifying himself as a better risk, a better employee, a borrower more likely to repay, then we say he is <u>signalling</u>."(Emphasis in the original).

In his Nobel lecture, Stiglitz considers the issue of equilibrium in the insurance market. Though insurance markets exist, they are far from complete. In addition, the market exhibits instability. Regulation of rate setting may help stabilise the market. Further, the market is far from as rational as the theory would suggest and there is less experience rating. Competition is thwarted by "significant search costs" and "considerable uncertainty" about how easily one can get a claim. He opines: Self-selection is still relevant, but the model of monopoly or some version of monopolistic competition may be more relevant than the model of perfect competition. He also argues that even small search costs could make a large difference to the behaviour of product and labour markets. In support of this conclusion, he cites Diamond's 1971 paper which showed lack of robustness of competitive equilibrium theory.

Contrary to the traditional theory that positive competitive market equilibrium leads to Pareto efficient allocation of resources, economies with information imperfections would not be Pareto efficient, even when costs of obtaining information are considered. That is, government interventions in the market could make all parties better off. The case for free capital markets is based on their price—discovery function. Stiglitz contends that this is largely redistributive, with the gains of those obtaining the information occurring at the expense of others. Further, information can have unfavourable effects on volatility and can lead to destructive markets, in a way which results in lowering of welfare. As mentioned in the earlier part of the chapter, markets with information asymmetries and other information imperfections are far from efficient. In the case of models with moral hazard, there results a negative externality. Market failures are pervasive. Moreover, it is not possible to decentralise efficient market solutions and impairment of the efficiency of competitive processes where markets are interlinked over time.

Stiglitz deals with agency problems-one of the sources of market failure. The extent of agency problems and of market failures depends on wealth distribution as noted in the discussion of share-cropping. It is therefore clear that one cannot separate out issues of equality and efficiency. This was earlier pointed out by Mirrlees. He argued that all redistributive taxation is distortionary.

From the above discussion, Stiglitz draws the conclusion that the second welfare theorem, asserting the possibility of separating issues of distribution, is not valid. Further, Stiglitz in his work co-authored with Arnott supported the conclusion that only under very special circumstances markets could be shown to be efficient.

41.2.2 NEW THEORY OF THE FIRM AND FOUNDATIONS OF MODERN ECONOMICS

There was widespread dissatisfaction with Keynesian economics with its lack of microeconomic foundations. The microeconomic foundations to repair the lacuna by using the traditional perfect competition paradigm were found to be unsatisfactory. Stiglitz's major preoccupation during the past two decades or more was to construct a macroeconomic model which includes the consequences of imperfections of information in labour, product and capital markets. At the heart of the model is the new theory of the firm for which the theory of asymmetric information provides the foundations. It is Stiglitz's opinion that the modern theory of the firm rests on three pillars—the theory of corporate finance, the theory of corporate governance and the theory of organisational design. His work (with different co-authors) shows how the willingness to buy or to sell shares conveys information. Hence, how firms raise capital makes a difference. Firms are found to rely heavily on debt-finance. Therefore, failure of firms to meet debt obligations leading to bankruptcy (the factor that was ignored by Modigliani and Miller in their work) matters. Firms act as though they are risk—averse because of the bankruptcy costs and limitation in the design of managerial incentive schemes.

Further, with credit rationing or potential credit rationing the firm's net worth or market value of its assets matters as also its asset structure including liquidity. In this connection, Stiglitz points out the importance of the distinction between lack of liquidity and insolvency that depends on asymmetries of information. The neo-classical theory of investment postulated that investment depends upon the real rate of interest and firm's estimation of expected returns on the investment. The firm's cash flows and net worth are not considered important. The work of Stiglitz and others on asymmetric information reveals that, particularly for small and medium enterprises, those variables are crucial. In traditional theory there was no "corporate veil" as Stiglitz observes. What is going on inside the firm is known. It makes no difference for an investor except for tax reasons whether the firm distributes profits or retains them in the firm for future investment. Once it is accepted that there is imperfect information regarding what is going in the firm, there is a corporate veil that cannot be pierced easily.

According to Stiglitz, the next issue which has to be considered for developing a new macroeconomic paradigm concerns corporate governance. The traditional theory hypothesised that firms attempt maximisation of expected present discounted value of profits which equalled market value. How firm's decisions matter does not count much. Modern corporations in which there is divergence of ownership and control, (agents) managers can take actions which promote their interests at the expense of the interests of owners or shareholders (principal). Likewise, majority shareholders can advance their interests ignoring the interests of minority shareholders. As such, corporate governance is quite important. Stiglitz is of the opinion that the problem of corporate governance comes up not only from the problems of imperfect information but also from the public good nature of management. Likewise, decisions in regard to take-over of other firms are also important. He does not agree with the argument that firms maximise the market value of the stock.

The third pillar of the modern theory of the firm, according to Stiglitz, is organisational design which is of little importance in a world of perfect information. On the basis of the research work, Stiglitz and his co- authors suggest "that in a variety of circumstances, especially when there is a scarcity of good projects, decentralised polyarchical organisational structures have distinct advantages."

Stiglitz, in his Nobel lecture, states that the central macroeconomic issue is that of unemployment and much of macroeconomics is concerned with dynamics, with economic fluctuations. His work with co-authors shows how the theories of asymmetric information provide explanations of these macroeconomic phenomena. Particularly, capital market imperfections result in risk-averse behaviour of firms and in cash flow constraints affecting firms and households. Additionally, imperfections of capital markets and incomplete contracting provide part of the explanation of observed key macro phenomena. Stiglitz asserts that wages and prices are not perfectly flexible, neither are they perfectly rigid as was interpreted in many versions of Keynesian economics. The problem is not only with price rigidity. Even excessive down side price flexibility could create problems through redistributive changes, among others. Redistributive changes may create significant real effects which could not be insured against because of capital market imperfections. Stglitz argues that large shocks could result in bankruptcy and with bankruptcy – "especially when it results in firm liquidation, there was a loss of organizational and informational capital." It has to be remembered that in traditional economic theories, bankruptcy hardly played any role. When such shocks do not lead to bankruptcy, they can affect ability and willingness of firms to take risks affecting aggregate supply and investment demand. More importantly, the work of Stiglitz and co—authors has emphasised the supply side effects of shocks, the interrelationships between supply and demand side effects and the importance of finance in "propagating" fluctuations.

In the reformulation of macroeconomics by Stiglitz and others, monetary economics received particular focus. In modern economics, credit is mainly required for transaction purposes and not money as in traditional theories. Further, most transactions involve exchange of assets, therefore not directly related to GDP. As such, in modern economies what is important is the availability of credit and the terms on which it is available. Stiglitz emphasises: "Information is at the heart of monetary economics. The ability of and willingness of banks to bear risks (they are also risk averse) in lending out funds crucially depends on their net worth which can be adversely affected by shocks mentioned above giving rise to large adverse macroeconomic consequences." The theory stresses the importance of regulatory instruments, such as risk-adjusted capital adequacy requirements, in addition to traditional monetary instruments like reserve requirements. Monetary policy can therefore be used to impact the supply of credit, interest rate charged, and bank's risk portfolio. Stiglitz sounds a warning: excessive reliance on capital adequacy requirements could be counter-productive.

The policy implications of the theory developed by Stiglitz and his co-authors have been referred to in his lecture. He asserts that it provides a "new basis for a 'liquidity trap'" explaining why monetary policy may be relatively ineffective in severe economic downturns. He cites the policy failures-- Fed to forestall the 1991 recession and the failures of IMF in East Asia in 1997.

Another important point emphasised by Stiglitz concerns credit inter-linkages—firms receiving credit from other firms, providing at the same time credit to still other firms. He draws a disturbing conclusion: As a result of these general inter-linkages... a shock to one firm gets transmitted to others, and when there is a large enough shock, there can be cascade of bankruptcies. A fore-warning of sub- prime mortgage crisis?

In addition to the analysis of implications of imperfections in credit markets due to information problems for cyclical variations, Stiglitz and co-authors worked on problems relating to growth and development. For the growth of firms, capital is required and how they raise it is crucial. In this connection Stiglitz states: In particular, "equity rationing" -- especially important in developing countries, where informational problems are even greater--impedes firms' willingness to invest and undertake risks and thus growth slows down. To improve economic growth, appropriate changes in economic policy which encourage firms to bear more risk would be helpful. In contrast, IMF's intervention policies in which interest rates are raised to "very high levels," discouraged the use of debt and affected growth.

Investment in research is very crucial for helping the pace of growth. The results of the work by Stiglitz reveal that "market economies in which research and innovation play a crucial role are not adequately taken into account in the standard competitive model and that the market equilibrium, in the absence of government intervention, is not, in general, Pareto efficient; that is, there is a potentially important role for government. In this context, Stiglitz refers to the issue of taxation." An analysis, for instance, of the incidence of taxation which is predicated on perfectly competitive markets with perfectly informed consumers and risk neutral firms, is likely to go astray."

In the concluding part of the Nobel lecture, Stiglitz explores the difficulties citizens have of controlling their government and the problems posed to government in the conduct of business in the face of information asymmetries. In regard to the latter, he deals with three key areas: Taxation, regulation and production. Redistribution of income is one of the functions of the government. Even if it does not redistribute income, government has to raise sufficient revenues to finance public goods. The collection of revenues has to be done in an equitable manner which requires that government be able to identify such individuals that can make a greater contribution. The crucial question for the design of a tax system then thus boils down to "what is observable" in the face of information asymmetries. Stiglitz observes that the government's problem of maximising social welfare subject to information constraints is "closely analogous to that of the monopolist," maximising private profit subject to information constraints. He comments: That is why Mirrlees's (1971) paper on optimal taxation, though not couched in information-theoretic terms, was an important precursor to the Stiglitz and his co-authors' work.

As in taxation, in regulation government faces the same problem posed by information asymmetries. Stiglitz refers to a movement in the 1980s towards privatisation of state enterprises, even in areas where there existed a situation of a natural monopoly. This led to government regulation replacing government ownership. Even with government ownership, problems exist; the theories of imperfect information suggest that "even the best designed regulatory system would work imperfectly." He concludes that their work showed that only under extremely restrictive conditions would privatisation improve social welfare.

In his comprehensive Prize lecture, Stiglitz sums up his arguments by stating that not only the competitive model was not robust and could not explain important economic phenomena but also gave rise to "misguided" policy prescriptions. His and his co-authors' work, while remaining broadly within the standard framework, altered only one assumption—the assumption relating to perfect information. This modification has "drastic consequences;" he realised that an alternative paradigm that is robust and possessed "great explanatory power" could be constructed. Addressing to the problems of development, he realised that development means a significant transformation of society, including a change in preferences and attitudes, acceptance of change, and abandoning many traditional ways of thinking. More importantly, Stiglitz is convinced that "the dynamics of change may not be well described by equilibrium models.... Information economics has alerted us to the fact that history matters.... Random events... have consequences that are irreversible. Dynamics may be better described by evolutionary processes and models than by equilibrium processes. Further, one cannot predict where the economy will be by knowing preferences, technology, and initial endowments." There can be a "high level of indeterminancy."

In a broader framework, Stiglitz turns his attention as to how imperfections and asymmetries, which are pervasive in every aspect of life and society, affect political processes. Here, it is to be noted that political processes necessarily involve information asymmetries. Here exists the standard principal—agent problem as there is a delegation of responsibility for day to day decision-making in a democracy. Stiglitz notes that in economic processes, take-over mechanism is an imperfect check and electoral processes provide an imperfect check. He sounds a pertinent warning: one has to be concerned with abuses, as in the political processes there exist limited "exit" options. Further, "ensuring public good (public management) is itself a public good." Stiglitz asserts that as more transparency reduces scope for action, there are strong forces for those in government to reduce transparency. There is also another rationale for secrecy: secrecy is artificially created scarcity of information. He observes: "... like artificially created scarcities, it gives rise to rents, rents which in some countries are appropriated through outright corruption (selling information), but in others are part of a "gift exchange" in which reporters not only provide puff pieces praising the government official who has given the reporter privileged information.... Without unbiased information, the effectiveness of the check that can be provided by the citizenry is limited; without good information, the contestability of the political processes can be undermined."

41.2.3 OTHER CONTRIBUTIONS OF JOSEPH STIGLITZ

In the opening remarks for his Prize acceptance, Stiglitz said: I hope to show that information economics represents a fundamental change in the prevailing paradigm within economics. Further, in an interview in 2001 he explained: The theories that I (and others) helped develop explain why unfettered markets often not only not lead to social justice but do not even produce efficient outcomes. Interestingly, there has been no intellectual challenges to the refutation of Adam Smith's invisible hand. Individuals and firms in pursuit of their self-interest, are not necessarily or in general, lead as if by an invisible hand, to economic efficiency.

Besides his significant work on economics of information, Stiglitz has important contribution to public economics, especially the theory of optimal taxation, industrial organisation and the economics of natural resources. Stiglitz's research has provided the foundation for the emergence of modern development economics. Many insights from the economics of information have been included in it. Stiglitz's sharecropping model and Akerlof's lemons model have provided the basis for explaining institutional relationships between landlords and tenants. Further, the dichotomy between modern and traditional sectors in developing economies could be classified using the arguments based in their works. Lofgren, Persson and Weibull note: "[Kasushik Basu (1997)] is an example of a modern advanced textbook in development economics that builds heavily on the economics of information."

41.3 CONCLUDING OBSERVATIONS

Stiglitz states in his Prize lecture: "I entered economics with the hope that it might enable me to do something about unemployment, poverty, and discrimination. As an economic researcher, I have been lucky enough to hit upon some ideas that I think do enhance our understanding of these phenomena. As an educator, I have been lucky enough to have had the opportunity to reduce some of the asymmetries of information.... And to have had some first rate students who themselves have pushed the research agenda forward." He also admits that he had good fortune to translate his ideas into practice as a public servant in the American government and at the World Bank. Admitting that living in democracies and enjoying academic freedom which involve responsibility, Stiglitz concludes with a fond hope that the responsibility to use that freedom "to do what we can to ensure that the world of the future be one in which there is not only greater economic prosperity, but also more social justice."

41.4 SELECT BIBLIOGRAPHY OF JOSEPH STIGLITZ'S WORKS

41.4.1 BOOKS

1977 (with P. Dasgupta et al.), An Economic Analysis of the Conservation of Depletable Natural Resources, Federal Energy Administration, Washington, D.C.

1980 (with A. B. Atkinson), Lectures in Public Economics, McGraw-Hill, New York.

1981 (with D. Newbery), The Theory of Commodity Price Stabilization, Oxford University Press, New York.

1986 Economics of the Public Sector, W. W. Norton, New York.

1989 The Economic Role of the State, Basil Blackwell, Oxford.

1992 (with R. Sah), Peasants versus City-Dwellers: Taxation and the Burden of Economic Development, Clarendon Press, Oxford .

1993 (with K. Hoff and A. Braverman eds.), The Economics of Rural Organization: Theory, Practice, and Policy, Oxford University Press, New York.

1994 Whither Socialism?, MIT Press, Cambridge, MA.

2001 a (with G.M .Meir eds.), Frontiers of Development Economics: The Future Perspective, Oxford University Press, New York.

b (with R. Holzmann eds.), New Ideas about Old Age Security, World Bank, Washington, D.C.

c (with S. Yusuf eds.), Rethinking the East Asian Miracle, World Bank and Oxford University Press, New York.

d (with G. Caprio et al. eds.), Financial Liberalization: How Far, How Fast, Cambridge University Press, Cambridge.

2002 Globalization and its Discontents, W.W. Norton, New York.

2003 The Roaring Nineties, W.W. Norton, New York.

2004 (B. Greenwald), Towards a New Paradigm for Money Economics, Cambridge University Press, Cambridge.

2005 (with A. Charlton), Fair Trade for All, Oxford University Press, New York.

2006 a Making Globalization Work, W.W. Norton, New York.

b Stability with Growth: Macroeconomics, Liberalization, and Development, Oxford University Press, New York.

2008 (with L. Blimes), The Three Trillion Dollar War: The True Cost of the War in Iraq, W.W. Norton, New York and Penguin, London.

2009 The Selected Works of Joseph E. Stiglitz, Vol. I: Information and Economic Analysis, Oxford University Press, New York.

2010 Free Fall: America, Free Markets, and the Sinking of the World Economy, W. W. Norton, New York.

2011 (P. Bolton et al.), Sovereign Wealth Funds and Long-Term Investing, Columbia University Press, New York.

2012 a The Price of Inequality: How Today's Divided Society Endangers Our Future, W.W. Norton, New York.

b (with O.J. Blanchard et al.) In the Wake of the Crisis, MIT Press, Cambridge, MA.

41.4.2 ARTICLES

1967 a (with K. Shell) "Allocation of Investment in a Dynamic Economy," QJE, Vol.81, Nov.

b "A Two-Sector, Two Class Model of Economic Growth," RES, Vol.34, April.

1968 (with R. Solow), "Output, Employment and Wages in the Short Run," QJE, Vol.82, Nov.

1969 a "Allocation of Heterogeneous Capital Goods in a Two Sector Economy," IER, Vol.10, No.3.

b "Behavior Toward Risk With Many Commodities," Econometrica, Vol.37, No.4.

c (with K. Shell and M. Sidrauski), "Capital Gains, Income and Savings," RES, Vol.36, Jan.

d (with G. A. Akerlof), "Capital, Wages and Structural Unemployment," EJ, Vo.79, June.

e "The Effects of Income, Wealth and Capital Gains Taxation on Risk-Taking," QJE, Vol.83, May.

f "A Re-Examination of the Modigliani-Miller Theorem," AER, Vol.59, No.5.

1970 a "A Consumption Oriented Theory of the Demand for Financial Assets and the Term Structure of Interest Rates," RES, Vol.37, No. 3.

b "Factor Price Equalization in a Dynamic Economy," JPE, Vol.78, No.3.

c (with D. Cass), "The Structure of Investor Preferences and Asset Returns, and Separability in Portfolio Allocation: A Contribution to the Pure Theory of Mutual Funds," JET, Vol.2, No.1.

d (with M. Rothschild), "Increasing Risk: I. A Definition," JET, Vol.2, No. 3.

1971 (with M. Rothschild), "Increasing Risk: II. Its Economic Consequences," JET, Vol.5, No.1.

1972 a "On the Optimality of the Stock Market Allocation of Investment," QJE, Vol.86, No.1.

b "Some Aspects of the Pure Theory of Corporate Finance: Bankruptcies and Take-Overs," Bell JE, Vol.3, No.2.

c "Taxation, Risk Taking, and the Allocation of Investment in a Competitive Economy," in Studies in the Theory of Capital Markets, M. Jensen (ed.), Praeger, New York.

1973 a "Approaches to the Economics of Discrimination," AER, Vol.63, No.2.

b "Taxation, Corporate Financial Policy and the Cost of Capital," JPubE, Vol.2, Feb.

c "Education and Inequality," Annals of the American Academy of Political and Social Sciences, 409, Sep.

1974 a "Alternative Theories of Wage Determination and Unemployment in L.D.C.'s: The Labor Turnover Model," QJE, Vol.88, No.2.

b "Growth With Exhaustible Resources: The Competitive Economy," RES, Vol.41, Mar.

c "Incentives and Risk Sharing in Sharecropping," RES, Vol.41, No.2.

d (with P. Diamond) "Increases in Risk and in Risk Aversion," JET, Vol.8, No.3.

e "On the Irrelevance of Corporate Financial Policy," AER, Vol.64, No.6.

f "Theories of Discrimination and Economic Policy," in Patterns of Racial Discrimination, G. von Furstenberg, et al. (eds.), D.C. Heath and Company (Lexington Books), Boston, MA.

1975 a "Incentives, Risk and Information: Notes Toward a Theory of Hierarchy," Bell JE, Vol.6, No.2.

b "Information and Economic Analysis," in Current Economic Problems, J.M. Parkin and A.R. Nobay (eds.), Cambridge University Press, Cambridge.

c "The Theory of Screening, Education and the Distribution of Income," AER, Vol.65, No.3.

1976 a "The Efficiency Wage Hypothesis, Surplus Labor and the Distribution of Income in L.D.C.'s", OEP, Vol. 28, No.2.

b (with M. Rothschild), "Equilibrium in Competitive Insurance Markets: An Essay on the Economics of Imperfect Information," QJE, Vol.90, No.4.

1977 a "Monopoly, Non-Linear Pricing and Imperfect Information: The Insurance Market," RES, Vol.44, No.3.

b (with S. Grossman), "On Value Maximization and Alternative Objectives of the Firm," JF, Vol. 32, No.2.

c "Symposium on the Economics of Information: Introduction," RES, Vol.44, No. 3.

1979 a "Equilibrium in Product Markets with Imperfect Information," AER, Vol. 69, No.2.

b "On Search and Equilibrium Price Distributions," in Economics and Human Welfare: Essays in Honor of Tibor Scitovsky, M. Boskin (ed.), Academic Press New York.

1980 (with S. Grossman), "On the Impossibility of Informationally Efficient Markets," AER, Vol.70, No.3.

1981 a (with A. Weiss), "Credit Rationing in Markets with Imperfect Information," AER, Vol.71, No.3.

b "Pareto Optimality and Competition," JF, Vol. 36, No.2.

1982 a "Alternative Theories of Wage Determination and Unemployment: The Efficiency Wage Model," in The Theory and Experience of Economic Development: Essays in Honor of Sir Arthur W. Lewis, M. Gersovitz, et al. (eds.), London.

b "The Inefficiency of the Stock Market Equilibrium," RES, Vol.49, No.2.

c "Information and Capital Markets," in Financial Economics: Essays in Honor of Paul Cootner, W. F. Sharpe and C. Cootner (eds.), Prentice Hall, Englewood-cliffs, NJ.

d "Ownership, Control and Efficient Markets: Some Paradoxes in the Theory of Capital Markets," in Economic Regulation: Essays in Honor of James R. Nelson, K. D. Boyer and W. G. Shepherd (eds.), Michigan State University Press, Michigan.

e "Self-Selection and Pareto Efficient Taxation," JPubE, Vol. 17, No.2.

f (with A. Braverman), "Sharecropping and the Interlinking of Agrarian Markets," AER, Vol.72, No.4.

g "Utilitarianism and Horizontal Equity: The Case for Random Taxation," JPubE, Vol. 17, No.2.

1983 a "Risk, Incentives and Insurance: The Pure Theory of Moral Hazard," Geneva Papers, 8(No.26, Jan 1983).

b (with A. Weiss), "Alternate Approaches to the Analysis of Markets with Asymmetric Information," AER, Vol. 73, No.1.

c "Information, Screening and Welfare," in Bayesian Models in Economic Theory, M. Boyer and R. Khilstrom (eds.), Elsevier Science, Amsterdam.

d (with P. Neary), "Towards a Reconstruction of Keynesian Economics: Expectations and Constrained Equilibria," QJE, Vol.98, Supplement.

1984 a (with A. Weiss and B. Greenwald), "Informational Imperfections in the Capital Markets and Macroeconomic Fluctuations," AER, Vol. 74, No. 2.

b "Price Rigidities and Market Structure," AER, Vol. 74, No.2.

1985 a "Credit Markets and the Control of Capital," JMBC, Vol. 17, No.2.

b "Equilibrium Wage Distributions," EJ, Vol.95, No.379.

c "Information and Economic Analysis: A Perspective," EJ, Vol.95, Supplement.

1986 a (with A. Braverman), "Cost Sharing Arrangement Under Sharecropping: Moral Hazard, Incentive Flexibility and Risk," Journal of Agricultural Economics, Vol. 68, No.3.

	b	(with B. Greenwald), "Externalities in Economies with Imperfect Information and Incomplete Markets," QJE, Vol. 101, No. 2.
	c	"The New Development Economics," World Development, Vol.14, No.2.
	d	"Theories of Wage Rigidities," in Keynes' Economic Legacy: Contemporary Economic Theories, J.L. Butkiewicz, et al. (eds.), Praeger Publishers, New York.
	e	"Theory of Competition, Incentives and Risk," in New Developments in the Analysis of Market Structure, J. E. Stiglitz and F. Mathewson (eds.), MacMillan/MIT Press, London.
	f	"Toward a More General Theory of Monopolistic Competition," in Prices, Competition, & Equilibrium, M. Peston and R. Quandt (eds.), Philip Allan/Barnes & Noble Books, Oxford.
1987	a	"The Causes and Consequences of the Dependence of Quality on Prices," JEL, Vol.25, No.1.
	b	"Competition and the Number of Firms in a Market: Are Duopolies More Competitive Than Atomistic Markets?" JPE, Vol. 95, No.5.
	c	(with B. Greenwald), "Imperfect Information, Credit Markets and Unemployment", European Economic Review, Vol.31, No.1-2.
	d	(with D. Sappington), "Information and Regulation," in Public Regulation, E. Bailey (ed.), MIT Press, London.
	e	"Sharecropping," in The New Palgrave: A Dictionary of Economics, MacMillan Press, London.
1988	a	"Economic Organization, Information, and Development," in Handbook of Development Economics, H. Chenery and T.N. Srinivasan (eds.), Elsevier, Amsterdam.
	b	(with R. Arnott), "The Basic Analytics of Moral Hazard,", ScandJE, Vol. 90, No. 3.
	c	(with B. Greenwald), "Examining Alternative Macroeconomic Theories," BPEA, No.1.
	d	"Money, Credit, and Business Fluctuations," Economic Record, Vol.64, No.18.
	e	"On the Relevance or Irrelevance of Public Financial Policy," in The Economics of Public Debt, Macmillan, London.
	f	"Why Financial Structure Matters," JEP, Vol.2, No. 4.
	g	(with B. Greenwald), "Pareto Inefficiency of Market Economies: Search and Efficiency Wage Models," AER, Vol.78, No.2.

1989 a "Financial Markets and Development," Oxford Review of Economic Policy, Vol.5, No.4.

b "Imperfect Information in the Product Market," in Handbook of Industrial Organization, 1, Elsevier, Amsterdam.

c "Markets, Market Failures and Development," AER, Vol. 79, No.2.

d "Monopolistic Competition and the Capital Market," in The Economics of Imperfect Competition and Employment - Joan Robinson and Beyond, G. Feiwel (ed.), New York.

e "Principal and Agent," in The New Palgrave: Allocation, Information and Markets, MacMillan, London.

f "Rational Peasants, Efficient Institutions and the Theory of Rural Organization: Methodological Remarks for Development Economics," in The Economic Theory of Agrarian Institutions, P. Bardhan (ed.), Clarendon Press, Oxford.

1990 a (with B. Greenwald), "Asymmetric Information and the New Theory of the Firm: Financial Constraints and Risk Behavior," AER, Vol.80, No.2.

b (with D. Jaffee), "Credit Rationing," in Handbook of Monetary Economics, B. Friedman and F. Hahn (eds.), Elsevier, Amsterdam.

c (with K. Hoff), "Imperfect Information and Rural Credit Markets: Puzzles and Policy Perspectives," World Bank Economic Review, Vol.4, No.3.

d (with B. Greenwald), "Macroeconomic Models with Equity and Credit Rationing," in Asymmetric Information, Corporate Finance, and Investment, R. B. Hubbard (ed.), University of Chicago Press, Chicago, Ill.

e (with R. Arnott), "The Welfare Economics of Moral Hazard," in Risk, Information and Insurance: Essays in Memory of Karl H. Borch, H. Louberge (ed.), Kluwer Academic, Norwell, MA.

1991 a "Another Century of Economic Science," EJ, Vol.101, No.404.

b "Introduction to Symposium on Organizations and Economics," JEP, Vol.5, No.2.

c (with R. Arnott), "Moral Hazard and Non-Market Institutions: Dysfunctional Crowding out or Peer Monitoring," AER, Vol.81, No.1.

d (with B. Greenwald), "Toward a Reformulation of Monetary Theory: Competitive Banking," Economic and Social Review, Vol.23, No. 1.

1992 a "Capital Markets and Economic Fluctuations in Capitalist Economies," European Economic Review, Vol. 36, No.2-3.

b "Contract Theory and Macroeconomic Fluctuations," in Contract Economics, L. Werin and H. Wijkander (eds.), Basil Blackwell, Oxford.

c "Methodological Issues and the New Keynesian Economics," in Alternative Approaches to Macroeconomics, A. Vercelli and N. Dimitri (eds.), Oxford University Press, Oxford.

d "Prices and Queues as Screening Devices in Competitive Markets," in Economic Analysis of Markets and Games: Essays in Honor of Frank Hahn, D. Gale and O. Hart (eds.), MIT Press, Cambridge, MA.

1993 a "The Role of State in Financial Markets," Proceedings of the World Bank Conference on Development Economics, World Bank, Washington D.C.

b "Perspectives on the Role of Government Risk-Bearing within the Financial Sector," in Government Risk – bearing, M. Sniderman (ed.), Kluwer Academic, Norwell, MA.

1994 a (with R. Arnott and B. Greenwald), "Information and Economic Efficiency," Information Economics and Policy, Vol.6, No.1.

b "Reflections on Economics and on Being and Becoming an Economist," in The Makers of Modern Economics, Vol. II, A. Heertje (ed.), Harvester wheat sheaf, New York.

c (with A. Weiss), "Sorting Out the Differences Between Screening and Signaling Models," in Mathematical Models in Economics, M.O.L. Bacharach, et al. (eds.), Oxford University Press, Oxford.

1995 (with B. Greenwald), "Labor Market Adjustments and the Persistence of Unemployment," AER, Vol. 85, No.2.

1997 a "The Role of Government in the Economies of Developing Countries," in Development Strategy and the Management of the Market Economy, E. Malinvaud and A.K. Sen (eds.), Oxford University Press, Oxford.

b (with M. Rothschild), "Competition and Insurance Twenty Years Later," Geneva Papers on Risk and Insurance Theory, Vol.22, No.2.

1999 a "Interest Rates, Risk, and Imperfect Markets: Puzzles and Policies," Oxford Review of Economic Policy Vol.15, No.2.

b "Toward a General Theory of Wage and Price Rigidities and Economic Fluctuations," AER, Vol.89, No.2.

2000 a (with T. Helmann and K. Murdoch), "Liberalization, Moral Hazard in Banking and Prudential Regulation: Are Capital Requirements Enough?" AER, Vol.90, No.1.

b "The Contributions of the Economics of Information to Twentieth Century Economics," QJE, Vol.115, No.4.

2001 "Principles of Financial Regulation: A Dynamic Approach," The World Bank Observer, Vol.16, No.1.

2002 "Information and Change in Paradigm in Economics, Nobel Lecture," AER, Vol. 92, No.3.

2003 "Globalization of Growth in Emerging Markets? The New Economy Policy Making," JPM, Vol.25, No.5.

2005 "Integration of Un Insurance with Retirement Insurance," JPubE, Vol.89, No.11-12.

2006 "Helping Infant Economies Grow: Foundations of Trade Policies for D.Cs," AER, Vol.96, No.2.

2007 "Credit Chains and Bankruptcy Propagation in Production Networks," JEDC, Vol.31, No.6.

2008 "Exiting a Lawless State," EJ, Vol. 118, No.531.

2009 "Dividend Taxation and Inter-temporal Tax Arbitrage," JPubE, Vol.93, Nos. 1-2.

2010 a "Equilibrium Fictions: A Cognitive Approach to Societal Liquidity," AER, Vol.100, No.2.

b "Leverage and Asset Bubbles: Averting Armageddon with Chapter 11?" EJ, Vol. 120, No. 544.

c "Risk and Global Economic Architecture: Why Full Financial Integration May be Undesirable?" AER, Vol. 100, No.2.

2011 "Rethinking Macroeconomics: What Failed, And How to Repair It?" Journal of the European Economic Association, Vol.9, No.4.

41.5 WORKS OF OTHERS

Arrow, K.J. (1973), "Higher Education as a Filter," JPubE, Vol. 2, No.3.

Basu, K. (1997), Analytical Development Economics, MIT Press, Cambridge, MA.

Lofgren, K.G, T. Persson and J.W. Weibull, (2002), "Markets with Asymmetric Information: The Contributions of George Akerlof, Michael Spence and Joseph Stiglitz," ScandJE, Vol.102, N0.2.

Mirrlees, J. (1971), "An Exploration in the Theory of Optimum Income Taxation," RES, Vol. 38, No.2.

CHAPTER 42

VERNON LOMAX SMITH

(1927 –)

Vernon Smith shared the 2002 Nobel Memorial prize for Economic Sciences with Daniel Kahneman. The Royal Swedish Academy of Sciences specifically refers to Smith's efforts at establishing laboratory experiments as a tool in empirical economic analysis, especially in the study of alternative market mechanisms, while Kahneman was given the award for having integrated insights from psychological research into economic science, especially concerning human judgment and decision-making under uncertainty. Kahneman's relevant contributions have been summarised in chapter 54. This chapter covers Smith's major contributions to economic science.

Traditionally, economics has been viewed as a non-experimental science that had to rely exclusively on field data. In this context, Advanced Information supplied by the Royal Swedish Academy of Sciences gives the following quote from the text book on economics by Samuelson and Nordhaus: "Economics... cannot perform the controlled experiments of chemists or biologists because [it] cannot easily control other important factors. Like astronomers or meteorologists, [economists] generally must be content largely to observe." It is felt that tests of economic theory would remain restricted unless controlled experiments are carried out. This is perceived as an obstacle to the continued development of the subject. It is further felt that on the basis of field data, it is difficult to decide whether and when a theory fails, and to identify the aspects responsible for this failure. It is clear that new findings based on experiments suggest new theories; likewise, new theories suggest new experiments. In the absence of the feedback mechanism between theory and observation under controlled conditions, this route for the development of a subject seemed to be largely unavailable to economics. This view has been profoundly challenged by the development of a growing research field, namely experimental economics. The potential for drawing causal inferences from observed data has been bolstered by availability of new sets of panel data and by advancement in econometrics by works of Heckman, McFadden and others. Experimental economists study human behaviour under controlled laboratory conditions and that in pure and simplified forms simulate those encountered in markets and other forms of economic interactions. It is still being debated as to the extent to which the results of such experiments can be generalised to real market situation. Nevertheless, the view that results from laboratory experiments relating to microeconomic behaviour can essentially inform the development of economic theory is importantly the same as the view that laboratory results concerning small-scale phenomena in physics can basically inform the development of theoretical physics.

The Royal Swedish Academy of Sciences traces the early predecessors of experimental research in economics, such as Edwin Chamberlin, John Nash and Reinhard Selten. Chamberlin, in his attempt to test the neo-classical theory of perfect competition used the experimental method. John Nash with his colleagues conducted early studies on the predictive power of game theory in an experimental setting. Reinhard Selten in association with Sauerman conducted early experimental studies of price formation in oligopoly markets. However, the foremost researcher in the experimental tradition in economics undoubtedly is Vernon Smith. He not only made the most important early contributions, but has also remained a major figure in the field to date. Furthermore, Smith has educated, and collaborated with, a number of young researchers in experimental economics.

Before attempting a summary of Vernon Smith's contributions to the subject, a brief biographical sketch of Smith may be given.

42.1 A SHORT BIOGRAPHICAL SKETCH: VERNON SMITH

Vernon Lomax Smith was born in Wichita, Kansas, United States, on January 1, 1927, in the year leading to Great Depression. His mother's first husband Grover Bougher, a fireman, was killed in a train accident on September 17, 1918. His father Vernon Chessman Smith, a machinist married the widow, Lulu Belle Lomax. The life insurance money provided to her was invested in a farm located near Wichita, which was to become the family's sole means of survival "during the difficult years, 1932-1934". In his autobiographical note Vernon Smith states: "The farm brought hard work and hard times for my parents... [and it proved] an invigorating childhood with ample opportunity for daily, fatherly lessons in 'how things work' - an interest I have carried the breadth of my life."

At age six, Smith took his place alongside more seasoned farm children for primary education in the "classic rural one-room schoolhouse... There were only three subjects - reading, writing and arithmetic." After his "stellar first grade academic achievements", he continued to perform well in the city primary schools. Smith began his first wage work when he was in the ninth grade.

He started attending North High School in 1941 and graduated from the school in January 1944. In the summer of 1943, at age 16, he started working for Boeing Aircraft. He resigned his job in August 1944 to begin college. He joined Caltech, "the best college in the United States" at that time, in September 1945. According to Smith's autobiographical note "Caltech was a meat grinder like I could never have imagined." He studied night, day, weekends and survived hundreds of problems; "what a joy to take freshman chemistry from Linus Pauling, hear physics lectures by J. Robert Oppenheimer on his frequent visits to Caltech, attend a visiting lecture by Bertrand Russell,.... "Smith was majoring in physics, but switched to electrical engineering, as a senior. He received his BS in Electrical Engineering in 1949.

As a senior, Smith took an economics course and found it very "intriguing". Curious about advanced economics, he went to the Caltech library, stumbled upon two books, Samuelson's Foundations, and von Mises's Human Action. Smith states "From the former, it was clear that economics could be done like physics, but from the latter there seemed to be much in the way of reasoning that was not like physics. I also subscribed to the Quarterly Journal of Economics, and one of the first issues had a paper by Hollis Chenery on Engineering Production Functions. So, economics was also like engineering! I had not a hint then as to how much those first impressions would be changed in my thinking over the decades to follow." After graduating in engineering, Smith went to the University of Kansas to get an M.A. in economics "as a vehicle for allowing me to decide if I wanted to continue in economics." At the University of Kansas, he took classes from Dick Howey, in, among other subjects, a full year course in the Development of Economic Thought. Smith remarks: "Howey was a surviving member of an endangered species, a History of Economic Thought scholar... it was from him that I learned what scholarship really meant.... With Dick [Howey] as a mentor, I decided economics was for me, and I continued by pursuing an economics Ph.D. at Harvard beginning in 1952." Alvin Hansen ("the foremost American Keynesian"), Gottfried Haberler ("his dry wit"), Wassily Leontief ("his sarcasm") Guy Orcutt ("his deeply serious search for the messages hidden in all data") were some of his teachers at Harvard. Smith observes "Schumpeter was no longer alive, but his ghost was lurking in the halls." For microeconomics, Smith supplemented with courses Samuelson taught down the Charles River at MIT.

Smith obtained his Ph.D. degree in 1955, and got his first teaching post at Purdue University. With suitable modifications Smith continued with the experimental method initiated by Chamberlin. Over the years 1956-1960, Smith brought many variations in the experimental method, changing the supply and demand environment, examining the shifts in demand or supply, altering the trading rules and introducing cash rewards showing that they made a difference. He states: "I gradually became persuaded that the subjects, without intending to, had revealed to me a basic truth about markets that was foreign to the literature of economics." During these years, he was engaged in research and teaching capital and investment theory, and related pricing problems. In 1961-1962, Smith was a visiting associate professor at Stanford, where he met Sydney Siegel "a truly powerful experimental intellect -- who had also been doing experimental economics. Unknown to both of us at the time, Reinhard Selten had also been pioneering economics experiments in Germany."

Smith's research in experimental economics grew over time and resulted in his initiating a graduate seminar in experimental economics at Purdue in 1963, which continued until his departure in 1967. He got in 1967 tenured professorship at Brown

University, then in 1968 at the University of Massachusetts. In 1974 Caltech offered him Sherman Fairchild Distinguished Scholar position for one year, and stayed on there in 1974-1975 with joint appointment at Caltech and University of Southern California. He moved to University of Arizona in 1975 and continued there for 26 years before leaving for George Mason University. At the time Nobel Prize was awarded to him, Smith was Professor of Economics and Law at George Mason University, a research scholar in the interdisciplinary centre for Economic Sciences and Fellow of Mercatus Center, all in Arlington, Virginia.

Smith received a number of honours and awards. He serves or has served on the Board of Editors of American Economic Review, Journal of Economic Behaviour and Organization, Journal of Risk and Uncertainty, Economic Theory, Economic Design, Games and Economic Behaviour and Journal of Economic Methodology. He is past president of Public Choice Society, the Economic Science Association and the Western Economic Association. He was a Ford Foundation Fellow, Fellow of the Centre for Advanced Study in the Behavioral Sciences and a Sherman Fairchild Distinguished Scholar at the California Institute of Technology (Caltech). He received an Honorary Doctor of Management degree from Purdue University, is a fellow of the Econometric Society and a Distinguished Fellow of the American Economic Association. The Smith Prize for the Advancement of Austrian Economics is named after him and is sponsored by the European Centre of Austrian Economics.

The award to Vernon Smith was for his contributions as a researcher in the "experimental tradition" and is considered a key figure in the field of experimental economics. His contributions are surveyed here under the following heads.

1. Market Mechanisms;
2. Tests of Auction Theory;
3. Issue of Rationality; and
4. Experiments Regarding Public Goods.

42.2 A BRIEF SUMMARY OF VERNON SMITH'S CONTRIBUTIONS

42.2.1 MARKET MECHANISMS

Controlled market experiments, as mentioned above, were believed to have been initiated by Edwin Chamberlin. In his autobiographical note Smith states: "Many generations of Harvard graduate students had been exposed to E. H. Chamberlin's beginning graduate course in Monopolistic Competition. On the first day he would set the stage for the semester using a classroom demonstration experiment showing that competitive price theory was an unrealistic idealization of the real world. He gave half the class buyer reservation values, and the other half seller reservation costs.... Chamberlin... had the buyers and sellers circulate, form pairs, and bargain over a bilateral trade; if successful, the price was posted on the blackboard; if not successful, each would seek a new trading partner. This continued until the market was closed. The prices in sequence were volatile and failed to support the equilibrium prediction. Chamberlin used this first-day exercise to set the stage for his Theory of Monopolistic Competition." Chamberlin reported the results of the experiment in the *Journal of Political Economy* (1948) in which he remarked: "... economists may have been led unconsciously to share their unique knowledge of the equilibrium point with their theoretical creatures, the buyers and sellers who, of course, in real life have no knowledge of it whatsoever." Theodore Bergstrom remarks: "Looking at Chamberlin's article today, it is remarkable that such a fascinating and provocative line of research could have been ignored by almost the entire economics profession. In fact it appears that this jewel was almost lost. According to the Social Science Citation Index, Chamberlin's paper was cited by other authors only four times between its publication in 1948 and its revival in 1962 by Vernon Smith."

The revival of the experimental tradition by Smith described in his Papers in *Experimental Economics* as quoted by Bergstrom throws good light: ".... I had insomnia one night and... I found myself thinking about the classroom experiment that Ed Chamberlin used to perform with the Harvard graduate students to prove the impossibility of perfect competition. I didn't take Chamberlin course.... But I did observe and participate in Chamberlin's little 'experiment'. The scuttlebutt among the Harvard graduate students was that the whole exercise was sort of silly.... So there I was, wide awake at 3 am, thinking about Chamberlin's silly experiment.... The thought occurred to me that... you should choose an institution of exchange that might be more favourable to yielding competitive equilibrium.... This led to two ideas: (1) Why not use the double oral auction procedure used on the stock and commodity exchanges? (2) Why not conduct the experiment in a sequence of trading 'days' in which supply and demand were renewed to yield functions that were daily flows?"

Smith's research work in the area encompassed experiments with competitive markets, evolution of different auction forms and the design of what is referred to as "induced-value" method. The procedure for conducting the experiment may be outlined here. Participants were assigned the roles of buyer and seller randomly. Each seller is given one unit of the good to be sold and its reservation price. Assume that the reservation price was 'v' for the unit of good, (known only to her/him or what is called private information) below which the seller was not allowed to sell. If the seller sells the unit at a price p>v, he would earn p-v rupees. Likewise, each buyer was assigned a private reservation price, w, and the highest price at which he was allowed to buy a unit of the good. Purchases at a price p<w, would result in his earning of w-p rupees. Smith could draw a supply and a demand schedule based on his distribution of reservation prices, and locate the competitive equilibrium price as the intersection of the schedules. The participants in the experiment, of course, did not posses this information and were, therefore, not able to compute the theoretical equilibrium prices. Surprisingly, actual trading price was close to the theoretical equilibrium price. The profit earned by subjects (buyers and sellers) were, like in Chamberlin's experiments, only "hypothetical"; no cash changed hands. Smith

draws the conclusion that the experiments which were initially supposed to be rejected, supported the traditional microeconomic theory. Smith concludes,"...there are strong tendencies for a... competitive equilibrium to be attained as long as one is able to prohibit collusion and to maintain absolute publicity of all bids, offers, and transactions.... Changes in the conditions of supply and demand cause changes in the volume of transactions per period and the general level of contract prices. These latter correspond reasonably well with the predictions of competitive price theory."

Smith also found the convergence of double oral auction results towards competitive equilibrium robust

(a) to variations in the shape of demand and supply curves;

(b) to asymmetries in the distribution of profits between buyers and sellers; and

(c) to various permutations in research design.

Further, Smith observed that convergence to competitive equilibrium occurs even with a small number of participants, with as few as six to eight agents. On the basis of the results of the experiments, Smith draws an important conclusion—that the results of the experiments seem to extend the applicability of supply and demand theory beyond the "frictionless, price-taking environment assumed by conventional economic theory."

In Smith's original design of experiment in which sellers and buyers were allowed to change prices continuously during a trading period, there was a slower convergence towards the theoretical equilibrium price. The experimental approach of Smith made it possible to hold constant the "market environment" (distribution of reserve prices) while varying the "market institution" (rules of price adjustment) in a controlled fashion.

In a subsequent (published) experiment, actual monetary payoffs were permitted in place of hypothetical profits. The effect of monetary rewards on the performance of the subjects investigated by Smith in another subsequent work (2000) shows that inexperienced subjects converge toward "rational" behaviour much more rapidly as the size of the rewards is increased . He underscores the point that monetary incentives should be adequate in order to make subjects try to maximise the payoffs stated by the experimenter. Smith emphasises the importance of using monetary rewards to achieve what he calls "salience".

Smith's experiments during 1960s and 1970s were "low-tech" in that there was no special equipment for conducting the experiments except the use of pencil and paper in the classroom. In 1975, at the University of Arizona, however, Smith in collaboration with a colleague, designed and programmed for carrying out the double-auction method in which participants or subjects would interact through computer terminals in a well–monitored laboratory environment.

Smith extended his investigations to examine the performance of a wide variety of alternative market institutions, operating with similar fundamentals of buyer values and seller costs. He explored the operation of many double auction designs that are possible, with the computer managing the queuing of bids, offers, and transactions. He and his co-researchers found that the system that maintains a "rank queue" in which offers are accepted and placed in a queue, with the lowest not-yet accepted bid automatically extended as the correct standing bids and offers works best in terms of price stability and market efficiency. These features designed by Smith and other researchers are similar to procedures followed by the New York Stock Exchange. Critics remark that evolutionary forces in real world stock markets helped create market design aimed at promoting efficiency and stability.

Vernon Smith experimented also with one–sided markets to examine whether outcomes are sensitive to who could make offers: buyers only; sellers only; or both. While the results in one-sided markets are somewhat different from double-auction markets, the magnitudes of price difference are not large. His conclusion is that the outcomes from one-side markets are as efficient as those from double–auctions.

Leon Walras's tatonnement process, with which economists are quite familiar, is one of the alternative mechanisms to double-auction method. With tatonnement, no trading is permitted until an equilibrium price is arrived at (that is until a price is found at which the demand and supply for a period are equal). With the double auction, however, continuous trading takes place between agents who, not knowing the equilibrium price, may trade at non-equilibrium prices. Smith and his co-authors modified the Walrasian system by allowing individual traders to engage in multiple transactions and allowing change in demand and supply conditions between periods. Their experiments revealed that the modified tatonnement mechanism consistently performed less efficiently than the continuous double-auction mechanism. Further, they found that sellers and buyers seemed "to engage in strategic withholding of trade." As a consequence, there were fewer trades than would be efficient.

The wide range of experiments with alternative market mechanisms, by Smith and his co-authors prompted Smith to conclude that "institutions do matter" in ways that a prior economic theory would not have predicted. Critics have noted that the work of Smith and his co-authors had the healthy effect of inducing economists to pay much greater attention to the influence of institutional structure on economic results.

One must also recognise that Smith with several collaborators had used experimental markets to study inter-temporal asset markets. One such experiment relates to the study of a "two-season market." In each round of the two round experiments, a good is demanded and supplied in each of the two periods. With storage of good not allowed, the equilibrium is revealed to be higher in the second period than in the first one. In contrast, if the storage of good is allowed at zero cost, the competitive price is same in both periods and quantities traded are fairly close to the levels predicted by competitive theory. It is beneficial for some buyers to purchase and store the good at zero cost either for resale or for their own use. No information is provided to the subjects regarding total demand for or total supply of good in each of the two periods. Further, the convergence to competitive outcomes occurs with a small number of subjects even though no individual trader has "perfect knowledge" of conditions in the market.

The experimental work of Smith and his collaborators has been able to produce laboratory–induced stock market bubbles. They find that when the traders are inexperienced, trading over the life time of a stock exhibits "dramatic price bubbles;" that is, stock prices rise much above the fundamental values (determined on the basis of their dividend payments) and then fall back to their fundamental values at some time later in the stock in life time. The bubbles tend to disappear with traders becoming more experienced and spot prices approaching those predicted by rational expectations model. In a recent article, Smith has concluded: "Financial theorists and economic theorists in the rational expectations mode will tell you... that those bubbles should not happen.... psychologists... love the bubbles because they see bubbles as violating the rationality of expectations. Both the theorists and the psychologists, however, are wrong in thinking that rational expectations are falsified by the experiments.... A rational expectations equilibrium, if attained, cannot be instantaneous; there must be a process whereby people go from wherever they start to the ending equilibrium.... As we view it, the experiments provide the theory with a dynamic learning directive. Rational expectations theory does not define a process whereby agents come to have rational expectations."

In most market experiments, controlling of the subjects' preferences is a must to test the hypothesis in question. At the same time, it is very difficult for the researcher to directly observe the subjects; idiosyncratic evaluations of gains and losses influence selling and buying in the market. Chamberlin was the first economist to address this problem. He suggested a method for resolving it, basically by providing the subjects with the "right" monetary incentives-- the method is referred to as "induced- value" method. The method was further refined and developed by Vernon Smith which has now become a "standard tool" in experimental economics.

42.2.2 TESTS OF AUCTION THEORY

Since the early 1960s, auction theory has emerged as one of the most successful developments in microeconomic theory and game theory. Auctions, as the term is commonly understood, may appear to be of very little importance in real world economics. However, employment of different auction forms has helped deepen our understanding of the functioning of real world markets. It is observed that some of the simple auction forms studied in theory are extensively used in practice, particularly in the context of deregulation and privatisation of natural monopolies, public procurement, sale of government bonds or securities and so on. As noted in the chapter on William Vickrey, a number of theoretical results for a variety of auction forms were developed by him, followed by other researchers.

Vernon Smith started experimental testing of many of those propositions and published a number of articles on the subject. More importantly, he initiated the employment of controlled laboratory experiments as wind tunnel (a laboratory set up used to test prototypes for aircraft) tests of designing of new auctions prior to their practical use. Critical to Smith's experimental work on auctions are the established theoretical predictions for certain forms of auctions commonly used in the sale of a single object. Such auctions are conventionally categorised into four types:

1. English or Ascending Auction;
2. Dutch Auction or Descending Auction;
3. First Price-Sealed-Bids Auctions; and
4. Second Price–Sealed-Bid Auctions.

A brief explanation of each type of auction may be in order.

In the first type or English auction, buyers announce their bids sequentially and in an increasing order, until no higher bid is submitted, while in the Dutch auction a high initial bid by the seller is gradually lowered in fixed steps at fixed times controlled by a clock until one of the buyers shows "buy" where upon the clock stops. Both the English and Dutch auctions are normally oral, and the trading price is the last (first) bidder's bid. In the other two auction forms, all the bidders simultaneously submit their bids in sealed envelopes and the unit for sale is given to the highest bidder. In the first price-sealed-bid auction, the highest bidder pays his bid to the seller, where as in the second-price-sealed-bid auction, the highest bidder pays only the second highest bid. All the four auction forms are equivalent if all buyers are assumed to be risk-neutral.

Microeconomic theory also draws a distinction between auctions with private values and auctions with common values. The value to each buyer in both cases is treated as a random variable. In the case of former, that is, in the case of private values, the valuations are statistically independent across the population of potential bidders. In the latter, which is in the case of auctions with common components, however, the value to the buyer has a common component such as resale market value or conditions in some related market. Examples of the latter type include spectrum auctions and telecommunication markets.

A large variety of experiments which test the theoretical propositions of auction theory were conducted by Smith and other experimental research workers. The studies identified a number of regularities. The following have been culled out by Theodore Bergstrom:

(a) English auctions and second-price-sealed-bid auctions which are theoretically isomorphic in private value environments, produce very similar results in the experimental laboratory;

(b) Dutch auctions and first-bidder-sealed- bid auctions (the two are theoretically isomorphic in private goods environment) do not produce the same results in the laboratory;

(c) Nash equilibrium models that assume identical attitudes towards risk by all participants are rejected in laboratory experiments;

(d) In laboratory experiments, as predicted by auction theory, English and second-bidder auctions result in more efficient outcomes than Dutch and first- bidder-sealed - bid auctions.

Dealing with the auction theory and the laboratory experiments, Smith says: "... modeling of auctions is directly predicated upon the allocation and message rules of alternative markets institutions.... In environments in which alternative auction institutions are equivalent, the institution-free property is derived as a theorem, instead of an implicit assumption. Auction theory does more than begin with the extensive form of a game; it begins with various extensive forms we observe in the economy.... Consequently it is able to guide empirical testing programs.... Where theory fails under experiments... it is easier to see which part of the theory has failed and to see where the theory needs improvements."

Another significant contribution of Smith as mentioned earlier, relates to the use of laboratory as a 'wind tunnel'- a laboratory set up used to test prototypes for aircrafts. His use of laboratory as a wind tunnel has the purpose of studying the performance of suggested institutional mechanisms for deregulation and privatisation of public goods. The usefulness of the experimental methods used by Smith can be assumed from the fact that these institutional mechanisms are generally so complex that existing theory does not give accurate predictions.

Smith's work, in addition to providing significant results on markets and auctions, has had immense impact on methodology. His 1976 article "Experimental Economics; Induced-Value Theory" outlined a practical and detailed guide to the design of economic experiments in a laboratory. Besides, in recent years, it has served as a paradigm for experimental researchers in economics. Smith's experimental method designing experiments has been helpful in making repeated trials to make subjects familiar with and comprehend the experimental situation.

The Nobel Foundation draws an important and clear distinction between methods employed by psychologists and those of Smith. Whereas psychologists have been largely interested in individual behaviour, Smith's main purpose in designing his experiments is the analysis of market outcomes.

In recent years, economists have been helping policy- makers in designing auctions appropriate to a number of institutional and technical settings. Experimental economics has contributed, in no small measure, to the growth of and enrichment of policy decisions. In this context, Bergstrom reported the part played by economists in organizing the British government's sale of spectrum licenses for the 3G mobile phone technology. The auction in March and April 2000 is reported to have raised about 2.5 per cent of the year's British GNP.

42.2.3 ISSUE OF RATIONALITY

There has been considerable discussion regarding the rationality or otherwise of economic agents. While traditional economic theory conducted analysis on the assumption of rational behaviour of market participants, experimental psychologists and behavioural economists dispute this claim. The latter group maintains that people in real life are not nearly so rational and buttress their contention with large information accumulated from experiments in which people make decisions that are inconsistent with rational decision theory. Vernon Smith claims that neither side has got the story quite right. According to him experimental economics offers "a third view which documents a growing body of evidence that is consistent with rational models, although there are many exceptions." Smith believes that on the basis of the evidence gathered by him and his co-workers psychologists need to abandon or at least revise their unstated premises on which there is implicit agreement between psychology and mainstream theory. The evidence accumulated by Smith and his co-workers shows:

(i) "Prices and allocations converge quickly to the neighborhood of the predicted rational expectations competitive equilibrium ; and

(ii) These results generalize to a wide variety of posted-price, sealed-bid, and other institutions of exchange, although convergence rates tend to vary and can be influenced by extreme parameter distributions."

Such convergence to outcomes predicted by rational behaviour occurs even though subjects have very little understanding of the economic processes at work. Furthermore, Smith argues that many of the perceived behavioural anomalies will either disappear or be much less pronounced when framed in a market context.

An economy's institutional structure, its market environment and behaviour of agents will determine its performance. It is argued by Smith that the rules that govern the exchange are defined by the institutional structure, while tasks of agents and endowments of resources and information define the market environment, whereas the agents and trading strategy influences the behaviour of agents. Gode and Sunder, who replaced human traders by computers with the purpose of isolating the effect of market rules and agents' behaviour on market performance, argue that "allocative efficiency of a double auction derives largely from its structure, independent of traders' motivation, intelligence or learning. Adam Smith's invisible hand... can generate aggregate rationality not only from individual rationality but also from individual irrationality."

However, it is to be noted that in slightly more complex inter- temporal models that Vernon Smith studied, markets made up of zero–intelligence traders or programs that Gode and Sunder have experimented with, would not perform efficiently. Yet, after a few rounds of trading, human subjects reach efficient outcomes close to those predicted by competitive theory. Even then, the time path of prices and the environments where zero-intelligence traders operate differ significantly from those observed among human traders; moreover, there is greater variation in prices in the former than in the latter.

42.2.4 EXPERIMENTS REGARDING PUBLIC GOODS

Economists for long have been concerned with the issue of efficient provision of public goods, equitable methods of paying for their production and search for an institutional mechanism for this purpose. In this context, Knut Wicksell was a pioneer followed by Erik Lindahl. It may be recalled that Wicksell suggested an equitable and efficient system of public finance which provides for simultaneous voting for incremental change in public expenditures along with a tax regime to cover the cost. More importantly, Wicksell stipulated the adoption of such changes if only there is unanimity among taxpayers in this regard. A slight variant of this proposal was put forward by Lindahl. His scheme envisaged that the supply of public goods and related tax rates must be such that the quality of public goods supplied receives voters' endorsement. Modern economists have been sceptical whether any voting scheme can be found which would be able to give a Pareto-efficient provision of public goods, what with the self–interested citizens.

Smith and his collaborators designed a series of experiments in search of a workable scheme. They tested alternative mechanisms for determining the quantum of public goods to be supplied and the method of financing them. Smith put forward a mechanism for this purpose which is in the spirit of Wicksell's unanimity principle. He calls it the "Action Method" for the provision of public goods. He reports results of his experiment in a number of research papers. He reports that "with quasi-linear utility and with groups of 5-8 participants, quantities of public goods selected are fairly close to efficient, but the distribution of costs is not very close to Lindahl equilibrium."

Smith also carried out some more experiments with other mechanisms for provision of public goods. In regard to the issue of wholesale economic design, he has the following comment to make: "Like languages, economic institutions... are not the product of our mind or someone else's logical experimental design, but are the product of thousands of minds over many generations of trial-and error filtering combined with a societal memory for those arrangements that are in some sense best, or good enough.... Can we consciously design new and better property-right-exchange systems? There is good reason to be sceptical about whether any of us professionals knows or understands enough about the elements of institutional success to allow an affirmative answer to this question. But it is also true that we have made significant progress in the last quarter of a century in our abstract and empirical understanding of incentives in institutions."

42.2.5 OTHER EXPERIMENTS

Smith and other writers conducted many other interesting experiments such as ultimatum games and dictator games. In the former type of games, subjects are matched anonymously and one agent, the first mover, is asked to propose division of a fixed sum of money between him and the other agent - the second mover. The second mover can either accept or reject the proposed division. If the proposed division is accepted, then each subject gets the agreed amount. If the proposed division is not accepted, then both get zero. Rational (selfish) behaviour dictates that in this one-shot game, the second mover would accept any small amount of money to accepting zero (if the proposal is rejected). Therefore, the first mover would offer a very small amount to the second mover and keep the rest for himself. A large number of experiments with the one-shot ultimatum game revealed that in almost all of them, the first player's proposals tend to be more generous than those that would be offered by rational self- interested agents.

The results from experiments obtained by Smith and others pose a direct challenge to rational-choice game theory. The question that needs to be answered is: If people do not behave as rational agents motivated by self-interest in a laboratory experiment as simple as the ultimatum game, how can game theory guide people in making decisions in real-world situations? There are many suggestions to explain away the conflict, of which the following two are noteworthy.

(i) The results of ultimatum game experiments suggest that consumers possess a streak of altruism; or

(ii) Consumers, perhaps, possess a "taste for fairness" that traditional economists have failed to recognise.

As Bergstrom observes: "In a one shot ultimatum game, there is no question that a second mover will maximize his pay off by any positive share." Therefore, if he is rational, selfish and truly believes that the game is a one-shot game, he will not refuse a contract that gives him a positive pay off, however small. On the other hand, the best strategy for the first mover depends on his belief about how the second mover will respond. "

In a bid to help untangle the motives of first movers, a simpler game was devised by Forsythe and others. In this game, called the "dictator game," the second mover has no choice but to accept the first mover's proposal for a division of a fixed sum of money between himself and an anonymous second mover. It was found in this "dictator game" that the first movers are, on average, much less generous than in the ultimatum game, but a substantial proportion of the "dictators" seem to continue to offer 30 percent to 50 percent of the fixed sum to the other (anonymous) player. Smith and co-authors replicate these results.

42.3 CONCLUDING OBSERVATIONS

The outstanding accomplishment of Vernon Smith and his fellow experimentalists is to impress upon the economic professionals that economics can be an experimental science. A large and growing community of economic researchers is seen conducting laboratory experiments in economics. It is reported that Economic Science Association, an organisation of experimental economists founded by Vernon Smith and a few others, currently has about 200 members. According to Bergstrom "perhaps the most significant measure of the impact of experimental economics is the way that experimental results have reshaped the thinking of those who work in game theory, in the theory of consumer choice, and in applied areas such as public economics, industrial organization, resource economics, labour economics and finance. Experimental economists have initiated another new branch of economics-the science of experimentally tested economic design-that promises to assume greater importance.

Smith's research suggests that competitive theory works well to predict outcomes in laboratory over a much broader class of environments than those assumed by economic theorists. These results are obtained even without full information or the presence of a large number of traders.

In this context Smith's observations deserves to be quoted in full.

"At the heart of economics is a scientific mystery. How is it that the pricing system accomplishes the world's work without anyone being in charge.... The pricing system... is a scientific mystery as deep as that of the expanding universe or forces that bind matter. For to understand it is to understand something about how the human species got from hunter-gathering through the agricultural and industrial revolutions to a state of affluence."

42.4 SELECT BIBLIOGRAPHY OF VERNON SMITH'S WORKS

42.4.1 BOOKS

1958 (with K. Davidson and J. Wiley), Economics: An Analytical Approach, Richard D. Irwin, Homewood, Ill.

1961 Investment and Production, Harvard University Press, Cambridge, MA.

1977 Economics of Natural and Environmental Resources, Gordon and Breach.

1979 (editor) Research in Experimental Economics, Vol.1, JAI Press, Greenwich.

1982 (editor) Research in Experimental Economics, Vol.2, JAI Press, Greenwich.

1985 (editor) Research in Experimental Economics, Vol. 3, JAI Press, Greenwich.

1990 (editor) Schools of Economic Thought: Experimental Economics, Edward Elgar Publishing, London.

1991 Papers in Experimental Economics, (1962-1988), Cambridge University Press, New York.

1993 (with R. Day eds.), Experiments in Decision, Organization and Exchange, Elsevier Science, Amsterdam.

2000 Bargaining and Market Behavior: Essays in Experimental Economics (1990-1998), Cambridge University Press, New York.

2008 a (With C. Plott eds.), Handbook of Experimental Economics: Results, Elsevier Science, Amsterdam.

b Rationality in Economics: Constructivist and Ecological Forms, Cambridge University Press, New York.

42.4.2 ARTICLES

1959 "The Theory of Investment and Production," QJE, Vol.73, No.1.

1962 a "An Experimental Study of Competitive Market Behavior," JPE, Vol.70, No.2.

b "The Theory of Capital," AER, Vol.52, No.3.

1964 "Effect of Market Organization on Competitive Equilibrium," QJE, Vol.78, No.2.

1965 "Experimental Auction Markets and the Walrasian Hypothesis," JPE, Vol.73. No 4.

1976 "Experimental Economics: Induced Value Theory," AER, Vol.66, No.2.

1977 "The Principle of Unanimity and Voluntary Consent in Social Choice," JPE, Vol. 85, No.6.

1980 "Experiments With a Decentralized Mechanism for Public Good Decision," AER, Vol. 70, No.5.

1982 a (A. Williams, et al.), "Competitive Market Institutions: Double Auctions versus Sealed Bid Offer Auctions," AER, Vol. 72, No.1.

b "Microeconomic Systems as an Experimental Science," AER, Vol. 72, No.5.

1984 (with A. Williams), "Cyclical Double Auction Markets With and Without Speculators", JB, Vol.57, No.1.

1985 "Individual Rationality, Market Rationality, and Value Estimation," AER, Vol.75, No.2.

1987 "Experimental Methods in Economics," in The New Palgrave: A Dictionary of Economic Theory and Doctrine, Macmillan, London.

1988 (With G. Suchanek and A. Williams), "Bubbles, Crashes and Endogenous Expectations in Experimental Spot Asset Markets," Econometrica, Vol.56, No.5.

1989 "Theory, Experiment and Economics," JEP, Vol.3, No.3.

2003 "Constructivist and Ecological Rationality in Economics," Nobel Lecture, AER, Vol.93, No.3.

2005 "Hayek and Experimental Economics," The Review of Austrian Economics, Vol.18, No.2.

2007 " Sustaining Cooperation in Trust Games," EJ, Vol.117, No.522.

2011 "Exchange, Specialization, and Property as a Discovery Process," HOPE, Vol. 43, No.2.

42.5 WORKS OF OTHERS

Bergstrom, T. C. (2003), "Vernon Smith's Insomnia and the Dawn of Economics as Experimental Science," ScandJE, Vol. 105, No.2.

Chamberlin, E. (1948), "An Experimental Imperfect Market," JPE, Vol. 56, No.2.

Forsythe R., J. Horowitz, et al. (1994), "Reciprocity, Fairness and Pay in Experiments with Simple Bargaining Games," GEB, Vol. 6, No.3.

Kagel, J and A.E Roth (1995), Hand book of Experimental Economics, Princeton University Press, Princeton, NJ.

Lindahl, E.(1958), "Just Taxation- A Positive Solution," in Classics in the Theory of Public Finance, R. Musgrave and A. Peacock, (eds.), Macmillan, London.

Vickrey, W. (1961), "Counterspeculation, Auctions and Competitive Sealed Tenders," JF, Vol. 16, No.1.

Wicksell, K(1958), "A New Principle of Just Taxation," in Classics in the Theory of Public Finance, R. Musgrave and A. Peacock, (eds.), Macmillan, London.

CHAPTER 43

LEONID HURWICZ, ERIC STARK MASKIN & ROGER BRUCE MYERSON

(1917 – 2008),
(1950 –) &
(1951 –)

The Royal Swedish Academy of Sciences has awarded the Nobel Memorial Prize in Economic Sciences, 2007, jointly to three American economists, Leonid Hurwicz of University of Minnesota, Minneapolis, Eric Stark Maskin of Institute for Advanced Study, Princeton and Roger Bruce Myerson of University of Chicago, Chicago. The prize has been awarded to them for having laid the foundations of Mechanism Design Theory. The scientific background note outlined by the Royal Swedish Academy observes that markets, or market-like institutions, facilitate occurrence of economic transactions and generally help efficient allocation of goods and services. The traditional economic theory of perfect competition by decentralised price mechanism with private ownership of resources demonstrates how such an economic system, under fairly restrictive assumptions, satisfies the criteria of Pareto efficiency. In perfectly competitive markets with wide dispersion of information about technology, endowments and preferences among households and firms, each market participant takes decisions relating to his/her production and trading activities which are coordinated by market signals. This corresponds to Adam Smith's invisible hand which refers to how the market mechanism, under ideal conditions, ensures efficient allocation of the economy's scarce resources. But in real world such ideal conditions do not exist. Competition is not free, consumers and firms are not perfectly informed, market participants have asymmetric information and privately desirable production and consumption may give rise to social costs and benefits. Moreover, many transactions may not take place in open markets. Instead, buyers and sellers may bargain and fail to trade. Social projects which are beneficial to society at large may sometimes be not undertaken because of failure of beneficiaries to reach an agreed sharing of the project costs. For instance, in case of insurance market, with a view to hike the premium on sickness insurance policy, the insurers may claim that their costs are high. Economic theory tries to understand the institutional and allocative mechanisms that are geared to minimise economic losses generated by private information. A number of questions arise for which answers have to be given. Some of them may be spelt out here. What trading mechanisms would result in largest gains from trade? What collective decision making procedures facilitate implementation of desirable joint projects while, at the same time, denying funds for socially undesirable projects? Which insurance schemes would provide the best risk cover without encouraging misuse? These and such other issues need satisfactory answers.

Mechanism Design theory originally developed by Hurwicz and refined and applied by Maskin and Myerson provides answers to the above questions as also to other similar ones by providing tools that are helpful for analysing them. Taking game-theoretic approach, the theory specifically provides answers as to how prices are fixed. Further, Mechanism Design theory shows that double auctions, where buyers and sellers post their bid-and ask-prices can be efficient trading institutions for allocation of private goods among a given group of potential buyers. It also shows what auction format will maximise the seller's expected revenue. With the increase in number of traders, the double auction mechanism will more efficiently aggregate privately held information, and eventually all information is reflected in equilibrium prices. These results lend support to Frederich Hayek's contention that markets efficiently aggregate relevant private information.

While at one extreme is the free market economy with decentralised price mechanism outlined above, centrally planned economy or socialist economy is at the other extreme. In such an economy, resources are owned by the state and the central planner decides production targets and resource allocation for production of goods and services. Economic agents have a very limited role in this framework. They may "communicate" their consumption preferences to the central planner who, on the basis of such information, may fix detailed quantitative production targets for mangers of firms or planner may adopt methods of planning guided by prices fixed by him.

Dilip Mookerjee, in an article in the Scandinavian Journal of Economics, traces the origin of the Mechanism Design approach to debates in the 1930's about the possibility of efficient resource allocation in a socialist society. Also referred to as the principle-agent problem, Mechanism Design theory concerns with the problem faced by a principal or planner in designing a "mechanism by which a set of agents with productive capacities of consumption needs and preferences will interact with one another to produce resource allocation outcomes." The central feature of the theory is information dispersion among agents because of which there is a need for the economic system to design systems of communications and an authority to take decisions as well as rewards. Realising the deficiencies and shortcomings of market-based systems such as prevalence of externalities and increasing returns, economic theorists began to study alternative decentralised processes that obviated such deficiencies.

In this context, it is pertinent to quote from Hurwicz's 1973 Richard T. Ely Lecture to American Economic Association. "Oscar Lange's contribution to the debate in 1930's is well known, but there was a remarkable earlier reply by Jacob Marshack in 1924. While Lange's line was to be that socialism is as capable of playing the perfectly competitive game as is capitalism, Marshack took the opposite view; Capitalism is not a world of prefect competition, but of monopolies and cartels, which (in a Schumpeterian spirit) has its good points, especially in the realm of dynamics. Marshack expected similar phenomena under the brand of democratic 'socialism' he had in mind and was not depressed by the prospect. He felt that the advantages of imperfect competition would carry over into collectivism. The real issues would not be rational economic calculation but motivation, stimulation of initiative and intensity of effort [in other words, incentives] under an egalitarian system where managers would be democratically elected."

More importantly, no market mechanism may result in a fully efficient resource allocation in some cases. As for example, Samuelson in his 1954 article "The Pure Theory of Public Expenditure" showed that because of the selfish interest of "each person to give false signals, to pretend to have less interest in a given collective activity than he really has.... No resource allocation mechanism can bring about a fully efficient level of public goods such as national security and clean air." In such cases, Mechanism Design theory is helpful in analysing the economic efficiency of alternative institutions for providing public goods, "ranging from markets and consensual collective decision making through majoritarian decision rules all the way to dictatorship...." A key insight is that decision making through consensus is generally incompatible with economic efficiency, lending support to government financing of public goods through government taxation. Furthermore, Mechanism Design theory provides important advances in a number of other areas of economics including corporate finance, regulation and taxation theory.

It is commonly admitted that the development of Mechanism Design theory began with the work of Leonid Hurwicz. He defined mechanism as a communication system or a game in which the participants send messages to each other and/or to a "message center," and where a pre-specified rule assigns an outcome, such as an allocation of goods and services to every collection of received messages. These messages may contain private information such as an individual's (true or false) willingness to pay for a public good. Given the assumptions about participants' beliefs and preferences, each rule gives one or more predicted outcomes or equilibria. Within this framework, it is possible to compare the predicted outcomes associated with markets, and market-like institutions with those of a number of alternative trading institutions. In this connection, a reference needs to be made to the pioneering work relating to the theory of teams by Marshack and Radner. However, it is realised that in a number of situations, providing incentives to the participants is a key issue, which was tackled again by Hurwicz. In his 1972 work, he incorporated the key concept of "incentive-compatibility," permitting the analysis to include incentives of self-interested participants. Specifically, it facilitates a rigorous analysis of economies, where agents who have private information, are self-interested.

Significant advances in Mechanism Design theory were possible in the 1970s with the formulation of what is referred to as "revelation principle." This principle (in its greatest generality) was developed by Roger Myerson and pioneered its application to important areas in economics such as regulation and auction theory. The principle suggests that a researcher, trying to find out the best possible mechanism to solve a given problem, can confine his focus to a small subclass of mechanisms, namely the so called direct mechanisms that satisfy Hurwicz's conditions of incentive compatibility.

Even with the development of revelation principle, a hurdle remained, namely one mechanism may give several different equilibria. Moreover while achieving one equilibrium, which is the best outcome, there may exist other equilibria that may be inferior. Then the question arises: can a mechanism be designed such that all equilibria are optimal. The first general solution to this issue was provided by Eric Maskin by his "implementation theory," which has become an element of modern mechanism design.

As this year's prize is awarded for the development of Mechanism Design theory, the contributions of Hurwicz, Myerson and Maskin are being covered in this chapter, as it has been done in the case of Kydland and Prescott in an earlier chapter. A short biographical sketch of each of the three prize winners is given prior to summarising their contributions to the topic.

43.1 A SHORT BIOGRAPHICAL SKETCH: LEONID HURWICZ

Leonid Hurwicz was born in Moscow, Russia, on August 21, 1917 before the October Bolshevik revolution. After the Communists came to power in Russia, Leonid Hurwicz's family returned to Warsaw, Poland, his father's home; his mother was also Polish.

His father was a lawyer, with a degree from the Sorbonne in Paris. To practice law in Warsaw, a five-year internship was necessary. While completing internship, his father taught history. Hurwicz didn't begin formal schooling until the age of nine, when he started studies at a private institution attended and staffed mostly by Jews. At that time Europe was experiencing "pogroms." Though his family was not seriously affected, Hurwicz recalled some strange, random attacks. Specifically one year, the University in Warsaw had decided that the Jewish community had not contributed its share of corpses to the medical school. When a group tried to force Jewish students to sit in a segregated section of their classrooms, the university rector failed to intervene. For the entire year the Jewish students, including Leonid, stood in the back of the room. The protest succeeded and the following year Jewish students were seated with other students again.

Hurwicz recalled: "I experienced harassment during this period but I never was beaten or attacked personally. And with my professors, I felt no discrimination."

Hurwicz graduated in 1938, with a degree in law (LL.M. degree) from Warsaw University with an intention to follow in his father's footsteps. However, beginning in his second year of law school, he had taken some obligatory courses in economics and became more interested in this discipline. Hurwicz observed: "I had the belief that many troubles... on the European continent were due to politicians not understanding economic phenomena. Even if they had good intentions, they didn't have the skills to solve problems." Hitler's rise to power in Germany made Jews across Eastern Europe uneasy. Hurwicz's father, sensing the changing tides, suggested that his older son apply to the London School of Economics rather than set up a law practice at home.

Hurwicz went to London in the fall of 1938. He studied at London School of Economics with Nicholas Kaldor and Frederich Hayek. His troubles began in the spring of 1939 when the British refused to extend his visa. So, Hurwicz went to France and then to Switzerland on a transit visa. He arrived in Berne in August 1939. With the outbreak of World War II, his parents and brother were arrested and taken to a labour camp in Arctic European Russia. Hurwicz spent months in Geneva, enrolled as a part-time student, hoping for news of his family.

He had decided to go to America, where in Chicago he had cousins. For this purpose, he booked passage on an Italian boat. In the mean time, Mussolini joined Hitler. Hurwicz's ticket to America became worthless because no Italian ship could enter American ports. To cut the long story of Hurwicz's troubles short, he finally landed in Chicago. He lived with his cousins and audited courses at the University of Chicago with the great economist, Ludwig von Mises. Finally, he got an offer of a job at the Massachusetts Institute of Technology (MIT) from Paul Samuelson. The job was as a teaching and research assistant for only one semester, "a term no self-respecting graduate student would accept."

According to Hurwicz: "... I had no other offers. In fact, it was a miracle I had this one." At MIT, Hurwicz tested a hypothesis about how firms fix prices for their goods and services. He returned to Chicago in mid-June 1941, and was research assistant to Oscar Lange at the University of Chicago, where he got appointment with the Institute of Meteorology of Chicago. In 1942, at the Cowles Commission for Research in Economics at the University of Chicago (now the Cowles Foundation at Yale University), Hurwicz had Jacob Marshack and Tjalling Koopmans as Advisors.

Hurwicz had a short academic stint at Iowa State University and then at the University of Illinois. In 1951, he joined the economics department at the University of Minnesota where he would develop the idea that would win him the Nobel Memorial Prize.

At the University of Minnesota, he became a professor of Economics and Mathematics in the School of Business Administration. He was Regent's Professor of Economics at the University. He was visiting professor at Stanford University, Harvard University, North Western University, University of California at Berkley and University of Michigan among others. Hurwicz also taught at Bangalore University in 1965. He worked as a consultant to the Rand Corporation and to the U.S Bureau of Budget.

Among the awards and honours Hurwicz received, mention may be made of Guggenheim Fellowship. He was elected fellow of the Econometric society (1947) and was its president in 1969. He was inducted into the American Academy of Arts and Sciences, National Academy of Sciences, U.S.A and was named a Distinguished Fellow of the American Economic Association. Hurwicz received the National Medal of Sciences in 1990 in Behavioral and Social Science from the president of the U.S. He also served on the editorial boards of several journals. He presented Fisher-Schultz, Richard T. Ely, David Kinley and Colin Clark Lectures. Hurwicz also received honorary doctorate from six universities, including University of Chicago and North Western University.

Hurwicz observed: "When you talk about the economic process of a society, sometimes we separate it into two stories. One is about monetary variables. But then, we very often assume the underlying arrangement, the other variable, is 'perfect competition,' which means people do whatever they are supposed to do. But actually, there is usually some chapter, not too long, which tells you there are different mechanisms that operate in a particular economy.... My question was what other systems or mechanisms or variables are possible?" He answered these questions by developing Mechanism Design to help businesses and other organisations arrive at solutions that combine truthfulness, individual rationality, and social welfare. Hurwicz stated: "The way I describe it is, there are two kinds of games in economics.... One is the game where people use only legal moves. Then there is the true game, the one like real life, where the strategies and moves people make, some of them contain illegal gains. So you take into account when you write the rules of the game that the players will try to cheat."

A critic comments: "The basic premise underlying Hurwicz's theory may seem obvious now. But when he began working on it in the 1960's, the idea of factoring in the self interest of players in business transactions was considered cutting edge. He and his colleagues believed that incentives could encourage players to arrive at the best possible outcome not only for themselves but for the other players in the game."

Leonid Hurwicz was too frail to make the trip to Sweden to personally receive the award. He received Nobel award from Swedish Ambassador to the United States in the University of Minnesota on December 10, 2007. To date, he was the oldest recipient of the Nobel Prize.

Hurwicz died at the age of 90 on June 26, 2008 in Minneapolis.

43.2 A SHORT BIOGRAPHICAL SKETCH: ERIC MASKIN

Eric Maskin was born in New York City, but grew up across the Hudson River in Alpine, New Jersey. He attended junior high and high school in the town of Tenafly, three miles down the road. Maskin says he was lucky to have some dedicated teachers; he was particularly indebted to his calculus instructor, "who opened his eyes to the striking beauty of mathematics." Maskin became mathematics major at Harvard College. Almost by accident, he wandered at one point into a course on "Information Economics" taught by Kenneth Arrow, later Maskin's Ph.D. advisor. According to Maskin "the course was a hodgepodge of topics from the frontiers of economic theory, but a good part of it was devoted to Leonid Hurwicz's work in the nascent field of mechanism design. This work was a revelation to me: it had the precision, rigor, and sometimes the beauty of pure mathematics and also addressed problems of real social importance" an irresistible combination. In fact, I ended up essentially an economics Ph.D. The degree was nominally in applied mathematics."

Maskin acknowledges his indebtedness to Kenneth Arrow in these words: "as an advisor Ken Arrow, was amazingly generous with his time; and I learned an immense amount from our many one-on-one discussions in his office...." Maskin has showed in his Ph. D. dissertation that, on any domain of preferences, "the problem of finding a social welfare function satisfying the Arrow axioms is solvable if and only if the problem of finding an unmanipulable mechanism is also solvable."

Frank Hahn, helped Maskin get a post-doctoral research fellowship at Jesus College in Cambridge University. Maskin admits that, that year was a marvellous experience in every way. "Cambridge college life, London theater, and touring around Europe. However, the true highlights were weekly tutorial sessions with Frank, and the opportunity to start research projects and lifelong friendships with Jean-Jacques Laffont and Partha Dasgupta." While in England, Maskin started research on a problem inspired by Hurwicz's work: under what circumstance is it possible to design a mechanism or game that implements a given social goal or a social choice rule? After struggling for almost one year, he realised that the key is monotonicity--referred to as "Maskin monotonicity." A social choice rule is not implementable if it does not satisfy monotonicity.

However if the social choice rule satisfies the property of monotonicity, it is implementable, provided no veto power holds. He showed how it is possible to explicitly design an implementing mechanism, which was later simplified in the paper titled "Nash Equilibrium and Welfare Optimality."

Maskin joined MIT's economics department as assistant professor in 1977. At that time the department was small. He says that the luncheon meeting at the faculty club each day was always a treat: "on any given day, Paul Samuelson and Franco Modigliani might hold forth, with frequent interjections by Bob Solow." However, Maskin says that, he learned most at MIT by teaching and working with Peter Diamond. Maskin was of the opinion that MIT was notable not only for its faculty but also for its students-- noted for its bright students.

Although MIT was the best place for his first teaching job, Harvard seemed a more natural long-term fit for the sort of work Maskin was doing. He joined the economics department at Harvard University in 1985. In his autobiographical note, Maskin states that as at MIT he was lucky to have a "succession of terrific students at Harvard some of them became long-term collaborators and friends." After fifteen years at Harvard, he was feeling the pressure of over-scheduling: too many courses, too many students, and "worst by far" too many committee meetings. Therefore when an offer came for a position at the Institute for Advanced Study, Princeton University in 2000, Maskin took it. Since 2000, he was Albert O. Hirschman Professor of Social Science there. The Institute has provided everything he had hoped for: first-class working conditions, stimulating colleagues, interaction across disciplines, and blessed freedom. He concludes the autobiographical sketch: "I was exceptionally lucky to have discovered economics in the first place, to have entered the field at a time when mechanism design was just beginning to bloom, and, most crucially, to have had a succession of remarkable teachers, students, colleagues, and friends in the profession. Finally, in a world where so many people dislike their jobs, I am lucky to be spending my days working hard at something I love." Maskin returned as professor of economics at Harvard University in 2011. He is a visiting lecturer with the rank of professor at Princeton University.

Maskin received a large number of fellowships, awards and honours, besides Nobel Prize in Economics. Among them must be mentioned Guggenheim Fellowship (1980-81) and National Science Foundation Graduate Fellowship. He was elected Corresponding Fellow, British Academy. He received National Science Foundation Research Grants, Economic and Social Science Research Council Grants, and elected member National Academy of Sciences. He was elected fellow Econometric Society (1981) and was its president 2003. He was elected President of Game Theory Society. He functioned twice as member of the Nominating Committee and as chair, search committee for editor, American Economic Journal: Microeconomics, 2006. Maskin was editor, Quarterly Journal of Economics, 1984-1990, editor, Economic Letters since 1992 and Advisory Editor, International Journal of Game Theory since 2007. In 2010, Maskin was awarded Harvard University Centennial Medal.

43.3 A SHORT BIOGRAPHICAL SKETCH: ROGER B. MYERSON

Roger Myerson was born in Boston, Massachusetts, on March 29, 1951. In his autobiographical note, Myerson states that a scholar's greatest asset is his or her intuition about what questions to study and with what methodology. Further, he observes that the interests that shape one's adult life generally have deep roots in childhood. Myerson grew up in a comfortable suburb of Boston with a fine public school system. His family greatly valued reading and scientific learning.

From a young age, Myerson was aware of the threat of nuclear war which was widespread in the 1950s. When he was twelve, Myerson read a classic science-fiction novel that described a future where advanced mathematical social science provided the guidance for a new Utopian civilisation. He states that he hoped that fundamental advances in the social sciences might help find better ways of managing the world's problems, as fundamental advances in the physical sciences had so dangerously raised the stakes of social conflict in our time.

While Myerson was interested in history, he had greater interest in analytical subjects. He began reading Paul Samuelson's basic economics textbook in high school vacation. When he joined college, he concentrated in economics and applied mathematics. In the spring of 1972, as a third-year student in Harvard College, Myerson took a course on decision analysis from Howard Raiffa. At the end of the course, Raiffa stated that game theory is concerned with the analysis of interactions among two or more rational utility-maximising decision-makers, and that the theory had not progressed much. In his autobiographical note Myerson observes: "This negative assessment provided a positive focus for my studies thereafter.... I started reading a book on game theory that summer." As at that time there were no regular courses on game theory at Harvard, he started studying books, journals and articles about game theory. When he came across John Harsanyi's 1963 paper that defined a general cooperative solution concept, sometime in the fall of 1972 Myerson felt that he had found the research programme that he wanted to join.

After studying Harsanyi's and Selten's papers on modelling games with incomplete information, Myerson identified an important issue in game theory that "has not yet been addressed in the literature." He has desired to extend the two player cooperative game solution concepts to games with more than two players who have incomplete information about each other. He took up for dissertation research the issue of predicting what might happen when cooperative agreements are negotiated among rational individuals who have different information. That is, he tried to build a theory of cooperation under uncertainty. He completed his research work under his dissertation advisor, Kenneth Arrow.

In 1976, Myerson was appointed an assistant professor by the School of Management (later to be designated as Kellogg School of Management) at North Western University. He states: "The... department was probably the only academic department in the world where game theory and information economics were not viewed as peripheral topics but as central strengths of the department. I had great colleagues...." Myerson's first papers were largely about cooperative game theory.

In them, he showed how simple principles of equity between pairs of individuals could be consistently extended to situations where many individuals cooperate in coalitions. Myerson's ultimate goal was developing a "coherent general methodology for game-theoretic analysis." In this effort, as stated in his autobiographical note, he was especially influenced by "three classic ideas" of game theory: (i) von Neumann's principle of strategic normalisation for reducing dynamic games; (ii) Nash's approach of subsuming cooperative games into non-cooperative game theory; and (iii) Schelling's focal-point effect for understanding games with multiple equilibria.

For any dynamic extensive game theory, the principle of strategic normalisation facilitates construction of an equivalent one-stage game in strategic form, where the players choose strategies independently which determine every player's expected pay-off.

For the purpose of analysing games in strategic form, Nash defined a general concept of equilibrium, in which the predicted behaviour of each player must be his or her best response to the predicted behaviour of all other players. However, it is found that there is no unique equilibrium when Nash's approach is followed. Even simple games can have multiple equilibria; hence, a predictive theory cannot be determined without some principles for selecting among such equilibria. In this situation Schelling's work suggested a way out. He argued that, in a game that has many equilibria, anything that focuses the players' attention jointly on one equilibrium can cause them to expect it and act rationally according to it, as a self-fulfilling prophecy. In the words of Myerson: "The focal factors that steer the players to one particular equilibrium can be derived from the players' shared cultural traditions, or from the coordinating recommendations of a recognized social leader or arbitrator, or from any salient properties that distinguish one equilibrium as the focal equilibrium that everybody expects to play." However, Myerson was of the view that it is appropriate to devise some general principles for eliminating some Nash equilibria that turn out to be irrational. He has recognised that such irrational equilibria could be ignored by accepting the possibility that those players making mistakes with some "infinitesimally small probability." He prepared a paper on "proper equilibria." At roughly the same time Reinhard Selten's 1975 paper on perfect equilibria was published. Myerson comments: "...perfect and proper equilibria were attempts to recognize in strategic form the equilibria that would be sequentially rational in the underlying dynamic games."

Issues relating to information and incentives, particularly relating to Leonid Hurwicz's ideas of incentive compatibility interested Myerson and influenced his search for a cooperative theory of games with incomplete information. He could see that Alan Gibbard's early formulation of the revelation principle for implementation of dominant-strategy could be extended to Harsanyi's Bayesian model. Myerson states: "The revelation principle basically says that, for any equilibrium of any communication system, a trustworthy mediator can create an equivalent communication system where honesty is a rational equilibrium for all individuals." He wrote the Econometrica paper (1979) demonstrating how the revelation principle for Bayesian incentive compatibility could be extended that simplifies the feasible set for Harsanyi's and Selten's bargaining solution for two person games with incomplete information.

His research efforts resulted in a number of research papers dealing with issues such as maximisation of seller's expected revenue, optimal regulation of a monopolist with private information about costs, efficient mechanism for mediation of bilateral trading problems, derivation of revenue–equivalence theorems and extension of revelation principle to problems involving both adverse selection and moral hazard. He also extended the revelation principle to dynamic multi-stage games where sequential rationality is needed in all events.

Myerson's later work attempted at extending economic concepts of efficiency to situations where people have private information as also to the problem of defining general cooperative bargaining for Bayesian games where players have different information. In late 1980s, he concentrated on writing a text book on game theory which was published in 1991. He also began to work on game-theoretic models of politics. Since 1996, Myerson has several papers on the history of game theory.

Myerson joined the economics department at the University of Chicago in 2001. He observes: "... After 25 years in one school [North Western] it seemed time for a change, especially when the alternative... was a university with another outstanding tradition of scholarship in economics." Regarding the award of Nobel Prize, Myerson has to state: "... I am very proud to have my name so prominently linked with Leo's [Leonid Hurwicz] and Eric's [Eric Maskin], and with the advances in analysis of coordination mechanisms and incentive constraints...."

Myerson is Glen A. Lloyd Distinguished Service Professor of Economics at the University of Chicago. He is a member of the American Academy of Arts and Sciences and of the National Academy of Sciences. He has served for 10 years as editorial board member of the International Journal of Game Theory. He has made contributions as an economist, as an applied mathematician and as a political scientist.

43.4 A SUMMARY OF MECHANISM DESIGN THEORY

Mechanism Design is defined by Roger Myerson in the New Palgrave Dictionary of Economics on Line as follows: "A mechanism is a specification of how economic decisions are determined as a function of information that is known by individuals in the economy. Mechanism theory shows that incentive constraints should be considered equally with resource constraints in the formulation of the economic problem. Where individuals' private information and actions are difficult to monitor, the need to give people an incentive to share information and exert efforts may impose constraints on economic systems just as much as the limited availability of raw materials. Mechanism is the fundamental mathematical methodology for analyzing economic efficiency subject to incentive constraints."

The origin of the Mechanism Design Theory, as mentioned earlier, can be traced to the discussions in the 1930's about the possibility of efficient resource allocation in a socialistic society. According to Hurwicz, the debate was essentially "provocated" by von Mises's scepticism as to even a theoretical feasibility of rational allocation of resources in an economy under socialism. In his Richard Ely lecture to the American Economic Association, Hurwicz summarised the origins of the debate. He said: "In 1930's two major lines of development are relevant. One line was the work of Lange, Lerner and others on resource allocation in a socialistic economy, the slightly earlier 1929 paper by F.M Taylor on trial and error methods, Hotelling's contribution on marginal cost pricing and consumer-producer surplus, and " new welfare economics" of Hicks, Kaldor, Scitovsky, and others. The line of development, started in the 1940's, was the mathematization of "Classical welfare economics" by Lange, Allais, Debreu and Koopmans ...."

Hurwicz was also of view that with the phenomenal growth of private enterprise and governmental units, issues such as motivation, stimulation of initiative and intensity of effort arise in determining the relationship between the central office of a firm and its divisions or a ministry and its components. Further, there is a close relationship with information theory and with problems of administrative organisation. He gave important credit to Marschak for his development of economic theory of information and to Herbert Simon for his work on organisation and economic behaviour. The design of mechanism was stimulated by the following developments of the 1940's referred to by Hurwicz in his Ely lecture.

1. Activity Analysis and Linear Programming including the simplex method developed by Dantzig, Kantorovich and Koopmans.
2. Game theory including the iterative solution procedures- most important contributions of von Neumann and Morgenstern.
3. Linking linear and non-linear programming to two person zero-sum games. Work of Gale, Kuhn and Tucker is associated with this development.

Goal conflicts because of multiplicity of consumers form the essence of economics, programming --whether linear or non-linear--deals generally with a single well–designed objective function to be, say, maximised. That is, it corresponds to an economy with only one consumer. Hurwicz comments, "...mechanisms designed under the influence of programming theory dealt to a large extent with one-objective function problems and thus failed to face the crucial issue of goal conflict." However, these mechanisms designed are an important step on the road to the more difficult multi-objective problems. Pointing out the limitations of mechanisms designed using a variant of the programming approach, Hurwicz specifically mentions computational difficulties and problems relating to information transfer. In this context, he recalls one of Hayek's important points while summing up the state of the debate concerning the feasibility of centralised socialist solution. Hayek stated that in view of a large number of variables and equations, it would be difficult to solve the equations. However, decisions would have to be made continuously. Further, Hayek discussed some informational aspects which have become more important now. Specifically, Hurwicz referred to the difficulty of placing all the relevant information in the hands of a single agency (may be Central Planning Board), because of the dispersal of information throughout the economy. The exercise may be either impossible, in the sense that much information would be lost in the process of transfer of information from consumers, producers and resource holders to a single agency or too costly in the light of accuracy requirements. Nevertheless, if the economic units which initially are the only ones with information about themselves are capable of carrying out calculations then it is possible to employ computing procedures that would not need information transfers and also distribute the tasks of calculation. Hurwicz observed that this is what informationally decentralised procedures are meant to accomplish.

Further developments in this genre may be ignored and we may attempt at outlining the contributions of Hurwicz and others in 1970s and in subsequent years. Hurwicz began his Ely lecture by stating that traditionally economic analysis treated the economic system as one of the "givens;" that is, the structure of the economic system is to be regarded as unknown. There is, therefore, a need to finding a "superior" system – a superior mechanism. He conceded that one could get by without finalising the meaning of a resource allocation mechanism. However, in our search for alternatives to existing mechanisms for non-classical situations, such as increasing returns, indivisibilities, externalities and public goods, it would be desirable to have a rigorous formulation of an allocative mechanism. Any good resource allocation mechanism must serve the purpose of guiding economic agents, such as consumers, producers and financial intermediaries in decisions that determine the flow of resources. Further, the mechanism should guide economic agents toward feasible actions though classical welfare economics requires efficiency or optimality, in addition to feasibility. Hurwicz stated: "... We are fairly clear on our options- from efficiency in production (as defined by Koopmans) through optimality (introduced by Pareto...), to the maximization of social welfare function (as defined by Bergson, Samuelson, or Arrow)... they are defined independently of the mechanism."

In his Ely lecture, Hurwicz discussed mechanisms that are analogous to the tatonnement process where a period of dialogue without actions is followed by decisions regarding flow of resources, specifically, production and exchange. However, he was of the view that a more general theory is needed in which dialogue, decisions and actions overlap in time as in the non-tatonnement processes. The participants in the dialogue include not only producers and consumers etc., but may also include governments, planning bodies or trade or employee's unions. Exchange of messages between participants constitutes a dialogue. Messages may contain proposals of actions, bids, offers or plans for resource flow for the entire economy or may comprise information regarding preferences, technology and resource endowments. Hurwicz termed aggregate of messages permissible under a given mechanism its language. The mechanism stipulates what are called "response rules" governing message response to messages previously received and also specifies the actions to be taken, given the course of dialogue outcome rule. According to Hurwicz the rules may be probabilistic or deterministic; mathematically, they are expressed as functions. Both market phenomena and command systems can be accommodated into this schema. Each resource allocation mechanism contains an adjustment process specified by its language, response rules and the outcome rule. The adjustment process, of course, must yield feasible outcomes. He formulated the basic set of performance requirements for processes to be considered: that they be non-wasteful, unbiased and basically single valued. These three requirements Hurwicz called Pareto-satisfactoriness.

Whether the requirements are met or are not met by a given process very much depends on the environment in which it is to operate. Hurwicz opined that the competitive process is Pareto-satisfactory over classical environments which are free from externalities or indivisibilities, their sets are convex, and increasing returns are ruled out. The next question is whether we find Pareto-satisfactory processes for non-classical environments also. Hurwicz felt that some restrictions need to be imposed on the information or incentive structure of the processes to be considered. He acknowledged the seminal work of Jacob Marschak and Roy Radner on the theory of teams in which there is recognition of the role played by the information structure. Taking inspiration from that work, Hurwicz drew a distinction between information obtained directly by participants (such as by one's own observation) and through messages received. He postulated that participants have direct information only about themselves, not about others. He termed the direct information, privacy of the adjustment process. Hurwitz observed: "The totality of these and certain other conditions.... I have labeled informational decentralization." He stated that it is possible to construct processes that are informationally decentralised for all decomposable environments, that is, for the class of all environments that are free of externalities.

It is clear from the above discussion that it is possible to design process rules which, if followed, would have certain desirable consequences. The next question is whether the participants could be expected to follow the rules, since there is a possibility of individual departures from prescribed norms or outright collusions. To consider the first situation (that is, where there is individual departures from the rules), Hurwicz used non-cooperative game theory without side payments. He adopted the concept of Nash equilibrium and observed that a configuration of behaviour patterns constituting Nash equilibrium is referred to as individual incentive–compatible. Such a configuration is present if no participant finds it beneficial to deviate from behaviour pattern so long as others do not. In the alternative, one could assume existence of an enforcement system (carrots or sticks) that makes it unattractive for the participants openly to violate the stipulated rules. Without openly violating the rules, a participant may resort to "cheating"-- he could "pretend" to be poorer than he really is, or less efficient, or less eager for certain goods. In his 1964 article Samuelson dealt with this issue, in the context of the allocation problem for public goods. In fact, a similar problem is present in a "non-atomistic" world of pure exchange of exclusively private goods. Hurwicz argued that the rules of perfect competition are not incentive-compatible. He concluded his Ely lecture thus: "... in a non-atomistic exchange economy, there can be no incentive-compatible mechanism with optimal equilibria and the no-trade option, even though there are no public goods!"

In an economy with production, the possibility of successful false revelation of individual characteristics is particularly important. Hurwicz showed that in a production economy again, perfect competition is not incentive compatible. However, unlike under pure exchange, it is possible here to devise a reward scheme that would eliminate the incentive toward misrepresentation on the part of the participant. In Ely lecture, Hurwicz noted that the major unsolved problem in the theory of Mechanism Design related to the proper integration of the information and the incentive aspects of resource allocation models. However, he expressed satisfaction that economic analysis has broken out of its traditional limits in at least two important ways: (1) designing specific new mechanisms; and (2) exploring the constraints and trade-offs to which the design of mechanisms is subject.

Dwelling on the subject in his Prize lecture titled "But who will Guard the Guardians?" Hurwicz observed: "Viewing the economic process as a non-cooperative game in which the strategy of each participant is a statement (not necessarily truthful) about his/her preferences and the 'payoff' is the utility of outcome for that participant (designed in Samuelson's analysis by the Lindahl formula), Samuelson's first point can be formalised as the proposition that truthful revelation of preferences is not a Nash equilibrium in the Lindahl game. That is, if all other players have told the truth, and it is now your turn, you will in general gain by misrepresenting your preferences. So, Samuelson's first point turned out to be correct: Truth is not a Nash equilibrium. As regards Samuelson's second point, that illegal behaviour would be advantageous in any decentralised system, different criteria can be used for judging performance by the system (like Pareto optimality or degree of income inequality and different kinds of decentralised mechanisms), not necessarily revelations of one's preferences, Hurwicz's conclusion was that Samuelson's second (impossibility) point cannot be accepted. Hence optimism replaces pessimism. However, the issue of enforcement remains-- whether Nash equilibria are self-enforcing? Those who agree that they (equilibria) are self–enforcing contend that by definition, in a Nash equilibrium, no player can profit by a unilateral departure from his/her equilibrium strategy. More importantly, collusion is not feasible in non- cooperative games. As such, there is no need or possibility for enforcement. In Hurwicz's view, enforcement is a valid question to pose even in Nash equilibria. A need for enforcement implies the possibility of violating the rules of the game. Hurwicz classified the set of all feasible actions by players as legal and illegal and referred to that set the "true strategy domain." He clarified: "The set of true strategies consists of two feasible and disjoint subsets, that of legal strategies and that of illegal strategies. Participants are playing the 'true game' whose game form may contain both legal and illegal strategies. Some persons might risk and may choose an illegal strategy. However, since the decision produces consequences, it is necessary to know what the true outcome function is."

Hurwicz in his Prize lecture defined successful enforcement of the rules. In later part of the lecture he classified implementation as a more general concept than enforcement. According to him, the outcomes of the true game ensure that illegal strategies are less attractive than legal strategies. While it is possible to formulate strong or weak form of successful enforcement, Hurwicz had preference for a weak formulation-- that is, a player at least would be no worse off by "staying within the law." Then the next issue is the exposition of implementation idea. He considered that implementation was successful if equilibrium outcomes correspond to those of the desired game as envisaged by, say, legislation. In this framework, Nash equilibrium is not self-enforcing because it may be profitable in the absence of enforcement, to move to illegal strategies. Likewise, Nash equilibria are not self–implementing because implementation actions are necessary to ensure that the true outcome is the same as the legal outcome. On the basis of causal empiricism, he stated that there are many situations where rules are "substantially (if not perfectly) implemented or enforced." He concluded his lecture with observations that legal behaviour is not incompatible with rational, self–interested behaviour. Further, it may be possible to create systems in which rational self–interest, due to a variety of rewards and punishments may lead to legal and ethical behaviour. At the end Samuelson's second conjecture that there may be no successful implementation for public goods under decentralisation remains an open question.

Eric Maskin has refined and carried forward the development of the Mechanism Design theory. In his Prize lecture he offers "a brief introduction to the part of mechanism design called implementation theory, which, given a social goal, characterises when we can design a mechanism whose predicted outcomes (i.e., the set of equilibrium outcomes) coincide with the desirable outcomes, according to that goal." While much of economic theory is devoted to understanding the extant economic institutions and attempts at explaining or predicting outcomes that the institutions generate, the mechanism design, according to Maskin, reverses the direction. That is, it begins by identifying desired outcomes and asks whether mechanisms or institutions could be designed to achieve the desired outcomes or goods and, if so, what forms would institutions take? He explains the terms used in mechanism design, namely outcomes, goals and mechanisms. The meaning of each term depends on the context. For example, for a government that has to deliver public goods, an outcome consists of the quantities provided of such goods (e.g., national defence, public education) as also the means of financing them. Likewise, for an auctioneer intending to sell a group of assets, an outcome signifies an allocation of those assets across potential buyers as also with the payments that these buyers make.

In a like manner desirability or optimality of an outcome will be judged by the context. For the purpose of evaluating public good choices, the criterion of maximisation of net social surplus would be used. In the case of auctioning of assets, Maskin suggests employment of two different criteria: (i) whether the allocation is efficient in the sense that the assets are given to the highest bidders, and alternatively (ii) whether it has resulted in seller's revenue maximisation.

As regards mechanism that is a game or procedure or an institution for determining outcomes, who is the mechanism designer, depends upon the setting. Public goods are normally expected to be provided by the government which also decides the provision and the methods of financing. For sale of assets, the typical mechanism is auction where rules of auction are set by the seller. Maskin asserts: "...in the public goods framework, if government knows at the outset which choice of public good is optimal, then, there is a simple indeed trivial mechanism for achieving the optimum, the government has only to pass a law mandating this outcome." Similarly, in the case of auction of assets, if the auctioneer has prior knowledge of who is the highest bidder, he can directly award them to him.

However, the problem is not simple. The government or auctioneer does not have this information. That is the reason for theoretical interest in Mechanism Design. For instance, in the case of public goods, the government should have information on citizens' preferences for such good. It is obvious that the government will not have the required information. As such, the government cannot decide in advance which outcomes are optimal. The problem is further complicated as "... the individuals who do have this critical information- the citizens in the public good case or the buyers in the asset-selling example- have their own objectives and so may not have the incentive..." to reveal the information. It is, therefore, necessary that the mechanism is "incentive- compatible," as posited by Hurwicz. Maskin states the fundamental difficulty mechanism designers face is their lack of knowledge, at the outset, as to optimal outcomes. They, therefore, have to proceed indirectly; that is, designing mechanisms that themselves generate the required information.

The work in mechanism design developed by Hurwicz, Maskin, Myerson and others basically directed at three main questions. In the words of Maskin, the questions are:

When is it possible to design incentive-compatible mechanism for attaining social goals?

What form might these mechanisms take when they exist? and

When is finding such mechanisms ruled out theoretically?

For understanding the issue involved, Maskin has given the following simple concrete example in his Prize lecture.

Consider a society with two consumers of energy A and B. The energy authority has to choose one of the four available public energy sources- gas, oil, nuclear power and coal. Assume that there are two possible states of the world.

In state 1, consumers consider that the future is relatively less important; that is they have comparatively high temporal discount rates.

In state 2, consumers consider future to be more important in that their discount rates are correspondingly low.

Further, assume A gives greater importance to convenience and in state 1 favours gas over oil, oil over coal and coal over nuclear power. And in state 2 favours nuclear power over gas, gas over coal and coal over oil. He expects technical advantages to make gas, coal and nuclear power easier to use in future compared with oil.

In contrast, B cares more about safety and prefers in state 1 nuclear power over oil, oil over coal and coal over gas, while in state 2, he favours oil over gas, gas over coal and coal over nuclear power. His preferences are dictated by disposal of nuclear waste which may be difficult; as such, gas is considered safer.

Table 43.1 given below summarises, the consumers' ranking of the energy sources in the two states.

Table 43.1 Consumers' Ranking of Energy Sources

State 1		State 2	
A	**B**	**A**	**B**
Gas	Nuclear Power	Nuclear Power	Oil
Oil	Oil	Gas	Gas
Coal	Coal	Coal	Coal
Nuclear Power	Gas	Oil	Nuclear Power

Assume further that the energy authority is interested in choosing the energy source that both consumers (A, B) are 'reasonably happy' with.

Reasonably happy is interpreted as getting one's first or second choice. It is clear that oil is the optimal choice in state 1 and gas in state 2. Thus if 'f' is the social choice rule, then

f (state 1) = oil:

F (state 2) = gas.

But, suppose the authority does not know the state and so does not know what the optimal choice is. In that case, the authority could ask each consumer to announce the state. A has an incentive to say state 2 irrespective of the actual state and regardless of what B says. By saying state 2, A raises the probability of his preferred outcome (namely, gas) from 0 to 0.5, if B says state 1 and from 0.5 to 1.0, if B says state 2. As such, we could expect A to report state 2 in both states. Likewise, B would always report state 1 because he prefers oil to gas in either state. Taken together, the outcome is 50-50 randomisation between oil and gas. Hence, simply asking consumers to reveal actual state results rather in naïve mechanism.

The authority, instead, can ask consumers to participate in the mechanism given in the following Table 43.2.

Table 43.2 Optimal Outcome

B

A	**Left**	**Right**
Top	Oil	Coal
Bottom	Nuclear	Gas

Hence, A can choose either the top row or bottom row now. B can choose either the left column or right column. The outcome of these choices is given in the corresponding entry of the matrix (see Table 43.2). It is seen that in state 1, B is better off choosing left column irrespective of what A chooses. If A choose top row, then left column leads to oil as the outcome, the preference of B. If A chooses bottom row, then nuclear power (B's preferred outcome) is the consequence of choosing left column. Thus, left column is the 'dominant strategy' for B in state 1. Further, given that B's choice is left column, A is better off choosing top row rather than the bottom row, since A prefers oil to nuclear power. As such, in state 1, it is better for A to choose top row and B to choose left column. Top, left is the unique Nash equilibrium. Furthermore- and this is the critical point- the resulting outcome, oil is social optimum in state 1. Similarly in state 2, bottom row is the dominant strategy for A; if B chooses left column, he is better off with bottom row rather than top row, as he prefers nuclear power to oil. If B chooses right column, then bottom row leads to gas, which is preferred to coal. When A chooses bottom row, B is better off choosing right column, as he prefers gas to nuclear power. Thus, in state 2, bottom row and right column is the unique Nash equilibrium. Moreover, gas is the social optimum.

Thus, in either state, mechanism achieves social optimum, even though "(I) the mechanism designer (the energy authority does not even know the actual state), and (ii) A and B are interested in their own preferences, not those of the authority." As the above Nash equilibrium outcomes "coincide with the optimal outcomes in each state, we say that the mechanism implements the authority's social choice rule in Nash equilibrium." (Emphasis in the original)

Three questions were raised by Maskin in his Prize lecture about incentive-compatible mechanisms recounted earlier. He rephrases those three questions in the language of implementation theory which are given below.

Under what conditions can a social choice rule be implemented?

What form does an implementing mechanism take?

Which social choice rules cannot be implemented?

As an answer to these questions, he puts forward a property called "monotonicity" (sometimes referred to as Maskin monotonicity) which is the key to implementation of Nash equilibrium. He explains the concept of monotonicity with reference to Table 43.1 and Table 43.2 given earlier. They have shown that oil is the optimal outcome in state 1; further, oil is ranked higher than coal and nuclear power by A in state 1. However, the opposite is true in state 2. In state 2, gas but not oil is optimal does not violate monotonicity. Further, gas is ranked higher, relative to both coal and nuclear power by B in the move from state 2 to state 1. As such, though gas is optimal in state 2 but is not optimal in state 1 is also not in conflict with monotonocity. Maskin states: That is, the authority's social choice rule satisfies monotonocity and thus the possibility of implementing it does not contradict the following theorem:

Theorem 1. If a social choice rule is implementable, then it must be monotonic.

Maskin, however, contends that not all monotonic social choice rules are implementable. Nevertheless, if there are at least three individuals in society, monotonicity guarantees implementability. One more condition is to be imposed. There should be no "veto" power. More importantly, if there are three or more individuals, no veto power condition is satisfied automatically. Maskin draws a general result on the possibility of implementing social choice rules and formulates the following theorem.

Theorem 2: Suppose there are at least three individuals. If the social choice rule satisfies monotonicity and no veto power, then it is implementable.

While concluding his lecture, Maskin says that he presented his work that was done thirty years ago; it may give an "antique flavour." He concludes on a satisfactory note: "... an especially gratifying aspect of the theory is that almost fifty years after Hurwicz (1960), the subject remains intellectually vibrant and important: New implementation papers appearing all the time. It will be interesting to see where the field goes in the next fifty years."

Roger Myerson in his Prize lecture "Perspectives on Mechanism Design in Economic Theory" presents his work relating to Revelation Principle after providing a brief historical perspective. He defines Revelation Principle in the New Palgrave Dictionary of Economics on line as follows:

"In any economic institution, individuals must be given appropriate incentives to share private information or to exert unobserved efforts. The revelation principle is a technical insight that allows us to make general statements about what allocation rules are feasible, subject to incentive constraints, in economic problems with adverse selection and moral hazard. The revelation principle tells us that, for any general coordination mechanism, any equilibrium of rational communication strategies for the economic agents can be simulated by an equivalent incentive-compatible direct-revelation mechanism, where a trustworthy mediator maximally centralizes communication and makes honesty and obedience rational equilibrium strategies for the agents."

Myerson outlines the development of economics as an analytical social science by concentrating on production and allocation of material goods, methodologies of national income accounting and price theory. Focussing on resource allocation, Classical economics defined economic problem as human's ability to satisfy their desires constrained by scarce resources. It was also argued that since available limited resources cannot improve every one's welfare, free trade among countries can achieve allocative efficiency. Starting with Cournot, the focus shifted from resource allocation to analysis of incentives. In 1930's the debate about capitalism versus socialism, proved to be inconclusive and the limitations of price theory for evaluating non-price institutions like socialist command economy were realised. In a highly influential paper (1945) in the American Economic Review(rated as one the best twenty papers in the American Economic Review in the first 100 years) – "The Use of Knowledge in Society"-- Hayek argued that economic theory to be useful for analytical comparison of fundamentally different forms of economic organisation must recognise that economic institutions of all kinds should serve an essential function of communicating widely dispersed information about the desires and the resources of different individuals in society. Myerson says that different economic institutions should be compared as mechanisms for communication. It is commonly agreed that the pivotal moment occurred when in 1972 Hurwicz posed the fundamental question of incentives to communicate information and introduced the general concept of incentive-compatibility which is covered in the earlier part of the chapter.

Myerson observes that given the information, preferences and resources that people have in a society, different social coordination mechanisms could give rise to different games, each of which could have different equilibria. However, the "Revelation Principle" developed by Myerson among many others facilitates characterisation of the set of all possible equilibria of all possible games. He asserts: "With the revelation principle, the feasible set essentially coincides with the set of incentive-compatibility mechanisms, which satisfy certain incentive constraints. These incentive constraints express the basic fact that individuals will not share private information or exert hidden efforts without appropriate incentives." (Emphases in the original) Mechanism theory has widened our understanding of the economic problem by including resource constraints as well as incentive constraints. In economic analysis we employ new concepts of incentive efficiency for evaluating the rules by which allocation of resources takes place, taking into account incentive constraints also.

An important aspect that needs to be considered in this connection is the actual feasibility of the kind of social coordination plans. A number of different social institutions can implement a feasible social coordination plan. Myerson starts his discussion with a centralised institution where every individual communicates separately and confidentially with a reliable central mediator. The mediator, on the basis of all the reports of private information communicated individually to him, recommends to each individual the actions to be undertaken by him under the plan. If we suppose that individuals can be dishonest or disobey the mediator's instructions, the social plan, as Hurwicz suggested, must grant people incentives to share information and to act according to the social plan. Myerson terms the problem of getting people share private information honestly as "adverse selection." He defines moral hazard as the problem of making people to act obediently to a social plan for which an incentive may have to be given to the people. He considers a plan incentive-compatible if it is a rational equilibrium for everyone to be honest and obedient to the central mediator implementing social coordination plan.

Such incentive-compatible coordination plans can be characterised by a set of inequalities called incentive constraints. Further, Myerson says that the Revelation Principle asserts that any rational equilibrium of individual behaviour in any social institution must be equivalent to an incentive–compatible coordination plan. He observes "...without loss of generality, a trustworthy mediator can plan to make honesty and obedience the best policy for everyone.... If any individual had any incentive to be dishonest or disobedient to the mediator under this plan, then he would have had an incentive also to be dishonest or disobedient to himself under his given equilibrium strategy in the given mechanism. But in a rational equilibrium, nobody can gain by lying to himself or disobeying his own optimal strategy."

In the Prize lecture, Myerson provides three examples to demonstrate the power of mechanism design theory--one example of trading in a pure exchange economy with one buyer and one seller (a case of adverse selection); second, a production example involving moral hazard in management, and a third example that introduces politics into a productive economy, involving moral hazard in government. The second and third examples involving moral hazard exemplify what Hayek argued as practical disadvantages of socialism. While discussing the first example, Myerson makes a reference to Coase's argument regarding transaction costs; that is, irrespective of the initial allocation of property rights, allocative efficiency can be achieved through free trade of resources and property rights, provided there are no transaction costs. Myerson states that information-incentive constraints can be considered as a source of Coasean transaction costs. He therefore concludes: "The theory of mechanism design gives us an analytical framework, where the initial allocation of property rights can affect the probability of achieving an outcome that is allocatively efficient."

Through the second example (production economy involving moral hazard in management), he demonstrates situations with potential advantages of socialism and those with potential disadvantages of socialism. Lower private property rights are available in socialism compared with free-market capitalism. He contends that in the latter, honest communication may be difficult, increasing the informational problems of adverse selection. In contrast, the former set up may reduce problems of adverse selection while, at the same time, increasing problems of moral hazard.

As regards the third example, involving moral hazard in the government, Myerson argues that costs of unbridled central power can be viewed as problems of moral hazard in the government. Free market, he observes, may be viewed as the "antithesis of centralized political control of the economy." From this angle one may rationalise the free market economy. He shows through the example that even an autocratic ruler may grant private property rights even though such a grant may lead to the ruler losing his power ultimately. However a bountiful endowment of natural resources in his ruled territory may bring down the ruler's incentive to liberalise. The conclusion that is drawn is "a nation may be cursed by too many natural resources."

Myerson concludes his lecture as to how mechanism design theory altered the primary objective of economic analysis from allocation of given resources "to the social plan or allocation mechanism that specifies how resource allocations should depend on people's information."

43.5 CONCLUDING OBSERVATIONS

Kenneth Arrow speaking at a luncheon meeting of the American Economic Association referred to Leonid Hurwicz as a "transforming figure in modern economic theory." He makes references to Hurwicz's "rigorous mind:" a "perfectionist." Arrow also mentions Hurwicz's other important contributions – general formulation of the concept of identification and for the issue of integrability relating to consumer demand theory. Arrow finally refers to Hurwicz's "breadth and strength of interests and feelings" especially his broad cultural interests and deep and penetrating political insights. In Myerson's words "mechanism design and other areas of game theory have contributed to a fundamental change in the scope of economics.... In the quest for better analytical understanding of how the wealth of nations may depend on their institutions, economic analysis has returned to the breadth of vision that characterized the ancient Greek philosophers who first gave economics its name."

43.6 SELECT BIBLIOGRAPHY OF WORKS ON MECHANISM DESIGN BY HURWICZ, MASKIN AND MYERSON

43.6.1 LEONID HURWICZ

43.6.1.1 Books

1958 (with K. J. Arrow and H. Uzawa, eds.), Studies in Linear and Non- Linear Programming, Stanford University Press, Stanford, Ca.

1977 (with K.J. Arrow eds.), Studies in Resource Allocation Process, Cambridge University Press, Cambridge.

1985 (with D. Schmeidler and H. Sonnenschen, eds.), Social Goals and Social Organization, Cambridge University Press, Cambridge.

43.6.1.2 Articles

1944 "Stochastic Models of Economic Fluctuations," Econometrica, Vol.12, No.2.

1945 "The Theory of Economic Behavior," AER, Vol.35, No.5.

1946 a "Theory of the Firm and of Investment," Econometrica, Vol. 14, No.2.

b "What Has Happened to the Theory of Games?" AER, Vol.36, No.2.

1947 (with K.J. Arrow), "Gradient Methods for Constrained Maxima," Operations Research, Vol.5, No.2.

1956 (with K.J. Arrow), "Reduction of Constrained Maxima to Saddle point Problems," in Proceedings of Third Berkley Symposium, J. Neyman (ed.) Berkley, Ca.

1960 "Optimality and Informational Efficiency in Resource Allocation," in Mathematical Methods in Social Sciences, Arrow, K.J. et al., (eds.), Stanford University Press, Stanford, Ca.

1969 "On the Concept and Possibility of Informational Decentralization," AER, Vol.59, No.2.

1972 "On Informationally Decentralized Systems," in Decision and Organization, C.B. McGuire and R.R Radner (eds.), North Holland, Amsterdam.

1973 "The Design of Mechanism for Resource Allocation," AER, Vol.63, No.2.

1977 "On the Dimensional Requirements of Informationally Decentralized Pareto-Satisfactory Processes," in Studies in Resource Allocation Process, K. J. Arrow and L. Hurwicz (eds.), Cambridge University Press, Cambridge.

1978 (with D. Schmeidler), "Construction of Outcome Functions Guaranteeing Existence and Pareto–Optimality of Nash Equilibria," Econometrica, Vol.46, No.6.

1979 a "Outcome Functions Yielding Walrasian and Lindahl Allocations at Nash Equilibrium Points," RES, Vol.46, No.2.

b "On Allocations Attainable Through Nash Equilibria," JET, Vol.21, No.1.

1986 a "Incentive Aspects of Decentralization," in Handbook of Mathematical Economics, K. J. Arrow, M.D. Intriligator (eds.) III, North Holland, Amsterdam.

1995 a "What is the Coase Theorem?" Japan and the World Economy, Vol.7, No.1.

b (with E. Maskin and A . Postle Waite), "Feasible Nash Implementations of Social Choice Rules when the Designer Does not know Endowments or Production Sets," in The Economics of Informational Decentralization: Complexity, Efficiency and Stability, Essays in Honor of Stanley Reiter, J. Ledyard (ed.)Kulwer Academic Publishers, Boston, MA.

c "Implementation and Enforcement," in Political Economy, Institutions, Competition and Representation, W. A. Bernell et al.(eds.), Cambridge University Press, Cambridge.

1996 "Institutions as Families of Game Forms," Japanese Economic Review, Vol. 47, No.1.

1999 "Mechanism Design without Games," Journal of Economic Public Theory, Vol.1, No.2.

2008 "But Who Will Guard the Guardians", Prize Lecture, AER, Vol.98, No.3.

43.6.2 ERIC MASKIN

43.6.2.1 Books

1992 (with P. Dasgupta et al. eds.), Economic Analysis of Markets and Games: Essays in Honor of Frank Hahn, MIT Press, Cambridge, MA.

2000 (with A. Simonovits, eds.), Planning, Shortage, and Transformation: Essays in Honor of Janos Kornai, MIT Press, Cambridge, MA.

43.6.2.2 Articles

1979 (with P. Dasgupta and P. Hammond), "The Implementation of Social Choice Rules: Some General Results on Incentive Compatibility," RES, Vol.46, No.2.

1984 a (with J. Riley), "Optimal Auctions with Risk-Averse Buyers," Econometrica, Vol.52, No.6.

b (with J. Riley), Monopoly with Incomplete Information," Rand JE, Vol.15, No.2.

1985 a (with J. Riley), "Auction Theory with Private Values," AER, Vol.75, No.2.

b "The Theory of Implementation in Nash Equilibrium: A Survey," in Social Goals And Social Organization, (H. Hurwicz et al. eds.), Cambridge University Press, Cambridge.

1986 (with D. Fudenberg), "The Folk Theorem in Repeated Games with Discounting or with Complex Information," Econometrica, Vol. 54, No.3.

1992 "Auctions and Privatization," in Privatization: Symposium in Honor of Herbert Girsh Mohor, H. Siebert (ed.), Sieseck, Tubingen.

1999 a "Nash Equilibrium and Welfare Optimality," RES, Vol.66, No.1.

b (with J. Moore), "Implementation and Renegotiation," RES, Vol.66,No.1.

c (with J. Tirole), "Unforeseen Contingencies and Incomplete Contracts," RES, Vol.66, No.1.

2000 (with P. Dasgupta), "Efficient Auctions," QJE, Vol.115, No.2.

2002 (with T. Sjöström), "Implementation Theory," in Handbook of Social Choice and Welfare, Vol.1, (K. J. Arrow, A. Sen, and K. Suzumura (eds.)), Elsevier Science, Amsterdam.

2003 (with S. Baliga), "Mechanism Design for the Environment," in Handbook of Environmental Economics, K.G. Mäler, and J. Vincent (eds.),Vol.1, Elsevier Science, Amsterdam.

2005 (with P. Dasgupta), "Uncertainty and Hyperbolic Discounting," AER, Vol.95, No.4.

2008 "Mechanism Design: How to Implement Social Goals," Prize Lecture, AER, Vol.98, No.3.

2011 "Commentary: Nash Equilibrium and Mechanism Design," GEB, Vol.71, No.1.

43.6.3 ROGER MYERSON

43.6.3.1 Articles

1977 "Two-Person Bargaining Problems and Comparable Utility," Econometrica, Vol.45, No.7.

1979 "Incentive Compatibility and the Bargaining Problem," Econometrica, Vol.47, No.1.

1981 a "Utilitarianism, Egalitarianism, and the Timing Effect in Social Choice Problem," Econometrica, Vol.49, No.4.

b "Optimal Auction Design," Mathematics of Operations Research, Vol.6, No.1.

1982 "Optimal Coordination Mechanisms in Generalized Principal-Agent Problems," Journal of Mathematical Economics, Vol.10, No.1.

1983 a "Mechanism Design by an Informed Principal," Econometrica, Vol.51, No.6.

b (with M. A. Satterthwaite) "Efficient Mechanisms for Bilateral Trading," JET, Vol.29, No.6.

1985 "Bayesian Equilibrium and Incentive Compatibility," in Social Goals and Social Organization, L. Hurwicz, D. Schmeidler, and H. Sonnenschein, (eds.), Cambridge University Press, Cambridge.

1986 a "Negotiation in Games: A Theoretical Overview," in Essays in Honor of K. J. Arrow, (W.P Heller, R. Starr, and D. Starrett eds.), Cambridge University Press, Cambridge.

b "Multistage Games with Communication," Econometrica,Vol.54, No.2.

1989 "Mechanism Design," in The New Palgrave: Allocation, Information, and Markets, (J. Eatwell, et al.eds.), Norton, New York.

1994 "Communication, Correlated Equilibria, and Incentive Compatibility," in Handbook of Game Theory with Economic Applications, R. J. Aumann and S. Hart (eds.), Elsevier Science, Amsterdam.

1996 "John Nash's Contribution to Economics," GEB, Vol.14, No.2.

1999 "Nash Equilibrium and the History of Economic Theory," JEL, Vol.37, No.3.

2001 a "Learning Game Theory from John Harsanyi," GEB, Vol. 36, No.1.

b "Review of "Incentives and Political Economy," by Jean-Jacques Laffont," JEL, Vol.39, No.4.

2006 "Fundamental Theory of Institutions: a Lecture in Honor of Leo Hurwicz," Presented at The North American Meetings of Econometric Society.

2007 (with P. Braguinsky), "Capital Growth with Oligarchic Property Rights," Review of Economic Dynamics, Vol. 10, No.4.

2008 a "Perspectives on Mechanism Design in Economic Theory," Noble Lecture, AER, Vol. 98, No.3.

2012 "A Model of Moral-Harzard Credit Cycles," JEP, Vol. 120, No.5.

43.7 WORKS OF OTHERS

Coase, R. (1960), "The Problem of Social Cost," JLawE, Vol. 7, pp.1-44.

Lange, O. (1936), "On the Economic Theory of Socialism," RES, Vol. 4, pp.53-71.

Von Hayek, F. (1945), "The Use of Knowledge in Society," AER, Vol. 35, No.4.

SECTION - VI
INTERDISCIPLINARY RESEARCH

CHAPTER 44

SIMON KUZNETS

(1901-1985)

The Nobel Memorial Prize in Economic Sciences for the year 1971 was awarded to Professor Simon Kuznets of Harvard University, U.S.A., for "his empirically founded interpretation of economic growth which has led to new and deepened insight into the economic and social structure and process of development." The citation refers to his attempts at understanding the processes of economic and social development by giving quantitative precision to relevant economic entities. In this work, Kuznets "identifies, documents and analyses the emergence of a new epoch in economic history" which he christened as modern economic growth. In the process of this effort, he developed methods for estimating the size and changes of national income by collecting substantial statistical material and carefully analysing it. While Kuznets had used models explaining the relation between strategic elements in the economic system, he showed almost no sympathy for abstract and radically generalising models which give limited opportunities for empirical testing. In his attempts at coherent interpretation of phenomena of economic growth and business cycles, he included in his models, besides relevant economic data, institutional and non-economic factors – such as demographic changes, industrial structure and marketing forms as endogenous variables.

44.1 A SHORT BIOGRAPHICAL SKETCH: SIMON KUZNETS

Simon Kuznets was born in Pinsk, Russia on 30th April, 1901, of Jewish parents and died in Cambridge, Massachusetts, U.S.A, on 9th July, 1985. After a brief stint as the head of a statistical office in Ukraine under the early Soviet regime, he migrated to the United States in 1922 to join his father. Kuznets's university studies began in Russia and were completed at Columbia University, New York. From Columbia University, he received his B.Sc. in 1923, M.A. in 1924 and Ph.D. in economics in 1926. At Columbia University's graduate school, he first met Wesley C. Mitchell with whom he was associated for many years at the National Bureau of Economic Research (NBER), New York.

After completion of graduate studies at Columbia University, Kuznets spent a year and half (1925-26) as Research Fellow of the Social Science Research Council in the work that led to preparation of the monograph, Secular Movements in Production and Prices. A large part of his scientific contribution was as a member of the research staff of the NBER from 1927 to the early 1960's. His work during this period was mostly in the fields of national income and capital formation in the United States. During 1949-1968, when Kuznets was Chairman of the Social Science Research Council Committee on Economic Growth, his work was mainly comparative quantitative analysis of economic growth of nations. He held Professorial appointments at a few Universities -- Professor of Economics and Statistics at University of Pennsylvania, Philadelphia, part-time between 1931 and 1936 and full time from 1936 to 1954, Professor of Political Economy at the John Hopkins University between 1954-1960 and Professor of Economics at Harvard University, 1960-1971. Even after his retirement, Kuznets continued to be an active researcher for another decade.

44.2 A SUMMARY OF KUZNETS'S CONTRIBUTIONS

Kuznets was a prolific writer. A bibliography of Kuznets's work lists over 200 titles – around 30 books and major essays of at least 100 pages each, covering about 9,000 pages all told. His contribution to Economics is summarised under the following four heads.

1. Studies of National Income;
2. Problems Relating to Savings and Investment;
3. Studies of Economic Growth; and
4. Findings on Modern Economic Growth.

44.2.1 STUDIES OF NATIONAL INCOME

Kuznets is considered the foremost pioneer in conceptualisation and measurement of national income and its components. In sheer volume of achievement in the field of national income, no other scholar comes anywhere near him. Richard A. Easterlin of the University of Pennsylvania makes this succinct observation: "...so great are his accomplishments in the measurement of national income and so close the identification of national income with his name that American economists frequently cite this work as the basis for his Nobel award. Certainly, there is no doubt that this work too is a landmark in the evolution of economic science." Erik Lundberg provides an important clarification in regard to Kuznets's contribution: "...Kuznets did not take part in developing concepts and methods for the layout of complete national accounting systems and national budgets. The pioneering work in these fields was done in Great Britain (Richard Stone and James Meade) and Norway (Ragnar Frisch)."

Kuznets started his national income studies in 1930s and the first results of his studies, National Income 1929-32, were published by the U.S. Department of Commerce in 1934. His most important contribution in this field was the voluminous National Income and its Composition, 1919-38, published in 1941. His studies in the field of national income provided material for empirical research by a large number of research scholars into different aspects of the U.S. economy, such as consumption and savings functions, structural changes in production and consumption, and the vital importance of capital formation in the economic growth process. The large body of work in the field of Keynesian macroeconomic analysis carried out by researchers was made possible by Kuznets's estimates of national income, its size and composition.

Incidentally, Keynes in his General Theory makes a reference to Kuznets's work on U.S. national income.

Besides taking initiative for making comprehensive estimates of the U.S. national income, Kuznets had inspired national income studies in other countries and was a driving force behind efforts at estimating national income in a number of countries in 1940's and 1950's as evidenced by the series of Studies in Income and Wealth.

44.2.2 PROBLEMS RELATING TO SAVINGS AND CAPITAL FORMATION

Kuznets, in his 1926 volume on Cyclical Fluctuations, postulated the relation between consumption expenditures and income in a way which, according to some economists, foreshadowed Keynes with a lead-time of roughly a decade. Kuznets also showed, with the imperfect statistical data available at that time, how consumption and saving of a family move with income fluctuations and how the consumption-income ratio seems to vary with the business cycle, showing an increase during a period of depression and a tendency to fall in the period of a boom. Kuznets's studies of national income had clearly demonstrated that the average consumption ratio at around 88 percent remained secularly stable as the average propensity to consume of households in the U.S. likewise showed secular stability. In the opinion of observers like Lundberg "it is easy to take quotations from this book [1926 work on Cyclical Fluctuations] to show that Kuznets was fully aware that the observed relation between consumption and income, in combination with an investment change, could give rise to a cumulative process in the development of income and employment" which is nothing but Keynes's multiplier.

While in a number of his works, Kuznets dealt with the problems of capital formation, we must make a specific reference to his Capital in the American Economy (1961), wherein he provided plausible explanations of observed long-run stability in savings-income ratio. He also made attempts at disaggregating nation's savings with breakdowns for households, government, corporate business units and other firms. In this work, Kuznets provided a comprehensive discussion of the vexed issue of whether in the long run a nation's investment activity is constrained by the available supply of savings and answers in the affirmative. In his view, a nation's propensity to save acts as a determinant of the size and stability of the aggregate investment ratio over time. He also hinted at the concept of forced savings. The light thrown from his studies of capital formation include secular decline of net investment ratio, development of capital-output ratios for the economy as a whole and for different industries and comparisons of average and marginal capital-output ratios and their development between different countries.

Kuznets assigned relatively low importance to the growth of capital and high investment ratio in a country's growth process. He gave greater weight to factors such as improved quality of labour force, current supply of consumer goods, technological development and structural changes. He observed: "For a country's greatest asset is its people, with their skill, experience, and drive toward useful economic activity.... The effects of a high standard of living, assured by an adequate flow of perishable and other commodities, and of the skills generated by such a 'perishable' service as education are, of course, immense."

Kuznets had studied the rate of increase in productivity and the factors that explain it. At the same time, he pointed out that increased productivity is not an unmixed blessing. The growth process creates social costs through rapid urbanisation and expansion of the public sector. He also explored the effect of innovations and technological change on increases in productivity and structural changes in production. He attempted at measuring the effect of structural change on the long-run economic growth of a nation. He emphasised the role played by certain growth industries in this process and focused on the important role played in structural change by the relative fall in prices of products belonging to these growth sectors as also the high-income elasticity. On the other hand, improved productivity recorded by the traditional activities, such as, agriculture and manufacture of textiles, comes as a consequence of transfer of resources from these sectors to the rapidly growing sectors. On the basis of the analysis, he came to a conclusion that it is not the aggregate investment rate that determines a country's growth but rather the share of resources in labour, capital etc. channelled into the growth industries.

44.2.3 STUDIES OF ECONOMIC GROWTH

Kuznets did not develop a formal model exhibiting the mechanism of economic growth. Instead, he attempted at drawing "some suggestions from the empirical record about the identity and relative importance of and inter-connections among the determining factors...." He had laid particular emphasis on factors such as size, age and occupational distribution of population, structural changes, innovations, quality and skill endowments of labour force, composition and quality of capital, international trade, movements of capital and changes in social environment and market forms. In the long run, Kuznets took factors, such as demographic development, technological changes, structure of industry and market forms as endogenous variables. In Lundberg's opinion, Kuznets had played an original and partly pioneering role in respect of the following topics:

1. Kuznets's cycles and their relation with business cycles and demographic movements;
2. Problems of saving and investment;
3. Connection between structural change and productivity growth;
4. Growth and income distribution; and
5. Comparison between countries as regards national income and growth.

In his studies since the early 1950's, Kuznets had considered changes in income distribution over time from many different angles and the relationship of such changes with processes of growth and business cycles, with focus on the U.S. Important findings of these studies were reported by Kuznets in Quantitative Aspects, VII and in a later volume Modern Economic Growth published in 1966. He had demonstrated how the functional distribution of income changes in the long run to the benefit of labour. He also showed how the redistribution of income in favour of labour takes place when wage rate rises relative to the cost of capital services. Of much greater interest, however, were his studies of size distribution of income, appearing in Quantitative Analysis, VIII as also in Shares of Upper Income Groups in Income and Saving (1953). He showed the way in which mobility of income-earners between various income classes increases with the structural change accompanied by acceleration of the growth rate. Furthermore, he showed that the skewness of personal distribution of income exhibits a secular decline.

In addition to studies devoted to estimating national income, savings, capital formation and growth of the U.S., Kuznets made strenuous efforts to make the results comparable with those relating to other countries. His attempts at making international comparisons were a part of his quest for identifying common patterns of growth, and discern similarities and differences between countries at different levels of development. He had championed the view that the determinants and consequences of economic growth are largely identical for different countries. He was conscious of many 'disparate sources of error' that are likely to surface in international comparisons of per capita national income and growth rates and discussed them in his work. For instance, the level and growth of output in developed industrial countries tend to be overestimated by including in the output of goods and services the output of some industries, the rationale for the production of which is to offset the deleterious consequences of industrialisation. Likewise, the level of output in developing countries may suffer from underestimation mainly because of the variations in the extent to which the market mechanism operates in different countries. Similarly, foreign exchange rates may be poor and misleading indicators of the relative purchasing power of goods and services in different countries. Despite such sources of error and despite the problems associated with international comparisons of economic data, Kuznets advocated taking a critical view of as to how important such sources of error are in different kinds of comparisons instead of outright rejection of comparative national income data.

44.2.4 FINDINGS ON MODERN ECONOMIC GROWTH

In his Nobel Banquet speech on December 10, 1971, Kuznets in humility observed: "the award of a Nobel Memorial Prize honors not only the individual scholar but, implicitly, also a special field or a distinctive method." He summarised his findings and reflections on modern economic growth, a succinct summary of which will throw some light on his lifetime's scholarly work.

After defining a country's economic growth as a long-term rise in capacity to supply increasingly diverse goods to its population, Kuznets stated that advancing technology and the institutional and ideological adjustments help in the secular rise in such capacity. The sustained rise in the supply of goods is the result of economic growth. While he conceded the possibility of the ability of some small countries to raise per capita income by selling fortuitous gifts of nature and obtaining a large and increasing rent by exploiting a resource such as minerals, Kuznets's interest lay only in the study of nations that derive abundance by using advanced contemporary technology. Advancing technology is a permissive source of economic growth, a necessary but not a sufficient condition for growth. For efficient and wide use of technology and for the stimulating technological advance by proper use of innovations generated by the burgeoning stock of human knowledge, he stipulated presence of appropriate institutional and ideological adjustments. Further, Kuznets noted that the pace at which technological progress, particularly in production sectors, was achieved and economic growth advanced differed over time (in fact, centuries) and among world's regions.

Kuznets termed as epochal innovations those major break-throughs or achievements in the advance of human knowledge that resulted in sustained growth over long periods and spread to a substantial part of the world. He suggested that, on the basis of epochal innovations with the distinctive characteristics of growth that it generated, we may subdivide into economic epochs, the changing course of economic history. He asserted that modern economic growth represents such a distinct epoch – growth dating back to the late eighteenth century and limited (except in significant partial effects) to economically developed countries.

In his Nobel lecture, Kuznets talked of six characteristics of modern economic growth that have emerged in the analysis of conventional estimates of national income and its components, population, labour force and the like. Two quantitative characteristics relate to aggregate growth rates, another two relate to structural transformation and the last two relate to international spread.

The first characteristic is the high rates of growth of per capita product and of population in the developed countries.

Second, the high rate of rise in productivity; that is, of output per unit of all inputs. The major productive factor, of course, is labour.

Third, the high rate of structural transformation; Kuznets discussed here the major aspects of structural change. They include a shift away from agriculture to non-agricultural pursuits, and 'recently' away from industry to services, a shift in the scale of productive units and a related change from small personal enterprise to "impersonal organization of economic firms, with a concomitant change in the occupational status of labour."

Fourth, rapid change in the closely related and significantly important structures of society and its ideology; for example, urbanisation and secularisation as components of what sociologists call the process of modernisation.

Fifth, the process of globalisation promoted by economically developed countries. The developed nations have been able to do this by means of increased power of technology, specifically in transport and communications.

Last, but not the least. The spread of modern economic growth (in spite of its partial effects around the world) is limited to economically developed countries. The economic performance of the rest of the world, which accounts for three quarters of world population, still falls short of the minimum levels feasible with the potential of modern technology.

Kuznets emphasised the inter-related aspect of these six characteristics. He illustrated such inter-relations among them and termed them as 'most significant.' He concluded: "Thus, modern economic growth reflects an inter-relation that sustains the high rate of advance through the feedback from mass applications to further knowledge. And unless some obstacle intervenes, it provides a mechanism for self-sustaining technological advance, to which, given the wide expanse of the universe (relative to mankind on this planet) there are no obvious proximate limits."

Dwelling on the situation in developing countries, Kuznets stated that two major factors appear to have limited the spread of modern economic growth to them.

1. Absence of a stable but flexible political and social framework capable of accommodating rapid structural change and resolving the conflicts that it generates, while encouraging growth-promoting groups in society.
2. Policies that developed countries have followed, ranging from the imposition of colonial status to other limitations on political freedom as a result of which developing countries have given top priority to achieving political independence rather than economic advance.

Kuznets, in his lecture, noted some interesting preliminary findings regarding developing countries.

The developing countries are characterised by specific common features such as a low per capita product, a large share of agriculture or other extractive industries and small-scale production units.

The developing countries suffer from a combination of greater backwardness and seemingly greater backlog of technology, which account for the significant differences between the growth position of the developing countries today and that of developed countries when they were entering the modern economic growth process.

Finally, modern technology with its emphasis on labour-saving inventions may not be appropriate and suitable to countries with abundant labour but a scarcity of other co-operant factors, such as land and water. Modern institutions may not be suited to the traditional patterns of life of agricultural communities predominating in the developing countries.

On the basis of his diagnostic analysis, Kuznets made a bold suggestion that for achieving a substantial economic advance, developing countries may have to bring in the available pool of material technology and "probably even greater innovations in political and social structures. It will not be a matter of merely borrowing existing tools, material and social; or of directly applying past patterns of growth, merely allowing for the difference in parameters. The innovational requirements are likely to be particularly great in the social and political structures."

After noting that the conventional measures of the national product and its components do not reflect many costs of adjustment in economic and social structures to the channelling of major technological innovations as also their positive returns, Kuznets commended the efforts being made by developing countries to expand the national accounting framework to take into account the so far hidden but important costs, for instance, in education as capital investment, in the shift to urban life in the pollution and other negative aspects of mass production. He believed these efforts will bring out some so far unmeasured positive returns, in the way of better health and greater longevity, grater labour mobility, more leisure and lower inequalities of income.

For the developing countries, however, he outlined different tasks of economic research. The imperative need is a wider supply of tested data, that is, data that have been scrutinised in the process of their use for economic analysis. The stock of data and of economic analysis is "far poorer for these countries than that for developed countries;" however, there has been in recent years, rapid accumulation of data for many of them. Kuznets observed that the lag has been in the analysis of these data by economists and other social science scholars. The economic research of the developing countries has to deal with "quantitative basis and institutional conditions of their performance, in addition to those concentrating on what appear to be their major bottlenecks and the seemingly optimal policy prescriptions."

44.3 CONCLUDING OBSERVATIONS

In his research, Kuznets had invariably aimed at imparting quantitative precision to those economic magnitudes that are necessary for understanding the processes of social development. Easterlin considers that Kuznets's work on national income played a crucial role "in the transition of economics from a deductive to a quantitative science. The transition required a union of theory, economic measurement and statistical methodology. In the 1930's, the new macroeconomic theories of...Keynes [and] Kuznets' concurrent and independent effort to develop measures of consumption, savings and investment components of national income provided the empirical counterparts of the Keynesian concepts. This advance in economic measurement and its concordance with new theoretical formulations was a key step in the development of econometrics."

Kuznets believed that it is important to make efforts to improve and strengthen empirical knowledge : "The time lag may be long between establishment of empirical findings and their absorption into tested theory....Yet...there is a clear need for more, not less, such empirical knowledge; longer, not shorter historical perspective; for a more detailed, not a more aggregated structuring of empirical evidence; for wider interspatial and inter- temporal comparisons rather than concentration on a single country and period."

44.4 SELECT BIBLIOGRAPHY OF KUZNETS'S WORKS

44.4.1 BOOKS

1926 Cyclical Fluctuations, Retail and Wholesale Trade, United States, 1919-1925, Adelphi, New York.

1930 Secular Movements in Production and Prices: Their Nature and their Bearing upon Cyclical Fluctuations, Houghton Mifflin, Boston, MA.

1933 Seasonal Variations in Industry and Trade, NBER Books, NBER, New York.

1934 a National Income, 1929-32, Senate Document No.124, 73rd Congress, Second Session, Government Printing Office, Washington D.C.

b Gross Capital Formation, 1919-1933, NBER Books, NBER, New York.

1937 National Income and Capital Formation, 1919-1935, NBER, New York.

1941 (Assisted by L. Epstein and E. Jenks), National Income and Its Composition, 1919-1938, 2 Vols., NBER, New York.

1945 (With Milton Friedman) Income from Independent Professional Practice, NBER, New York.

1946 a (Assisted by L. Epstein and E. Jenks), National Income since 1869, NBER, New York.

b National Income: A Summary of Findings, NBER, New York.

1953 a (Assisted by E. Jenks), Shares of Upper Income Groups in Income and Savings, NBER, New York.

b Economic Change: Selected Essays in Business Cycles, National Income and Economic Growth, W. W. Norton, New York.

1959 Six Lectures on Economic Growth, Free Press, Glencoe, Ill.

1961 (Assisted by E. Jenks), Capital in the American Economy: Its Formation and Financing, Princeton University Press, Princeton, NJ.

1965 Economic Growth and Structure: Selected Essays, W. W. Norton, New York.

1966 Modern Economic Growth: Rate, Structure, and Spread, Yale University Press, Newhaven, Conn.

1968 Towards a Theory of Economic Growth with Reflection on the Economic Growth of Modern Nations, W. W. Norton, New York.

1971 Economic Growth of Nations: Total Output and Production Structure, Harvard University Press, Cambridge, MA.

44.4.2 ARTICLES

1930 "Monetary Business Cycle Theory in Germany," JPE, Vol.38, pp.125-163.

1941 "Statistics and Economic History," JEH, Vol.1, No.1.

1947 "Measurement of Economic Growth," JEH, Vol.7, No.1.

1951 "The State as a Unit in Study of Economic Growth," JEH, Vol.11, No.1.

1952 "National Income Estimates for the United States Prior to 1870," JEH, Vol.12, No.2.

1973 "Modern Economic Growth: Findings and Reflections," AER, Vol.63, No.3.

1976 "Demographic Aspects of the Size Distribution of Income: An Essay," Econ Dev & Cult Chng, Vol.25, No.1.

1977 "Two Centuries of Economic Growth: Reflections on U.S. Experience," AER, Vol.67, No.1.

1980 "Driving Forces of Economic Growth: What Can We Learn from History?" Review of World Economics, Vol.116, No.3.

1982 "Children and Adults in the Income Distribution," Econ Dev & Cult Chng, Vol.30, No.4.

44.5 WORKS OF OTHERS

Easterlin, R. A. (1987) The New Palgrave: A Dictionary of Economics, Macmillan, London.

Lundberg, E. (1971) "Simon Kuznets' Contribution to Economics," Swedish JE, Vol.73, No.4.

CHAPTER 45

FRIEDRICH AUGUST VON HAYEK

(1899 – 1992)

Friedrich August von Hayek, who shared the 1974 Nobel Memorial Prize for Economic Sciences with Gunnar Myrdal, was credited with contributions in the field of economic theory. The Swedish Academy cites Hayek's analysis of the functional efficiency of different economic systems as one of his most significant contributions to economic research. He presented new ideas regarding basic difficulties in 'socialist calculating,' and investigated the possibilities of achieving effective results by decentralised 'market socialism.' While comparing various economic systems, his approach was to study how efficiently the knowledge and information disseminated among individuals and business enterprises were utilised. His prime conclusion was that only by far reaching decentralisation in a competitive market system characterised by free price-fixing is it possible to make effective and full use of knowledge and information.

Hayek's analyses of the competence of economic systems which were published in the 1940's and 50's provided significant impetus to the growing field of research in comparative economic systems. The Swedish Academy makes particular reference to Hayek's research on business cycles. His theory of business cycles and his exposition of the effects of monetary and credit policies on business cycles evoked much discussion and debate. He made strenuous attempts at penetrating more deeply into the mechanism of business cycles and was one of the few economists who sounded timely warning of the possibility of a major economic crisis before the onset of the great crash in the autumn of 1929. Hayek specifically showed how expansion of money supply, accompanied by lending which exceeded the rate of voluntary saving, could lead to a misallocation of resources, specifically impacting the capital structure.

45.1 A SHORT BIOGRAPHICAL NOTE: FRIEDRICH HAYEK

Hayek was born on May 8, 1899 in Vienna into an academic family. His father, Dr. August von Hayek was Professor of Botany at the University of Vienna. The junior Hayek entered the University of Vienna (following military service as an artillery officer in World War I), where he attended the lectures of Firedrich von Wieser, and obtained doctorates in law and political science. After spending a year for doing post-graduate work in New York University in 1923-1924, Hayek returned to Vienna where he joined the famous Private

Seminar conducted by Ludwig von Mises. In 1927, Hayek became the first Director of Austrian Institute for Trade Cycle Research.

On an invitation from Lionel Robbins, he lectured at the London School of Economics (LSE) in 1931 and subsequently he accepted the Tooke Chair in Economic Science and Statistics at the LSE, where he continued till 1950. During the 1930's, he actively participated in the contemporary debates in England in the fields of monetary theory, business cycle theory and capital theory. He was also one of the principal figures in the "celebrated controversies" with John Maynard Keynes, Frank Knight and Piero Sraffa. During the late 1930's and early 1940's, Hayek's research was focused on a number of important issues, such as role of knowledge and discovery in market processes and the methodological underpinnings of the Austrian School.

In 1950, Hayek shifted to the United States, joining the Committee on Social Thought at the University of Chicago, accepting Professorship of Social and Moral Science. He remained there till 1962 when he returned to Europe accepting Professorship first at the University of Freiburg, West Germany and then in 1969 at the University of Salzburg in Austria. He was visiting Professor at various dates at Universities such as Stanford, Virginia, Los Angeles (California) in the U.S. and Capetown in South Africa. He received honorary degrees from a few universities. He was Fellow of the British Academy (1944) and Honorary Fellow, London School of Economics (1972).

Hayek died in the year 1992.

45.2 A BRIEF SURVEY OF HAYEK'S CONTRIBUTION TO ECONOMICS

Hayek's scholarly output spans about seven decades and includes 18 books, 25 pamphlets, 235 articles and 16 books edited or introduced. While his contributions cover, besides economics, other social sciences, his writings in the field of economics are proposed to be surveyed here. These are covered under the following heads.

1. Economics as a Coordination Problem;
2. Price System as a Communication Network;
3. Monetary Theory and Trade Cycle Theory;
4. Inter-temporal Capital Structure;
5. Critique of Keynes's Theory and Policy; and
6. Methodological Issues.

45.2.1 ECONOMICS AS A COORDINATION PROBLEM

A central concern of economic theory has been the analysis of efficiency in the context of resource allocation. It is a crucial element of modern microeconomic theory. The provision of goods and services to satisfy human wants is considered the end of all economic action. The supply of goods and services through production and exchange is constrained by technology and scarcity of resources in an economy. In this context, efficiency connotes "going as far as possible" in the satisfaction of wants within the constraints of resources and technology, expressed by Pareto optimality. Since knowledge about human wants, technology and resources is widely dispersed, efficient outcomes can be realised only by coordination of economic activity.

According to O'Driscoll, Hayek's writings reflected his general conception of economics as a coordination problem. Hayek in his 1945 American Economic Review article emphasised the role of knowledge or information, particularly in the context of prices and markets in coordinating economic activity. A careful study of market economies reveals that they are characterised by a more complex and intricate order than can be explained in terms of deliberate efforts to realise coordination among individual activities. Hayek pointed out that the institutional mechanism of markets and prices performs the function of communicating information dispersed among economic agents so as to bring about coordinated economic action. Hayek contended that a large part of modern economics fails to understand the nature of economic problem facing society by ignoring the problems raised by the fact of dispersed information. Hayek observed that it is the existence of the "spontaneous order" that provides the subject matter of economics.

However, market economies are not fully coordinated which gives rise to the coordination problem. That the plans of consumers and producers of a particular good are not adequately coordinated is evidenced by an oversupply of or excess demand for that good. Sometimes it is noticed that there are significant economy-wide failures in market economies. Hayek had focussed his early research on identifying the circumstances or "the sequence of events" that could give rise to such failures--what he calls inter-temporal discoordinations over time compared to coordination in a given period of time. It is obviously difficult to coordinate individual activities. In an economy, production takes time; as such, producers must take decisions now in anticipation of decisions of other producers and ultimately the consumers will make in future. This introduction of the element of time may enhance the possibility of "erroneous" investment decisions and may lead to "cumulative investment errors." A number of inter-temporally discoordinated investments, caused by disturbances of monetary or real nature will create a boom. An eventual detection of the discoordination, will cause a bust.

The study of business cycles by Hayek adopted a two-pronged approach. Dealing with the issue of economy-wide failure of coordination, Hayek remarked: "before we explain why people commit mistakes, we must first explain why they should ever be right." He attempted at delineating the role of price system as a communication network and as an efficient user of economic information. Hayek had to extend monetary theory so as to include relative price effects associated with changes in money supply. Likewise, he had to modify capital theory to take into account inter-temporal substitutability and complementarity of individual elements of the capital structure. Thus, Hayek had contributed substantially to these three fields of study. His outstanding achievement, however, lay in his integration of the three fields, i.e. price theory, monetary theory and capital theory and put forward a cohesive account of a market process "that tends towards inter-temporal coordination and of central bank policies that can interfere with that process in such a way as to cause artificial economic booms which are inevitably followed by economic busts." Edmund Phelps draws our attention to Hayek's 1928 article in German language in which the concept of inter-temporal equilibrium was introduced. In that article Hayek drew an analogy between inter-temporal trade and the national (or inter-spatial) trade; prices of the same thing at two different times or places are not generally equal; though they may be pushed up or pulled down together.

45.2.2 PRICE SYSTEM AS A COMMUNICATION NETWORK

Hayek emphasised the important role the price system plays in promoting social well-being by its ability to transmit information from one segment of the market to another. The information contained in prices results from market competition. Competition is thus a discovery process. As the information is dispersed throughout the society (as mentioned above), the need for such a communication network is clear. The nature of prices as market signals, as stressed by Hayek, has come to be widely recognised.

In his discussions regarding the use of knowledge in society, Hayek talked of two kinds of knowledge. The first category is the scientific or technical knowledge with which the economist is concerned. The second one with which the market participants are concerned relates to the particular circumstances of time and place. According to him, failure to recognise this important "division of knowledge" can lead to erroneous conclusion either that the "rational planning" can perform better than or as well as the market itself or that "rational expectations" can nullify the systematic effects of changes in monetary policy.

Hayek recognised that a fully adjusted system of equilibrium prices must depend on a prior groping process of market discovery. According to him, markets are not in equilibrium; the free market competitive process involves continuous flux: such a process results in the discovery of possibilities and preferences. These insights of Hayek concerning knowledge and process of market discovery have profound influence on the development of economic theory since then. As one perceptive observer comments: "The tremendous drift away from macroeconomic controls and policies to allowing the micro processes to lead to their own aggregate results is also in a way a tribute to Hayek's perception." He was foremost a defender of freedom and decentralisation.

45.2.3 MONETARY THEORY AND TRADE CYCLE THEORY

Hayek's monetary theory attempted at integrating the function of money as a medium of exchange with the idea of the price system as a communication network. In his business cycle theory, Hayek aimed at integrating monetary theory with his capital theory in which was emphasised the system of inter-temporal prices, a particular aspect of the price system. He argued against the received doctrine that the focus of the monetary theory is on the relationship between the quantity of money and the general price level. Instead, he argued in favour of moving beyond proportionality explanation implying a relatively stable velocity of circulation of money.

Hayek introduced the well-known concept of "neutral money" which characterises a monetary system in which money facilitates the coordination of economic activities without itself being a source of discoordination. He argued that neutrality of money requires the absence of what he called "injection effects." The injection of new money resulting in a rise in the quantity of money temporarily distorts relative prices making the price system communicate information, about consumer preferences and resource availabilities, which turns out to be false. Hayek's assessment of the U.S. monetary policy during the prosperous decade of 1920's that the injection of new money through credit markets must result in resources misallocation despite near-constant price level had prompted him to predict that the "money-induced boom would eventually lead to a bust."

Hayek's theory of trade cycle was based upon the idea that injections of new money can have a systematic effect on the inter-temporal pattern of prices. The Austrian theory of trade cycle was first formulated by Mises in 1912. The main contribution of Hayek to the theory in his 1935 work Prices and Production was founded upon the time consuming production process. The components of the structure of production consists of time dimension of the production structure or the degree of roundaboutness of production, money value of the consumer goods resulting from the production process, stages of production and the money value of the incomplete production process. The actions of entrepreneurs influenced by price signals result in allocation of resources among different stages of production.

However, because of the distinct temporal dimension of the production structure, the supplies of and demands for resources connected with different stages of production are "differentially sensitive" to interest rate changes. Hayek made a vital distinction between changes in interest rate emanating from changes in inter-temporal preferences of consumers and changes in interest rates attributable to the policy of a central bank. In the first case, actions of business and the consequential changes in the price pattern permit the production structure to be modified in line with altered preferences of consumers. In the latter case, however, similar changes in the price pattern brought about by injection of new money through credit markets denote false 'signals' leading to a resources misallocation among the stages of production. As a result of (artificially) low rate of interest caused by injection of new money through credit markets, an unsustainable boom is created. In the conditions of boom, too many resources are allocated to the early stages of production resulting in starting of more production projects than can possibly be completed. However, this cannot last and what Hayek called a 'self reversing process' ensues, characterised by scarcity of resources turning the artificial boom created by injection of new money into a bust.

The subsequent economic recovery is accompanied by liquidation of 'malinvestments' and reallocation of resources in line with actual inter- temporal preferences and resource availabilities. Thus, Hayek observed that expectations about future interest rate changes and interpretations of inter- temporal price movements by entrepreneurs would have significant impact on the course of the trade cycle. In essence, "prices are signals, not marching orders" as remarked by Garrison and Kirzner. They further point out: "...Hayek did not assume, as some modern economists do, that falsified price signals plus 'rational' expectations are equivalent to unfalsified signals: such an equivalence would require that market participants make use of knowledge of the kind that they cannot plausibly possess."

45.2.4 INTER-TEMPORAL CAPITAL STRUCTURE

Fritz Machlup evaluated Hayek's contribution to the development of capital theory as his fundamental and path- breaking achievement. It is commonly agreed that Hayek's 1928 work (in German, translated into English by Hayek himself and published in 1984) Inter Temporal Price Equilibrium and Movements in the Value of Money inspired many subsequent contributions by economists in this area, most importantly those of Sir John Hicks.

In his 1935 work, Prices and Production, Hayek put forward the concept of triangles for describing the changes in the inter-temporal pattern of capital structure. The problem of inter- temporal coordination is that it gains particular significance because of two factors--the important element of time involved in the production process of the economy and the complexities embedded in the structure of capital. Producers must draw up production plans which require the commitment of resources now by individual producers. These plans must be mutually compatible and jointly consistent with the availability of resources. The market process characterised by implementation of his plan by each producer determines as to how far such mutual compatibility of plans and the consistency of the plans with the resource availability actually exists. The degree of inter-temporal coordination or discoordination of the capital structure is revealed only when each producer tries to secure additional capital required to execute his plan and with the passage of time. If discoordination is found out by some producers, they have to revise their production plans.

Hayek had thrown further light on the subject in his 1941 publication, Pure Theory of Capital. In this work, he elaborated the characteristics of capital goods in terms of reproducibility, durability, specificity, substitutability and complementarity and how the relationships among them determine the whole structure of production to be characterised by a longer or shorter period of production, a greater or lesser degree of "roundaboutness." The market rate of interest determines the degree of "roundaboutness" of production, "the extent to which the production process ties up resources over time." Hayek conceived the market rate of interest as the terms of trade between present goods and future goods, or goods that will be available in the future. Inter- temporal preferences of market participants are translated into production plans by the market process. For example, an increased willingness of public to forgo present goods for future goods, resulting in a fall in the rate of interest, prompts producers to adopt more roundabout production processes.

45.2.5 CRITIQUE OF KEYNES'S THEORY AND POLICY

Hayek found fault with Keynes for the latter's failure to identify the market process that could bring about inter-temporal coordination. Hayek commented: "Mr. Keynes's aggregates conceal the most fundamental mechanism of change." Keynes, by emphasising the characteristics of money as a liquid asset rather than on money's function as a medium of exchange, could not see the harm caused by expansion of money supply through policies of injecting new money through credit creation or direct spending on public projects through fiscal policy measures. Hayek underlined the function of money as a medium of exchange, money constituting "a kind of loose joint in a self-equilibrating apparatus of the price mechanism which is bound to impede its working – the more so, the greater the play in the loose joint" and sounded a warning in regard to Keynesianism that "the existence of such a loose joint is no justification for concentrating attention on that loose joint and disregarding the rest of the mechanism, and still less making the great possible use of short-lived freedom from economic necessity which the existence of this loose joint permits."

Garrison and Kirzner making a brief survey of the subsequent developments remark: "In the decades that followed the debate between Hayek and Keynes, economic theory was dominated by Keynesianism and the corresponding macroeconomic policies consisted precisely of those measures that Hayek had warned against: monetary manipulation for political advantage.... The political exploitation of the monetary loose joint contains an inherent inflationary bias.... Monetary injections through the commercial banking system can stimulate the economy by triggering an artificial boom...the cumulative effects of the play-off between political advantage and economic necessity is the theme of Hayek's critique to Keynesianism."

45.2.6 METHODOLOGICAL ISSUES

Hayek's perception of the subject-matter of economics, i.e., economic phenomena as spontaneous order was reflected in his methodological norms. According to him, fundamental institutions in society reflected the "results of human action but not of human design." The outstanding example of spontaneous order is the use of money, the most commonly accepted medium of exchange. There would be no scope and need for social sciences if the only order in society is consciously designed. The task of social sciences in a world of spontaneous order is to explain those aspects of the social order that were not consciously designed.

Hayek was not in favour of applying uncritically the methods of physical sciences to the phenomena of social sciences – he employs the terms 'scientism' for such 'inappropriate' use. In his 1952 book, The Counter-revolution of Science: Studies on the Abuse of Reason, he advocated the case of subjectivism and methodological individualism in the social sciences in these words: "It is probably no exaggeration to say that every important advance in economic theory during the last hundred years was a further step in the consistent application of subjectivism." While classical economists had concentrated on the objects being valued, the Austrian school of economists especially Menger, Mises and Hayek shifted the focus to the subjects engaged in valuation. Hayek's subjectivist outlook and his consistent adherence to the rules of methodological individualism are 'mutually reinforcing.' In Hayek's own words: "it is the concepts and the views held by individuals which are directly known to us and which form elements from which we must build up, as it were, the more complex phenomena."

45.3 CONCLUDING OBSERVATIONS

Hayek made important contributions to other social sciences too. He qualified at Vienna in Law and Economics. His 'transmutation' into a philosopher was relatively straight forward. His anglophilia explains many of the implicit assumptions of his work, particularly in The Road to Serfdom — 'an important and scholarly book.' Hayek's fundamental moral standard was freedom as was pointed out by D.P.O. Brien. According to Hayek it was freedom, which allowed the development of social organization as well as economic organisation and of individuals within a society and protected individuals from the threat of a government's arbitrary action. He was clearly of the view that the essence of rules of just conduct in a society was that all power should be limited. When people pursued their own ends subject to such rules, a spontaneous order is the result.

Hayek recognised a substantial legitimate role for government and even advocated that government should provide a wide range of public goods. He even discussed such important issues as market failure and externalities. He was against overall tax burden being progressive though he did not rule out individual taxes, such as income tax, being progressive. Hayek's approach to government regulation of private sector was that such regulation should be according to rules and not a matter of discretion. As such, he rejected price controls since they are necessarily discretionary. In contrast, factory legislation was perfectly acceptable to him.

In Law, Legislation and Liberty, Hayek put forward proposals for 'denationalisation' of the money supply, particularly because government had 'shamelessly abused' the money supply in order to obtain command over real resources. He suggested that control over money supply should be removed from the purview of government. While this proposal of Hayek was 'remarkably short of detail' and largely controversial, O'Brien sees an important point to be noted. The proposal may have helped to strengthen the case of those who have advocated independence of central banks from government. As a matter of fact, recent research has demonstrated a negative association between the degree of independence of a central bank and the propensity of government to debase the currency.

It is very necessary to mention here that in 2011, Hayek's article "The Use of Knowledge in Society" was selected as one of the top 20 articles published in The American Economic Review during its first 100 years.

Sylvia Nasar in her book "Grand Pursuit: The Story of Economic Genius" comments: "In 1974, the Swedish Academy of Sciences plucked Hayek out of obscurity by awarding him a Nobel Prize.... Ironically, he shared it with Swedish socialist Gunnar Myrdal.... In the early 1990s, the collapse of the Soviet Union and the spread of free market reforms in Eastern Europe and Asia made him a hero among conservatives around the globe."

45.4 SELECT BIBLIOGRAPHY OF HAYEK'S WORKS

45.4.1 BOOKS

1941 The Pure Theory of Capital, University of Chicago Press, Chicago, Ill.

1944 The Road to Serfdom, University of Chicago Press, Chicago, Ill.

1949 Individual and Economic Order, Routledge and Kegan Paul, London.

1952 The Counter-Revolution of Science: Studies on the Abuse of Reason, Free Press, Glencoe, Ill.

1967 Prices and Production, 2nd edition, Auguustus M. Kelley, New York.

1972 The Constitution of Liberty, Henry Regnery & Co, Chicago, Ill.

1975 a Monetary Theory and the Trade Cycle, A.M. Kelley, New York.

b Profits, Interest and Investment, A. M. Kelley, New York.

1976 Denationalization of Money, Institute of Economic Affairs, London.

1984 a Money, Capital and Fluctuations: Early Essays, R. McCloughly (ed.), University of Chicago Press, Chicago, Ill.

1989 The Collected Works of F.A. Hayek (W. W. Bartley et.al.) University of Chicago Press, Chicago, Ill.

45.4.2 ARTICLES

1931, 1932 "Reflections on the Pure Theory of Money of Mr. J M Keynes I-II," Economica, August 1931 and February 1932.

1937 "Economics and Knowledge," Economica, (n.s.), Vol.4, Feb.

1945 "The Use of Knowledge in Society", AER, Vol. 35, No. 4.

1968 "Competition as a Discovery Procedure," in New Studies in Philosophy, Politics, Economics and the History of Ideas, University of Chicago Press, Chicago.

1984 "The Future Monetary Unit of Value," in Money in Crisis: The Federal Reserve, the Economy and Monetary Reform, B. Siegel (ed.), Ballinger, MA.

45.5 WORKS OF OTHERS

Garriison R. W. and I. M. Kirzner (1987), The New Palgrave: A Dictionary of Economics, Macmillan, London.

Machlup, F. (1976), "Hayek's Contribution to Economics," in Essays on Hayek, F. Machlup (ed.), Hillsdale College Press, Hillsdale, Mich.

Nasar, S. (2011), Grand Pursuit: The Story of Economic Genius, Fourth Estate, London.

O'Driscoll, G. (1977), Economics As a Coordination Problem: The Contribution of Friedirch A. Hayek, Sheed Andrews & McMeel, Kansas City.

CHAPTER 46

GUNNAR MYRDAL

(1898 – 1987)

The Royal Swedish Academy of Sciences awarded the 1974 prize for Economic Sciences in memory of Alfred Nobel jointly to Professor Gunnar Myrdal and Professor Friedrich von Hayek "for their pioneering work in the theory of money and econopmic fluctuations and for their penetrating analysis of the interdependence of economic, social and institutional phenomena." In the estimation of the Academy, Myrdal and von Hayek have not only significantly contributed to central economic theory but also successfully carried out important interdisciplinary research. They both started their research careers with important contributions in the field of pure economic theory – in the fields of the theory of economic fluctuations and monetary theory. Thereafter, they have widened their research horizons to include broad aspects relating to social and institutional phenomena.

Specifically, Myrdal had sought to link economic analysis to such important concerns as social, demographic and institutional conditions. This is particularly seen in Myrdal's in depth study of Negro problem in the USA and the poverty of the developing countries. Hayek had extended his field of study to encompass questions relating to the legal framework of economic systems as also issues embracing the way of functioning of social systems, organisations and individuals. As both Myrdal and Hayek were deeply interested in economic policy problems, they extended their studies to include changes in the organisational, institutional and legal conditions prevailing in contemporary societies. One of the prime consequences of the above-mentioned widening of their research horizon and of their well-documented ability to find new and original ways of posing questions and putting forward new ideas on causes and policies, is their being controversial.

In the present chapter, we undertake a review of prime contributions of Myrdal to economic science, which brought him the award; Hayek's contribution is summarised in the preceding chapter.

46.1 A BRIEF BIOGRAPHICAL NOTE: GUNNAR MYRDAL

Gunnar Myrdal was born in Gustaf's parish, Sweden, on December 6, 1898. He graduated from the Law School of Stockholm University in 1923 and began practising law while continuing his studies at the university. He received his juris doctor degree in economics in 1927. He was a student of giant figures in economics, Knut Wicksell, David Davidson, Eli

Heckscher and above all Gustav Cassel. His personal friendship was warmest with Cassel to whose chair (Lars Hierta Chair) of Political Economy and Public Finance at Stockholm University he succeeded in 1939.

From 1925 to 1929 he studied in Germany and Britain, followed by his first trip to the United States in 1929-1930 as a Rockefeller Fellow, following the crash of 1929. On his return to Europe, Myrdal first served for one year as Associate Professor in the Post Graduate Institute of International Studies, Geneva, Switzerland. After his appointment to Lar Hierta Chair at the University of Stockholm he, with his wife Alva, became active in Swedish politics. Gunnar Myrdal was elected to the Senate as member of the Social Democratic Party. Together they pioneered the modern population policy. His involvement in Swedish politics between 1931 and 1938 turned him from a theoretical economist into a political economist and what he himself describes as an 'institutionalist.'

In 1938, the Carnegie Corporation of New York commissioned Myrdal to direct a major investigation of the Negro problem in America, a project which resulted in the volume An American Dilemma: The Negro Problem and Modern Democracy, published in 1944. He returned to Sweden in 1942 and got involved in politics for a period of five years. He was re-elected to Swedish Senate in 1942, served as a member of the Board of the Bank of Sweden, and was Chairman of the Post-war Planning Commission. From 1945 to 1947, Myrdal was Sweden's Minister for Trade and Commerce. As minister, he arranged for a highly controversial treaty with the then Soviet Union. In 1947, he became Executive Secretary of the United Nations Economic Commission for Europe. After a decade with the Commission in Geneva, he embarked on a ten-year comprehensive study of economic trends and policies in South Asian countries for the Twentieth Century Fund, the result of which was the monumental Asian Drama: An Inquiry into the Poverty of Nations and The Challenge of World Poverty: A World Anti-poverty Program in Outline.

Myrdal was appointed Professor of International Economics at the Stockholm University in 1961 in which year he founded the Institute for International Studies at the University. He was Chairman of the Stockholm International Peace Research Institute (SIPRI). During the year 1973-1974, he was visiting Research Fellow at the Center for Study of Democratic Institutions at Santa Barbara, California, and during the next year Distinguished Professor at New York University. Myrdal was recipient of more than thirty honorary degrees including Harvard University in 1938. He received many awards and prizes. He was member of the British Academy, American Academy of Arts and Sciences, Fellow of the Econometric Society and honorary member of American Economic Association.

Gunnar Myrdal was married to Alva Reimer who held high posts in the UNO and UNESCO and was Swedish Ambassador to India. Myrdal died in the year 1987.

46.2 MYRDAL'S MAJOR CONTRIBUTIONS TO ECONOMICS

Throughout his life, Myrdal devoted his attention to methodological questions. We can see his concern for them in Myrdal's early work Political Element in the Development of Economic Theory. In his doctoral dissertation on price formation and economic change,

Myrdal systematically brought in the concept of expectations into the analysis of prices, profits and changes in value of capital. His microeconomic analysis dealt with planning by firms. In his work on macroeconomics, for example Monetary Equilibrium, he employed some of these ideas.

A common thread running through his three important works, namely, The Political Element in the Development of Economic Theory, An American Dilemma; The Negro Problem and Modern Democracy, and Asian Drama: An Inquiry into the Poverty of Nations, is his effort to "purge" economic thinking of systematic biases and his stress on realistic and relevant research.

His ideas can be surveyed around the following three themes.

1. Notion of Cumulative Circular Causation;
2. Rejection of faith in Lassiez-faire; and
3. Introduction of the Concepts of ex-ante and ex-post.

46.2.1 CUMULATIVE CIRCULAR CAUSATION

Myrdal believed that no social science is adequately equipped for making a comprehensive study of any social problem. For the purpose of understanding social behaviour of individuals one has to analyse together a number of factors – economic, sociological, legal, historical and psychological forces. Thus, social development cannot be analysed by using any one factor as the prime determinant.

Paul Streeten traces the circular or cumulative causation to Wicksell who, in Interest and Prices, had analysed divergence between the natural and the market rates of interest in terms of upward or downward cumulative processes, until the elimination of the divergence. The concept of vicious or virtuous circle was used by Myrdal synonymously with cumulative circular causation. Myrdal's analysis implied that any action exercised on one variable will not only affect that variable but also has spread effects on other variables, which, in turn, have a backwash effect or feedback effect on the former. Thus, the aggregate effect of an initial action on one variable is cumulated by taking account of the spread and backwash effects through several rounds. This cumulative process involves time dimension. It is suggested that a simultaneous action on each variable producing upward effects is perhaps more effective than relatively strong action on a single variable. The magnitude of the aggregate effect depends, of course, on circular effects therefrom. Myrdal also argued that in social sciences, while studying a change, the distinction between a determinate variable and determinant variable was not valid.

By using the Principle of Cumulative Causation, one can show movements away from a position of equilibrium as an outcome of the interaction of several variables. While some writers have suggested that any form of circular causation is cumulative and hence disequilibrating, in Myrdal's opinion this need not be so. A series of mutually caused events may, after a disturbance, quickly converge on the initial or some other point of stable equilibrium. For example, an increase in consumption, by increasing the aggregate demand will raise incomes which, in turn, will raise consumption and so on. However, as long as the marginal propensity to consume is less than one, the infinite series will converge on a finite value.

Myrdal applied the idea of cumulative causation fruitfully to price expectations and to the relations between regions. He demonstrated the manner in which the advantages of 'growth poles' can become cumulative, while the backward region may remain relatively or, in some case, even absolutely impoverished. Myrdal applied the notion to sociological variables, such as the prejudices against blacks in the U.S. and their performance levels (low skills, crime, disease, etc), to economic variables; and to the interaction of economic and non-economic variables. He argued that the inclusion of non-economic variables in the analysis "opens up the possibility of numerous cumulative processes" which conventional economic analysis could not capture. It also guards against uni-causal explanations. Paul Streeten states: "The revolutionary character of the concept of cumulative causation is brought out by the fact that the interaction takes place not only within a social system in which the various elements interact, but also in time, so that memory and expectations are of crucial importance." The history of a variable determines the responses to any given variable. What distinguishes Myrdal's approach from that of general equilibrium economists is this dynamic feature of his analysis and its implications for policy.

Myrdal made use of the concepts 'backwash' and 'spread' effects in his Economic Theory and Underdeveloped Regions and also in Asian Drama to analyse the movement of regions or whole countries at different stages of development and the effects of unification.

46.2.2 REJECTION OF LAISSEZ-FAIRE

Another major contribution of Myrdal was his rejection of faith in laissez-faire or market process. He did not believe that the market process would lead to total social development, particularly in underdeveloped countries. Government interventions at several points continuously are necessary for underdeveloped countries to move up. For bringing about "induced change" in the underdeveloped countries, he introduced the notion of what he called 'social engineering' as an instrument.

Myrdal underlined, like Marxists, the unequal distribution of power and property as hindrance to equity as well as efficiency and growth. In the words of Paul Streeten: "He [Myrdal] regards a direct planning of institutions and shaping of attitudes (what Marx regarded as part of the super structure) as necessary, though very difficult, partly because he believes that attitudes and institutions are inert, and partly because the policies which aim at reforming attitudes and institutions are themselves part of the social systems, part of the power and property structure." In Asian Drama, he called the kind of government functioning in the underdeveloped countries as 'soft state.' They are 'soft' in the sense they are not willing to resort to coercion for the purpose of implementing declared policy goals. He ascribed this tendency to two factors – first, a gap between real intentions and declared professions and, second, reflection of the extant power structure. He wanted the underdeveloped countries to be transformed from 'soft states' to socially disciplined hard states.

In the analysis of the simultaneous existence of inflationary situation and widespread unemployment in developed countries in the west in the 1970s, Myrdal termed it a situation of 'stagflation,' one of the first to use the term. He cited a number of factors which contributed to this situation. They are the market structure, methods of oligopoly pricing, organisation of producers as pressure groups, relatively comparative weakness of consumer groups, the tax system which encourages speculative expenditures, and so on. He considered inflation as a socially highly divisive force.

Myrdal is opposed to the approach of capitalist laissez- faire as well as the then Soviet system. Myrdal's view put forward in both Asian Drama and An American Dilemma is that when there is a conflict between ideals and reality, one of them must give way whereas traditional economic theory attempts at concealing that conflict.

46.2.3 EX-ANTE AND EX-POST CONCEPTS

The lack of distinction between anticipation and results had caused considerable confusion in economic theory. Ex-ante and ex-post concepts are the most popular terminological innovations developed by the famous Stockholm School in 1930s which helped clear the confusion to a large extent. Myrdal is credited with the development of these concepts and introducing them into macroeconomic theory that has helped clarify the discussion of savings, investment and income and their impact on prices in an economy. Ex-ante savings or planned savings can diverge from planned investment. After the event or ex-post, they must be identical since the community can save only by accumulating real assets. It is the process by which anticipations are adjusted so as to bring about the book-keeping identity ex-post that explains un-anticipated gains and unexpected losses as also fluctuations in prices. Ex-ante savings are equal to ex-ante investment only in equilibrium.

Paul Streeten emphasises: "By bringing in expectations into the analysis of economic processes, Myrdal made a significant contribution to freeing economics from the shackles of static theory in which the picture is like the past." Myrdal thus paved the way for economic dynamics, in which time, uncertainty and expectations enter in an important way. The popularisation of the method of ex-ante and ex-post is due to Bert Ohlin's seminal article in the Economic Journal, 1937, which made it generally accepted over the whole world "with a rapidity unusual to economics."

46.3 CONCLUDING OBSERVATIONS

Apart from his work on expectations, on racial problems and problems of underdeveloped regions, Myrdal is best known for his critique of mainstream economic theory. His criticism of conventional economic theory ran on five lines. First, his appeal for realism in the sense of what he called 'opportunistic ignorance' – ignoring relevant issues and selecting largely irrelevant issues. Second, the conventional theory's definitions of economic development, economic growth and welfare. Third, narrow definitions and limits of disciplines. Myrdal advocated institutional approach for the purpose of bringing to bear all relevant knowledge and techniques on the analysis of a problem. Fourth, spurious objectivity. That is, concealment of political valuations and interests under the mask of scientific analysis. Fifth and last, his criticism of biases and twisted terminology.

In his Nobel Prize lecture titled "The Equality Issue in World Development" in which Myrdal dwelt upon the economic, financial, social, psychological and political conditioning of our thinking about the issue, which, he said, is "at bottom, a moral issue." Going over the issues that he studied since 1930's and tracing the recent developments on those issues, he approvingly quoted what he asserted in the middle of 1950's in the volume primarily on redistribution of wealth and income. "Indeed, aid can only be a very small part of a rational international equalization program.... None of the schemes which have been propounded for capital aid for development of underdeveloped countries has ever amounted to taking away more than a tiny fraction of the yearly increase of national income per head in the rich countries, which implied that no real solution has ever been envisaged. A wholesale income equalization by redistribution between nations is both impossible and, I am inclined to believe, an unimportant objective."

In the current world situation, Myrdal asserted, there are certainly "moral and rational reasons for a new world order and, to begin with, for aid on a strikingly much higher level. In particular, people in the rich countries should be challenged to bring down their lavish food consumption.... The blunt truth is that without rather radical changes in the consumption patterns in the rich countries, any pious talk about a new world economic order is humbug."

Myrdal's prescription was that the developing countries have to bring about fundamental changes in the conditions in which they are living and working which imply both greater equality and increased productivity at the same time. "To these imperatively needed radical changes belong, first, land reform, but also a fundamental redirection of education and health work. And the 'soft state' must be made efficient, and corruption, which is now almost everywhere increasing, must be exterminated on all levels."

46.4 SELECT BIBLIOGRAPHY OF MYRDAL'S WORKS

46.4.1 BOOKS

1939 Monetary Equilibrium, Hodge, London.

1940 Population: A Problem for Democracy, Harvard University Press, Cambridge, MA.

1944 An American Dilemma: The Negro Problem and Modern Democracy, Harper, New York. (Paperback Edition, McGraw-Hill, New York, 1964).

1953 The Political Element in the Development of Economic Theory, Trans P. Streeten, Routledge & Kegan Paul, London.

1956 a Development and Underdevelopment: A Note on the Mechanism of National and International Inequality, National Bank of Egypt, Cairo.

b An International Economy: Problems and Prospects, Routledge & Kegan Paul, London.

1957 Economic Theory and Underdeveloped Regions, Duckworth, London.

1958 Value in Social Theory: A Selection of Essays in Methodology, P. Streeten (ed.), Routledge & Kegan Paul, London.

1968 An Asian Drama: An Inquiry into the Poverty of Nations, Twentieth Century Fund, New York.

1970 The Challenge of World Poverty: A World Anti-Poverty Program in Outline, Pantheon, New York.

1972 Against the Stream: Critical Essays in Economics, Pantheon, New York.

46.4.2 ARTICLES

1970 "The 'Soft State' in Underdeveloped Countries," in Unfashionable Economics, P. Streeten (ed.), Weidenfeld and Nicholson, London.

1974 "The Equality Issue in World Development," Nobel Lecture, Nobel Lectures Economics, 1969-1980, Ed. Assar Lindbeck(ed.), World Scientific Publishing Co., Singapore, 1992.

46.5 WORKS OF OTHERS

Streeten, P. (1987) "Myrdal, G.," The New Palgrave: A Dictionary of Modern Economics, Macmillan, London.

CHAPTER 47

HERBERT ALEXANDER SIMON

(1916 – 2001)

The 1978 Alfred Nobel Memorial Prize in Economic Sciences was awarded by the Royal Swedish Academy of Sciences to Professor Herbert A. Simon, Carnegie-Mellon University, Pittsburgh, Pennsylvania, U.S.A., "for his pioneering research into the decision-making process within economic organizations."

Simon's research interests and scientific output go far beyond the disciplines in which he held academic positions (professorships), namely political science, administration, psychology, computer science and artificial intelligence. He is universally regarded as one of the founders of Artificial Intelligence. He had conducted research and made contributions in a number of fields – theory of science, applied mathematics, statistics, operations analysis, business administration, besides economics. Simon's development of ideas in these fields helped other researchers to use those ideas as a basis for empirical research. The Nobel Award Committee specifically states that "he is, first and foremost, an economist – in the widest sense of the word." Most of all, his name is associated with publications on "structure and decision-making within economic organizations, a relatively new area of economic research."

In traditional economics and economic studies, no distinction was drawn between enterprises and entrepreneurs. Further, it was assumed that enterprises or entrepreneurs had a single goal: maximisation of profit. The main purpose of this "classic and rather rudimentary theory of the firm" was to serve as a basis for studies of aggregate market behaviour – not of the behaviour of individual firms. As long as these firms are small, patriarchally run units, their activities rather remained relatively uninteresting. However, as enterprises, firms and corporates grew in size, operating them became more and more separated from owning them – divergence of ownership from management and control. In addition, as employees began to form labour unions, as the rate of expansion increased and as price competition between many producers was replaced by competition in regard to quality and service between a few, the behaviour of individual companies "attained quite another degree of interest."

Influenced by the organisational research that was being conducted in other social sciences in the 1930s, economists began to look at the structure of corporates and the process of decision-making in companies in an entirely new manner. For their new line of development in economics, Simon's work was of the utmost importance. In his epoch-making book, Administrative Behavior and in a number of subsequent works, Simon described the company as an "adaptive system of physical, personal and social components that are held together by a network of inter-communications and by the willingness of its members to cooperate and to strive towards a common goal." The most important idea characterising Simon's work was his rejection of the assumption made in classical theory of the firm as an omniscient, rational, profit-maximising entrepreneur. He replaced this entrepreneur by a number of cooperating decision-makers, whose capacities for rational action are limited both by a lack of knowledge about the total consequences of their decisions and by personal and social ties. Since these decision-makers cannot choose the best alternative, as can the entrepreneur in the classical theory, they have to be content with a satisfactory alternative. Therefore, individual corporates, according to Simon, strive not to maximise profits but to find acceptable solutions to acute problems. This might mean reaching, at the same time, a number of partly contradictory goals. Each decision-maker in such a company attempts to find a satisfactory solution to his set of problems and takes into consideration how others are solving them.

In the Nobel Memorial presentation speech Professor Sune Carlson summarises the essence of Simon's contribution: Herbert Simon has questioned the appropriateness of classical approach that assumes "a lone decision-maker with infallible foresight, with complete rationality and with profit-maximization as his permanent aim. He argued that a study of the structure and the decision-making of a firm is important. Simon's work has been of the most importance in this new line of development."

Simon's theories and observations regarding decision-making in organisations apply remarkably well to the systems and techniques of planning, and budgeting and control that are used in modern business and public administration. The award citation concedes that these theories of Simon may be less elegant and less suited to overall economic analysis than the classic profit-maximising theory. But they provide greater possibilities for understanding and prediction in a number of areas. They have been used extensively to explain and predict such diverse activities as the distribution of access to information and decision-making within corporate organisations, market adjustment to limited competition, choice of investment portfolios and choice of a country in which to establish a foreign investment. Modern business economics and administrative research are largely based on Simon's ideas.

While Simon was awarded 1978 prize in economics for his research into the process of decision-making within economic organisations, he had also made other notable contributions to economic science. For example, his interest in simplifying and understanding situations involving complex decision-making had led him at an early stage to the problem of breaking down complex equation systems. His studies of "causal order" in such systems have been of immense importance.

47.1 A SHORT BIOGRAPHICAL NOTE: HERBERT SIMON

Herbert Alexander Simon was born in Milwaukee, Wisconsin, U.S.A., on June 15, 1916. His father, after earning his electrical engineering diploma in Germany, migrated to the United States in 1903. After completing school education in Milwaukee, Simon entered University of Chicago in 1933. Simon thought that social sciences "need the same kind of rigor and the same mathematical underpinnings that had made the 'hard' sciences so brilliantly successful, I would prepare myself to become a mathematical social scientist." His most "important mentor" at Chicago was the econometrician and mathematical economist, Henry Schultz.

Simon's career was "settled at least as much by drift as by choice." An undergraduate field study for a term paper developed his interest in decision-making in organisations. On graduation in 1936, the term paper led to a research assistantship in the field of municipal administration, carrying out investigations that would now be classified as operations research. The research assistantship led to the directorship from 1939 to 1942, of a research group at the University of California, Berkley, engaged in the same kind of studies. By arrangement with the University of Chicago, he took his doctoral examinations by mail and "moonlighted" a dissertation on administrative decision-making during his three years at Berkley. He earned a doctorate in political science in 1943 from the University of Chicago.

In 1942, Simon joined Illinois Institute of Technology, Chicago, in the Department of Political Science. He became Professor of Political Science there in 1947. He used to be a regular participant in the work of the Cowles Commission for Research in Economics. He reminisces: "That started me on a second education in economics, supplementing the Walrasian theory and Neymann-Pearson statistics. I had learned earlier from Henry Schultz ....With a careful study of Keynes's General Theory (made comprehensible by the mathematical models proposed by Meade, Hicks, and Modigliani), and the novel econometric techniques introduced by Frisch...." He joined Jacob Marschak and others in a study of the "Prospective Economic Effects of Atomic Energy." The project was his "real baptism in economic analysis."

During 1950 to 1955, Simon worked out the relations between causal ordering and identifiability, discovered and proved (with David Hawkins) the Hawkins-Simon theorem on the conditions for the existence of positive solution vectors for input-output matrices and developed (with Albert Ando) theorems on near decomposability and aggregation. Simon was appointed Professor of Administration and Psychology at the Carnegie Institute of Technology (now Carnegie Mellon University), becoming Professor of Computer Science and Psychology in 1955. He, along with Charles Holt, and later with Franco Modigliani and John Muth, developed dynamic programming techniques for aggregate inventory control and production smoothing. Simon in collaboration with Holt had derived the rules for optimal decision under uncertainty and proved a certainty-equivalence theorem that permitted the technique to be applied under conditions of uncertainty.

Herbert Simon was Richard King Mellon University Professor of Computer Science and Psychology at Carnegie Mellon University. He had an illustrious 52-year career in artificial intelligence, psychology, administration and economics.

Simon received world-wide acclaim and numerous honours besides Nobel Memorial prize. They include A.M. Turing Award (1975) and National Medal of Science (1986). In 1993, he won the American Psychological Association Award for Outstanding Lifetime Contributions to psychology. In 1994, Simon was one of only 14 foreign scientists ever to be inducted into the Chinese Academy of Sciences. He was inducted into the American Hall of Fame because of his pioneering work in the field of artificial intelligence.

Herbert Simon died on February 9, 2001.

47.2 A BRIEF SURVEY OF SIMON'S CONTRIBUTIONS

As mentioned earlier, Herbert Simon's contributions are quite vast and diverse. They include philosophy and methodology of science, applied mathematics, economics, political science, computer science, cognitive psychology, management science and study of human behaviour in regard to solving problems. His work is truly remarkable in that it is fundamental and original in all these areas, marked by precision and clarity, which enabled him and others to conduct empirical research. As Albert Ando remarks: "....In many of these areas, we can recognize the characteristic of Simon's work in their basic body of knowledge."

It is not possible to summarise given the space constraint and given the diversity and vastness of Simon's contribution, even if there were no intellectual constraint limiting the author's ability to comprehend all the varied contributions. Simon's contributions are summarised here under the following heads. (The classification is due to William Baumol and Albert Ando).

1. Organisational Behaviour : Satisficing as opposed to Maximising;
2. Criterion for Positive-Valued Solutions to Input-Output Model: Hawkins-Simon Theorem;
3. Certainty Equivalent Theorem;
4. Adaptive Behaviour and Dynamic Adjustment Process; and
5. Validation and Discovery of Scientific Hypotheses.

47.2.1 ORGANISATIONAL BEHAVIOUR: SATISFICING VERSUS MAXIMISING

This is one of Simon's most significant contributions to economics. The basic assumption of microeconomic theory since Cournot has been maximisation of some objective function by the decision-maker, either a consumer or producer/firm. The firm is posited to maximise profit. As an alternative, some of the later writers hypothesised that the management seeks to maximise something (total sales revenue, rate of growth of assets, probability of survival or managerial perquisites). The fact of human behaviour was not considered specifically.

It is, of course, true that Herbert Simon is not the first one to question the neo-classical model of rational human behaviour. There were some economists in the nineteenth century who, on the basis of evidence from psychology, questioned the validity of the assumption of rationality but could not demonstrate that maximisation model does not fit facts.

As Baumol observes, maximisation by definition requires a process of comparison of available alternatives, in the absence of which a decision-maker cannot be said to be maximising anything – be that profit, or production or utility. Simon in his Nobel lecture asserted: "Evidence that consumers actually distribute their purchases in such a way as to maximize their utilities, and hence to equate marginal utilities is non-existent." The empirical data confirm that demand curves have negative slopes. Simon argued that "negatively sloping demand curves could result from a wide range of behaviors satisfying the assumptions of bounded rationality rather than those of utility maximization." He quoted Gary Becker in support of his contention. Becker categorically states: "...The fundamental theorem of traditional theory – that demand curves are negatively inclined – largely results from the change in opportunities alone and is largely independent of the decision rule." Becker is more explicit in the following quote: "Not only utility maximization but also many other decision rules incorporating a wide variety of irrational behavior, lead to negatively inclined demand curves because of the effect of a change in prices or opportunities."

Simon carefully and painstakingly elaborated the requirements of a classical model. It calls for knowledge of all the alternatives that are open to choice. It calls for complete knowledge of "or ability to compute" the consequences that will follow on each of the alternatives. It calls for certainty in the decision-maker's present and future evaluation of these consequences. Simon observed "...a strong positive case for replacing the classical theory by a model of bounded rationality begins to emerge when we examine situations involving decision-making under uncertainty and imperfect competition."

Rationality is said to be bounded when it falls short of omniscience. According to Simon "...the failures of omniscience are largely failures of knowing all the alternatives, uncertainty about relevant exogenous events, and inability to calculate consequences." In this connection the following quote from Peter Bernstein is relevant: "The information you have is not the information you want. The information you want is not the information you need. The information you need is not the information you can obtain. The information you can obtain costs more than you want to pay". A theory of bounded rationality must incorporate a theory of search. However, utility maximisation was not essential to the search scheme. Instead, Simon postulated that the decision-maker had formed some aspiration as to how good an alternative he should locate. As soon as he finds an alternative for choice meeting his desired level of aspiration, he would end his search and choose that alternative. Simon called this mode of selection 'satisficing. ' Aspiration levels are not, of course, static, but tend to rise and fall in line with changing experiences.

Simon illustrated this process with an example – the search for needle in a haystack. The haystack is known to contain a number of needles. He contrasted two different processes of search. The first seeks to find the sharpest needle in the haystack – a process of maximisation. The second is a search for the first needle that can be found and which happens to be sharp enough for the person who is looking to complete some sewing. This was termed 'satisficing' by Simon.

Baumol gives an economic analogy: it is the business enterprise whose management takes a set of decisions that yield 30 per cent return on investment to the firm. It might be, however, aware that there exists alternative decisions of a character unknown to the firm that might yield higher profits. The decision-maker rests content "with the first acceptable decision he happens to stumble upon and makes no further attempt to see if there exists something even better." Satisficing criteria terminate search when satisfactory problem solutions have been found.

In his Nobel lecture, Simon specifically stated that the micro-assumptions of the theory of the firm – the assumptions of perfect rationality – are contrary to fact. It is not a question of approximation; they do not even remotely describe the processes that human beings use for making decisions in complex situations. The alternative theories that are available, in one way or another, incorporate the notions of bounded rationality: the need to search for decision alternatives, the replacement of optimisation by targets and satisficing goals, and mechanisms of learning and adaptation. Simon concluded his Nobel lecture with the following sum up: "...We do understand today many of the mechanisms of human rational choice. We do know how the information processing system called Man, faced with complexity beyond his ken, uses his information processing capacities to seek out alternatives, to calculate consequences, to resolve uncertainties, and thereby – sometimes, not always – to find ways of action that are sufficient unto the day, that satisfice."

47.2.2 HAWKINS-SIMON THEOREM

The mere formulation of an input-output system does not guarantee that it has a meaningful general solution. One of the fundamental requirements to the solution of an input-output system is that none of the outputs be assigned a negative value. Otherwise, there is an implication that negative outputs of some commodities are necessary to achieve the targets of final consumption. In a note in 1949 Econometrica, David Hawkins and Herbert Simon made the basic contribution concerning this issue – the Hawkins-Simon Theorem. The operational form of the theorem is expressed in terms of the signs of a sequence of determinants in a system of simultaneous relationships in a multiplicity of variables. However, the theorem is easy to understand if we discuss an input-output structure involving two independent industries. We may use here a simple model Baumol presents in the Scandinavian Journal of Economics. The two simple input-output equations are the following.

$$X_a = k_{ab} X_b + t_a \quad .....(1)$$

$$X_b = k_{ba} X_a + t_b \quad .....(2)$$

Where

X_a : Output of good a

X_b : Output of good b

k_{ab} : Quantity of good a used as input per unit of good b

k_{ba} : Quantity of good b used as input per unit of good a

t_a : Target of net output of good a

t_b : Target of net output of good b

The product k_{ab} k_{ba} has the following interpretation: In order to produce one unit of good a we have to use k_{ba} units of b which, in turn, needs k_{ab} units of good a. Thus, to produce one unit of commodity a, we have to use up indirectly the quantity of $k_{ab}k_{ba}$ of commodity a. Now if we suppose $k_{ab}k_{ba}>1$, it implies that to produce one unit of gross output of good a, more than one unit of commodity a must be used up in the process of production. The conclusion which one has to draw from this situation is that an economy fails to meet the Hawkins- Simon test and cannot exist over the long run because "it must live off its own capital forever."

A number of other applications, some of them very important of Hawkins-Simon conditions, have been developed by economists. Samuelson's correspondence principle suggests that an economy characterised by such "misbehaviour in the production system which was just described will also run into misbehaviour in the dynamics of its structure." Samuelson in his 1959 Quarterly Journal article "A Modern Treatment of Ricardian Economy," demonstrated the wide applicability of Hawkins-Simon conditions. The importance of Hawkins-Simon conditions becomes more pronounced in large Leontief input-output models where such conditions become crucial for interpretation and analysis.

47.2.3 CERTAINTY EQUIVALENT THEOREM

Simon discussed the transport of optimisation techniques from economics into management science and the invention and development of new optimisation techniques, especially, linear programming. It is necessary that the decision tools employed in management science are capable of actually making or recommending decisions, taking as their inputs the kinds of empirical data that are available in the real world and performing calculations with the existing facilities of 'practical computability.'

In the real world, for example, a manager has to decide how many workers to hire and at what level production in the factory should be maintained for the initial period. A theorist would summarise the expected future sales into a joint probability distribution and assuming a cost function would formulate a dynamic programming problem in which the aggregate expected cost is minimised subject to the probability distribution of sales.

Taking the relation between production and needed work force and identity of production, sales and inventory, the theorist can formulate a set of conditions under which a solution to the problem exists.

Simon suggested that in such a situation, to simplify the problem, the cost function can be approximated by a quadratic function and the probability distribution of the expected future sales can be replaced by the mean of the distribution. This proposition has been referred to as the "Certainty Equivalence Theorem." Though the result for the problem seems to have been obtained by the application of the maximising principle, it is not. It is not known how good the quadratic approximation to cost really is. Further, it is not known whether the particular quadratic equation chosen by the researcher is the 'best' among all possible quadratic functions. Thus, the solution by Simon and his co-authors was not a solution to the maximisation problem of the classical economics variety, but a satisficing solution. He observed in the Nobel lecture: "...decision makers can satisfice either by finding satisfying solution for a more realistic world... by giving up optimization, a richer set of properties of the real world can be retained in the models." In principle, unattainable optimisation is sacrificed for, in practice "attainable satisfaction."

Thus, the body of the theory that had developed in management science shares with the body of theory in descriptive decision theory a central concern with the ways in which decisions are made, and not just with the outcomes of decisions. Simon stated, "...these are theories of how to decide rather than theories of what to decide." (Emphases in the original).

47.2.4 ADAPTIVE BEHAVIOUR AND DYNAMIC ADJUSTMENT PROCESS

It is generally assumed that individuals and organisations can understand and respond to their environment and with no limit. It is further taken that if some change occurs in the environment, the behaviour of the concerned decision-makers reflects the change immediately and fully. The comparative static analysis of economics depends on this assumption. The same assumption underlies the discussion of growth paths outlined in neo-classical economics.

It is, however, common knowledge, that economic agents do not respond to changes in environment instantaneously and completely, at least some of the time. In some cases, the delay in response may be because of the inability of the decision- makers to properly understand the change in order to compute the new maximising response and take suitable action. Ando reflects: "This...type of delay is the prime cause of the dynamic adjustment process of economics, and it is the type of behaviour which applied econometricians are forced to deal with often, without much guidance from economic theory for its proper functioning."

As economists traditionally postulated decision-making behaviour of economic agents as a constrained optimisation problem, the complexity introduced by the dynamic adjustment response of economic agents is taken care by formulating a more complex constrained maximisation problem and specify that the cost of adjustment to a change in environment is a function of the speed of adjustment, among others. This type of augmented constrained optimisation problem does not truly reflect the situation and is found to be inadequate, may be even incorrect.

Recognising the complexity of the problem, Simon suggested a different theory of human behaviour which specifically takes into account the limitations of human ability to adapt to changes in environment. His findings and theoretical underpinnings thereof regarding individual behaviour were formulated on the basis of laboratory experiments and hence could not be of much use in comprehending the behaviour of economic agents in real markets and in complex situations. However, Simon had initiated "organizing an analytical framework, for comprehending the important elements of delayed and partial responses of economic agents to complex changes in the environment facing the decision-makers." The work of Simon co-authored with Newell and reported in the volume, Human Problem Solving is rated as an "unique and singularly important contribution" to the understanding of dynamic adjustment processes in society.

In Simon's opinion, such complex systems could as well be simplified for the purpose of analysis by dividing the entire system into a number of sub-systems. Then, each sub-system could be analysed independently of the others. Simon observed that this kind of simplification is commonly employed in natural sciences. The possibility of such simplification depends upon the ability of the researcher to arrange elementary variables of the system in a way such that each elementary variable belongs to one, and only one group of these variables. Relationships among the variables within a group are much stronger than relations between any pair of variables not belonging to the same group.

If we agree that the environment of man is decomposable, then, as the system gets more complex, the number of variables the decision-maker has to contend with at any one time need not necessarily increase. It may result only in increase in the number of layers the decision-maker has to take up for analysis. Simon believed that man's environment could be decomposed most of the time and, as such, ordinary decision- makers could cope with their environment.

47.2.5 VALIDATION AND DISCOVERY OF SCIENTIFIC HYPOTHESES

A scientific hypothesis is formulated by finding some regularity in the nature-generated data. Such a generalisation is rarely exactly true, but is a rough approximation to the reality. Having formulated a hypothesis or a simple generalisation, the scientist attempts to find out if the degree of approximation of the hypothesis to the reality is good enough for the purpose at hand, or what factors cause the discrepancies noticed between the hypothesis and observed facts. In order to get answers to such questions, the scientist uses the methods of standard statistical testing; "it is almost certain that any hypothesis of this type will generally be rejected at any level of significance, as the sample size increases, however close the original approximation may have been."

Faced with this methodological problem, natural scientists either perform more carefully controlled experiments with more accurate measuring instruments, or, "organize an explanation why the hypothesis should fit the observed facts under a set of ideal conditions." For economists, it is not possible to make initial generalisation and then systematically improve them in the light of observed facts.

Recognising this problem quite early in his career, Simon proposed informal guidelines that social scientists could observe in their empirical researches which is the subject-matter of the essay "On Judging the Plausibility of Theories." Ando notes: "Beginning in the mid 1950's, Simon undertook a research project on size distribution of, among other things, firm sizes, city sizes, income of individuals and word counts.... The observations that size distribution of many things can be very accurately described by certain types of skew distribution...." Simon constructed an explanation for this phenomenon and suggested chance operating through the probability laws as "a plausible candidate for explaining this regularity." Ando commends: "...Simon's is the only theory for the explanation of observed skew distribution of size frequencies that seems plausible and is internally consistent."

47.3 CONCLUDING OBSERVATIONS

A brief sum up of Simon's work is contained in this quote:

"In the light of his epoch-making book Administrative Behavior, personal and social components, that are held together by a network of communications and by the willingness of members to cooperate and to work towards a common goal, he [Simon] argues that the firm must strive towards an equilibrium not only in relation to the outside world--the economic thinking for a long time--but also internally between the various components of the organisation."

It is generally accepted that Herbert Simon possessed an original and creative mind. Measured either in volume or in substance, his contributions over the years have been 'enormous' and 'impressive.' Baumol pays the following compliment "...that he is not an economist but a Professor of Computer Science and Psychology, and the magnitude of his contribution to our discipline [economics] becomes all the more remarkable. Surely, if even there was a case where interdisciplinary strengths have borne fruit in economics, this is it."

Another angle for the assessment of his contribution is provided by Albert Ando. From the point of view of economics, Simon's contribution lay in his analysis of the implications of recognising the limitation of man "to comprehend, to adapt to, and to affect" his environment completely and instantaneously, as was essentially assumed in classical economics. Simon had attempted to modify and to generalise classical economic theory so that it conforms better to the behaviour of man and his organisations in the real world. Ando evaluates the quality of Simon's contribution: "In the process, Simon exhibited almost unparalleled originality, profound analytical insight, and an extraordinary ability to extract information from quantity of data." Comparing the nature of Keynes's contribution to that of Simon, Ando comments: "...Simon has paid much closer attention and devoted a great deal more time and energy to the development of methodology and to actual empirical work, and therefore it is much easier for serious economists to take advantage of Simon's initiative and build on it than it was in the case of Keynes.... His contribution has been and will be, directly and indirectly, an important ingredient in every future economist's knowledge...."

47.4 SELECT BIBLIOGRAPHY OF SIMON'S WORKS

47.4.1 BOOKS

1947 Administrative Behavior, Macmillan, New York; 4th edition, 1997, Free Press, New York.

1957 Models of Man, Wiley, New York.

1958 (with J. G. March), Organizations, Wiley, New York.

1960 (with C. C. Holt et.al.), Planning Production, Inventories and Workforce, Prentice-Hall, Englewood Cliffs, NJ.

1972 (with A. Newell), Human Problem Solving, Prentice-Hall, Englewood Cliffs ,NJ.

1977 (with Y. Ijiri), Skew Distributions and the Sizes of Business Firms, North Holland, Amsterdam.

1979 Models of Thought, Vols.1 and 2, Yale University Press, New Haven, CT.

1982, 1997 Models of Bounded Rationality, Vols.1, 2, and 3., MIT Press, Cambridge, MA.

1991 Models of My Life, MIT Press, Cambridge, MA.

47.4.2 ARTICLES

1949 (with D. Hawkins). "Some Conditions of Macroeconomic Stability," Econometrica, Vol.17, July-Oct.

1951 "A Formal Theory of the Employment Relationship," Econometrica, Vol.19, July.

1952-53 "A Comparison of Organization Theories," RES, Vol.20, No.1.

1955 "A Behavioral Model of Rational Choice," QJE, Vol.69, Feb.

1956 a "Dynamic Programming under Uncertainty with a Quadratic Criterion Function," Econometrica, Vol. 24, Jan.

b (with R .M. Cyert and D. B. Trow) "Observation of a Business Decision," JB, Vol.29, Oct.

1959 "Theories of Decision Making in Economics and Behavioral Science," AER, Vol.49, No.3.

1961 (with A. Ando), "Aggregation of Variables in Dynamic Systems," Econometrica, Vol.29, Apr.

1962 "New Developments in the Theory of the Firm," AER, Vol.52, No.2.

1963 (with F .K. Levy). "A Note on the Cobb-Douglas Function," RES, Vol.30, June.

1971 (with Y. Ijiri), "Effects of Mergers and Acquisitions on Business Firm Concentration," JPE, Vol.79, No.2.

1976 "From Substance to Procedural Rationality," in Method and Appraisal in Economics, S. J. Latsis (ed.) Cambridge University Press, Cambridge.

1978 "Rationality As Process and As Product of Thought," Richard T .Ely Lecture delivered before the American Economic Association, AER, Vol.68, No.2.

1979 a "On Parsimonious Explanations of Production Relations," ScandJE, Vol.81, No.4.

b "Rational Decision-Making in Business Organizations," Nobel Lecture, AER, Vol. 69, No.4.

1984 "On the Behavioral and Rational Foundations of Economic Dynamics," JEBO, Vol.5, No.1.

1986 "Rationality in Psychology and Economics," JB, Vol.59, No.4.

1991 a "Organization and Markets," JEP, Vol.5, No.2.

b "Altruism and Economics," AER, Vol.81, No.2.

47.5 WORKS OF OTHERS

Ando, A. (1979) "On the Contributions of Herbert A. Simon to Economics," ScandJE, Vol. 81, No.1.

Baumol, W. J. (1979) "On the Contributions of Herbert A .Simon to Economics," ScandJE, Vol. 81, No.1.

Becker, G. S. (1962) "Irrational Behavior and Economic Theory," JPE, Vol.70, No.1.

Bernstein, P. L. (1998), Against the Goods: The Remarkable Story of Risk, Wiley, New York.

CHAPTER 48

JAMES McGILL BUCHANAN JR.

(1919 – 2013)

The Royal Swedish Academy of Sciences has awarded the 1986 Alfred Nobel Memorial Prize in Economic Sciences to Professor James McGill Buchanan, George Mason University, Virginia, U.S.A., for his development of the "contractual and constitutional bases for the theory of economic and political decision-making and public economics."

Traditional economic theory has concerned itself with explaining in great detail how consumers and entrepreneurs make decisions regarding purchase of goods and services, choice of work and leisure, production, savings and investments and so on. In a series of studies, Buchanan had developed a corresponding theory of decision-making in the public sector. This comprehensive theoretical formulation that came to be known as, "Public Choice" or the New Political Economy, lies on the boundary between economics and political science and has its origins in the work of the well-known Swedish economist, Knut Wicksell. In his A New Principle of Just Taxation, Wicksell pronounced: "The science of public finance should always keep...political conditions clearly in mind. Instead of expecting guidance from a doctrine of taxation that is based on the philosophy of bygone ages, it should instead endeavour to unlock the mysteries of the spirit of progress and development."

One of Buchanan's main contributions was the transfer of the concept of gain derived from mutual exchange between individuals to the realm of political decision-making. The political process thus becomes a means of cooperation for achieving reciprocal advantages. But the result of this process essentially depends on "rules of the game;" that is, the constitution in a broad sense. This, in turn, underlines the crucial importance of the formulation of constitutional rules and the possibility of constitutional reforms. Buchanan was against advising politicians or trying to influence the outcome of specific issues as in a given system of rules, the outcome is determined upon established political constellations. A relevant example is that those who would like to correct individual tariffs should concentrate instead on the fundamental rules of international trade such as GATT or WTO regulations.

For over forty years, James Buchanan had devoted himself to a systematic development of the contractual and constitutional bases for the theory of economic and political decision-making, in the process becoming the leading researcher in the field, which has come to be known as "public choice theory."

For a long time, traditional economics did not have an independent theory of political decision-making. Modern welfare theory often relied on the assumption that public authorities could apply relatively mechanical methods to correct different types of so-called market failures. Keynesian or monetarist theory of stabilisation policy seemed to assume that political authorities endeavoured to achieve certain macroeconomic or socioeconomic goals relating to inflation, employment, or growth rates. Buchanan and others belonging to the Public Choice School have not accepted this simplified view of political life. Instead, they have sought explanations for political behaviour that are similar to those used to analyse behaviour on markets.

Individuals who behave selfishly on markets can hardly behave wholly altruistically in political life. This leads to analyses which indicate that political parties or authorities that act out of self-interest (at least to some extent) will try to obtain as many votes as possible in order to reach positions of power or secure large allocations of budget. This type of analysis has become common in recent years and is perhaps the most widely known aspect of public choice theory.

Buchanan had attempted at extending the parallels between economic and political decision-making even further. It is widely accepted that market behaviour is premised primarily on voluntary agreements and free exchange of goods and services which give rise to mutual advantage for agents in market transactions. An essential pre-requisite of the market system, however, is the setting up of a legal system that protects rights of ownership and the enforcement and realisation of contractual agreements. The political system may also be regarded as a system based on voluntary agreements.

Starting with Swedish economist Knut Wicksell's early analysis of the relation between public expenditure and taxes, Buchanan had formulated a theory of public sector and political decision-making based on the principle of unanimity. It is therefore possible to interpret decisions concerning the dimensioning and financing of collective efforts as the outcome of voluntary agreement among citizens. In theory, every citizen would receive a welfare gain if the value to him/her of collective measures exceeds what he must forego in the form of taxes.

In this perspective, the political process becomes mainly a method of cooperating to achieve mutual benefit, and not a means for redistributing resources among individuals. However, because of high costs of arriving at decisions, the principle of unanimity is difficult to apply in practice. The costs of making decisions based on a high degree of mutual agreement have to be weighed against the costs an individual faces when the majority decision goes against him. It thus becomes crucially necessary to distinguish between fundamental decisions regarding the rules, which govern future decisions on all types of issues, and the decisions themselves.

Buchanan contended that once constitutional rules are adopted, the outcome on specific issues is often given by the internal dynamics of the political system. Thus, the design of constitutional rules and the possibility of constitutional reforms take on great importance. Attempts to advise politicians or affect the outcome of particular issues are often futile; for any given system of rules, the outcome is determined largely by prevailing "political constellations."

According to the citation of the Royal Swedish Academy, Buchanan's foremost achievement is that he had consistently and tenaciously emphasised the importance of fundamental rules and applied the concept of the political system as an exchange process for the achievement of mutual advantages. He had used his method with great success in the analysis of numerous specific problems and issues. Long before large budget deficits became common in a number of countries, he demonstrated how debt financing breaks the relation between government expenditures and taxes in the decision-making process. Buchanan, however, said the prize highlighted his long struggle for a concept. He stated: "I have faced a sometimes lonely and mostly losing battle of ideas for some 30 years now in efforts to bring academic economists' opinions into line with those of the man on the street. My task has been to 'uneducate' the economists."

Developments over the last few decades have confirmed Buchanan's predictions. Governments have become bigger than ever. Tax revenues have been falling far short of needs of public programmes. More importantly, borrowing, public as well as private borrowing, has "become a way of life. Politicians still act in their own interests, while espousing the public good, and national deficits have soared into trillions. Governments had grown so vast and complex that it was no longer possible for elected officials to make more than a fraction of the policy decisions that genuinely affect the people." According to Buchanan, much discretionary power is actually wielded by civil functionaries who can manipulate priorities, impose barriers to entitlements and pressure legislators for rules and budgets favourable to their own interests.

Buchanan's realistic view of the scope of economic policy and the importance of continuously reconsidering fundamental rules of the game, while retaining stable rules was largely vindicated. Economists currently working in the field of stabilisation policy have been showing greater interest in fixed rules than they were a few decades ago when "fine tuning" was in fashion. Earmarked taxes and qualified majority as methods of achieving better correspondence between public expenditures and taxes have now become topical questions than they were, say, forty years ago, when as little as possible attempts were focussed on restructuring the political administrative decision-making process.

48.1 A BRIEF BIOGRAPHICAL OUTLINE: JAMES BUCHANAN

James McGill Buchanan was born in Murfreesboro, Tennessee, U.S.A., on October 3, 1919. After academic studies at Middle Tennessee State College and obtaining B.A. degree from there in 1940, he obtained M.S. degree from University of Tennessee in 1941. Buchanan received his doctorate from University of Chicago in 1948. He described how he came into economics as a dedicated socialist and was converted into a strong advocate of the market economy "through a mere six-week exposure to Frank Knight."

Between 1956 and 1968, he served as Professor at the University of Virginia where he directed the Thomas Jefferson Center for Studies in Political Economy and Social Philosophy. After a short stint at the University of California in Los Angeles, he became Professor at the Virginia Polytechnic Institute in Blacksburg in 1969, where, with Gordon Tullock, he founded and led the Center for Study of Public Choice. In 1983 Buchanan moved to George Mason University, Fairfax, Virginia, where the Center was moved.

Buchanan was Ford Foundation Fellow, 1959-1960, visiting professor, Cambridge University, England, 1961-1962 and was visiting professor at the London School of Economics and Political Science. He was a recipient of numerous honours and awards. He received honorary doctorate from University of Bucharest, City University of London, University of Zurich and George Mason University. He received Distinguished Alumnus Award, American Association of State Colleges and Universities and Distinguished Fellow, American Economic Association. Buchanan served as Vice-President and President of Western Economic Association, as President of the Southern Economic Association and as Vice-President of the American Economic Association.

Buchanan died on January 9, 2013 in Blacksburg, Virginia, U.S.A., at the age of 93.

48.2 A SURVEY OF BUCHANAN'S CONTRIBUTIONS TO ECONOMICS

As mentioned above, the award announcement acknowledges the role of the writings of Wicksell in the development of Buchanan's thinking. Buchanan himself had stated that the origins of the Public Choice, date to the mid-twentieth century. It would be useful to summarise here the background in which the theory of Public Choice was developed, as it would put in proper perspective the contribution of Buchanan.

In the aftermath of World War II, nations, including Western democracies, were allocating between one-third and one-half of their aggregate product through political institutions rather than through markets. Buchanan noted that economists, however, were devoting their efforts almost exclusively to understanding and explaining the market sector. His entry into the subject in 1949 was just a call for those economists who examined taxes and public spending "to pay some attention to empirical reality and thus to politics."

According to Buchanan, the great Swedish economist Knut Wicksell was "the most important of all precursory figures in Public Choice." In his dissertation published in 1896, Wicksell was concerned with "both the injustice and inefficiency resulting from unfettered majority rule in parliamentary assemblies. Majority rule seemed quite likely to inflict net costs or damages on large segments of citizens or taxpayer groups. The question then arises as to why members of such groups of minorities, facing discrimination, lend their support to democratic political structures. Unless all groups benefit from the ultimate exchange with the government, how can overall stability be maintained in a nation?"

These considerations led Wicksell to question the efficacy of majority rule. He therefore advocated modification of the majority rule in the direction of unanimity. If the agreement of all persons in the voting group is required (as in the solution of unanimity) to implement collective action, it would guarantee that all persons secure net gains and further that the approved actions would yield benefits in excess of costs. At the same time, Wicksell had recognised that, if applied in a liberal voting setting, a requirement of unanimity would produce stalemate. This recognition, however, does not reduce the value of the unanimity rule "as a bench-mark for collective evaluation." In his suggestions for practical reforms, Wicksell supported changes in voting rules from simple to qualified or super majorities; for example, a requirement of five-sixths approval for collective proposals.

Buchanan was also prompted to enter into the area of Public Choice by the work of contemporary economists. Working simultaneously, but independently, Kenneth Arrow and Duncan Black have shown that democracy, interpreted as majority rule, could not work to promote any general or public interest. Arrow's famous "Impossibility Theorem," put forward in 1951 stimulated an extensive discussion. Buchanan observed: "the suggestion of this analysis [Arrow's and Black's] was that majoritarian democracy is inherently unstable" as elections rotate all the time in continuous cycles or "majority cycles" with no equilibrium.

Buchanan questioned as to whether "majority cycles" are not the most desirable outcome of a democratic process. He contended: "After all, any attainment of political equilibrium via majority rule would amount to the permanent imposition of the majority's will on the outvoted minority." His concern was the "prevention of discrimination against minorities, rather than a stability of political outcomes." He suggested that from the perspective of an economist the question is how to obtain a combination of efficiency and justice under majority rule.

A second major influence on Buchanan's work, according to A. B. Atkinson, was the Italian School of Public Finance theory. The Italian influence is particularly important in the case of Buchanan's work on the topic of burden of the national debt. Buchanan had acknowledged: "...the Italian approach to the whole problem of public debt was instrumental in shaping my views."

The contributions of Buchanan may be summarised under the two broad topics mentioned below.

1. Public Choice; and
2. Public Debt.

Most of the attention is on the first topic, while the second one is covered very briefly.

48.2.1 PUBLIC CHOICE

Buchanan in his Nobel lecture outlines as to how there was failure on the part of economists for a long time to recognise that the value-maximising perspective (in the sense that individuals who choose and act in the market generate outcomes that under the specified constraints, can be judged to be value-maximising for participating individuals) cannot be extended from the market to politics since the latter does not directly possess the incentive-compatible structure of the market. Simply put, there is no political counterpart to Adam Smith's invisible hand.

Elaborating on this basic argument, Buchanan talked of "methodological individualism." He described how economists start their analysis with individuals as evaluating, choosing and acting in a decision environment for individuals who have to make selections from among the available alternatives. The focus is on individual choice irrespective of the possible complexity of the processes or institutional structures from which outcomes emerge. Economists presume that individuals as buyers and sellers of goods and services are able to choose (between, say, oranges and apples) according to their preferences, whatever these may be. The economist does not deem it necessary to enquire into the content of these preferences or "the arguments in individuals' utility functions." Individual economic units are the sources of evaluation and the task of the economist is to offer an explanation of the "process through which these unexamined preferences are ultimately translated into a complex outcome pattern."

Buchanan submitted: "The relationship between the positively valued results of market processes and the institutional characteristics of these processes themselves emerged as a source of ambiguity when 'the market' came to be interpreted functionally, as if something called 'the economy' existed for the purpose of value maximization." Efficiency in resources allocation is defined independently of the processes through which individual choices are exercised. Economists generally have failed to recognise that individuals who exercise their choices in the market bring about outcomes that, under the specified constraints, can be taken as value-maximising for participating individuals, "without the necessity of introducing an external evaluative criterion." The nature of the process itself ensures maximisation of individual values. Buchanan contended that if the maximisation exercise is confined to individual choice-making "without extending to the economy as an aggregation," there is no problem in analysing individual choice behaviour under differing institutional settings and in making predictions regarding how these varying settings will influence the outcome of the interaction processes. The individual who makes a choice between oranges and apples remains the same person who chooses between candidate "A" and candidate "B" in the polling booth. It is obvious that the choice behaviour may be crucially affected by differing institutional structures themselves. Public Choice theory seeks to explain these relationships.

If predictions are sought to be made regarding the effects of shifts in constraints on individual choice behaviour, it is necessary to make "some identification and signing of the arguments" in individual utility functions. Buchanan then cited some examples from individual's economic behaviour. If both oranges and apples are positively valued goods, and if the price of apples falls relative to the price of oranges, more apples tend to be purchased relative to oranges. Likewise, if income is a positively valued good, and if marginal rate of tax on income source A increases relative to that on income source B, more effort at earning income will be diverted to source B. Similarly, if pecuniary rents are positively valued by individuals and if a political agent's discretionary power to distribute rents increases, individuals in the hope of securing these rents will "invest" more resources in an attempt at influencing the agent's decisions. Thus, we can see that identification and signing of the arguments in individual utility functions "takes us a considerable way towards operationalization without prior specification of the relative weights of the separate arguments. There is no need to assign net wealth or net income dominating motivational influence or behavior in order to produce a fully operational economic theory of choice behavior, in market or political interaction."

The difference that has been drawn above, between the identification and signing of arguments on one side and the weighing of these arguments on the other, needs greater attention when it is proposed to extend the model of individual rational behaviour to politics. The minimal critical assumption for the explanatory power of economic theory of politics is only that "identifiable economic self-interest (e.g. net wealth, income, social position) is a positively valued 'good' to the individual who chooses." This assumption does not put economic interest in a dominating position. In The Reason of Rules, which Buchanan co-authored with Brennan, this assumption had been defended by the authors that in political decisions an individual will act like homo- economicus. They were not saying that people will act in narrow self-interest. In fact, in his earlier writings Buchanan had dealt with the richness of individual motives in voting behaviour. Nor did Buchanan impute evil or malicious motives to political actors. Buchanan claimed that this theory remains on all forms with the motivational structure of the standard economic theory. The differences in predicted results emanating from market and political action come about from differences in the structure of those two institutional settings rather than "any switch in the motives of persons as they move between institutional roles."

Markets are institutions facilitating exchange of goods and services and persons enter markets to exchange one thing for another. Buchanan asserted that persons do not enter markets to promote or achieve "some supra-exchange or supra-individualistic result. Markets are not motivationally functional; there is no conscious sense on the part of individual choosers that some preferred aggregate outcome, some overall 'allocation' or 'distribution' will emerge from the process."

We cannot extend this exchange conceptualisation to politics. It is open to question whether persons participate in politics through some common search for good that is defined independently of the values of the participants. Wicksell and modern Public Choice theorists led by Buchanan contend that the relevant difference between markets and politics does not lie in the kinds of values/interests that persons pursue, but in the conditions under which they pursue their various interests. Buchanan argued: "Politics is a structure of complex exchange among individuals, a structure within which persons seek to secure collectively their own privately defined objectives that cannot be efficiently secured through simple market exchanges. In the absence of individual interest, there is no interest. In the market, individuals exchange oranges for apples; in politics, individuals exchange agreed-on shares in contributions toward the costs of that which is commonly desired, from the services of the local fire station to that of the judge."

The commonly noticed coercive elements in the activities of the state appear to be hard to reconcile with the model of voluntary exchange among individuals. It is pertinent to quote here Wicksell's observation: "It would seem to be a blatant injustice if someone should be forced to contribute towards the costs of some activity which does not further his interests or may even be diametrically opposed to them." For example, coercing or forcing people who are believers in pacifism and peace to pay taxes for financing war. Furthermore, Public Choice theorists ask: Coercion to what purpose? Why must individuals accept or acquiesce in the coercion of the state or of politics unless the "ultimate constitutional exchange" furthers their interests.

For the purpose of formulating a normative theory of economic policy, it is important to make exchange conceptualisation of politics. Whether there is improvement in working of politics is to be judged not in terms of moving closer to some externally defined, supra-individualistic ideal but in terms of the satisfaction of that objective that is desired by an individual, whatever that objective may be. It is possible that which is desired by an individual may be the same for many persons. The basic difference between market exchange and political exchange is in the sharing of objectives in the political exchange. The idealised agreement on the objectives of politics does not permit any supersession of individual evaluation. In Wicksell's words: "...whether the benefits of the proposed activity to the individual citizens would be greater than its cost to them, no one can judge this better than the individuals themselves." Commonly shared agreement among individual citizens has to be importantly distinguished from any externally defined definition or description of that "good" upon which persons should agree.

Buchanan had observed: "...the restrictive implications for a normative theory of economic policy are severe." It is not possible to evaluate directly any policy as there is no criterion which facilitates such evaluation. We may therefore have to resort to an indirect evaluation based on some measure of the degree to which the political process helps the translation of "expressed individual preferences into observed political outcomes." In this connection, Buchanan had drawn a distinction between the Wicksellian approach and the orthodox normative economics. In the former, the constitution of policy rather than policy itself becomes the relevant object for reform. Buchanan illustrated the difference with a simple game analogy. The Wicksellian approach focussed on reform in the rules, as against improvement in strategies of play for particular players within defined or existing rules. In the standard theory of choice in markets, there is no concern with the "constitution" or the choice environment in that there is no institutional barrier between the revealed expression of preference and direct satisfaction. The presumption is that the individual is able to implement his preferences. Efficiency in market interaction directly follows if the market participants are given the same choice options.

In political exchange, there is no decentralised process that allows "efficiency" to be evaluated "deontologically" similar to the evaluation of a market. In political exchange, individuals cannot adjust their own behaviour to "common terms of trade." Public choice theory stipulates that the political analogue to decentralised trading among individuals must be "agreement" among the individual participants. According to Buchanan "the unanimity rule for collective choice is the political analogue to freedom of exchange of partitionable goods in markets. If 'efficiency' is accepted as a desired criterion, normative improvement in process is judged by movement towards the unanimity requirement."

If, as mentioned earlier, majority rule produces injustice and inefficient outcomes and if political stability can only be obtained by discrimination against minorities, how can democracy claim normative legitimacy? Wicksell's criterion for achieving justice and efficiency in collective action, requiring shift from majority rule toward unanimity, does not seem to be practical institutionally. But in the absence of some such reform, how could taxpayers be assured that their participation in the democracy would yield them net benefits? Buchanan in collaboration with Gordon Tullock wrote a well known book The Calculus of Consent (which Arrow describes as a work of major importance) in which it is argued that the Wicksellian unanimity principle has a special claim on our attention. They observed that majority voting has been elevated to an undeserved status, being at best "one among many practical expedients made necessary by the cost of securing widespread agreement" and that the unanimity rule had been dismissed too readily without considering the issue whether unanimity may be brought about by debate and bargaining even when there is no unanimity initially.

The book distinguishes different levels of decisions and suggests a two-level structure of collective decision-making. The authors differentiated between "ordinary politics", consisting of decisions made in legislatures and "constitutional politics" comprising decisions made about the rules for ordinary politics. In support of the distinction they had drawn, they cite how constitutional law has long been distinguished from statute law in legal theory and practice. The authors brought this distinction into economic analysis. From the perspective of both justice and efficiency, majority rule may be permitted to operate in the realm of ordinary politics, provided "there is generalized consensus on the constitution, or on the rules that define and limit...what can be done through ordinary politics." However, in arriving at this constitutional framework, Wicksell's idea requiring unanimity or at least super majorities may be practically incorporated. To the extent that individuals reckon that a constitutional rule will remain applicable over a long period, with many in-period choices to be made, they are necessarily placed behind, what Buchanan termed, a partial "veil of uncertainty" regarding the effects of any rule on their own predicted interests. Buchanan argued: "Choice among rules will, therefore, tend to be based on generalizable criteria of fairness, making arrangements more likely to occur than when separable interests are more easily identifiable."

According to Wicksell, the ultimate goal "is equality before the law, greatest possible liberty, and the economic well-being and peaceful cooperation of all people." Buchanan stated that as the basic Wicksellian construction is shifted to the choice among rules or constitutions and as a veil of uncertainty is used to facilitate the potential bridging of the difference between identifiable and general interest, "the research program in political economy merges into that of contractarian political philosophy, both in its classical and modern variations; the familiar construction of John Rawls, who utilises the veil of ignorance along with the fairness criterion to derive principles of justice that emerge from a conceptual contractual agreement as a stage prior to the selection of a political constitution."

The constitutional approach had been developed further by Brennan and Buchanan in The Reason of Rules, published in 1985. Atkinson particularly refers to the discussion of the modelling of individual behaviour "where the authors defended their assumption that in political decisions an individual will act like homo economicus. They are not claiming that people will act in narrow self-interest." Buchanan further contended that individuals may calculate that they are better off for their membership in the constitution order, even while evaluating the effect of ordinary political actions inimical to their interests. A loose way of putting this, according to Buchanan, is: in a constitutional democracy, persons owe loyalty to the constitution, rather than to the government.

48.2.2 PUBLIC DEBT

Buchanan, in his Public Principles of Public Debt mounted an attack on what he called the "new orthodoxy" that the creation of public debt does not involve any transfer of real burden to future generations and that no analogy can be drawn between individual debt and public debt. He had also taken issue with the prevalent view among economists that there is a sharp distinction between internal and external debt. He saw the importance of distinguishing different definitions of the burden of public debt, especially with regard to the unit of analysis. He did not agree with those economists who devoted their attention to a consideration of the impact on the economy as a whole. He emphasised that the focus of attention in a democratic society ought to be on the individual sacrifice or burden.

In his Nobel lecture, he had the following to say in regard to public debt. Referring to the deficit financing regimes in modern democratic polities, he said: "It is almost impossible to construct a contractual calculus in which representatives of separate generations would agree to allow majorities in a single generation to finance currently-enjoyed public consumption through the issue of public debt that insures the imposition of utility losses on later generations of taxpayers. The same conclusion applies to the implicit debt obligations that are reflected in many of the inter-generational transfer programs characteristic of the modern welfare state."

48.3 IMPACT OF PUBLIC CHOICE THEORY

From the umbrella of Public Choice theory has emerged the concept of "rent-seeking," particularly developed by Gordon Tullock and Anne Krueger. It seeks to extend the idea of the profit motive from the economic sphere to the domain of collective action. The idea of rent-seeking presupposes that if there is a value to be gained through politics, persons will put or invest resources in efforts to garner this value. In the perspective of aggregate value, this investment is, of course, wasteful. Tullock considers the example of monopoly, tariff and theft in the context of rent-seeking. Another relevant example may be cited. If the government has got the power to sanction monopoly rights or tariff to a particular group at the expense of the general public or "designated losers," potential beneficiaries will compete for the 'prize.' Much of the modern politics is interpreted as consisting of rent-seeking activities. Public Choice theory explains much of the growth of bureaucratic or regulatory sector of government in terms of the competition between political agents for constituency support through the employment of discriminatory transfers of wealth.

Therefore, "Welfare Economics" in traditional economic theory offered theories of market failure. The question that has been raised by Buchanan and others is: Failure in comparison to what? The implicit presumption has always been that politicised corrections for market failures would work perfectly. That is, market failures are set against the idealised politics. In regard to the problem of externalities, Buchanan, in his article on "Politics, Policy and the Pigovian Margins," had challenged the Pigovian welfare prescriptions, on grounds different from those of Coase. Buchanan argued: "...any attempt to replace or modify an existing market situation...characterized by serious externalities, will produce solutions that embody externalities which are different, but precisely analogous, to those previously existing." Further, Buchanan contended that if the principle of majority voting is followed, and people act in individual self-interest, the majority can impose costs on the minority in just the same way as a polluter can impose costs. On the other hand, if people identify their own interest with that of the group as a whole, then both the social costs and benefits will be taken into account in private actions and no government intervention is necessary.

As regards the application of the public choice approach to the field of welfare economics, Buchan's article "Positive Economics, Welfare Economics, and Political Economy" needs to be specifically mentioned as it provides a useful example to illuminate the removal of a tariff. Atkinson states: "Buchanan distinguished three roles. First, there is the 'positive economist,' who makes the predictions of the consequences of the tariff's removal. Second, there is 'positive political economist' who attempts to construct a plan for its removal which will be approved by an overwhelming majority (Wicksell's approximate unanimity). Third, the 'normative economist' may introduce his own ethical valuations. These distinctions are valuable, but appear to exclude a fourth possibility, which is that the 'welfare economist' may postulate particular evaluations, not necessarily his own, in order to explore their implications."

The Public Choice theory has provided analyses of behaviour of persons acting politically – whether they be voters, politicians or bureaucrats. In a sense, Public Choice has become a set of theories of government failures, as an "offset" to the theories put forward by Buchanan in Vienna in 1976. Public Choice is "politics without romance." He refuted the suggestion that Public Choice is an anti-government ideology. Public Choice analysis brings "a more critical attitude towards politicized nostrums to alleged socio-economic problems. It disallows any presumption that bureaucratic corrections for market failures will accomplish the desired objectives."

There are critics who criticise Public Choice as being "immoral." According to Public Choice theorists the source of the charge lies in the application to politics of the assumption that individuals in the market place behave in order to achieve their self-interests. Further, critics of Public Choice argue that people acting politically, for example, as voters or legislators, do not behave as they do in markets. That is, individuals are differently motivated when they are "choosing for the public" rather than for themselves in capacities involving private choice. Buchanan stated that people act from many motives and the economic model concentrates its attention on only one of the possible forces behind human actions. He was categorical that Public Choice theory incorporates the presumption that persons do not readily become "economic eunuchs" as they shift from market to political participation. "Those who respond predictably to ordinary incentives in the market place do not fail to respond at all when they act as citizens."

Public Choice theorists claim that the structure of ideas that was adduced in support of the "emerging Leviathan Welfare State" was logically flawed and could have been maintained only "through long-continued illusion." Public Choice theory has offered a foundation for a "coherent understanding and interpretation of what could be everywhere observed -- over-reaching of government everywhere" in modern times. People could clearly observe the failure of collectivistic schemes, failure of politicisation to make promised correctives for any or all social ills and failure of government intrusions to make things better rather than worse. Aimed with insights from Public Choice, persons could understand why, once established, bureaucracies tend to grow with no limit and with no connection to initially promised functions. They could understand "why there seems to be a direct relationship between the overall size of the government and the investment in efforts to secure special rent-seeking concessions, why the tax system is characterized by the increasing number of special credits, exemptions and loopholes, why balanced budgets are hard to secure and why some industries secure tariff protection."

48.4 CONCLUDING OBSERVATIONS

Buchanan was a prolific writer. According to Atkinson, Buchanan authored (by 1987) over 20 books and more than 300 articles. Buchanan's work has been widely praised as marked by the highest standards of scholarship. Public Choice theory for the development of which Buchanan has been rightly given the credit has evolved and matured over the course of more than half a century. His work clearly demonstrates "an impressively wide knowledge of the writing of his predecessors in the field." Furthermore, his career "amply demonstrates that such knowledge is neither unnecessary nor a barrier to originality."

The purpose of and the highest motivation for Buchanan's work is clearly stated in his Nobel lecture: "I have never been tempted to make pronouncements on this or that policy issue.... I have never felt an urge to save the world or, indeed, to treat myself to be more responsible in a civic sense than any other person. On the other hand, I also recognize that unless someone, somewhere, takes the lead in promulgating constitutionalist ideas that are inherently "public," then we could scarcely expect such ideas to enter into public consciousness. We shall not secure the social order that is within the realm of the possible if each of us sits by and waits for the process of social evolution to work its will. There is, for me, a categorical distinction to be made between the presumptive arrogance of anyone, Nobel Laureate or anyone else, who takes it on himself to tell others what they should do, and the attitude of someone who actively enters as a participant in a discussion of social change with all persons treated as reciprocating contributors."

The following quote from one of the lectures of Buchanan lends support to the last part of the above lecture.

"Public Choice is like a small boy who said that the king really has no clothes. Once he said this, everyone recognized the king's nakedness, but no one had really called attention to this fact."

In a post script to the Nobel lecture written in 1999, Buchanan stated: "The arguments developed [in the Nobel lecture] now seem more important than they did a decade earlier. I am deeply concerned about the apparent apathy of citizens everywhere, about the absence of outrage at the sometimes petty intrusions of governments into our lives.... In the new Century, more than ever, we must attend to the rules of the game."

In a write up in the New York Times, Tyler Cowen sounded a timely warning that "his colleague Dr. Buchanan had accurately forecast that deficit spending for short-term gains would evolve into 'a permanent disconnect' between government outlays and revenue. We end up institutionalizing irresponsibility in the federal government, the largest and most central institutions in our [U.S.] society."

48.5 SELECT BIBLIOGRAPHY OF JAMES BUCHANAN'S WORKS

48.5.1 BOOKS

1954 (with C. L. Allen and M. R. Goldberg), Prices, Income, and Public Policy, McGraw Hill, New York.

1958 Principles of Public Debt, Richard D. Irwin, Homewood, Ill.

1960 a The Public Finances, Richard D. Irwin, Homewood, Ill.

b Fiscal Theory and Political Economy, University of North Carolina Press, Chapel Hill, Nc.

1962 (with Gordon Tullock), The Calculus of Consent: Logical Foundations of Constitutional Democracy, University of Michigan Press, Ann Arbor, Mich.

1966 Public Finance in Democratic Process: Fiscal Institutions and Individual Choice, University of North Carolina Press, Chapel Hill, Nc.

1968 Demand and Supply of Public Goods, Rand-McNally, Chicago, Ill.

1969	Costs and Choice: An Inquiry in Economic Theory, Markham Publishing Co., Chicago, Ill.
1972	(with Robert Tollison, eds.), Theory of Public Choice: Political Applications of Economics, University of Michigan Press, Ann Arbor, Mich.
1975	The Limits of Liberty: Between Anarchy and Leviathan, University of Chicago Press, Chicago, Ill.
1977	(with R.E.Wagner), Democracy in Deficit: The Political Legacy of Lord Keynes, Academic Press, New York.
1978	Freedom in Constitutional Contract: Perspectives of a Political Economist, Texas A&M University, College, Tx.
1980	(with G. Brennan), The Power to Tax: Analytical Foundations of a Fiscal Constitution, Cambridge University Press, New York.
1984	(with R. Tollison eds.), The Theory of Public Choice –II, University of Michigan Press, Ann Arbor, Mich.
1985	(with G. Brennan), The Reason of Rules – Constitutional Political Economy, Cambridge University Press, New York.
1986	Liberty, Market, and State: Political Economy in the 1980s, New York University Press, New York.
1992	Better than Plowing and Other Personal Essays, University of Chicago Press, Chicago, Ill.
1999	(with R.A. Musgrave), Public Finance and Public Choice: Two Contrasting Visions of the State, MIT Press, Cambridge, MA.
2000	(with G. Brennan), The Reason of Rules, Cambridge University Press, New York.

48.5.2 ARTICLES

1949	"The Pure Theory of Government Finance: A Suggested Approach," JPE, Vol.57, Dec.
1950	"Federalism and Fiscal Equity," AER, Vol.40, No.4.
1954	"Social Choice, Democracy and Free Markets," JPE, Vol.62, Apr.
1956	"Private Ownership and Common Usage: The Road Case Re-examined," SEJ, Vol.22, No.1.
1959	"Positive Economics, Welfare Economics, and Political Economy," JLawE, Vol.2, Oct.

1961		"Simple Majority Voting, Game Theory, and Resource Use," Canadian Journal of Economics and Political Science, Vol.27, Aug.
1963		"The Economics of Earmarked Taxes," JPE, Vol.71, Oct.
1964		"What Should Economists Do?" SEJ, Vol.30, No.1.
1967		"Cooperation and Conflict in Public Goods Interaction," WEJ, Vol.5, Mar.
1968	a	"A Public Choice Approach to Public Utility Pricing," Public Choice, Vol.5 Fall.
	b	"Social Insurance in a Growing Economy," National Tax Journal, Vol.21, Dec.
1970		"Notes on the Economic Theory of Socialism," Public Choice, Vol.8, Spring.
1972		(with C. J. Goetz), "Efficiency Limits of Fiscal Mobility," JPubE, Vol.1.
1973		"The Coase Theorem and the Theory of the State," National Resources Journal, Vol.13, Oct.
1975	a	(with W. J. Samuels), "On Some Fundamental Issues in Political Economy: An Exchange of Correspondence," JEI, Vol.9, Mar.
	b	"Public Finance and Public Choice," National Tax Journal, Vol.28, Dec.
1976	a	"Taxation in Fiscal Exchange," JPubE, Vol.6, No.1-2.
	c	"The Justice of Natural Liberty," Journal of Legal Studies, Vol.5, Jan.
	d	"A Hobbesian Interpretation of Rawlsian Difference Principle," Kyklos, Vol.29, No.1.
1977		(with G. Brennan), "Towards a Tax Constitution for Leviathan," JPubE, Vol.8, Dec.
1978		(with G. Brennan), "Tax Instruments as Constraints on the Disposition of Public Revenues," JPubE, Vol.9, June.
1979		(with G. Brennan), "The Logic of Tax Limits: Alternative Constitutional Constraints on the Power to Tax," National Tax Journal, Vol.32, June.
1980	a	(with R. Faith), "Subjective Elements in Rawlsian Argument on Distributional Rules," Economic Inquiry, Vol.18, Jan.
	b	(with G. Brennan), "The Logic of the Ricardian Equivalence Theorem," Finanzarchiv, Vol.38, No.1.
	c	(with A. P. Barbosa), "Convexity Constraints in Public Goods Theory," Kyklos, Vol.33, No.1.
1981	a	"Revenue Implications of Money Creation under Leviathan," AER, Vol.71, No.2.

	b	(with R. Faith), "Entrepreneurship and the Internalization of the Externality," JLawE, Vol.24, Mar.
	c	(with R. Faith), "Towards a Theory of Yes-No Voting," Public Choice, Vol.37, No.2.
	d	(with G. Brennan), "The Normative Purpose of Economic 'Science': Rediscovery of an Eighteenth Century Method," International Review of Law and Economics, Vol.1, Dec.
1982		(with D. R. Lee), "Tax Rates and Tax Revenues in Political Equilibrium: Some Simple Analytics," Economic Inquiry, Vol.20, July.
1983		(with G. Brennan), "Predictive Power and Choice among Regimes," EJ, Vol.93, Mar.
1984	a	"The Ethical Limits of Taxation," ScandJE, Vol.86, No.2.
	b	(with G. Brennan), "Voter Choice: Evaluating Political Alternatives," American Behavioral Scientist, Vol.28, No.2.
	c	(with L. Lomasky), "The Matrix of Contractarian Justice," Social Philosophy and Policy, Vol.2, Autumn.
1986	a	(with D. R. Lee), "Vote Buying in a Stylized Setting," Public Choice, Vol.49, No.1.
	d	(with V. J. Vanberg), "Organization Theory and Fiscal Economics: Society, State, and Public Debt," Journal of Law, Economics and Organization, Vol.2, No.2.
1987	a	"The Economizing Element in Knight's Ethical Critique of Capitalist Order," Ethics, Vol. 98, Oct.
	b	"The Constitution of Economic Policy," Nobel Lecture, AER, Vol.77, No.3.
	c	"Towards the Simple Economics of Natural Liberty: An Exploratory Analysis," Kyklos, Vol.40, Jan.
	d	(with J. Roback), "The Incidence and Effects of Public Debt in the Absence of Fiscal Illusion," Public Finance Quarterly, Vol.15, Jan.
	e	"Tax Reform as a Public Choice," JEP, Vol.1, No.1.
1988	a	"Is Public Choice Immoral? The Case for the 'Nobel' Lie," Virginia Law Review, Vol.74, Mar.
	b	(with V. Vanberg), "Rational Choice and Moral Order," Analyse & Kritik, Vol.10, Dec.
	c	"Economists and the Gains from Trade," Managerial and Decision Economics, Special Issue, Vol.9, No.5.

1989 a "On the Structure of an Economy: A Re-emphasis of Some Classical Foundations," Business Economics, Vol.24, Jan.

b (with V. Vanberg), "A Theory of Leadership and Deference in Constitutional Construction," Public Choice, Vol.61, Apr.

1990 "The Domain of Constitutional Economics," Constitutional Political Economy, Vol.1, No.1.

1991 a "Economics in the Post-Socialist Century," EJ, Vol.101, Jan.

b (with V. Vanberg), "The Market as a Creative Process," Economics and Philosophy, Vol.7, No.2.

1992 (with D. R. Lee), "Open Markets in the Transfer State," SEJ, Vol.59, No.1.

1993 (with D. Fand), "Monetary Policy: Malpractice at the Fed," Critical Review, Vol.6, No.4.

1994 a "The Political Efficiency of General Taxation," National Tax Journal, Vol.46, No.4.

b "Choosing What to Choose," Journal of Institutional and Theoretical Economics, Vol.150, No.4.

1995 (with Y.J. Yoon), "Rational Majoritarian Taxation of the Rich: With Increasing Returns and Capital Accumulation," SEJ, Vol.61, No.4.

1996 "An Ambiguity in Sen's Alleged Proof of the Impossibility of a Pareto Libertarian," Analyse & Kritik, Vol.18, No.1.

2002 "Game Theory, Mathematics, and Economics," Journal of Economic Methodology, Vol.8, No.1.

2008 a "Let us Understand Adam Smith," Journal of History of Economic Thought, Vol.30, No.1.

b (with Y. J. Yoon), "Public Choice and the Extent of the Market," Kyklos, Vol.61, No.2.

48.6 WORKS OF OTHERS

Arrow, K. J. (1951, 1963), Social Choice and Individual Values, Yale University Press, New Haven, Conn.

Atkinson, A. B. (1957), "James M. Buchanan's Contributions to Economics," Scand JE, Vol.89, No.1.

Coase, R. H. (1960), "The Problem of Social Cost," JLawE. Vol.3.

Wicksell, K. (1958), "A New Principle of Just Taxation," in R. A. Musgrave and A. T. Peacock (eds.), Classics in the Theory of Public Finance, Macmillan, London.

The New York Times, January 10, 2013.

CHAPTER 49

RONALD HARRY COASE

(1910 – 2013)

The 1991 Nobel Memorial Prize in Economic Sciences was awarded to Professor Ronald Coase, University of Chicago, U.S.A., for his discovery and explanation of the significance of transaction costs and property rights for the institutional structure and functioning of the economy.

Until recently, basic economic analysis had its focus on studying the functioning of the economy in the framework of an institutional structure which is taken as given. It was considered that efforts to explain the institutional structure were "either unnecessary or futile." For instance, the existence of firms is self-evident. Likewise, observed variations in the forms of contract in the economic sphere were considered as a given fact. Similarly, laws and rules of the legal system were perceived as an externally imposed setting for economic activity.

By means of a radical extension of microeconomic theory, Coase succeeded in putting forward principles for explaining the institutional structure of the economy. He had thus made contributions to improve our understanding of the way the modern economy functions. His achievements are highly significant specifically in an inter-disciplinary context, since they have provided legal science, economic history and organization theory with powerful impulses. Coase's contributions are the outcome of methodical research work, where each segment was gradually added to the next over a period of many years. It took a very long time for his approach to be accepted and gain a foothold. The breakthrough was finally emphatic which occurred during the 1970's and 1980's. The citation observes: "Today Coase's theories are among the most dynamic forces behind research in economic science and jurisprudence."

Coase demonstrated that traditional basic microeconomic theory was incomplete in that it neglected the costs of entering into and executing contracts and managing organisations; it considered only production and transport costs. The costs that are ignored by the traditional theory are known as transaction costs and they form a considerable share of the total resource use in the economy. When these costs are taken into account, it is possible to give relatively simple explanations for the existence of firms, different corporate forms, and even for the fundamental features of the legal system. By taking different types of transaction costs into account, Coase had facilitated a systematic analysis of institutions in the economic system and helped in explaining their significance.

Coase also showed that the power and precision of microeconomic analysis can be improved if the analysis is carried out in terms of rights to use goods and factors of production instead of the goods and factors themselves as was being done in the traditional analysis. These rights, which came to be called property rights in economic analysis, may consist of full ownership, different kinds of usership rights, or specific and limited decision and disposal rights, defined by clauses in contracts or by internal rules in organisations. The definition of property rights and their distribution among individuals by law, clauses in contracts and other rules determine economic decisions and their outcome. Coase argued that every given distribution of property rights among individuals tends to be reallocated through contracts, provided it is to the mutual advantage of the parties and is not discouraged by transaction costs and that institutional arrangements other than contracts would tend to emerge if they imply lower transaction costs. These arrangements also encompass modifications of legal rules by courts and legislatures. Property rights thus constitute a basic component in analyses of the institutional structure of the economy. The Nobel Award citation observes: "In perhaps somewhat pretentious terminology, Coase may be said to have identified a new set of 'elementary particles' in the economic system." Subsequently, other researchers have also enriched the field of property rights.

The press release announcing the award makes reference to the stages in Coase's contributions. The first stage refers to his major study "The Nature of the Firm." In this 1937 study Coase posed two questions which were not till then subjected to strict economic analysis and "lacked robust and valid solutions." The questions are: why are there organisations of the type represented by firms? And, why is each firm of a certain size? The traditional microeconomic theory showed that the price system or what is called the market mechanism has the ability to coordinate the use of society's resources in the process of production. However, the applicability of this theory is naturally diminished by the fact that in a modern economy a large proportion of total use of resources was deliberately withheld from price mechanism in order to be coordinated administratively within firms.

By introducing transaction costs in this analysis, Coase illustrated their importance. Beside production costs, the firms have to incur costs for preparing, entering into and monitoring the execution of all kinds of contracts as well as costs for implementing resource allocative measures within firms in a corresponding way. By taking all these circumstances into consideration Coase concluded that a firm originates when allocative measures are carried out at a total lower cost (total of production, contract and administrative costs) within the firm than the cost involved by the use of market mechanism (i.e. by means of purchases and sales on the market). Likewise, a firm expands to the point where an additional allocative measure costs more internally than it would through a contract on markets. If the transaction costs are zero, no firm would arise. All allocations of resources would take place through simple contracts between individuals using the market mechanism.

An important element in the model is the existence of two types of contracts: contracts that stipulate the total obligations (or rights) of parties and those which are deliberately kept incomplete by not specifying all obligations, but intentionally allow a free margin for unilateral decisions by one of the parties. Such 'open' agreements may be exemplified by employment contracts which usually leave room for direction and order-giving. In Coase's theory, the firm is characterised by the scope for decision created by a particular cluster of such open contracts. The firm, in fact, consists of this assortment of contracts and is linked with the rest of the world by other fully specified contracts regarding purchases of inputs, products sales and loans under prescribed terms.

The formulation of the theory of the firm by Coase has proved to be exceedingly practicable and has generated efforts at intensively examining the contractual relations characterising firms. It has become obvious that every type of firm comprises a distinctive contract structure and thereby specific distribution of rights and obligations or property rights. Coase's work concerning the theory of the firm has formed the basis for rapidly expanding research on principal- agent relations. It has also influenced vital aspects of financial economics, such as the lively research dealing with the explanation of the pattern of financial intermediaries and financial intermediation.

The second stage is Coase's other major study entitled "The Problem of Social Cost." In this work, he introduced the concept of property rights as part of the institutional structure of the economic system. He postulated that if a property right is well defined, if it can be transferred and if the transaction costs in an agreement that transfers the rights from one holder to another are zero, then the use of resources does not depend on whether the right was initially allotted to one party or another, except, of course, for the difference which can arise if the distribution of wealth between the two parties is affected. Even if the initial holding entailed an unfavourable total result, the better result would be brought about spontaneously through a voluntary contract, as both parties to the contract gain from it and it can be executed at zero cost. In other words, all legislation aimed at granting rights to individuals would be meaningless in terms of resource use since parties would "agree themselves around" every given distribution of rights if it is to their mutual advantage. According to Coase's formulation, a large amount of legislation would serve no material purpose in a world of no transaction costs. This thesis is a direct parallel to the conclusion in "The Nature of the Firm" that firms, under the same conditions, are superfluous. All resource allocations could be effectuated through simple, uncomplicated agreements without administrative features, i.e. through frictionless markets.

Coase concluded that non-zero transaction costs in real world explain the institutional structure of the economy, including variation in forms of contracts and many kinds of legislation. To be more precise, the institutional structure of the economy may be explained by the relative costs of different institutional arrangements, combined with efforts of parties to minimise total costs. Alongside price formation, the formation of the institutional structure is regarded as an integral step in the process of resource distribution. Hence, economic institutions do not require a separate theory. It is sufficient to render existing theory complete and formulate it in terms of the primary components, i.e. property rights.

These conclusions regarding the radical effects of ever prevailing transaction costs are thus the main result of the analysis of Coase. The citation states: "Somewhat paradoxically, circumstances have ordained that it is the preceding conclusion about the consequences of overlooking transaction costs which has come to be called the 'Coase theorem.'" It is necessary to recall Coase's categorical statement in this regard: "The world of zero transaction costs has often been described as a Coasian world. Nothing could be further from the truth."

It is clear that the situation without transaction costs is only a hypothetical norm of comparison, to facilitate the analysis of real world conditions. It may also inspire studies of contracting which can actually be observed, in areas where earlier theory, without any investigation, took it for granted that transaction costs are so high that contracts are inconceivable. Further examination by Coase himself, or students and others inspired by him, have shown that in some such cases, transaction costs are not so high as to preclude a contract. Such contracts are found to have strong peculiarities, created by the parties in order to alleviate the drawbacks of high transaction costs. These findings are in line with Coase's main conclusion. That is, in cases where transaction costs absolutely prevent a contract, there is a tendency for other institutional arrangements to emerge, for example a firm or amended legislation. The circle is closed – this is exactly the message conveyed by "The Nature of the Firm."

As regards legislation, in "The Problem of Social Cost," Coase developed a hypothesis concerning the behaviour of courts where two or more parties dispute rights and where agreements are impossible or extremely difficult because of high transaction costs. Coase argued that courts probably try to distribute the rights among the parties so as to realise the solution which would have been the outcome of an agreement, if such an agreement were possible. That is, common pleas courts serve as an extension of the market mechanism to areas where it cannot function due to transaction costs. This hypothesis has become extremely important because, along with the general formulation in terms of property rights, it has created the impetus for developing the new discipline of "law and economics" and, in extension, for renewal of many aspects of legal science.

49.1 A SHORT BIOGRAPHICAL SKETCH: RONALD COASE

Ronald Coase was born on 29th December 1910 in Willesden, Middlesex, England. His father was a telegraphist in the local post office. As a young boy, Coase suffered from a weakness in his legs, "which necessitated, or was thought to necessitate," the wearing of irons on his legs. As a result, he went to the school for physical defectives run by the local council. He studied at Kilburn Grammar School from where he passed the matriculation examination in 1927.

It was then possible to spend the two years after matriculation at the Kilburn Grammar School studying for the intermediate examination of the University of London as an external student, which covered the work which would have been taken during the first year at the university as an internal student. "I then had to decide what degree to take. The answer was in fact determined by one of those accidental factors which seem to have shaped my life." Coase's inclination was to take a degree in history. To do this he would have to know Latin; there was no possibility of studying Latin at his school. He therefore started to study for a science degree, specialising in chemistry. "However, I soon found that mathematics, a requirement for a science degree, was not to my taste and I switched to the only other degree for which it was possible to study at the Kilburn Grammar School, one in Commerce."

After passing the Intermediate examination in 1929, Coase went to the London School of Economics to continue his studies for a Bachelor of Commerce degree. In 1930, he passed Part I final examination. "In Part II, I specialized in the Industry group. I then had an extraordinary stroke of luck, another accidental factor which would affect everything I was to do subsequently." It is the appointment of Arnold Plant as Professor of Commerce at the London School who introduced Coase to Adam Smith's "invisible hand." He made Coase aware of how a competitive economic system could be coordinated by the pricing system. Plant did not merely influence Coase's ideas; Plant changed his life. As a result of Plant's influence, the University of London awarded Coase a Sir Ernest Cassel Travelling Scholarship. In Coase's words: "...although I did not know it, I was on the road to becoming an economist."

Coase spent the academic year 1931-1932 on Travelling Scholarship in the United States, studying the structure of American industries with the aim of discovering why industries were organised in different ways. His enquiries led to the introduction of a new concept into economic analysis, transaction costs, and an explanation of why there are firms. These ideas became the basis of his article "The Nature of the Firm" published in 1937, cited by the Royal Swedish Academy of Sciences in awarding the Nobel Memorial Prize.

Coase held a teaching position at the Dundee School of Economics and Commerce from 1932 to 1934, at the University of Liverpool from 1934 to 1935 and at the London School of Economics from 1935. In 1940, after Second World War broke out, he entered government service doing statistical work, returning to London School in 1946.

In 1951, Coase migrated to the United States. He was Professor at University of Buffalo between 1951 and 1958 and after a year at the Center for Advanced Study in the Behavioral Sciences, he joined the Economics department of the University of Virginia in 1959, where he stayed till 1964. He taught regulated industries and economic analysis and public policy. During the year at the Center for Advanced Study in the Behavioral Sciences, Coase made a study of the Federal Communications Commission which regulated the broadcasting industry in the U.S. In 1964, Coase moved to the University of Chicago and became Editor of the Journal of Law and Economics from 1964 to 1982. From 1964 to 1970, he was Professor of Economics at the University of Chicago. He was appointed Clifton R. Musser Professor of Economics from 1971 to 1981. Since 1982 he remained Clifton R. Musser Professor Emeritus of Economics and concurrently Senior Fellow in Law and Economics.

Coase received various honours and awards including honorary doctorates from Universite de Paris I, University of Birmingham, England, University of Dundee, Scotland, Yale University, Washington University in St. Louis and University of Cologne. Coase received D. Francis Bustin Prize, University of Chicago, 1988. He was Distinguished Fellow, American Economic Association, Honorary Fellow, London School of Economics, and Fellow, American Academy of Arts and Sciences. He was President, International Society for New Institutional Economics, 1997. In 2000, he became Research Advisor, Ronald Coase Institute, an organisation that seeks to encourage the study of markets, with particular support to researchers from developing countries. He was Fellow, the School of Global Studies, Arizona State University since 2006-till his death. Coase received an honorary doctorate from the Department of Economics, University of Buffalo in 2012. Coase died in Chicago on 2 September, 2013 (aged 102). He was praised across the political spectrum. The Washington Post called his work over eight decades "impossible to summarize."

49.2 A BRIEF SURVEY OF COASE'S CONTRIBUTIONS

When Coase celebrated his 100th birthday on 29th December 2010, The ECONOMIST (London) paid a fitting tribute. It said: "For philosophers the great existential question is: 'why is there something rather than nothing?' For management theorists the more mundane equivalent is: 'Why do firms exist? Why isn't everything done by the market?"

Tracing the development of Coase's ideas The ECONOMIST notes: "Today most people live in a market economy and central planning is remembered as the greatest economic disaster of the 20th century. Yet most people spend their working lives in centrally planned bureaucracies called firms. They stick with the same employer for years rather than regularly returning to the jobs market.... We have these 'islands of conscious cooperation' to borrow a phrase from D. H. Robertson", Stating that Classical economists had little to say about this question, the weekly refers to Adam Smith's 'wonderful description' of the division of labour in a pin factory in The Wealth of Nations, and remarks: "...but he said nothing about the bosses who hired the pin-makers or the managers who organised them. Smith's successors said even less either ignoring the pin factory entirely or treating it as a tedious black box. They preferred to focus on the sea rather than the islands." Coase had restored the pin factory to its rightful place at the 'heart of economic theory.'

In the Nobel Prize lecture, Coase said: "My contribution to economics has been to urge the inclusion in our analysis of features of the economic system so obvious that...they have tended to be overlooked. Nonetheless, once included in the analysis, they will...bring about a complete change in the structure of economic theory, at least in which it is called price theory or microeconomics." He then refered to the "principal theme" of The Wealth of Nations of Adam Smith, namely government regulation or centralised planning were not necessary to make an economic system function in an orderly way. The economy could be coordinated by a system of prices (the "invisible hand") and, furthermore, "with beneficial results." Economists since then have been engaged in formalising this proposition and propose changes designed to bring about conditions necessary for achieving the outcome. He further argued that economists have neglected consideration of the internal arrangements within organisations but only in what happens on the market, the purchase of factors of production and the sale of the goods that these factors produce; what happens in between is largely ignored.

This neglect of other aspects of the system has been helped "by the growing abstraction of the analysis." According to Coase what is studied is a system "which lives in the minds of economists but not on earth;" he called the result "blackboard economics." The firm and market appear by name but they lack substance. The firm in mainstream economic theory has often been described as a "black box" and "so it is." Coase considered this neglect as "extraordinary," given that most resources in a modern economic system are employed within firms, with the way the resources are used dependent on administrative decisions and not directly on the operation of a market. As such, the efficiency of the economic system depends to a large extent on the way these organisations conduct their affairs, particularly the modern corporates. More surprising is the neglect of the institutional arrangements that govern the process of exchange in the market. Coase wanted to provide answers to these important issues.

In Karl Brunner's view, Coase, in his work, made three far-reaching propositions that form an integral part of economics and law.

Firms exist because there are costs of using the price mechanism or markets.

Courts have been "internalizing externalities" for a long time by assigning property rights. Existence of externalities does not justify or warrant either legislative or government's administrative action. In a regime of no transaction costs, the use of resources is independent of the specific assignment of property rights to individuals by the courts.

Coase's contributions to economics are surveyed under two broad heads indicated by his two outstanding articles.

1. The Nature of the Firm or the Theory of the Firm.
2. The Problem of Social Cost or the Coase Theorem.

49.2.1 THE NATURE OF THE FIRM

Coase anchored the existence of the firm in the presence of transaction costs; that is, the fact that markets cannot function without an input of resources. The market mechanism or price mechanism does not operate without any cost. Potential market transactions impose substantial information and transaction costs. The opportunity for avoidance of costs is provided by a firm. The question is: how far is it productive to substitute conscious management of resources for market allocation of resources. A firm provides a framework which eliminates the daily renegotiation for the resource-use. For example, one can compare substitution of a long-term contract for a series of short-term contracts to acquire labour services for an extended period. It is likely that a reduction in transaction costs may result from the substitution of a single long-term contract for multiple short-term contracts. However, entering into a single long-term contract involves conscious management of resources in the process of production since the future productive use of an employee is characterised by uncertainty. For a reduction in transaction costs to obtain through a long-term contract, the employee under such an arrangement must be willing to permit his future activities to be supervised within certain limits.

Coase identified substitution of conscious management of resources for the price system as the substitution of the firm for the market. The degree of substitution (in the case of substituting a long-term agreement in place of short-term contracts for acquiring labour services) is determined by comparing the cost of managing with the cost of transacting.

Taking a similar view for resource inputs other than labour, Coase stated that "make within the organization" or "buy in the market" decision crucially depends on a comparison of the cost of using a market. He, thus, argued that the existence of transaction costs leads to the emergence of the firm. He also discussed the pervasive effects of transaction costs in the economy. Transaction costs have to be taken into account by businessmen in their ways of doing business and on what to produce. Transaction costs affect not only contractual arrangements but what goods and services are produced in the economy and prevent activities involving unproductive division of labour. He mentioned one part of economics in which transaction costs have been used to explain a major feature of the economic system and that relates to the evolution and use of money. Coase concluded that what we think of as economic activity is, in fact, designed to accomplish what high transaction costs would otherwise prevent or to reduce transaction costs so that individuals can freely negotiate and take advantage of the diffused knowledge.

Coase, extending his analysis to the issue of the size of the firm, considered its two dimensions. The firm expands its operations of any particular product until marginal costs equal the costs of market transactions. But a firm may also vary the number of products integrated into the firm. "Vertical integration of the production process is called for if the cost of managing the production of the input is less than the cost of transacting to buy it.

Increasing cost of entrepreneurial coordination ultimately limits the shift of further transactions to the firm from the market."

The principal results concerning these aspects are summarised by Coase as follows: "Other things being equal, therefore, a firm will tend to be larger:

The less the cost of organizing and the slower these costs rise with an increase in the transactions organized.

The less likely the entrepreneur is to make mistakes and the smaller the increase in mistakes with an increase in the transactions organized.

The greater the lowering (or less the rise) in the supply price of factors of production to firms of larger size."

Harold Demsetz comments: "Coase's 'The Nature of the Firm' appeared in 1937. It attracted some attention shortly after its publication but...it then largely ceased to affect work done by economists.... The neglect...did end, however, and it is now widely cited and very influential, nowhere more so than in the new institutional economics.... It remains one of only a few pillars upon which the new institutional economics is built." Dealing with this long neglect of his concept of transaction costs and the failure of its incorporation into a general theory as has been argued by Oliver Williamson (another Nobel Laureate), Coase, in his Prize lecture, offered a reply: "...incorporating transaction costs into standard economic theory which has been based on the assumption that they are zero, would be very difficult and economists who, like most scientists, as Thomas Kuhn has told us, are extremely conservative in their methods, have not been inclined to attempt it." Another reason for this failure in Coase's own words is: "...the interrelationships which govern the mix of market and hierarchy...are extremely complex and in our present state of ignorance it will not be easy to discover what these factors are. What we need is more empirical work."

49.2.2 THE PROBLEM OF SOCIAL COST

Coase's seminal insight on social cost appeared in print in his 1959 paper "The Federal Communications Commission." Radio stations in the U.S. were initially free to broadcast on whatever frequency they wished which resulted in chaos, as stations were occupying frequencies so close to each other as to interfere with each others' transmissions. This unsatisfactory situation led to the establishment in 1927 of a regulatory body, which in 1934 became the Federal Communications Commission to allocate frequencies administratively. The issue Coase was directly concerned with is "...those actions of business firms which have harmful effects on others." That is, in the case of the problem of allocation of radio frequencies, Coase was clear that Radio Station B must be in operation; if it is to be damaged by Station A, and that station A's interference with station B's operation implies interference in the opposite direction as well. It is obvious that the damaged party is as responsible for the damage as is the damaging party; thus, the position of the parties is symmetrical. He argued that even conceptually it is impossible to assign the roles 'victim' and 'offender' or damaged and damaging party in a causal sense since damage always results from actions of both parties.

In the then dominant Pigovian tradition, the situation was identified as a market failure requiring direct government intervention (a tax on the offender or the damaging party). Before summarising Coase's solution to the problem, it may be useful to refer to the externality doctrine and the four propositions that are offered by the work of Pigou. Harold Demsetz summarises the propositions as follows:

A divergence between social cost and private cost (or between social benefit and private benefit) can arise even if markets are competitive;

Resource allocation will be inefficient if this divergence occurs;

There is a specific party who is responsible for creating this divergence; and

To achieve efficiency, this party should be taxed in accord with, or should be held liable for, the damages this party's activity causes.

Coase did not accept the view that allocation of radio frequencies by government discretion makes the most sense. In his view the problem does not arise from competition. "Instead, the real cause of the trouble was that no property rights were created in these scarce frequencies. If property rights were assigned, chaos disappears and so does the government except that a legal system to define property rights and to arbitrate disputes is of course necessary." This market solution was commended by Coase as it has the merits of allocating the rights to the highest bidder which eliminates the windfall profits otherwise reaped by those broadcasters fortunate enough to be selected by the Federal Communications Commission and resources do not go to those with the most money but to those who are willing to pay the most for them.

The 1959 paper "The Federal Communication Commission" attracted attention in a quarter that turned out to be crucial both for Coase personally and for the field of economics. George Stigler recalls: "Ronald Coase criticized Pigou's theory rather casually, in the course of a masterly analysis of the regulatory philosophy underlying the Federal Communications Commission's work. Chicago economists could not understand how so fine an economist as Coase would make so obvious a mistake. Since he persisted, we invited Coase (he was then at the University of Virginia) to come and give a talk on it. Some twenty economists from Chicago and Ronald Coase assembled one evening at the home of Aaron Director.... In the course of two hours of argument the vote from twenty against and one for Coase to twenty one for Coase. What an exhilarating event!"

The article "The Problem of Social Cost" was a response of Coase to the encouragement provided by the Chicago encounter to elaborate and refine his analysis. The article was explicitly motivated as an attack on Pigou's treatment of externalities. In his Prize lecture, Coase stated: "I thought I was exposing the weaknesses of Pigou's analysis of the divergence between private and social products, an analysis generally accepted by economists.... Pigou's conclusion and that of most economists using standard economic theory was, and perhaps still is, that some kind of government action (usually the imposition of taxes) was required to restrain those whose actions had harmful effects on others, often termed negative externalities." He demonstrated that externalities would not exist if transaction costs were zero and Pigou's doctrine could not be relied on to give a correct solution if positive transaction costs create a divergence between private and social cost.

Coase made the economic profession question the validity of Pigou's four propositions listed earlier and the article is considered "a classic of water-shed calibre for having done so." Specifically, what Coase showed in that article was that in a regime of zero transaction costs, an assumption of standard economic theory (as also of Pigou), negotiations between the parties would lead to those arrangements being made which would maximise wealth and this is irrespective of the initial arrangement of rights. Coase considered that the Theorem named after him is a stepping stone on the way to an analysis of an economy with positive transaction costs. In such an economy government actions, such as government operation, regulation or taxation, including subsidies, could not produce a better result than relying on negotiations between individuals in the market. Coase urged economists to study the world of positive transaction costs taking into account what 'real' governments actually do and not by studying 'imaginary' governments.

Moving from a regime of zero transaction costs to one of positive transaction costs, we realise the crucial importance of the legal system in the new world. The article on Social Cost explains that what are traded on the market are not "physical entities" but the "rights to perform certain actions" and the rights which individuals possess are established by the legal system. In such a world, any attempt by parties to an exchange to negotiate for changing any provision of the law would be extremely expensive and unprofitable. Because of this, the rights individuals possess, with their duties and privileges will be largely determined by law. Therefore, Coase contended, the legal system will have a profound effect on the working of the economic system and may in certain respects be said to control it. As such, it is clearly desirable that these rights are assigned to those that can use them most productively and with incentives that encourage them to do so. Furthermore, to facilitate this outcome and to discover and maintain such a distribution of rights, the costs of their transference have to be low, through clarity in the law and by making the legal requirements for such transfers "less onerous." According to Coase, this desirable situation can come about only if there is an appropriate system of property rights and strict enforcement of such rights. He concluded: "...it is easy to understand why so many academic lawyers...have found so attractive the task of uncovering the character of such a property right system and why the subject of 'law and economics' has flourished in American law schools. Indeed, work is going forward at such a pace that I do not consider it over-optimistic to believe that the main outlines of the subject will be drawn within five or ten years."

In his Prize lecture, Coase remarked that till recently most economists did not betray their awareness of the relationship between the economic system and the legal system. Economists often cite the examples of stock and commodity exchanges for perfect or near-perfect competition. However, these exchanges regulate in great detail the activities of traders on those exchanges apart from any public regulation. The authorities of the exchange stipulate in detail what can be traded on the exchange, when it can be traded, the terms of settlement and so on; all these rules and regulations, Coase termed "private law." Further, "when trading takes place outside exchanges (and this is almost all trading) and where the dealers are scattered in space and have very divergent interests, as in retailing and wholesaling, such a private law would be difficult to establish and their activities will be regulated by the laws of the State. It makes little sense for economists to discuss the process of exchange without specifying the institutional setting within which the trading takes place since this affects the incentives to produce and the costs of transacting." He advocated serious study by economists of the process of contracting in a real world setting which would make them aware of the richness of the institutional alternatives between which they have to and can choose.

Demsetz observes: "A count of footnote citations from judicial opinions and law review articles reveals that "The Problem of Social Cost" is the most cited law article of all time, and by a wide margin." This observation is buttressed by David De Meza's conclusion: "PSC [The Problem of Social Cost] is cited even more frequently in law journals than in economic journals." He also states that "PSC appears to have been cited more often between 1981 and 1996 than any other paper written by an economist..." The article provided for lawyers a systematic and coherent set of principles with which "to explain the consequences of different legal rules, and to appraise their desirability." The article shows that the impact of the law on resource allocation is not clear in a straight forward manner, but it provides many clues as to how to approach the issue. Coase himself put it in his 1993 article: "Legal scholarship...moves forward in a new spirit. Ernest Rutherford said that science is either physics or stamp collecting, by which he meant, I take it, that it is either engaged in analysis or in operating a filing system. Much, and perhaps most, legal scholarship has been stamp collecting. Law and Economics, however, is likely to change all that and, in fact, has begun to do so."

Coase's perspective in regard to the policy implications of the problem of social cost is contained in his following prescription: "Even when it is possible to change the legal delimitation of rights through market transactions, it is obviously desirable to reduce the need for such transactions and thus reduce the employment of resources in carrying them out."

49.3 CONCLUDING OBSERVATIONS

The ECONOMIST (a reference to the write-up therein has been made earlier in this chapter) appropriately observes: "The economics profession was slow to recognise Ronald Coase's genius. He first expounded his thinking about the firm in a lecture in Dundee in

1932, when he was just 21 years old. Nobody much listened. He published 'The Nature of the Firm' five years later. It went largely unread. But Mr.Coase laboured on regardless; a second seminal article on 'The Problem of Social Cost' laid the intellectual foundations of the deregulation revolution of the 1980's. Eventually, Mr.Coase acquired an army of followers, such as Oliver Williamson, who fleshed out his ideas...."

Summarising the essence of Coase's contribution, The ECONOMIST says: "His central insight was that firms exist because of going to the market all the time can impose heavy transaction costs.... A firm is essentially a device for creating long-term contracts when short-term contracts are too bothersome." The issue that crops up when the markets are so inefficient is "... why don't firms go on getting bigger forever?" Mr.Coase pointed out that these planned societies impose transaction costs of their own which tend to rise as they grow bigger. The proper balance between hierarchies and markets is constantly recalibrated by the forces of competition: entrepreneurs may choose to lower transaction costs by forming firms but giant firms eventually become sluggish and uncompetitive.

In addition to the seminal papers discussed above, there are other examples which demonstrate Coase's scholarship. For example, in his 1946 article "The Marginalist Controversy," he recommended the use of a multipart tariff to obviate pricing problems that inhere in natural monopoly situations. In the 1972 paper "Durability and Monopoly," Coase showed that the competitive price will prevail for a durable good regardless of the number of sellers. The paper attests to Coase's "subtle theoretical mind and his skill in relating a theoretical issue to institutional aspects." As a third example, we may cite his exploration of the issue of "The Lighthouse in Economics" (1974). From the 19th Century onwards, it is a well established belief in economics that lighthouses have to be under government operation, financed exclusively by government as the private operators would not be able to capture the revenues from the operation of a light house. Coase had shown the invalidity of this argument and suggested a deeper study and further analysis. To quote Demsetz again: "The end points of these empirical explorations are theoretical generalizations that Coase believes to be consistent with the facts he has uncovered."

It is appropriate to mention here an important contribution of Coase— what has come to be referred to as the "Coase Conjecture." It refers to Coase's "informal argument" that monopolists in durable goods do not have market power because they are not able to commit to not lowering their prices in future periods. Coase is reported to have coined an adage that is often misquoted: "If you torture the data long enough, it will confess."

Coase's theorisation is primarily about firms and markets, the two institutions central to the functioning of a capitalist economy. He does not employ mathematical or econometric techniques to develop and expound his ideas. In his Prize lecture he categorically stated his position: "My remarks have been interpreted as implying that I am hostile to the mathematization of economic theory. This is untrue. Indeed, once we begin to uncover the real factors affecting the performance of the economic system, the complicated inter-relations between them will clearly necessitate a mathematical treatment, as in the natural sciences...." Further, he said; "...a scholar must be content with the knowledge that what is false in what he says will soon be exposed and, as for what is true, he can count on ultimately seeing it accepted, if only he lives long enough."

As regards the quality of his contribution, Demsetz has to say: "Even if Coase's other fine articles and books are set aside, this accomplishment [upsetting Pigou's doctrine regarding the problem of externality with Coase's Social Cost article] is grand enough to merit the Nobel Prize." He had explored questions that have been neglected or misunderstood by economists. His approach to economics has been marked by a sense of utility and significance.

It needs to be noted that Coase's theory continues to explain some of the most puzzling problems in modern business. The case of large diversified business groups, like Tatas is sought to be explained by companies stretching their brands over many industries, particularly where trust in established institutions is scarce. The ECONOMIST further argues that where capital and labour markets are inefficient "... it makes equal sense for companies to allocate their own capital and train their own loyalists." While Coase's narrow focus on transaction costs offers only a partial explanation of firms's power, attempts have been made by what is referred to as "neo-Coasian school" to widen the explanation. The school argues that "activities are conducted within firms not only because markets fail but also because firms succeed." They can marshal a wide range of resources–particularly "nebulous ones, such as corporate culture and collective knowledge—that (Markets) cannot access."

We may end this essay by quoting Brunner's evaluation of Coase as an old-fashioned scholar: "...Ronald Coase must be counted as one of the most influential scientists of the 20th century. His impact on economics, where he is the patriarch of the burgeoning 'new institutional economics' has been remarkable. His influence on the study of law could in the long run be even more remarkable."

49.4 SELECT BIBLIOGRAPHY OF RONALD COASE'S WORKS

49.4.1 BOOKS

1950 British Broadcasting: A Study in Monopoly, London School of Economics and Political Science and Longmans Green & Co., London.

1988 The Firm, The Market and the Law, University of Chicago Press, Chicago, Ill.

1994 Essays on Economics and Economists, University of Chicago Press, Chicago, Ill.

2012 (with N. Wang), How China became Capitalist, Palgrave Macmillan, London.

49.4.2 ARTICLES

1935 "The Problem of Duopoly Reconsidered," RES, Vol.2, No.2.

1937 a "Some Notes on Monopoly Price," RES, Vol.5, No.1.

b "The Nature of the Firm," Economica (n.s.), Vol.4, No.16. Also in American Economic Association Readings in Price Theory, (K. E. Boulding and G. J. Stigler, eds.), R. D. Irwin, Chicago, Ill, 1952.

1939 "Rowland Hill and the Penny Post," Economica (n.s.), Vol.6, No.24.

1946 a "The Marginal Cost Controversy," Economica (n.s.), Vol.13, No.51.

b "Monopoly Pricing with Interrelated Costs and Demands," Economica (n.s.),Vol.13, No.52.

1947 "The Economics of Uniform Pricing Systems," Manchester School of Economics and Social Studies, Vol.15, No.2.

1948 "The Origin of the Monopoly of Broadcasting in Great Britain," Economica (n.s.), Vol.14, No.55.

1959 "The Federal Communications Commission," JLawE, Vol.2, Oct.

1960 "The Problem of Social Cost," JLawE, Vol.3, Oct. Also in Readings in Microeconomics, (W. Breit & H. M. Hochman eds.), 1968.

1966 "The Economics of Broadcasting and Government Policy," AER, Vol.56, No.2.

1968 "Consumer's Surplus," in International Encyclopaedia of Social Sciences, Macmillan and Free Press, New York.

1970 "The Theory of Public Utility Pricing and its Applications," BellJE, Vol.1, No.1.

1972 "Durability and Monopoly," JLawE, Vol.15, No.1.

1974 a "The Lighthouse in Economics," JLawE, Vol.17, No.2.

b "The Market for Goods and the Market for Ideas," AER, Vol.64, No.2.

1976 "Adam Smith's Views of Man," JLawE, Vol.19, No.3.

1978 "Economics and Contiguous Disciplines," The Journal of Legal Studies, Vol.7, No.2.

1981 "The Coase Theorem and the Empty Core: A Comment," JLawE, Vol.24, No.1.

1987 "Arnold Plant," in The New Palgrave: A Dictionary of Economics, Macmillan, London.

1988 "R. H. Coase Lectures: The Nature of the Firm. 1. Origin, 2. Meaning 3. Influence," Journal of Law, Economics, and Organization, Vol.4, No.1.

1992 "The Institutional Structure of Production," Nobel Lecture, AER, Vol.82, No.4.

1993 "Law and Economics at Chicago," JLawE, Vol.36, No.1.

1995 "My Evolution as an Economist," in Lives of the Laureates, (W. Breit and R. W. Spencer, eds.), 3rd edition, MIT Press, Cambridge, MA.

1998 "The New Institutional Economics," AER, Vol.88, No.2.

2012 "Saving Economics from the Economists," HBR, Dec.

49.5 WORKS OF OTHERS

Barzel, Y and L. A. Kochin (1992), "Ronald Coase on the Nature of Social Cost as a Key to the Problem of the Firm," ScandJE, Vol.94, No.1.

Brunner, K. (1992), "Ronald Coase: Old Fashioned Scholar," ScandJE, Vol.94, No.1.

De Meza, D. (1987), "Coase Theorem," in the New Palgrave: A Dictionary of Economics, Macmillan, London.

Demsetz, H. (1987), "Coase Ronald Harry," in the New Palgrave: A Dictionary of Economics, Macmillan, London.

Demsetz (1997), "The Firm in Economic Theory: A Quiet Revolution," AER, Vol.87, No.2.

Kahnemann, D., J.L. Knetsch, and R. H. Thaler (1990), "Experimental Tests of the Endowment Effect and the Coase Theorem," JPE, Vol.98, No.6.

Pigou, A. C. (1932), The Economics of Welfare, 4th edition, Macmillan, London.

Stigler, G. J. (1988), Memoirs of an Unregulated Economist, Basic Books, New York.

The Economist (London), December 16, 2010.

CHAPTER 50

GARY STANLEY BECKER

(1930 – 2014)

Professor Gary S. Becker, University of Chicago, U.S.A., was awarded the 1992 Alfred Nobel Memorial Prize in Economic Sciences. The Royal Swedish Academy of Sciences has awarded the Prize to Professor Becker "for having extended the domain of microeconomic analysis to a wide range of human behavior and interaction, including non-market behavior!"

Gary Becker's pioneering research contribution comprises extension of the domain of economic theory to those aspects of human behaviour which had previously been dealt with, if at all, by other social science disciplines such as sociology, demography and criminology. In so doing, he had stimulated economists to enter new areas and tackle new problems.

Becker's research used the economic approach to analyse social issues that go beyond those usually considered by economists. His research programme was founded on the idea that an individual's behaviour adheres to the same fundamental principles and is driven by a much richer set of values and preferences in a number of different areas. Thus, according to Becker, the same explanatory model is applicable in analysing highly diverse aspects of human behaviour. The explanatory model he had chosen to work with is based on what he called an economic approach, which he had applied to issues in one area after another. This approach is characterised by the fact that individual agents – whether they be households, firms, or other organisations – are assumed to behave rationally (that is, purposefully) and that their behaviour can be described as if they maximise welfare, as they conceive it, whether they be "selfish, altruistic, loyal, spiteful or masochistic." In other words, their behaviour can be described as if they maximised a specific objective function, such as utility or wealth. Becker had applied the principle of rational, optimising behaviour to areas where researchers formerly assumed that behaviour is habitual and often downright irrational. He had borrowed an aphorism from George Bernard Shaw to describe his methodological philosophy: "Economy is the art of making the most of life."

Becker's applications of his basic model to different types of human behaviour, according to Royal Swedish Academy press release, can be fruitfully analysed by distinguishing among four research areas:

(i) Investments in Human Capital;

(ii) Behaviour of the Family or Household, including Distribution of Work and Allocation of Time in the Family;
(iii) Crime and Punishment; and
(iv) Discrimination on the Markets for Labour and Goods.

Gary Becker's most noteworthy contribution is in the area of human capital, that is, human competence, and the consequences of investments in human capital. While the theory of human capital is considerably older than Becker's work in the field, his foremost achievement is in formulating and formalising the micro foundations of the theory. In doing so, he had developed the human-capital approach into a general theory for determining the distribution of labour income in an economy. He is credited with the formulation of the so-called human capital-earnings functions which specify the relation between earnings and human capital. Becker's theoretical and empirical contributions in this area are contained in his 1964 book, Human Capital.

The theory of human capital has created a uniform and generally applicable analytical framework for studying wage differentials and wage profiles over time, in addition to return on education and on-the-job training. The theory has found various other applications made by economists including a breakdown into components of the factors underlying economic growth, migration as well as investments and earnings in the health sector. The human-capital approach also helped explain trade patterns across countries. In fact, differences in the supply of human capital among countries had been shown to have more explanatory power than differences in the supply of real capital.

The increased availability of micro data, such as panel data on wages and different characteristics of labour, has dramatically facilitated practical applications of the theory of human capital. The micro data availability has, in turn, been stimulated by Becker's theoretical and empirical studies. The award citation observes: It is hardly an overstatement to say that the human capital approach is one of the most empirically applied theories in economics today.

A more radical extension of the application of economic theory by Gary Becker concerned his analysis of relations among individuals outside of the market system. The most notable example is his work relating to the analysis of the functions of the family summarised in his 1981 publication A Treatise on the Family.

Becker's basic idea was his view that a household can be regarded as a "small factory," which produces what he calls basic goods, such as meals, a residence, entertainment and so on, using time and input of ordinary market goods and "semi-manufactures" which the household purchases on the market. In this analysis, prices of basic goods have two components – first, direct cost of purchasing intermediate goods on the market, and second, time spent for production and consumption of the good in question. For a specific good, this time spent is equivalent to wages multiplied by the time spent per unit of the good produced in the household. An important implication of this approach is: an increase in the wage of one member of the household gives rise not only to changed incentives for work on the market, but also to a shift from more to less time-intensive production and consumption of goods produced by the household, that is, basic goods. Instead of an analysis in terms of the traditional dichotomy between work and leisure, Becker's model provided a general theory for the household allocation of time; for example in his 1965 essay "A Theory of the Allocation of Time." This approach has been found useful for examining numerous issues associated with household behaviour.

Becker had gone further and formulated a general theory for the behaviour of the family, including not only the distribution of work and the allocation of time in the family, but also decisions regarding marriage, divorce and children. As real wages increase, coupled with the possibilities of substituting capital for labour, labour is released in the household so that it becomes more and more uneconomical to let one household member specialise wholly in household production (for instance, child care). As a consequence, some of the family's previous social and economic functions are shifted to other institutions such as firms, schools and other agencies. In a 1986 article, Becker had argued that these processes explain not only the increase in married women's job participation outside the home, but also the rising tendency towards divorce.

In addition to the analysis of the distribution of labour and allocation of time in a household, Becker's most influential contribution in the context of the household and family is, perhaps, his studies on fertility, starting with the 1960 essay "An Economic Analysis of Fertility." Parents are assumed to have preferences regarding both the number and educational level of their children, where the educational level is influenced by the amount of time and other resources that parents spend on their children. Investments in children's human capital may then be derived as a function of income and prices. As wages rise, parents increase their investments in human capital, combined with a decrease in the number of children. By using this theory, Becker explained the historical decline in fertility in industrialised countries, as well as the variations in fertility among different countries and between urban and rural areas. The Award press release states that the highly extensive family policy in Sweden suggests the merits of an economic approach to the analysis of these issues.

The next area in which Becker has applied the theory of rational behaviour and human capital is "Crime and Punishment." A criminal, with the exception of a limited number of psychopaths, was assumed to react to different stimuli in a rational predictable way, both with respect to returns and costs, such as in the form of expected punishment. Becker analysed criminality as rational behaviour under uncertainty, instead of regarding criminal activity as irrational behaviour associated with the specific psychological and social status of an offender as can be gleaned from his 1968 essay, "Crime and Punishment: An Economic Approach" and his 1974 publication entitled Essays in the Economics of Crime and Punishment.

Empirical studies based on this approach indicate that the type of crime committed by a certain group of individuals may largely be explained by an individual's human capital and education. These studies also reveal that the probability of getting caught has a more deterrent effect on criminality than the term of the punishment.

Another example of Becker's unconventional application of the theory of rational, optimising human behaviour concerned his analysis of discrimination on the basis of race, gender and so on. Discrimination was defined as a situation where an economic agent is prepared to incur a cost in order to refrain from an economic transaction or from entering into an economic contract, with someone who is characterised by traits other than her/his own with respect to race or gender. Becker showed that such behaviour, in purely analytical terms, acts as a "tax wedge" between social and private economic rates of return. The explanation is that the discriminating agent behaves as if the price of good or service purchased from the discriminated agent were higher than the price actually paid, and the selling price to the discriminated agent is lower than the price actually obtained. Becker concluded that discrimination thus tends to be economically detrimental not only to those who are discriminated against, but also to those who practice discrimination.

Gary Becker's analysis has been controversial and at the outset met with scepticism and even distrust. Not discouraged by the reception, he persevered in developing his research, gradually gaining increasing acceptance among economists for his ideas and methods. His work also influenced those working in other social sciences; for example, fertility and other aspects of demography. Other examples include his research on discrimination in labour market and criminology. The award citation concludes: "...Becker has also had an indirect impact on scientific approaches in social sciences other than economics; more frequently than in the past, sociologists and political scientists work with models based on theories of 'rational choice.'"

50.1 A BRIEF BIOGRAPHICAL NOTE : GARY BECKER

Gary Becker was born on December 2, 1930 in Pottsville, Pennsylvania, U.S.A. His father, who owned a small business, moved to Brooklyn, New York, when Gary Becker was four or five. Becker went to elementary school and high school in Brooklyn. By the time he finished high school, Becker's interest in mathematics was beginning to compete with a desire to do something useful for society. Becker says: "These two interests came together during my freshman year at Princeton, when I accidentally took a course in economics, and was greatly attracted by the mathematical rigor of a subject that dealt with social organization...my heavy investment in mathematics at Princeton prepared me well for the increasing use of mathematics in economics."

Becker, after earning a B.A. at Princeton University in 1951, decided to go to the University of Chicago for graduate work in economics. His first encounter with Milton Friedman's course on microeconomics renewed his excitement about economics. Becker stated: "He [Friedman] emphasized that economic theory was not a game played by clever academicians, but was a powerful tool to analyze the real world. His course was filled with insights both into the structure of economic theory and its application to practical and significant questions. That course and subsequent contacts with Friedman had a profound effect on the direction taken by my research."

While Friedman who clearly was "the intellectual leader," Chicago had a first class group of economists who were doing innovative research. Especially important to Becker were Gregg Lewis's use of economic theory to analyse labour markets, T. W. Schultz's pioneering research on human capital, Aaron Director's application of economics to anti-trust problems, and industrial organisation more generally, and L. J. Savage's research on subjective probability and the foundations of statistics. Becker received a doctoral degree at the University of Chicago in 1955.

Becker taught at Columbia University from 1957 to 1968 and then returned to Chicago. For twelve years, he divided his time between teaching at Columbia and doing research at the National Bureau of Economic Research, (NBER), New York. His book on human capital was the outcome of his first research project for NBER. During this period, he wrote frequently cited articles on the allocation of time, crime and punishment and irrational behaviour. During 1968-1969, he was Arthur Lehman Professor of Economics, Columbia University. In 1969-1970, he was Ford Foundation Visiting Professor of Economics at the University of Chicago before joining the Department of Economics there in 1970. In 1983, the Department of Sociology at Chicago offered Gary Becker a joint appointment. He was appointed University Professor, Department of Economics and Sociology, 1970-1983. Becker served as Chairman, Department of Economics during 1984-1985. From 1983 he served as University Professor, University of Chicago, Department of Economics, Graduate School of Business and Sociology.

Becker was a Senior Fellow, Hoover Institution, Stanford University, since 1990. He wrote a monthly column for Business Week from 1985 to 2004, alternating with liberal Princeton economist, Alan Blinder. Becker received a number of honours and awards. He received honorary doctorates from Hebrew University, Jerusalem, State University of New York at Stony Brook, Princeton University, Columbia University, Warsaw School of Economics and Harvard University among others. He was elected Fellow, American Statistical Association, 1965, Fellow, Econometric Society, 1967 and Vice President and President, Western Economic Association. He was awarded John Bates Clark Medal of the American Economic Association in 1967. Becker served on the Editorial Board of American Economic Review during 1968-1971 and served as Vice-President, 1974 and President of the American Economic Association, 1987. He became Distinguished Fellow of the American Economic Association, 1988. He received John Von Neumann Award in 2004 and Presidential Medal of Freedom in 2007. He received University of Chicago 2010 Alumni Medal.

Gary Becker died in Chicago, aged 83, on May 3, 2014.

50.2 A BRIEF SURVEY OF GARY BECKER'S CONTRIBUTIONS

As mentioned in the announcement of the Nobel Memorial award, Becker's research is founded on his view that economic theory can be fruitfully applied to a wide range of issues in the social sciences beyond those usually considered by economists. The economic approach Becker followed was defined by him as follows: "The combined assumptions of maximizing behavior, market equilibrium, and stable preferences, used relentlessly and unflinchingly, form the heart of the economic approach as I see it." He further made an important clarification that the economic approach he refers to does not assume that individuals are motivated solely by selfishness or gain. There is no assumption about particular motivations. The economic approach that Becker adopted, had prompted him to take up problems that were previously not considered to be appropriate subjects for economists, such as racial discrimination and crime, in addition to broadening the theoretical foundations for well-established subjects, such as labour supply and population growth.

The contributions of Gary Becker to economics are summarised under the following heads.

1. Human Capital;
2. Economics of Household and Economic Demography;
3. Economics of Discrimination; and
4. Economic Analysis of Crime and Punishment.

50.2.1 HUMAN CAPITAL

The concept of human capital has had a long intellectual history, though the name did not remain the same throughout. The subject has been discussed by some of the great economists of the past, such as Adam Smith and Alfred Marshall. Becker recognised that the "sophisticated analyses" of investments in education and training by Smith and Marshall in the past and Friedman in modern times were not integrated into discussions of productivity and that until 1950's economists generally assumed that "labour power was given and not augmentable." While the analysis of the implication of investments in human capital for economic growth and other related questions was pioneered by T. W. Schultz and others earlier, Becker had put forward a coherent, far-reaching and empirically fruitful theory.

Human Capital analysis starts with the assumption that individuals decide on their education, training, health and medical care by considering the benefits and costs. Benefits include "cultural and other non-monetary gains" along with improvements in occupations and increases in earnings, while costs comprise basically the foregone value of the time spent on these investments. Becker, in developing a coherent theoretical structure, had brought together several disparate strands of research on human capital. In his work, he raised almost all the principal economic questions on the topic that were raised till that time.

In 1950's and 1960's there was considerable hostility to the approach that was taken in order to analyse human capital. The very concept of human capital was taken to be "demeaning" because it treated people as machines. In his Prize lecture Becker noted: "To approach schooling as an investment rather than a cultural experience was considered unfeeling and narrow."

Becker's work attempted a more systematic study of the topic, considerably strengthened its microeconomic foundations and suggested numerous interesting and influential applications. From the individual point of view, education and vocational training can be considered as an investment as it helps him/her in getting into better occupations giving higher earnings. The costs of developing human capital include, besides direct monetary costs of education such as fees etc., the value of earnings foregone by not working during the period of time it takes to acquire the education. From the individual's point of view, education can be considered a profitable investment if the net present value of benefits over costs is positive. Furthermore, to the extent that wages reflect real marginal product of labour, investment in human capital is also real investment from the society's point of view. Becker's work on human capital began with an effort to calculate private rate of return as also social rate of return to various social groups, such as men, women and blacks from investment in different levels of education. His analysis of human capital had also helped explain many regularities in labour markets and the economy at large. In Becker's opinion it is possible to develop a more general theory of human capital that included not only individuals but also firms and that could consider its macroeconomic implications.

Economists have raised some problems with the formulation of the human capital theory. For example, education and training activities do not enter individuals' utility functions. The application of separation theorem is invoked. While individuals make investment decisions with the objective of maximising the present value of the expected future stream of income, preferences play a role only in decision regarding the allocation of consumption over time. According to Sandmo "ignoring the consumption value of educational activities is an obvious simplification, and Becker is naturally aware of this...the defence for this assumption is in terms of simplicity and its power to generate fruitful hypotheses...."

The second problem relates to Becker's assumption of a perfect capital market in his formal presentation of the theory; that is, when the individual faces a given rate of interest and no quantity constraints on lending and borrowing. However, in his applications of the theory, for example, in regard to problems of income distribution, Becker underlined the importance of capital market imperfections, such as credit rationing, though he did not modify the theoretical formulation. With imperfect capital markets, the separation theorem cannot be invoked and consumption preferences influence investment decisions of individuals. However, one has to admit that this problem is not peculiar to human capital theory only but is generally applicable to all investment decisions. Critics point out that "it is particularly conspicuous in decisions where the object of investment is the personal skill level of the individual himself."

Becker was among the first economists to examine the link between measured ability and education since more able people in the society tend to acquire education. The important question is the way to disentangle the effects of ability and human capital investment. Becker in his empirical work found the resulting "ability bias" (that part of the school effect that was actually capturing an unmeasured ability effect) to be rather small. These findings have been confirmed by later research work in this area. Sherwin Rosen, who is one of the researchers in the area, observes: "There is now strong consensus that measured rates of return to human capital investments do not masquerade for unobserved ability. The development of educational signalling, where education is a pure ability signal rather than a socially productive investment, is an interesting extension of these ideas, but of little general validity; the small direct effects of measured ability on earnings detected in the data, and the strong cross country associations between economic development and education both support the standard model." Becker concluded: "Ability corrections did not seem very important but large changes in adult mortality and sizeable rates of economic growth did have big effects" on rates of return to education.

One of the most influential theoretical concepts in human capital analysis and one of the most fruitful applications of the theory is the distinction between general and specific training or knowledge. General training is useful in all firms and is expected to raise the overall level of skill of the individual and therefore increase his marginal and average product in many lines of production. As regards general training, since there is no guarantee that the employee will use his augmented skill in the employer's business, the employer has little or no incentive to provide it. It is therefore expected that specialised institutions provide general training and it has to be paid for by the individual or state. On the other hand, specific training or firm-specific knowledge is useful only in the firms providing it by raising the individual's productivity in the business of the employee only. In the Prize lecture, Becker stated: "This distinction helps explain why workers with highly specific skills are less likely to quit their jobs and are the last to be laid off during business downturns. It also explains why most promotions are made from within a firm rather than through hiring (workers need time to learn about a firm's structure and "culture") and why better accounting methods would include the specific human capital of employees among the principal assets of most companies."

The human capital theory that Becker had developed is able to satisfactorily explain the empirical observation of the greater geographical mobility of young workers compared to the old. Assuming that the costs of moving are roughly the same, the explanation is that older workers have a shorter time within which to capture the benefits of moving to a new place of work. This explanation is more meaningful and makes much more sense than the very vague speculations about inertia induced by age, which were common prior to the development of human capital literature. More importantly, the human capital approach provides a specific formula by which net present value of a move to a new work place can be computed for different age groups.

Human capital theory has facilitated satisfactory explanations of empirical observations that were previously thought to contradict basic economic theory. Sandmo refers to the famous example of the Leontief Paradox in international economics. In his 1954 empirical work, Leontief found that United States tended to export labour-intensive products, contrary to what Hecksher-Ohlin theory of international specialisation predicts. Sandmo states: "A resolution of this paradox is that the United States is in fact particularly well endowed with human capital, which is embodied in the labour price but not taken into account in econometric studies based on national accounts data...human capital theory has made an important contribution to the interpretation of data on factor endowments and specialization. Similar remarks apply to its contribution to studies of economic growth and capital accumulation." While there was for a while neglect of the study of the relation of human capital to growth, human capital has been brought to the forefront of discussions with the revival of more formal models of endogenous growth; for example, 1986 article of Romer, 1988 paper of Lucas and Becker's 1990 article "Human Capital, Fertility and Economic Growth" co-authored with Murphy and Tamura.

While there is no doubt that human capital theory has made a very significant contribution to economics and Becker's contribution to our understanding of human capital approach has been very important, there have been alternative explanations, such as Arrow's theories of screening and Spence's work on market signalling. These explanations of the relationship between education and income are "to some extent" in direct conflict with the insights provided by human capital theory. Becker's reply is: "schooling as screening...is a relatively minor influence in determining earnings differentials by education."

In his Prize lecture, Becker summed up the important empirical insights that the human capital approach had provided. The theory of human capital investments establishes inequality in earnings to differences in talents, family background and bequests and other assets. Many empirical studies regarding the relation of income to schooling and training have relied on human capital concepts. The "sizeable" growth in earnings' inequality in the U.S. during the 1980's is largely explained by higher returns to the more educated and better trained. Furthermore, "Human Capital theory gives a provocative interpretation of the so-called "gender gap" in earnings. Traditionally, women have been far more likely than men to work part-time and intermittently, partly because they usually withdraw from the labour force for a while after having children. As a result, they had fewer incentives to invest in education and training that improved earnings and job skills." There has been a sea-change during the last three decades. Becker argued: "The decline in family size, the growth in divorce rates, the rapid expansion of the service sector where most women are employed, the continuing economic development that raised the earnings of women along with men, and civil rights legislation encouraged greater labour force participation by women and hence greater investment in market-oriented skills. In practically all rich countries, these forces significantly improved both the occupations and relative earnings of women."

In more recent years, Becker had extended his human capital approach to cover social aspects and developed the concept of what he called "social capital." He considered social forces important for many aspects of market behaviour. For most behaviour, people are influenced by what others around them are doing. Social phenomena are important in markets, and economists need to put more efforts in using economic analysis to incorporate social forces. While social influences affect individual behaviour, social influences are themselves built up from individual behaviour. While human capital usually looks at a person, her knowledge or her skills, social capital looks at a person's link to other individuals. That is why it is social. It is capital because it has some durability, where depreciation rate may be endogenous. Becker refered to the book Social Economics which he wrote with Kevin Murphy as "a small beginning." He hoped the small beginning will encourage others to make bigger advances as they recognize the importance of this kind of capital (social capital).

50.2.2 ECONOMICS OF HOUSEHOLD AND ECONOMIC DEMOGRAPHY

Becker's work on human capital, identified the family as major financier of human capital investments. Becker dealt with allocation of resources within families inclusive of direct and market provision of human capital and bequests. The most important applications of economic analysis as it relates to non-market behaviour concern his work on the economics of household and studies relating to economic demography.

The economic approach to the family by Becker interpreted marriage, fertility, divorce and relationship among family members through the lens of utility-maximising forward-looking behaviour. Becker stated that "the family is arguably the most fundamental and oldest of institutions – some authors trace its origin to more than 50,000 years ago." His A Treatise on the Family attempted an analysis of not only Western families but also those in other cultures and changes in family structure during the past several centuries. His initial work in the field was concerned with the economic analysis of fertility which analysed the role of parental choice in determining the quantity as well as the quality of their children. The term quality in Becker's model stands for parental investments in the human capital of children, broadly interpreted to include education and skill development as well as health. The analysis of fertility, according to Becker, has a long and honourable history. Economic models of behaviour have been used to study fertility ever since Malthus. Knut Wicksell was attracted to economics by his belief in the Malthusian predictions of overpopulation.

The failure of Malthus's simple model of fertility persuaded economists that decisions regarding family size lay beyond economic calculus. It is Becker's view that the trouble with the Malthusian approach was its use of economics inappropriate for modern life. It ignored the fact that the time spent on child care becomes more expensive as countries become more productive. The higher value of time raises the cost of children and thereby reduces the demand for large families. The Malthusian approach also fails to consider that the greater importance of education and training in developed industrialised economies encourages parents to invest more in the skills of their children which also raises the cost of large families. Becker concluded that the growing value of time and the increased importance given to school and other human capital help explain the decline in fertility as countries develop (contrary to Malthus's conclusion) and many features of birth rates in modern economies.

The 1960 paper of Becker emphasised a vital idea, that child quality is the other side of the quantity. Furthermore, the positive effect on demand for children takes the form of substituting greater quality per child for a larger quantity of children. The conclusion is clear and significant. On the whole, more aggregate resources are invested in children in higher income families and developed industrialised countries through greater per-child investments, even though the number of children is smaller. Furthermore, the article argued that the decision to have children can be modelled on lines similar to the demand for durable goods.

Another paper on the topic is "A Theory of the Allocation of Time" which has formulated a general theory of the family leading to the "reintegration" of economics and demography. It was shown that the quantity-quality substitution is reinforcing, as "greater per-child investment made each child even more costly and further reduced the demand for numbers."

Becker had extended, over time, the economics of household in a number of directions. His work on the theory of marriage and social interactions analysed the problem of family allocation of resources when family members are linked together altruistically. This formulation required Becker to consider interdependent preferences, the area in which he had done sustained and important work.

Becker's most ambitious work in this area is the 1981 book A Treatise on the Family. In this work, he combined his earlier theoretical contributions such as, theory of human capital formation, theory of household production and allocation of time and further extended his theoretical framework to multi-person households. He provided a complete economic theory of the family, its formation and dissolution.

Becker's analysis was also devoted to problems of division of labour and the nature of the marriage contract. He identified biological differences as the basis of the division of labour and the marriage contract as reinforcing it where woman gives birth to and raises children in return for protection and "insurance." Specifically, Becker had considered an important issue: why in almost all societies have "married women specialized in bearing and rearing children and in certain agricultural activities, whereas married men have done most of the fighting and market work?" His explanation was a combination of biological differences between men and women and discrimination against women in market activities, partly through "cultural conditioning." Since the return from investing in a skill is greater when more time is spent utilising the skill, a married couple could benefit considerably from a sharp division of labour – the husband specialising in some types of human capital and the wife in others. His theory also explained in a satisfactory manner why women entered labour force as "families became smaller, divorce more common, and earning opportunities for women improved."

One of the most well known ideas in the book, originally introduced by Becker in his 1974 article "A Theory of Social Interactions," is the "Rotten Kid Theorem" which is concerned with the role of altruism in the family. Becker observed that relations among members of a family differ radically from those among employees of firms and members of other organisations. The interactions among family members are more likely to be motivated by love, obligation, guilt and a sense of duty than by narrowly interpreted self-interest. The issue can be illustrated with an example. Assume that the head of a family, the benefactor, is an altruist, and takes into account utilities of other members of the family. Take the case of another member of the family – the beneficiary – who is selfish and is only interested in his own income. Since the latter takes the reaction of the benefactor into account, he will behave towards the benefactor and the other members of the family in a way which is indistinguishable from altruism, acting so as to maximise family income, though the immediate effect of it may be to reduce his own income. Sandmo observes: "A further implication of this result is that the utility function of the family will be that of the benefactor; on the assumptions underlying the rotten kid theorem, there is no problem of aggregation over individuals in the household."

The "Rotten Kid Theorem," thus shows how the behaviour of selfish individuals is affected by altruism. Under certain conditions, even selfish beneficiaries – most parents believe that the best example of this is selfish children with altruistic parents – are induced to act as if they are altruistic toward their benefactors because that raises their own selfish welfare. They act this way because otherwise gifts from their benefactors would be reduced enough to make them worse off. Becker had shown earlier that altruism within families enormously alters how they respond to shocks and public policies that redistribute resources among members. He had also demonstrated "that exogenous redistribution of resources from an altruist to her beneficiaries (or vice versa) may not affect the welfare of anyone because the altruist would try to reduce her gifts by the amount redistributed." In a 1974 paper, Robert Barro derived the result in an intergenerational context, casting doubt on the common assumption that government deficits and related fiscal policies have real effects on the economy.

In the analysis of divorce, Becker adopted an approach similar to the one that he adopted for analysing marriage, namely considerations of the incomes of each spouse inside and outside marriage. He explained the increase in divorce rate in the U.S. by the increase in market wages of women and in social security payments to single mothers. Becker employed the same factors for explaining the decline in the number of children per family and for explaining the relative rise in illegitimate children. Becker's A Treatise on the Family has been hailed by critics as "a high point in the economic research of the family and a demographic phenomena associated with it." The book is considered "...a pioneering exploration of the theory and evidence" and as a major contribution to the conceptual foundation of the subject.

Becker in collaboration with Barro had, in recent years, put forward models of fertility choice and intergenerational transfers within the framework of a neoclassical growth model. They employed a "dynastic" utility function in which the utility of the present generation depends on the utilities of all future generations. This formulation forms the basis of the theory of intergenerational transfers and fertility. Sandmo states: "Because the equilibrium over time can be seen as the outcome of a maximization problem, a number of results follow for the dependence of the equilibrium of exogenous variables like the rate of interest, the rate of technical progress, the cost of raising children, the tax and social security system, etc." Becker and Barro argued that the implications of their analysis are closer to the actual experiences of modern economies.

In the Prize lecture, Becker commented: "It is much less appreciated that altruistic parents who leave bequests also tend to invest more in their children's skills, habits, and values. For they gain from financing all investments in the education and skills of children that yield a higher rate of return than the return on savings. They can indirectly save for old age by investing in children, and then reducing bequests when elderly. Both parents and children would be better off when parents make all investments in children that yield a higher return than that on savings, and then adjust bequests to the efficient level of investment." He demonstrated this proposition in the Appendix to the lecture. Carrying the argument further, Becker stated that both the parents and children would be better off if the parents agreed to invest more in the children in return for a commitment by the children to care for the parents when the latter need help. Economists and lawyers usually suggest a written agreement to ensure commitment and compliance. Becker ruled out this option. He said in his lecture: "Part of my current research considers an indirect way to generate commitments when promises and written agreements are not binding...it carries the economic approach to the family unto uncharted ground related to the rational formation of preferences within families." He opined that economic theory needs to incorporate guilt, affection and related attitudes into preferences in order to have a deeper understanding of when commitments are credible and provides a formal discussion in the appendix to the lecture. Becker therefore recommended extending the traditional analysis of individual rational choice to incorporate into the theory a much richer class of attitudes, preferences and calculations.

50.2.3 ECONOMICS OF DISCRIMINATION

Becker's seminal and first important work in this area was the 1957 book The Economics of Discrimination originating in his doctoral dissertation at the University of Chicago. He admited that discrimination against outsiders had always existed, but with the exception of a few discussions of the employment of women, there was not much of writing on this subject by economists. To define discrimination, he used the economic concept of willingness to pay. Discrimination comes from prejudice which Becker translated into a monetary unit – how much one is willing to pay. The starting point of his analysis is that discrimination occurs when economic agents have a prejudice or a preference against women, or against blacks or Hispanics, or Chinese or Asians or foreigners, whatever the group may be. As a result, economic agents reveal a willingness to pay to not entering into contracts with other agents possessing different characteristics, say with a different colour of their skin. Becker used the concept of "discrimination coefficient" – a measure of how much a person is willing to pay. To cite an example, a white employer faces a money wage rate W for black labour. In his hiring decision, the white employer acts as if the true wage cost of labour were W (1+d), where d (a positive number) is the employer's "discrimination coefficient." Likewise, it is possible to define discrimination coefficients for white employees' willingness to work with a black employee, white consumers' willingness to purchase goods produced by black labour and so on.

Discrimination coefficients incorporate the influence of race, gender and other personal characteristics on tastes and attitudes, instead of making the common assumptions that employers only consider the productivity of employees, that workers ignore the characteristics of those with whom they work and that customers only care about the qualities of the goods and services provided. According to Becker, it is only through widening of the usual assumptions that it is possible to understand the obstacles to advancement encountered by minorities. The actual discrimination in a market place against a minority group depends, according to Becker, on the combined discrimination of employers, workers, consumers, schools and governments. He also pointed out that discrimination by the majority in the market place is effective because members of the minority cannot provide various skills in sufficient quantities to companies that would specialise in using these workers.

An important contribution of Becker's study was to point out that discrimination may actually harm both groups – black and white in this case. To demonstrate this, he used a simple international trade model, where the two communities – white and black – trade in factors of production and where the role of tariffs is played by discrimination coefficients. He then showed that a state of discrimination resulted in an inferior equilibrium from also the point of view of community which has a taste for discrimination. "Discrimination – like protection – is unfair to non-discriminating free trade."

In the Prize lecture, Becker commented: "When the majority is very large compared to the minority – in the United States whites are nine times as numerous and have much more human and physical capital per capita than blacks – market discrimination by the majority hardly lowers their incomes but may greatly reduce the incomes of the minority. However, when minority members are a sizable fraction of the total, discrimination by the majority injures them as well."

He illustrated the proposition citing the case of South Africa where blacks were four to five times as numerous as whites, the Afrikaner discrimination imposed sizeable cost on whites (except some white groups which benefited), leading to its eventual breakdown. He also noted with satisfaction the evidence accumulated "during the past twenty-five years" from many countries on the earnings, employment and occupations of blacks, women, religious groups, immigrants and others. He made particular reference to the work of Arrow and Phelps which suggests that the beliefs of employers, teachers and other influential groups that members of minority groups are less productive can be largely self-fulfilling, since these beliefs may cause minorities to underinvest in education, training and work skills which make them less productive.

Becker's work on discrimination has been subjected to criticism such as adhocism of his theoretical analysis and far from convincing nature of the empirical work. However, his book is considered a major contribution which opened up a new area of research for economists. Becker is considered far ahead of his time. His work has strong influence on labour economics for its "inventive use of the equalizing difference apparatus," encouraging others to further study the question. Critics are of the opinion that Becker's work stands alongside Myrdal's work as one of the leading contributions to the subject.

50.2.4 ECONOMIC ANALYSIS OF CRIME AND PUNISHMENT

The initial inspiration for Becker's work on the economics of crime came while searching for a parking spot in New York City. The true story as he had recounted in his Prize lecture: "I began to think about crime in the 1960's after driving to Columbia University for an oral examination of a [Ph.D] student in economic theory. I was late and had to decide quickly whether to put the car in a parking lot or risk getting a ticket for parking illegally on the street. I calculated the likelihood of getting a ticket, the size of the penalty, and the cost of putting the car in a lot. I decided it paid to take the risk and park on the street. (I did not get a ticket). As I walked the few blocks to the examination room, it occurred to me that the city authorities had probably gone through a similar analysis. The frequency of their inspection of parked vehicles and the size of the penalty imposed on violators should depend on their estimates of the type of calculations potential violators like me would make. Of course, the first question I put to the hapless student was to work out the optimal behavior of both the offender and the police, something I had not yet done." After he finished the examination, Becker said: "Gee, this is an interesting topic." He started working on it seriously at that point.

Intellectual discussions of crime in the 1950's and 1960's were dominated by the opinion that criminal behaviour was the result of mental illness and social oppression and those criminals were helpless victims. These attitudes determined the social policy, leading to changes in laws aimed at expanding the rights of criminals. These changes led to reduction of apprehension and conviction of criminals and provision of less protection to the law – abiding population.

Becker was not sympathetic to the assumption that criminals had radically different motivations from everyone else. Instead, he applied mainstream economic ideas of costs and benefits to understand unlawful behaviour. He analysed criminal acts as the outcome of rational choice under conditions of uncertainty. The implication is that similar to all other rational decisions of economic agents, criminal behaviour responds positively to its gains and negatively to its costs (costs include the probability of detection and quantum of penalties if detected). Becker clarified that rationality does not necessarily imply narrow materialism. Rationality recognises that many people are constrained by moral and ethical considerations, and economic agents do not commit crimes even when they were profitable and there is no danger of detection. However, Becker agreed, police and jails would be unnecessary if such attitudes always prevailed. Rationality implies that some individuals become criminals since financial rewards from crime compared favourably to legal work, taking into account the likelihood of apprehension and conviction and the severity of punishment.

In Becker's approach, the amount of crime in a society is determined by the rationality and preferences of would be criminals as well as by the economic and social environment created by public policies, including expenditures on maintenance of police force, punishments meted out for different crimes and opportunities for employment, schooling and training programmes.

The economics of crime is basically considered a problem of welfare economics. Contrary to the use of a social welfare function as is done in welfare economics, Becker introduced a social loss function, which has as its arguments the damage to the society from offences and costs of conviction and punishment to society. As the social loss function reflects the loss to the society as a whole and as it depends only on aggregate measures of costs and damages, the function is neutral with respect to the distribution of costs and damages among individuals in the society thus "reflecting only efficiency concerns." Becker's simplified framework yielded a number of interesting results; for example, on the margin, it should be true that "crime does not pay." That is, criminal activities should appeal only to "risk lovers."

It is the view of Becker that aggregate spending on fighting crime could be reduced, while keeping the mathematical expectation of punishment unchanged, by offsetting a cut in expenditures on catching criminals with a sufficient increase in the punishment to those convicted. However, risk-loving individuals are more deterred from crime by a higher probability of conviction than by severe punishments. Therefore, "optimal behaviour by the state would balance the reduced spending on police and courts from lowering the probability of conviction against the preference of risk-preferring criminals for a lesser certainty of punishment." At the same time he sounded a very valid warning: "The State should also consider the likelihood of punishing innocent persons."

Dwelling on the topic of crime and punishment, Becker in his Prize lecture admited that in the early stages of his work on crime, he was puzzled by why theft is socially harmful since it appears merely to redistribute resources, usually from wealthier individuals to poorer individuals. He resolved the puzzle (as given in his 1968 paper) by recognising "that criminals spend on weapons and on the value of the time in planning and carrying out their crimes, and that such spending is socially unproductive – it is now what is called 'rent-seeking' – because it does not create wealth, only forcibly redistributes it." He further added: "The social cost of theft was approximated by the number of dollars stolen since rational criminals would be willing to spend up to that amount on their crimes. (I should have added the resources spent by potential victims protecting themselves against crime.)"

There is gradual acceptance of the economic approach to crime, in large part due to efforts of Gary Becker, and a voluminous literature has grown on the topic over time.

Becker noted with satisfaction in his Prize lecture that studies of crime that use the economic approach have become common during the past quarter century, which include "analysis of the optimal marginal punishments to deter increases in the severity of crimes – for example, to deter a kidnapper from killing his victim (the modern literature starts with Stigler [1970]), and the relation between private and public enforcement of laws (see Becker and Stigler [1974], and Landes and Posner [1975])."

Becker prefered fines to imprisonment and other types of punishment, as they are more efficient. In addition, with a fine, the punishment to offenders is also revenue to the State. Empirical work regarding the effects of crime rates, of prison terms, conviction rates, unemployment levels, income inequalities and so on has been taken up by other researchers in the field.

The economic approach to crime initiated by Becker has become influential primarily because of the applicability of the analytical apparatus to study enforcement of a variety of laws and regulations, such as minimum wage legislation, clear air acts, insider trading and other violations of security laws and evasions of income tax. Since very few laws are self-enforcing, they require expenditures on conviction and punishment to deter violations. The basic cost-benefit approach adopted by Becker has been extended to a number of cases such as civil disputes, administrative law, dispute settlement, out-of-court settlement and behaviour of prosecutors using simple game-theoretic tools.

Finally, while there is a general acceptance of Becker's economic approach to crime, it is not as though there are no critics. The approach has been strongly criticised by Stern. In this context, it is appropriate to quote Sandmo's verdict: "It is unreasonable to expect those who say the first words on a subject also to say the last. Becker has clearly made a major contribution in laying the foundations for a new era of theoretical and empirical research."

50.3 CONCLUDING OBSERVATIONS

Gary Becker's singular contribution lay in broadening the reach of economics into spheres previously neglected by economists and to thereby transform those fields as well as economics. The areas to which he has applied the analytical tools of micro economics include preference formation, the family, discrimination and addiction. He has explored each of these phenomena with the underlying assumption that "humans behave rationally – attempting to maximize their utility, however they define it, under whatever constraints they may face." His work was initially viewed "with skepticism and often with disdain" by the economic establishment. But one has to note that Becker's "elegant theoretical models, testable hypotheses and uncannily accurate predictions" eventually won him the respect of his critics. Observers do not fail to note that over time, his initially controversial views became a vital part of the "cannon of modern microeconomics" and his methods of analysis have now become common practice in various social science fields such as law, criminology, demography, family social science and so on.

Besides the areas covered in the earlier pages, Becker had made contributions in other areas as well. He is considered one of the founders of the 'new' theory of consumption or the theory of household production along with Kelvin Lancaster and John Muth. Becker had made contributions to the economics of political decision-making. In his early work, he made a significant point that observation of market failure was not sufficient to recommend public policy intervention and in the absence of a positive theory of public decision-making, there is no guarantee that collective action would lead to improvement in resource allocation.

In regard to the new field of behavioural economics for the development of which Richard Thaler (his colleague at Chicago) made important contribution, he expressed his major differences. He said: "One can get excellent suggestions from experiments, but economic theory is not about how people act in experiments, but how they act in markets. And those are very different things.... The theory is not about how people answer questions. It is a theory about how people behave in market situations.... Economists have a theory of behavior in markets, not in labs and the relevant theories can be very different. One reason is the division of labor in markets."

Regarding the issue of rationality, Becker offered an important clarification: "The important point is that markets are more "rational" than individuals...markets have a lot more rationality than any one person does. Economists are really analyzing markets and how they work...economics is a theory of markets. The theory of the individual is just a way of attacking market problems."

One cannot but fail to note the innovative nature of Becker's work. Rosen describes Gary Becker as "one of the greatest risk takers in all the social sciences" in that he has consistently chosen to work on problems that were out of the economic mainstream. He is considered a great visionary. Rosen further observes: "An interesting footnote for the philosophy of science is the extent to which Becker has influenced economists younger than himself, who were not trapped by received ideas, modes of thinking, and prior beliefs. But that is the way with all revolutionaries in a scientific field. Becker is now firmly part of the establishment."

50.4 SELECT BIBLIOGRAPHY OF GARY BECKER'S WORKS

50.4.1 BOOKS AND MONOGRAPHS

1957 The Economics of Discrimination, University of Chicago Press, Chicago, Ill. (Second Edition, 1971).

1964 Human Capital, Columbia University Press for the NBER, New York. (Second Edition, 1975. Third Edition, 1993).

1967 Human Capital and the Personal Distribution of Income: An Analytical Approach, University of Michigan, Ann Arbor, Michi.

1971 Economic Theory, A. Knopf, New York.

1974		(edited with W.M. Landes), Essays in the Economics of Crime and Punishment, Columbia University Press for NBER, New York.
1975		(with G. Ghez), The Allocation of Time and Goods over the Life Cycle, Columbia University Press for NBER, New York.
1976	a	(edited) Essays in Labor Economics in Honor of H. Gregg Lewis, Special Supplement to JPE, Vol.84, No.2, Part 2.
	b	The Economic Approach to Human Behavior, University of Chicago Press, Chicago, Ill.
1981		A Treatise on the Family, Harvard University Press, Cambridge, M.A. Expanded Edition 1991.
1993		Human Capital: A Theoretical and Empirical Analysis, with Special Reference to Education, University of Chicago Press, Chicago, Ill.
1996	a	Accounting for Tastes, Harvard University Press, Cambridge, MA.
	b	(with G. N. Becker), The Economics of Life, McGraw Hill, New York.
2001		(with K. M. Murphy), Social Economics: Market Behavior in a Social Environment, Harvard University Press, Cambridge, MA.

50.4.2 ARTICLES

1952		(with W. J. Baumol), "The Classical Monetary Theory: The Outcome of the Discussion," Economica, Vol. XIX, Nov.
1957		(with M. Friedman), "A Statistical Illusion in Judging Keynesian Models," JPE, Vol.LXV, No.1.
1960		"An Economic Analysis of Fertility," in Demographic and Economic Change in Developed Countries, Conference of the Universities – National Bureau for Economic Research (NBER), A Report of the NBER, Princeton University Press, Princeton, NJ.
1962	a	"Irrational Behavior and Economic Theory," JPE, Vol.LXX, No.1.
	b	"Investment in Human Capital: A Theoretical Analysis," JPE, Vol. LXX, No.5: Part 2.
1965		"A Theory of Allocation of Time," EJ, Vol. LXXV, No.299.
1968		"Crime and Punishment: An Economic Approach," JPE, Vol.76, Pages 169.
1973	a	(with H.G. Lewis), "On the Interaction between the Quantity and Quality of Children," JPE, Vol.81, No.2, Part 2.
	b	"A Theory of Marriage: Part I," JPE, Vol.81, No.4. Reprinted in T. W. Schultz (ed.), Economics of the Family, University of Chicago Press, Chicago, Ill. 1974.

1974 a (with G. J. Stigler), "Law Enforcement, Malfeasance and Compensations of Enforcers," Journal of Legal Studies, Vol.III, No.1.

b "A Theory of Marriage: Part II," JPE, Vol.82, No.2: Part 2. Reprinted in T. W. Schultz (Ed.), Economics of the Family, University of Chicago Press, Chicago, Ill.

c "A Theory of Social Interactions," JPE, Vol.82, No.6.

1976 "Altruism, Egoism, and Genetic Fitness: Economics and Sociology," JEL, Vol. XIV, No.3.

1977 (with E. M. Landes and R.T. Michael), "An Economic Analysis of Marital Instability," JPE, Vol.85, No.6.

1979 (with N. Tomes), "An Equilibrium Theory of the Distribution of Income and Intergenerational Mobility," JPE, Vol.87, No.6.

1981 "Altruism in the Family and Selfishness in the Market Place," Economica, Vol.103, Feb.

1985 a "Human Capital, Effort and the Sexual Division of Labor," Journal of Labor Economics, Vol.3, No.1, Part 2.

b "An Economic Analysis of the Family," Seventeenth Geary Lecture, The Economic and Social Research Institute, Dublin, Ireland.

1986 (with N. Tomes), "Human Capital and the Rise and Fall of Families," Journal of Labor Economics, Vol.4, No.3: Part 2.

1988 a (with R. J. Barro), "A Reformulation of the Economic Theory of Fertility," QJE, Vol. 103, No.1.

b (with K. M. Murphy), "A Theory of Radical Addiction," JPE, Vol.96, No.4.

1989 a "Family Economics and Macro Behavior," Presidential Address to the American Economic Association, AER, Vol.79, No.1.

b (with R. J. Barro), "Fertility Choice in a Model of Economic Growth," Econometrica, Vol.57, No.2.

1990 (with K. M. Murphy and R. Tamura), "Human Capital, Fertility and Economic Growth," JPE, Vol.98, No.5: Part 2.

1991 (with M. Grossman and K. M. Murphy), "Rational Addiction and the Effect of Price on Consumption," AER, Vol.81, No.2.

1992 a "Habits, Addictions and Traditions," Kyklos, Vol.45, No. 3.

b "Fertility and the Economy," Journal of Population Economics, Vol.5, No.3.

c (with K. M. Murphy), "The Division of Labor, Coordination, and Knowledge," QJE, Vol.107, No.4.

1993 "The Economic Way of Looking at Behavior," Nobel Lecture, JPE, Vol.101, No.3.

1994 (with M. Grossman and K. M. Murphy), "An Empirical Analysis of Cigarette Addiction," AER, Vol.84, No.3.

1997 (with C. B. Mulligan), "The Endogenous Determination of Time Preference," QJE, Vol.112, No.3.

1998 (with T. J. Philipson), "Old-Age Longevity and Mortality – Contingent Claims," JPE, Vol.106, No.3.

1999 (with E. L. Glaser and K. M. Murphy), "Population and Economic Growth," AER, Vol.89, No.2.

2005 a (with T. Philipson and R. Soares), "The Quantity and Quality of Life and the Evolution of World Inequality," AER, Vol.95, No.1.

b (with K. M. Murphy and I. Werning), "The Equilibrium Distribution of Income and the Market for Status," JPE, Vol.113, No.2.

2007 (with L. Rayo) "Habits, Peers, and Happiness: An Evolutionary Perspective," AER, Vol. 97, No.2.

2010 (with W. H. J. Hubbard and K. M. Murphy), "The Market for College Graduates and the World Wide Boom in Higher Education of Women," AER, Vol. 100, No. 2.

50.5 WORKS OF OTHERS

Arrow, K. J. (1973), "Higher Education as a Filter," JPubE, Vol.2, No.3.

Lancaster, K. J. (1966), "A New Approach to Consumer Theory," JPE, Vol.74, Apr.

Leontief, W. W. (1954), "Domestic Production and Foreign Trade: The American Position Re-examined," Economic Internationale, Vol.7, Feb.

Muth, R. F. (1966), "Household Production and Consumer Demand Functions," Econometrica, Vol.34, No.3.

Rosen, S. (1993), "Risks and Rewards: Gary Becker's Contributions," ScandJE, Vol.95, No.1.

Schultz, T. W. (1966), "Investment in Human Capital," AER, Vol.51, No.1.

Spence, M. (1974), "Market Signalling," Harvard University Press, Cambridge, MA.

Stern, N. (1978), "On the Economic Theory of Policy towards Crime," in J.M. Heineke (ed.) Economic Models of Criminal Behavior, North-Holland, Amsterdam.

CHAPTER 51

ROBERT WILLIAM FOGEL

(1926 – 2013)

The Royal Swedish Academy of Sciences has awarded the 1993 Alfred Nobel Memorial Prize in Economic Sciences jointly to Professor Robert W. Fogel, University of Chicago, Chicago, U.S.A., and Professor Douglass C. North, Washington University, St. Louis, U.S.A., "for having renewed research in economic history by applying economic theory and quantitative methods to explain economic and institutional change."

For the fourth year in a row, the Nobel Memorial Prize in Economic Sciences went to works that extended economic analysis to an applied field. The economic sociology of education and the family, law and industrial organization, finance and now economic history have been recognized as important subfields of the discipline. Incidentally, it is the first time the Economics prize has been given to economic historians.

The contribution of modern economic historians to the development of economic sciences has been in two directions – by combining economic theory with quantitative methods and by creating new databases by constructing and reconstructing economic data bases. This has enabled modern economic historians to question and re-evaluate earlier results that have helped augment our knowledge of the past; it has also helped eliminate "irrelevant" theories. Modern economic historians have shown that in order to gain an understanding of economic growth, there is need to modify or supplement traditional theories. It is well known that economic historians often consider complex problems, requiring an integration of economics, sociology, statistics and history. Robert Fogel and Douglass North, this year's Nobel Prize winners, are the economic historians who have best achieved such a scientific integration. They are commonly recognised as pioneers in the branch of economic history that has been called the "new economic history" or "cliometrics;" that is, research that combines economic theory, quantitative methods, hypothesis testing, counterfactual alternatives and traditional techniques of economic history, to explain economic growth or decline in a country. In fundamental areas of research, their work has enhanced our knowledge and understanding as to how, why and when economic changes occur.

Robert Fogel studied the role of the railroads in the economic development of the United States, the importance of slavery as an institution and its economic role in the U.S. and historical demography.

The press release announcing the award to Douglass North makes reference to the study of long-term economic development in Europe and the United States and his recent work devoted to the analysis of the role of institutions in economic growth.

Robert Fogel's contributions to economics are summarised in this chapter, while Douglass North's contributions will be surveyed in the next.

The Royal Swedish Academy makes particular mention of Robert Fogel's scientific breakthrough in his 1964 book on the role of the railroads in the American economy. There was a general agreement with Joseph Schumpeter's and Walt W. Rostow's earlier assertion that modern economic growth and development were a result of certain important discoveries. Fogel rejected this hypothesis after testing it with "extraordinary exactitude." Instead, Fogel had shown that the recorded economic development was determined by a sum of many technical changes rather than by a few great innovations. The explanation that the great transport systems have a decisive impact on development seems intuitively plausible. Fogel constructed a hypothetical alternative (a so-called counterfactual historiography). He compared actual occurrences with a hypothetical course of events with a view to assess the importance of the railroads. He found that they were not absolutely necessary in explaining the U.S. economic development and that their effect on the growth of American GDP was less than three per cent. Few books in economic history have made such an impression as Fogel's. He also became an innovator in the methodology of economic history through his use of counterfactual arguments and cost-benefit analysis.

Fogel's painstaking interpretation of his sources, along with the use of innumerable and highly varied historical data, made it difficult for his critics to argue against him on purely empirical grounds. As he pointed out, a greater problem facing the researchers often is the lack of relevant data rather than the lack of relevant theory. Fogel's use of counterfactual analysis and his expert command of quantitative techniques in combination with economic theory have had a significant influence on our understanding of economic change.

The second important book of Fogel on slavery as an institution and its role in the economic development of the United States received considerable attention and created bitter controversies. According to Fogel, the established opinion that slavery was an ineffective, unprofitable and pre-capitalist organisation was "erroneous." Slavery as an institution did not disintegrate due to its economic weakness, but because of political decisions. He showed that despite its inhumanity, the system had been economically efficient.

Fogel's careful testing of all conceivable sources and his innovative methodological approach have increased our knowledge of the activities of institutions as well as their decay and have renewed our methods of research. His books on the railroads and on slavery have forced researchers to reconsider previous, generally accepted, results and few books in economic history have been scrutinised in such detail by critical colleagues.

Another area of research of Fogel concerned economic demography and, in particular, changes in mortality rates over long periods of time and their relation to changes in standards of living in the past few centuries. This work is less controversial than the other two, and is both interdisciplinary and international, including collaboration with colleagues from many countries. His conclusion was that less than half of the decrease in mortality can be explained by improved nutritional standards prior to modern medical breakthroughs. Thus, a significant part of the decline in mortality remains unexplained. Fogel was of the view that a systematic analysis requires an integrated study of mortality rates, morbidity rates, nutritional intake and individuals' height and weight. According to the press release of the Royal Swedish Academy, Fogel was in the process of integrating bio-medical and economic techniques. The release further adds that it is already apparent that his analyses will affect many levels of research in economic history.

51.1 A BRIEF BIOGRAPHICAL NOTE: ROBERT FOGEL

Robert William Fogel was born in New York City in 1926 to immigrant parents from the city of Odessa in Russia. He had his education in the public schools of New York City between 1932 and 1944. It was excellent preparation for a life in sciences. He aspired to a career in science. Fogel received B.A. degree from Cornell University, Ithaca, New York State. It was at Cornell that his scientific interests shifted from physics and chemistry to economics and history. In his own words "the switch in focus was precipitated by the widespread pessimism about the future of the economy during the second half of the 1940's, when forecasts about the imminent return to the massive unemployment of the Great Depression were rife." He began his graduate training in Columbia University with the "naïve belief" that by combining the study of economics and history he would "quickly discover" the fundamental forces that had determined technological and institutional changes over the ages and that such knowledge would help in finding solutions to the problems of economic instability and inequity the nation was then facing. He soon realised as to how little was actually known about these large processes and their interconnections leading him to conclude that much greater use had to be made of quantitative evidence. Fogel, therefore, had set out to master the most advanced analytical and statistical methods that were then taught in the economics department of Columbia University. Fogel stated: "It was only later that I discovered that the training program I had worked out for myself was unorthodox for an economic historian."

The two teachers who influenced Fogel most at Columbia were George J. Stigler (1982 Nobel Laureate in Economics), who taught the graduate microeconomic sequence and Carter Goodrich, who taught the sequence in American economic history. Fogel bestowed high praise on both of them. Stigler, while making microeconomic theory come alive, emphasised "not its elegance but its applicability to a wide range of issues in economic policy." Stigler continually moved between theory and evidence; he often considered when, with what model, and under what implicit assumptions one could draw a particular inference from a given body of data. Goodrich impressed Fogel not only with his knowledge of the literature of American economic history, but with his willingness to identify the gaps in the profession's collective knowledge of key issues. It was to Goodrich that Fogel turned for advice on his master's thesis; the topic related to Union Pacific Railroad which was also Fogel's first published book. Goodrich also suggested that, given Fogel's substantial interests and quantitative approaches to economic history, Simon Kuznets at John Hopkins University was "probably the best economist to guide my future training."

Simon Kuznets (1971 Nobel Laureate in Economics), who supervised Fogel's doctoral dissertation at John Hopkins was "by far the most influential figure in his graduate training." Soft spoken and of moderate stature, one did not have to be in his class very long to discover that he was a towering intellect, erudite not only in economics, but also in history, demography, statistics, and the natural sciences. Kuznets's course was valuable not only for the substance of the material but also for the way that he "used the material to transmit the art of measurement." Fogel received his Ph.D. from John Hopkins University in 1963.

Fogel taught at John Hopkins (1958-1959), the University of Rochester (1960-1965 and 1968-1975), the University of Chicago (1961-1975) and Harvard University (1975-81). In the Graduate School of Business, University of Chicago, he succeeded George J. Stigler as the Charles R. Wallgreen Professor of American Institutions in 1981. He also worked as Director of the Centre for Population Economics, University of Chicago.

Robert Fogel died at Oakland, U.S.A on June 11, 2013.

51.2 A SUMMARY OF ROBERT FOGEL'S CONTRIBUTIONS

In his monumental work, History of Economic Analysis, Joseph Schumpeter argued for the role of economic history in economics. He stated: "What distinguishes the 'scientific economist' from all the other people who think, talk and write about economic topics is a command of techniques that we class under three heads: history, statistics, and 'theory.' The three together make up what we shall call Economic Analysis." But for a long time economists neglected economic history and became self-sufficient in its comparative statics and dynamics "without any relation to history." As McCloskey observes "economics has always wavered between the blackboard and the archive." Prior to the 1960's, economics and economic history had grown apart. In the words of Eichengreen, "Samuelson's Foundations (1947) was a landmark on a route along which research in economics became progressively more abstract, formal and mathematical.... Economic history increasingly became the domain of scholars of a more traditional methodological bent situated largely outside of economics departments."

Roger Fogel was a key figure in the development of the "new economic history" by introducing the methods of modern economics into the study of economic history. Fogel and North are the first of the new school of "Cliometricians" to be recognised by the Royal Swedish Academy of Sciences. Cliometricians are the practitioners of an economic history characterised by the explicit use of economic theory, quantification and formal hypothesis tests. Fogel is considered the Napoleon of the Cliometric revolution. Eichengreen talks about how "crosspollination between cliometrics and the older historical tradition has given birth to a mature "new economic history" that successfully marries theory, statistics and econometrics to traditional historical methodologies." To this transformation, Fogel had immensely contributed by his discourses on methodology as also by the example set by his research. He asserted that all history had some kind of theory implicit in it and the best history spells out the underlying model facilitating the checking of its logical consistency, identifying its critical assumptions and testing of its principal propositions. Fogel remarked: "The belief that the older economic history is solidly grounded in fact is an illusion. Actually it is permeated with untested covert models and subliminal mathematical assumptions."

Furthermore, in reply to the arguments advanced by the traditional school of economic history scholars that historical data are of inadequate quality and reliability to support statistical tests and that even where the data are adequate, historical questions cannot be answered on the basis of statistical tests, Fogel stated: "...all of the pitfalls of econometrics and econometric history are also present in the old economic history. Indeed, these pitfalls are more dangerous in the old work than in the new because they are more deeply concealed." He had also pioneered the use of large-scale cross-sectional and longitudinal data sets gathered from historical sources to obtain answers for questions of current policy interest and of historical relevance. The sources he had used included census manuscripts, family genealogies, church records, slave manifests, certificates of freedom for former slaves, military records, farm accounts and tax assessments. Fogel's work epitomises another distinguishing feature of Cliometrics, namely "policy-oriented." The research was motivated by and considers issues of current policy concern.

Fogel's main contributions belong to three main substantive areas in which he significantly advanced the state of knowledge. They are as follows.

1. The Transportation Revolution and the 19th Century Economic Development of the U.S;
2. Slavery as an Economic System; and
3. Relationship between Nutrition and Standards of Living.

51.2.1 THE TRANSPORTATION REVOLUTION AND THE 19th CENTURY ECONOMIC DEVELOPMENT OF THE U.S.

Fogel's first publication was The Union Pacific Railroad (1960) which is a pioneering attempt to calculate private and social returns on construction costs. However, his first significantly important work is the 1964 book The Railroads and American Economic Growth. This work was an effort to "transform economic history from a discipline based on implicit, weakly specified and untested theories to one based on rigorously specified and empirically warranted theories." The important role played by railroads in the economic development of America in the 19th century is generally highlighted. The growth process was promoted by railroads by sharply reducing transportation costs, bringing about a national market by integrating the extant separate regional economies, by allowing regions to specialise in the production of commodities in which they had a comparative advantage dictated by the region's resource endowments. In addition, railroads stimulated output growth in a number of sectors like coal, iron, etc. by consuming vast quantities of iron, fuel, machinery and capital. There is an implied suggestion that the government bond guarantees and land grants that subsidised railroad construction must have yielded "impressive" social rates of return. Rostow in his The Stages of Economic Growth (1959) had argued that an economy to take off into a stage of sustained economic growth needs a leading sector to propel the rest of the economy and also highlighted the importance of the government to extend support to the leading sector. Furthermore, Rostow assigned these critical functions to the railroads and the grant of government subsidies for railroad construction in the 19th century United States.

Fogel basically challenged the conventional wisdom relating to the railroads as well as the traditionally accepted economic history. He did this by posing an explicit counterfactual questioning: by what percentage the level of the GNP in the U.S. would have differed in 1890 if there were no railroads. In the absence of railroads, there would have been much heavier utilisation of alternative modes of transportation, such as canals and horse-drawn wagons. The "social savings" or addition to national income attributable to the railroad depended on "observed cost differentials" between rail transport and these alternative modes of transportation. Fogel's conclusion was that these social savings were "surprisingly small." U.S. GNP in 1890 would have been only 5 percent lower. According to him, rail traffic could have been diverted to the available alternative modes of transportation, particularly canals, at relatively low cost, "and all but 4 percent of the existing agricultural land could still have been economically cultivated." More Importantly, Fogel drew our attention to some important implications such as concentration of land taken out of cultivation would have been primarily located in the west and to a lesser degree in the Midwest and that in the absence of railroads, the GNP would not have been affected very much and, "the composition and the locale of economic activity would not have been very much different." The basic conclusion of Fogel was that there would not have been much of difference in the early economic history even in the absence of railroads.

Eichengreen identifies the following distinctive characteristics of Fogel's research on Railroads and American Economic Growth.

It was the output of a scholar of prodigious energy. Fogel deployed numerous historical factors and a large number of "ramifications, qualifications and implications of the central counterfactual explored."

Fogel was able to handle an exceptionally ambitious research agenda by making simplifying assumptions and applying appropriate economic theory. Eichengreen significantly observes: "The concept of social savings [which Fogel argues were quite small] allowed the debate over the contribution of the railroad to American economic growth to be significantly advanced by the calculation of a single statistic."

Another important feature of Fogel's work was the presentation of his estimated results in a fashion common in natural sciences "that encouraged replication, allowed refutation and facilitated comparisons with other country cases." His way of presentation of the results allowed other researchers in the subject to alter Fogel's assumptions in order to challenge the robustness of his results. Likewise, other scholars could use his approach to the historical experience of other countries. Moreover, it encouraged sensitivity analysis which, in Fogel's words, is "the knife that Cliometricians use to cut the Gordian knot created by long string of inferences." Eichengreen remarks: "if provoking a large subsequent literature is evidence of a research project with impact, then Fogel's work on the railroads surely qualifies."

Fogel spelt out the implications of the findings of his study for economic theory and applied economics. He generalised his rejection of the significant contribution to the economic growth of the U.S. into a rejection of "the axiom of indispensability," suggesting, according to Eichengreen, "...that the capacity of market economies to substitute on various margins is fundamentally subversive to arguments about the essential nature of any single technological innovation, casting doubt on the case for government support for 'leading sectors' and applying these insights to the U.S. space program."

As mentioned above, Fogel introduced the important concept of social savings which is the difference in social costs between the real and counterfactual worlds. It is an important research tool; from a methodological viewpoint, it is equally important as Fogel defined it operationally.

While summing up the importance of Fogel's work on Railroads, Lance Davis specifically mentions the following four important innovations that were to have a major influence on the nature of research in economic history.

(i) Providing an operational definition of social savings;

(ii) Explicit use of counterfactual. By an appropriate counterfactual, what is meant is that what the world would have been like, had there been no railroads;

(iii) The use of formal economic model to estimate what the costs would have been had the decisions been taken by economic man; and

(iv) The economic man's choice, when it is necessary to make assumptions regarding the actual world, of assumptions that were biased against Fogel's central findings.

51.2.2 SLAVERY AS AN ECONOMIC SYSTEM

Another area of Fogel's research, which was very controversial, related to a study of American slave system before the American Civil War. The research was carried out by him largely in collaboration with Stanley Engerman of the University of Rochester. Before Fogel took up this work, there was considerable growth of literature on the subject. Conrad and Meyer's 1958 article "The Economics of Slavery in the Antebellum South," was prominently mentioned though critics noted its lack of "detailed historical dimension of Fogel and Engerman's work." Eichengreen observes: "Two economic historians, William

Parker and Robert Gallman, had pioneered the construction of machine-readable micro-data sets, drawing from the 1860 Census of Agriculture a sample of cotton-belt farms that formed a major data source for Fogel and Engerman's Time on the Cross...[by which they] galvanized the debate by undertaking a research program of exceptional scale and scope."

The traditional interpretation of the economics of slavery in the U.S. was "long and complex." Fogel and Engerman had summarised the principal conclusions in their Time on the Cross. The propositions are the following.

1. Slavery was generally an unprofitable investment.
2. Slavery was economically moribund.
3. Slave labour, and agricultural production employing slave labour, was economically inefficient.
4. Slavery was responsible for the economy of the U.S. South to stagnate or, at least, impeded its growth.
5. For the typical slave, slavery provided extremely harsh material conditions of life.

Fogel and Engerman challenged the prevalent view that American Slavery was an economically backward institution by employing economic theory and statistics. They assembled evidence to show that slavery was an efficient and profitable economic system and that slave owners were rational and profit-seeking. To drive home their points, Fogel and Engerman conducted extensive economic analyses such as, estimation of total factor productivity on plantations in the South and farms in the North in the U.S., estimation of rates of return on investment in slaves and demonstrating that per capita income in the U.S. South rose as rapidly as the American average growth in per capita income between 1840 and 1860.

The main conclusions of their study were presented as "principal corrections of the traditional characterization of the slave economy." They are given by Thomas Weiss in a Review Essay on the book.

Slavery was not a system kept in existence irrationally by owners failing to perceive or indifferent to their best economic interests. Purchase of a slave was a profitable investment that yielded a rate of return comparable favourably with the best investment opportunities in manufacturing.

As argued by earlier historians, the system of slavery was not economically moribund at the time of the American Civil War. Slavery as an economic system was very strong as the Civil War approached; in fact, the trend was for the entrenchment of the system. Further, no evidence was available to conclude that economic forces by themselves, without political intervention, would have soon brought the collapse of slavery.

On the eve of the Civil War, slave owners were experiencing a wave of optimism, anticipating an "era of unprecedented prosperity."

Slave agriculture compared very favourably with free agriculture. Economies of scale, effective management and intensive utilisation of labour and capital made Southern slave agriculture 35 percent more efficient than the Northern system of free family farming.

The typical slave labour on farm was "not lazy, inept and unproductive." In fact, on average, he was more hardworking and more efficient than his white counterpart.

There was no evidence to show that slavery was not compatible with an industrial system or that slaves found it difficult to cope with an industrial regimen. In regard to diligence and efficiency, slaves employed in industry compared favourably with free workers. The demand for slaves in urban areas was showing a rapid increase compared to the demand in the countryside.

The family was the basic unit of social organisation under slavery. The belief that the black family was destroyed by slave-breeding, sexual exploitation and promiscuity is a false notion. As the economic interests of slave-owners dictated encouragement of slave families, most of the slave owners did so.

In contradistinction to psychological conditions, the material conditions of the lives of slaves compared favourably with those of free industrial workers. This should not be construed as good by modern standards.

It is true that slaves were exploited in that a part of the income produced by them was expropriated by slave-owners. The rate of expropriation, however, was lower than has generally been presumed. According to Fogel's estimates, the typical slave labour on farm received over the course of his lifetime 90 percent of the income he produced.

There was rapid economic growth in the South before the Civil War, as against the early historians' verdict that the economy stagnated. Fogel and Engerman estimated that between 1840 and 1860, per capita income in the South increased more rapidly than in the rest of the nation. By 1860, the level of per capita income attained by the South was high by the standards of the time.

What followed Fogel and Engerman's work was an "avalanche of criticism." The authors were lambasted from every direction. However, in Thomas Weiss's words: "There is no question this was a seminal work, if by that one means it was responsible for bringing forth further work. In this case it did so in abundance." The surprising conclusion of Fogel and Engerman that the efficiency of agriculture in South was the joint product of shrewd capitalistic planters and hard working slaves contained the seeds of controversy as they argued that the slaves worked hard because they were rewarded for the work, not because they were driven to it by slave owners. However, Fogel and Engerman admitted that force was used by slave owners and it "could and often did, lead to cruelty." They tried to rationalise the use of force and the carrot and stick policy followed by slave owners: "Planters being capitalistic businessmen used force for exactly the same purpose as they used positive incentives – to achieve the largest product at the lowest cost. Like everything else, they strove to use force not cruelly, but optimally." They also emphasised the hardworking nature of slaves and the superior quality of slave labour. According to them, the efficiency of Southern farms "was not due to some special way in which land or machinery was used, but to the special quality of plantation labor." Ordinary slaves, according to them, were "imbued like their masters with a Protestant ethic."

Fogel and Engerman's work should not be construed as defence of slavery as a social institution. The work of Fogel must be interpreted as a strong attack on the traditional view of the nature of slave life and the profitability of slave agriculture. In the opinion of Eichengreen the work "...bore the hallmarks of Fogel's application of scientific methodology to questions of economic history." It made extensive use of economic theory, and deployed a wide array of quantitative historical sources. Another important feature of the work is the exploration of the extent to which data can be said "to speak for themselves versus the extent to which their informational content is filtered by the observer's formulation of the problem and interpretation of the evidence."

51.2.3 NUTRITION AND STANDARD OF LIVING

Since the 1980's, the focus of research of Fogel shifted to examining the relationship between changes in nutrition and health on the one hand and economic, social and demographic behaviour on the other. Extensive studies by economists show that human capital investment has a significant impact on the growth of productivity of labour and per capita incomes in the 20th century. However, while the focus of research works relating to developed countries concerns education as a determinant of human capital, studies on developing countries have devoted special attention to factors such as nutrition, public sanitation and health. The secular decline in mortality rates and reduction in the depreciation of human capital have been brought about by improvements in nutrition and public health. Fogel's research effort since the mid-1980's was aimed at carefully examining the historical data on nutrition, mortality rates and health to have a better understanding of the factors that promote modern economic growth and its consequences.

In this research, Fogel employed theoretical and statistical models from other fields, such as anthropometric literature connecting physical stature to nutrition and the medical literature linking nutrition to health. Further, the work of Fogel in collaboration with others had shown in a 1982 report that "native-born Americans reached modern heights and, by inference, modern nutritional standards by the time of the American Revolution." This is in contrast to European countries such as France. This American experience is a result of abundance of land and a relatively equal distribution of income. Eichengreen observes: "They suggest that improvements in living standards [in the U.S.] prior to industrialization helped to eliminate problems of inadequate nutrition that had previously inhibited the transition to modern economic growth based on intensive factory labor."

The trends witnessed in nutrition have important implications for morbidity and mortality. The Prize lecture of Fogel entitled "Economic Growth, Population Theory and Physiology: The Bearing of Long-Term Processes on the Making of Economic Policy" sketched a theory of the secular decline in morbidity and mortality that took account of changes induced in physiological functioning early on. In Fogel's own words: "The synergism between technological and physiological improvements has produced a form of human evolution, biological though not genetic, rapid, culturally transmitted, and not necessarily stable, which is still ongoing in both OECD and developing countries." The lecture also considered the impact of the thermodynamic and physiological aspects of economic growth on growth rates and the implications of this theory for forecasting population, national income measurement, demand for leisure, pension policies and demand for health care.

Fogel observed that sizeable decline in mortality rates during the early decades of the twentieth century "...delivered a major blow to the Malthusian theory of population.... Efforts to reconcile Malthusian doctrine with the observed mortality decline, to modify it, or to replace it" pushed research in three directions. First, a concerted effort was made to develop time series of death rates with a view to determine when the decline in mortality began. Second, an analysis of available mortality rates was undertaken to specify factors that might explain the decline as well as to establish patterns that would facilitate predictions of the future course of mortality. Third, there was a serious effort to identify the relationship between food supply and mortality rates. This effort has several dimensions such as discovery of the synergy between nutrition and infection, attempt by writers in development economics after World War II at closing the "yawning gap" in income, health and life expectancy between the industrialised nations and the developing nations and the combined effort of economic and demographic historians to study the role of mortality crises and their relationship to famines during the seventeenth and eighteenth centuries.

The analyses of French and English time series revealed that the elimination of "crisis mortality," whether related to famines or not, accounted for less than 10 percent of the secular decline in mortality rates. Fogel commented: "By demonstrating that famines and famine mortality are a secondary issue in the escape from the high mortality rates of the early modern era, these studies shifted attention to the neglected issue of chronic malnutrition as the principal pathway through which malnutrition contributed to the high mortality rate of the past." Recent research, integrating recently developed bio-medical techniques with economic techniques, indicates that for many European nations before the middle of the nineteenth century, the food output was quite low and that the high disease rates of the period were "not merely a cause of malnutrition but undoubtedly, to a considerable degree, a consequence of exceedingly poor diets."

On the basis of his analysis, Fogel remarked that rather than one level of subsistence, as Malthus originally used it and as is still widely used today, there are numerous levels at which a population and a food supply can be in equilibrium, "in the sense that they can be indefinitely sustained." Malthus also believed that malnutrition manifested itself in the exceptional – in periodic famines and in the excess mortality prevalent among the ultra-poor of his day that lived in misery and vice. He thought that persons near the middle of the social order, the sturdy agricultural labourer or the town artisan, were generally well fed, healthy, and lived normal life spans. The evidence Fogel analyses showed that "famines accounted for less than 4 percent of the premature mortality of Malthus's age, and that the excess mortality of the ultra-poor...accounted for another sixth of premature mortality. About two-thirds of all premature mortality in Malthus's time came from the part of the society that Malthus viewed as productive and healthy."

As regards the implications of Fogel's work for developing countries, the Prize lecture points out that the childhood stunting and wasting has a long reach, predicting chronic disease rates at young adult and later ages. The relevant information on such conditions in developing countries is not generally available as it is not collected. Fogel's insightful observation in this regard is important: "...the long reach of childhood malnutrition in rich countries, both now and when they were much poorer than they are today, suggests that a similar inter-connection also exists in developing countries."

The work of Fogel and others clearly point out that we are in a much different world than that of Malthus. The issue now is not whether or not to provide food to poor who might otherwise die, but how to distribute services, such as health care and pensions, that have proved successful in raising the quality of life of the aged and in extending life expectation. In Fogel's opinion, the growing opportunities to improve health of the young, to reduce the incidence of chronic diseases at later ages, and to alleviate the disabilities associated with chronic diseases raises two other population issues. First, the impact of improved health on the size of population and the connected policy issues such as health care costs and pension costs. Second, the growing and income inelastic demand for leisure. These policy issues need to be satisfactorily tackled both by developed nations as well as developing countries.

In the concluding part of the Prize lecture, Fogel observed: "Focusing on the thermodynamic and physiological aspects of economic growth calls attention to the long lags that frequently occur between the time that certain investments are made and the time that their benefits occur.... Failure to take account of these extremely long lags between investments and payoffs leads to puzzling paradoxes." In this category of investments with long lags are included such public health investments as the construction of facilities to improve the supply of water, streamlining the milk supply, the draining of swamps, the development of effective systems of quarantines and the sprucing of the slums.

Fogel called upon economists to take account of long-run dynamic processes through a study of history which requires an enormous investment in time and effort. He sounded an appropriate warning. A superficial knowledge of the work of economic historians is at least as dangerous as a superficial knowledge of theory.

The impact of Fogel's research work in this area is equally great as is evidenced by the number of other scholars who have followed him into this field. Eichengreen, tracing how the work of scholars in this area connects to Fogel's earlier research projects observes:

"...the finding that the stature of nineteenth-century American slaves was closer to that of European aristocrats than to that of European peasants...is consistent with the arguments in Time on the Cross concerning the nutritional standards of slaves."

51.3 CONCLUDING OBSERVATIONS

It is increasingly being realised that many of the important questions facing economies are fundamentally historical.

McCloskey provides examples of issues which are intrinsically historical. How do great Depressions happen? How is the income structure determined? How, as Wicksell put it, did the earlier conception, "so repellent to our minds, of a workman as a mere beast of burden" change in about one hundred fifty years to the free worker? Stating that economic history has contributed significantly to the formulation of economic theory, Fogel stated that Smith, Malthus, Marx, Marshall, Keynes, Hicks, Arrow, Friedman, Solow and Becker (the last five are Nobel Laureates in Economics) have found history an important source for their ideas. Furthermore, he emphasised: "Nowhere is the need to recognize the role of long-run dynamics more relevant than in such pressing current issues as medical care, pension policies, and development policies."

Lance Davis traces the roots of "Clio" in Cary Brown's work "Fiscal Policy in the Thirties: A Reappraisal" and in Alfred Conrad and John Meyer's "The Economics of Slavery in Antebellum South." According to him, Cliometrics, however, did not really begin to flower until the publication of Fogel's study of the impact of railroads on the Nineteenth Century American economic growth. Fogel's study has inspired "at least five parallel studies" of Russia, Brazil, Mexico, England and Scotland. More importantly, Fogel's study of the impact of railroads provided a methodological foundation for the systematic study of economic history and long-term economic growth.

The steadily growing reliance on historical evidence in studies of economic growth, inequality of incomes, wage and price flexibility, the transmission of business cycles among others bears testimony to the influence of Fogel's work. Eichengreen observes that no appreciation of Robert Fogel would be complete without mentioning a particular quality of the man himself. "It is impossible to think of another economist whose students regard him with more admiration, esteem he elicits by the care he so clearly evinces as well as by the example of prodigious energy he sets."

51.4 SELECT BIBLIOGRAPHY OF FOGEL'S WORKS

51.4.1 BOOKS

1960 The Union Pacific Railroad: A Case in Premature Enterprise, John Hopkins University Press, Baltimore, Md.

1971 (with S. L. Engerman et al.), The Reinterpretation of American History, Harper and Row, New York.

1972 a Railroads and American Economic Growth: Essays in Economic History, John Hopkins University Press, Baltimore, Md.

b (with W. O. Aydelotte et al.), The Dimension of Quantitative Research in History, Princeton University Press, Princeton, NJ.

1974 a (with S. L. Engerman), Time on the Cross: The Economics of American Negro Slavery, Little, Brown and Company, Boston, MA.

b (with S. L. Engerman), Time on the Cross: Evidence and Methods, Little, Brown and Company, Boston, MA.

1989 Without Consent or Contract: The Rise and Fall of American Slavery, W. W. Norton, New York.

1992 a (with others), Without Consent or Contract: The Rise and Fall of American Slavery: Evidence and Methods, W. W. Norton, New York.

b (with others), Without Consent or Contract: The Rise and Fall of American Slavery: Markets and Production: Technical Papers, Vol.1. W. W. Norton, New York.

c (with others), Without Consent or Contract: The Rise and Fall of American Slavery: Conditions of Slave Life and the Transition to Freedom, W. W. Norton, New York.

2000 The Fourth Great Awakening and the Future of Egalitarianism, University of Chicago Press, Chicago, Ill.

2003 The Slavery Debates, 1952-1990: A Retrospective, Walter Lynwood Fleming Lectures in Southern History, Louisiana University Press, Baton Rouge.

2004 The Escape from Hunger, and Premature Death, 1700-2100; Europe, America and the Third World, Studies in Population, Economy and Society in the Past, Cambridge University Press, New York.

2011 (with R. Floud), The Changing Body Health, Nutrition, and Human Development in the Western World since 1700, Cambridge University Press, New York.

51.4.2 ARTICLES

1962 "A Quantitative Approach to the study of Railroads in American Economic Growth: A Report of Some Preliminary Findings," JEH, Vol.22, No.2.

1964 a "A Provisional View of the 'New Economic History,'" AER, Vol.54, No.2.

	b	(with S. L. Engerman), "A Model for the Explanation of Industrial Expansion during the Nineteenth Century: With an Application to the American Iron Industry," JPE, Vol.72, June.
1965		"The Reunification of Economic History with Economic Theory," AER, Vol.55, No.2.
1966		"Railroads as an Analogy to the Space Effort: Some Economic Aspects," EJ, Vol.76, Mar.
1967		"The Specification Problem in Economic History," JEH, Vol.27, No.3.
1971		(with A. Fishlow), "Quantitative Economic History: An Interim Evaluation: Past Trends and Present Tendencies," JEH, Vol.31, No.1.
1975	a	"The Limits of Quantitative Methods in History," American Historical Review, Vol.80, No.2.
	b	"Three Phases of Cliometric Research on Slavery and its Aftermath," AER, Vol.65, No.2.
1977		(with S. L. Engerman), "Explaining the Relative Efficiency of Slave Agriculture in the Antebellum South," AER, Vol.67, No.3.
1979		"Notes on the Social Saving Controversy," JEH, Vol.39, No.1.
1986		"Nutrition and Decline in Mortality since 1700: Some Preliminary Findings," in Studies in Income and Wealth, Vol.51, University of Chicago Press, Chicago, Ill.
1989		"Some Notes on the Scientific Methods of Simon Kuznets," in S. Kuznets, Economic Development, the Family, and Income Distribution: Selected Essays, Cambridge University Press, London.
1991		"The Conquest of High Mortality and Hunger in Europe and America: Timing and Mechanisms," in Favorites of Fortune: Technology, Growth and Economic Development Since the Industrial Revolution, D. Landes et al.(eds.), Harvard University Press, Cambridge, MA.
1993		"Second Thoughts on the European Escape from Hunger: Famines, Chronic Malnutrition, and Mortality Rates," in Nutrition and Poverty, S. R. Omani (ed.), Clarendon Press, Oxford.
1994		"Economic Growth, Population Theory and Physiology: The Bearing of Long Term Processes on the Making of Economic Policy," Noble Prize Lecture, AER, Vol.84, No.3.
1997	a	"The Contribution of Improved Nutrition to the Decline in Mortality Rates in Europe and America," in The Economics of Population: Key Modern Writings, J. L. Simon (ed.) Elgar Reference Collection,

International Library of Critical Writings in Economics, Vol.78, Elgar, Cheltenham.

b "New Findings on Secular Trends in Nutrition and Mortality: Some Implications for Population Theory," in Handbook of Population and Family Economics, M. R. Rosenzweig and O. K. Stark (eds.), Handbooks in Economics, Vol.14, Elsevier North Holland, Amsterdam.

1998 "Douglass C. North and Economic Theory," in The Frontiers of the New Institutional Economics, J. N. Drobak and J. V. C. Nye (eds.) Harcourt Brace Academic, Sandiego, CA.

1999 "Catching Up with the Economy," AER, Vol.89, No.1.

2004 "Health, Nutrition and Economic Growth," Econ Dev & Cult Chng, Vol.52, No.3.

51.5 WORKS OF OTHERS

Conrad. A. H. and Meyer, J.R. (1958), "The Economic Slavery in the Antebellum South," JPE, Vol.66, No.2.

Davis, L. (2000), "Review Essay by Lance Davis:" Review of Robert W. Fogel's Railroads and American Economic Growth: Essays in Econometric History, Economic History Services, July 1, 2000, URL.

Eichengreen, B. (1994), "The Contributions of Robert W. Fogel to Economics and Economic History," ScandJE, Vol.96, No.2.

Fishlow, A. (1965), Railroads and the Transformation of the Antebellum American Economy, Harvard University Press, Cambridge, MA.

McCloskey, D. N. (1976), "Does the Past Have Useful Economics?" JEL, Vol.14, No.2.

McCloskey, D. N. (1994), "Fogel and North: Statics and Dynamics in Historical Economics," ScandJE, Vol.96, No.2.

Rostow, W. W. (1959), The Stages of Economic Growth, Cambridge University Press, New York.

Samuelson, P. A. (1947), Foundations of Economic Analysis, Harvard University Press, Cambridge, MA.

CHAPTER 52

DOUGLASS CECIL NORTH

(1920 –)

Professor Douglass Cecil North, Washington University, St. Louis, U.S.A., has shared the 1993 Nobel Memorial Prize in Economic Sciences with Professor Robert W. Fogel. The Prize was jointly awarded to them "for having renewed research in economic history by applying economic theory and quantitative methods to explain economic and institutional change." Douglass North has studied long-term economic development in Europe and the United States and in his recent work has analysed the role of institutions in economic growth.

North, in his 1961 book, The Economic Growth of the United States, 1790-1860, introduced an explanatory model for American economic growth before 1860. North's model has distinctly influenced the direction of research in the U.S. and elsewhere. Employing an export-base model that he had formulated in his earlier work, North has shown how one sector – cotton plantations – stimulated development in other sectors and advanced to specialisation and inter-regional trade.

In his article entitled "Sources of Productivity Change in Ocean Shipping, 1600-1850," North has demonstrated that organisational changes had more vital effects than technical change. This article has become very influential in the profession and has become one of the most quoted studies in economic history. North has increasingly argued that, besides economic factors, political and social factors also have to be considered for the purpose of understanding the emergence of institutions that have had an impact on economic growth. He has also drawn our attention as to how such institutions have been influenced by ideological and non-economic factors. He maintains that if economics is a theory of choice under certain specific assumptions, then the purpose of economic history is to theorise about the development of these concepts.

North has warned that if the time factor and social conflicts are ignored in conducting economic analyses, there is a danger that the analyses may become "ahistoric." Systematic reintroduction of institutional explanations into historical analysis is an attempt to correct this deficiency.

North, as one of the pioneers in the new institutional economics, has shown the important role of institutions, including property rights in a number of his works. He has argued that new institutions emerge when groups in society find a possibility of availing themselves of profits that cannot be realised under extant institutional conditions. New institutional arrangements tend to develop when external factors allow an increase in income but is prevented by the prevailing institutional factors. Testing his hypotheses on development in the U.S. during the nineteenth century, he has shown in his 1971 publication, Institutional Change and American Economic Growth, how agricultural policy, developments in banking, transport etc., could be explained by institutional arrangements. In a subsequent work, he has considered the economic development of Western Europe since the Middle Ages upto the eighteenth century and has shown that economic incentives founded on individual property rights were a pre-requisite for economic growth. Institutional changes in Western Europe were brought about by changes in relative prices and variations in population growth. England and the Netherlands experienced a relatively rapid industrialisation due to the fact that certain conservative institutions, such as guilds, were weak. Private property rights were also guaranteed in these countries in contrast to the case of Spain, where absence of institutional innovations led to a century of stagnation. North does not consider innovations, technical changes and other generally accepted factors as sufficient explanations of growth but are themselves part of the growth process and therefore cannot explain it. According to him, effective economic organisations are the key to economic change. In his words: "Institutions are sets of rules, compliance procedures, and moral and ethical behavior of individuals in the interest of maximizing the wealth or utility of principals."

In a recent publication, Institutions, Institutional Change and Economic Performance, North raises the fundamental issue as to why some countries are rich and others poor. His answer is: "Institutions provide the basic structure by which human beings throughout history have created order and attempted to reduce uncertainty in exchange. Together with the technology employed, they determine transaction and transformation costs and hence the profitability and feasibility of engaging in economic activity." Large scale institutional changes occur rather slowly since institutions are the result of historical change, which has modelled individual behaviour. The greater the institutional uncertainty, the higher the transaction costs. North contends that the lack of opportunities to enter into binding contracts and absence of other institutional arrangements is a cause of economic stagnation, in both developing countries and the erstwhile socialist states. He has tried to explain the difficulties that confronted these countries by focussing his analysis on the political and legal framework for economic growth. He also raises basic questions concerning the relation between economic change, technical development and institutional conditions. North demonstrates the disadvantages of neoclassical economic theory as a means of explaining growth as well as the advantages of using this theory in combination with the approaches he has proposed. The Royal Swedish Academy's press release comments: "North has forced economists to rethink, to become aware of when economic 'laws' are sufficient as an explanation for a given problem and when other factors have to be taken into account."

Both Fogel and North have inspired a large number of researchers. North's unswerving emphasis on the importance of rigorous theory and the role of institutions has influenced not only economic historians, but also economists and political scientists. Fogel is an empiricist, leaving no source unexplored. North inspires and produces ideas by identifying new problems and showing how economists can solve the old problems more effectively.

Thus, in different ways, both Fogel and North have renewed research in economic history by endowing it with rigour and theoretical awareness.

52.1 A SHORT BIOGRAPHICAL SKETCH: DOUGLASS NORTH

Douglass North was born in Cambridge, Massachusetts, U.S.A., on November 5, 1920. His father was a manager at the Metropolitan Life Insurance Company in a town near Cambridge. North went to elementary school in Ottawa, Canada, and then to a private secondary school. He completed high school education at the Choate School in Wallingford, Connecticut. North graduated from the University of California, Berkley. While he was there, he became a convinced Marxist and engaged in a variety of student liberal activities. He received the B.A. degree from the University of California, Berkley, in 1942. In his autobiographical note North says: "My record at the University of California as an undergraduate was mediocre to say the best. I had only slightly better than a "C" average, although I did have a triple major in political science, philosophy and economics."

When World War II started, because of his strong feeling against killing anybody, North joined the Merchant Marine after his graduation from Berkley. He went back to the University of California for graduate work with the clear intention that "what I wanted to do with my life was to improve societies, and the way to do that was to find out what made economies work the way they did or fail to work. I believed that once we had an understanding of what determined the performance of economies through time, we could then improve their performance. I have never lost sight of that objective."

North wrote his Ph.D. dissertation on the history of life insurance in the United States and had had a Social Science Research Council (S.S.R.C) Fellowship to go to the East Coast and do the spadework. It turned out to be a productive year. He sat on Robert Merton's seminars in sociology at Columbia and got deeply involved in the Entrepreneurial School of Arthur Cole at Harvard. The result was that Joseph Schumpeter had a strong influence upon him. North received his Ph.D. degree in economics from the University of California, Berkley, in 1952. His early work and publications centered on expanding the analysis of life insurance in his dissertation and its relationship to investment banking. Prior to finishing his Ph.D., North had also been a semi-professional photographer.

For a period of thirty-two years, North was associated with the University of Washington at Seattle where he was Director of the Institute for Economic Research for five years and Chairman for twelve years. For a year (1981-82), he was Professor at Cambridge University, England. He joined the faculty of Washington University in St. Louis in 1983 as the Henry R. Luce Professor of Law and Liberty in the Department of Economics and served as the Director of the Center in Political Economy from 1984 to 1990.

North was Peterkin Professor of Political Economics at Rice University in the fall of 1979, Pitt Professor at Cambridge University in England in 1981-1982 and Visiting Fellow of the Center for Advanced Studies in Behavioral Sciences at Stanford University in 1987-1988. North received numerous honours and awards including Editorship of the Journal of Economic History for 5 years and Presidentship of Economic History Association in 1972. He was a twenty-year member of the Board of Directors of National Bureau of Economic Research until 1986. In 1987, he was elected to the American Academy of Arts and Sciences. In 1992, he became the first economic historian ever to win one of the economics profession's most prestigious honours, the John R. Commons Award. Along with Ronald Coase and Oliver Williamson, North helped found the International Society for the New Institutional Economics that held its first meeting in St. Louis in 1997.

North received a Ford Faculty Fellowship under which he spent a year, 1966-67 in Geneva. He was elected a fellow of the British Academy in July 1996 and was selected for the Spencer T. Olin Professor in Arts and Sciences at Washington University in St. Louis in October 1996. He is a Bartlett Burnal Senior Fellow of Hoover Institution. North was elected Fellow of the British Academy, 1996. He acted as economic consultant to a number of countries including Russia, Argentina, Peru and Czech Republic.

52.2 A BRIEF SUMMARY OF DOUGLASS NORTH'S CONTRIBUTIONS

Any student of the history of economic analysis would notice that the early writers, especially in the 18th century focussed on understanding the interaction of human beings. With the formulation of the idea of a "spontaneous order" and with the introduction of the notion of the "invisible hand" achieving the desired result without an authority giving central commands, there was a neglect of other methods coordinating interaction among a multitude of human beings. Walras's construction of a model of general equilibrium led to the price mechanism occupying the centre stage in economic analysis. The refinement in the analysis attempted in the works of Hicks, Samuelson, Arrow and Debreu (all Nobel Laureates in Economics), has resulted in totally ignoring the forms of human relations and interactions other than the price system. This exclusive focus on the price system to the neglect of the other aspects relating to human interrelations was challenged by Ronald Coase (another Nobel Laureate in Economics) who argued for including transaction costs into the economic analysis. Property rights and transaction costs are put on the research agenda of economists by the work of Alchian, Demsetz and Cheung, besides the work of Coase. Inspired by the work of his precursors relating to the theory of institutions, Douglass North realised the relevance of institutions and their importance for economic history. He developed and refined a theory of institutions and analysed economic history by applying it.

It is the view of Myhrman and Weingast that "the contribution by Douglass North does not revolve on one theoretical idea which is applied in several fields." Instead, he put in continuous efforts to improve and expand a basic idea and demonstrated its relevance and explanatory power in a wide range of contexts in economic history. The sustained efforts of North have resulted in the development of a new approach to economic growth and development and to the theory of institutions.

North's contributions can be summarised under four heads with a focus on his important publications through time. They are summed up as under.

1. Economic Growth of the United States, 1790-1860 and Institutional Change and American Economic Growth;
2. The Rise of the Western World: A New Economic History;
3. Structure and Change in Economic History; and
4. Institutions, Institutional Change and Economic Performance.

52.2.1 INSTITUTIONAL CHANGE AND ECONOMIC GROWTH OF THE U.S.

A number of early contributions of North had their focus on American economic history; these include: "Capital Accumulation in Life Insurance between the Civil War and the Investigation of 1905," "The Spatial and Inter-regional Framework of the United States Economy: An Historical Perspective," "International Capital Flows and the Development of the American West," and "The Estimation of Shipping Earnings in Historical Balance of Payments Studies." North's first major research publication, The Economic Growth of the United States, 1790-1860 is considered "one of the founding" contributions to cliometrics and the new economic history. The book was in the tradition of neo-classical economics and had examined the role of exports and regional specialisation in American economic growth. The volume analysed how markets work in the context of an export staple model of growth. It, however, introduced certain research innovations, such as the relationship between a large decline in transportation costs and trade flows within the regions.

In 1966-1967, North decided to switch from American to European economic history and therefore went to Geneva under a Ford Faculty Fellowship. There he decided to "re-tool" as he was convinced that the tools of neo-classical economic theory "were not upto the task of explaining the kind of fundamental societal change that had characterized European economies from medieval times onward." In the long search for a framework that would provide new tools of analysis, North's interest and concern with the new institutional economics evolved. He thus made "a major conceptual leap" with Institutional Change and American Economic Growth co-authored with Lance Davis. While the neo-classical economic analysis takes as given property rights, institutional arrangements and rules of the economic game, North and Davis have shown in the volume that changes in property rights and invention of new forms of economic organisation and new institutional arrangements are often required for reaping gains from exchange. They could demonstrate that the factors which facilitated growth in the U.S. economy were not only factor accumulation; the growth is also "because of a complementary process of institution evolution" by changing the rules.

The United States had gone through a "transportation revolution" in the early 19th century in which canals played a leading role. Canals, being a cheaper mode of transport, had substantially lowered transportation costs which, in turn, enhanced the extent as well as the scope of the market. Canals opened up vast new regions to specialisation, production and trade. By the end of the period of the study of North and Davis, the then Northwest region of the U.S.A. was exporting a large part of its food produce to East Coast besides Europe.

While canals had brought down the transportation costs, investment in canals did not occur through individual financing. The investment required was heavy as well as risky and therefore could not be financed by citizens. The success of the Erie Canal in the mid-1820s had encouraged many states in the U.S. to chalk up new institutional arrangements for financing the canals. Myhrman and Weingast comment: "The institutional arrangements by which these investments occurred were thus of considerable importance to the economic growth of the United States, and yet, as political decisions, their creation is beyond the purview of neoclassical economics." Similar logic is employed by North in his examination of the other institutional changes required for economic growth, including evolution of capital markets, the formulation of rules and passing of legislation enabling setting up of corporations that promoted pooling of capital and risk as also risk distribution, public support for educational activities and institutional changes in service industries. Myhrman and Weingast pertinently observe: "As is obvious from the study of developing countries, new institutional arrangements do not automatically arise simply because they yield improvements in social welfare. Institutional evolution thus remains outside the scope of what is normally considered the 'market' because it had to do with how the market is defined. Understanding how and when institutional arrangements occur requires a set of tools different from those used in neoclassical economics."

From a study of the American economic growth, North has concluded that the growth was largely fostered by economic and political arrangements and facilitated by design of new institutions. For formulating a general theory which will be able to explain why some countries developed while others had failed, North had decided to study economic history of Europe.

52.2.2 THE RISE OF THE WESTERN WORLD: A NEW ECONOMIC HISTORY

North has noted that while Rome was the centre of Europe's power and wealth two thousand years ago, China was world's richest country a hundred years ago. The rise and fall of these powerful countries cried for a suitable explanation. There is a need to explain the phenomenon of West's vast accumulation of wealth during the last few hundred years. There was a long secular growth in Europe which resulted in a substantial rise in living standards of all segments of population. The economic historian has to provide satisfactory answers to the main questions: How and why did the growth begin and more importantly why at the time at which it began?

Traditional explanations ascribed the growth in the West to a combination of random inventions of the steam engine and spinning jenny and the founding and expansion of the British Empire. Employing the tools developed by North in association with Lance Davis in the earlier book, namely, The Theory of Institutional Arrangements, North, in collaboration with Robert Thomas, provided a new explanation in The Rise of Western World: A New Economic History. According to them, the key factor in the phenomenal growth of wealth in the West was the efficient organisation of the economy.

North and Thomas point out that factors, such as capital accumulation, technological development and scale economies, which were considered by traditional theories as having promoted growth, are not the primary causes of economic growth of the West but are inherent parts of the growth process. Instead, they argued that the causes of growth are "the incentives for efficient organization, the ability of society to implement institutional arrangements that make the return to individuals equal to the return to society." The question that immediately crops up is whether essaying for efficiency implies that institutional arrangements are always optimal for which the answer of North is a clear 'no'. The arrangements are not always optimal since there are two problems – free rider problem and the problem of transaction costs. The first problem is illustrated by the fact that everyone would not share in the cost of an institutional arrangement. The second problem can be explained with reference to property rights such as the costs of defining and enforcing the rights of buyer and seller in potential settlements.

A major finding of the study of the economic history of Western Europe from 900 to 1800 by North and Thomas is that the serfdom is an efficient organisation under the then prevailing conditions. The relationship between the serf and the landlord was akin to a contract regulated by customary law under which the serf and his family were protected against other feudal lords and bandits in return for his performing the landlord's work. This arrangement is related to the lack of an organised market for labour and commodities.

Another significant conclusion of their study is that the medieval world was not characterised by a stationary state, as was the traditional interpretation. Instead, demographic and technological changes have spurred economic change. The changed conditions altered relative prices inducing new institutional arrangements between 900-1200. They also found growth of population in Europe, bringing of more new land under cultivation, expansion of trade and founding of new townships in Europe. According to Myhrman and Weingast, this perspective has two important implications. First, as a result of population growth and relative scarcity of land becoming more pronounced, there was a change in the labour relationship between landlords and serfs. The serfs had to put in longer hours of work for accomplishing the tasks assigned by landlords leaving them with less time to cultivate their own land. Second, the black plague, by making labour the scarce factor, "...forced rights and obligations to adjust, resulting in, most notably, a freeing of the serfs in many areas of Western Europe."

North and Thomas compare the growth experience of the Netherlands with that of England on one hand and France and Spain on the other. Their analysis reveals that the Netherlands had used trade as the vehicle for wealth creation in the absence of natural resources. With the objective of promoting commercial interests, the Dutch rulers mitigated domestic regulations, reduced the power of guilds and encouraged merchants and exchange. As a result of these positive steps taken by the rulers, the Dutch economy prospered, outperforming other European nations in the 17th century.

The case of England was somewhat different. Besides developing new institutions of trade and commerce, curbs were placed on the rule of government monopolies; patent protection was granted and private property rights were protected. England encouraged setting up and growth of banks and maintained price stability through a stable currency for over three centuries. North and Thomas demonstrated that development of institutions including an orderly political system, securing private property rights and encouraging individualism helped England's rise to rank as the richest nation in the world. In contrast, the burden for the decline of Spain and France was placed by them at the doorstep of the failure of the two countries to design efficient institutional arrangements that could help economic growth. They noted that these countries often did exactly the opposite, confiscating the wealth of their citizens, and impairing the development of a vibrant, private economy. Myhrman and Weingast conclude: "Development is therefore not primarily a matter of a timeless production function, as in neoclassical economics, but the result of path-dependent development of growth-promoting institutions which, in turn, are the result of the forces exerted by the participants in the political system."

52.2.3 STRUCTURE AND CHANGE IN ECONOMIC HISTORY

In his autobiographical note, North concedes that the earlier two books – Institutional Change and American Economic Growth and The Rise of the Western World were his tentative attempts to develop the tools of institutional analysis in order to apply them to economic history. The framework was still neo-classical. It was posited that institutions were efficient, however defined. No attempt was made to explain why "inefficient" rules tend to exist and be perpetuated. Another serious flaw in the analysis is the failure to recognise that individual beliefs were obviously important to the choices people make. It is, therefore, necessary to admit that ideas, ideologies and prejudices mattered which the economists have failed to understand because of extreme myopia. North, therefore, has argued that one has to reckon with the fact that the choices people make are determined by ideologies and ideas that they possess. The economic historian, in the final analysis, has to evolve a framework, taking into account all these considerations, in order to develop a view of institutions that would explain why institutions produced results that, in the long run, did not manage to produce economic growth.

In Structure and Change in Economic History, North has abandoned the idea that institutions were efficient. However, he persisted with the neoclassical theory of the state which could explain why the state could frame rules that did not encourage economic growth. According to North, State was a ruler who maximises his own benefits subject to constraints (the ultimate constraint being his replacement by another ruler) and was provider of a number of primary services, frames and enforces the rules of the economic game and political institutional set up. This framework does not rule out a conflict between the objective of maximising the ruler's revenues and maximising the social output. North demonstrates how the ruler's interests may be served better by creating monopolies and other modes of extractions rather than creating conditions for emergence of competitive markets.

North contends that the theory of organisation of a society and institutions must have a theory of ideology as a supplement. It is also argued that there has to be a "moral system of norms to support the formal rules." The degree of legitimacy that the system possesses determines the cost of running an economic system. Thus, one can see "...a trade off between the pecuniary cost of achieving a certain result and the moral imperative necessary to achieve the same result without a pecuniary reward." This trade off is vital for the method of functioning of societies and the trade off may vary over time. North introduces such factors as state and ideology into the neoclassical model in order to analyse the historical development and the processes of change at different periods of time. Applying the new framework developed by him, North interprets the divergence of economic development in the Netherlands and England on the one hand and in Spain and France on the other, during the 16th, 17th and 18th centuries.

Myhrman and Weingast succinctly summarise North's conclusions. In the Netherlands and England "the interests of merchant classes led to a range of institutions underpinning specific temporal transactions and more efficient economic exchanges." These countries by shoring up property rights paved the way for an era of economic growth that has "continued into our age with unsurpassed continuity." Not only that, they had seen that the attitude towards the design of property rights was spread to their colonies. As an example, one can cite the case of the British colonies in North America where meticulous observance of private property rights promoted strong economic growth.

In complete contrast to the situation in the Netherlands, Britain and British colonies, the economic stagnation witnessed in France and economic retardation suffered by Spain stand out. The crucial factor which caused stagnation or retardation was the government encroachment on private property rights in those countries because of "the seemingly constant need for government revenues" which prompted strengthening of guilds and others in order to obtain revenues.

52.2.4 INSTITUTIONAL CHANGE AND ECONOMIC PERFORMANCE

In his Prize lecture "Economic Performance through Time," North clarifies that economic history is about the performance of economies through time. He spells out the crucial objective of research in the field as "not only to shed light on the economic past but also to contribute to economic theory by providing analytical framework that will enable us to understand economic change." He categorically states once again that the neo-classical economic theory is an "inappropriate tool" to analyse and prescribe policies that will induce development. Neo-classical economic theory is concerned with the operation of markets, not with how markets develop. It models a frictionless and static world. In the analysis of economic performance through time "it contains two erroneous assumptions, one that institutions do not matter and two that time does not matter." North suggests that the analytical framework of neo-classical theory be modified by relaxing the assumption of rationality and introducing the dimension of time and retaining its fundamental assumption of scarcity and hence competition and the analytical tools of macroeconomic theory.

North states that "institutions are the humanly devised constraints that structure human interaction." They are made up of formal constraints such as rules, laws and constitutions, informal constraints (as, for example, norms of behaviour, conventions and self-imposed codes of conduct) and their enforcement features. Together, they define the incentive structure of societies and specifically of economies. The transaction and transformation costs that add up to the production costs are determined by the institutions and the technology employed. North acknowledges Ronald Coase's contribution by critically connecting institutions, and transactions to the neo-classical theory. The neo-classical result of efficient markets obtains only in a world with no transaction costs. In a regime of transaction costs, including information costs, institutions do matter and it is costly to transact. Most decision problems are characterised by inter-temporal transaction costs. In an empirical study, Wallis and North have shown that 45 per cent of the U.S. GNP was devoted to the transactions sector in 1970.

According to North, in the real world, "individuals act on incomplete information and with subjectively derived models that are frequently erroneous; the information feedback is typically insufficient to correct these subjective models. Institutions are not necessarily or even usually created to be socially efficient; rather, they or at least the formal rules, are created to serve the interests of those with the bargaining strength does not affect the efficiency of outcomes; but in a world of positive transaction costs it does."

If it is exceptional to find efficient economic markets, it is almost impossible to find efficient political markets. An important conclusion of North is: economic markets in the past and present are typically imperfect and beset by high transaction costs. Further, he observes: "it is the interaction between institutions and organizations that shapes the institutional evolution of an economy." If institutions are rules of the game, organisations and their entrepreneurs are the players. Organisations comprise groups of individuals bound together for achieving certain objectives. They may be political bodies, economic bodies, social bodies or educational bodies. The organisations that come into existence reflect the opportunities presented by the "organizational matrix."

Economic change, which is an incremental and ongoing process, is brought about by daily choices economic agents make. The decisions might be under the existing rules or in some cases may involve modification of rules, necessitating institutional changes. The more important long run source of change concerns learning of organisations by individuals and entrepreneurs. According to North, while the speed of economic change is determined by the rate of learning, the direction of that change is influenced by the expected pay-offs to acquiring different kinds of knowledge. There is a need to re-examine the rationality assumption in order to constructively approach the nature of human learning. The framework of rational choice is patently inappropriate in making choices under conditions of uncertainty. In this context, North approvingly quotes Herbert Simon, 1978 Nobel Laureate in Economics, who focussed on the issue. Simon stated: "If...we accept the proposition that both the knowledge and the computational power of the decision maker are severely limited, then...we must construct a theory (and test it empirically) of the process of decision. Our theory must include not only the reasoning processes but also the processes that generated the actor's subjective representation of the decision problem, his or her frame."

Stating that the analytical framework that is to be built must originate in an understanding of how human learning takes place, North takes the help of cognitive science to develop a tentative approach in this direction. The mental models that are developed by humans may have to be continually redefined with new experiences. Furthermore, North believes that a common cultural heritage permits us to reduce the divergence in the mental models that people have and facilitates inter-generational transfer of unifying perceptions. Mental models get transformed into societal and economic structures by institutions as well as by both formal rules and informal norms of behaviour.

North admits that the beliefs and institutions that evolve through time need not necessarily produce economic growth. In fact, most societies throughout history are found to have got "stuck in an institutional matrix" that failed to evolve into the impersonal exchange necessary to capturing productivity gains derived from division of labour and specialisation. North clarifies that the concept of time indicates not only current experiences and learning of individuals but also cumulative experience of past generations that is embodied in culture. The transmission in time of an accumulated stock of knowledge is termed "collective learning" by Hayek.

Thus, learning is an incremental process that determines the perceived pay-offs. North observes that societies which got stuck, embody belief systems and institutions that fail to confront and solve new problems of societal complexity. The incentives to acquire pure knowledge, the basic foundation of modern economic growth, are determined by monetary rewards and punishments. They are also basically affected by a society's tolerance of creative developments. North remarks that a major influence in the economic development of Western Europe was the "gradual perception" of the utility of research in pure science. He concedes that explaining the pace and direction of economic change in a country throughout history poses a major puzzle. The institutional/cognitive approach adopted by North to explain the very uneven pattern of economic performance of countries indicates that there is nothing automatic about the evolving of conditions that will permit low cost transacting in the impersonal markets that are essential to productive economies.

North observes that the institutional/cognitive approach to contemporary problems of economic development enables us explain the rise and decline of Soviet Union and World Communism, while the tools of neo-classical analysis cannot. He draws the following implications of the approach.

The economic performance of a country is shaped by "the admixture of formal rules, informal norms and enforcement characteristics." North, therefore, concludes that a transfer of formal political and economic rules of successful Western market economies to Third World and Eastern European economies is not a sufficient condition for good economic performance. Privatisation is not a panacea for solving poor economic performance.

Polities generally shape economic performance since they define and enforce the economic rules. As such, a crucial component of development policy is the creation of polities that will create and enforce efficient property rights.

The key to long run economic growth is adaptive efficiency, not allocative efficiency. The creation of institutional infrastructure that promotes growth requires long gestation. There is no clear-cut answer as to how adaptive efficiency can be created in the short run.

He concludes the Prize lecture by indicating the new directions for future research in the field.

52.3 CONCLUDING OBSERVATIONS

Douglass North underlines the fact that wide divergences in economic growth performance across countries and over time cannot be adequately explained merely by different factor endowments, differences in factor productivities and differences in saving behaviour. For a satisfactory explanation, one has to take recourse to explaining the emergence and non-emergence of certain institutions that promote growth. A wider approach going beyond the neo-classical approach by including technology, population, institutions, ideology and politics and further integrating economics with history, political analysis and even sociology is needed. In this context, one has to recall the perceptive comment of Myhrman and Weingast: "Schumpeter's vision finally seems to be fulfilled. Douglass North's work...points towards a way of reintegrating several of the social sciences."

Furthermore, drawing a distinction between the work of Fogel and North in economic history, McCloskey comments that the real difference is that between statics and dynamics. The studies of Fogel and other historical economists practice comparative statics. "They are snapshots of the rationale for institutions at a single time." The work of North advocates dynamics – moving pictures. The note may be concluded with the following quote of McCloskey regarding Fogel's and North's studies: "The one is synchronic, a cross section; the other diachronic, a time series. The one is precise, but sacrifices historical movement. The other is storytelling, but imprecise."

52.4 SELECT BIBLIOGRAPHY OF DOUGLASS NORTH'S WORKS

52.4.1 BOOKS

1961 — The Economic Growth of the United-States, 1790-1860, Prentice-Hall, Upper Saddle River, NJ.

1966 — Growth and Welfare in the American Past: A New Economic History, Prentice-Hall, Upper Saddle River, NJ.

1968 — (edited with R. P. Thomas), A Documentary History of American Economic Growth, 1607-1860, Harper & Row, New York.

1971 a — (with R. L. Miller), The Economics of Public Issues, Harper & Row, New York.

b — (with L. E. Davis), Institutional Change and American Economic Growth, Cambridge University Press, London.

1973 — (with R. P. Thomas), The Rise of the Western World: A New Economic History, Cambridge University Press, London.

1974 — Growth and Welfare in the American Past, Prentice-Hall, Upper Saddle River, NJ.

1981 — Structure and Change in Economic History, W. W. Norton & Co., New York.

1989 — Institutions and Economic Growth: An Historical Introduction, Cambridge University Press, London.

1990 — Institutions, Institutional Change and Economic Performance, Cambridge University Press, London.

1996 — (with L. Alston and T. Eggertsson eds.), Empirical Studies in Institutional Change, Cambridge University Press, London.

2005 — Understanding the Process of Economic Change, Princeton University Press, Princeton, NJ.

2009 — (with J. J. Wallis and B.R. Weingast), Violence and Social Order: A Conceptual Framework for Interpreting Recoded Human History, Cambridge University Press, New York.

52.4.2 MONOGRAPHS

1960 — The United States Balance of Payments 1790-1860, Trends in the American Economy in the Nineteenth Century, 24th Conference on Income and Wealth, NBER, Princeton University Press, Princeton, NJ.

1961 Four Lectures in Regional Economic Analysis, Presented at the Getulio Vargas Institute, Rio Janeiro, Revista Brasilaira de Economica, September.

52.4.3 ARTICLES

1952 "Capital Accumulation in Life Insurance between the Civil War and the Investigation of 1905," Men in Business, W. Miller (ed.), Harvard University Press, Cambridge, MA.

1954 "Life Insurance and Investment Banking at the time of the Armstrong Investigation," JEH, Vol.14, No.3.

1955 "Location Theory and Regional Economic Growth," JPE, Vol.63, No. 3.

1956 "International Capital Flows and the Development of the American West," JEH, Vol.16, No.4.

1958 "Ocean Freight Rates and Economic Development, 1750-1910," JEH, Vol.18, No.4.

1960 a (with A. Heston) "The Estimation of Shipping Earnings in Historical Balance of Payments Studies," Canadian Journal of Economics and Political Science, 1960, May.

b "The United States in the International Economy, 1790-1950," in American Economic History, S. Harris (ed.), McGraw-Hill, New York.

1963 "Quantitative Research in American Economic History," AER, Vol.53, No.1: Part I.

1964 a "Industrialization in the United States," Cambridge Economic History, Vol.VI, Cambridge University Press, Cambridge.

b "Capital Formation in the United States during the Early Period of Industrialization: A Re-examination of the Issues," Proceedings of the Second International Conference in Economic History, 1962, International Economic History Association.

1965 "The State of Economic History," AER, Vol.55, No.2.

1968 a "Economic History," International Encyclopaedia of Social Sciences, MacMillan, London.

b "Sources of Productivity Change in Ocean Shipping, 1600-1850," JPE, Vol.76, No.4.

1970 (with L. E. Davis), "Institutional Change and American Economic Growth: A First Step towards a Theory of Institutional Innovation," JEH, Vol.30, No.1.

1974 "Beyond the New Economic History," JEH, Vol.34, No.1.

1975 "The New Economic History After Twenty Years," American Behavioral Scientist, Nov-Dec.

1978 a "Evaluating Three Schools of Economic History," JEH, Vol.38, No.1.

b "Structure and Performance: The Task of Economic History," JEL, Vol.16, No.3.

1982 (with J. Wallis), "American Government Expenditures: An Historical Perspective," AER, Vol.72, No.2.

1984 "Transaction Costs, Institutions and Economic History," JITE, Vol.11, No.1.

1985 "The Growth and Government in the United States: An Economic Historian's Perspective," JPubE, Vol.28, No.3.

1986 "The New Institutional Economics," JITE, Vol.13, No.1.

1987 a (with J. Wallis), "Measuring the Transaction Sector in the American Economy, 1870-1970," in Income and Wealth: Long Term Factors in American Economic Growth, Engerman, S. L. and R. E. Gallman (eds.) University of Chicago Press, Chicago, Ill.

b "Institutions, Transaction Costs and Economic Growth," Econ Inq, Vol.25, No.3.

1989 "Institutions and Economic Growth: An Historical Introduction," World Development, Vol.7, No.9.

1991 "Institutions," JEP, Vol.5, No.1.

1994 a (with A. T. Denzau), "Shared Mental Models: Ideologies and Institutions," Kyklos, Vol.47, No.1.

b "Economic Performance through Time," Noble Prize Lecture, AER, Vol.84, No.3.

1997 "Cliometrics – Forty Years Later," AER, Vol.87, No.2.

2000 a "Big-Bang Transformation of Economic Systems – An Introductory Note," JITE, Vol.27, No.1.

b (with B. R. Weingast), "Introduction: Institutional Analysis and Economic History," JEH,Vol.60,No.2.

52.5 WORKS OF OTHERS

Coase, R. (1960), "The Problem of Social Cost," JLawE, Vol.3, No.1.

Hayek, F. A. (1960), The Constitution of Liberty, The University of Chicago Press, Chicago, Ill.

McCloskey, D. N. (1994), "Fogel and North: Statics and Dynamics in Historical Economics," ScandJE, Vol. 96, No.2.

Myhrman, J. and B. R. Weingast (1994), "Douglass C. North's Contributions to Economics and Economic History," ScandJE, Vol.96, No.2.

Schumpeter, J. A. (1954), History of Economic Analysis, Oxford University Press, New York.

Simon, H. A. (1986), "Rationality in Psychology and Economics," in Hogarth, R.M. and M. W. Reder (eds.), Rational Choice, The University of Chicago Press, Chicago, Ill.

CHAPTER 53

AMARTYA SEN

(1933 –)

The Bank of Sweden Prize in Economics in memory of Alfred Nobel for the year 1998 was awarded by the Royal Swedish Academy of Sciences to Professor Amartya Sen, Trinity College, Cambridge, U.K, for his contributions to Welfare Economics. The Academy's press release while announcing the award makes reference to Sen's several key contributions to the research on fundamental problems in welfare economics - axiomatic theory of social choice, definitions of welfare and poverty indexes and empirical studies of famine. These are closely connected to his general interest in issues of distribution and a particular interest in the most impoverished members of society. Sen is particularly remembered for classifying the conditions which allow aggregation of individual values into collective decisions and the conditions which permit rules for collective decision-making that are consistent with a sphere of rights for the individual. By taking into account the available information about welfare of different individuals when collective decisions are made, Sen has not only improved the theoretical foundation for comparing different distributions of society's welfare but also defined new and more satisfactory indexes of poverty. In empirical studies, the applications of his theoretical approach have improved our understanding of the economic mechanisms underlying famines.

A number of questions arise in connection with a study of the broad area of applied welfare economics. They include the following.

Is it possible to aggregate values which individual members of society attach to different alternatives to derive values for society as a whole in a manner that is fair and theoretically sound? Is the decision of the majority feasible as a decision rule? In which way can inequality of income be measured? When and how can we compare the distribution of welfare in different societies? What is the best way of determining the decline in poverty? What factors trigger famines? By answering questions such as these, Sen has made significant contributions to the main fields of economic science. Furthermore, he opened up new fields of study for subsequent generations of teachers and researchers. His attempts at combining the tools from economics and philosophy, has restored an ethical dimension to the discussion of key economic problems.

The press release from the Royal Academy covers the main contributions of Sen to welfare economics under three major heads. They are:

1. Individual Values and Collective Decisions;
2. Indexes of Welfare and Poverty, and
3. Welfare of the poorest.

53.1 INDIVIDUAL VALUES AND COLLECTIVE DECISIONS

The choices made by the society are non-controversial when there is general agreement. However, when opinions differ, methods have to be found for bringing together different opinions in decisions which concern everyone. The link between individual values and collective choices is the main concern of the theory of social choice. The main issues in this context are whether, and, if so, how to derive consistent preferences for the whole society from preferences of its members. The answers to these are important for the feasibility of ranking or otherwise evaluating different social states thereby constructing meaningful measures of social welfare.

Though the rule of majority is a measure that is commonly followed for making collective decisions, serious deficiencies are found in this measure. Besides, the majority rule may lead to suppression of a minority. Moreover, it is possible to manipulate the order in which different alternatives are voted upon or to vote strategically, such as refrain from voting for a preferred alternative. Sometimes, a clear result in a group may not emerge, when voting is between pairs of alternatives. An example of non-transitivity may illustrate the problem. A majority of the group may prefer alternative M to alternative N, whereas a second majority may prefer N to P, while a third majority prefers P to M. In such a situation of 'intransitivity,' the decision rule fails to clearly select any alternative that is best for any majority. Sen has the distinction of having specified general conditions that eliminate intransitivities of majority rule.

In the chapter on Kenneth Arrow, a reference has been made to his examination of possible rules for aggregating individual preferences (values or votes). He has considered the majority rule as one of the alternatives and came to the "pessimistic" conclusion that no aggregate (decision) rule exists that satisfies all the five axioms or conditions, each of which appears very reasonable on its own. The so-called impossibility theorem seemed to be an obstacle to progress in the normative branch of economics. The moot question was the way by which individual preferences could be aggregated and different social states could be evaluated in a theoretically satisfactory fashion. Sen's contributions from mid-1960's onwards helped alleviate the pessimism. His work enriched the principles of social choice theory. In addition, it opened up new and important fields of study. His monograph Collective Choice and Social Welfare proved to be very influential and provided inspiration to many researchers to examine once again basic welfare issues. The Swedish Academy specifically observes: "Its style, interspersing formally and philosophically oriented chapters, gave the economic analysis of normative problems a new dimension. Sen's work during the period (mid-1960's onwards) dealt with crucial problems relating to the subject of social welfare such as majority rule, individual rights and availability of information about individual welfare."

Any collective decision rule should not reflect the values of any single individual-- that is, it should be non-dictatorial. The decision rule should aim at protecting individual rights. It implies that the rule should respect individual preferences of at least some people in at least some dimension, for instance relating to their personal sphere. The press release states: Sen pointed to a fundamental dilemma by showing that no collective decision rule can fulfil such a minimal requirement on individual rights and the other axioms in Arrow's impossibility theorem. This finding gave rise to extensive scientific discussion on the extent to which a collective decision rule can be made consistent with a sphere of individual rights.

The only assumption of the theory of social choice traditionally was that every individual can rank different alternatives. No assumption was made in regard to interpersonal comparability, thereby shirking the issue of whether the utility individuals attach to different alternatives can really be compared. In the process; it did not say anything important about the problem of inequality.

In his work, Sen demonstrated how different assumptions regarding interpersonal comparability impinge upon the possibility of finding a consistent, non-dictatorial rule for collective decisions. Through his work, he started a new field of research in the theory of social choice. Later developments in social choice greatly rely on Sen's analysis of the information about individual utilities and their interpersonal comparability.

53.2 INDEXES OF WELFARE AND POVERTY

An important application of the theory of social choice relates to the construction of some kind of index that measures differences in welfare or income. Such type of index is useful to compare distributions of welfare in different countries or to study changes over a period of time in the distribution of welfare within a given country. The reasoning behind the construction of such indexes is that inequality indexes are closely linked to welfare functions representing the society's values. Around 1970, Sen (as also some other researchers) have clarified the relation between Lorenz curve describing income distribution and Gini coefficient that measures the degree of income inequality and societal ordering of different distributions of income. Sen has also made valuable contributions by defining welfare indicators such as poverty indexes.

Traditionally, poverty in a society is measured by the proportion of population with income below a certain, pre-fixed poverty line with no clear theoretical foundation for such a measure. The measure also skirted the issue of poverty among the poor. To improve the measurement of poverty, Sen suggested five axioms from which a poverty index can be constructed.

$$P = H\,[I + (1-I)\,G]$$

Where

P: Poverty Index

H: Share of population below poverty line

I: a measure (between 0 and 1) of the distribution of income computed only for individuals below the poverty line.

G: Gini coefficient, computed again for individuals below the poverty line.

Sen also suggested when such poverty index can and should be applied. He also clarified that welfare comparisons can be made even when data problems exist, which are true in case of developing countries. Sen's poverty index has subsequently been applied extensively by others. Some researchers have suggested alternative indexes.

A commonly used indicator for comparing welfare of different societies is per capita income, which takes into account only the average conditions. Sen has developed alternative indicators which cover income distribution. He suggested an alternative measure which, like poverty index discussed above, is derived from a number of axioms. The measure is

$$y\,(1-G)$$

Where,

y: Income per capita,

G: Gini coefficient.

For suggesting the above welfare indicator, Sen advanced an argument that what creates welfare are not goods as such but the activity for which they are needed. Income is important as it creates opportunities. However, Sen argues that actual opportunities and capabilities also depend on a number of other factors, such as health. While measuring welfare, these factors have also to be taken into account. The press release points out those alternative welfare indicators, such as the UN's Human Development Index, that are constructed precisely in this spirit.

Sen concedes that the distribution problem can never be fully solved as equality in some dimension invariably implies inequality in others, while all well-founded ethical principles presuppose equality among individuals in some respect. The way we evaluate different dimensions of welfare determines the dimensions in which we advocate equality and those in which we accept inequality. In line with his approach to measurement of welfare, Sen argues that individual capabilities constitute the principal dimension in which we should strive for equality. However, in this regard, we have to contend with a problem. Individuals make decisions which determine their capabilities at a later stage.

53.3 WELFARE OF THE POOREST

Sen's early work on choice of production techniques suggests that almost all his work deals with development economics and often devoted to the welfare of the poorest of the poor. In line with his theoretical approach to welfare measurement, Sen has also systematically studied actual famines. In his work, Sen has controverted prevalent common view that the most important explanation for famine was a shortage of food. He has identified explanatory factors on the basis of a study of a number of such famines in India, Bangladesh and Saharan countries from 1940's onwards. He showed that famines have occurred even when the supply of food was not significantly lower than during the previous non-famine years or that famine-stricken areas have sometimes even exported food. Sen argues that a good understanding of famine has to be based on a thorough analysis of how various economic and social factors influence different groups in society and determine their actual opportunities or capabilities. Later work by Sen discusses how to prevent a famine or how to limit the effects of famine once it has occurred. Sen's work on famines is rated as a key contribution to development economics.

53.4 A SHORT BIOGRAPHICAL NOTE: AMARTYA SEN

Amartya Sen was born in 1933 in Santiniketan, Calcutta in Bengal, India. His family is from Dhaka - now the capital of Bangladesh. His father Ashutosh Sen taught chemistry at Dhaka University. In his autobiographical note, Sen says that his field of study varied a good deal in his younger years and between the ages of three and seventeen. He "seriously" flirted with Sanskrit, Mathematics and Physics, before settling for the "eccentric charms" of economics. He states: "But the idea that I should be a teacher and a researcher of some sort did not vary over the years. I am used to thinking of the word "academic" as meaning "sound," rather than the more old-fashioned dictionary meaning: "unpractical," "theoretical" or "conjectural."

During the childhood years--between the ages of 3 and 6 he was in Mandalay in Burma, (now Myanmar) where his father was a visiting professor. Sen began his formal education at St. Gregory's School, Dhaka. He however, soon moved to Santiniketan, and it was mainly in Tagore's school that "my educational attitudes were formed." The emphasis in the school was "on fostering curiosity rather than competitive excellence, and any kind of interest in examination performance and grades was severely discouraged."

Another important point in the autobiographical note of Sen is that Tagore and his school constantly resisted "the narrowly communal identities of Hindus or Muslims or others." He further states: Some of my own disturbing memories as I was entering my teenage years in India in the mid-1940's relate to the massive identity shift that followed divisive politics.... I had to observe, as a young child, some of that mindless violence. One afternoon in Dhaka, a man came through the gate screaming pitifully and bleeding profusely. The wounded person, who had been knifed on the back, was a Muslim daily labourer.... He had come for some work in a neighbouring house [of a Hindu family] – for a tiny reward. As he was being taken to the hospital by my father, he [said that] he had to go out in search of work and earning because his family had nothing to eat. The penalty of that economic unfreedom turned out to be death...."

Sen joined Presidency College, Calcutta (Kolkata now), for the B.A. programme. He was captivated by its educational excellence. He says "My interest in economics was amply rewarded by quite outstanding teaching. I was particularly influenced by the teaching of Bhabatosh Datta and Tapas Majumdar...." He had also "wonderful" classmates including (Late) Sukhamoy Chakravarty. He states that his intellectual horizon was radically broadened. The student community of Presidency College was also politically most active. Sen was impressed by the "quality of sympathy" and egalitarian commitment of the "left."

Sen was at Presidency College during 1951 to 1953. The memory of the Bengal famine of 1943, in which between two and three million people had died, and which he had watched from Santiniketan, was fresh in his mind. He states: "I had been struck by its thoroughly class-dependent character.... It was not a famine that afflicted even the lower middle classes -- only people much further down the economic ladder, such as landless rural labourers." In his autobiographical note, Sen admits: "... as I look back at the fields of academic work in which I have felt most involved throughout my life (and which were specifically cited by the Royal Swedish Academy of Sciences in making their award), they were already among the concerns that were agitating me most in my undergraduate days in Calcutta. These encompassed welfare economics, economic inequality and poverty, on the one hand (including the most extreme manifestation of poverty in the form of famines), and the scope and possibility of rational, tolerant and democatic social choice, on the other...."

After obtaining a B.A degree from Calcutta University (with economics major and mathematics minor), Sen moved to Cambridge University to study at Trinity College. Despite having B.A degree, Cambridge enrolled him for another B.A. in pure economics to be quickly done in two years. According to Sen the style of economics at the-then Cambridge was much less mathematical than in Calcutta. Notable fellow students of Sen at Cambridge included L.Pasinetti, P.Garegnani, Samuel Brittain and Mahabub ul Haq.

The major debates in political economy in Cambridge were geared to the pros and cons of Keynesian economics and the diverse contributions of Keynes's followers at Cambridge such as Richard Kahn, Nicholas Kaldor and Joan Robinson on the one hand, and of "neo-classical" economists sceptical of Keynes, such as Dennis Robertson, Harry Johnson, Peter Bauer and Michael Farrell on the other. The debates centred on macroeconomics but later moved to capital theory, with the neo-Keynesians strongly against any use of "aggregate capital" in economic modelling.

Sen opines that Kaldor was the most tolerant of the neo-Keynesians at Cambridge: Richard Kahn was in general the most bellicose. Sen states: "... the stern reproach that I received often for not being quite true to the new orthodoxy of neo-Keynesianism came mostly from my thesis supervisor - the totally brilliant but vigorously intolerant Joan Robinson."

Sen reminisces: "In this desert of constant feuding, my own college, Trinity, was a bit of an oasis...three remarkable economists of very different political views coexisted there. The Marxist Maurice Dobb and the conservative neo-classicist Dennis Robertson did joint seminars, and Trinity also had Piero Sraffa, a model of scepticism of nearly all the standard schools of thought. I had the good fortune of working with all of them and learning greatly from each." Though there existed a nice "practice" of democratic and tolerant social choice at Trinity, he could not get anyone in Trinity, or in Cambridge, very excited in the theory of social choice. After completing B.A, Sen therefore had to choose quite a different subject for his research thesis—"the Choice of Techniques" --which interested Joan Robinson as well as Maurice Dobb. The regulations of the University stipulated that a student for submitting the thesis must be registered for a period of three years. Sen sought a two-year leave from the university to come to India. When in India he was appointed to a chair in Economics at Jadavpur University which he accepted. Further, he submitted the thesis for a Competitive Prize Fellowship.

Sen has taught economics at Jadavpur University, Calcutta (now Kolkata) and at the Delhi School of Economics (where he completed his Magnum Opus, Collective Choice and Social Welfare in 1970). He was a Professor at Delhi School of Economics from 1961 to 1972. In 1972, he joined the London School of Economics as a Professor of Economics, where he taught till 1977. From 1977 to 1986, he taught at the University of Oxford, where he was first a Professor of Economics at Nuffield College, Oxford and then Drummond Professor of Political Economy and a Fellow of All Souls College, Oxford. In 1986, he joined Harvard University as the Thomas W. Lamont Professor of Economics. In 1998, he was appointed as Master of Trinity College, Cambridge (1998-2004). He is the first Indian and first Asian academic to head an Oxbridge College. In January 2004, Sen returned to Harvard and is currently Thomas W. Lamont Professor and Professor of Economics and Philosophy at Harvard University. He is also a senior fellow at the Harvard Society of Fellows, distinguished fellow of All Souls College, Oxford and a fellow of Trinity College, Cambridge. Between 1960- 1961, Sen was a visiting Professor at MIT. He was also a visiting Professor at University of California—Berkley, Stanford University and Cornell University.

Sen has served as President of the Econometric Society (1984), The International Economic Association (1986-1989), The Indian Economic Association (1989) and the American Economic Association (1994). He has served as the President of the Development Studies Association (1980-1982) and continues to be an Honorary Vice-President of Royal Economic Society, London (since 1988). He presently serves as Honorary Director of Centre for Human and Economic Development Studies at Peking University in China. Sen is also a board council member of the Prime Minister of India's Global Advisory Council of Overseas Indians.

Sen has received a number of awards and honours. He received Bharat Ratna, the highest civilian award in India given by the President of India in 1999. He was awarded Companion of Honour (CH), U.K., in 2000. In 1981, he was elected a foreign honorary member of the American Academy of Arts and Sciences. He was awarded Leontief Prize for his outstanding contributions to economic theory. Sen has received over 90 honorary degrees from universities around the world including Harvard, Yale and Columbia universities and University of Oxford and University of Edinburgh. Sen's works have been translated into more than thirty languages over a period of 40 years. He is a trustee of Economists for Peace and Security. In 2010, Time Magazine included him in their "100 most influential persons in the world." The New Statesman listed him in their 2010 edition of "World's 50 most Influential People Who Matter."

53.5 AMARTYA SEN'S CONTRIBUTIONS: A BRIEF SUMMARY

Amartya Sen is an outstanding economic theorist. His research work encompasses an unusually wide range of areas. As A.B Atkinson has observed, he is a world authority on social choice and welfare economics, a leading contributor to the area of development economics, who did outstanding work on evaluating the investment projects in developing countries and a world leader in economic analysis of famines. Sen's work has significant influence on international organisations, such as the World Bank, ILO, and U.N agencies. He broadened the economist's areas of interest to Philosophy. Sen was both Professor of Economics and Professor of Philosophy at Harvard University. His contributions appeared not only in economic journals but also in the Journal of Philosophy. However, the press release from Royal Swedish Academy refers specifically to social choice, welfare distributions and poverty, which itself is a vast area. On one count, Sen has published more than twenty books and 250 articles. Arrow observes that Sen's work has nevertheless "a very considerable degree of unity." In view of the large volume of Sen's work, it is well nigh impossible to do even a semblance of justice to his contributions due to constraints of space and also to maintain some balance in the total volume of work of the Nobel Laureates. It is proposed to briefly summarise here his contributions to the theory of social choice, measurement of inequality and poverty and his notable contributions to development economics.

53.5.1 THEORY OF SOCIAL CHOICE

A large part of Sen's work was devoted to the theory of social choice. Arrow, as discussed in the chapter relating to his contributions, has put forward the basic paradigm in this field. He has shown that there is no social welfare function satisfying the conditions laid down by him: Pareto principle, independence of irrelevant alternatives and non–dictatorship. Arrow's the so-called Possibility Theorem inspired a large amount of literature to which Sen has been an outstanding contributor. Sen comments: "...Arrow's powerful 'Impossibility Theorem' invites engagement, rather than resignation." Sen states in his Nobel lecture that the motivating issue that inspires social choice theory is: how can it be possible to arrive at cogent aggregative judgments about the society, say about social welfare or aggregate poverty, given the diversity of preferences, concerns, and predicaments of different individuals within the society? Further, is reasonable social choice possible at all, given as Horace observed there may be as many preferences as there are people? Sen's lecture is devoted to "some general questions" about social choice as a discipline--its content, its relevance and reach. More importantly he posed a few problems in social choice theory such as: When would majority rule yield clear and consistent decisions? Taking into account the disparate interests of its different members, how can we judge how well society as a whole is doing? Given varying predicaments and miseries of diverse people that the society is made up, how do we measure aggregate poverty? How can rights and liberties of persons be accommodated, recognising at the same time, their preferences? How to appraise social valuation of public goods such as the natural environment? Sen comments: The reach and relevance of public choice theory can be very extensive.

Sen observes that prior to Arrow, the motivation that influenced the early choice theorists included the avoidance of both instability and arbitrariness in arrangements for social choice. He further notes that Arrow is very concerned with difficulties of group decisions and inconsistencies to which they may lead. Though Arrow should be credited with putting the discipline of social choice in a structured framework, he "deepened the pre-existing gloom by establishing an astonishing–and apparently pessimistic result of ubiquitous reach." Sen comments: Social appraisals, welfare economic calculations and evaluative statistics would have to be, it seemed, 'inevitably' arbitrary or irremediably despotic. The question that is to be put is whether the pessimism associated with "Arrowian" structures in social choice theory must be seen to be devastating for welfare economics as a discipline. Welfare economics has been influenced by utilitarianism, which neglected distributional issues. By 1930's, economists were convinced by Lionel Robbins's arguments that inter-personal comparisons of utility had no scientific basis.

As a consequence, the so called new welfare economics was developed from the 1940's onwards, which employed only one basic criterion of social improvement-- Pareto comparison. This criterion was considered inadequate as it does not take interest in distributional issues. A need was felt to have another criterion which would improve the reach of the social welfare judgments. This demand has led to Arrow's important work that related social preferences or decisions to the set of individual preferences-- a relation that is called a "social welfare function."

Arrow's formulation requires "unrestricted domain" emphasising that the procedure of social choice must work for every conceivable cluster of individual preferences. He explored the possibility of placing adequate restrictions that would ensure consistent majority decisions. Sen, in his Nobel lecture, asserts: "So far as welfare economics is concerned, majority rule and voting procedures are particularly prone to inconsistency, given the centrality of distributional issue in welfare economic problems." Further, voting--

based procedures are quite unsuitable for many problems of social choice; for example, to obtain an aggregate index of social welfare. Furthermore, we have to consider Arrow's dictum that inter-personal comparison of utilities has no meaning.

In this regard Sen observes: "I would like to report that inter-personal comparisons of various types can be fully axiomatized and exactly incorporated in social choice procedures (through the use of 'invariance conditions') in a generalized framework, formally constructed as social welfare functionals...indeed, inter--personal comparison need not be confined to 'all or none' dichotomies. We may be able to make inter-personal comparison to some extent, but not in every comparison, nor of every type nor with tremendous exactness...." He argues for "partial comparability" and contends that quite often rather limited levels of partial comparability will be adequate for making social decisions. In addition, he states that "even weaker forms of comparability would still permit making consistent social welfare judgments, satisfying all of Arrow's requirements, in addition to being sensitive to distributional concerns...."

In Sen's opinion, the distributional issue is closely connected with the need to go beyond voting rules as the basis of social welfare judgments. In his view utilitarianism is also distribution-indifferent; it seeks maximisation of the sum of total utilities, without considering how unequally that total may be distributed. He concludes that the broad approach of social welfare functional contained in his work enables use of many different types of social welfare rules, which differ in the treatment of equality as well as efficiency and also their informational requirements. The rejection of inter-personal comparisons of utilities in welfare economics and the theory of social choice was grounded in interpreting them solely as comparisons of mental states. Instead, Sen suggests taking into consideration, incomes or commodity bundles or resources more generally in judging a person's advantage. He argues for judging individual advantage in terms of the respective "capabilities" which the person has, to live the way he has reason to value. The advantage of this approach is its focus on substantive freedom that people have, rather than only on particular outcomes with which they end up. Sen, thus, advocates use of partial comparability based on evaluation of capabilities as the informational basis of reasoned social judgments. Atkinson comments: He [Sen] recognizes that the capability may generate utility, but argues that it is the capability to function that comes closest to the notion of standard of living.

53.5.2 MEASUREMENT OF INEQUALITY AND POVERTY

Arrow notes: "Sen's general concern about the meaning of social policy and individual variations in the capacity for functioning has found application in developing appropriate measure of income inequality." Sen basically formalises Dalton's transfer principle; that is, a transfer from a rich person to a poor person is to be considered a reduction in inequality. The key concept in the measurement of inequality is that of "dominance," taken from stochastic dominance theory. A distribution of income, say A, is said to dominate another, say B, if and only if, social welfare is greater for A for all possible social welfare functions in some given class. Sen has demonstrated, among others, that the class of social welfare functions which it is natural to consider is that of non- decreasing, 's' – concave functions. It is also shown that "for constant total income and population, dominance of distribution A or distribution B for the class w2 [class of social welfare functions] is equivalent to it being possible to reach distribution A from distribution B by making a series of mean preserving equalising transfers." Atkinson comments: "This mathematical result links the welfare economic approach to two practical intuitive measures— [the Lorenz Curve and Gini Coefficient]." The dominance approach leads to "inequality" as a quasi-ordering. Sen states that it is possible "to arrive at a partial order on the basis of the rule of going by the congruence of different complete orderings; for example, the shared ranking of complete orders generated by different statistical measures of inequality." A partial order is useful to locate the areas of disagreement.

Atkinson further makes a reference to Sen's 1976 article on real national income in the Review of Economic Studies and rates it as one his Top Twelve list as it demonstrates not only Sen's contribution to welfare economic theory but also a deep concern for implementation. The article addresses the multi--dimensional nature of commodity bundles. Further, it suggests comparisons of real incomes in terms of "named – goods vectors," treating the same commodity going to a different person as a different good.

Measures of poverty, the subject to which Sen has made outstanding contributions, are closely related to measures of inequality. Poverty measures have played an important role in evaluation of domestic and international public economic policies. In studies of poverty, particular attention is paid to the bottom of the income distribution. The topic of poverty is highly controversial including the definition of the poverty line itself and the choice of the poverty indicator. Poverty studies generally use the head count measure of the proportion of population below the poverty line. In his Nobel lecture, Sen raises two questions in regard to this approach. First, is poverty adequately seen as low income? Second, even so, is the aggregate poverty of a society best characterised by the index of the head--count measure? He sees poverty as a "serious deprivation of certain basic capabilities, though lowness of income can be very important in many contexts." He then raises a crucial question. Is deprivation not ultimately a lack of opportunity "to lead a minimally acceptable life?" This depends not only on personal income but also physical and environmental characteristics, and variables such as the availability and costs of medical and other facilities. He suggests that we look beyond "income poverty." He observes that there are at least four different sources of variation. (i) "personal heterogeneities, as for example, proneness to illness; (ii) diversities of environment, as for example, living in a flood –prone or storm-prone area; (iii) variations in social climate, as for example, prevalence of crime in the area; and (iv) differences in relative deprivation, as for example, being relatively impoverished in a rich society." He concedes that the perspective of poverty as income deprivation cannot be given up; in many contexts, use of income information may be an immediate approach to the empirical study of severe deprivation. In this context, Sen refers to the causation of famines and remarks that the causation may be seen in terms of a steep decline in real incomes of a section of the population resulting in starvation and death. This may be contrasted with an exclusive focus on agricultural production and food supplies in earlier studies on famines. He remarks: "The shift in informational focus from food supply to entitlements (involving incomes as well as supply, and the resulting relative prices) can make a radical difference, since famines can occur without any major decline...of food production and supply... starvation occurs when some people cannot establish entitlement over an adequate amount of food." He concludes that an approach involving income-sensitive entitlement provides a better explanation of famines compared to the one with exclusively production-oriented view. Arrow comments: "His [Sen's] careful analysis of four famines brings out clearly that neither variation in food supply due to natural causes nor physical obstacles to food distribution played significant roles in these famines. Rather, they were due to shifts in the real income distribution, particularly a lowering of incomes of the very poor. It was inability to afford the purchase of food that caused hunger and famine on massive scales."

In regard to the second question, aggregate poverty of a society, Sen expresses the view that one has also to consider as to how far below the poverty line the poor individuals are and more importantly how the deprivation is shared and distributed among the poor. Sen cites 'relative deprivation'-- "the lower a person in the welfare scale, the greater his sense of poverty." To get an informative and usable measure of aggregate poverty, the social data on the respective deprivation of the individuals constituting the poor in a society have to be aggregated. This, he considers, is a social choice problem and expresses his preference to Sen-Shorrocks measure over the original Sen Index (discussed in the earlier part).

Sen then refers to various distribution-sensitive poverty measures that have been developed. He also makes a mention of gender inequality and deprivation of women in traditionally unequal societies. Further, he observes that the socially cultivated sense of commitment and serenity may even affect the perception of morbidity illness. Sen, therefore, concludes that mental reactions, the mainstay of classical utility, can be a very defective basis for the analysis of deprivation. In understanding inequality and poverty, one has to look at real deprivation and not merely at mental reaction to that deprivation.

Atkinson sums up the impact of Sen's work on poverty on the profession. "Sen's 1976 article was the catalyst for the theoretical analysis of poverty measures.... It has however, less impact on official statistical practice.... While there may be agreement on the need to use a measure sensitive to the depth of poverty, it has proved difficult to convince policymakers of the salience of the particular approach adopted by Sen, with its emphasis on a person's rank in the distribution."

53.5.3 DEVELOPMENT ECONOMICS

The contribution of Sen to Development Economics is rated high. It is observed by critics that right from the start of his career, Sen has been motivated "by the challenge of applying cool, yet concerned, analysis to economic development." Sen's Cambridge doctoral work, "Choice of Techniques" was his first foray into the area. The issue that was hotly debated at that time was whether a developing country which has abundant labour and scarcity of capital should use more labour-intensive methods of production that could be profitable at the market wage rate. That is, whether it should use a "shadow" wage rate that is lower than the market wage. Sen uses the example of cotton weaving, where handlooms have the highest output per unit of capital but factory power looms generate a larger surplus, that can be used for future investment. He brought clarity to the debate by his contribution. In Atkinson's word's "Sen's contribution was to provide an analytical framework within which these issues could be discussed, a framework that combines elegance of theory with a concern for practical application. The solution is given by the shadow price for labour obtained from formulating the problem as an exercise in constrained optimization."

While the notion of shadow prices was debated extensively in 1930's and 1940's, Sen has refined it as a practical tool for making appraisal of investment projects. He, in collaboration with others, has contributed to the literature on project appraisal. This work, together with the work of Little and Mirrlees, has wielded enormous influence in showing how divergences between market and social values have to be tackled in investment decisions. In this context, Sen has introduced the concept of "control areas." Elucidating this, Atkinson observes: The decision- maker is part of a political machinery and is constrained by a complex structure within which he has to operate...successful policy making requires an understanding of the constraints that in fact hold and clarity about the precise area in which the person in question can exercise effective control...it is an illustration of pioneering contribution by Sen to what is today called 'Political Economy'."

Sen's development of capability approach, a reference to which has been made earlier, has been, particularly helpful in the definition of poverty in the context of economic development. It has helped him sort out the "absolute--relative disputation" in the conceptualisation of poverty. He says that poverty is an absolute notion in the space of capabilities; however, it takes a relative form in the space of commodities or characteristics. According to him, relative deprivation in the space of incomes can lead to absolute deprivation in the space of capabilities.

The empirical implementation of the capability approach has attracted much interest. Sen's concept has been used in developing the Human Development Index published by the United Nations Development Program (UNDP) based on parameters such as life expectancy at birth, literacy and per capita real income. Sen, in one of his lectures, argues that mortality information can be used to throw light on some of the coarsest aspects of gender-related inequality.

53.6 CONCLUDING COMMENTS

Amartya Sen's contributions encompass a wide spectrum of economics. He is a prodigious writer with a large number of publications – books as well as articles. Arrow acknowledges the "very high quality" of Sen's work and his important contributions to our understanding and to the formation of economic policy. He is credited with opening and defining new fields of research "with strong results." Sen's attack of Samuelson's revealed preference approach to consumer behaviour for its narrow view was well received. Sen has also questioned the assumption of economic man as "purely economic man indeed close to being a social moron. Economic theory has been much preoccupied with this rational fool." Atkinson underlines the integrated view of the subject that runs through Sen's work in different fields and links the research at different stages of his career. This is apparent from the way in which the essays on development economics interlock with those on justice. Sen's concern with famines is linked to that with poverty. He draws from his work on philosophical investigations in his writings on the measurement of poverty. Sen's work on individual choice behaviour is closely connected with that on social choice theory. Atkinson draws our attention to Sen's views on the role of social values impinging on individual behaviour and the need for recognising the complexity of individual motivations in analysing the implications for the formation of social judgements.

While praising Sen as a "Complete Economist," Atkinson mentions a few more distinguishing characteristics of Sen's contributions. One of them is Sen's criticism of narrowing boundaries of modern economics involving, as Sen remarks, partitions that classical economists, such as Smith or Marx could not easily have recognised and his strenuous attempts to "reverse" the narrowing of scope. Another distinguishing characteristic of Sen's contributions relates to his challenging conventional economics (Atkinson's remark: he does so with relish) and his willingness to tackle uncomfortable subjects. Yet another characteristic is that of scholarship: (in Atkinson's words increasingly rare). Sen generously acknowledges contributions of other scholars giving testimony to what Sugden terms as Sen's extraordinarily wide reading in economics. In this connection Sugden's observation: "In acknowledging what he (Sen) has learned from this literature-including what he has learned from his opponents-he is characteristically generous."

In conclusion we reproduce here the assessment of Atkinson. He says: "...One of his key contributions is to legitimize the investigation of certain topics-- such as famine- that had previously regarded by many as outside the profession's concerns. His own central position in the discipline has meant that when he has ignored the conventional lines of demarcation, then graduate students have had the image to follow."

53.7 SELECT BIBLIOGRAPHY OF AMARTYA SEN'S WORKS

53.7.1 BOOKS

1960 a Choice of Techniques, Basil Blackwell, Oxford.

b (editor), Growth Economics, Penguin Books , Hammondsworth.

1970 Collective Choice and Social Welfare, Holden Day, San Francisco, CA.

1972 (with P. Dasgupta and S. A. Marglin), Guidelines for Project Evaluation, UNIDO, United Nations, New York.

1973 On Economic Inequality, Clarendon Press, Oxford. (Extended edition 1997).

1976 Employment, Technology, and Development, Oxford University Press, New Delhi.

1982 Poverty and Famines: An Essay on Entitlement and Deprivation, Oxford University Press, New Delhi.

1983 Choice, Welfare and Measurement, Oxford University Press, New Delhi.

1985 Resources, Values and Development, Oxford University Press, New Delhi.

1987 a Commodities and Capabilities, Oxford University Press, New Delhi.

b The Standard of Living, Tanner Lectures with Rejoinders by Bernard Williams and Others, (G. Hawthorne, ed.), Cambridge University Press, Cambridge.

1989 (with J. Drèze), Hunger and Public Action, Clarendon Press, Oxford.

1990 On Ethics and Economics, Oxford University Press, New Delhi.

1994 Inequality Re examined, Clarendon Press, Oxford.

1995 (with J. Drèze), India: Economic Development and Social Opportunity, Clarendon Press, Oxford.

2002 a Rationality and Freedom, Harvard University Press, Harvard, Cambridge. MA.

b (with J. Drèze), India: Development and Participation, Oxford University Press, New Delhi.

2005 The Argumentative Indian, Penguin Books, U.S.A.

2006 Identity and Violence: The Illusion of Destiny, Penguin Books, New Delhi.

2009 The Idea of Justice, Harvard University Press, Cambridge, MA; Allen Lane, London.

2010 (with J. E. Stiglitz and J. P. Fitoussi), Mismeasuring our Lives; Why GDP Doesn't Hold Up? The New Press.

2011 (ed.) Peace and Democratic Society, Open Book Publishers, Cambridge, MA.

2013 (with. J. Dreje), An Uncertain Glory: India and its Contradictions, Allen Lane, Penguin, New Delhi.

53.7.2 ARTICLES

1957 a "A Note on Tinbergen on the Optimum Rate of Saving," EJ, Vol.67, Dec.

b "Some Notes on the Choice of Capital-Intensity in Development Planning," QJE, Vol.7l, Nov.

1958 "A Note on the Mahalanobis Model of Sector Planning," Arthaniti, May.

1959 a "Choice of Capital-Intensity Further Considered," QJE, Vol.73, Aug.

b "The Choice of Agricultural Techniques in Underdeveloped Countries," EDCC, Vol.7, Apr.

1961 a "On Optimizing the Rate of Saving," EJ, Vol.7l, Sep.

b (with K. N. Raj), "Alternative Patterns of Growth under Conditions of Stagnant Export Earnings," OEP, Vol.13, Feb.

1962 "On the Usefulness of Used Machines," RES, Vol. 44, Aug.

1963 a "Neo-Classical and Neo-Keynesian Theories of Distribution," Economic Record, Vol. 39, Mar.

b "The Money Rate of Interest in the Pure Theory of Growth," in Theories of the Rate of Interest, F. Hahn and F. Brechling, (eds.), Macmillan, London.

c "Distribution, Transitivity and Little's Welfare Criterion," EJ, Vol.73, Dec.

1964 a "Preferences, Votes and the Transitivity of Majority Decisions," RES, Vol. 3l, Apr.

b "The Efficiency of Indirect Taxes," in Problems of Economic Dynamics and Planning: Essays in Honour of M. Kalecki, Warsaw.

c "Size of Holdings and Productivity," Economic Weekly, Annual Number, 16.

1966 a "A Possibility Theorem on Majority Decisions," Econometrica, Vol. 34, No.2.

b "Labour Allocation in a Cooperative Enterprise," RES, Vol. 33, July.

1967 a "Isolation, Assurance and the Social Rate of Discount," QJE, Vol. 81, Feb.

b "The Pattern of British Enterprise in India 1854-1914: A Causal Analysis," in Social and Economic Change, B. Singh and V. B. Singh (eds.), Allied Publishers, Bombay.

c "Surplus Labour in India: A Critique of Schultz's Statistical Test," EJ, Vol. 77, Mar.

1968 "General Criteria of Industrial Project Evaluation," in Evaluation of Industrial Projects, UNIDO, United Nations, New York.

1969 a "Quasi-transitivity, Rational Choice and Collective Decisions," RES, Vol. 36, July.

b "Choice of Techniques: A Critical Survey of Class of Debates," in Planning for Advanced Skills and Technologies, Industrial Planning and Programming Series No. 3, United Nations, New York.

1970 a "The Impossibility of a Paretian Liberal," JPE, Vol. 78, No.1. Reprinted in F. Hahn and M. Hollis, (eds.), Philosophy and Economic Theory, Oxford University Press, Oxford.

b "Interpersonal Aggregation and Partial Comparability," Econometrica, Vol. 38, May, "A Correction," Econometrica, Vol. 40, Sep 1972.

1973 a (with P. Dasgupta and D. Starrett), "Notes on the Measurement of Inequality," JET, Vol. 6, Apr.

b "On Ignorance and Equal Distribution," AER, Vol. 63, Dec.

1974 a "Informational Basis of Alternative Welfare Approaches: Aggregation and Income Distribution," JPubE, Vol. 3, No. 4.

b "Poverty, Inequality and Unemployment: Some Conceptual Issues in Measurement," Sankhya: The Indian Journal of Statistics, Vol. 36, June and Dec.

c "On Some Debates in Capital Theory," Economica, Vol. 4l, No. 163.

1975 "The Concept of Efficiency," in Contemporary Issues in Economics, (M. Parking and A. R. Nobay eds.) Manchester University Press, Manchester.

1976 a "Real National Income," RES, Vol. 43, Feb.

b "Poverty: An Ordinal Approach to Measurement," Econometrica, Vol. 44, Mar.

c (with M. Majumdar), "A Note on Representing Partial Orderings," RES, Vol. 43, Oct.

d "Famines as Failures of Exchange Entitlements," EPW, Special Number, 11.

1977 a "Social Choice Theory: A Re-Examination," Econometrica, Vol. 45, No.1.

b "On Weights and Measures: Informational Constraints in Social Welfare Analysis," Econometrica, Vol. 45 , Oct.

c "Non-linear Social Welfare Functions," in Logic, Methodology and Philosophy of Science, R. Butts and J. Hintikka, (eds.), Reidel, Dordrecht.

d "Rational Fools: A Critique of the Behavioural Foundations of Economic Theory," Philosophy and Public Affairs, Vol.6, Summer.

	e	"Starvation and Exchange Entitlements: A General Approach and Its Application to the Great Bengal Famine," CJE, Vol.1, Mar.
1978	a	"Welfare Theory," in Encyclopedic Handbook of Mathematical Economic Sciences, (Beckmann et al. eds.), Gabler.
	b	"Ethical Measurement of Inequality: Some Difficulties," in Personal Income Distribution, W. Krelle and A. F. Shorrocks, (eds.), North-Holland, Amsterdam.
	c	"On the Labour Theory of Value: Some Methodological Issues," CJE, Vol. 2, No.2.
1979	a	"Strategies and Revelation: Informational Constraints in Public Decisions," in Aggregation and Revelation of Preferences, J. J. Laffont(ed.), North-Holland, Amsterdam.
	b	"The Welfare Basis of Real Income Comparisons," JEL, Vol.17, Mar.
	c	"Issues in the Measurement of Poverty," ScandJE, Vol. 8l, No.2.
	d	"Personal Utilities and Public Judgments: Or What's Wrong with Welfare Economics?" EJ, Vol. 89, Sep.
	e	"Utilitarianism and Welfarism," Journal of Philosophy Vol. 76, Sep.
1980	a	"Interpersonal Comparisons of Welfare," in Economics and Human Welfare, M. Boskin (ed.), Academic Press, New York.
	b	"Famine Mortality: A Study of the Bengal Famine of 1943," in Peasants in History, (E. J. Hobsbawm et al. eds.) Oxford University Press, London.
	c	"Equality of What?" in Tanner Lectures on Human Values, Vol.1, S. McMurrin (ed.), Cambridge University Press, Cambridge.
1981	a	"Ingredients of Famine Analysis: Availability and Entitlements," QJE, Vol.95, Aug.
	b	"Public Action and the Quality of Life in Developing Countries," Oxford Bulletin of Economics and Statistics, Vol.43, Nov.
1983	a	"Poor, Relatively Speaking," OEP, Vol. 35, Aug.
	b	(with S. Sengupta), "Malnutrition of Rural Children and the Sex Bias," Economic and Political Weekly, Annual Number, 18.
1985	a	"Social Choice and Justice: A Review Article," JEL, Vol.23, Dec.
	b	"Rationality and Uncertainty," Theory of Decision, Vol.18, No.2.
	c	"Goals, Commitment and Identity," Journal of Law, Economics and Organization, Vol.1, Fall.

d "The Moral Standing of the Market," Social Philosophy and Policy, Vol.3. Reprinted in E. F. Paul, et al., (eds.), Ethics and Economics, Blackwell, Oxford.

1986 a "Foundations of Social Choice Theory: An Epilogue," in Foundations of Social Choice Theory, J. Elster and A. Hylland (eds.), Cambridge University Press, Cambridge.

b "The Concept of Well-Being," in Essays on Economic Progress and Welfare: In Honour of I.G. Patel, (S. Guhan and M. Shroff, eds.), Oxford University Press, Oxford.

c "Information and Invariance in Normative Choice," in Social Choice and Public Decision Making: Essays in Honor of K. J. Arrow, Vol. I, W. P. Heller et al. (eds.), Cambridge University Press, Cambridge.

d "Prediction and Economic Theory," Philosophical Transactions of the Royal Society of London, Vol. 407.

1987 a "Social Choice," In The New Palgrave: A Dictionary of Economics, Macmillan, London.

b "Justice," In The New Palgrave: A Dictionary of Economics, Macmillan, London.

c "Rational Behaviour," in The New Palgrave: A Dictionary of Economics, Macmillan, London.

1988 a "Freedom of Choice: Concept and Content," European Economic Review, Vol. 32, No. 2-3.

b "Family and Food: Sex-Bias in Poverty," in Rural Poverty in South Asia, (P. Bardhan and T.N. Srinivasan eds.) Columbia University Press, New York.

c "The Concept of Development," in Handbook of Development Economics, (H. Chenery and T. N. Srinivasan (eds.)) North Holland, Amsterdam.

d "Property and Hunger," Economics and Philosophy, Vol.4, No.2.

1989 "Food and Freedom," Text of Sir John Crawford Memorial Lecture, Washington, D C. Reprinted in World Development, Vol.17, June.

1991 a "Welfare, Preferences and Freedom," Journal of Econometrics, Vol. 50, No. 1-2.

b "The Nature of Inequality," in Issues in Contemporary Economics: Markets and Welfare, (K. J. Arrow, ed.), Macmillan, London.

c "Utility: Ideas and Terminology," Economics and Philosophy, Vol.7, No.2.

d "Capability and Well-Being," in The Quality of Life, (M. Nussbaum and A. Sen, (eds.)), Clarendon Press, Oxford.

1992 “Missing Women,” British Medical Journal, Vol. 304, Mar.

1993 a “Internal Consistency of Choice,” Econometrica, Vol. 61, Mar.

b “Markets and Freedoms,” OEP, Vol. 45, No.4.

c “On the Foundations of Welfare Economics: Utility, Capability and Practical Reason,” in Ethics, Rationality and Economic Behavior, F. H. Hahn, et al., (eds.), Oxford University Press, Oxford.

d “Life Expectancy and Inequality: Some Conceptual Issues,” in Development and Change, (P. K. Bardhan et al.eds.) Oxford University Press, Oxford.

1994 a “Markets and the Freedom to Choose,” in The Ethical Foundations of the Market Economy, (H. Siebert ed.), J. C. B. Mohr, Tubingen.

b “The Formulation of Rational Choice,” AER, Vol.84, No.21.

c “Growth Economics: What and Why?” in Economic Growth and the Structure of Long-term Development, (L. Pasinetti and R. Solow, eds.), Macmillan, London.

1995 “Rationality and Social Choice,” AER, Vol.85, No.1.

1997 a “Individual Preference as the Basis of Social Choice,” in Social Choice Re-examined, (K. J. Arrow et al. eds.), Macmillan, London.

b “From Income Inequality to Economic Inequality,” SEJ, Vol.64, No.2.

c “Maximization and the Act of Choice,” Econometrica, Vol. 65, No.4.

1998 “Mortality as an Indicator of Economic Success and Failure,” EJ, Vol. 108, No.448.

1999 “The Possibility of Social Choice,” AER, Nobel Lecture, Vol. 89, No.3.

2000 a “Merit and Justice,” in Meritocracy and Economic Inequality, K. J. Arrow, et al. (eds.), Princeton University Press, Princeton, NJ.

b “Social Justice and the Distribution of Income,” in Handbook of Income Distribution, A.B. Atkinson and F. Bourguignon, (eds.), Elsevier, Vol.1, Amsterdam.

2003 “Sraffa, Wittgenstein, and Gramci,” JEL, Vol. 41, No.4.

2006 “Conceptualizing and Measuring Poverty,” in Poverty and Inequality, D. Grusky and R. Kanbur, (eds.), Stanford University Press, Stanford.

53.8 WORKS OF OTHERS

Arrow, K. J. (1999), "Amartya K. Sen's Contributions to the Study of Social Welfare," ScandJE, Vol. 101, No.2.

Atkinson, A. B. (1999), "The Contributions of Amartya Sen to Welfare Economics," ScandJE, Vol. 101, No.2.

Rao, B. S. R. (1974), "A Theoretical Exercise: Book Review," On Income Inequality, Amartya Sen, Oxford University Press, New Delhi, Economic Times, Dec 22, 1974.

CHAPTER 54

DANIEL KAHNEMAN

(1934 –)

The Royal Swedish Academy of Sciences has awarded the Bank of Sweden Prize in Economic Sciences in memory of Alfred Nobel for the year 2002, jointly to Daniel Kahneman of Princeton University, U.S.A, and Vernon L. Smith of George Mason University, U.S.A. The award citation states that Kahneman is given the prize for having integrated insights from psychological research into economic science, especially concerning human judgment and decision-making under uncertainty. In the case of Vernon Smith, the citation refers to his establishment of laboratory experiments as a tool in empirical economic analysis, particularly in the study of alternative market mechanisms.

Traditionally, economic research is basically depended on the assumption of an economic man, who is motivated by self-interest and is credited with a capability to making rational decisions. Further, economics has been till recently considered a non-experimental science, relying on observation of real world economies rather than on controlled laboratory experiments. In recent times, however, research in economics has taken off in new directions, modifying and testing postulates, that is pure self-interest, complete self control and unbounded rationality. Moreover, economic research in recent years has started increasingly relying upon data collected in the laboratory rather than on more traditional field data—that is, data obtained from observations of real economies. The press release of Royal Swedish Academy announcing the award specifically observes: "... recent research has its roots in two distinct, but currently converging, areas: The analysis of human judgment and decision-making by cognitive psychologists [for instance, Kahneman and Tversky] and the empirical testing of predictions from economic theory by experimental economists [such as, Vernon Smith and Charles Plott]. We notice that behavioural economics and experimental economics have become some of the most active fields in economics as is evident from research publications in major economic journals, new doctoral dissertations, seminars, workshops and conferences." The Academy states that this year's laureates-- Kahneman and Smith-- are pioneers in these two fields of research.

One of the key standard assumptions in economics is the rationality of the decision–makers. Nevertheless, it is generally observed that human decision-making deviates, in one way or another, from this rationalistic paradigm. If such deviations from rationality and self interest were small and purely idiosyncratic, they are expected to cancel out and prediction of outcomes for large aggregate of economic agents by economic theory would not be wide off the mark. A revision of prevalent economic theory is called for, however, in case such deviations from rationality and self-interest were systematic. The award notification states: Following the lead of Daniel Kahneman and the late Amos Tversky, early studies of human decision-making of cognitive psychologists can be seen as testing hypotheses of systematic deviation from rationality. Kahneman's work has laid the basic foundation for what has come to be known as behavioural economics.

Typically, economics assumes that market behaviour is motivated importantly by material incentives. Further, it is assumed, as mentioned above, that self interest and rationality govern economic decisions of the people. Rationality is interpreted as decision-makers using all available information in a logical and systematic way, assessing the state of the economy and the consequences of their behaviour by processing the information using standard statistical principles. This process is expected to lead people to making optimal choices, given the alternatives at hand and the objective to be achieved. It is supposed that decision-makers fully take into account future consequences of current decisions. In other words, human economic behaviour is supposed to be shaped by what is called "extrinsic incentives."

Specifically, economists have regarded decision maker's preferences over available alternatives as fixed and given. He or she is assumed to form probabilistic beliefs or expectations about the state of the nature and the consequences of his actions. The approach of the standard economic theory is to formulate axiomatically expected utility maximisation as founded by von Neumann and Oscar Morgenstern and extended by Leonard Savage. Formally. it is presumed that for every decision-maker there exists some real-valued function, u, defined on the relevant set X of outcomes $x_1, x_2, \ldots x_n$, such that if one available action 'a' results in probabilities p_i over the outcomes x_i (for i=1,…,n) and another available action 'b' results in probabilities q_i over the same outcomes, then the decision-maker strictly prefers action 'a' to action 'b,' if and only if, expected value of this 'utility function' u, is greater under *'a'* than under *'b.'* That is,

$$\Sigma_i\, p_i\, u(x_i) > \Sigma_i\, q_i\, u(x_i)$$

Given the existing market conditions defining the choice set available to the decision-maker, he or she is assumed to correctly assign probabilities to relevant random events and choose an action that maximised the expected value of resulting utility to him.

By contrast, cognitive psychologists consider that decision-making is an interactive process influenced by several factors in a non-trivial way. The factors include perception, (following its own laws) and mental models or beliefs (for interpreting situations as they arise). A human decision may also be influenced by intrinsic motives, such as emotions (the decision maker's state of mind) and attitudes (stable psychological tendencies to relate to a given phenomenon in one's environment). Furthermore, a strong influence on current decision-making is a strong cognitive function, the memory of previous decisions and their consequences. Given this complex view, cognitive psychologists regard human behaviour as locally conditioned to a given situation. Typically, behaviour is adaptive, dependent on the context and transitory perceptual conditions.

Given these differences between psychology and standard economics, there is difference in research methodology of the two as well. Experiments in economics often emphasise the generality of a situation and consist monetary rewards and repeated trials whereas psychologists attempt at capturing intrinsic motivations and the mental processes at work in a particular decision situation, commonly referred to as framing of a decision problem.

Historically, decision-making as a research topic for psychologists was introduced by W. Edwards in 1954. Prior to that, Maurice Allais outlined a positive theory of choice under uncertainty based on psychology. Herbert A. Simon suggested in 1956 an approach to processing of information and decision-making based on bounded rationality. The Royal Swedish Academy remarks that research in cognitive psychology did not come into its own until Daniel Kahneman and Amos Tversky published their findings on judgment and decision-making. Though Kahneman's research has been based in the discipline of cognitive psychology, it was also addressed to economists as can be seen that a number of his articles have been published in economic journals. Further, one of the articles of Kahneman and Tversky has the distinction of highest citation count of all articles published in the Econometrica. Kahneman is credited with building a bridge between research in economics and psychology. The Royal Swedish Academy highlights the existence of two bridges between economics and psychology: one, built around experimental methods and the other around theoretical modelling. Both these bridges serve as the basis for the current wave of research work in "behavioural economics."

The assumption of economic rationality, at least in situations of complex decisions, has been called into question by extensive behavioural evidence collected by Kahneman and other researchers which documented a large amount of deviations from such an assumption. It is demonstrated that decision makers in real world do not invariably evaluate uncertain prospects according to probability laws. Furthermore, sometimes they make decisions which violate the principles of maximisation of expected utility.

An important notion underlying much of the early research of Kahneman and Tversky (1973-1996) is that people in general are unable to analyse situations involving economic and probabilistic judgments. In such situations, humans resort to heuristics or short cuts and such judgments are sometimes systematically biased. Thus, contrary to the postulate of rationality in traditional economic theory, human judgment under uncertainty may be biased. Kahneman and Tversky find that humans violate the law of large numbers in probability theory; instead, they appear to use law of small numbers attributing the same probability distribution to the empirical value of mean form small as from large samples. As people believe the psychological law of small numbers, that is the mean value from a small sample also has a distribution concentrated at the expected value of the random variable, they resort to "over-inference" from short sequences of independent observations. A pertinent example of the law of small numbers is when an investor observing a fund manager, performing above-average for two years in a row concludes that the fund manager is better than average while the true statistical implication is very weak and hence the investor's conclusion is unwarranted.

Kahneman and Tversky found representativeness (which is related to the law of small numbers) as an important ingredient in human judgment. They illustrated the function of this heuristic in several experiments. The same heuristic can also prompt people to believe that the joint probability distribution of two events is larger than the probability of one of the constituent events, which contradicts a fundamental principle of probability, the conjunction rule. It is also argued by some researchers that the law of small numbers and representativeness explain certain anomalies in financial markets.

Another bias that is found by Kahneman and Tversky in probabilistic judgment is availability. People assign disproportionately high weight to salient or easily remembered information. Yet another finding in cognitive psychology relates to the belief that familiar information that is more easily accessible from memory is more relevant or real. Familiarity and availability may therefore serve as cues for accuracy and relevance. Thus, mere repetition of certain information in the media, whether it is accurate or not, is falsely perceived to be more accurate.

Thus, the empirical validity of one of the fundamentals of traditional economic theory has been seriously questioned by such evidence on human judgment. It has demonstrated that human reasoning systematically violates basic laws of probability. The accumulated evidence indicates that human judgment departs in a systematic way from traditional economic theory. More importantly, decision-making under uncertainty diverge from the predictions of expected utility theory. In this context, reference has to be made to the work of Maurice Allais, which showed decisions under uncertainty departing from the von Neumann – Morgenstern – Savage Expected Utility Theory, referred to in the literature as "Allais Paradox." For example, many individuals prefer a certain gain of Rs 3,000 to a lottery giving Rs 4,000 with 80 percent probability and zero percent otherwise. However, some of these same individuals also choose winning Rs 4,000 with 20 percent probability to winning Rs 3,000 with 25 percent probability, even though the probabilities for the gains were scaled down by the same factor, 0.25, in both alternatives (from 80 percent to 20 percent, and from 100 percent to 25 percent). Such preferences violate the substitution axiom of expected-utility theory. It may be recalled that by this axiom, if a decision-maker prefers lottery A to B, he should also prefer a probability mixture $\rho A + (1-\rho)C$ to the probability mixture $\rho B + (1-\rho)C$, for all lotteries C.

Kahneman has provided extensive evidence of departures from the predictions of expected utility theory. One key finding of Kahneman and others is that people are often much more sensitive to the way an outcome differs from some non-constant reference level such as the status quo, rather than to the outcome measured in absolute terms. This focus on changes rather than levels is considered related to well-established psychophysical laws of cognition.

Moreover, people appear to be more averse to losses, relative to their reference level, than attracted by gains of the same size. That is, Kahneman found that people's preferences appear to be characterised by local loss aversion. The finding of apparently risk-loving behaviour with respect to large losses is inconsistent with the assumption of risk–aversion in traditional economic theory.

Kahneman and Tversky are not merely critical of traditional economic theory. They suggest an alternative modelling framework in their seminal article, "Prospect Theory: An Analysis of Decisions under Risk," which is summarised below. While expected-utility theory is axiomatic, their Prospect Theory is descriptive, developed by induction from empirical observations. In a later article, they suggested the need for two theories: Expected-utility theory to characterise rational behaviour and Prospect theory to describe actual human behaviour.

The contributions of Daniel Kahneman are surveyed in this chapter. Vernon Smith's contributions in economic sciences are summarised in chapter 42. Before covering Kahneman's contributions, an attempt is made here to provide a brief biographical note.

54.1 A BRIEF BIOGRAPHICAL NOTE: DANIEL KAHNEMAN

Daniel Kahneman was born in Tel Aviv, in what is now Israel, in 1934. His parents, who were Lithuanian Jews, migrated to France in the early 1920's and settled in Paris. In his autobiographical note, Kahneman confesses that the family's roots in France were shallow, and the family never felt completely secure. Whatever vestiges of security the family had were lost when Germany invaded France in 1940 (in the Second World War). According to Kahneman "... what was probably the first graph I ever drew, in 1941, showed my family's fortunes as a function of time - and around 1940 the curve crossed into the negative domain." From his experience with a German soldier in a street, Kahneman was convinced that his mother was right: people were endlessly complicated and interesting. After his father's death in 1944, the family moved to Palestine.

He had grown up "intellectually precocious and physically inept." At age seventeen, he had decided to defer his military service until he completed his first degree by applying to a unit that entailed spending the summers in officer-training school. By that time, he had decided "with some difficulty" that he would be a psychologist. When he went for vocational guidance psychology emerged as the top recommendation, with economics "not too far behind." Kahneman obtained his first degree from Hebrew University in Jerusalem in two years, with a major in psychology and a minor in mathematics. He admits that he was "mediocre" in mathematics. As a first-year student, he "encountered the writings of the social psychologist Kurt Lewin" and "fascinated" by his early exposures to new psychology.

In 1954, he was drafted for military service. In the second year of military service Kahneman was assigned to the Psychology branch of the Israel Defense Forces. During the periods of military experience from 1954 to 1956, Kahneman coined terms, such as: "The illusion of validity," which have been made into the technical literature of cognitive psychology.

The illusion of validity referred to compelling experience of insight. In his autobiographical note, Kahneman calls it "first cognitive illusion." He developed a statistical technique for analysis of multi-attribute heteroscedastic data for evaluating soldiers in military units. This technique provided the material for his first published article. Kahneman reminisces that that was the beginning of a lifelong interest in the statistics of prediction and description. During the period, he also developed a structural interview schedule for the purpose of evaluating the potential of military recruits. On the basis of this, Kahneman got the seed of the paper on the psychology of intuitive prediction: "... that Tversky and I published much later." Further, he observes: "... with B.A. in the appropriate field, I was the best-trained professional psychologist in the military."

After coming out of the Army in 1956, Kahneman went to the University of California at Berkley for doing Ph.D. on a fellowship from Hebrew University so that he would be able to return and teach in the Psychology Department. He states that his experience of graduate school was quite different from that of students today. He was an eclectic student. He wrote his dissertation in 1961, in eight days. He recollects: "... that was probably the last time I wrote anything without pain. The paper itself ... was so convoluted and dreary that my teacher ... memorably described the experience of reading it as 'wading through wet mush'."

Kahneman loved teaching undergraduates and he considered himself as good at it. He started teaching first-year statistics class and, for some years, taught that course and the second-year course in research methods, which also included a large dose of statistics. To teach effectively he did a lot of serious thinking about valid intuition on which he could draw and erroneous intuitions that he should teach students to eschew. He remarks: "I had no idea...that I was laying the foundations for a program of research on judgment under uncertainty." His research achievements in the early years, in his own judgment, were quite "humdrum" but he was excited by several opportunities to bring psychology to bear on the real world. Teamed with others, Kahneman designed training programs for various groups of people, such as, immigrants and flight instructors of the Air Force. While teaching flight instructors, Kahneman once made a statement that praise is more effective than punishment for promoting skill-learning which was contradicted by a seasoned instructor in the audience. About this experience Kahneman says: "... understood an important truth about the world: because we tend to reward others when they do well and punish them when they do badly, and because there is regression to the mean, it is part of the human condition that we are statistically punished for rewarding others and rewarded for punishing them."

Kahneman states that his first experience of truly successful research came in 1965, when he was on sabbatical leave at the University of Michigan, where he joined Jerry

Blum. Blum had a laboratory in which volunteer participants performed various cognitive tasks while in the grip of powerful emotional states induced by hypnosis.

When he returned in 1967, Kahneman was "finally" a well–trained research psychologist. In 1969, he taught at a graduate seminar on applications of psychology to real world problems. Kahneman refers to what turned out to be a life-changing event; he asked Tversky to tell the class about what was going on in his field of judgment and decision–making. This resulted in their writing a joint paper. More importantly, they remained a team for well over a decade. Kahneman notes: "The Nobel Prize was awarded for work that we produced during that period of intense collaboration—and probably much of its success—came from ability to elaborate each other's nascent thoughts...." They published eight journal articles during their peak period, 1971-1981, of which five had been cited more than a thousand times by 2002.

Kahneman and Tversky's collaborative effort resulted in an article in Science (1974) dealing with the prevalence of systematic biases in intuitive assessments and predictions that could possibly be of interest to scholars outside psychology. Essentially, the article was conceived with an interesting issue: "The susceptibility to erroneous intuitions of intelligent, sophisticated and perceptive individuals...." According to Kahneman: "... the article soon became a standard reference as an attack on the rational–agent model, and it spawned a large literature in cognitive science, philosophy and psychology." He claims that they had shown that some judgments relating to uncertain events are mediated by heuristics, which sometimes produce predictable biases. The work has been interpreted as a broad attack on human rationality rather than as a critique of the rational–agent, which was the authors' attempt. Kahneman asserts: "I am now quick to reject any description of our work as demonstrating human irrationality. I carefully explain that research on heuristics and biases only refutes an unrealistic conception of rationality, which identifies it as comprehensive coherence."

After the publication of 1974 article in Science, Kahneman and Tversky decided to work together on the topic of decision-making. It involved construction of a theory that would explain Allais's paradox "parsimoniously." The task was to set aside the issue of rationality and to develop a theory of the preferences that people actually have, whether or not these preferences can be justified. They had realised that all problems of choice were formulated in terms of gains and losses whereas the utility functions that were supposed to explain the choices were drawn with wealth as the abscissa. This seemed to them "unnatural" and psychologically "unlikely." They, therefore, decided to shift from wealth to changes and/or differences in wealth as "carriers of utility." This is particularly significant because of a property of preferences that Kahneman and Tversky later labelled loss-aversion. They argue: "... the response to losses is consistently much more intense than the response to corresponding gains, with a sharp kink in the value function at the reference point." Kahneman rightfully claims in his autobiographical note: "The concept of loss aversion was, I believe, our most useful contribution to the study of decision making. The asymmetry between gains and losses solves quite a few puzzles."

While the draft of Prospect Theory was ready in 1975, which they called "Value Theory" at that time, it was sent after revisions to Econometrica. Later Kahneman developed concepts such as "Framing" and "Mental Accounting." In association with Richard Thaler, Kahneman developed a list of phenomena, called "Mental Accounting" that describes how people violate rationality by failing to maintain a comprehensive view of outcomes, and by failing to treat money as fungible. Kahneman observes: "Our interaction with Thaler eventually proved to be more fruitful than we could have imagined at the time, and it was a major factor in my receiving the Nobel Prize." The committee cited me "for having integrated insights from psychological research into economic science...." Kahneman submits that "the work of integration was 'actually done' mostly by Thaler and the group of young economists that quickly began to form around him."

In the later part of the autobiographical note, Kahneman says that the focus of his research for the past fifteen years has been the study of various aspects of "experienced utility." It is the measure of the utility of outcomes as people actually live them. He states that the concept of utility he is interested in was the one that Bentham and Edgeworth had in mind. Further, Kahneman states that their evidence contradicts the standard rational model, which does not distinguish between experienced utility and decision utility. He presented it as a new type of challenge to the assumption of rationality.

Kahneman held Professorships at Hebrew University, Jerusalem, (Israel), University of British Columbia (Canada) and University of California at Berkeley. Since 1993, he is Eugene Higgins Professor of Psychology and Professor of Public Affairs at Princeton University, U.S.A. He has received numerous awards including Distinguished Scientific Contributor Award of the American Psychological Association (jointly with Amos Tversky). Hilliard Award for life time contributions to General Psychology, Schelling Prize for intellectual contributions to public policy, Harvard University, Frank P. Ramsey medal of Decision Analysis Society (jointly with Amos Tversky), Distinguished Life Time Contribution Award, American Psychological Association and John McGovern Lecture, The American Association for the Advancement of Science. He received honorary doctorates from many prestigious Universities and other higher educational institutions including, University of Pennsylvania, Harvard University, The New School, University of East Anglia, Univerite de Paris, University of British Columbia and University of Alabama. He was elected Fellow of American Psychological Society and member of the Econometric Society, American Academy of Arts and Sciences, National Academy of Sciences, American Philosophical Society and Society of Experimental Psychology.

54.2 A SUMMARY OF DANIEL KAHNEMAN'S CONTRIBUTIONS TO ECONOMICS

Alfred Marshall in his Principle of Economics defined the scope of the subject: "Economics... is on the one side a study of wealth; and, on the other, and more important side, a part of the study of the man." (Emphasis supplied). We can observe that the more important side, the study of man, has largely been neglected till recently. The traditional economic theory posits as Bernstein remarks: "Investors have no difficulty in making optimal choices in the bewildering jumble of facts, rumors, discontinuities, vagueness, and black uncertainty that make up real world around us.... How much do we know about how people in the real world arrive at decisions and make choices? How great are the differences between the theoretical assumptions [of human rationality] and the real world? And do these differences matter?" The work of Daniel Kahneman and Amos Tversky laid foundations of Behavioural Economics/Behavioural Finance and are in the forefront of creating a competing vision to the rational model of how people make decisions under conditions of uncertainty. The essence of their work is a study of human behaviour or a study of man. Kahneman states that the research work cited by the Noble Committee was done jointly with the late Amos Tversky (1937-1996) during a "long and close collaboration." They worked together primarily on the issue of rationality. In his Prize lecture, Kahneman covers three major topics of their joint work, heuristics of judgment, risky choice, and framing effects.

Traditionally, as stated earlier, standard economic theory, postulated and most of the economic research conducted on assumptions that economic decision-making is largely rational and motivated by self interest. In recent times, however, widespread attempts have been made to test basic economic assumptions and to modify them wherever felt necessary. In early 1950's Edwards, Allais and Simon had made pioneering attempts in this direction. While Allais outlined a psychology-based positive theory of choice under uncertainty, Edwards suggested human decision-making as a research topic for psychologists and provided an agenda for future research. Simon introduced the concept of bounded rationality and proposed an approach to processing of information and human decision-making based on it. In this context it is appropriate to refer to the recommendation of Paul Krugman as his first rule of research to young economists as quoted by Matthew Robin: "Listen to the Gentile.... Pay attention to what intelligent people are saying, even if they do not have your customs or speak your analytical language." Krugman advises economists conducting research on topics in international trade to pay attention to the field of geography: "Geographers and regional scientists have amassed a great deal of evidence on the nature and importance of localized external economies, and organized that evidence intelligently if not rigorously." Robin estimates that the joint work of Kahneman and Tversky "... is surely one of the biggest boons to the social sciences in recent decades that they have launched this research program so relevant for economics, doing so with an ability and willingness to address economists in economic language and venues and with an emphasis on the implications of their research for economic questions."

It is proposed to cover here Kahneman's main contributions to economics. His contributions are summarised under the following heads.

1. Heuristics of Judgment under Uncertainty;
2. Loss Aversion and Reference- Based Preferences;
3. Prospect Theory;

4. Framing Effects;
5. Fairness Judgments; and
6. Preferences and Hedonics.

54.2.1 HEURISTICS OF JUDGMENT UNDER UNCERTAINTY

In economics, it is assumed that people make decisions under conditions of uncertainty, on the basis of assessments using subjective probability estimates. Kahneman and Tversky's first joint research program was concerned with various types of judgments about uncertain events. They tried to show as Kahneman states "...[that] people rely on a limited number of heuristic principles which reduce the complex tasks of assessing probabilities and predicting values to simpler judgmental operations. In general, these heuristics are quite useful, but sometimes they lead to severe and systematic errors. The subjective assessment of probability resembles the subjective assessment of physical quantities such as distance or size. These judgments are all based on data of limited validity, which are processed according to heuristic rules." The concept of heuristics was illustrated by the role of the blur of contours as a potent determinant of the perceived distance of mountains. In this case, reliance on blur to determine the distance cue will result in overestimation of distances on foggy days as a result of poor visibility and underestimation of distances on clear days because of good visibility. This is a good example of a heuristic-induced bias. Such biases are also noticed in the intuitive judgment of probability.

Human beings, it is stated, are subject to judgmental imperfections and illusions and when and how such imperfections matter and when and how they can be ignored needs to be studied carefully. Critics consider that such judgmental biases are particularly important to the issue of bounded rationality. The research by Kahneman and his associates emphasises the predictable nature of such errors. Their research underlines the departure of probability judgments from the standard model of perfect rationality assumed by economists. However, they do not question the assumption that people are generally "intelligent and purposive" in their decision–making. They argue that for discussions in economics there is a need to consider separately the "bounded" component and "rationality" component of the concept of bounded rationality.

Kahneman in his Prize lecture specifies three heuristics of judgment namely, representativeness, availability and anchoring. He states that prior to his 2002 paper with a co-author, no adequate definition of judgment heuristics was available. The article provides an explicit definition of a generic heuristic process of attribute substitution. A judgment is said to be mediated by a heuristic when the individual assesses a specific target attribute of a judgment object by substituting a related heuristic attribute that comes more readily to mind. This may be (i) an availability heuristic, for example; when a person is asked: "What proportion of long-distance relationships break up within a year?" he may answer as though he were asked "Do instances of swift breakups of long-distance relationships come readily to mind?" or (ii) relative strength heuristic. For example: When a person was asked to assess the probability that team A will beat team B in a cricket match, he may answer by "mapping" an impression of the relative strength of the two teams on the probability scale. The first is an example of a substitute related to the target while the second is a case of substituting a highly accessible one to the target. Thus, the definition heuristic is used in two senses. While heuristic as a noun refers to the cognitive process, the adjective heuristic attribute clearly identifies the substitution that is used in a specific judgment. Further, Kahneman clarifies that the representative heuristic is defined by the use of representativeness as a heuristic attribute to judgment probability.

The important biases identified by Kahneman and Tversky are termed by them under the head representative heuristics. The representativeness heuristic is defined by the use of representativeness as a heuristic or a short cut attribute to judge probability. An example will illustrate this. Suppose a person behaves "more like a criminal (shifty eyes etc.), we think it "more likely he is a criminal." However, the reason given by Kahneman and others for this judgment is that people tend to over-use "representativeness" in assessing probabilities and under–use base rates. "If we see somebody who looks like a criminal, our assessment of the probability that he is a criminal tends to under-use knowledge about the percentage of people who are criminals." They provide another example: "... if a certain medical test always comes out positive among people with a rare disease, and only occasionally among people without the disease, people tend to exaggerate the likelihood of having the disease given a positive result. Given the rarity of the disease, the total number of false positives may be far greater than the number of true positives."

In his Prize lecture, Kahneman provides the result of a study from heuristics and biases literature illustrating what is called the "conjunction fallacy."

Linda is 31 years old, single, outspoken and very bright. She majored in philosophy. As a student she was deeply concerned with issues of discrimination and social justice and also participated in anti-nuclear demonstrations. Respondents were shown the description of Linda and a list of eight possible outcomes relating to her present employment and activities. Two key statements on the rest were: Linda is a bank teller, and the conjunction item, the other statement was Linda is a bank teller and active in the feminist movement; some respondents ranked the eight outcomes by representativeness; others ranked the same outcomes by probability. The correlation between the mean rankings was 0.99. Over 85 percent respondents judged it likely that Linda was both bank teller and feminist than she was a bank teller. Kahneman remarks: "Linda does resemble the image of a feminist bank teller more than she resembles a stereotypical bank teller. However, the reliance on representativeness as a heuristic attribute yields a pattern of probability judgments that violate monotonicity, and has been called the 'conjunction fallacy'."

Tversky and Kahneman find a fundamental bias or another evidence of representative heuristic in that individuals appear to use what they call the "law of small numbers." By using the law of small numbers, individuals attribute the same probability distribution to the empirical mean value for small samples as for large samples. By doing this, they violate the law of large numbers in probability theory. Belief in the law of small numbers gives rise to a number of errors that may be significant for economics. When people do not know the probability distribution, they may "over-infer" the probability distribution from "short sequences." A financial analyst who correctly forecasts market movements for three years in a row may be judged a financial genius. It may not be correct; the analyst may be simply lucky. This may lead to "wrong perception of regression to the mean." As a result of reading too much into pattern that deviates from norm, we may fail to expect further observations that deviate from the norm. Matthew Robin sounds a valid warning after giving another example: If a student performs well on a mid- term examination but poorly in the final, teachers are prone to over-infer that the student has slacked off. Such misrepresentation can lead to all sorts of errors in the design of incentives, and hence can influence organisational design.

Kahneman and Tversky recognise a number of other heuristic biases and give relevant evidence; such as hindsight bias. Observers have recognised the slow penetration of cognitive biases into economics. However, a breakthrough can be seen in the areas of behavioural finance and behavioural economics.

54.2.2 LOSS AVERSION AND REFERENCE–BASED PREFERENCES

In Kahneman's early research in collaboration with Tversky on decision–making under uncertainty, it was assumed that in the context of facts of perpetual adaptation, people are expected to evaluate the decision outcomes to be reference–dependent. However, they noted that reference-dependence is compatible with prevailing theoretical model of Expected Utility Theory. When Daniel Bernoulli presented the Expected Utility Theory (the dominant model of risky choices), his purpose was to formalise the intuition that it is eminently reasonable for the poor to buy insurance and for the rich to sell it. The basis of his argument is that the increment of utility associated with an increment of wealth is inversely proportional to the initial wealth. He, therefore, posited a logarithmic utility function for wealth. He further argued that a sensible decision rule for choice that involves risk is to maximise the expected utility of wealth. He thus explained people's attitude of risk aversion as also differential risk attitudes of the rich and of the poor. According to Kahneman, Bernoulli's theory is prescriptive (what is sensible or reasonable to do). It is not meant to describe the choices of reasonable men. He further remarks: "There is no acknowledgement of any tension between prescription and description in Bernoulli's essay." This "error" of Bernoulli that decision-makers evaluate outcomes by the utility of the final asset position has been retained in economic analysis for almost 300 years.

Kahneman criticises Bernoulli's model as flawed as it is reference-independent. That is, "it assumes that the value that is assigned to a given state of wealth does not vary with the decision maker's initial state of wealth." Kahneman contends, on the basis of an analogy in psychology, that the carriers of utility are likely to be gains and losses rather than states of wealth. He says that this contention is buttressed by evidence of experimental and observational studies of choice. Moreover, Bernoulli's error (that is, his assumption that the carriers of utility are final states is the error of reference-independence) is not confined to decision-making under risk, but is built into the customary representation of indifference maps. Kahneman observes: "It is puzzling to a psychologist that these maps do not include a representation of the decision maker's current holdings of various goods – the counterpart of the reference in Prospect Theory." The Prospect Theory is discussed in the next section.

It follows from Tversky and Kahneman's arguments, that in the context of utility theory, that instead of assuming that the consumer's utility at time t, u_t, depends exclusively on current consumption, c_t, it also depends on a "reference level" r_t, which is determined, in turn, by factors such as past consumption or expectations of future consumption. The utility function better be formulated in a more general form, $u_t(c_t, r_t)$. It is, of course, true that the function of reference levels in decision-making may be inconsistent with full rationality assumption, though effects of reference levels can be captured within the utility theory framework. Kahneman and Tversky put forward the view that preferences and choices are influenced in two ways. First, people are loss-averse; that is, they are averse to losses relative to their reference level than they are allured to gains of equal size. They, in fact, suggest in one of their articles that people, in general, value moderate losses roughly twice as much as same-sized gains. Second, people exhibit diminishing sensitivity. They contend that diminishing sensitivity demonstrates a vital characteristic of human cognition and motivation. In their words: "Many sensory and perceptual dimensions share the property that the psychological response is a concave function of the magnitude of physical change.... We propose that this principle applies in particular to the evaluation of monetary changes. Thus, the difference between a gain of 100 and a gain of 200 appears to be greater than the difference between a gain of 1,100 and a gain of 1,200. Similarly, the difference between a loss of 100 and a loss of 200 appears greater than the difference between a loss of 1,100 and a loss of 1,200 unless the larger loss is intolerable. Thus, we hypothesise that the value function for changes of wealth is normally concave above the reference point... and often convex below it.... That is, the marginal value of both gains and losses generally decrease with their magnitude."

A significant sequel of a broad definition of loss aversion is the endowment effect, first specified by Richard Thaler and developed by Kahneman in association with Thaler and others. A person when he possesses a good, values it more than prior to its possession. They provide an example to illustrate the concept. A decorated mug valued at about $5 was placed before one-third of a group of students. The other group of students were supposed to be sellers of the mug. Information about prices at which they were willing to sell their mugs was obtained in a way that they would not have any incentive to be untruthful. The two groups of students face the same choice; however, the reference level is different. For sellers, selling the mug is a loss, while for "choosers" there was no loss. The average selling price was roughly $7.00. For choosers, the average exchange value was about $3.50. The difference noticed between these two amounts exhibit the effect of owning the mug on its valuation. This is what is called "endowment effect," conceptualised as a case of loss aversion. Endowed mugs are considered a part of individuals' reference levels; subsequent non-possession of the mug is treated as a loss: on the other side, individuals without mugs initially, consider not having a mug as remaining at the same reference point.

Economists consider endowment effect as qualitatively similar to models of habit persistence. Matthew Robin refers to research work of Genesove and Mayer who studied the market downtown Boston condominium (building containing a number of individually owned flats) sold between 1990 and 1997 and comments: "Genesove and Mayer provide very strong evidence that loss aversion matters a lot in the housing market." Further, Robin observes that Kahneman, Thaler and others show that loss aversion permeates people's notion of fairness and many examples of framing effects (discussed below) revolve around loss aversion. Robin also observes: "Loss aversion is implicated in the strong resistance to cuts in (nominal) wages, for instance, and such attitudes are clearly economically important. The salience of losses relative to the status quo is a big fact about human judgment, preferences and behaviour, with pervasive implications for economics."

54.2.3 PROSPECT THEORY

As pointed out earlier, in the standard economic theory Expected Utility Theory (EUT) is the basis for decision making under uncertainty. It is applied as a descriptive model of economic behaviour; it is also used as a normative model of rational choice of people. Decision-making here is a process of choosing between different prospects or gambles. That is, choosing from out of a number of possible outcomes along with their associated probabilities. The theory is, however, found wanting in explaining widely observed violations of monotonicity, transitivity and invariance.

EUT model is basically a model of preference maximisation. It is assumed that economic agents behave as if they are optimising some underlying preference function. Behavioural models attempt at modelling the psychological processes that lead to choice. These are referred to as "procedural theories;" Prospect Theory, one such theory developed by Kahneman and Tversky, has been undoubtedly very influential and one of the authors of the theory, Daniel Kahneman, is one of the recipients of Nobel Memorial Prize for Economic Sciences in 2002.

The Prospect Theory was developed originally in 1979 in Kahneman's paper co-authored with Amos Tversky. The same authors extended the paper in "Cumulative Prospect Theory" (1992). The theory stipulates a two- phase process. The first phase involves coding while the second phase is concerned with evaluation of each of the edited prospects.

Offered prospects are analysed with the objective of obtaining a simple representation to facilitate the process of evaluation. For the purpose of evaluating the options, certain heuristic rules and operations may be employed to narrow down the options. Such operations normally include, according to Kahneman and Tversky, coding, combination, segregation, cancellation, simplification and the detection of dominance among the prospects.

After evaluating each of the edited prospects, the decision-maker is supposed to choose the prospect with the highest value. The overall value of the edited prospect (V) is expressed in terms of two scales, v and π. For each outcome, the first scale, v, assigns a number x, v (x), reflecting the subjective value of that outcome. The second scale, π associates with each probability p a decision weight, **π (p)** indicating the impact of p on the overall value of the prospect.

54.2.4 ESSENTIALS OF PROSPECT THEORY

Assume a simple prospect according to which one receives x with probability p, y with probability q and nothing with probability 1–p–q, where $p + q \leq 1$,. That is, the prospect is of the form (x, p; y, q) which has at most two non-zero outcomes. A prospect is considered strictly all positive if its outcomes are positive; that is

If, $x, y > 0$ and $p + q = 1$

A prospect is strictly negative if its outcomes are all negative.

A prospect is regular if it is neither strictly positive, nor strictly negative.

The overall value of regular prospects are determined by the way v and π are combined in the basic equation of the theory.

If(x, p; y, q) is a regular prospect, that is either $p+ q <1$, or $x \geq 0 \geq y$, or

$x \leq 0 \leq y$, then

$$V (x, p; y, q) = \pi (p) v(x) + \pi (q) v (y) \quad .....(1)$$

Where $v (0) = 0, \pi (0) = 0$, and $\pi (1) = 1$

As can be seen, V is defined on prospects, whereas v is defined on outcomes. In the case of sure prospects, the two scales coincide, where

$$V (x, 1.0) = V (x) = v(x).$$

A numerical example would be useful to understand.

Assume a coin is tossed, where the outcome of heads results in gain of \$20 while the outcome of tails results in a loss of \$10. The utility of this regular prospect can be expressed as follows:

$$V (20, .5; -10, .5) = \pi (.5) v (20) + \pi (.5) v (-10)$$

In case of strictly positive and strictly negative prospects, a different rule is followed for evaluation. Such prospects are segregated into two components:

(i) The riskless component , that is the minimum gain or loss which is certain to be obtained or occurred;

(ii) The risky component, that is the additional gain or loss that is actually at stake. The equation given below shows the evaluation of such prospects.

If $p + q = 1$ and either $x > y > 0$, $x < y < 0$, then

$$V(x,p;y,q) = v(y) + \pi(p)\,[v(x) - v(y)] \qquad \text{.....(2)}$$

In words, the value of a strictly positive or a strictly negative prospect equals the value of the riskless component plus the value–difference between the outcomes, multiplied by the weight associated with the more extreme outcome. An illustrative example is given below.

$$V(400, .25; 100, .75) = v(100) + \pi(.25)\,[v(400) - v(100)]$$

As can be seen in eq. (2), a decision weight is applied to the value-difference, v (x)- v(y) (representing the risky component of the prospect) but not to v(y) representing the riskless component.

We may note that in Prospect Theory, outcomes are defined relative to a reference point, which serves as a zero point of the value scale. In equations (1) and (2), v measures the value of the deviations from the reference point-- that is, gains and losses. Kahneman and Tversky state: "This assumption is compatible with basic principles of perception and judgment. Our perceptual apparatus is attuned to the evaluation of changes or differences rather than to the evaluation of absolute magnitudes. When we respond to attributes such as brightness, loudness or temperature, the past and present context of experience defines an adaptation level, or reference point and stimuli are perceived in relation to this reference point."

While the current status of wealth or welfare of an individual is frequently assumed to be the relevant reference point for evaluating gains and losses, it need not necessarily be so. The appropriate reference point may be the expected status rather than the current status. Reference point may be influenced by expectations or by status of others in the society. Reference point may not correspond to the current wealth position, in case the person has not yet adapted to it. An example was given in the 1979 paper. Imagine a person who is involved in a business venture, has already lost 2,000 and is now facing a choice between sure gain of rupees 1,000 and an even chance to win 2000, or nothing. If he has not yet adapted to his losses, he is likely to code the problem as a choice between (–2,000,0.50) and (–1,000) rather than as a choice between (2,000, 0.50) and (1000).

Another key element of the Prospect Theory is loss aversion. In their paper Kahneman and Tversky observe: "A salient characteristic of attitudes to changes in welfare is that losses loom larger than gains. The aggravation that one experiences in losing a sum of money appears to be greater than the pleasure associated with gaining the same amount." In mathematical terms, this phenomenon is expressed as

$$v(x) < -v(-x), \text{ where } x > 0 \qquad \text{.....(3)}$$

This phenomenon of loss aversion can be discussed with consumers' price elasticities observed in the market. Loss averse consumers do not like price increases more than they like the gains from price cuts. They are observed to reduce purchases more when prices rise than their increase in purchases when the prices fall. That is, price elasticities of demand for consumer goods which are observed to be asymmetric, implies loss aversion of consumers. The extent of loss aversion is generally measured in terms of a coefficient of loss–aversion, which is computed by taking the ratio of loss and gain disutilities.

By using the concept of loss aversion, some of the anomalies in finance can be explained; for example, the so-called disposition effect. It is observed that investors tend to hold on too long to shares that have lost value compared to their purchase price, whereas they are anxious to dispose of shares that have risen in price. This phenomenon can be explained on the basis of both loss aversion and reference point, with the purchase price of the share serving as reference point. Similarly, Prospect Theory can explain the phenomenon commonly observed in racetrack betting, namely the end of the day effect. It is noticed that in horse races, bettors tend to shift their bets toward long–shots, and away from favourite horses, later in the racing day. This can be explained by Prospect Theory; both loss aversion and reference point are involved here. Likewise endowment effects are explained by Prospect Theory.

Another important element of the Prospect Theory concerns what is called "value function." In (economics) literature we come across three other utility functions. The shapes of the utility functions may be noted here. The standard economic model employs concave utility function. The shape is a result of the law of diminishing marginal utility of wealth. As the traditional concave function fails to explain observed phenomena, such as gambling, Friedman and Savage in their 1948 paper proposed a utility function, which is concave then convex and concave again. That is, the shape of the function has two concave regions and a convex region between the two. Failure of this function to explain empirical data prompted Markowitz to propose a utility function which is S- shaped in the region of both gain and loss and revere S- shaped in the middle region of small gains and losses. The shape of the function suggested by Markowitz indicates that people tend to be risk- seeking for small gains, explaining most gambling behaviour and risk –averse for small losses, explaining people purchasing insurance. Further, people would be risk- seeking for large losses and risk – averse for large gains.

Kahneman and Tversky in their 1979 paper presented a utility function which features what they call diminishing marginal sensitivity for both gains and losses. The marginal value of both gains and losses generally decreases with their magnitude. What they call the value function for changes of wealth is usually concave above the reference point and convex below it. Mathematically,

$$V''(x) < 0 \text{ for } x > 0, \text{ and}$$

$$V''(x) > 0 \text{ for } x < 0$$

The relationship is depicted in Fig. 54.1.

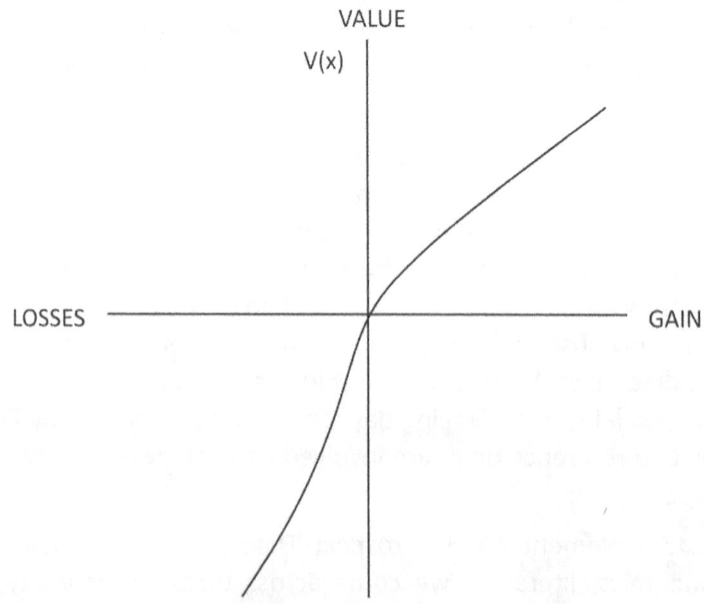

Fig. 54.1 Value Function

For example, when faced with the prospects of (200, 0.5) and (100), people generally choose the latter, sure gain, the reason being that the gain of 200 does not usually have twice as much utility as the gain of 100. That is,

v (200) < 2v (100). In the reverse situation, however, people generally prefer the prospect (– 200; 0.5) to (–100). In this situation, people are willing to gamble, as the loss of 200 does not usually have twice as much disutility as the loss of 100. That is, –v (200) < – 2v (100).

They call this phenomenon, "reflection effect." Reflection effect implies that the preference between negative prospects or losses is the mirror image of the preference between positive prospects or gains. In this connection, they examine the attitudes of a sample of 95 respondents to positive and negative prospects. They present the following results. Between the prospects (4000, .80) and (3000), 80 percent of the sample preferred a sure gain – the second prospect. However, between the prospects (–4000, .80) and (–3000), 92 percent of the sample preferred the first prospect, implying willingness to take a risk of making a greater loss. Markowitz in his 1952 'Utility of Wealth' article also noted this phenomenon.

Another element of Kahneman – Tversky model pertains to "decision weighting." As regards this, Kahneman and Tversky's 1992 "Advances in Prospect Theory: Cumulative Representation of Uncertainty" is a revision of their original 1979 paper and is applicable to situations involving uncertainty as well as to those involving risk. Specifically, the principle of diminishing marginal sensitivity is applied in the 1992 paper to weighting functions as well as to the utility function. They state: "Diminishing sensitivity entails that the impact of a given change in probability diminishes with its distance from the boundary." For example, an increase of 0.1 in the probability of winning a given prize has more impact when it changes the probability of winning from 0.9 to 1.0 or from 0 to 0.1, than when it changes the probability of winning from .3 to .4 or from .6 to .7. Diminishing sensitivity, therefore, gives rise to a weighting function that is concave near 0 and convex near 1. The weighting function for both gains and losses has inverted S-shape.

Nick Wilkinson draws practical implication of the modifications to the weighting function. Instead of having a simple two-fold attitude to risk involving risk aversion for gains and risk–seeking for losses, a more complex four-fold pattern emerges. That is, risk–aversion for gains and risk-seeking for losses of high probability and risk–seeking for gains and risk-aversion for losses of low probability. It is found that the refined model (1992) fits better with empirical observations. A number of studies in a variety of fields provide "general support" for Cumulative Prospect Theory (1992). Particularly, according to Camerer. "Prospect theory can... explain why people buy full insurance...."

The Prospect Theory has been criticised on a number of grounds, such as, lack of normative status, regarding the nature of the utility function, relating to the determination of reference points, regarding endowment effects and the market experience and the nature of framing effects.

54.2.5 FRAMING EFFECTS

The assumption that preferences are not affected by variations of irrelevant features of options or outcomes has been called "extensionality" by Arrow and "invariance by Kahneman and Tversky." Kahneman and Tversky contend that invariance is a key feature of rationality, which is violated in "demonstrations of framing effects such as Asian disease problem." They illustrate it with the following problem (given in Kahneman's Nobel lecture).

Imagine that the United States is preparing for the outbreak of an unusual Asian disease, which is expected to kill 600 people. Two alternative programmes to combat the disease have been proposed. Assume that the exact scientific estimates of the consequences of the programmes are as follows:

If Program A is adopted, 200 people will be saved.

If Program B is adopted, there is a one-third probability that 600 people will be saved and a two-thirds probability that no people will be saved.

Which of the two programs would you favour?

In this version of the problem, a substantial majority of respondents favour program A, indicating risk aversion. Other respondents, selected at random, receive a question in which the same cover story is followed by a different description of the options:

If Program A is adopted, 400 people will die;

If Program B is adopted, there is a one-third probability that nobody will die and a two-thirds probability that 600 people will die

A clear majority of respondents now favours program B, the risk-seeking option.

Kahneman comments: "Although there is no substantive difference between the versions, they evidently evoke different associations and evaluations. This is easiest to see in the certain option, because outcomes that are certain are over-weighted relative to outcomes of high or intermediate probability. Thus, the certainty of saving people is disproportionately attractive, and the certainty of deaths is disproportionately aversive. These immediate affective responses respectively favour A over B and B over A."

After reviewing a few research efforts on the topic, Kahneman observes that the ease with which framing effects can be demonstrated displays a significant limitation of the human mind. Moreover, framing effects are not restricted to decision-making but is also observed in the domain of problem-solving. He raises the important issue of human rationality. In this context, he says that important doubts arise about the "descriptive realism" of models of rational choice because of the issue of invariance. In this context, he states: "Highly accessible features will influence decisions while features of low accessibility will be largely ignored. Unfortunately there is no reason to believe that the most accessible feature is also the most relevant to a good decision."

54.2.6 FAIRNESS JUDGMENTS

The advance information provided by the Royal Swedish Academy refers to Kahneman's contributions to the areas of behavioural economics. It makes particular mention of his joint work with Knetsch and Thaler on the importance of considerations of fairness. This is an issue on which economists have discussed for long-- whether there exists preferences that deviate from pure self interest and economic implications of such behaviour. The work of Kahneman with his associates was of a positive nature, not normative. They have studied, using survey method, what a typical economic agent might assess as a fair or as an unfair behaviour rather than studying normative standards of what policy-makers might reckon, as fair allocation or proper social welfare functions. For example, Kahneman and co-authors put questions to subjects to ascertain their views on fairness of reducing wages of current employees as against employing fresh hands at lower wages. They found that the first one was considered unfair while the second one, that is, talking advantage of market conditions to fix lower wages for fresh hands as fair. It was also found from surveys that economic actors find firms raising prices or lowering wages in response to current shifts in their costs acceptable but not in response to demand shifts or short supply.

Kahneman's joint article with Thaler and others is considered unique in that it tries to draw out people's fairness judgments about real world market scenarios. Reference levels and loss aversion play an important role in judgments of fairness. The authors explain the phenomena of medium-run price and wage stickiness observed in macroeconomic studies as due to delay in adjustments of fairness judgments.

It is relevant to note here that, till very recently, it is generally considered that economists have not to concern themselves with a systematic study of actions deviating from self-interest. The Royal Swedish Academy's note underlines the work of Kahneman and others in this regard. The field has become a lively research field as evidenced by the work carried out by a number of researchers demonstrating that a variety of market behaviours can be gleaned from considerations of fairness and reciprocity. Through this and other work, Kahneman is credited with being a major source of inspiration behind the recent explosion of research in newly developing areas such as behavioural economics and behavioural finance.

54.2.7 REFERENCES AND HEDONICS

In his autobiographical note, Kahneman states that the focus of his research for the past fifteen years has been the study of various dimensions of what he calls "experienced utility" – the measure of the utility of outcomes as people actually live them. He argues: "... it may be rash to assume as a general rule that people will later enjoy what they want now. The relation between preferences and hedonic consequences is better studied than postulated. These considerations suggest an explicit distinction between two notions of utility. The experienced utility of an outcome is the measure of the hedonic experience of that outcome.... The decision utility of an outcome, as in modern usage, is the weight assigned to that outcome in a decision." (Emphases in the original). Kahneman states that the concept of experienced utility is the one that he is interested and that it is the one that Bentham and Edgeworth had in mind. This has largely disappeared from economic discourse in the last century in favour of a notion that he calls decision utility, which is inferred from choices and is used to explain choices. According to him, the distinction could be of no great relevance for fully rational agents, who "presumably" maximise experienced utility as well as decision utility. He contends that if rationality cannot be assumed, the quality of consequences becomes worth measuring and the maximisation of experienced utility becomes a testable proposition. More significantly, he claims that in the experiments carried out by him and his colleagues, this proposition was "falsified." These experiments employed a simple rule that administered the assignment of remembered utility to past episodes in which an agent is passively exposed to a pleasant or unpleasant experience. He states that, recollected or remembered utility happens to be determined essentially by the "peak" intensity of the pleasure or discomfort experienced during the event and by the intensity of pleasure or discomfort at the end of the event – what is referred to as the "Peak and End Rule". Kahneman provides a useful summary of his findings on how retrospective evaluation of episodes compares to their "experienced well–being." In his words;

"The results... support two empirical generalizations.

1. **The Peak and End rule:** Global evaluations are predicted with high accuracy by a weighted combination of the most extreme effect recorded during the episode and of the effect recorded during the terminal moments of the episode. Here again, as in the context of decision utility, the evaluations of particular moments appear to be used as a proxy for the evaluations of a more extended period of time.
2. **Duration Neglect:** The retrospective evaluation of overall or total pain or (pleasure)

> is not independently affected by the duration of the episode. In the colonoscopy study, for example, the duration of the procedure varied from 4 to 69 minutes in a sample of 101 patients. Surprisingly, these variations of duration had no significant effect on retrospective evaluations. The ratings of both patients and attending physicians were dominated by the intensity of pain at its worst, and by the intensity of discomfort during the last few minutes of the procedure. Duration neglect is not immutable.... In general, however, effective peaks and endings are more salient than duration in the cognitive representation of events."

The evidence of Kahneman and his co-workers contradicts,the standard rational model that does not distinguish between experienced utility and decision utility. Kahneman thus presents it as a new type of challenge to the assumption of rationality. Matthew Robin in his evaluation of Kahneman's contribution notes: "Recognizing the possibility that there are potential flaws in how people go about managing their flows of utility, Kahneman and others have launched research that may help to move economics towards a more realistic approach to welfare analysis. It will let us continue applying revealed preference theory in the many domains where doing so gets things right, but also allows engaging in careful and systematic scientific inquiry into when and how there is a separation between people's choices and what brings them satisfaction.... Kahneman is a leader in the exciting new focus in social sciences on the direct empirical study of what makes people happy."

54.3 CONCLUDING OBSERVATIONS

The importance of Vernon Smith's and Daniel Kahneman's enormous contributions has gained recognition – may be rather slowly– and the award (Nobel Memorial Prize) is an appropriate recognition of that. A current wave of research draws on the combined tradition of psychology and experimental economics which is potentially important for all areas of economics and finance. The Royal Swedish Academy concedes that the combined contributions of Kahneman and Smith--though their research agenda differs in many respects--have already changed the direction of economic science. Further, it is their achievement that many, nay most, economists today consider psychological insights and experimental methods as essential ingredients in modern economics. A challenging task in financial economics is to evaluate the extent to which the effects of systematic non-rationality on asset prices will be weeded out by market arbitrage.

54.4 SELECT BIBLIOGRAPHY OF DANIEL KAHNEMAN'S WORKS

54.4.1 BOOKS

1973 Attention and Effects, Prentice-Hall, Englewood-Cliffs, NJ.

1982 (with P. Slovic, and A. Tversky, (eds.), Judgment under Uncertainty: Heuristics and Biases, Cambridge University Press, New York.

1999 (with Diener, and N. Schwarz, (eds.)), Well-being: The Foundations of Hedonic Psychology, Russell Sage Foundation, New York.

2000 (with A. Tversky (eds.), Choices, Values and Frames, Russell Sage Foundation and Cambridge University Press, New York.

2002 (with T. Gilovich and D. Griffin eds.), Heuristics and Biases: The Psychology of Intuitive Judgment, Cambridge University Press, New York.

54.4.2 ARTICLES

1971 (with A. Tversky), "Belief in the Law of Small Numbers," Psychological Bulletin, Vol.76, No.2.

1974 (with A. Tversky), "Judgment under Uncertainty: Heuristics and Biases," Science, Vol.185, Sep.

1979 (with A. Tversky), "Prospect Theory: An Analysis of Decisions under Risk," Econometrica, Vol. 47, No.2.

1981 (with A. Tversky), "The Framing of Decisions and the Psychology of Choice," Science, Vol. 211, Jan.

1984 (with A. Tversky), "Choices, Values and Frames," American Psychologist, Vol.39, No.4.

1986 a (with J. L. Knetsch and R.H Thaler), "Fairness as a Constraint on Profit Seeking: Entitlements in the Market," AER, Vol. 76, No.4.

b (with J. L. Knetsch and R.H Thaler), "Fairness and the Assumptions of Economics," JB, Vol.59, No.4.

c (with A. Tversky), "Rational Choice and the Framing of Decisions," JB, Vol.59, No.4.

1990 a (with J. L. Knetsch and R.H Thaler), "Experimental Tests of the Endowment Effect and the Coase Theorem," JPE, Vol.98, No.6.

b (with A. Tversky and P. Slovic), "The Causes of Preference Reversal," AER, Vol.80, No.1.

1991 a (with R. H. Thaler), "Economic Analysis and the Psychology of Utility: Applications to Compensation Policy," AER, Vol.81, No.2.

b (with J. L. Knetsch and R. H. Thaler), "Anomalies: The Endowment Effect, Loss Aversion, and Status Quo Bias," JEP, Vol.5, No.1.

c (with A. Tversky), "Loss Aversion in Riskless Choice: A Reference-Dependent Model," QJE, Vol.106, No. 4.

1992 a "Reference Points, Anchors, Norms, and Mixed Feelings," Organizational Behavior and Human Decision Processes, Vol. 51, No.2.

b "Advances in Prospect Theory: Cumulative Representation of Uncertainty," Journal of Risk and Uncertainty, Vol. 5, No.4.

c (with J. L. Knetsch), "Valuing Public Goods: The Purchase of Moral Satisfaction," Journal of Environmental Economics and Management, Vol. 22, No.1.

1994 a "New Challenges to the Rationality Assumption," JITE, Vol. 150, No. 1.

b (with I. Ritov), "Determinants of Stated Willingness to Pay for Public Goods: A Study in the Hedonistic Method," Journal of Risk and Uncertainty, Vol.9, No. 1.

1997 (with P. P. Walker and R. Sarin), "Back to Bentham? Explorations of Experienced Utility," QJE, Vo.112, No.2.

1998 (with D. A. Sachkade and C. R. Sunstein), "Shared Outrage and Erratic Awards: The Psychology of Punitive Damages," Journal of Risk and Uncertainty, Vol.16, No.1.

1999 (with I. Ritov and D. Sachkade), "Economic Preferences or Attitude Expressions? An Analysis of Dollar Responses to Public Issues," Journal of Risk and Uncertainty, Vol.19, No.1-2.

2001 (with Kunreuther and N. Novemsky), "Making Low Probabilities Useful," Journal of Risk and Uncertainty, Vol. 23, No.2.

2003 a "A Psychological Perspective on Economics," AER, Vol. 93. No.1.

b "Maps of Bounded Rationality: Psychology for Behavioural Economics," Nobel Lecture, AER, Vol. 93, No.5.

2004 (with A. B. Krueger et al.), "Towards National Well-being Accounts," AER, Vol. 94, No.2.

2005 a (with R. Sugden), "Experienced Utility as a Standard of Policy Evaluation," Environmental and Resource Economics, Vol.32, No.1.

b (with F. Bateman et al.), "Testing Competing Models of Loss Aversion: An Adversarial Collaboration," JPubE, Vol.89, No.8.

c (with S. Frederick,), "A Model of Heuristic Judgment," in The Cambridge Handbook of Thinking and Reasoning, (K. J. Holyoak and R. G. Morrison (eds.)), Cambridge University Press, New York.

d (with N. Novemsky), "The Boundaries of Loss Aversion," Journal of Marketing Research, Vol.42, No.2.

2006 a (with R. H. Thaler), "Anomalies: Utility Maximization and Experienced Utility," JEP, Vol.20, No.1.

b (with A. B. Krueger), "Developments in the Measurement of Subjective Well-being," JEP, Vol.20, No. 1.

2008 (with P. Dolan), "Interpretations of Utility and their Implications for the Valuation of Health," EJ, Vol. 118, No. 525.

2009 "The Myth of Risk Attitudes," Journal of Portfolio Management, Vol.36, No.1.

2010 (with S. Frederick and D. Machon), "Elaborating a Simple Theory of Anchoring," Journal of Consumer Psychology, Vol. 20, No.1.

54.5 WORKS OF OTHERS

Bernstein, P. L. (1990), Against the Gods: The Remarkable Story of Risk, John Wiley, New York.

Bernstein, P. L. (2007), Capital Ideas Evolving, John Wiley and Sons, Hoboken, NJ.

Robin, M. (2003), "The Nobel Memorial Prize For Daniel Kahneman," ScandJE, Vol. 105, No.2.

Simon, H. A. (1987), "Behavioural Economics," The New Palgrave: A Dictionary of Economics, MacMillan, London.

CHAPTER 55

OLIVER EATON WILLIAMSON

(1932 –)

Oliver Eaton Williamson shared the Nobel Memorial prize in Economic Sciences for 2009 with Elinor Ostrom, "for his analysis of economic governance, especially the boundaries of the firm." Economic governance is defined by Avinash Dixit as "the structure and functioning of the legal and social institutions that support economic activity, and support economic transactions by protecting rights, enforcing contracts, taking collective action to provide physical and organizational infrastructure.... Good economic governance thus underpins the whole Smithian process whereby individuals specialize in different tasks and then transact with one another to achieve the full economic potential of the society."

According to Williamson markets and hierarchical organisations, such as firms, represent alternative governance structures. Each of them helps in resolving conflicts of interest. However, each of these has strengths as well as drawbacks. The main drawback of markets is that they involve haggling and disagreement. Haggling costs can be substantial. Moreover, there is no guarantee that the final agreement will be either efficient or immediate. The hierarchical organisations, such as firms, facilitate cheaper resolution of conflicts. A chief executive of a firm is empowered to decide, in case two employees quarrel about the allocation of tasks or the distribution of revenues. The primary drawback of firms is that authority which reduces conflict or contention can be abused. The perceived advantage of competitive markets is that they function well because both buyers and sellers can search for other trading partners in case of disagreement. However, when market competition is limited, firms perform better in the sense they are better suited for conflict resolution than markets. On the basis of his early work, Williamson predicted which received empirical support that economic agents prefer to conduct their transactions inside the boundaries of a firm when it is cheaper to do so or when their assets possess features that are relationship specific.

The press release of the Royal Swedish Academy notes that this argument may give an impression that all transactions have necessarily to take place in "a single giant firm." This does not represent reality or real life situation. Outsourcing is a good example of the opposite. As is clear, outsourcing creates a market transaction supplanting an internal transaction. There is a general impression that hierarchical organisation is costly as it involves administrative costs. Williamson has not subscribed to this view as the boundaries of a firm can be moved without any change in administrative routines. Instead, in Williamson's view the most important problem with hierarchical organisations is the possibility of the abuse of executive authority- for example, extraction of "surplus from subordinates in unproductive ways."

Williamson tried to find an answer to the issue of the importance of conflict resolution. According to him, the value of conflict resolution depends mainly on two factors. First, if disagreement is costless, there is no need to resolve conflicts. The firm is not necessary, if both buyer and seller can without difficulty find some other suitable trading partner. There is no question of resolving conflicts that do not arise. Future transactions can be regulated easily and cheaply through contracts; in such a case, there is almost no need for a firm. Therefore, according to Williamson, the emergence of hierarchical organisations is contingent upon the complexity of transactions and on mutual dependence of parties. A very relevant example of mutual dependence is that parties have assets, either physical assets or knowledge, which are only valuable inside a relationship.

The benefits of vertical integration which is the result of incompleteness of contracting were emphasised by initial contributions of Williamson. Later, his research work has related to "Transactions Cost Economics," of which he is considered the founder and chief developer.

55.1 A SHORT BIOGRAPHICAL SKETCH: OLIVER WILLIAMSON

Oliver Williamson was born in Superior in Wisconsin State on September 27, 1932. He was the second child of his parents both of whom were high school teachers. His father who later joined in the family real estate business was a successful small businessman and served as president of the local City Council. Williamson attended public school in Superior and he remarks that it was a very egalitarian experience. He candidly states in his autobiographical essay. "I was a good student, a mediocre athlete, and had many good high school friends.... Many of them remain close friends to this day."

His initial thoughts of becoming a lawyer changed in high school since he became more attracted to mathematics and science. He entertained ideas of becoming an engineer. He enrolled in Ripon College, which had a "combined plan" with MIT. He remarks: "That 'combination worked out well'." His first job after graduation was as a project engineer for G.E. and later with the U.S. government in Washington, D.C. In 1958, he applied to and was accepted into the Ph.D. program at the Graduate School of Business at Stanford University. According to Williamson, his engineering training in mathematics and statistics and model building was very useful. More importantly, his engineering training gave him a "much more grounded foundation than would most undergraduate programs in any of the social sciences."

In his autobiographical note, Williamson draws a distinction between engineering and economics. He particularly states that in economics assumptions of "functionlessness (of which the standard assumption of zero transaction costs was one)... were involved asymmetrically." While markets are subject to failures, corrective public policy measures were prescribed; however, there was no corresponding provision for failures in the public sector. He asserts that a more symmetrical approach would be to recognise the existence of positive transaction costs and to accept the fact that all forms of organisation experience such costs in varying degree. He observes: "I credit my engineering background with giving me a receptive attitude towards transaction costs, to include an interest in pinning down and working out the organisational ramifications of such costs."

Williamson moved from business into economics as a result of advice of his teachers including information supplied about the interdisciplinary programme in economics and organisation theory at Carnegie University. His decision was also helped by the award of a portable three-year fellowship by the Ford Foundation. In Carnegie, Williamson found his "niche": "the combination of economics and organization theory as taught by the small but remarkable faculty... to classes with a small but remarkable group of students. Seven Nobel Prizes in Economics have since been awarded to faculty and students at GSIA [Graduate School of Industrial Administration] in its halcyon years." He approvingly quotes Jacques Dreze's observation: "Never since have had I experienced such intellectual excitement." Williamson's Ph.D. dissertation on "The Economics of Discretionary Behavior: Managerial Objectives in a Theory of the Firm" was completed in 1963 and, as a winner in the Ford Foundation dissertation competition, was published by Prentice-Hall in 1964. In 1963 (Fall) he joined the faculty of the Economics Department at the University of California at Berkeley. He was hired into the industrial organisation field. The field of industrial organization, especially its public policy applications to antitrust and regulation, had fallen on hard times in the 1960s.

According to Williamson, this situation was related to three misconceptions. First, there was overreliance on the neoclassical theory of the firm according to which the firm including the modern corporation, is a "black box" for transforming inputs into outputs according to the laws of technology. Second, the firm's internal organisation which was inconsequential could be ignored. Third misconception relates to the assumption of zero transaction costs. In the industrial organization and public policy courses at Berkeley and at University of Pennsylvania, Williamson introduced two propositions; that (1) organisation is often important; and (2) economics and organisation theory need to be joined if we have to develop a deeper understanding of complex contracts and internal organisation. His experience as Special Economic Assistant to the Head of the Antitrust Division of the U.S. Department of Justice was very helpful; what he describes as "the defining event." The then prevailing opinion was economies could be only of a technological kind. Economies from organisational and contractual design were ruled out. Vertical integration and vertical market restrictions were regarded as "especially problematic." He, therefore, resolved to re-examine the antitrust ramifications of vertical integration when he resumed teaching and research at the University of Pennsylvania.

Stating that teaching can be learning, “especially if student curiosity with the question, ‘What’s going on here?’ can be elicited.” Williamson observes: “This was a recurrent question in the graduate seminar that I organized to examine the literature on vertical integration and vertical market restraints.” He reformulated vertical integration from the perspective of combining economics and organisation theory providing positive transaction costs. This resulted in preparing a paper and publishing it in 1971. In his later research work, Williamson developed the theory further providing momentum to transaction cost economics resulting in a number of publications in the field.

In his Prize lecture, Williamson states: My appointment with economics department at the University of Pennsylvania was expanded to include appointments to the faculty of Law School and School of Public and Urban Policy in the late 1960s. It turned out to be a productive mixture with many good colleagues and students in all three places. He was Charles and William L. Day Professor of Economics and Social Science during 1977-1983. In 1983, he was appointed at Yale University as joint professor in (1) School of Organization and Management, (2) the Law School, and (3) the Economics Department. He served as founding editor of the Journal of Law, Economics, and Organization. He was Golden B. Tweedy Professor of Economics, Law and Organization at Yale University. Because of considerable complexities involved in Yale appointment, Williamson left Yale and returned to the University of California, Berkeley in 1988 where he has been since. At Berkley, he was professor of the Graduate School (Economics and Law) between 1988 and 2004. Simultaneously, he was professor at Haas School of Business for a decade (1988-1998) and from 1998 till 2004 (where he retired from teaching in 2004 but continues to remain active in research). He was Edgar F Kaiser professor of Business Economics at the same School of Business of the University of California, Berkeley. Since 2004, Williamson has been Edgar F. Kaiser Professor Emeritus of Economics and Law at Berkeley.

Williamson has received numerous fellowships, awards and honours. Among them, the following may be mentioned: Guggenheim Fellowship (1977-78), Fellow, Center for Advanced Study in the Behavioral Sciences (1977- 1978), Fellow, American Academy of Political and Social Science (1997) and Member, National Academy of Sciences (1994). He is Distinguished Fellow, American Economic Association (2007), and Distinguished Fellow, Industrial Organization Society (2005). Williamson has received numerous visiting academic appointments. He was Vice-President of American Economic Association in 2001. He was awarded Honorary Doctorate by Nice University, University of Chile, St. Petersburg University, Russia and Norwegian School of Economics and Business Administration. Williamson received John von Neumann Award, Budapest University and Alexander Henderson Award for Excellence in Economic Theory, Carnegie-Mellon University. He was founding Honorary Editor, Journal of Law, Economics and Organization and Honorary Editor, Journal of Economic Behavior and Organization. He was President, American Law and Economics Association, 1997-1998, President, Western Economic

Association, 1999-2000 and President, International Society for New Institutional Economics, 1979-2002. He worked for some time as Consultant to the RAND Corporation, U.S Department of Justice and Federal Trade Commission.

55.2 A SUMMARY OF WILLIAMSON'S RESEARCH WORK ON ECONOMIC GOVERNANCE

In his Prize lecture, Williamson observes that the work for which he was awarded the prize is referred to as the "economics of governance," "the economics of organization," and "transaction cost economics." Further, through transaction cost economics, he breathed life into the overreaching concept of governance and into the operational content of an organisation. According to him, the inspiration for his work came from Ronald Coase's 1937 article in Economica in which he raised an important issue; what efficiency factors determine when a firm produces a good or service to its own needs rather than outsource? In Coase's words: "Why does the entrepreneur not organise one less transaction or one more?" or as Williamson questions in his concluding part of the lecture: what explains the boundaries of a firm? Williamson reformulates it as a contracting problem and explores the issue: When and why should a firm acquire a technologically separate component by outsourcing instead of producing it to its own needs, that is, contracting out rather than contracting within. He has explored this as a question of efficiency by "selectively combining economics with organization theory."

In the course of his research effort, Williamson has examined economic organisation "through the lens of contract," discarding the "neoclassical lens of choice." Thus, his research turned out to be inter-disciplinary in nature combining the disciplines of economics, organisation theory, law and transactions, the last one neglected in economic analysis. His research necessitated a re-examination of neoclassical economic theory and a re-look into the leading institutional economists in the first half of the last century, John R. Commons's formulation of the problem of economic organisation. Commons formulated the problem as quoted by Williamson: "The ultimate unit of activity... must contain in itself the three principles of conflict, mutuality, and order. This unit is a transaction." Institutional economics makes transaction as the basic unit of analysis. Commons recommended (again as quoted by Williamson) that "theories of economics center on transactions and working rules, as problems of organization, and on the... [ways] the organization of activity is stabilized."

Williamson observes that compared to the approach of Commons to the subject, neoclassical paradigm of resource allocation differs in two crucial aspects. The latter neglected both the organisation and the continuity of contractual relations; instead, its focus was on prices, output, supply and demand. Furthermore, as the price-theoretic approach to economics prevailed during the 20th century, institutional economics was consigned to the history of economic thought. According to Williamson, institutional economics "ran itself into the sand."

James Buchanan, drawing a distinction between lens of choice and lens of contract approaches to economic organisation, contended that economics as a discipline went on a wrong track by concentrating on the science of choice and the associated optimisation technique. He further argued that if mutuality of advantage from voluntary exchange is crucial of all understandings in economics, then the lens of contract approach is an "under-used perspective." Robert Gibbons in his 2011 article, discussing Williamson's contributions, remarks: "The 2009 Noble Memorial Prize was special moment for the study of economic governance (and there have been others such as earlier prizes to Buchanan, Coase, and North) because the institutions of economic governance explicitly affect or implicitly underlie huge parts of both economic activity and economics literature. We need institutions not only to support simple exchanges in markets, but also to conduct both non-market transactions (in firms, communities, governments, and elsewhere) and complex transactions in markets (via contracts and other governance structures that are not simple exchanges). When considering settings beyond simple exchanges, including those analysed by Ostram and Williamson, one sees why Buchanan...argued that economics comes closer to being a 'science of contract' than a 'science of choice'."

Williamson dissenting from the view of the neoclassical theory that the firm transforms inputs into outputs according to the laws of technology, approvingly quotes Harold Demsetz who expressed the view that the then extant theory did not study the inner workings of a real firm. Demsetz, however, does not suggest joining of economics and organisation theory in order to understand firm and market organisation. Williamson decided to take up the issue for research. It was, as mentioned earlier, Ronald Coase who was the first to bring the concept of transaction costs to bear on the study of firm and market organization and emphasised the need to explain the basis on which, in practice, a decision is made in regard to choosing between firm and market as a method of coordinating production. According to Williamson, the missing concept is transaction cost. He states that internal organisation is substituted for market exchange because of "transactional failures" in the operation of markets for intermediate goods. Arrow also in his 1969 article has emphasised the need to consider positive transaction costs in regard to market failures and in conjunction with intermediate product market contracting. Arrow further observes: "the existence of vertical integration may suggest that the costs of operating competitive markets are not zero, as is usually assumed in our theoretical analysis."

From a study of vertical integration of production, Williamson has concluded that efficient intermediate product market exchange is usually well served by simple market contracting, provided the assets are generic. However, it is advantageous to operate in a firm because of asset specificity giving rise to bilateral dependency and the resulting risk of costly maladaptations. He has realised that vertical integration paradigm would be appropriate for studying complex contract and economic organisation. Williamson states: "The combination of incomplete contracts, bilateral dependency (contingent on asset specificity) and defection from the norm of coordinated adaptation when a contract experiences significant disturbances (for which the stakes are great) had application to a wide range of phenomena...."

For developing a comprehensive theory, Williamson developed three "clusters:" (i) Key conceptual moves, (ii) key operational moves, and (iii) applications. Further, there is a need to examine economic organisation at a more micro analytic level of analysis. At a conceptual level, attributes of human actions, adaptation and contract laws have to be elaborated. Following Herbert Simon, Williamson also accepts human behaviour that is "intently rational, but only limitedly so;" in other words, "bounded rationality." Williamson asserts: "Human actors are neither hyper rational nor irrational but are attempting effectively to cope with complex contracts that are incomplete." He puts forward the idea that routines describe the behaviour of most individuals most of the time; opportunism is the operative condition at other times.

The main purpose of economic organisation has been differently viewed by Chester Bernard and Friedrich Hayek: empirical testing. While the former refers to "coordinated adaptation," Hayek refers to the "marvel of the market" where autonomous adaptations are implemented simultaneously in response to changes in relative prices. Economics of governance has to recognise that both kinds of adaptations are important and to make selective provisions for each. According to Williamson, Transaction Cost Economics (TEC) recognises that the two are alternative models of governance. Each of the two has a distinctive role to play in a well-functioning economy.

The third basic move for the development of the theory, as indicated above, is to introduce contract laws. Contrary to the standard practice of one all-purpose law of contract, it is envisaged that "the major importance of legal contract is to provide... a framework which almost never accurately indicates real working relations, but which affords a rough indication of around which such relations vary, an occasional guide in case of doubt, and a norm of ultimate appeal when the relations cease in fact to work." Williamson sums up: "... adaptations (of autonomous and coordinated kinds), are taken to be the central purpose of organization: and viable modes of governance differ in contract law respects."

After outlining the above summarised conceptual moves, Williamson specifies three key operational moves for studying organisations. They are (i) to name the attributes of the unit of analysis, (ii) to name the attributes for modes of governance, and (iii) to advance the efficient alignment hypothesis. Williamson recommends the transaction as the unit of analysis in the transaction cost economics set up, in line with the suggestion of Commons and Coase. For the purpose of economising transaction costs, the key dimensions of transactions are (a) complexity, (b) the condition of asset specificity, and (c) disturbances to which a transaction is subject. Of the three, the last two are the most important for understanding the governance of contractual relations.

Williamson, in his Prize lecture, underlines the wide reach of asset specificity. He observes that different types of hazards accrue to different forms of asset specificity.

These variations have important organisational ramifications. Specifically, those assets cannot be redeployed to alternative uses and users without sacrificing their productive value. In this connection, one has also to reckon with inter-temporal considerations.

As regards modes of governance, Coase in his 1937 paper has referred to two polar opposites of governance-- markets and hierarchies. Williamson introduced transaction cost economics and the hybrid mode to interpret a wide range of commercial and some non-commercial phenomena.

In order to predict which transactions go where, transaction cost economics follows the efficient alignment hypothesis. Transactions which are generic in the sense that they do not involve asset specificity and the adaptive needs can be gathered and implemented automatically will be procured in the market. On the other hand, transactions that are supported by substantial investments in transaction-specific assets and are subject to incompleteness are implemented by hierarchy. This is because such transactions benefit from unified ownership and coordinated adaptations.

Economic theories would be considered more useful when the predictions made by the theory are supported by empirical verification. Further, they gain significance when variations in the original theme are worked out and when "public policy ramifications accrue and are displayed." Transaction cost economics makes predictions and those are subjected to empirical testing.

Williamson, in his Prize lecture, states that empirical testing of transaction cost economics in one year, 2006, number over 800 and they have been broadly supportive; as such, it has been quite influential. Besides in the field of industrial organization, transaction cost economics has found application in many fields of economics such as, public finance, labour, economic development among others. Likewise, there have been applications in business; for instance, management and accounting. There are applications also in other social sciences, such as sociology and political science. Williamson observes that while there have been a number of applications of transaction cost economics in public policy relating to business, such as anti-trust regulation and corporate governance, it is, "in my judgment, an under-used public policy perspective."

In his 2008 paper, "Transaction Cost Economics: The Precursors," Williamson states that theories generally progress through four stages from informal to pre-formal to semi-formal and fully formal. In the period 1920-1970, the first stage of natural progression, especially during the decade of 1930's, economists, organisation theorists and legal scholars dissented from the "overuse of resources allocation paradigm" according to which firms were supposed to be "production functions whereby inputs were transformed into outputs according to laws of technology." Further, markets functioned as simple market exchanges where "faceless buyers and sellers meet for an instant to exchange standardized goods at equilibrium prices." The focus of attention was prices and output, supply and demand. Organisation theory was "relegated" to sociologists and organisation theorists. Williamson states that it takes a theory to beat a theory. New theories of the firm and market organisation were developed of which Transaction Cost Economics was one. In the words of Williamson "contrary to standard assumption in economic theory circa 1970 that the transaction costs were zero, Transaction Costs Economics makes express provision for positive transaction costs." Furthermore, instead of viewing the assumption in applied microeconomics that "non-standard and unfamiliar contractual practices and organizational structure" are meant to gain monopoly power, it is assumed specifically that they are for the purpose of promoting organisational efficiency. He points out: "Economizing on transaction costs becomes the basic engine of analysis. A huge number of economic phenomena are reinterpreted in the process." The crucial issue is the implementation of the new thinking in the proliferation of types of transaction costs.

Williamson, in the above cited paper, outlines the three conceptual moves in that direction. They are (i) use of the lens of contract/ governance, (ii) express provision for economising transaction costs as these relate to adaptation, and (iii) selective appeal to contiguous social sciences.

55.3 CONCLUDING OBSERVATIONS

Robert Gibbons states: "Williamson's contributions to TCE [Transaction Cost Economics] are a counter example to Krugman's...dictum (originally composed for economic geography but equally applicable across most of economics): 'Like it or not... the influence of ideas that have not been embalmed in models soon decays'.... We economists are so used to seeing our theory in formal models.... There are three familiar benefits of formal modeling." The internal consistency of informal arguments can be verified through formal models. Further, formal models can be useful for specifying and interpreting empirical results of informal arguments. Sometimes, formal models give results that cannot be anticipated without the help of a model. More importantly, we can understand what the theoretical flaw is when fresh evidence shows the original theory is defective. Gibbons concludes: "... for all of the [above reasons]... it could be very helpful to have a formal theory that captures Williamson's TCE arguments."

55.4 SELECT BIBLIOGRAPHY OF WILLIAMSON'S WORKS

55.4.1 BOOKS

1964 The Economics of Discretionary Behavior: Managerial Objectives in a Theory of the Firm, Prentice-Hall, Englewood Cliffs, NJ. (Reprinted 1971).

1970 Corporate Control and Business Behavior: An Inquiry into the Effects of Organization Form on Enterprise Behavior, Prentice-Hall, Englewood Cliffs, NJ.

1975 Markets and Hierarchies: Analysis and Antitrust Implications, Free Press, New York.

1985 The Economic Institutions of Capitalism: Firms, Markets, Relational Contracting, Free Press, New York.

1990 a (Editor and contributor), Organization Theory: From Chester Barnard to the Present and Beyond, Oxford University Press, New York.

b (Editor and contributor), Industrial Organization, Edward Elgar, London.

1991 (Co-editor and contributor), Transaction Cost Economics, Vols.I and II, Edward Elgar, Brookfield, Vt.

1993 (Co-editor with S.G Winter and contributor), The Nature of the Firm: Origins, Evolution and Development, Oxford University Press, New York.

1996 The Mechanisms of Governance, Oxford University Press, New York.

55.4.2 ARTICLES

1963 a "Selling Expenses as a Barrier to Entry," QJE, Vol.77, No.1.

b "Managerial Discretion and Business Behavior," AER, Vol.53, No.5.

1965 a "Innovation and Market Structure," JPE, Vol.73, No.1.

b "A Dynamic Theory of Inter-firm Behavior," QJE, Vol.79, No.4.

1967 "Hierarchical Control and Optimum Firm Size," JPE, Vol.75, pp.123-138.

1968 "Economies as an Antitrust Defense: The Welfare Trade-Offs," AER, Vol.58, No.1.

1969 "Allocative Efficiency and the Limits of Antitrust," AER, Vol.59, No.2.

1971 "The Vertical Integration of Production: Market Failure Considerations," AER, Vol.61, No. 2.

1973 "Markets and Hierarchies: Some Elementary Considerations," AER, Vol.63, No.5.

1976 "Franchise Bidding for Natural Monopolies-in General and with Respect to CATV," BellJE, Vol.7, No.1.

1979 "Transaction Cost Economics: The Governance of Contractual Relations," JLawE, Vol. 22, No.2.

1981 a "The Economics of Organization: The Transaction Cost Approach," American Journal of Sociology, Vol. 87, No.3.

b "The Modern Corporation: Origins, Evolution, Attributes," JEL, Vol.19, No.4.

1983		"Credible Commitments: Using Hostages to Support Exchange," AER, Vol.73, No. 4.
1984		"Corporate Governance," Yale Law Journal, Vol. 93, June.
1987	a	"Vertical Integration," in The New Palgrave: A Dictionary of Economics, Macmillan, London.
	b	""Antitrust," in The New Palgrave: A Dictionary of Economics, Macmillan, London.
1988	a	"Corporate Finance and Corporate Governance," JF, Vol. 43, No.3.
	b	"Opportunistic Behavior in Contracts," in The New Palgrave Dictionary of Economics and the Law, Macmillan, London.
	c	"The Logic of Economic Organization," Journal of Law, Economics, and Organization, Vol.4, No.1.
1991		"Comparative Economic Organization: The Analysis of Discrete Alternatives," Administrative Science Quarterly, Vol.36, No.2.
1992		"Markets, Hierarchies, and the Modern Corporation: An Unfolding Perspective," JEBO, Vol.17, No.3.
1993	a	"Contested Exchange Versus the Governance of Contractual Relations," JEP, Vol.7, No.1.
	b	"The Evolving Science of Organization," JITE, Vol.49, Mar.
1994	a	"Visible and Invisible Governance," AER, Vol.84, No.2.
	b	"Evaluating Coase," JEP, Vol.8, No.2.
1995		"Hierarchies, Markets, and Power in the Economy: An Economic Perspective," Industrial and Corporate Change, Vol.4, No.1.
1996		"Transaction Cost Economics and the Carnegie Connection," JEBO, Vol. 31, No.2.
1998	a	"The Institutions of Governance," AER, Vol.88, No.2.
	b	"Opportunistic Behavior in Contracts," in The New Palgrave Dictionary of Economics and the Law, Macmillan, London.
1999		"Public and Private Bureaucracies: A Transaction Cost Economics Perspective," Journal of Law, Economics, and Organization, Vol.15, No.1.
2000	a	"The New Institutional Economics: Taking Stock, Looking Ahead," JEL, Vol.38, No.3.

	b	"Ronald Harry Coase: Institutional Economist/Institution Builder," in Institutions, Contracts, and Organizations, Claude Menard, (ed.), Edward Elgar, London.
2001	a	"Transaction Cost Economics and Property Rights," Encyclopaedia of the Social and Behavioral Sciences, Elsevier Science Ltd., Oxford.
	b	"Hierarchies and Markets," Encyclopaedia of the Social and Behavioral Sciences, Elsevier Science Ltd., Oxford.
2002	a	"The Lens of Contract: Private Ordering," AER, Vol.92, No.2.
	b	"The Theory of the Firm as Governance Structure: From Choice to Contract," JEP, Vol.16, No.3.
2003		"Examining Economic Organization through the Lens of Contract," Industrial and Corporate Change, Vol.12, No.4.
2005	a	"The Economics of Governance," AER, Vol. 95, No.2.
	b	"Transaction Cost Economics and Business Administration," Scandinavian Journal of Management, Vol.21 , No.1.
2008	a	"Transaction Cost Economics: The Precursors," Economic Affairs, Vol.28, No.3.
	b	"Corporate Boards of Directors: In Principle and in Practice," Journal of Law, Economics, and Organization, Vol.24, No.2.
2009	a	"Pragmatic Methodology: A Sketch with Applications to Transaction Cost Economics," The Journal of Economic Methodology, Vol.16, No.2.
	b	"Opening the Black Box of Firm and Market Organization: Antitrust," in The Modern Firm, Corporate Governance and Investment, Per-Olaf Bjuggren and D. C. Mueller, (eds.), Edward Elgar, Northampton, MA.
2010		"Transaction Cost Economics," "The Natural Progression," Nobel Prize Lecture, AER, Vol.100, No.3.

55.5 WORKS OF OTHERS

Arrow, K. J. (1969), "The Organization of Economic Activity: Issues Pertinent to the Choice of Market Versus Non-Market Allocation" in The Analysis and Evaluation of Public Expenditure: The PPB System, Vol.1, Joint Economic Committee, 91st Congress, U.S. Government Printing Office, Washington, D.C.

Buchanan, J. (1975), "A Contractarian Paradigm for Applying Economic Theory," AER, Vol.65, No.2.

Coase, R. H. (1937), "The Nature of the Firm," Economica, N.S, Vol.4, No.16.

Coase, R. H. (1960), "The Problem of Social Cost," JLawE, Vol.3, No.1.

Coase, R. H. (1992), "The Institutional Structure of Production," AER, Vol.82, No.4.

Demsetz, H. (1983), "The Structure of Ownership and the Theory of the Firm," JLawE, Vol. 26, No.2.

Dixit, A. (1996), The Making of Economic Policy: A Transaction Cost Politics Perspective," MIT Press, Cambridge, MA.

Gibbons, R. (2010), "Transaction Cost Economics: Past, Present, and Future?" ScandJE, Vol. 112, No.2.

Jensen, M. and W. Meckling (1976), "The Theory of the Firm: Managerial Behavior, Agency, Costs, and Ownership Structure," JFE, Vol.3, No.4.

Knight, F. H. (1921), Risk, Uncertainty and Profit, Houghton Mifflin, New York.

Lewellyn, K. N. (1931), "What Price Contract?, An Essay in Perspective," Yale Law Journal, Vol.40, No.5.

Schultz, G. (1995), "Economics in Action: Ideas, Institutions, Policies," AER, Vol.85, No.2.

Solow, R. M. (2001), "A Native Informant Speaks," Journal of Economic Methodology, Vol. 8, No.1.

CHAPTER 56

ELINOR OSTROM

(1933 – 2012)

The Nobel Memorial Prize for Economic Sciences for the year 2009 was awarded by the Royal Swedish Academy of Sciences jointly to Elinor Ostrom, Indiana University, Bloomington, USA and Oliver Eaton Williamson, University of California, Berkeley, USA. While Ostrom was awarded the Prize "for her analysis of economic governance, especially the commons," Williamson received the Prize "for his analysis of economic governance, especially the boundaries of the firm." Economic transactions take place under many institutional arrangements in markets, within firms, associations, households and agencies. However, traditional economic theory has basically dealt with transactions in markets, highlighting the virtues and limitations of the markets. Thus, economic theory has been essentially a theory of markets, more specifically, about market prices. For some time, it is felt that economic science should go beyond price theory. At least two reasons can be cited in support of this stand. First, considerable economic activity takes place outside of markets, in a number of organisations, such as within households, firms, agencies and associations. Second, proper functioning of markets does not take place in the absence of formulation and enforcement of suitable contracts. There is, therefore, a need to understand institutions that support markets.

The essential purpose of a country's institutional structure is to facilitate production and exchange. Thus, institutions are sets of rules that control human interactions. Institutions that influence human prosperity by facilitating production and exchange of goods and services include political government, laws and business organisations. Research relating to economic governance covers good understanding of the nature of such institutions in the context of underlying economic problems they are called upon to handle.

The rules of the market, that is, legal rules and enforcement mechanisms aimed at protecting property rights and facilitate property trading, are one set of institutions. There exist also institutions that support production and exchange outside markets, such as transactions that are effected inside business firms. In modern times, governments actively organise production and funding of pure public goods like national defence and upkeep of public spaces. In this connection, a number of issues crop up. Which mode of governance is appropriate for what type of transactions? Likewise, the assessment of the relative efficiency of various modes of governance is equally important.

A number of natural resources such as lakes, ground water basins, woods, pastures and fish stocks are managed as common property as many users have access to the resource in question. According to conventional wisdom, common property is poorly managed leading to degradation of our natural environment. There were also instances in the past of collapses of stocks of natural resources. It is, therefore, advised that we should benefit from the successes and failures of common property-regimes. There have been suggestions that common property should be completely privatised or regulated by governmental authorities in order to ensure proper management and utilisation of scarce natural resources. It is generally argued that common ownership of resources result in excessive utilisation of the resource. As such, it is advisable to reduce utilisation either by imposing government regulations such as taxes or quotas or by completely privatising the resource. The theoretical argument runs as follows: Each user of the resource weighs private benefits against private costs, thereby ignoring the negative impact on other users.

Elinor Ostrom challenged this argument that common property is badly or poorly managed on the basis of numerous empirical studies of natural resource management. In fact, her conclusion is that very often common property is surprisingly well managed. A scrutiny of a number of empirical studies of user-managed fish stocks, pastures, woods, lakes and ground water basins led Elinor Ostrom to conclude that the actual outcomes are often better than predicted by standard theories. According to her, the perspective of these traditional theories is static and hence fails to capture the sophisticated institutions for decision-making and rule enforcement that have emerged to deal with conflicts of interest in user-managed common property around the world. It is also observed that resource-users, by and large, develop sophisticated mechanisms for decision-making and rule enforcement to tackle conflicts of interest. She found that more recent theories, which are dynamic in nature, could explain observed institutions as equilibrium outcomes of repeated games. Nevertheless, it is difficult to reconcile other rules and types of behaviour with the theory under the common assumption that players are selfish materialists who only punish others violating rules when it is in their own interest. In the field studies and laboratory experiments conducted by Elinor Ostrom and other researchers, it is found that individuals' willingness to punish defectors tends to be greater than predicted by such a model. These observations are significant to the study of management of natural resources, besides to the general study of human behaviour.

Oliver Williamson, in his research work starting from 1971, has contended that markets and hierarchical organisations like firms should be viewed as alternative governing structures that differ in their approach to resolving conflicts of interest. Williamson focuses on the drawbacks of markets in that they often involve haggling and disagreement. In case of firms, these problems are minor since conflicts of interest can be settled through the use of authority. Such authority, which is helpful in mitigating disputes, is, however, susceptible to misuse or abuse. Competitive markets function reasonably well because buyers and sellers can search for other trading partners in case of disagreement. But when market competition is limited, firms are in a better position to resolve conflicts of interest than markets. An important prediction of Williamson's theory, which received empirical support, is that the greater the mutual dependence the greater the propensity of economic agents to conduct their transactions inside the boundary of a firm. How is the degree of mutual dependence determined? Williamson's answer is that it is largely determined by the specificity of assets or by the extent to which assets can be redeployed outside the relationship. The example is given of a coal mine and a plant generating electricity, which is near the mine. In this case, it is more likely to be jointly incorporated the greater the distance to other mines and electric generating plants.

The contributions of Williamson and Ostrom are considered complementary. While Williamson deals with the problem of regulating transactions that comprise detailed contracts or legal rules, Ostrom focussed on the issue of enforcement of rules. They apply themselves squarely to the issues raised by Ronald Coase. He put forward the argument that firms tend to emerge whenever transaction costs (such as costs of exchanging goods, services and money) are lower inside the firm than in the corresponding market. It is true that while economists were convinced by Coase's arguments about the need to look inside the boundaries of firms, no full-fledged theory of the firm emerged. It was felt that in the absence of clear spelling out of determinants of costs associated with administrative decision-making, Coase's statement does not lead to formulation of a clear theory that would yield refutable predictions. The question remained unanswered: What precisely do organisations, such as firms and associations achieve that cannot be achieved in markets? In his path-breaking 1971 paper and in his later work, Williamson provided the answer by developing a detailed and comprehensive theory of the firm in the Coasean spirit. Briefly, Williamson's answer is: Where arranging transactions within firms are more desirable and when transactions are complex and when physical and human assets are strongly relationship-specific, a firm emerges. His theory has the required empirical content since both complexity and specificity are capable of measurement.

The contributions of Elinor Ostrom are summarised in this chapter after a brief biographical sketch; Williamson's major contributions have been covered in the preceding chapter.

56.1 A BRIEF BIOGRAPHICAL NOTE: ELINOR OSTROM

Elinor Ostrom was born in Los Angeles, California, on August 7, 1933, and grew up during the Great Depression. Her childhood was spent learning and doing the traditional activities of a girl during the 20th century. Her major recreational activity was swimming, which helped her earn money by becoming a swimming teacher. The money she could save from her earnings helped her go through college.

Elinor attended Beverly Hills High School: "Poor kid in rich kids school." In junior year of high school, she joined the debate team and participated actively in speech competitions around the state. She observed: "Learning debate was an important early impact on my ways of thinking. You are taught that there are always at least two sides to public policy questions, and you have to learn a good argument for both sides as well as knowing how to critique both sides." She also got benefited by participating in team efforts. Since 90 percent of the students in the High School went to college it appeared to Ostrom that going to college was natural. However, her mother saw no reason to support her during her college years. Ostrom financed her college education by working in the library, at retail stores and at the book store. Further, since the semester fees were low, she could complete her undergraduate degree without going into debt. Ostrom took a number of courses across the social sciences; in her last year as an undergraduate, she "graded Freshmen Economics."

When Ostrom started looking for a job after graduation, she was shocked by the future employers enquiring whether she had typing and shorthand skills. The presumption in those days was that the appropriate job for a woman was as a secretary or as a teacher in a grade school or high school. After a brief stint as an export clerk, Ostrom applied for admission to a Ph. D. programme and research assistantship in the University of California at Los Angeles (UCLA). Her discussions with the Economics Department at UCLA about obtaining a Ph.D. in Economics were pretty discouraging, as she had not taken mathematics at the undergraduate level. The Political Science department was skeptical about admitting any woman to their Ph.D. program as they feared that only a city college would employ a woman with a Ph.D. That was not a good placement for building the reputation of the UCLA department. Elinor Ostrom was, however, admitted in a class of 40 students with three other women. She stated: "Fortunately, our fellow male graduate students were friendly and encouraged us all to continue in our program."

In her graduate work, Elinor Ostrom participated in a research team studying the water industry in Southern California. She admitted: "Without knowing, I was studying a common-pool resource problem, I became very familiar with the kinds of problems that users of a common-pool resource face in trying to manage such a resource." The title of her Ph.D. dissertation was "Public Entrepreneurship: A Case Study in Ground Water Management." In 1965 she defended her Ph.D. dissertation. When her husband, Vincent Ostrom (whom she married in 1963) was offered an attractive position as full time professor at Indiana University, Bloomington, she tagged along as it was very hard for any department to hire a woman in those days. After working for a year as a Visiting Assistant Professor in the department of Political Science of the University, she moved to regular appointment as a Graduate Advisor.

After fifteen years of extensive research on police industry structure and performance, Elinor returned to her basic area of research interest--namely studying the commons, but this time with the recognition of what she was studying. The National Research Council created a special committee in the mid-1980s to review the empirical research written about common-pool resources. There was recognition that much research on this topic had been conducted but was divided by discipline, sector, and synthesised. This taught

Ostrom a major lesson. She understood that the way the modern American university was organized resulted in fragmentation of knowledge badly.

In association with Vincent Ostrom, Elinor established an "effective research center;" named it the Workshop in Political Theory and Policy Analysis. The workshop was composed of a variety of scholars across economics, political science, and other disciplines working together to understand "how institutional arrangements in a diverse set of ecological and social economic political settings affected behavior and outcomes." With the support of FAO (Food and Agricultural Organisation) the Ostroms, with the same workshop philosophy developed a collaborative network to study forest conditions and forest policy by scholars living in different countries. Elinor Ostrom significantly observed: "...if one is trying to understand and test theory in the field and in the experimental lab and to really pursue in-depth studies of diverse institutional arrangements around the world, then working with colleagues located in diverse settings at various stages of their careers is crucial for making scientific progress."

At the time of the Nobel award, Elinor Ostrom was Arthur F Bentley Professor of Political Theory and Policy Analysis (later senior research professor of the workshop) and part-time professor of Public and Environmental Affairs and Co-Director, Centre for the Study of Institutions, Population, and Environmental Change (CIPEC), Indiana University, Bloomington. Later, she became Distinguished Professor, Indiana State University. She was founding Director for the Study of Institutional Diversity, Arizona State University, Tempe. She had received a number of awards and honours, which include Fellow, American Academy of Arts and Sciences, (since 1991), President, American Political Science Association (1996-97), Member, Committee on National Urban Policy, National Academy of Science/National Research Council (1985-88), and President, Public Choice Society (1982-84). She received Honorary Doctorates from Michigan State University, East Lansing and McGill University, Canada. Ostrom received the University Medal, Indiana University (2010) and Galbraith Award, American Agricultural Economics Association.

Elinor Ostrom died of pancreatic cancer on June 12, 2012 at the age of 78. On the day of her death, she published her last article, "Green from the Grassroots."

56.2 A SUMMARY OF ELINOR OSTROM'S CONTRIBUTIONS

In his definitional article of 1954, "The Pure Theory of Public Expenditure," Paul Samuelson categorised goods produced in an economy as private goods and public goods. Buchanan in his 1965 article added a third type of good, which he called "club goods." In the light of further theoretical and empirical research, Elinor Ostrom and her husband Vincent Ostrom, proposed further modifications to the classification of goods, "to identify fundamental differences which affect the incentives facing individuals." They suggested four broad types of goods that "differentially affect the problem individuals face in devising institutions to enable them to provide, produce and consume diverse goods." They suggested replacing the term "rivalry of consumption" with "substractability of use" in the case of pure private goods. Further, they conceptualised substractability of use and excludability of goods to vary from low to high rather than characterising as either present or absent. They also substituted the name "toll" good instead of a "club" good. Finally, they added a fourth category of goods–common-pool resources. These goods share the difficulty of exclusion with public goods and the characteristic of substractability with private goods. In the last category of goods were included forests, water resource systems, fisheries and global atmospheres.

Commons or Common-pool resources (CPRs) are resources that are characterised by access to more than one individual and each person's use reduces availability of the resource to others. A number of examples are given such as fish stocks, pastures, and woods, as well as water for drinking or irrigation. In this context, the problem is the overuse of such resources, which has been the concern of social thinkers for a very long time. Such common pool resources may be overused since there exist strong private incentives for this type of action which is detrimental to the group as a whole. The scientific back ground note released by the Royal Swedish Academy makes reference to the early formal analysis by Warming and Gordon regarding open access of resources; that is, where there is entry of users of the resource till the marginal benefit equals the marginal cost to the last entrant. The biologist Garrett Hardin, in an article (1968) with a catchy title "The Tragedy of the Commons" refers to the rapidly increasing overexploitation of common pool of resources throughout the world and sounds a timely warning. "Ruin is the destination towards which all men rush; each presuming his own best interest in a society that believes in the freedom of commons. Freedom in a commons brings ruin to all." Bergstrom in his 2010 article comments that economists view it "as a one shot'n'player game in which each player chooses the intensity with which he exploits the commons. The pay-off to each player is an increasing function of the total exploitation by all n-players. Given plausible assumption, such a game has a unique Nash equilibrium." However it is not an efficient equilibrium as all players could be made better off, provided each player reduced his exploitation.

Two main solutions were suggested in economics to the common-pool problem. Pigovian solution involves central government ownership of the resources and extractions of revenue by levying a tax. This solution involves disenfranchisement of original users. Further, under ideal circumstances, the taxes would be equal to efficient market prices. Dasgupta and Heal suggest that under such ideal circumstances, there is also an equivalent solution to the problem based on quotas. An alternative approach, called property rights approach, suggests elimination of common access and establishment of marketable property rights with exclusive claim to the use of relevant resources by individual owners. Given that property rights are unequally settled and in the absence of transaction costs, rational individuals will arrive at a Pareto-efficient allocation through negotiated agreements. This proposition is the essential principle of the property rights school. Those who subscribe to the property rights argument, no doubt agree that it may be difficult in the face of transaction costs to establish property rights. Bergstrom gives an example to illustrate this. Shopping centres may permit their parking lots to remain a commons as expenses incurred for fixing parking meters is uneconomical. Coase also refers to the significance of transaction costs in real-world applications. Further, in his Nobel Prize lecture, he states that establishment of private property rights is not a general solution. Coase, in fact, suggests further study of the problem. He states "...it does not imply, when transaction costs are positive, that government actions... could not produce a better result than relying on negotiations between individuals in the market. Whether this would be so could be discovered not by studying imaginary governments but what real governments actually do. My conclusion: let us study the world of positive transaction costs."

A third solution was put forward by Ostrom. Bergstrom considers her solution as a response to Coase's above suggestion for studying the world of transaction costs. To retain the resource as common property, the system of governance is set up by the users themselves. This solution was given up earlier by economists. Ostrom did not agree with the presumption that the governance of common property invariably implies a tragedy. She asserted: "It is difficult to know exactly what analysts mean when they refer to the necessity of developing private rights to some common pool resources.... Even when particular rights are utilized, quantified and salable, the resource system is still likely to be owned in common rather than individually."

It is suggested that it is advantageous to distinguish a variety of forms of partial property rights that may be connected with the use of common pool resources. Ostrom suggested that it would be useful to distinguish a number of types of partial property rights connected to the use of common-pool resources, such as access, withdrawal, management, exclusion and alienation. She provided many examples of arrangements involving partial property rights. In Swiss Alps, peasant villagers maintained private plots of land in the valley. The work relating to the maintenance on the summer pastures was shared by villagers on the basis of the number of cows they pastured in summers. The irrigation canals in Spanish river valleys were maintained locally subject to the rules framed by local groups regulating withdrawal of wealth. The rules have been in force for about 500 years. Elinor Ostrom in collaboration with co-researchers studied 127 local systems located in Nepalese irrigation systems--a small proportion of them were managed by government agencies and about two-thirds were organised by local farmers. These systems shared a common technological feature. If there is no agreement, first access to scarce irrigation water was available to farmers located upstream who plant highly water intensive rice crops. As a result, land located downstream generally suffers from inadequate irrigation waters. This is not an efficient outcome. It is to be noted that while usage of water is decided by local groups, the rules for utilisation of water is agreed upon after bargaining among farmers. Ostrom and her co-author contended that since to maintain the canal system the contributions of labour by groups located downstream is crucial, the two groups (that is those located upstream and downstream) reach agreements that are more efficient and favourable to the latter than the "default outcome." They also came to a conclusion that the performance of water districts managed by agencies of the government was inferior to that of farmer-managed systems. They measured the performance of water systems by the fraction of water that reaches users at down streams.

The background material provided by the Royal Swedish Academy observes that a few case studies rarely permit broad generalisations. It states: "The key to Ostrom's breakthrough insights was... the realization... there exist thousands of detailed case studies of the management of CPRs, [Common-Pool Resources] and that most of them were written by authors interested in only one or a small set of cases. By collecting and comparing these isolated studies, it should be possible to make substantially stronger inferences." Her examination of a large number of case studies, showed that in most of the cases, local communities had successfully managed CPR's, sometimes for centuries. Ostrom also studied unsuccessful cases and found instances in which resources collapse. She concluded that local organisation can be remarkably efficient. Ostrom's study of case studies highlights conditions under which local government is feasible, but also reveals conditions under which neither privatisation nor state ownership works well as standard economic analysis suggests.

For better interpretation of cases study material, Ostrom made extensive use of concepts from non-cooperative game theory, especially the theory of repeated games, associated with Robert Aumann. However, no specific game–theory model could be employed for Ostrom's data. The difficulty did not prevent her from using game theory adeptly and effectively in formulating and describing the problems that are associated with common pool resources. The application of the theory of repeated games is considered quite appropriate in situations connected with common-pool resources. For instance, in the case of irrigation or pasturing, every year is basically a repetition of the previous year's conditions. Ostrom gave examples of Swiss pasturing commons and irrigation systems in Spain, referred to earlier.

It is observed that repeated game reasoning suggests that as the size of the group increases, or the time horizon of the users decreases, cooperation among users of the resources becomes rather difficult. The game-theoretic predictions, such as these, are largely supported by Ostrom's empirical studies. In her Prize lecture, Ostrom stated that "...moving up a level in generality, I tried to understand the broader institutional regularities among the systems that were sustained over a long period of time and were absent in the failed systems."

To characterise these regularities, she used the term "design principle." In her words: "The effort was to identify a set of core underlying lessons that characterized the long sustained regimes as contrasted to the cases of failure." She gave a brief updated list (of what Ostrom has provided in her work) as developed by Cox, Arnold, and Villamayor-Tomás, after analysing over 100 studies. The list given in her Prize Lecture is given below.

Clear and locally understood boundaries between legitimate users and non-users are present.

Clear boundaries that separate a specific common pool resource from a larger social-ecological system are present.

Appropriation and provision rules are congruent with local social and environmental conditions.

Appropriation rules that are congruent with provision rules; the distribution of costs is proportional to the distribution of benefits.

Most individuals affected by a resource regime are authorised to participate in making and modifying its rules.

Individuals who are users or who are accountable monitor the appropriation and provision levels of the users and also the condition of the resource.

Sanctions for rule violations start very low but become stronger for a repeated violation of rules by the user.

There must exist rapid, low-cost, local arenas for resolving conflicts among users or with officials.

Government has to recognize rights of local users to make their own rules.

When a common-pool resource is closely connected to a larger social-ecological system, governance activities are organised in multiple nest layers.

Ostrom commented: The design principles appear to synthesize core factors that affect the probability of long-term survival of an institution developed by the users of a resource.

In addition to using game-theoretic models, Ostrom and her colleagues conducted experiments to study common-pool resource problems. According to Ostrom "the existence of a large number of cases where users had overcome social dilemmas in order to sustain long-term use of common-pool resources successfully challenged the presumption that it was impossible. Many variables simultaneously affect these outcomes in the field. Developing game–theoretical models of common–pool resource situations... has been one strategy we have used to assess the theoretical outcomes of a set of variables we have observed in the field. We have also thought it was important to examine the effect of precise combinations of variables in an experimental setting." The experiments revealed that the opportunity for repeated face-to-face communication among subjects was "extremely successful" in increasing joint returns. Further, in many field settings, it was found that resource users have devised a variety of formal or informal ways of sanctioning one another, if rules are broken. In addition, it was observed that sanctioning was mainly directed at those who defected. The experiments revealed that the predictions of non-cooperative game theory are roughly supported only "when participants in a laboratory experiment do not know the reputation of others involved in a common-pool resource dilemma and cannot communicate with them." However, when subjects communicate face-to-face, they substantially increase their returns by frequently agreeing on joint strategies and abiding by their agreements. It was also found that communication to decide on and design a sanctioning system facilitates those choosing this option to achieve near optimal returns. Experiments conducted by Ostrom and other researchers strengthen Ostrom's argument that a proper understanding of human cooperation requires a more nuanced analysis of individuals' motives than has been usual in economic science, especially regarding the nature and origin of reciprocity.

Dealing with the current position subsequent to a half century of extensive empirical research, Ostrom observed in her Prize lecture that "the earlier theories of rational, but helpless, individuals who are trapped in social dilemmas are not supported by a large number of studies using diverse methods." At the same time, we cannot be overly optimistic and presume that dilemmas will always be solved by those involved. More importantly, simple policy prescriptions to hand over resources to a government, or to privatise or to decentralise may not succeed. She concluded this part of the discussion with a timely alert: "... We have a difficult task of developing the theories further to facilitate our understanding and predicting when those involved in a common–pool resource dilemma can self-organize and how various aspects of the broad context they face impact their strategies, the short term success of their efforts, and the long term robustness of their initial achievements." There is a vital need to develop a better theoretical understanding of human behaviour as also the impact of the diverse contexts that humans face. Human behaviour is determined by individual differences over time; it is also influenced by the context of interactions. Ostrom emphasised the need for social scientists to recognise that individual behaviour is strongly influenced by the context in which interactions take place; it is not simply a result of individual differences.

Ostrom endorsed Arrow's view of the crucial role of trust among participants as the most efficient mechanism to enhance transactional outcomes. This is based on empirical studies, which confirm the important role of trust in overcoming social dilemmas. She summarised the empirical results of studies relating to micro situations in these words: "The central core of the findings is that when individuals face a social dilemma in micro settings, they are more likely to cooperate when situational variables increase the likelihood of gaining trust that others will reciprocate." In regard to broader socio-ecological systems, she stated that "a set of ten variables have been identified across many field studies as impacting the likelihood of users self-organizing in order to overcome a common-pool resource dilemma.... These include: the size, productivity and predictability of the resource system; the extent of mobility of the resource units; the existence of collective-choice rules that the users may adopt authoritatively in order to change their own operational rules; and four attributes of users (the number, the existence of leadership/entrepreneurship, knowledge about the SES [Socio Ecological Systems], and the importance of the SES to the users)."

Concluding her lecture, Ostrom spelt out the most important lesson for public policy analysis. The lesson is: Contrary to what was postulated in rational choice theory, the motivational structure of humans is more complex and possesses better capability to solve social dilemmas. Further, the extensive empirical research suggests that a key goal of public policy should be to facilitate the development of institutions that bring out the best in humans and help achieve "more effective, equitable and sustainable outcomes at multiple scales." Furthermore, we have to be willing to deal with complexity, instead of rejecting it.

56.3 CONCLUDING OBSERVATIONS

Elinor Ostrom is a political scientist, as observed by Steven Levitt "both by training and her career – one of the most decorated political scientists around." In her autobiographical note she mentioned that she and her husband, Vincent Ostrom, established workshop in Political Theory and Policy Analysis. She had stated: "The logic of our workshop has always been that there would be a variety of scholars across economics, political science and other disciplines who worked together trying to understand how institutional arrangements in a diverse set of ecological and social economic political settings affected behaviour and outcomes." Bergstrom in his 2010 article observes: "The fact that they [Professors Levitt and Krugman, both distinguished scholars with strong interest in the economics of public policy] were unacquainted with Ostrom's work is, as Professor Levitt suggests, evidence of a remarkable lack of communication between subcultures of the academic world." Bergstrom also advises economists to consider spending some time with her [Elinor Ostrom's] work. The reasons given by him for this advice are reproduced here.

1. They will learn much that is useful and interesting about institutions that manage common property resources.
2. They are likely to become more skeptical about simplistic solutions to social dilemmas like the tragedy of commons.
3. They will see an example of how to integrate a field research with cleanly designed laboratory experiments.
4. They will find a role model for incorporating work from other academic disciplines into their economic research.
5. They might learn to read lists all the way to the end.

In conclusion, it may be said that Elinor Ostrom's work was associated with the new institutional economics and has caused the resurgence of political economy.

56.4 SELECT BIBLIOGRAPHY OF WORKS OF ELINOR OSTROM

56.4.1 BOOKS

1990 Governing the Commons: The Evolution of Institutions for Collective Action, Cambridge University Press, New York.

1992 (with P. Benjamin and G. Shivakoti) Institutions, Incentives and Irrigation in Nepal, Indiana University Press, Bloomington, IN.

1994 (with R. Gardner and J. Walker), Rules, Games and Common-Pool Resources, University of Michigan Press, Ann Arbor, Mi.

1995 (With R. Keohane, eds.), Local Commons and Global Interdependence: Heterogeneity and Cooperation in Two Domains, Sage, London.

2000 (with C. Gibson et al.), People and Forests: Communities, Institutions and Governance, MIT Press, Cambridge, MA.

2002 (with G. Shivakoti eds.), Improving Irrigation Governance and Management in Nepal: ICS Press, Oklahoma.

2003 a (with J. Walker eds.), Trust and Reciprocity: Interdisciplinary Lessons from Experimental Research, Russell Sage Foundation, New York.

b (with T. K. Ahn, eds.), Foundations of Social Capital, Edward Elgar, Cheltenham.

c (with N. Dolšak eds.), The Commons in the New Millennium: Challenges and Adaptations, MIT Press, Cambridge, MA.

2005 a (with E. Moran, eds.), Seeing the Forest and Trees: Human- Environment Interactions in Forest Ecosystems, MIT Press, Cambridge, MA.

b (with C. Gibbon et al.), The Samaritan's Dilemma: The Political Economy of Development Aid, Oxford University Press, Oxford.

c (with G. Shivakoti, et al.), Asian Irrigation in Transition: Responding to Challenges, Sage, New Delhi.

d Understanding Institutional Diversity, Princeton University Press, Princeton, NJ.

2006 (with B. Guha-Khasnobis et al.), Linking the Formal and Informal Economy: Concerns and Policies, Oxford University Press, Oxford.

2007 (with C. Hess, eds.), Understanding Knowledge as a Commons: From Theory to Practice, MIT Press, Cambridge, MA.

2010 (with A. R. Poteete, et al.), Working Together: Collective Action, The Commons and Multiple Methods in Practice, Princeton University Press, Princeton, NJ.

2011 a (With W. F. Lam et al.), Improving Irrigation in Asia: Sustainable Performance of an Innovative Invention in Nepal, Edward Elgar, Cheltenham.

b (with D. H. Cole, eds.), Property in Land and Other Resources, Lincoln Institute of Land Policy, Cambridge, MA.

56.4.2 ARTICLES

2000 "Collective Actions and Evolution of Social Norms," JEP, Vol. 14, No.3.

2001 (with A. Agarwal), "Collective Actions, Property Rights, and Decentralization in Resource Use in India and Nepal," Politics and Society, Vol. 29, No.4.

2008 "Institutions and Environment," Economic Affairs, Vol.28, No.3.

2009 a (with J. Cox et al.), "Trust in Private and Common Property Experiments," Southern Economic Journal, Vol.75, No.4.

b "Engaging with Impossibilities and Possibilities," in Arguments for Better World: Essays in Honour of Amartya Sen, Vol. II, Society, Institution and Development, K. Basu and R Kanbur (eds.), Oxford University Press, Oxford.

2010 a "Beyond Markets and States: Polycentric Governance of Complex Economic Systems," AER, Vol. 100, No.3. (Revised Version of Noble Lecture).

b "Revising Theory in Light of Experimental Findings," Journal of Economic Behavior and Organization, Vol. 73, No.1.

2011 "Reflections on 'Some Unsettled Problems of Irrigation'," AER, Vol.101, No.1.

56.5 WORKS OF OTHERS

Andersen, P. (1983), "On Rent of Fishing Grounds: A Translation of Jens Warming's 1911 Article, with an Introduction," HOPE, Vol.15, No.3.

Bergstrom, T. C. (2010), "The Uncommon Insights of Elinor Ostrom," ScandJE, Vol.112, No.2.

Buchanan, J. (1965), "An Economic Theory of Clubs," Economica, Vol. 32, No.125.

Coase, R. H. (1960), "The Problem of Social Cost," JLawE, Vol.3, No.1.

Das Gupta, P. S., and G. M. Heal (1979), Economic and Exhaustible Resources Theory, Cambridge University Press, Cambridge.

Gordon H. S. (1954), "The Economic Theory of Common Property Resources: The Fishery," JPE, Vol. 62, No.2.

Harding, G. (1968), "The Tragedy of Commons," Science, Vol.162.

Pigou, A. C. (1932), The Economics of Welfare (4th edition) MacMillan, London.

Samuelson, P. A. (1954), "The Pure Theory of Public Expenditure," REStat, Vol.36, No.4.

SECTION - VII
GAME THEORY

CHAPTER 57

JOHN FORBES NASH, Jr.

(1928 –)

The Royal Swedish Academy of Sciences has awarded the Bank of Sweden Prize in Economic Sciences in Memory of Alfred Nobel for the year 1994, jointly to the following:

Dr. John F. Nash, Jr. of Princeton University, New Jersey, U.S.A.

Professor John C. Harsanyi of University of California, Berkley, California, U.S.A., and the names are belong the other Professor Reinhard Selten of Professor Wilhelms Rheinische Freedrich- Universitat, Bonn, Germany. for their path-breaking pioneering analysis of equilibria in the theory of non-cooperative games.

Game Theory or Interactive Decision Theory (a more descriptive name suggested by Aumann, Economics Nobel Laureate, 2005) emanates from the formal resemblance of interactive decision problems to parlour games such as chess, poker, monopoly, diplomacy, or battleship. The term also underlines the "rational, cold, calculating nature of the analysis." In these games, players are required to think and plan a strategy based on expected counter- moves from other player or players or decision-makers. According to Aumann, the major applications of game theory are to economics, political science, tactical and strategic military problems, evolutionary biology and most recently computer science. The theory has important connections with statistics, foundations of mathematics, accounting, social psychology, epistemology and ethics. As many economic situations are characterised by such strategic interactions, game theory has been found to be very useful in economic analysis.

For studying strategic market interactions, economists like Cournot devised methods more than 170 years ago (1838). However, these methods focussed on specific situations and, for a long time, no overall method existed. The foundations for using game theory in economics were introduced in a monumental study by John von Neumann and Oskar Morgenstern entitled Theory of Games and Economic Behavior. It is pertinent to note that von Neumann had laid the mathematical foundation of the theory of games in his 1928 paper. von Neumann-Morgenstern work, first published in 1944, is considered the first systematic attempt to analyse strategic interactions in a unified framework. Their work has given economists a new tool for analysis of economic problems. It is commonly accepted that Morgenstern, was the first economist who had "clearly and explicitly" recognised that economic agents while making their decisions should take into consideration the interactive nature of economics. The importance of von Neumann-Morgenstern's contribution to economic analysis can be appreciated by noting that classical economic theory by assuming perfectly competitive markets, had sidestepped the game theoretic aspects of economic behaviour; that is, classical economic theory's postulation that every buyer and seller in the market is too small to make any impact on market prices by his actions. Each economic agent takes that the prices at which he can buy his inputs including labour and at which he can sell his outputs or services are given. Harsanyi observed: "This will make his choice of inputs and of outputs into a one person simple maximization problem, which can be solved without game-theoretic analysis." (Emphasis in the original).

It has been increasingly realised that the assumption of perfect competition for most parts of the economic system is patently unrealistic. A large number of industries around the world now are dominated by a small number of large firms (oligopolistic market) while labour is largely organised in large labour unions. Further, in many countries, including developed ones, governments or their agencies are important players as buyers or sellers, as regulators or as tax authorities or agencies providing subsidies. It is, therefore, necessary to use game theory for any realistic economic analysis. The press release of the Royal Swedish Academy of Sciences observes that non-cooperative game theory, that is, the branch of game theory that excludes binding agreements has had great impact on economic research. The key aspect of non-cooperative game theory is the concept of equilibrium which is used to make predictions about the strategic interaction. Specifically, the release mentions the eminent contributions made by John F. Nash, John C. Harsanyi and Reinhard Selten to this type of equilibrium analysis.

The press release sums up: through their contributions to equilibrium analysis in non-cooperative game theory, the three laureates constitute a natural combination: Nash provided the foundations for the analysis, while Selten developed it with respect to dynamics, and Harsanyi with respect to incomplete information.

Nash's contributions are summarised in this chapter; contributions of Harsanyi and Selten are briefly surveyed in the next two chapters.

57.1 A SHORT BIOGRAPHY: JOHN NASH

John Forbes Nash, Jr. was born on June 13, 1928 in Bluefield, West Virginia, U.S.A. His father John Nash, a Texan, was an electrical engineer and moved to Bluefield to work for an electrical utility company there while his mother was born in Bluefield. Nash went to the standard schools in Bluefield, a small city. By the time he was a student in high school, he was reading the classic, Men of Mathematics by E T. Bell. Nash's precocity can be judged by this statement in his autobiography: "I remember succeeding in proving the Classic Fermat theorem about an integer multiplied by itself p times where p is a prime."

On a full scholarship, called the George Westinghouse Scholarship, he entered Carnegie Tech (now Carnegie Mellon University) in Pittsburgh with the intention of majoring in chemical engineering. However, he later chose mathematics as a major, as a result of encouragement he received from mathematics faculty. In Nash's words: "And in the end I had learned and progressed so much in mathematics that they gave an M.S. in addition to my B.S. when I graduated."

When he graduated, Nash was offered fellowships for graduate studies by Harvard University as also by Princeton University. As Princeton was much nearer geographically to Bluefield and since the Princeton fellowship was somewhat more generous, Nash finally decided in 1948 to join Princeton for his graduate studies. He came to the Mathematics department with a one sentence letter of recommendation from R.L. Duffin of Carnegie. The letter said simply: "This man is a genius." Nash's thesis advisor, Professor A. W. Tucker was to write several years later: "At times I have thought this recommendation was extravagant, but the longer I've known Nash the more I am inclined to agree that Duffin was right."

When Nash was at Carnegie, he took an elective course in International economics and as a result of that exposure to economic ideas and problems he arrived at the idea that resulted in the paper "The Bargaining Problem" which was later published in Econometrica (1950). Further, this idea, in turn, when he was a graduate student at Princeton, led to his interest in the game theory studies at Princeton that had been stimulated by the work of von Neumann and Morgenstern. The results of these studies are reported in Nash's doctoral dissertation entitled "Non-Cooperative Games" (1950). In this connection, the remark of Kuhn of Department of Mathematics at Princeton University, at the Nobel Seminar on the work of John Nash in Game Theory, conducted on December 8, 1994, is significantly revealing. Kuhn states: "If we do the arithmetic of subtracting the date of Nash's arrival in Princeton, which was September 1948, from the date of submission...to the proceedings of the National Academy of Sciences of the main results of Nash's thesis, November 1949, we find the results for which he is being honored this week were obtained in his first fourteen months of graduate study." Kuhn comments that it is a fine goal to set before the graduate students who were then in the audience.

While doing the doctoral dissertation work, simultaneously Nash also made "a nice discovery" relating to manifolds and real algebraic varieties as he feared that the game theory work would not be regarded acceptable as a thesis in the mathematics department. In such an event, he could realise the objective of a Ph.D. thesis with the other results. Later, subsequent to the acceptance of his doctoral dissertation by the Mathematics Department of the University in May 1950, he wrote up "Real Algebraic Manifolds" and sent it for publication.

Regarding the doctoral work of Nash, Tucker, who was one of the two professors, who evaluated Nash's doctoral work, wrote: "This (the doctoral work) is a highly original and important contribution to the Theory of Games. It develops notions and properties of 'non-cooperative games,' finite n-person games which are very interesting in themselves and which may open up many hitherto untouched problems that lie beyond the zero-sum two-person case. Both in conception and in execution this thesis is entirely the author's own."

After obtaining his doctoral degree in 1950, Nash served as instructor at Princeton. In the summer of 1951, he accepted MIT's offer of C.L.E. Moore Instructorship on the mathematics faculty as "it seemed desirable more for personal and social reasons than academic ones to accept the higher-paying instructorship at MIT." During the academic year 1956-57, Nash received Alfred P. Sloan grant; he chose to spend the year as a temporary member of the Institute for Advanced Study in Princeton. During the academic sabbatical of 1956-57, he married Alicia who played a very important role in his eventual recovery from paranoid schizophrenia. It was reported: "On an April evening in 1959, a man struggles in vain as two plain-clothes police officers carry him to their car, which is parked in front of a house in a Boston suburb. They drive to the nearby small town of Belmont and take him to the Mclean Hospital, a large psychiatric clinic." This puts a temporary end to the career of John Nash, the best American mathematician of his generation, and it takes decades before he can lead a normal life again and reap the recognition he has earned for his work.

In his autobiographical note Nash states: Now I must arrive at the time of my change from scientific rationality of thinking into the delusional thinking characteristic of persons who are psychiatrically diagnosed as "schizophrenic" or "paranoid schizophrenic." His mental disturbances originated in the early months of 1959 (as mentioned in the earlier paragraph) when his wife, Alicia, was pregnant. Nash resigned his position as a faculty member at MIT. (He had been tenured there in 1958 – at the age of 29). He spent times of the order of five to eight months in hospitals. His autobiographical note says : "...when I had been long enough hospitalized...I would finally renounce my delusional hypotheses and revert to thinking of myself as a human of more conventional circumstances and return to mathematical research. In these interludes of...enforced rationality, I did succeed in doing some respectable mathematical research." By the time the Nobel award was announced and when he was penning the autobiographical note, Nash states that he seems to be thinking "rationally again in the style that is characteristic of scientists." He, however, admits: "...statistically, it would seem improbable that any mathematician or scientist, at the age of 66, would be able...to add much to his or her previous achievements." Nash's autobiographical piece ends on an optimistic note: "I have hopes of being able to achieve something of value through my current studies or with any new ideas that come in the future."

Nash was elected Fellow, Econometric Society. In 1978, Nash was awarded the John von Neumann Theory Prize for his "discovery" of non-cooperative equilibria, now called

Nash equilibria. He also won the Leroy P Steele Prize in 1999. He was awarded an honorary degree, Doctorate of Science and Technology from Carnegie –Mellon University in 1999.

57.2 A BRIEF SUMMARY OF JOHN NASH'S CONTRIBUTION TO ECONOMICS

Nash is not a prolific writer unlike many other economics laureates. His active career is "intensive but very short." His major works before the award of the Nobel Prize listed in his homepage are only five, all appeared in print between 1950 and 1953 – two of them in Econometrica, one each in Annals of Mathematics, in Annals of Mathematical Statistics and in Proceedings of National Academy of Sciences. However the award is in recognition of the quality of his work and the impetus his work has given to research in game theory since 1950's. As Rubinstein observes: the prize is also given to John Nash, the human being.

Aumann, describing the spirit of the time observes that the period of late 1940's and early 1950's was a period of excitement in game theory. "Giants walked the earth." Most of game theory is directed at answering the question as to given a game what outcome may be expected? In the case of two-person, zero-sum games, a clear answer is given: "the unique individually rational outcome; in almost all other cases, there is no unique answer." At Princeton, John Nash's contribution relates to laying the foundation for the general non-cooperative game theory and for the cooperative bargaining theory. Harsanyi recognised at least three fundamental important contributions to game theory by Nash in his four published brilliant papers.

Nash drew a clear distinction between cooperative and non-cooperative games. While in cooperative games, players can make "enforceable agreements" and can also make "irrevocable threats" to other players, i.e. commit themselves to specific strategies, no such self-commitment is envisaged in non-cooperative games.

He introduces the concept of "equilibrium points," now referred to as Nash equilibria, as a solution for non-cooperative games. He also proved the existence of equilibrium points in all finite games.

For two-person cooperative games, he suggested Nash bargaining solution for games with fixed threats as also for games with variable threats. In the case of games with variable threats, Nash established that the optimal strategies of the two players will have maximin and minimax properties.

Nash's 1951 paper opens by making a clear distinction between cooperative and non-cooperative games: "von Neumann and Morgenstern have developed a very fruitful theory of two-person zero-sum games in their book....[It] also contains a theory of n-person games of a type which we would call cooperative. This theory is based on an analysis of the inter-relationships of the various coalitions which can be formed by the players of the game...[this theory assumes that] coalitions will be enforced by an umpire. Our theory, in contradistinction is based on the absence of coalitions in that it is assumed that each participant acts independently, without collaboration or communication with any others."

Further, Nash states: "The notion of an equilibrium point is the basic ingredient in our theory. This notion yields a generalization of the concept of the solution of a two-person zero-sum game." According to Nash, an equilibrium of a strategic game is a pure or mixed strategy profile in which each player's strategy maximises his payoff given that the others are using their strategies.

In his dissertation on game theory, Nash presented the concept of a non-cooperative game and the optimal strategy subsequently named after him, the Nash equilibrium. One very popular example of such a game is what is referred to as the "Battle of Sexes." The game is elaborated as follows: "A man and a woman at different points in a city want to spend the evening together. Their mobile phones are out of order; so they can only set off with the guidance of common sense, hoping of course to find each other at the venue. They can choose either a football match which the man prefers, or a concert, the woman's preference. Who goes where? Nash's theory says there are two equilibria, two possible solutions that could save the evening: the man and woman see each other at the football match or at the concert. How they come to their decisions is left unconsidered.

It is simpler if the game is played several times in succession: a probability should emerge of the partners meeting as often as possible by going either to the stadium or to the concert hall. Nash equilibria exist where no participant can enhance his benefit by changing his own strategy."

Another simple example to understand the concept of Nash equilibrium provided in <u>The Concise Encyclopaedia of Economics</u> may be given.

Imagine that two beer manufacturing companies, Budweiser and Miller, are trying to decide where to place their beer stands on a beach that is perfectly straight. Assume also that sunbathers are located an equal distance from each other and they want to minimize the distance they walk to get a beer. Where then should Budweiser locate if Miller has not yet chosen its location? If Budweiser locates one-quarter of the way along the beach, then Miller can locate next to Budweiser and have three-quarters of the market. Budweiser knows this and thus concludes that the best location is right in the middle of the beach. Miller locates just slightly to one side or the other. Neither Budweiser nor Miller can improve its position by choosing an alternative location. This is a Nash equilibrium.

While developing non-cooperative games, Nash restricts himself to finite n-person games in strategic or normal form. He assumes that the payoff function of each player is a von Neumann-Morgenstern utility function. In a Nash equilibrium, all of the players' expectations are fulfilled and their chosen strategies are optimal. He provides two interpretations of the equilibrium concept. His first interpretation is based on rationality and the other on statistical populations.

According to the rationalistic interpretation, players are perceived to be rational and they possess all the information about the structure of the game including preferences of all the players regarding possible outcomes, where this information is common knowledge. Since all players have complete knowledge about each others' strategic alternatives and preferences, they can also compute each others' optimal choice of strategy for each set of expectations. In the words of Nash, "...by using the principles that a rational prediction should be unique, that the players should be able to deduce and make use of it, and that such knowledge on the part of each player of what to expect the others to do should not lead him to act out of conformity with the prediction ...." Then there are no incentives for anyone to change his strategy; Nash states that this is quite strongly a rationalistic and idealising interpretation. In general, Nash shows that for every game with a finite number of players, there exists an equilibrium in mixed strategies.

Using Brouwer's fixed point theorem in his doctoral work (in the 1950 Econometrica paper, Nash uses Kakutani's fixed point theorem), Nash derives an "quite elegant existence proof" of an equilibrium point. It may be noted that the early developments of general equilibrium theory, and the method of existence proofs for Walrasian equilibria were influenced by Nash's work. Arrow and Debreu employ Nash's method of proof; they observe: "...Nash has formally introduced the notion of an equilibrium point for a game. The definition can easily be extended to an abstract economy."

Nash's second interpretation of equilibrium concept, which is in terms of statistical populations, is found to be useful in what are called evolutionary games. The Nobel Award press release points out: "this type of game has also been developed in biology in order to understand how the principles of natural selection operate in strategic interaction within and among species."

A game may have no unique equilibrium point; it may have multiple equilibria. Recognising this fact, Nash introduces several concepts, such as inter-changeability and sub-solution to deal with the phenomenon of multiplicity. In this sense, a two-person, zero-sum game is solvable. Nash, however, admits that more general games need not be solvable. In such cases, he suggests finding a sub-solution that may be considered a set of mutually compatible equilibria, forming a coherent whole. In such unsolvable games, it is possible to find good heuristic reasons "for narrowing the set of equilibria to those lying in a single sub-solution." Eric van Damme and Jorgen W. Weibull provide an example of such a heuristic procedure in Nash's work on bargaining. Given a two-person (players A and B) game G = (I, A, U), Nash in his 1953 Econometrica paper builds a non-cooperative bargaining game that involves four stages that are given below:

"Each player, i, simultaneously commits to a mixed strategy in G which he will be forced to use in case they cannot come to an agreement in stage 2. This strategy ki is player i's threat." Nash states that it is essential for the success of the threat that A be compelled to carry out his threat if B fails to comply. Otherwise, the threat will have little meaning. For, in general, to execute the threat will not be something A would want to do, just for itself. Hence, Nash envisages the need for a sort of umpire, who will enforce contracts or commitments.

The players (A and B) inform each other of their threats.

Players independently express their utility demands – d_1 and d_2. d_1 and d_2 express the minimum utility levels the players would require to have.

If d_1 and d_2 can be simultaneously satisfied, that is, if there is a joint probability distribution or correlated strategy, then each player gets what he demanded. Otherwise, the threats must be executed. Then, player i's pay off is $U_i(t)$.

In this game, we have to first solve stage 2 sub-game induced by each pair t of threat strategies. Nash recognises that stage 2 game will have multiple equilibria: "...any pair of demands that is Pareto efficient in G and that Pareto dominate the threat point is an equilibrium." According to him, as different equilibria, however, have different stability properties, a unique equilibrium point can be selected by studying these relative stabilities.

As the pay-off function here is discontinuous, Nash suggests approximating this discontinuous function with a continuous one. After solving each sub-game in this fashion, each sub-game is replaced by its value. Nash notes that the resulting stage 1 game is strictly competitive. Since all stage 2 outcomes are Pareto efficient, one player can gain only if the other loses. As such, all equilibria are interchangeable. The bargaining problem is thus solvable.

Nash's contributions outlined above impacted game-theoretic research significantly. One notable effect was the development of theories of cooperative games and of non-cooperative games as virtually separate disciplines. Efforts were also made by game theorists to devise alternative solution concepts instead of developing the non-cooperative game theory further. During the decade of 1970-1980, there was significant increase of interest in non-cooperative games. There was simultaneous decrease in interest in cooperative solutions.

A number of factors influenced this perceived shift in interest. One factor that has important influence is what has come to be known as Nash program. It underpins axiomatic models in cooperative game theory with non-cooperative game models of an associated decision procedure. The Nash program involves modelling the offers and counter-offers leading to binding agreements as formal moves in a non-cooperative game. The 1951 paper of Nash in Annals of Mathematics contains the essence of this program. It states: A dynamic approach to the study of cooperative games based on reduction to non-cooperative form proceeds "... by constructing a model of the pre-play negotiation so that the steps of [this] negotiation become moves in a larger non-cooperative game...describing the total situation. This larger game is then treated in terms of the theory of this paper...and if values are obtained they are taken as the values of the cooperative game. Thus, the problem of analyzing a cooperative game becomes the problem of obtaining a suitable, and convincing, non-cooperative model for the negotiation."

Harsanyi and Selten made important contributions to the Nash program. Harsanyi's model is considered a dynamic n-person version of Nash's four stage bargaining model outlined above. The model developed by Harsanyi provides a better understanding of what are referred to as stable sets introduced by von Neumann and Morgenstern. Selten's model involves players successively making proposals for coalitions and payoff divisions until an offer is accepted by all coalition members. Harsanyi's and Selten's contributions to game theory are covered in the next two chapters.

The Nobel award recognises the central importance of game theory in current economic theory. The impact of Nash's contributions on economic theory is particularly highlighted in the press release awarding the Nobel Prize. The application of non-cooperative game theory in the analysis of oligopolistic market structures is highlighted in that trade legislation in many countries prohibits firms entering into binding contracts containing restrictive trade practices. The non-cooperative game theory is validly applicable for such situations. Further, in the design of government's tax policy, interaction among a government, special interest groups such as industry, agriculture and export-import groups and the general public is regarded as a non-cooperative game. Aumann considers the Nash equilibrium as, without doubt, the single game-theoretic solution concept that is most frequently applied in economics. According to him, economic applications include oligopoly, entry and exit, market equilibrium, search, location, bargaining, product quality, auctions, insurance, principal-agent problems, higher education, discrimination, public goods and so on. The press release also mentions the application of Nash equilibrium in macroeconomic policy, environmental and resource economics, foreign trade theory and information theory in order to improve our understanding of complex strategic interactions. The release also identifies new areas of research generated by non-cooperative game theory. It cites a specific example. In combination with the theory of repeated games, non-cooperative equilibrium concepts have been successfully used to explain the development of institutions and social norms.

The press release, while elaborating the usefulness of Nash's work, notes, at the same time, the problems associated with the concept of Nash equilibrium. If a game has several Nash equilibria (a reference has been made earlier to this), the criterion of equilibrium cannot be of immediate use in order to predict the outcome of the game. To remedy the situation, a number of refinements of the Nash equilibrium concept have been developed by later writers. Another limitation of the equilibrium concept is also noted. When interpreted in terms of rationality, the concept of equilibrium pre-supposes that each player has full information about the other players' situation. The contributions of Harsanyi and Selten have attempted to solve these problems.

57.3 OTHER CONTRIBUTIONS OF NASH

Nash's contribution to economics is, no doubt, significantly important. It is observed that ...on the conceptual side, he spawned much of the literature on non-cooperative game theory which has since grown at a prodigious rate-threatening, some claim, to overwhelm much of economics itself. His contributions to mathematics were no less remarkable. As an undergraduate at Princeton, Nash had "inadvertently (and independently)" proved

Brouwer's fixed point theorem. Later on, he solved Reimann's most perplexing mathematical conundrums.

Nash provided many breakthroughs in mathematics. In the interludes of what Nash calls "enforced rationality," he had done in his own words "some respectable mathematical research."

We should note that John Nash is rated a lot more brilliant mathematician and could have contributed a lot more to the field of mathematics, but for his battle with mental afflictions.

57.4 CONCLUDING OBSERVATIONS

Nash's influence on economic theory is widely acknowledged. As Kreps records "Nowadays one cannot find a field of economics... in which understanding of the concept of a Nash equilibrium is not nearly essential to the consumption of the recent literature. He is considered the master of Economic Modelling." According to Rubinstein "the art of economic theoretical modelling is the identification of simple structure which approximately represents the process by which people reason about a situation. Nash modelled interactive reasoning...[he] suggests a reasonable way to model such reasoning.... Nash demonstrates a clear principle: generalize the model only as long as the basic argument is not lost. Express the idea in a way that reveals the basic argument without trivialization of the proposition."

Maurice Preston states that the most fundamental parts of microeconomics are Nash equilibrium and the Kuhn-Tucker theorem. "The latter provides the basis for the whole theory of individual maximization and clarifies the concept of price, which is the essence of the decentralized markets." Nash offered a rigorous theory of equilibrium resulting from independent decision-making in a market context. "He offered a great leap along a path which started with Adam Smith and remained unfinished. To paraphrase Dr. Johnson, such a work of genius is so strongly embedded in literature, and taken so much for granted, that its originator, is forgotten." Preston's final assessment is that Nash's work meets the criteria of originality, significance and permanence. His bet for academic longevity is John Nash. However, Nash believes that he shared the 1994 Nobel Prize with Harsanyi and Selten for his "most trivial work."

We may give an extract from his Nobel Acceptance Speech.

"What truly is logic? Who decides reason? My quest has taken me to the physical, the metaphysical, the delusional and back. I've made the most important discovery of my career.... The most important discovery of my life. It is only in the mysterious equation of love that any logical reasons can be found. [Looking at Alicia] I'm only here tonight because of you. You're the only reason I am...You are all my reasons."

Nash's remarks about his madness and its consequences are sad, to say the least. Sylvia Nassar in her biography of Nash A Beautiful Mind, gives a poignant and vivid account of Nash, the tragedy of his personal life and the value of his contributions to economic theory. In Nassar's story, Alicia Nash, Nash's wife comes out as the true heroine. Nash associated his madness with living on an "ultralogical plane," "breathing air too rare" for most mortals and if being cured meant he could no longer do any original work at that level. Nash also sadly states that a remission from the disease might not be worthwhile in the end.

The chapter may be closed with a quote from Dryden's poem:

"Great wits are sure to madness near allied,

And thin partitions do their bounds divide."

57.5 SELECT BIBLIOGRAPHY OF NASH'S MAJOR WORKS

57.5.1 ARTICLES

1950 a "Equilibrium Points in N-Person Games," Proceedings of National Academy of Sciences, Vol.36.

b "The Bargaining Problem," Econometrica, Vol.18.

c (with L.S. Shapely), Annals of Mathematical Statistics, Vol.53.

1951 "Non-Cooperative Games," Annals of Mathematics, Vol.54, No.2.

1953 "Two-Person Cooperative Games," Econometrica, Vol.21, pp.128-140.

57.6 WORKS OF OTHERS

Arrow, K. and G. Debreu (1954), "Existence of Equilibrium for a Competitive Economy," Econometrica, Vol.22, No.3.

Aumann R. J. (1987), "Game Theory," in The New Palgrave: A Dictionary of Economics, The Concise Encyclopaedia of Economics (CEE), 2nd Edition, Macmillan, London.

Cournot, A. (1987), Researches into the Mathematical Principles of the Theory of Wealth, Macmillan, New York. (First published in 1838).

Damme, E. V. and J. W. Weibull (1995), "Equilibrium in Strategic Interaction: The Contributions of John C. Harsanyi, John F. Nash and Reinhard Selten," ScandJE, Vol.97, No.1.

Frangsmyr, T. (ed.) (1995), "The Work of John Nash in Game Theory," Les Prix Nobel, Nobel Foundation, Stockholm.

Harsanyi, J. (1994), "Games with Incomplete Information," Nobel Lecture, AER, Vol.85, No.3.

Nassar, S. (1998), A Beautiful Mind: A Biography of John Forbes Nash Jr., Simon & Schuster, New York.

Rubinstein, A. (1995), "John Nash: The Master of Economic Modeling," ScandJE, Vol.97, No.1.

CHAPTER 58

JOHN CHARLES HARSANYI

(1920 – 2000)

Professor John Charles Harsanyi shared the Nobel Memorial Prize in Economic Sciences for 1994 with John F. Nash Jr and Reinhard Selten for pioneering analysis of equilibria in the theory of non-cooperative games. Harsanyi was awarded the Prize for demonstrating how games of incomplete information could be analysed. His contribution lay in providing a theoretical foundation for a lively field of research - the economics of information – which focuses on strategic situations where different agents do not know each other's objectives. In games with complete information, all the players know the other players' preferences whereas in games with incomplete information, players do not have this knowledge, wholly or partially. No methods were available for analysis of games with incomplete information since the rationalistic interpretation of Nash equilibrium, as outlined in the preceding chapter, is based on the assumption that the players know each other's preferences. However in real world, games with incomplete information best reflect many strategic interactions.

Harsanyi published three articles in 1967- 1968 entitled "Games with Incomplete Information Played by Bayesian Players," which changed the situation radically. His approach to games with incomplete information may be viewed as the basis of nearly all economic analysis involving information, irrespective of whether the information is asymmetric, completely private or public.

According to Harsanyi, players in a game are of several "types." He postulated that every player belongs to one type or the other. Each type corresponds to a set of possible preferences for the player and a subjective probability distribution over the types of other players. In a game with incomplete information, every player chooses a strategy for each of his types. Under a consistency requirement on the players' probability distributions, Harsanyi showed that for every game with incomplete information, there exists an equivalent game with complete information. He then transformed games with incomplete information into games with imperfect information. Then, standard methods can be used for solving such games.

The press release provides an example of a situation with incomplete information. The example relates to trade-off between inflation and unemployment following Phillips Curve approach. The market cannot accurately predict the future interest policy of the central bank. As such, private firms and financial markets do not have precise knowledge of the central bank's preferences in regard to the trade-off between inflation and unemployment. The interactions between the formation of expectations by market participants and the central bank's policy can be usefully analysed employing the technique suggested by Harsanyi. In the simplest case, the policy of the central bank can be of two types with associated probabilities. The central bank may be planning to reduce unemployment by following lower interest rate policy or intends to combat inflation by pursuing a restrictive monetary policy. Another example where game theory using Harsanyi's technique can be applied pertains to regulation of a monopoly firm. As the regulator does not have accurate knowledge of the costs of the firm, the issue is what regulatory or contractual solution will yield a desirable outcome.

The main contributions of Harsanyi are outlined here. The joint contributions of Harsanyi and Selten are summarised in the next chapter. The press release announcing the award states that through their contributions to equilibrium analysis in non-cooperative game theory, the three laureates, Nash, Harsanyi and Selten constitute a natural combination.

58.1 A SHORT BIOGRAPHICAL NOTE: JOHN HARSANYI

John Charles Harsanyi was born in Budapest, Hungary on May 29, 1920. He studied in one of the best schools in Hungary with such distinguished alumni as John von Neumann and Eugene Wigner. In 1937, the year in which he passed out of the high school, Harsanyi won the first prize in Mathematics at the Hungary-wide annual competition for high school students.

When in 1937, he had to decide his field of study, he chose Pharmacy in line with his parents' wishes as they owned a pharmacy in Budapest. Additionally, he chose pharmacy since he (of Jewish origin) would obtain military deferment as a pharmacy student. He did have military deferment until the German army occupied Hungary in March 1944. Then he had to serve in a forced labour unit of the Hungarian army which was deported by the Nazi authorities from Budapest to an Austrian Concentration Camp "where most of my comrades eventually perished." Harsanyi was lucky to escape from the railway station in Budapest just before his train left for Austria. A Jesuit father gave him refuge in the cellar of their monastery. A clear picture of the tribulations Harsanyi passed through in that period is contained in the following write-up in The Concise Encyclopaedia of Economics: During his early years, Harsanyi escaped from two of the twentieth century's most vicious totalitarian regimes. He had wanted to study philosophy and mathematics but because he was of Jewish origin and saw Hitler's steady rising influence, Harsanyi took his parents' advice and became a pharmacy student, knowing that that would help him maintain a military deferment. In the language of game theory, he "looked forward and reasoned back." After the German army occupied Hungary, he worked in a "labour unit"--that is, he was a slave--from May to November 1944.When the German government tried to deport him to a concentration camp in Austria, Harsanyi escaped from the railway station in Budapest.

After the end of the Second World War, Harsanyi re-enrolled at the University of Budapest in order to obtain a Ph.D. in philosophy with minors in sociology and psychology. As he got credit for his prior studies in pharmacy, he got his Ph.D. in June 1947 after one more year of course work and after writing a dissertation in Philosophy.

Harsanyi worked as a junior faculty member at the University Institute of Sociology from September 1947 to June 1948. After Hungary became a communist country, he had to resign from the Institute because of his anti-Marxist views. In 1950, with his future wife, Harsanyi migrated to Australia where on January 2, 1951 he got married to Anne. As his English was not very good and as his Hungarian degrees were not recognised in Australia, Harsanyi had to work as a factory hand for several years. However, in the evening, he took economics courses at the University of Sydney. In his autobiographical note, Harsanyi stated: "I changed over from sociology to economics because I found the conceptual and mathematical elegance of economic theory very attractive." He received M.A. degree in economics in 1953 after two years of further coursework (he was given some credit for his Hungarian University courses) and after writing an M.A. thesis in economics.

Early in 1954, Harsanyi was appointed Lecturer in Economics at the University of Queensland in Brisbane. In 1956, he was awarded Rockefeller Fellowship to spend two years at Stanford University where Harsanyi got a second Ph.D. in Economics in 1959. In the autobiographical note, Harsanyi stated: "I had the good fortune of having Ken Arrow as advisor and dissertation supervisor. I benefited very much from discussing many finer points of economic theory with him. But I also benefitted substantially by following his advice to spend a sizable part of my Stanford time studying mathematics and statistics. These studies proved very useful in my later work in game theory."

Returning to Australia in 1958, Harsanyi got a very attractive research position at the Australian National University in Canberra. As game theory was virtually unknown at that time in Australia, he returned to U.S.A., as Professor of Economics at Wayne State University in Detroit. He got this appointment with the help of Arrow and Tobin. In 1964, he became at first a Visiting Professor and then Professor at Haas School of Business of the University of California in Berkley. Later in 1966, he accepted a joint appointment on the economics faculty of the University to the Department of Economics.

While still a student in early 1950's, Harsanyi published papers on the use of von Neumann-Morgenstern utility functions in welfare economics and in ethics and on the welfare economics of variable tastes. Harsanyi observed that his interest in game-theoretic problems "in a narrow sense" was first aroused by Nash's "four brilliant papers," published in the period 1950-1953, on cooperative and on non-cooperative games, on two-person bargaining games and on mutually optimal threat strategies in such games and on Nash equilibria.

As early as 1955, Harsanyi had pioneered the concept of "Veil of Ignorance;" though he did not give that name to the concept. The well-known philosopher, John Rawls, made famous this concept in his book, A Theory of Justice. Harsanyi was a strong votary of the rule of "utilitarianism" --the idea that the most ethical act is to follow the rule that will yield the most happiness.

In 1964, Harsanyi was asked to be one of ten game theorists to advise the United States Arms Control and Disarmament Agency on its negotiations with the then Soviet Union. The team found that it could not advise the U.S. negotiations effectively since neither side knows much about the other – it was a game of incomplete information. This led to Harsanyi developing a systematic procedure to convert any incomplete information game into an equivalent complete-information game containing random moves thereby significantly expanding the applicability of game theory to political and economic conflicts. In the late 1960's, he described this theory in a three-part article, "Games with Incomplete Information Played by Bayesian Players" which is now the basis for all work on games with incomplete information.

Harsanyi retired from University of California, Berkley, in 1990. He did path-breaking work in game theory; he made important contribution to the fields of ethics, social choice and welfare economics.

Harsanyi received a number of awards, besides Noble Memorial Prize for Economics. He was elected a Fellow of the Econometric Society. He was a Distinguished Fellow of the American Economic Association. In 1965-66, he was a Fellow of the Center for Advanced Study in the Behavioral Sciences at Stanford. He was a member of the National Academy of Sciences, U.S.A. Harsanyi was awarded honorary doctorates by many Universities around the world.

Harsanyi died of a heart attack on 9th August 2000 at his home in Berkley, California, at the age of 80 after suffering for a time from Alzheimer's disease.

58.2 AN OUTLINE OF HARSANYI'S CONTRIBUTIONS TO GAME THEORY

In the early stages of the development of game theory, each player is assumed to have full details of the rules of the game as also the pay-off functions of the other players; that is, the game-theoretic models were essentially confined to situations of complete information. Von Neumann and Morgenstern state in their book : "...[we assume] that all subjects of the economy under consideration are completely informed about the physical characteristics of the situation in which they operate and are able to perform all statistical and mathematical, etc. operations which knowledge makes this possible...we propose not to enter upon [the discussion of this assumption]. The question is too vast and too difficult and we believe that it is best 'to drive difficulties.'"

Luce and Raiffa in their book Games and Decisions highlight the importance of this restrictive assumption and remark that "...this is a serious idealization which only rarely is met in actual situations." While the restrictive nature of this full information assumption was noted, the non-availability of requisite tools for handling such situations prevented any advance in tackling it till late 1960's.

In the period 1965-1969, as mentioned earlier, the U. S. Army Control and Disarmament Agency, employed a group of about ten young game theorists as consultants. It was as a member of this group that Harsanyi developed a "simple" approach to the analysis of games with incomplete information. In his Nobel lecture "Games with Incomplete Information," Harsanyi explained that lack of information about the mathematical structure of a game may take many different forms. "The players lack full information about the other players' (or even their own) pay-off functions, about the physical or the social resources or about the strategies available to other players (or even to themselves), or about the amount of information the other players have about the various aspects of the game, and so on." He put forward Bayesian approach to the analysis of such games. Under the Bayesian approach, all uncertainty is explicitly spelled out and is quantified.

Harsanyi termed games with incomplete information as I-games (distinguished from C-games, games with complete information). In the case of the former, Harsanyi stated that two alternative assumptions can be made. The first one is player-centred interpretation of the I-game, whereas the other approach which he called type-centred in which the centres of activity are the various "types" of players. A player's type specifies all information that a player has about the game. Particularly, it specifies a probability distribution over the set of possible types of the other players involved in the game.

Damme and Weibull explain the game as given below.

"Harsanyi defines a Bayesian game as a tuple, I, S_i, T, U, P.

where

I is the player set,

S_i is the strategy set for player i,

T = $X_i T_i$ where T_i is the set of types of player I,

U = (U_i) I with U_i: SRT (R being the payoff function of this player; and

P_2 (P_i) with P_i (t-I, t_i) being the posterior belief of type t_i of Player I concerning the types t-I = (t_1..., t_{i+1}, t_{i+1},... t_n) of the other players.

A Bayesian (Nash) equilibrium specifies a strategy for each type such that each type maximises its conditional expected payoffs taking the other types' strategies as given."

Harsanyi suggested that a further simplification is possible if belief of the players about each others' types can be derived from a common prior distribution on the product space of types in the game; that is "...if there exists a probability distribution Q on T such that Q (t-i / ti) = Pi (t-i ; ti) for all t." It is referred to as a "consistent" case; there exists a simple game of complete, but imperfect information which is equivalent to the original game of incomplete information.

The distinction between games with perfect information and those with imperfect information has to be noted. In his Nobel lecture, Harsanyi explained this distinction. In games with perfect information, all players will have full information at every stage of the game about all moves made at earlier stages of the game, including "both personal moves and chance moves." In contrast, in games with imperfect information, "at some stage(s) of the game, the players or at least some of them, will have only partial information or none at all at some move(s) made at earlier stages." For example, games, such as chess and checkers, belong to the first category, as they are games with perfect information since the players are allowed to observe their own moves as well as the moves of the other player. In games, such as most card games, players are not permitted to see or observe the cards the other players have received from the dealer or to observe the discarded cards of other players with their faces down. Such games are games with imperfect information.

The simple consistent game of complete but imperfect information outlined above commences with a chance move that informs each player of his type; thereafter players choose actions. Since there exist differences in the information players have, the players have also differences in their beliefs. As a result, a carefully constructed model has to be consistent – this position is what is called Harsanyi doctrine. This consistent model has been widely applied.

An example of the application of the case is given by Damme and Weibull. Let us assume that two players, a buyer and a seller, are conducting negotiations for the sale of an asset. The buyer has information about the price he is willing to pay for the asset and the seller has information about his reservation value for the asset. A strategy plan for the two players can be shown to be a Bayesian (Nash) equilibrium if and only if each player maximises his expected revenue for each realisation of his own value. "In equilibrium the buyer 'shades' his offer below his true reservation price and the seller's strategy calls for a 'mark up,' with the consequence that not all possible gains from trade are exploited.... In fact, it can be shown that, no matter how one constructs the rules of the trading games, the gains from trade will not be fully exploited." In equilibrium, such a loss does not arise, in a corresponding game of complete information. Thus, it is clear that Harsanyi's method helps in identifying welfare losses on account of incompleteness of information in situations of strategic interaction.

The work of Harsanyi is regarded as the basis for nearly all economic analysis involving differential information, which is currently an active area in economic theory that underlines the greatness of Harsanyi's conceptual innovation for games with incomplete information. Furthermore, Harsanyi's construction of games with incomplete information has general application in that any incomplete information game can be represented by a Bayesian game.

Another important contribution to game theory by Harsanyi related to his providing a basis for mixed strategy equilibria. Sometimes rational play cannot in general be described by specifying a single pure strategy. Such a game is often non-deterministic with particular probabilities associated with each one of a specified set of pure strategies. Then the players have to employ mixed or randomised strategies, that is, probability distributions over pure strategies. When randomised strategies are used, expected pay-off replaces pay-off. The theory of expected utility was developed for using the concept of expected pay-off in this context, though the theory has been used elsewhere too.

For the purpose of establishing Nash equilibrium, Nash adopted the concept of mixed strategies; that is, probability distributions over pure strategies originally introduced by von Neumann and Morgenstern. The interpretation of mixed strategies as deliberate acts of active randomisation by players to decide on their actions has always had difficulties. Neumann observed: "Practically speaking, the idea that serious people would base important decisions on the flip of a coin [a randomising device] is difficult to swallow." There are conceptual problems as well. A player needs to randomise in equilibrium only for the purpose of keeping other players from deviating. "...He will do as well by choosing any pure strategy that appears with positive probability in this equilibrium mixed strategy."

L. J. Savage in his The Foundations of Statistics says that randomness represents the decision-maker's ignorance. A player 'I' associates a probability with every event in regard to which he is ignorant. What is important in strategy randomisation is that other players are ignorant of what player 'I' is doing and that they ascribe the appropriate probabilities to each of I's pure strategies. It is not necessary that player 'I' should actually make a strategic choice. Harsanyi was the first to break away from the idea of "explicit randomization." He gave a Bayesian interpretation of mixed strategies. According to him, a mixed strategy of player 'I' is seen as indicating the ignorance 'I's opponents have as to what 'I' is actually going to do. Harsanyi demonstrated that if the pay-offs of each player in a game are subject to "small independent random perturbations" known to player 'I' but not to other players, the resulting game of incomplete information has pure strategy equilibria that correspond to the mixed strategy equilibria of the original game. Aumann observes: "In plain words, nobody really randomizes. The appearance of randomization is due to the pay-offs not being exactly known to all; each player, who does not know his own pay-off exactly, has a unique optimal action against his estimate of what others will do." Thus, mixed strategies denote ignorance and should not be taken to be acts of conscious randomisation.

58.3 CONCLUDING OBSERVATIONS

The essentials of the main contributions to game theory have been summarized here. Harsanyi had also made important contributions to the foundations of welfare economics and to the area on the boundary between economics and moral philosophy.

In the banquet speech, Harsanyi expressed his great satisfaction at international recognition to game theory as an important branch of economic analysis. He also stated that up to the mid-1970's "...game theory was so little known by the educated public that one of the very distinguished university libraries actually classified von Neumann and Morgenstern's book under the surprising heading of 'Games and Physical Exercises.'"

On his death, flowing tributes were paid to Harsanyi. The Dean of Haas School with which he was associated had this to say: "John Harsanyi dedicated his life to employ the science of economics and game theory for the betterment of the human race.... He was a brilliant thinker, a gracious man, and a gentle soul...." Another tribute by a colleague: "...Harsanyi's work was instrumental in making economic theory 'fit' the imperfect world in which we live. His development of game theory showed how differences in the information available to economic actors affect market outcomes and economic welfare. His seminal works form the basis for all modern analyses of industrial organization, and they have real practical implications in business and government policy."

58.4 SELECT BIBLIOGRAPHY OF HARSANYI'S MAJOR WORKS

58.4.1 BOOKS

1976 Essays on Ethics, Social Behavior and Scientific Explanation, D. Reidel, Dordrecht.

1977 Rational Behavior and Bargaining Equilibrium in Games and Social Situations, Cambridge University Press, New York.

1982 Papers in Game Theory, D. Reidel, Dordrecht.

1988 (with R. Selten), A General Theory of Equilibrium Selection in Games, MIT Press, Cambridge, MA.

58.4.2 ARTICLES

1953 "Cardinal Utility in Welfare Economics and in the Theory of Risk-taking," JPE, Vol.61, pp.434-435.

1953-54 "Welfare Economics of Variable Tastes," RES, Vol.21, No.3.

1955 "Cardinal Welfare, Individualistic Ethics and Interpersonal Comparisons of Utility," JPE, Vol.63, pp.309-321.

1956 "Approaches to the Bargaining Problem Before and After the Theory of Games: A Critical Discussion of Zeuthen's, Hick's and Nash's Theories," Econometrica, Vol.24, No.2.

1963 "A Simplified Bargaining Model for the n-Person Cooperative Games," IER, Vol.4, No.2.

1967-1968 "Games with Incomplete Information Played by 'Bayesian' Players," Parts I to III, Management Science, Vol.14, Nos. 3, 5, & 7.

1973 a "Oddness of the Number of Equilibrium Points: A New Proof," International Journal of Game Theory, Vol.2, No.1.

b "Games with Randomly Distributed Pay offs: A New Rationale for Mixed Strategy Equilibrium Points," International Journal of Game Theory, Vol.2. No.1.

1975 a "The Tracing Procedure: A Bayesian Approach to Defining a Solution for n-Person Noncooperative Games," International Journal of Game Theory, Vol.4, pp.61-94.

b "Non-linear Social Welfare Function: Do Welfare Economists Have a Special Exemption from Bayesian Rationality?" Theory and Decision, Vol.6.

1978 "Bayesian Decision Theory and Utilitarian Ethics," AER, Vol.68, No.2.

1979 "Bayesian Decision Theory, Rule Utilitarianism, and Arrow's Impossibility Theorem," Theory and Decision, Vol.11.

1982 a "Solutions for Some Bargaining Games under the Harsanyi – Selten Solution Theory, Part I: Theoretical Preliminaries," Mathematical Social Sciences, Vol.3, No.2.

b "Solution for Some Bargaining Games under the Harsanyi-Selten Solution Theory, Part II; Analysis of Specific Bargaining Games," Mathematical Social Sciences, Vol.3, No.3.

1986 "Utilitarian Morality in a World of Very Half-Hearted Altruists," in Social Choice and Public Decision Making: Essays in Honor of K. J. Arrow, Vol.1, Heller, W. P. et al., (eds.) Cambridge University Press, New York.

1987 "von Neumann – Morgenstern Utilities, Risk Taking and Welfare," in Arrow and Ascent of Modern Economic Theory, Feiwel G. R. (ed.) New York University Press, New York.

1988 "Assessing other People's Utilities," in Risk, Decision and Rationality, Munier, B. E. (ed.) D. Reidel, Dordrecht.

1991 "Equality, Responsibility and Justice As Seen from a Utilitarian Perspective," Theory and Decision, Vol.31, No.2-3.

1995 a "Games with Incomplete Information," Nobel Lecture, AER, Vol. 85, No.3.

b "A New Theory of Equilibrium Selection for Games with Incomplete Information," Games and Economic Behavior, Vol.10, No.2.

c "Games and Decision Theoretic Models in Ethics," in Handbook of Game Theory, Vol.1, Aumann, R. J. and S. Hart (eds.), Elsevier, Amsterdam.

1996 "Utilities, Preferences and Substantive goals," Social Choice and Welfare, Springer, Vol.14, No.1.

58.5 WORKS OF OTHERS

Aumann, R. J. (1987), "Game Theory," in The New Palgrave: A Dictionary of Economics, Macmillan, London.

Damme, E. V. and J. W. Weibull (1995), "Equilibrium in Strategic Interaction: The Contributions of John C. Harsanyi, John F. Nash and Reinhard Selten," ScandJE, Vol.97, No.1.

Kreps, D. M. (1990), Game Theory and Economic Modelling, Oxford University Press, Oxford.

Luce, R. D. and H. Raiffa (1957), Games and Decisions, Wiley, New York.

Neumann, J. von and O. Morgenstern (1947), Theory of Games and Economic Behavior, Princeton University Press, Princeton, NJ. First edition 1944.

Savage, L. J. (1954), The Foundations of Statistics, John Wiley, New York.

Schelling, T. C. (1960), The Strategy of Conflict, Harvard University Press, Cambridge, MA.

The Concise Encyclopaedia of Economics (CEE), 2nd Edition.

CHAPTER 59

REINHARD SELTEN

(1930 –)

Professor Reinhard Selten shared the Nobel Memorial Prize in Economic Sciences for the year 1994 with John F. Nash and John C. Harsanyi for the pioneering analysis of equilibria in the theory of non-cooperative games. Selten was the first to refine the Nash equilibrium concept for analysing dynamic strategic analyses of competition with a few sellers – oligopoly market structure.

In the chapter on Nash, we have seen that a game can have several equilibria. This problem of numerous non-cooperative equilibria has generated a research program with a view to eliminating "uninteresting" Nash equilibria. This has been accomplished by using stronger conditions to reduce the number of possible equilibria besides avoiding equilibria that are unreasonable in economic terms. For this purpose, Selten introduced the concept of sub-game perfection. The concept may be explained by an example given in the press release announcing the award. Assume a monopoly market into which a potential entrant is deterred by threats of a price war. If the potential entrant or would-be competitor takes the threat seriously, his optimal strategy would be to stay out of the market or refrain from entering the market. The monopolist does not incur any cost as he need not carry out the threat. Then this may well be Nash equilibrium. If the monopolist faces substantial costs in a price war, then the threat is not credible. A potential competitor or potential entrant who realises this, will enter the market and the existing monopolist, confronted with fait accompli, will not start a price war. This situation is also a Nash equilibrium. Besides, it fulfils Selten's requirement of sub-game perfection. That is, sub-game perfection implies systematic formalisation of the requirement that only credible threats be taken into account.

Selten's concept of sub-game perfection has direct relevance in discussions of credibility in economic policy, the economics of information, analysis of oligopoly markets and so on. It is the most important refinement of Nash equilibrium. There are, however, situations where not even the requirement of sub-game perfection is sufficient. To tackle such situations, Selten has introduced a further refinement; that is referred to as the "trembling-hand" equilibrium. The analysis assumes that each player pre-supposes a small probability that a mistake will occur, "that someone's hand will tremble." A Nash equilibrium in a game is "trembling-hand perfect" if it is robust with respect to small probabilities of such mistakes. The press release states this as well as closely related concepts such as sequential equilibrium have proved to be very fruitful in several areas, including the theory of industrial organisation and macroeconomic theory for economic policy.

59.1 A BRIEF BIOGRAPHIAL SKETCH: REINHARD SELTEN

Reinhard Selten was born in Breslau (belonged to Germany then), now called Wroclaw, on 10th October 1930 in Lower Silesia, now in Poland to a Jewish father and Protestant mother. When he was born his father owned a business called a "reading circle," folders containing an assortment of magazines that were lent to customers for one week, then recollected and lent out again. Selten's father had to sell his firm because of his Jewish origin. Jews were forbidden to run a business connected to the press. The elder Selten died after a serious illness in 1942. In his autobiographical note, Selten states that it was not easy for him to live as a half-Jewish boy under the Hitler regime. At the age of 14, he had to leave high school and the opportunity to learn a trade was denied to him. The only career open to him was that of an unskilled worker. He says: "Fortunately it turned out that this did not matter much since after about half a year, my mother, my brothers and I left Breslau on one of the last trains before all outbound railway traffic stopped."

His situation as a member of an officially despised minority forced Selten to pay close attention to political matters very early in life. Moreover, he had to learn to trust his own judgement, rather than official propaganda or public opinion, which was a strong influence on his intellectual development. His continuing interest in politics and public affairs was one of the reasons for his interest in economics in his last school years.

After leaving Breslau, Selten and his mother with other members of the family moved as refugees from place to place settling down finally in Melsungen where he went to high school until 1951. In these years he developed a strong interest in mathematics. He had to walk to school which took about three and a half hours, then and back. When Selten finished highs school, he had decided to study mathematics. He studied mathematics at the University of Frankfurt from 1951 to 1957. Selten was permitted to take mathematical economics as a minor for the Master's degree – the first one to make this choice.

In his last high school year, Selten happened to read a popular article on game theory in Fortune magazine. He was immediately attracted to the subject matter. Later, when he studied mathematics, he read von Neumann and Morgenstern's book on game theory. Sometime later, Selten participated in a student seminar for economists on game theory headed by Professor Ewald Burger. Burger, who was a man of "extraordinary mathematical erudition and an excellent teacher," allowed Selten to write a master's thesis in cooperative game theory. Selten says that he owes much to Burger's guidance and his patient advice.

Selten's Master's thesis and later his Ph.D. thesis had the aim of "axiomatizing a value for e-person games in extensive forms." This enabled him to see the perfectness problem earlier than others and to write the contributions for which "I am now honored by the prize in memory of Alfred Nobel." After he received Master's degree in 1957, Professor Heinz Sauermann, an economist at the University of Frankfurt, helped Selten by associating him in his research, funded by the German counterpart of National Science Foundation of U.S. Selten became involved in economic laboratory experimentation. Selten observes: "...Sauermann was a remarkable man. He was one of the first to propagate Keynesianism in Germany. In spite of a lack of mathematical training he encouraged his students to work on formal models...[he] did much for the propagation of experimental economics. I owe much to him." In 1951, Selten published an article on oligopoly experiment, (An Experimental Approach to Oligopoly) written together with Sauermann.

Selten received his Ph.D. in mathematics at the University of Frankfurt. Oskar Morgenstern's visit to Frankfurt had facilitated Selten's participation in a game theory conference at Princeton, where he could interact with R.J. Aumann (Economics Nobel laureate) and M. M. Maschler. Impressed by H.A. Simon's (another Nobel laureate), Selten tried to construct a theory of boundedly rational multi-goal decision-making. Jointly with Sauermann, Selten worked out an "aspiration adaptation theory of the firm" published as a journal article in 1962. However, Selten was convinced that the structure of bounded by rational economic behaviour cannot be invented in armchair; it must be explored experimentally.

In his autobiographical note, Selten states: "In the early 1960's I had run experiments on oligopoly game with demand inertia. A game- theoretic analysis of this model proved to be too difficult but I was able to solve a simplified version." He found a natural equilibrium but the game has many other equilibria. In order to describe the distinguishing features of his solution, he defined sub-game perfectness. His paper, "An Oligopoly Model with Demand Inertia" was published in 1965. He states: "I did not suspect that it often would be quoted, almost exclusively for the definition of sub-game perfectness." In a paper published in 1975, he defined a refined notion of perfectness – referred to now as "trembling hand perfectness."

As mentioned in the Chapter on Harsanyi, Selten became a member of a group of game theorists, hired by a research firm MATHEMATICA (of which Harsanyi was a member) to work on projects for the Arms Control and Disarmament Agency. Selten worked in collaboration with Harsanyi on bargaining under incomplete information; he also worked on models of nuclear deterrence.

In Germany, for a career as a University teacher, after obtaining Ph.D. one is expected to work towards a "habilitation" presenting a habilitation thesis for this purpose. Selten prepared a monograph on multiproduct pricing which was published as a book in 1970. In the academic year 1967-1968, he was visiting professor at the business school of the University of California, Berkley. In 1969 he became professor of economics at Free University of Berlin in which he continued till 1972. In that year he moved to University of Bielefeld, attracted by plans to create a big Institute of Mathematical Economics.

Eventually a small institute with three professors of game theory was established because of paucity of funds.

Selten's years at the University of Bielefeld were productive. Though his experimental research progressed there, Selten mainly worked on game theory and its application to industrial organisation. Besides, jointly with Harsanyi, he worked on constructing a reasonable general theory of equilibrium selection in games. The work, which took 18 years, culminated in a book published in 1988. Prior to it, in 1974 he published a book on multiproduct pricing, the product of a collaborative effort with Tom Marschak of University of California, Berkley, where the first computerised laboratory for experimental economics was built up. The Centre for Inter- disciplinary Research at the University of Bielefeld facilitated his contact with biologists and in his development of a strong interest in biological game theory. One of Selten's important contributions to this field is the investigation of evolutionary stability in extensive games.

In 1984, Selten moved to the University of Bonn as Professor of Economics with the intention of building up there a computerised laboratory for experimental economics. At Bonn, Selten's and most of his assistants' work was concentrated on experimental economics. "It is a goal to build up a descriptive branch of decision and game theory which takes the limited rationality of human behavior seriously."

Selten holds several honorary doctoral degrees. He is currently Professor Emeritus at the University of Bonn.

59.2 A BRIEF SUMMARY OF SELTEN'S CONTRIBUTIONS

In game theory, reference is made to extensive and strategic forms of a game. The extensive form of a game, consists of a complete formal description of how the game is played, with a specification of the sequence of players' moves, the knowledge they have at the time of the move, the way chance occurrences enter the picture, and each player's pay-off at the end of play. The strategic form of a game, on the other hand implies, given strategies for each of the n players, the rules of the game determine a unique outcome as well as pay-off for each player.

According to von Neumann and Morgenstern the two forms of the game are equivalent since a rational player should have no difficulty in deciding in advance for all possible contingencies. As such, a researcher can choose to work with either. However, as the strategic form is analytically simple and is better suited for derivation of general theorems, the extensive form is beneficially used for analysis of particular games. Nash in his work has employed strategic form to prove the existence of equilibrium. As each game in extensive form can be represented in strategic form, there is an implication from Nash's existence theorem that any finite extensive form game has at least one equilibrium.

Selten disputed the equivalence of the two game forms. The essence of his argument is that players in an extensive game could not be committed to their strategies in advance and such commitment is to a certain extent assumed in any analysis of a strategic form game. Selten further contends that the impossibility of self commitment would lead to questioning certain Nash equilibria as reasonable solutions.

In support of the above argument, Selten gives an example (as given in Damme and Weibull's 1995 article in the Scandinavian Journal). It is illustrated below.

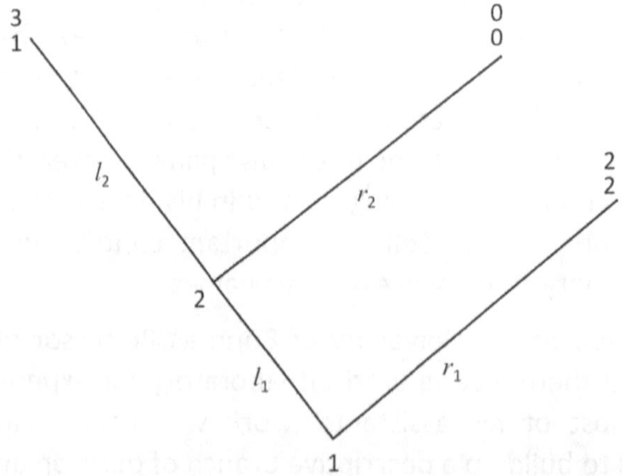

Fig. 59.1 Example of Sub-Game

The game proceeds as given here. Player 1 decides between strategies labelled ℓ_1 and r_1. If he chooses r_1, the game ends and each player receives pay-off 2. If, however, player 1 chooses alternative ℓ_1, player 2 has to choose between ℓ_2 and r_2. If player 2 chooses ℓ_2, player 1 receives 3 and player 2 receives 1. In case player 2 chooses r_2, each player has zero pay-off. It is seen that this game has two equilibria in pure strategies, namely, $L = (\ell_1, \ell_2)$ and $R = (r_1, r_2)$. Interpretation of equilibrium R requires that player 2 has to put forward a threat before the game commences that he could play r_2 with a view to inducing player 1 to play r_1. Since player 2 cannot commit himself to actually carrying out the threat, it is an empty threat. As the game is non-cooperative, player 2's self commitment is not possible. In view of player 1's choice of ℓ_1, player 2's optimal response is to play ℓ_2. Thus, only this equilibrium is "reasonable" as playing ℓ_1 is optimal for player 1.

The above example is what is called a sub-game; that is, it is a game by itself which is, however, part of a game. According to Selten, when players cannot commit themselves to a choice, behaviour in a game should amount to an equilibrium of the sub-game. "Otherwise, if there would exist a sub-game in which the solution does not constitute an equilibrium, then at least one player would have an incentive to deviate from that situation if the sub-game were actually reached, and the solution would not be self-enforcing." Selten calls them sub-game perfect equilibria. In Fig. 59.1 L is the only sub-game perfect equilibrium.

The concept of sub-game perfectness is used by Selten for solving an oligopoly game with demand inertia. According to him, the demand for the product of an oligopolistic firm depends not only on the prices set by firms in the current period but also on the market shares of the preceding period. Selten finds out a sub-game perfect equilibrium by using a dynamic programming technique for a finite horizon case; for the infinite horizon problem by investigating the limit of the finite horizon case. In establishing sub-game perfect equilibria, Selten uses what is called a backward induction procedure. It may be recalled that von Neumann and Morgenstern were against this approach as it presupposes rational behaviour of all players. They argued: "...if the superiority of 'rational behaviour' over any other kind is to be established, then its description must include rules of conduct for all conceivable situations-including those where the 'others' behaved irrationally."

Aumann observes: "In analyzing specific economic models using the strategic equilibrium...it was found that Nash's definition does not provide adequately for rational choices given one's information at each stage of an extensive game. Very roughly, the reason is that Nash's definition ignores contingencies 'off the equilibrium path.' To remedy this, various 'refinements' of strategic equilibrium have been defined, starting with Selten's (1975) 'trembling hand' equilibrium."

While recognising conceptual difficulties with the assumption of "persistent rationality," Selten contends that the concept of sub-game perfectness permits some "unreasonable" equilibria to survive. In the words of Damme and Weibull, "...Selten's ingenious suggestion for resolving both difficulties at once is to view the perfect rationality as a limiting case of incomplete rationality by introducing the possibility that players may make slight mistakes when implementing their desired actions." Selten argues: "There cannot be any mistakes if the players are absolutely rational. Nevertheless, a satisfactory interpretation of equilibrium points in extensive games seems to require that the possibility of mistakes is not completely excluded. This can be achieved by a point of view which looks at complete rationality as a limiting case of incomplete rationality."

The essence of Selten's argument is that players who are rational while making decisions, have to contend with the possibility of irrational play and the game which is termed a "perturbed game" takes the players' mistakes explicitly into account. Selten defines trembling hand perfect equilibrium "if it is the limit of some sequence of Nash equilibria in perturbed games in which the error probabilities tend to zero, hence, the equilibrium can be rationalized by some form of slight irrationality."

Dynamic games refer to games played in stages, with some kind of stationary time structure. They include repeated game with or without complete information, stochastic games, games of survival, recursive games and games with varying opponents. We may recall that the fathers of game theory, von Neumann and Morgenstern, stressed that their analysis refers to what they called "one-shot" games, games that are played just once, after which the players disperse, never to interact again. When this is not the case, according to Aumann, "one must view the whole situation – including expected future interactions of the same players – as a single larger game, and it, too, is to be played just once." This seems to be unreasonable. If it is taken literally, there would be need to analyse only one game "...whose players include all persons ever born and to be born." Savage in his discussion of one person decisions states that one should "envisage every conceivable policy for the government of his whole life in its most minute details, and decide here and now on one policy. This is utterly ridiculous...."

Repeated games model the psychological and informational side of ongoing relationships. The relevant theory predicts phenomena, such as cooperation, obtrusion, trust, revenge and punishment that are generally called subjective informational phenomena, as also objective informational phenomena like secrecy. While the former relates to information about players' behaviour, the latter concerns signalling of substantive information.

Selten's Prize lecture was titled "Multistage Game Models and Delay Supergames." He defined multistage game "as a structure built up of four constituents, a start s, a choice set function A, a probability assignment P, and a pay-off function h...." 's' represents the situation before the start of the game. The choices available to the players in every situation that may arise in the game are described by the choice set function (A). While P (the probability assignment) gives probabilities to random choice, the pay-off function (h) specifies the pay-offs at the end of the game.

That is, a multistage game,

$$G = (s, A, P, h),$$

where s, A, P and h are as defined above.

Further, Selten puts forward a definition of bounded multistage game. A multistage game G is called 'bounded' if in G the length of a path is bounded from above. "Obviously in such games a maximum length M of a path exists which implies that there is a random stopping condition: U = M, where U is a positive integer, as there are no pre-plays U with $|U| \geq M$.

In some game models, the players make simultaneous decisions on each of a number of successive stages, always fully informed regarding what has been done in the previous stages. Selten in his 1973 paper concerning oligopoly model posits that the players in the participation stage decide whether they desire to take part in cartel bargaining. This stage is followed by a cartel bargaining resulting in agreement on quota cartels. The third and last stage is a supply decision stage in which quantities of production are fixed and agreed upon. Selten argues that multistage games can be analysed using the concept of sub-game perfect equilibrium, the simplest refinement of ordinary game- theoretic equilibrium suggested by Nash's work. In the oligopoly model given above, Selten imposes additional selection criteria, such as symmetry and local efficiency and shows that "... upto 4 competitors always form a cartel whereas in the presence of 6 or more competitors, the probability of cartel formation is less than 2%."

Further, in some cases it may be appropriate to consider the stages of a multistage game model as decision points in time, while other models may not envisage treating decision-making in a fixed time order. For example, in the two stage duopoly model, production capacity decisions are made in the first stage while second stage decision involves imposing Bertrand price competition. This model, suggested by Kreps and Scheinkman, places capacity choice decisions in the first stage which are considered to be long term decisions that are fixed whereas price choice decisions which are placed in the second stage are considered short-term decisions. Selten remarks: "Term length than time is the basis for determining the order of stages.... The term length interpretation looks at multistage model as a condensed description of an ongoing situation in which stage decisions are not made once and for all. Strategic variables may change over time, but more short term decisions are in some way subordinated to more long term ones."

Selten observes that one could look at a multistage game model as representing the structure of a period in a super game, which implies that one sticks to the direct temporal interpretation of the order of stages. In the Prize lecture, he provides an explicit model of the underlying situation involved in the term length interpretation. There could be a number of interpretations for capacity decisions as long term and price decisions as short term. Selten, in his lecture offers an explanation which focuses on the delay between the time a decision is made and the time at which it becomes effective. The delay may be "two years" for capacity adjustments and only "one day" for price adjustments. The longer the delay the more long term the decision is considered to be. He elaborates the term length interpretation by looking at differences of delay in time required for a decision to become effective. The underlying ongoing situation is modelled by him as a "delay super game" in which "decisions on all strategic variables are made at the same time, period after period, but these decisions become effective with different delays." Thus in period t, decisions on the price in t+1 and capacity in t+1 may be made on both variables at the same time and simultaneously by all players. In addition, the players have full information about the play's previous history but not about simultaneous decisions made by other players. All decisions made by players in a period become publicly known at the beginning of the next period. For the analysis of delay super-games, the length of delays does not matter; what matters is the order of the decision variables with respect to the delay length.

According to Selten it is not necessary that the delay super-game be played for a fixed number of periods; the definition involves a probability distribution over the number of periods played. He draws a distinction between "bounded" delay super game and an "unbounded" one which is a game that is theoretically important. If the number of periods in which a game played has a finite upper bound, the game is called bounded delay super game; otherwise, it is an unbounded delay super game. Selten states: "Every sub-game perfect equilibrium of a bounded multistage game always generates a sub-game perfect equilibrium for every one of its bounded or unbounded delay super-games.... The generated equilibrium can roughly be described as the repeated application of the multistage game equilibrium strategies in every period played. In general, a delay super-game and especially an unbounded one may have many additional sub-game perfect equilibria.... Since normal form games are special multistage games with only one stage, super games are special delay super-games." This is the first main conclusion of the Prize lecture.

The second main conclusion is as follows: A sub-game perfect equilibrium set is a set of sub-game perfect equilibria all of which yield the same pay-offs not only in the entire game but also in each of its sub-games. A multistage game or delay super game is termed determinate when the set of all of its sub-game perfect equilibria is a sub-game perfect equilibrium set. In addition, every bounded delay super-game of a determinate bounded multistage game is determinate. Furthermore, Selten observes that under which conditions behaviour in a delay super-game converges to a sub-game perfect equilibrium of the underlying multistage game is an empirical question.

In their 1987 joint work A General Theory of Equilibrium Selection in Games, Harsanyi and Selten developed the theory for selecting one unique equilibrium from the set of all Nash equilibria, since, in general, a game may admit more than one Nash equilibrium. According to them "the basic task of game theory is to tell us what strategies rational players will follow and what expectations they can rationally entertain about each other...these problems must be solved jointly since for a player's strategy to be a rational strategy, it must be a best reply to his rational expectations about the other player's strategies." They argue that since these rational expectations are based entirely on the structure of the game and are "strictly endogenous," the game's solution must be independent of the context in which the game arises. They reiterate the applicability of the principle of sub-game consistency which is a strong form of the persistent rationality requirement. Thus, they show that the analyst can find the solution of an extensive form game by backward induction.

In case of games given in strategic form, Harsanyi and Selten put forward a theory the essence of which is a procedure helpful in selecting a unique equilibrium in each situation giving rise to two equilibrium candidates. The process consists of elimination and substitution grounded in dominance relationships between equilibria.

59.3 CONCLUDING OBSERVATIONS

Besides his main contributions to game theory outlined above, Selten has contributed powerful new insights relating to evolutionary games and experimental game theory.

The press release of Royal Swedish Academy of Sciences sums up the contributions of Nash, Harsanyi and Selten to the game theory. Through their contributions to equilibrium analysis in non-cooperative game theory, the three laureates constitute a natural combination: Nash provided the foundations for the analysis, while Selten developed it with respect to dynamics, and Harsanyi with respect to incomplete information. In this context, Damme and Weibull remark: "Reinhard Selten was the first to refine the Nash equilibrium concept for analysis of strategic dynamic interactions.... Selten's formalization of the requirement that only credible threats should be taken into account, the concept of sub-game perfect equilibrium, is widely used in the industrial organization literature and has led to important insight there as well as in other fields of economics." Furthermore, Harsanyi and Selten have been credited with the construction of the first coherent theory of equilibrium selection.

59.4 SELECT BIBLIOGRAPHY OF REINHARD SELTEN'S CONTRIBUTIONS

59.4.1 BOOKS

1974 (with T. Marshack), General Equilibrium with Price-Making Firms, Springer-Verlag, New York.

1988 a (with J. C. Harsanyi), A General Theory of Equilibrium Selection in Games, MIT Press, Cambridge, MA.

b Models of Strategic Rationality, Theory and Decision Library, Series C: Game Theory, Mathematic Programming and Operations Research, Kluwer Academic Publishers, Boston, MA.

1999 Game Theory and Economic Behavior: Selected Essays, 2 Vols, Edward Elgar Publishing, Cheltenham, Northampton, MA.

59.4.2 ARTICLES

1973 "A Simple Model of Imperfect Competition where 4 are Few and 6 are Many," IJGT, Vol. 2 (Reprinted in Selten, R.) Models of Strategic Rationality, 1988.

1978 "The Chain Store Paradox," Theory and Decision, Vol.9 (Reprinted in Selten, R. Models of Strategic Rationality), Kluwer Academic Publishers, Boston, MA.

1983 "Evolutionary Stability in Extensive Two-Part Games," Mathematical Social Sciences, Vol.5

1986 (with R. Stoecker), "End Behavior in Finite Prisoner's Dilemma Super-games," JEBO, Vol.7, No.1.

1987 (with M. Mitzkowitz and G. R. Uhlich), "Duopoly Strategies Programmed by Experienced Players," Econometrica, Vol.65, No.3.

1998 a "Multistage Game Models and Delay Super-games," Nobel Lecture, Theory and Decision, Vol.44, No.1.

b "Features of Experimentally Observed Bounded Rationality," EER, Vol.42, No.3-5.

2001 a (with M. H. Wooders), "Cyclical Games: An Introduction and Some Examples," GEB, Vol.34, No.1.

b "C. Harsanyi, System Builder and Conceptual Innovator," GEB, Vol.36, No.1.

2009 (with G. Sebastian), "Experimental Investigation of Stationary Concepts in Cyclical Duopoly Games," Experimental Economics, Vol.12, No.3.

59.5 WORKS OF OTHERS

Aumann, R. J. (1987), "Game Theory," in The New Palgrave: A Dictionary of Economics, Macmillan, London.

Damme, E. V., and J. W. Weibull (1995), "Equilibrium in Strategic Interaction: The Contributions of John C. Harsanyi, John F. Nash and Reinhard Selten," ScandJE, Vol.97, No.1.

Kreps, D. M. and J. A. Scheinkman (1983), "A Quantity Precommitment and Bernard Competition Yield Cournot Outcomes," Bell Journal of Economics, Vol.14, No.2.

Savage, L. J. (1954), The Foundations of Statistics, John Wiley, New York.

von Neumann, J. and O. Morgenstern (1944), Theory of Games and Economic Behavior, Princeton University Press, Princeton, NJ.

CHAPTER 60

THOMAS CROMBIE SCHELLING

(1921 –)

The 2005 Alfred Nobel Memorial Prize in Economic Sciences was awarded jointly to Thomas Crombie Schelling, University of Maryland, USA and Robert J. Aumann, Hebrew University, Jerusalem, Israel. The Royal Swedish Academy of Sciences, announcing the award, specifically mentions their contribution to enhance our understanding of conflict and cooperation. Schelling and Aumann have applied game theory, which is used for analysing strategic interaction among different human agents, to issues related to conflict and cooperation among agents. They have achieved this by extending and applying game theory concepts. Their work has contributed to usher in developments in non-cooperative game theory and making it applicable to analyse important issues in other social sciences, besides economics. In this process, Aumann and Schelling helped in transforming the social sciences far beyond the boundaries of economics.

To understand and appreciate the contributions of Schelling and Aumann, it is necessary to recall the attempts made over time by social scientists to understand important causes that lead to human conflict and cooperation. In the earlier chapters, reference has been made to the joint work of John von Neumann and Oscar Morgenstern in laying the foundations of game theory which resulted in publishing their book, "The Theory of Games and Economic Behavior" in 1944. Game theory basically involves analysis of all kinds of strategic interaction. Major contributions to the subject have been made by John Nash (who put forward what is referred to as Nash equilibrium), John Harsanyi and Reinhard Selten, whose major work has been summarised in the earlier chapters. The work of Nash, Harsanyi and Selten has developed solution concepts and provided valuable insights enriching the non-cooperative game theory leading to the enhancement of its usefulness and predictive power. To recall once again: A game consisting of a list of players, a set of available strategies to each player and a function for determining the pay-off consequences to all players of each strategy combination is called a non-cooperative game. Given a strategy combination – one strategy for each player, Nash equilibrium is attained, if each player's strategy is optimal against the other players' strategies. Harsanyi generalised the concept of Nash equilibrium to games of incomplete information while Selten showed how the concept could be refined to deal with dynamic games and for games where players make mistakes with infinitesimally small probabilities. Aumann and Schelling have attempted application of game-theoretic tools to vital societal issues.

The press release of the Royal Swedish Academy illustrates how even a two party human interaction may contain a number of alternative courses of action as well as a number of possible outcomes. In a two-party relation, assuming one party can choose one of the three alternative courses of action and the other can choose between the two alternative courses of action, the total number of possible outcomes would be six (3x2). The outcomes will be evaluated differently by the two parties and each party will act on the basis of which alternative he/she thinks the other party will choose. Furthermore, the game may become complex since many interactions may involve several steps over time and the interactions may be associated with asymmetric information.

Schelling and Aumann extended the application of methods of game theory to important issues which the society faces and the policies aimed at resolving them. The questions on which their research work was focussed include price formation on markets, security and disarmament policies and economic and political negotiations. Their approaches to the analysis differ from each other-- Schelling's approach was in the framework of economics while Aumann adopted the mathematical framework. In this context the press release observes: ".... Schelling showed that many familiar social interactions could be viewed as non-cooperative games that involve both common and conflicting interests and Aumann demonstrated that long-run social interaction could be comprehensively analyzed using formal non-cooperative game theory."

Schelling's contributions are summarised in this chapter. Aumann's contributions are briefly covered in the next chapter.

60.1 A SHORT BIOGRAPHY: THOMAS C. SCHELLING

Thomas Schelling was born in Oakland, California, U.S.A on April 14, 1921. His father John M. Schelling was a naval officer. Thomas Schelling attended the University of California, Berkley, graduating in economics in 1944. After spending a year and half in Washington, working as an analyst with the U.S Bureau of Budget, Schelling joined Harvard University. He completed his Ph.D. examinations in June 1948. He received a junior fellowship of the Society of Fellows from the University. He however, took leave to join the administration of the well-known Marshall plan, spending a year in Copenhagen, and a year and a half in Paris, eventually resigning his fellowship. Schelling joined the White House Staff of the foreign policy adviser to the U.S President in November 1950 and left the job in the fall of 1953 to join the economics faculty of Yale University. Schelling's Ph.D. dissertation was on National Income Behavior.

He gained experience in negotiations both in Washington and in his two stints abroad. At Harvard, Schelling became interested in bargaining strategy. He states: "... my government experience gave me much of the background I needed when later I decided to make bargaining theory my primary theoretical interest." His first two published articles when he was at Yale were "Essay on Bargaining" in 1956 and "Bargaining, Communication, and Limited War" in 1957. He believes that these two articles were considered by the Nobel Selection Committee as his contribution to understanding cooperation and conflict. By his own admission, he had more than a "smattering of acquaintance" with formal game theory. According to him, his first professional introduction to game theory was Raiffa and Luce's volume on Games and Decisions, published in 1957 on which he spent "at least a hundred, may be two hundred, hours." A fall out of this study was his preparing an article "Prospectus for a Reorientation of Game Theory" in 1958 when he was in London which was published as a whole issue of the Journal of Conflict Resolution. In the article, Schelling urged game theorists to devote more attention to strategic activities of players such as promises and threats, tacit bargaining, the role of communication, coordination tactics, the design of enforceable contracts and rules, the use of agents, and all the tactics by which individuals or firms or governments committed themselves credibly. Schelling candidly states: I don't think I had any noticeable influence on game theorists, but I did reach sociologists, political scientists and some economists.

While in London, he made acquaintance of several scholars and former military officers who were interested in the theory of deterrence and limited war. Schelling then realised the kind of game theory that can be usefully applied in military foreign policy, specifically nuclear weapons policy. He pursued his theoretical work when he was associated for a year as a guest of the Rand Corporation in California resulting in his producing two papers. The first one was "Surprise Attack and Disarmament." The other paper developed the idea of a probabilistic threat under the title "The Threat That Leaves Something to Chance." During that period, Schelling developed an idea that has come to be referred to as "focal point" or "Schelling point." He argued that the only viable convention regarding the use of nuclear weapons would be "no weapons," not some quantitative or qualitative limits. In his autobiographical note, Schelling states that this idea is the germ of his Nobel Memorial lecture. "The Astonishing Sixty Years: The Legacy of Hiroshima."

Schelling spent, in all, thirty one years at Harvard University, in the department of Economics and the Center for International Affairs. With the establishment of the J.F. Kennedy School of Government in 1969, he also worked there. He was permitted to write and to consult. Because of this permission, he was able to do advisory work for the government, particularly during summer months.

With a grant jointly given to Harvard and MIT, Schelling established a Center for Arms Control that would meet once in three weeks for dinner discussion. Further, in the summer of 1960, he organised a summer study of arms control financed by the Twentieth Century Fund. On the basis of the consensus reached by the group, Schelling, in association with M.H. Halperin of Yale, finished a book, Strategy and Arms Control published in 1961.

During nineteen seventies and eighties, Schelling mostly focused his research on two subjects. The first subject related to the behaviour of people who had habits or addictions or delinquencies, who made attempts, whether successful or not, to deal with themselves as they might deal with another's misbehaviour "attempting in effect to 'commit' themselves to avoiding the bad behavior or performing the good." Several essays on this topic are included in the two books published in 1984, and in 2006. The second subject that occupied him in 1970s was concerned with the ways individual behavioural choices could aggregate into social phenomena that were unintended or unexpected. In his autobiographical note, Schelling states that "without knowing it I was pioneering a field of study that later became known as 'agent-based computational modeling'." The work involved modelling spatial segregation "... the ways that people who differ conspicuously in binary groups-- e.g. blacks and whites, males and females... get separated spatially in residence, in dining halls, at public events." Much of the work was published in a volume in 1978.

In 1980s, Schelling was involved in the work on the Carbon Dioxide Assessment Committee of the National Academy of Sciences and prepared a chapter of the report on "Policy and Welfare Implications of Climate Change," which remained his major interest. He states in the autobiographical note: "Its relevance to my [Nobel] Prize is that mobilizing to do something about prospective global warming and climate change." This problem of global warming, according to Schelling, is going to be an important problem during the 20th century, "an immense challenge to cooperation amid conflict."

Schelling retired from Harvard University in 1990 and accepted appointment as Distinguished University Professor in the Department of Economics and the School of Public Policy at the University of Maryland. He continued his interest in nuclear weapons policy, climate change, or global warming, commitment and terrorism. At the time of the announcement of the Prize, he was Lucius N. Uttateur Professor of Political Economy, Emeritus, at Harvard University and Distinguished University Professor at the Department of Economics and School of Public Policy, Emeritus, at University of Maryland, College Park. He was also co-faculty at the New England Complex System Institute.

Among the honours and awards Schelling received, mention must be made of the NAS Award for Behavior Research relevant to the prevention of nuclear war in 1993 from the National Academy of Sciences, U.S.A., Honorary doctorate from Yale University and an honorary degree from the University of Manchester. The award given by the National Academy of Sciences, U.S., perhaps reflects the impact Schelling's work had on the behaviour of super powers.

60.2 A SUMMARY OF THOMAS C. SCHELLING'S MAJOR CONTRIBUTIONS

Schelling's Prize lecture titled "An Astonishing Sixty Years: The Legacy of Hiroshima," opens with a stunning statement: "The most spectacular event of the past half century is one that did not occur. We have enjoyed sixty years without nuclear weapons exploded in anger". For this stunning achievement or stunning good fortune, not a little was contributed by Schelling and his band of researchers. His work <u>The Strategy of Conflict</u>

provided the conceptual framework for the analysis of the nuclear arms race. He was at that time working as a consultant for government agencies at the Rand Corporation.

Corroborative statement regarding the danger of nuclear arms to global security came in 1960 from the British novelist C.P. Snow as mentioned in Schelling's Nobel lecture. Snow stated: "Unless the nuclear powers drastically cut down their nuclear armaments, thermonuclear warfare within the decade was a 'mathematical certainty." Schelling remarks in the lecture: "We now have that mathematical certainty compounded more than four times, and no nuclear war" and poses a pertinent question: "can we make it through another half dozen decades?" Applying the game-theoretic framework which he developed, Schelling offers an almost positive answer. His reasoning for drawing a comfortable conclusion is outlined here.

There has never been any doubt about the military effectiveness and potential for terror of nuclear weapons. Further, they were considered as unique and "a large part of their uniqueness derives from their being <u>perceived</u> as unique in contrast to conventional weapons" (Emphasis in the original). Schelling argues that an important part of its non-use has to be ascribed to the "taboo" that the then U.S secretary of State, John Foster Dulles, seemed to have attached to these weapons, though he deplored the taboo. His conjecture: "... nuclear weapons once introduced into combat, could not, or probably, could not be contained, confined, limited." Schelling, after tracing the development of this convention inhibiting the use of nuclear weapons, suggests that this attitude or convention, or tradition that took strong root and grew over (i.e., during the past five decades) is an asset to be treasured and preserved. He considers that preparing this tradition and helping to extend it to countries that may in future acquire nuclear weapons is important. Schelling comments: "I am particularly impressed by the '19 peril-filled years', [President] Johnson implied that for 19 years the United States had resisted the temptation to do what Dulles had wanted the United States to be free to do where nuclear weapons were concerned. He implied that the United States and other nuclear weapon states, had an investment, accumulated over 19 years, in the non-use of nuclear weapons; and these 19 years of quarantine for nuclear weapons were part of what would make any decision to use those weapons a political one of the highest order." Schelling finds it remarkable how these perceptual constraints and inhibitions cross cultural boundaries and categorically states that "the accumulating weight of tradition against nuclear use I consider... impressive and... valuable."

Referring to the discussion these days whether deterrence could be operative in future and whether it has a useful role in the U.S security, particularly in the context of the disintegration of the Soviet Union and acquisition of nuclear weapons by some other countries like India, Pakistan and other nations, Schelling expects that a new respect for deterrence would emerge. Furthermore, in the historical context of non-use by the USA and the erstwhile USSR, he feels that the prospect of nuclear retaliation made any initiation appear unwise. He makes a significant statement: "What nuclear weapons have been used for, effectively, successfully, for sixty years has not been on the battlefield nor on population targets: they have been used for influence." Schelling is hopeful that even terrorists may consider destroying large numbers of people as less satisfying than keeping the major nation at bay.

The foregoing analysis demonstrates how Schelling's ideas in regard to application of the game theory framework have direct relevance to political and diplomatic issues and military strategy in addition to economic, social and personal lives. Avinash Dixit observes: "Whether you want to improve the security of your country in the nuclear age, or want to make sure you don't hit the snooze button on your alarm clock too often in the morning, you should know and apply Schelling's analysis and conclusions." In this context, a reference may be made to what Schelling was reported to have told reporters as given by the BBC news on the day of the announcement of the award of the prize: "[Aumann] is a producer of game theory and I am a user of game theory." Dixit, however, is of the view that Schelling is being "excessively modest," particularly in the context of the latter's elucidation of many concepts and strategies of the game theory such as threats, promises, credibility, commitment, brinkmanship and focal points.

The information supplied by the Royal Swedish Academy of Sciences acknowledges that Schelling's vision of game theory has contributed to the unification of the frame work for the entire social science discipline. [His work was done in the context of the world's first nuclear arms race and his contributions were helpful in getting to understand its implications]. He moved away from zero-sum games as, in his view, almost all multi-person decision problems involve a combination of conflicting interests as also common interests which can be analysed by application of non-cooperative game theory. He argues that such combination of conflict and interest in game theory leads to the organisation of tacit coordination when interests are largely aligned. Schelling, considering that pure coordination is a game of strategy similar to a game of conflict, states: "It is a behavior situation in which each player's best choice depends on the action he expects the other to take, which he knows, depends, in turn, on the other's expectation of his own. This interdependence of expectations is what distinguishes a game of strategy from a game of skill." As an example, consider an oligopoly market structure whose member firms want to reach a tacit understanding to share the market. A solution to such problems involving tacit coordination crucially depends upon whether the expectations of players can converge on an outcome, called "focal point."

Such convergence of expectations needed for creating focal points lies outside the formal game theory frame. Dixit observes that some historical, cultural, linguistic "salience" is indispensable for the creation of convergent expectations in the mind of the players. He states: "This explains why people coming from different social or cultural backgrounds are often less successful in solving tacit coordination problems." Schelling conjectures: "The coordination game probably lies behind the stability of institutions and traditions." Moreover, if the players can make use of explicit communication such as overt bargaining with uninhibited speech, it no longer can be called a game.

Schelling's earliest work in game theory was concerned with analysis of behaviour in bilateral bargaining situations, where bargaining is broadly interpreted. In addition to situations in which explicit negotiations take place between parties, Schelling includes in bargaining cases such as when two trucks loaded with dynamite meet on a road wide enough for only one truck. Elaborating his contribution to the issue of bargaining, Schelling, while dealing with the tactics a player can employ to turn the outcome in his favour, points out that sometimes it may be advantageous to worsens one's own options for getting concessions from the opponent. An example where such tactics work is if an irreversible commitment is made. In order to make his commitment credible, a general in a war may wisely burn bridges behind his troops to indicate his lack of intention to retreat. Another example: making promises that would be embarrassing to break. However, in Schelling's opinion if the two parties make irreversible and conflicting commitments, harmful disagreement may be the consequence.

The Royal Swedish Academy of Sciences' release of advance information gives the following example to illustrate this type of game involving mobilisation of military forces or refraining from doing so in a dispute regarding a piece of territory, being claimed by both. The pay-off matrix, where one player chooses a row and the other simultaneously chooses a column is as given below. In each entry in the pay-off matrix, the row player's pay-off is given first.

	Mobilise	**Refrain**
Mobilise	0, 0	a, c
Refrain	c, a	b, b

If both countries mobilise, there would be a high probability of war. Further, the probability of reaching a peaceful agreement regarding the division of territory is low. If both countries mobilise military forces, the pay-off to each party or country is zero. Instead, if the two countries refrain from mobilisation, there is a high probability of a peaceful agreement about the division of the territory. In the latter case, each country gets expected pay-off 'b', a positive outcome. In case only one country mobilises its military forces, without war it can take control of the disputed territory, obtaining a pay-off 'a', while the other country's pay-off is c, where $a>b>c>0$. Thus it is seen that the worst outcome is war.

This game belongs to a class of games known as "chicken", also called "Hawk-Dove." Three Nash equilibria are possible in such games: two pure and one mixed. The pure equilibria result if only one country resorts to mobilisation of military forces; it is optimal for the other country to refrain from mobilisation. In case of "randomized" mobilisation by the two countries, the outcome is a positive probability of war – a case of mixed equilibrium. The pure equilibria are plausible in situations where the two countries have some means to coordinate on either equilibrium. Schelling is of the view that humans are capable of some such coordination in many situations. He states: "one cannot, without empirical evidence, deduce what understandings can be perceived in a non-zero sum game of manoeuvre any more than one can prove, by purely formal deduction that a particular joke is found to be funny." Instead, equilibrium selection is an area where experimental psychology can contribute to game theory.

Schelling draws a useful distinction between "mobilizing" and threatening to mobilize. Deterrence is not easy to analyse. Analysis of deterrence needs formulating a dynamic game with several stages. Dixit states that while traditional game theory posits complete specification of the game, the outcome of the game can be determined employing a particular equilibrium concept. Schelling formulates the game from the opposite angle. The players ask themselves the question that, given the outcome they would like to have, "is there anything I can do to bring it about?" This approach to a game involves all players in the game simultaneously planning to devise methods to engineer a change in its outcome in their favour. Modern game theory considers strategic moves of players as the first stage of a multi-stage game in which the available actions to the players at this stage are completely spelt out. The solution to the game is sub-game perfect Nash equilibrium which was discussed in the chapter on Selten. The opportunities available to the players may be identical or one player may have an advantage at the first stage. An example of the latter is the advantage an incumbent firm in an oligopolistic market may have while the other player may be intending to enter the market. In reality, however, as Dixit points out, "there is a whole continuum, from perceiving and playing a multi-stage game to a more fundamental alteration of the shared mental constructions of the players about the game they are playing and its equilibrium selection."

Players' commitments, threats and promises (referred to as strategic moves) need to be credible to be effective. In Dixit's words "the modern formal notion of credibility is sub-game perfectness; the outcome that the player making the strategic move wishes to achieve must be the result of a sub-game perfect equilibrium in the enlarged game." The analysis by Schelling of credible commitments shows that some Nash equilibria are more likely than others. This work of Schelling was ably carried further, introducing sub-game perfect refinements. The advanced information released by the Royal Swedish Academy of Sciences refers to Schelling's and Selten's work on strategic commitment carried further by others such as Avinash Dixit and Michael Spence. Reference may be made to analyses of strategic investment in oligopoly markets. The analyses demonstrate that a firm operating in an imperfectly competitive market can augment its profits by altering its cost structure, even if its unit cost of production rises in consequence. For example, a firm by investing in an expensive plant with low marginal cost and high volume of output may make a credible commitment though average costs may rise. This may lead to losses which can be outweighed by less aggressive behaviour of the competitors. Another instance of credible commitment is in entrusting monetary policy operation to an independent central bank. This action will influence the decisions of trade unions and firms since they take into account the expected monetary policy in fixing wages and prices.

Dixit in an article in the Scandinavian Journal of Economics specifically refers to Schelling's telling example of the game of chicken "where each of the two drivers heading toward each other wants to convince the other that he will not swerve, comes not from Hollywood movies, but Homer's vivid account of a chariot race between Antilochos and Menelaus, and he [Schelling] tells us how apparent irrationality, recklessness or unreliability can be a good way to achieve credibility and can therefore be strategically rational: "hotrods, taxis and cars with Driving School licence plates are given wide berths." Referring to brinkmanship, Schelling describes it as manipulation of shared risk. It is a richer and more realistic and dynamic version of chicken."

Schelling also studied what are referred to as pure coordination games which involve almost no clash of interest. In such games, all players would like to have a joint course of action, irrespective of the type of coordinated course of action. In experiments conducted with his students, Schelling found that they were able to coordinate well without communicating even in games with which they are not familiar and which had a number of Nash equilibria. It is, of course, true that coordination would be greatly facilitated when players can communicate with each other. Suppose two people are in a game which requires them to select a positive integer each. If they choose the same integer both get an award; no award is given if they choose different positive integers. In such a setting, it is likely that the two players select an identical integer number 1 as it is distinctive and is the smallest positive integer. Similarly, Schelling's experiments have revealed that the experimental subjects were able to utilise "contextual details joint references and empathy in order to identify 'focal' equilibria."

Another class of social decision problems involves interactions in which the players or participants distrust each other. Schelling provides an example in which the possibility of war arises solely because of mutual distrust, say between generals of two countries. The following example is given in the information supplied by the Royal Swedish Academy of Sciences. Suppose the following is the pay-off bi-matrix. The first number in each entry is the pay-off to the row player.

	War	**Peace**
War	2, 2	3, 0
Peace	0, 3	4, 4

Each player has two options --either go to war or refrain from it. The two pure strategy Nash equilibria are – (war, war) and (peace, peace). The most plausible outcome of the game would be peace, provided the two players are rational, having no uncertainty about the other player's pay-off; then, they carry out their plans perfectly. This equilibrium of peace, Schelling concedes, may be shattered if an iota of doubt exists about the other player's intentions.

Schelling also examines and analyses situations where one person may be playing against his own future self, showing that there need not be two persons to play a game of strategy. In a 1966 article "Coping Rationally with Lapses from Rationality," he observes that people who have difficulty concerning certain of their own behaviours may employ strategies to constrain their future choices. As Dixit states "we have all taken actions while our rational self was in charge, to guard against the temptations to which a future irrational or addicted or merely weak-willed self would succumb." This is a sort of commitment, meant to change one's own future action. Dixit provides a few examples of this kind. We may take steps to see that a portion of our salary payment be withheld and put in a pension plan for future financial security. This would avoid the temptation to buy a consumer durable. Likewise, a person may place the alarm clock on a desk far away from bed, obviating the possibility of hitting the alarm button in the morning. These efforts can be interpreted as a person's rational attempts to cope with some foreseeable lapse from full rationality. What happens during a "lapse" is not easy to describe. Further, it is not clear whether "succumbing" should be interpreted as rational or not; it is in dispute. However, Schelling refers to a number of conditions and behaviours for which a judgment about irrationality would be less problematic. He comments: They are important in their own right and also help to enlarge the class in which the more notorious addictive and compulsive behaviours can be fitted. He deals in the article with some of the preferences such as asleep, dowry, depressed, euphoric and drunk and extremes of motivation such as pain, fear and panic, phobias, temptations and compulsions. It is reported that Schelling's motivation for this research came from the problem of quitting smoking, as he had been a smoker himself. He got deeply immersed in the field. It is further reported that he ran a substantial smoking project at Harvard University for many years. His book Choice and Consequences appeared in one of those years.

Not only individuals, but societies also may experience similar problems. While in the case of individuals, action may be taken, in the case of societies, it may not be possible to coordinate necessary collective action; for example, people stranded as a result of natural disasters or affected by serious diseases. If preventive action was taken, the amount of resources that may be needed may be considerably less than amount needed to treat patients of such diseases or for rescuing people who are stranded by natural calamities. Moreover, Schelling states: "We often know who died for lack of safety; we rarely know who lived because of it." Dixit comments: "[Schelling's] essay offers a clear-headed but considerate analysis of the willingness to pay approach to the valuation of life and similar touchy issues."

60.3 OTHER CONTRIBUTIONS

Schelling also analysed how racially mixed societies and neighbourhoods can become segregated as the proportion of inhabitants of one race, gradually slides below a critical level. In an article that appeared in the American Economic Review, Schelling presents models of segregation. He observes that there is segregation by sex, age, income, language, colour, taste, comparative advantage and the accidents of historical location. "Some segregation is organized; some is economically determined....some results from the interplay of individual choices that discriminate." Schelling's paper is about the segregation that can result from discriminating individual choices. His ultimate concern was, of course, segregation by colour in the United States. He concludes: "Economists are familiar with systems that lead to aggregate results that the individual neither intends nor needs to be aware of, the results sometimes having no recognizable counterpart at the level of the individual." He gives a number of examples of this phenomenon; creation of credit by a commercial banking system, individual saving decisions causing depressions or inflations and Gresham's law. He conjectures that the inter-play of individual choices, where unorganised segregation is concerned, is a complex system with collective results that bear no close relation to individual intent.

60.4 CONCLUDING OBSERVATIONS

It is amply clear from Schelling's work that it is possible to clearly and cogently put difficult ideas in a simple and lucid style without the use of mathematics. The examples he gives are quite simple and easy to remember. In regard to Schelling's achievement in reorienting game theory, Michael Kinsley, Washington Post's OP.ED. Columnist and a former student of Schelling, has to say the following in an article celebrating Schelling's Nobel Prize for Economics: "[Y] ou're standing at the edge of a cliff, chained by the ankle to someone else. You'll be released, and one of you will get a large prize as soon as the other gives in. How do you persuade the other guy to give in, when the only method at your disposal – threatening to push him off the cliff would doom you both?

Answer: You start dancing, closer and closer to the edge. That way, you don't have to convince him that you would do something totally irrational: Plunge him and yourself off the cliff. You just have to convince him that you are prepared to take a higher risk than he is of accidentally falling off the cliff. If you can do that, you win."

Schelling is credited with coining the term 'ergonomics.' He used it in his paper "Ergonomics or the Art of Self-management" to describe self-management.

More importantly, Schelling is credited with developing many important concepts of modern game theory. Dixit observes that Schelling has given us game theory "to practice" and game theory "to remember." Further he says: Schelling stands as an exemplar of a research style that relies on deep integration between observations from life and theoretical thinking, where each motivates and enriches the other. Newcomers to research in economics and game theory could find no better role model."

In conclusion, it is said that the 'errant economist,' as Schelling called himself, has turned out to be a pre-eminent path-finder.

60.5 SELECT BIBLIOGRAPHY OF THOMAS C. SCHELLING'S WORKS

60.5.1 BOOKS

1951 National Income Behaviour: An Introduction to Algebraic Analysis, McGraw Hill, New York.

1958 International Economics, Allyn Bacon, Boston, MA.

1960 The Strategy of Conflict, Harvard University Press, Cambridge, MA.

1961 (with M. H. Halperin), Strategy and Arms Control, The Twentieth Century Fund, New York.

1966 Arms and Influence, Yale University Press, New Haven, Conn.

1978 Micromotives and Macrobehavior, W. W. Norton, New York.

1979 Thinking through the Energy Problem, Committee for Economic Development.

1984 Choice and Consequence, Harvard University Press, Cambridge, MA.

60.5.2 ARTICLES

1946 "Raise Profits by Raising Wages," Econometrica, Vol.14, No.3.

1947 "Capital Growth and Equilibrium," AER, Vol.37, No.5.

1948 "Income Determination: A Graphic Solution," REStat, Vol.30, No.3.

1949 "The Dynamics of Price Flexibility," AER, Vol.39, No.4.

1956 "An Essay on Bargaining," AER, Vol.46, No. 3.

1957 "Bargaining Communication and Limited War," Journal of Conflict Resolution, Vol.1, No.1.

1958 a "Design of the Accounts," in A Critique of the U.S. Income and Product Accounts, NBER Studies in Income and Wealth, Vol.22, NBER, New York.

b "The Strategy of Conflict: Prospectus for a Reorientation of Game Theory," Journal of Conflict Resolution, Vol.II, No.3.

1959 a "Surprise Attack and Disarmament," in NATO and American Security, (C. Knorr ed.), Princeton University Press, Princeton, NJ.

b "For the Abandonment of Symmetry in Game Theory," REStat, Vol.41, No.3.

1960 "Economic Reasoning and Military Science," The American Economist, Vol. IV, No.1.

1961 a "Reciprocal Measures for Arms Stabilization," Daedalus (Special Issue on Arms Control), Fall.

b "Arms Control will not cut Defence Costs," HBR, Mar/Apr.

c "Dispersal, Deterrence and Damage," Operations Research, Vol.9, No.3.

d "Experimental Games and Bargaining Theory," World Politics, Vol.XIV, No.1.

1962 "The Role of Deterrence in Total Disarmament," Foreign Affairs, Apr.

1963 "War without Pain and Other Models," World Politics, Vol. XV, No.3.

1966 "Uncertainty, Brinkmanship, and the Game of Chicken," in Strategic Interaction and Conflict, K. Archibald (ed.) Institute of International Studies, University of California, Berkley, Ca.

1967 a "The Strategy of Inflicting Costs," Issues in Defence Economics, NBER, Columbia University Press, New York.

b "What is Game Theory," in Contemporary Political Analysis, J. C. Charlesworth (ed.), The Free Press, New York.

1968 a "The Life You Save May be Your Own," in Problems in Public Expenditure Analysis, S. B. Chase Jr (ed.) The Brookings Institution, Washington D.C.

b "Game Theory and the Study of Ethical Systems," Journal of Conflict Resolution, Vol.XII, No.1.

1969 "Models of Segregation," AER, Vol.59, No.2.

1971 "Dynamic Models of Segregation," Journal of Mathematical Sociology, Vol.1, No.1.

1973 "Hockey Helmets, Concealed Weapons and Daylight Saving: A Study of Binary Choices with Externalities," Journal of Conflict Resolution, Vol. XVII, No.3.

1975 "A Framework for the Evaluation of Arms Control Proposals," Daedalus, Vol.104, Summer.

1978 a "Altruism, Meanness and Other Potentially Strategic Behaviors," AER, Vol.68, No.2.

b "Ergonomics, or the Art of Self management," AER, Vol.68, No.2.

1980 "The Intimate Contest for Self-command," The Public Interest, Vol.60, Summer.

1982 "Establishing Credibility: Strategic Consideration," AER, Vol.72, No.2.

1983 "Ethics, Law and the Exercise of Self-command," in The Tanner Lectures on Human Values, IV, S. M. McMurrin (ed.) University of Utah Press, Salt Lake City.

1984 "Self Command in Practice, in Policy, and in a Theory of Rational Choice," Richard T. Ely Lecture, AER, Vol.74, No.2.

1985 a "Enforcing Rules on Oneself," Journal of Law, Economics and Organisation, Vol.1, No.2.

b "Policy Analysis as a Science of Choice," in Public Policy and Policy Analysis in India, R. S. Ganapathy (ed.) Sage Publications, New Delhi.

c “What Went Wrong with Arms Control?” Foreign Affairs, Vol.64, No.2.

1987 “Value of Life,” The New Palgrave: A Dictionary of Economics, Macmillan Press, London.

1992 “Some Economics of Global Warming,” AER, Vol.82, No.1.

1995 “Intergenerational Discounting,” Energy Policy, Vol.23, No.4-5.

1996 “Coping Rationally with Lapses from Rationality,” Eastern Economic Journal, Vol.22, No.3.

1998 a “Costs and Benefits of Reducing Green House Gases,” American Enterprise Institute, Washington, D.C.

b “Commitment” in The New Palgrave: Dictionary of Economics and the Law, Macmillan, London.

2006 “An Astonishing Sixty Years: The Legacy of Hiroshima,” Nobel Lecture, AER, Vol.96, No.4.

2009 “International Coordination to Address the Climate Challenge,” in Innovations: Technology, Governance, Globalization, MIT Press, Vol.4, No. 4.

2010 “Game Theory: A Practitioner’s Approach,” Economics and Philosophy, Vol.26, No.1.

60.6 WORKS OF OTHERS

Dixit, A. (2006), “Thomas Schelling’s Contributions to Game Theory,” ScandJE, Vol.108, No.2.

Luce D. and H. Raiffa (1957), Decisions and Games, Wiley, New York.

Nash, J. (1950), “The Bargaining Problem,” Econometrica, Vol.18, No.2.

Nash, J. (1953), “Two-person Cooperative Games,” Econometrica, Vol.21, No.1.

Savage, L. (1954), The Foundations of Statistics, Dover, Mineola, NY.

Zeckhouser, R. (1989), “Distinguished Fellow: Reflections on Thomas Schelling,” JEP, Vol.3.

von Neumann J. and O. Morgenstern (1944), The Theory of Games and Economic Behavior, Princeton University Press, Princeton, NJ.

CHAPTER 61

ROBERT JOHN AUMANN

(1930 –)

The 2005 Nobel Memorial Prize in Economic Sciences was jointly awarded to Robert John Aumann and Thomas Schelling for their contribution to enhancing our understanding of conflict and cooperation. The advanced information provided with the announcement of the award by the Royal Swedish Academy of Sciences states that "war and other conflicts are among the main sources of human misery." It also observes that a minimum cooperation is a prerequisite for a prosperous society. The press release goes on to recall what Thomas Hobbes had said about living in an anarchic state of nature with its struggle of every man against every man as "solitary, poor, nasty, brutish and short."

To understand the fundamental factors causing conflict and cooperation have for long been studied by social scientists. In this effort, game theory has been found to be useful. As it is well known, John von Neumann and Oscar Morgenstern's work published in 1944 laid the foundation of game theory and provided fresh insights to the process of human conflict and cooperation. The usefulness of the theory was enhanced by research work of others. Prominent among them who provided new solution concepts and fresh insights are John Nash, John Harsanyi and Reinhard Selten. Their work which improved the usefulness and predictive power of non–cooperative game theory has been particularly distinguished and all of them were awarded 1994 Nobel Memorial Prize in Economic Sciences by the Royal Swedish Academy of Sciences. Nash equilibrium in which a strategy combination where each player's strategy is optimal against the strategies of other players is the most important solution. Harsanyi carried the theory further by demonstrating that this solution concept could be extended and generalised to games of incomplete information. Selten showed that the theory could be applied to dynamic games and for games in which players make mistakes with very small probabilities. These intellectual achievements would be of immense value, if the game-theoretic tools could be employed to deal with crucial societal issues. This task has been competently taken up by this year's awardees, namely Robert J. Aumann and Thomas C. Schelling. They further developed the non–cooperative game theory and applied it to deal with important issues in social sciences. The advanced information provided by the Royal Swedish Academy states: "Approaching the subject from different angles – Aumann from mathematics and Schelling from Economics – they both perceived that the game-theoretic perspective had the potential to reshape the analysis of human interaction." While Schelling demonstrated that many familiar social interactions could be considered as non-cooperative games characterised by both common and conflicting interests, Aumann attempted a comprehensive analysis of long run social interaction employing non-cooperative game theory.

Schelling's contributions have been outlined in the previous chapter. Aumann's major work in game theory has been briefly surveyed in this chapter.

61.1 A BRIEF BIOGRAPHICAL SKETCH: ROBERT AUMANN

Robert John Aumann was born on June 8, 1930 in Frankfurt, Germany, to an orthodox Jewish family. His father was a wholesale textile merchant, "rather well to do." His father's family lived in Germany for centuries and his father had fought in World War I for Germany and had been decorated. His mother grew up in London and obtained a B.A degree, a somewhat unusual feat for women in early 20th century. When in the nineteen thirties, the Nazi regime made life very difficult for Jews in Germany, Aumann's family left Germany and made its way to the United States in 1938. In that passage to New York, his parents lost all their assets, and had to work very hard to make a living. However, this mishap did not deter the family from giving their two children (Robert and his younger brother) excellent education and they had wonderful childhoods.

Robert Aumann went to Jewish parochial schools for elementary and high school education. In high school, Aumann had an extraordinary teacher of mathematics, who taught him to love the subject. In his autobiographical note, Aumann states: "What attracted me most were the axioms, theorems, proofs and construction of Euclid's geometry." When he joined City College of New York, Aumann decided to major in mathematics. He observes: "The vogue of pure mathematics – the 'purer', the better -- was at its height in the mid-twentieth century, and young and impressionable, I was drawn into it."

At the City College, in addition to mathematics, Aumann studied many other subjects, including economics. Economics baffled and bored him, and he dropped the subject after a few weeks. Aumann has praise for a marvellously broad undergraduate education in the United States. He obtained B.S. degree from City College in 1950. For graduate studies, Aumann entered the Massachusetts Institute of Technology (MIT) where he became interested in the modern branches of mathematics, like algebraic topology to which he was attracted by the excellent lectures of George Whitehead. He decided to do a Ph.D. with Whitehead in Knot theory. According to Aumann: "The whole subject was absolutely useless." He obtained Ph.D. in 1955 from MIT and his thesis was published in the Annals of Mathematics in 1956.

After completing Ph.D. Aumann went to work for an Operations Research consulting outfit, affiliated with the mathematics department of Princeton University. There he was assigned a problem which he figured, needs to be solved by the use of game theory. Aumann, therefore, studied "some game theory – just enough for this problem." He was attracted to the subject "in its own right."

In 1956, Aumann joined as instructor of mathematics at the Hebrew University, Jerusalem, and has been there ever since. The 1957 Luce–Raiffa book, Games and Decisions had made a great impression on him. The book has an "interesting – though inconclusive – discussion" of repeated games, and "this may have piqued my interest." In the autobiographical note, he recalls working on "Acceptable Points." In the course of that work he became aware of what later came to be known as the "Folk Theorem." At that time, it seemed to him that it did not have sufficient mathematical depth to merit publication. He realised later that it was a big mistake. Both "Acceptable Points" and the "Folk Theorem" are expressions of the relation between equilibrium behaviour in the repeated game and cooperative behaviour in the one-shot game; but while "Acceptable Points" is undoubtedly interesting, much deeper and more subtle, the "Folk theorem" is by far the more fundamental and important.

During his long academic career, Aumann was a research associate (1960-61) at Princeton University and visiting professor, Department of Statistics and Cowles Foundation for Research in Economics, Yale University. In 1968 he was appointed professor at Hebrew University of Jerusalem. He was Ford visiting research professor of Economics at University of California, Berkley, in 1971 and 1985. His other academic positions include, visiting professor of Economics, Stanford University in 1975-76 and 1980-81, visiting scholar, Cowles Foundation for Research in Economics, Yale University, Oskar Morgenstern visiting professor, North Western University and member of the Study of Rationality, The Hebrew University since 1991. Aumann retired from the Hebrew University to become Emeritus Professor in 2001.

Of a large number of awards and prizes, besides Nobel Memorial Prize in Economics Sciences that Aumann received, the following may be mentioned. Since 1974, he was a foreign honorary member, American Academy of Arts and Sciences, since 1985, member of National Academy of Sciences, U.S.A, and since 1995, corresponding Fellow, British Academy. He was a Fellow, Econometric Society since 1966, honorary member, American Economic Association since 1993 and President, Game Theory Society, 1998-2003.

Aumann received honorary doctorates from a number of Universities, including University of Chicago, City University of New York and University of Bonn. He delivered invited addresses at large international congresses including Second World Congress of Econometric Society, Cambridge, Walras-Bowley Lecture at the winter meeting of the Econometric Society, Toronto, International Congress of Mathematics, Fourth World Congress of Econometric Society and Presidential Address at the First World Congress of the Game Theory Society, 2000. He delivered endowed lectures at different Universities like Harvard University and Stanford University. He worked as associate editor of Journal of Economic Theory and member of the Advisory Board, Journal of Mathematical Economics.

61.2 A BRIEF SUMMARY OF ROBERT AUMMAN'S CONTRIBUTIONS TO GAME THEORY

Robert Aumann is widely regarded as an important figure in shaping game theory and placing it securely in modern economics. He has developed a unified view of game theory by effectively combining various disciplines such as economics, political science, statistics and philosophy. The Royal Swedish Academy of Sciences particularly notes Aumann's development of general methodologies to deal with various specific issues, such as deterrence, perfect competition, oligopoly, taxation and voting and investigated where these lead in each specific application. Furthermore, his research is marked by an "unusual combination of breadth and depth." Some of his contributions are characterised by "involved analysis" while others are technically simple though conceptually profound. The Swedish Academy sums up: His fundamental works have both clarified the internal logic of game–theoretic reasoning and expanded game theory's domain of applicability.

In an introduction to the comprehensive interview given by Robert Aumann, prior to the award of Nobel Prize, S. Hart (a former student of his) recounted the following as the major and significant contributions of Aumann. By far Aumann's greatest contribution was in the area of repeated games--that is, situations in which players encounter the same situation over and over again. Another key contribution is his introduction of the concept of correlated equilibrium in game theory. Compared to classical Nash Equilibrium, in non–cooperative games, correlated equilibrium is a more flexible one. Another first of Aumann was the introduction of common knowledge. He is also widely known for his "argument theorem." According to Aumann, argument theorem is one which under conditions specified by him, two Bayesian rationalists with common prior beliefs "cannot agree to disagree."

Hart, in an article subsequent to the announcement of the award, has classified the major contributions of Aumann under three heads.

1. ***Repeated Games***: The study of long term cooperation is the frame work of classical "selfish" utility maximisation.
2. ***Knowledge, Rationality and Equilibrium***: Aumann is known for his analysis of knowledge in multi–agent environments and for his laying of the foundation of rationality and equilibrium.
3. ***Perfect Competition***: Aumann has established perfect competition by introducing the concept of continuum of agents and established connection between price equilibria and cooperative outcomes.

61.2.1 REPEATED GAMES

Repeated games which involve modelling long-term interaction are considered a very important category of games. A great deal of interaction between agents and countries is long term in nature, sometimes of infinite duration. Examples include firms competing in the market may take monthly or more frequent decisions regarding production and prices taking into account past behaviour of competitors. Countries may have an opportunity to benefit at the expense of the neighbouring country. These examples and others underline the need to study recurrent interaction over a long period.

In his Prize lecture titled "War and Peace," Aumann discusses repeated games and how they relate to war and to other conflict situations such as strikes and all other interactive situations. He states that the theory underlying repeated games accounts for phenomena such as altruism, cooperation, trust, loyalty, revenge, self-destructive or non-self-destructive threats. Those phenomena may appear to be irrational, particularly when they are viewed in terms of "selfish" utility-maximising paradigm of game theory and neo-classical economics. Aumann clarifies that humans do not deliberately choose to take revenge or to act generously out of consciously self-serving, rational motives. Rather, humans, over time, have evolved norms of behaviour that are "optimal." It leads to strategic equilibrium.

The distinction between short-term interaction and long-term interaction is explained through the popular "prisoners' dilemma" game. The following pay-off bi-matrix can be used for this purpose. The first number in each entry is the pay-off to the row player and the second number the pay-off to the column player. The letters 'C' and 'D' denote cooperate and defect, respectively. The players choose their strategies simultaneously. As can be seen, each player's dominant strategy or optimal strategy, irrespective of the strategy chosen by the other player, is D. Even though this is an equilibrium outcome, it is worse for both players than the strategy pair where both cooperate (adopt strategy C). Both players gain by both choosing strategy C. Thus, it is seen that when the game is played once, there is one Nash equilibrium: both players defect (D).

	C	D
C	2, 2	0, 3
D	3, 0	1, 1

Now suppose the players play the "prisoners' dilemma" game (everyday) over and over again, with the objective of maximising the average daily pay-off stream over the infinite future. In such a situation, it is easily shown that cooperation in every period is an equilibrium outcome since players can now threaten to punish any deviation from cooperative play today by refraining from cooperating in the future. Thus, the reduction in gain in future cooperation outweighs short-term gain from defection today.

Aumann argues that in repeated games, strategic equilibrium is the outcome. He observes that strategic equilibrium expresses phenomena such as altruism, cooperation, trust, loyalty, revenge and threats. He defines that players in a game (such as the one outlined above) are said to be in strategic equilibrium or simply in equilibrium when their play is "mutually optimal;" that is, when the actions and plans of each player are rational in the given strategic environment; in other words, when each knows the actions and plans of others.

Aumann, in his Prize lecture, explains the concept of repeated games. Suppose game 'G' is played by the players, year after year. He observes that this situation can be considered as a "single big game" – super game of G, denoted G*, - whose rules are, 'play game G every year'. He states that the theory of repeated games that emerges from this process is "extremely rich and deep." He concludes that "repetition enables cooperation." The term "cooperative" is used by him to describe any possible outcome of a game, as long as no player can "guarantee" a better outcome for himself. In general, a cooperative outcome is not achievable in equilibrium. As is clear from the above cited example of the prisoners' dilemma game, the outcome in which neither player defects (D) is a cooperative outcome. It is better for both than the unique (Nash) equilibrium.

According to Aumann "the theory of repeated games of complete information is concerned with the evolution of fundamental patterns of interaction between people.... Its aim is to account for phenomena such as cooperation, altruism, revenge, threats etc, which may at first seem irrational...." Aumann presents in his Prize lecture the following simple example of a repeated game. Assume a game, H, in which R and C are two players. The game matrix is given below.

Acquiesce (A)	Punish (P)	
10 10	0 0	Divide Evenly (E)
1 100	0 0	Divide Greedily (G)

R must decide whether both she and C will receive the same amount – namely 10 – or whether she will receive ten times more, and C will receive ten times less. Simultaneously, C will have to decide whether or not to punish or take punitive action that will harm both, R and himself. If he decides to punish, the division is cancelled, and instead, each player gets nothing as shown in the above matrix. The cooperative outcome (E, A), giving 10 to each player (divide evenly, acquiesce), though not achievable in equilibrium, is interesting since no player can guarantee more for himself or herself. Such cooperative outcomes are achievable (by R and C) by contract or agreement, if contracts are enforceable; for example, in a nation with a legal system or a system with courts.

Aumann asserts that repetition of a game is like an enforcement mechanism that enables the emergence of cooperative outcomes in equilibrium – when everybody is acting in his own best interests.

If a game is a one shot game or it is played just once, then R is better off by dividing greedily (G) when C has no alternative but to Acquiesce, even though he does not like the outcome (G and A are in fact dominant strategies). But in a super game, H*, C can threaten to punish R "forever afterwards" if she divides greedily (G). This is, of course, Nash equilibrium. In such a situation, however, R chooses a strategy which is "play E (or divide evenly) forever. C's strategy is 'play A as long as R plays E; if R ever plays G, play 'P' forever afterwards." In this game as well as in such games, the equilibrium is maintained by threat of punishment. Aumann remarks: "if you like, call it 'MAD' – mutually assured destruction – the motto of the cold war. Only caveat to make this work is that the discount rate used for present value calculations should not be too high. He explains the work of this caveat. "The strategies that achieve cooperation in an equilibrium of the super game involve punishment in subsequent stages if cooperation is not forthcoming in the current stage. If the discount rates are too high, then the players are more interested in the present than in the future.... This vitiates the threat to punish in future stages."

The cooperative outcome (E, A) in the super game H* of the one shot game, H, is achievable in equilibrium. This is a special case of a much more general principle, commonly known as FOLK THEOREM, which says that any cooperative outcome of any game G (or H) is achievable as a strategic equilibrium outcome of its super game G* (or H*) – even if that outcome is not an equilibrium outcome of game G (or H). Conversely, every strategic equilibrium outcome of super game G* is a cooperative outcome of game G.

In the words of Aumann: "The significance of the Folk Theorem is that it relates cooperative behavior in the game G to non-cooperative behavior in its super game G*." He defines the Folk theorem as follows: "For any game G, the cooperative outcomes of G coincide with the equilibrium outcomes of its super game G*." In this context, Aumann recalls the concept of perfect equilibrium introduced by Reinhard Selten for which he was awarded Nobel Memorial Prize. Perfect equilibrium means that the threat of punishment is credible. That is, the player who resorts to punishment of the other player continues to be in equilibrium since he has no incentive to deviate. Aumann, in his Prize lecture, raises the question whether in the repeated game, can (E, A) be maintained not only in strategic equilibrium but also in perfect equilibrium. Aumann refers to his 1976 work with Lloyd Shapely and asserts that the answer is yes – this is referred to as <u>Perfect Folk Theorem</u>. He defines Perfect Folk Theorem thus: The cooperative outcomes of G coincide with the perfect equilibrium outcomes of its super game G*. Here again, repetition acts as an enforcement mechanism. He observes: "it makes cooperation achievable when it is not achievable in the one-shot game, even when one replaces strategic equilibrium as the criterion for achievability by the more stringent requirement of perfect equilibrium. In order for this to work, the discount rates of all agents must be low; they must not be too interested in the present as compared with the future." Then he sketches a simple proof of the result. He argues that any player who does not carry out a prescribed punishment is punished by the other player for not doing so. And he remarks: "Much of society is held together by this kind of reasoning."

In his Prize lecture Aumann explains the notion of "core" which plays a key role in application of game theory to economics. He states: "The core outcomes of G coincide with the strong equilibrium outcomes of its super game, G*." An outcome 'x' of a game is said to be in its "core" if no set' 'S' of players can improve upon it, that is, assure to each player in S an outcome that is better for him than what he gets at x. He posits: the core outcomes of an economy with many individually insignificant agents are the same as the competitive Walrasian outcomes – those defined by a system of prices for which the supply of each good matches its demand.

He also shows that the presence of asymmetric information hinders cooperation even when it is to the mutual advantage of both the players. The informed player, according to Hart, wants to convey his information, but he cannot do so credibly. Hart comments: "The study of repeated games of incomplete information... clarifies in a beautiful way the strategic use of information: how much to reveal, how much to conceal, how much of revealed information to believe."

Hart sums up the importance of Aumann's contribution of repeated games: The model of repeated games is an extremely simple, fundamental and universal model of multi-stage interactions. It allows participants truly to interact and react to one another; their behavior may be simple or highly intricate and complex. The analysis is deep and challenging, both conceptually and technically. In the end the results are elegant and most insightful; simple and natural behavior emerges.

61.2.2 CORRELATED EQUILIBRIUM

Aumann was the first to define the concept of correlated equilibrium. Correlated equilibria are mixed Nash equilibria, except that the players' randomisation need not be independent. Correlated equilibrium is considered "coarser" than Nash equilibrium. Assume that in a given and known game, each player that is playing the game, receives a certain signal that does not affect the pay-offs of the game. The question that needs to be answered is whether such signals can affect the outcome of the game. According to Aumann, players may use such signals to correlate their choices and effect the outcome of the game. He defines the notion of correlated equilibrium thus: It is a Nash equilibrium of the game with the signals. At one extreme, when the signals are stochastically independent, the game yields a Nash equilibrium. At the other extreme, when everyone receives the same "public signal" or when the signals are perfectly correlated, the outcome is an average of Nash equilibria or what is referred to as publicly correlated equilibrium. In other words, correlated equilibrium allows strategies of players to be statistically dependent and Nash equilibrium comes about in the case of statistical independence. In a correlated equilibrium, each player's conditioned choice is optimal, given the others' decision rules.

In the interview with Hart, Aumann argues that in "Battle of Sexes" game, if a player is going to select one equilibrium it has to be the mixed one. In that situation, a coin is tossed to decide on one of the pure equilibria and then it is to the advantage of both players to the equilibrium given by the toss of the coin. He states that the whole process, including the coin toss, is equilibrium. This equilibrium is definitely better than the unique mixed strategy equilibrium because it guarantees that the boy and the girl will definitely meet - either at the football match or at the concert – whereas with the mixed strategy equilibrium, they may well go to different places. With repeated games, one gets a similar result by alternating: one evening football match, the next evening concert. To conclude: correlated equilibria arise when the players get signals that need not be independent. Hart comments: "The notion of correlated equilibrium is most natural and arises in many setups. It is embodied in situations of communication and coordination, when there are mediators or mechanisms...."

61.2.3 COMMON KNOWLEDGE

Aumann explains subjective equilibrium where different players have different probabilities for the same event. Differences in probabilities can be ascribed to differences in information. But then, if a player knows that another player's probability is different from his, he might wish to revise his own probability. It is not clear whether this process of revision necessarily leads to the same probabilities for the players. This question was raised and left unanswered in Aumann's 1974 paper in the Journal of Mathematical Economics. In his 1976 paper "Agreeing to Disagree," he put forward what has come to be known as Agreement Theorem. That is, roughly, if the probabilities of two people for an event are commonly known by both, then they must be equal. This paper, as reported, became one of his two most widely cited papers. The Agreement Theorem as put forward by Aumann: Consider two people who start with the same prior beliefs and may receive different information. If their posterior probabilities for some event A are common knowledge, then those posteriors must be identical.

The introduction of the concept of common knowledge by Aumann has pioneered the field known as interactive epistemology – knowledge about others' knowledge. It enabled rigorous analysis of deep and complex issues such as rationality and what is needed for equilibrium. It led him back to correlated equilibrium. The idea of common knowledge facilitates the "right" formulation of correlated equilibrium. Correlated equilibrium is nothing more than just common knowledge of rationality, together with common priors. He puts forward the following theorem: Consider a game whose players start with the same prior beliefs and may receive different information. If it is common knowledge that all players are Bayesian rational, then they are playing a correlated equilibrium of the game. A player is said to be Bayesian rational if his action is optimal given his information. Aumann observes: It is remarkable that correlated equilibria are obtained from common knowledge of rationality and a common prior only; no assumptions of equilibrium behaviour are needed.

61.2.4 PERFECT COMPETITION

A central theme in economics is the market structure of perfect competition. Aumann introduced in his 1964 Econometrica paper the concept of markets with a continuum of traders; that is, modelling perfect competition by a continuum of agents. He states: "The influence of an individual participant in the economy cannot be mathematically negligible, as long as there are only finitely many participants. Thus a mathematical model appropriate to the intuitive notion of perfect competition must contain infinitely many participants. We submit that the most natural model for this purpose contains a continuum of participants, similar to the continuum of points on a line...." The continuum is an approximation to the "true" situation, in which the number of traders is large but finite. In 1966 Econometrica article, he dealt with the existence of a competitive equilibrium.

The idea of continuum of agents has contributed importantly to the advancement of economic theory. One of the significant results of Aumann's introduction of continuum of agents is the equivalence between competitive equilibria and core allocations in perfectly competitive markets: individual price-taking behaviour and social stability yield the same outcomes. Hart considers this as a "modern and rigorous formalization of the 'invisible hand' of Adam Smith and the limit contract curve of Edgeworth."

Aumann argues that in non-atomic games, in which there are only small players but no large players, no player by himself makes any significant contribution. An example of a non-atomic game is a large economy, consisting of small consumers and small businesses only, without large corporations or government interference. Another example given by Aumann is an election where no individual can effect the outcome. However, in a non-atomic game, though no individual player can effect the outcome, large coalitions can. The game theory concept of value is an a priori evaluation what a player or group of players can expect to get out of the game. Value of large economies is the same as competitive outcomes of a market. Hart observes: "The notion of value embodies standard economic ideas such as 'expected outcome' and 'marginal contribution'. Applying it to markets with a continuum of traders yielded a new equivalence result, this time between the price equilibria and the value allocations." In Aumann's own words: "perhaps the most remarkable single phenomenon in game and economic theory is the relationship between the price equilibria of a competitive market economy and all but one of the major solution concepts for the corresponding game...."

61.2.5 OTHER CONTRIBUTIONS

Aumann has made many other significant contributions to game theory including axiomisation, subjective probability and utility and non-transferable utility games. He advocates unified game theory. He says "game theory may be viewed as a sort of umbrella or 'unified field theory' for the rational side of social science, where 'social' is interpreted broadly to include human individuals (collectives such as corporations and nations....) Unlike other approaches to disciplines like economics or political science, game theory does not use different ad-hoc constructs to deal with various specific issues, such as perfect competition, monopoly, oligopoly, international trade, taxation, voting, deterrence. Rather, it develops methodologies that apply in principle to all interactive situations and then sees where these methodologies lead in each specific application."

He remarks: "Blaming game theory – or for that matter, economic theory- for selfishness is like blaming bacteriology for disease; game theory studies selfishness, it does not recommend it." His contributions to tactical military problems deserve particular mention. In his Prize lecture, Aumann states that war is not irrational, but must be scientifically studied in order to be understood, and eventually conquered. Further, he observes that simplistic peace making can cause war, while arms race, credible war threats and mutually agreed destruction can reliably prevent war. He concludes his Prize lecture on this cautious note: [Prophet] Isaiah is saying that "the nations can beat their swords into ploughshares when there is a central government – a Lord, recognized by all. In the absence of that, one can perhaps have peace – no nation lifting up its sword against another. But the swords must continue to be there – they cannot be beaten into ploughshares – and the nation must continue to learn war, in order not to fight". (Emphasis in the original).

Aumann is sceptical about behavioural economics. He says that practical decision-making is much more complex than our models. In practical decision-making one does not know the right decision until it is made. Most of behavioural economics deals with artificial laboratory set ups, "at best." At worst, it deals with polls, questionnaires etc, which are at a "double remove from reality." In behavioural economics people ask: "What would you do if...," it is not even a real set up, Empirical economics is a good way of finding out what people actually decide. He sums up: Behavioral economics is not really behavioral.

61.3 CONCLUDING OBSERVATIONS

Robert Aumann is a deeply religious man and possesses strong political views. Because of these and the use of his research to justify them, the decision to give him the Nobel Prize was criticised in the European press. A petition to cancel his prize garnered signatures from 1000 academics worldwide.

However, his contributions to game theory have helped shaping it into a conceptually profound and much of it mathematically deep discipline. Besides his own work, he has exercised significant influence and inspired generations of researchers and has been a driving force behind the development of many areas.

61.4 SELECT BIBLIOGRAPHY OF WORKS OF AUMANN

61.4.1 BOOKS

1974 (with L. Shapley), Value of Non-Atomic Games, Princeton University Press, Princeton, NJ.

1989 Lectures on Game Theory, Underground Classics on Economics, Westview Press, Boulder, Co.

1992, 1994, 2002 (with S. Hart (eds.), Handbook of Game Theory with Economic Applications, North Holland, Amsterdam.

1995 (with M. Maschler), Repeated Games of Incomplete Information, MIT Press, Cambridge, MA.

61.4.2 ARTICLES

1959 "Acceptable Points in General Cooperative n-person Games," in Contributions to the Theory of Games IV, Annals of Mathematics Study, Luce, R. P. and A. W. Tucker (eds.) Princeton University Press, Princeton, N.J.

1960 "Acceptable Points in Games of Perfect Information," Pacific Journal of Mathematics, Vol.10, pp.381-417.

1961 a "The Core of a Cooperative Game without Side Payments," Transactions of American Mathematical Society, Vol.98, pp.539-552.

b "Almost Strictly Competitive Games," Journal of the Society for Industrial and Applied Mathematics, Vol.9, No.4.

1962 "Utility Theory without the Completeness Axiom," Econometrica, Vol.30, No.3.

1963 (with F. J. Anscombe), "A Definition of Subjective Probability," Annals of Mathematical Statistics, Vol.34, No.1.

1964 "Markets with a Continuum of Traders," Econometrica, Vol.32, No.1-2.

1966 "Existence of Competitive Equilibria in Markets with a Continuum of Traders," Econometrica, Vol.34, No.1.

1967 "A Survey of Cooperative Games without Side Payments," in Essays in Mathematical Economics in Honor of Oscar Morgenstern, M. Shubik (ed.), Princeton University Press, Princeton, NJ.

1972 "Some Thoughts on Minimax Principle," Management Science, Vol.18, No.5.

1973 "Disadvantageous Monopolies," JET, Vol.6, No.1.

1974 "Subjectivity and Correlation in Randomized Strategies," JMathE, Vol.1, No.1.

1975 a "Cooperative Games with Coalition Structures," International Journal of Game Theory, Vol.4, pp.217-237.

b "Values of Markets with a Continuum of Traders," Econometrica, Vol.43, No.4.

1976 "Agreeing to Disagree," Annals of Statistics, Vol.4, pp.1236-1239.

1977 (with M. Kurz) "Power and Taxes," Econometrica, Vol.45, No.5.

1981 "Survey of Repeated Games," in Essays in Game Theory and Mathematical Economics in Honor of Oskar Morgenstern, Wissenschaftsverlag, Mannheim.

1983 (with M. Kurz and A. Neyman), "Voting for Public Goods," RES, Vol.50, No.4.

1985 "What is Game Theory Trying to Accomplish?" in Frontiers of Economics, K. J. Arrow and S. Honkapohja (eds.) Basil Blackwell, Oxford.

1987 a (with M. Kurz and A. Neyman), "Power and Public Goods," JET, Vol.42, No.1.

b "Correlated Equilibrium as an Expression of Bayesian Rationality," Econometrica, Vol.55, No.1.

c "Game theory," The New Palgrave: A Dictionary of Economics, Macmillan, Basingstoke.

1989 (with S. Sorin), "Cooperation and Bounded Recall," Games and Economic Behavior, Vol.1, No.1.

1992 "Irrationality in Game Theory," in Economic Analysis of Markets and Games, Essays in Honor of Frank Hahn, P. Dasgupta et al. (eds.), MIT Press, Cambridge and London.

1995 (with A. Bradenburger), "Epistemic Conditions for Nash Equilibrium," Econometrica, Vol.63, No.5.

1997 a (with S. Hart and M. Perry), "The Absent-Minded Driver," Games and Economic Behavior, Vol.20, No.1.

b "Rationality and Bounded Rationality," Games and Economic Behavior, Vol.21, No.1-2.

1998 "On the Centipede Game," Games and Economic Behavior, Vol.23, No.1.

1999 a "Interactive Epistemology I: Knowledge," International Journal of Game Theory, Vol.28, No.3.

b "Interactive Epistemology II: Probability," International Journal of Game theory, Vol.28, No.3.

2000 (with G. Werner), "Species Survival and Evolutionary Stability in Sustainable Habitats," JEvolE, Vol.10, No.4

2003 a "Presidential Address," Games and Economic Behavior, Vol.45, No.1.

b (with S. Hart), "Long Cheap Talk," Econometrica, Vol.71, No.6.

2005 "War and Peace," Nobel Prize Lecture, in Lex Prix Nobel, 2005, K. Grandin (ed.), Nobel Foundation, Stockholm, 2006.

2008 a (with R. Servano), "An Economic Index of Riskiness," JPE, Vol.116, No.5.

b (with J. H. Dreze), "Rational Expectations in Games," AER, Vol.98, No-1.

2009 (with J. H. Dreze), "Assessing Strategic Risk," American Economic Journal: Microeconomics, Vol.1, No.1.

61.5 WORKS OF OTHERS

Debreu, G. and H. Scarf (1963), "A Limit Theorem on the Core of an Economy," IER, Vol.4, No.3.

Hart, S. (2005), "An Interview with Robert Aumann," Macroeconomic Dynamics, Vol.9, No.5.

Hart, S. (2006), "Robert Aumann's Game and Economic Theory," ScandJE, Vol.108, No.2.

Luce, R. D. and H. Raiffa (1957), Games and Decisions, John Wiley, New York.

Selten, R. (1975), "Re-examination of the Perfectness Concept for Equilibrium Points in Extensive Games," International Journal of Game Theory, Vol.4, No.155.

Names of Journals: Abbreviations (Journal Index)

AER (American Economic Review)

Bell JE (Bell Journal of Economics)

BPEA (Brookings Papers on Economic Activity)

BPEA (Brookings Panel on Economic Activity)

Cambridge JE (Cambridge Journal of Economics)

Canadian JE (Canadian Journal of Economics)

Carnegie-Rochester (Conference Series on Public Policy)

Econ Dev & Cul Chang (Economic Development and Cultural Change)

EJ (Economic Journal)

GEB (Games and Economic Behavior)

HOPE (History of Political Economy)

IER (International Economic Review)

IJGT (International Journal of Game Theory)

JASA (Journal of American Statistical Association)

JDE (Journal of Development Economics)

JEBO (Journal of Economic Behavior and Organization)

JEDC (Journal of Economic Dynamics and Control)

JEH (Journal of Economic History)

JEL (Journal of Economic Literature)

JET (Journal of Economic Theory)

JEvolE (Journal of Evolutionary Economics)

JF (Journal of Finance)

JIE (Journal of International Economics)

JITE (Journal of Institutional and Theoretical Economics)

JLawE (Journal of Law and Economics)

JMathE (Journal of Mathematical Economics)

JMCB (Journal of Money, Credit and Banking)

JME (Journal of Monetary Economics)

JPE (Journal of Political Economy)

JPubE (Journal of Public Economics)

JRSS (Journal of the Royal Statistical Society)

OEP (Oxford Economic Papers)

QJE (Quarterly Journal of Economics)

Rand JE (RAND Journal of Economics)

RES (Review of Economic Studies)

REStat (The Review of Economics and Statistics)

RIE (Review of International Economics)

Scand JE (Scandinavian Journal of Economics)

SEJ (Southern Economic Journal)

WEJ (Western Economic Journal (later Economic Inquiry))

Name Index

A

B

C

D

H

I

J

K

M

S

W

X

Y

Z

Topic Index

C

D

E

F

N

O

P

Q

R

T

www.ingramcontent.com/pod-product-compliance
Lightning Source LLC
Chambersburg PA
CBHW061150240926
51846CB00006B/972
* 9 7 8 9 3 9 5 0 3 8 8 2 9 *